LAW AND CIVIL WAR IN THE MODERN WORLD

Law and Civil War in the Modern World

Edited by John Norton Moore

Published under the auspices of
the American Society of International Law
and the International Legal Research Fund
of the Columbia University School of Law
and prepared in collaboration with
Wolfgang G. Friedmann

The Johns Hopkins University Press
Baltimore and London

To Wolfgang G. Friedmann

Copyright © 1974 by The Johns Hopkins University Press
All rights reserved. No part of this book may be
reproduced or transmitted in any form or by any means,
electronic or mechanical, including photocopying,
recording, xerography, or any information storage and
retrieval system, without permission in writing
from the publisher.
Manufactured in the United States of America

The Johns Hopkins University Press, Baltimore, Maryland 21218
The Johns Hopkins University Press Ltd., London

Library of Congress Catalog Card Number 73-19338
ISBN 0-8018-1509-6 (clothbound)
ISBN 0-8018-1598-3 (paperbound)

Library of Congress Cataloging in Publication data
will be found on the last printed page of this book.

Contents

Acknowledgments

This volume of studies is the culmination of the Civil War Project of the American Society of International Law Panel on the Role of International Law in Civil Wars. Publication was made possible by the financial support of the Ford Foundation and the International Legal Research Fund of the Columbia Law School.

Although the study is a collaborative effort of the Civil War Panel, a few special debts stand out. Prior to his untimely death, Professor Wolfgang G. Friedmann, the Chairman of the Panel, assisted in mapping out the contents of this volume and in obtaining the financial support of the International Legal Research Fund. Professor Richard A. Falk, the former Chairman and Rapporteur of the Panel, conceived the initial outline of the study and set the stage by a series of case studies on the role of international law in civil wars that was prepared under his auspices as Chairman and published in two earlier volumes sponsored by the Panel: R. Falk (ed.), *The International Law of Civil War* (The Johns Hopkins University Press, 1972), and W. Kane, *Civil Strife in Latin America: A Legal History of U.S. Involvement* (The Johns Hopkins University Press, 1972). John R. Stevenson, formerly Legal Adviser to the Department of State, encouraged the Civil War Project both as President of the Society and as an early member of the Panel and was instrumental in obtaining initial funding for the Project. Stephen M. Schwebel both contributed his share of intellectual excitement as a member of the Panel and as Executive Vice-President of the Society shepherded the volume from inception to publication ·with his inevitable good judgment and aplomb.

I would also like to thank Linda Vlasak of the Johns Hopkins University Press for careful editorial attention in the preparation of the manuscript and Frederick S. Tipson of the University of Virginia School of Law who assisted with footnote revision and preparation of the Bibliography.

Finally, I would like to thank the American Society of International Law, whose unflagging dedication to scholarly inquiry and the free exchange of ideas has contributed immeasurably to the development of the ideas expressed in this volume. The American Society of International Law is an association of American and foreign international legal scholars, judges, and practitioners from more than one hundred countries. It is not affiliated with any government or committed to any ideology other than seeking the settlement of international disputes on the basis of law and justice. The views expressed in this volume are those of the individual authors and do not necessarily represent the views of the American Society of International Law, the International Legal Research Fund, the Ford Foundation, or any other institutional or governmental affiliation. The chapter and materials by me were written prior to appointment to the Department of State and do not necessarily represent the views of the United States Government or any agency thereof.

John Norton Moore

Introduction

THE SETTING

Revolutionary and counter-revolutionary violence has been a recurring problem throughout the history of the nation-state system. But since the end of World War II, the problem—together with its international counterpart, interventionary and counter-interventionary violence—has become a central world-order concern. A casual reading of the daily newspaper is sufficient to illustrate the seriousness of the problem. As this introduction was being prepared, the *New York Times* carried front-page stories on continuing civil violence in Northern Ireland and a bloody attempted coup and counter-coup in Burundi, where thousands of Hutus and Tutsis were slain in a contemporary incarnation of tribal warfare.[1] A few months earlier, the enormous tragedy of the Pakistan–Bangladesh Civil War, which ultimately resulted in Indian intervention, gave special poignancy to efforts to improve human rights in civil-war settings. And throughout the period, the Indo-China War, the attacks of Palestinian commando groups against Israel, the urban guerrilla warfare of the Tupamaros in Uruguay, and the guerrilla struggles in southern Africa—just to name a few of the more intransigent conflicts—continued to dominate the news. In fact, revolutionary violence has become so commonplace that it is repeatedly treated in political writing and more than occasionally used as a theme in literature, art, music, and even dress fashions.

Though the causes of this increase in revolutionary and interventionary activity remain obscure, a variety of likely contributing factors have been identified. These include both motivational factors (or factors making for heightened motivation for revolution and intervention) and opportunity factors (or factors making for increased opportunity for revolution and intervention). The most prominent among them are:

Motivational factors—

1. Rising demands for self-determination, human rights, and modernization, combined with a variety of intense ideological conflicts that center around communist and non-communist political ideologies;
2. Increasing complexity of social problems and bureaucratic organization that results in concomitant difficulties in effective governance and temptations to authoritarian or revolutionary "solutions;"
3. The demonstration effect inherent in a high frequency of revolutionary and interventionary activity;

[1] *N.Y. Times*, June 18, 1972, at 1, cols. 3 & 7.

This Introduction has been prepared on behalf of the Panel on the Role of International Law in Civil Wars by the Editor-Rapporteur.

4. Residual problems, stemming from political settlements and global transformations that followed World War II, particularly the continuing problem of cold-war divided nations; and

5. A pattern of formalized alliance systems which create pressure for external assistance.

Opportunity factors—

1. The great increase in newly independent nations, resulting from accelerated decolonization (from about 65 states immediately after World War II, the number has now grown to over 150);

2. The large number of weak governments and unstable national units resulting from the rapid increase in the number of new states and a sometimes haphazard process of decolonization;

3. The destabilizing effect of accelerated social change caused by technological and population explosions;

4. A high and rising level of interaction among nations (this factor is simultaneously a significant motivational factor);

5. Constraints of a balance-of-power system and the unacceptability of nuclear exchange between the superpowers that militate for limited and protracted conflicts and that deflect conflict to competitive interventions, covert operations, and proxy wars by client states;

6. A relatively low level of effective global organization for the control of revolutionary and interventionary violence;

7. Increased interventionary activities associated with governments which have recently come to power through revolution, coupled with the significant number and importance of such governments in the present international system; and

8. A rise in the number of private armies and ideological groupings transcending nation-state boundaries.

Since many of these factors are likely to be operative, if not accelerating, in the foreseeable future, it seems likely that revolutionary and interventionary violence will continue as principal world-order problems.[2]

The central challenges posed by revolutionary and interventionary violence are, first, how to encourage persuasive rather than coercive strategies for achieving needed social change and, second, as long as violence continues, how to moderate and confine it to minimize its destructiveness. Law, or the flow of decisions regarded by the community as authoritative and controlling, has an important role to play in meeting both challenges. Despite the decentralized nature of the present international legal system and despite the well-known difficulties in ensuring compliance with community decisions, there is a functioning network of international institutions and norms specialized to the production and allocation of all values

---

[2] *See generally* C. Black, *The Dynamics of Modernization* 166 (1966); C. Leiden & K. Schmitt, *The Politics of Violence: Revolution in the Modern World* 212 (1968); Young, "Intervention and International Systems," 22 *J. Int'l Aff.* 177 (1968); S. Huntington, *Political Order in Changing Societies* (1968).

and to the control of unauthorized coercion. Although law as an instrument of social change must respond to the challenge by providing more effective community procedures for realization of self-determination, human rights, and modernization, the most immediate challenge has been to the institutions and norms concerned more directly with the management of conflict.

There are five principal strands to the international law of conflict management. Each was developed primarily in response to conventional warfare across national boundaries, and each is in need of revision or supplementation to become more relevant to the problems posed by revolutionary and interventionary violence. They are:

1. Normative standards for distinguishing permissible and impermissible resort to force;
2. Institutions, organizations, and procedures for collective security and community management of conflict;
3. Laws of war, or the rules and structures for regulating the conduct of hostilities;
4. Rules and structures for the control of armaments; and
5. Standards and procedures for the ascription of personal responsibility for knowing violation of the major conflict-management rules. That is, standards and procedures for fixing criminal responsibility for the commission of crimes against peace, war crimes, or crimes against humanity.

An additional strand which might be added because of its significant transnational impact on conflict is:

6. Rules and practices within national legal systems concerning the allocation of authority for the use of the armed forces abroad.

The normative standards for differentiating permissible from impermissible resort to force have, like the other principal strands in the international law of conflict management, largely evolved in response to conventional warfare across national boundaries. Thus, for the most part, they provide only minimal guidance, if any, to normative judgment concerning conflicts purely within national boundaries. For example, what judgment, if any, should be made on the basis of the United Nations Charter concerning the permissibility of wars of secession? Such wars may present a conflict between the principle of self-determination, set out in Articles 1(2) and 55 of the Charter, and the principle of territorial integrity, set out in Article 2(4) of the Charter. Similarly, the principal normative standards are incomplete in responding to interventionary and counter-interventionary problems. Thus, Article 2(4) of the Charter prohibits the "use of force against the territorial integrity or political independence of any state," but it is unclear whether assistance to a widely recognized government, at its request, to suppress a purely internal insurgency would violate the "territorial integrity or political independence" of the state. The Charter also provides little guidance as to the legitimacy of "humanitarian intervention" for the prevention of gross denial of human rights as, for example, in the Pakistan–Bangladesh Civil War or the Burundi conflict. The potential conflict here is between the obligation to promote respect for human rights, embodied in Articles 1(3), 55, and 56 of the Charter, and the prohibition of the use of force against territorial integrity, embodied in Article 2(4) of the Charter. In the absence of a more complete Charter structure for the regulation of interventionary activity, a parallel set of more specialized "non-intervention" norms has evolved. One continuing theoretical need is for reconciliation of these parallel normative tracks.

The non-intervention norms themselves, and even more so the practices of states, have continued to reflect a fundamental ambivalence toward intervention which has rendered traditional norms of limited utility. Thus, states which vehemently oppose intervention when it proceeds against their interests will in another context favor external assistance to a widely recognized government at its request (or alleged request), assistance to "national liberation movements" (which may be vaguely and selectively defined), or intervention for the purpose of preserving "socialist self-determination" or deterring communist takeover. Aside from the obvious assertions of special interest lurking in many such inconsistent national positions, a fundamental difficulty remains that some interventions may in fact promote the common interest of the community while others (and probably most) do not. The need is for more responsive normative standards which will consistently (or, at least, on a more-often-than-not basis) separate those interventions which promote the common interest of the community from those which promote only special interests. Traditional rules, which included competing principles that prohibited external intervention in internal conflict and permitted assistance at the request of a widely recognized government—at least until some point at which "belligerency" was reached—did not meet the needs of providing clear criteria for separating interventions which promote common interests of the community from those which do not. More radical formulations, which would bar intervention except for "national liberation," have been similarly deficient. In recent years, a variety of newer proposals has been advanced, including an imaginative suggestion that permissibility should turn on whether the intervention involves participation in tactical operations.[3] Although neither this nor any other single test has yet

---

[3] Professor Tom Farer has suggested a "flat prohibition of participation in tactical operations, either openly or through the medium of advisors or volunteers," as a single rule for the regulation of intervention. Farer, "Intervention in Civil Wars: A Modest Proposal," 67 *Col. L. Rev.* 266, 275 (1967); Farer, "Harnessing Rogue Elephants: A Short Discourse on Foreign Intervention in Civil Strife," 82 *Harv. L. Rev.* 511 (1969). For a critique of the Farer proposal and a review of past standards and recent proposals, *see* Friedmann, "Intervention and International Law I," in L. Jaquet (Ed.), *Intervention in International Politics* 40 (1971); Moore, "The Control of Foreign Intervention in Internal Conflict," 9 *Va. J. Int'l L.* 205, 315–32 (1969), reprinted in J. N. Moore, *Law and the Indo-China War* 115, 251–74 (1972).

been or is likely to be accepted, there is a discernible trend toward a narrowing of the issues by a general consensus that some forms of intervention are impermissible, *i.e.*, intervention at the request of a government to suppress a popular internal insurgency and intervention on behalf of insurgents aimed at the overthrow of a representative government. Similarly, there are signs of a trend in agreement on the theoretical underpinnings of an adequate theory for the regulation of intervention. Many scholars would urge that development of an adequate theory requires an explicit statement of the values at stake in the decision to intervene, contextual differentiation of the variety of interventionary settings and claims, postulation of policy-responsive norms for regulation of similar groupings of claims, and continued testing and refinement of postulated norms by reference to the social effects of the decision.[4]

The institutions, organizations, and procedures for collective security and for community management of conflict also need revisions that would make them more relevant to problems of revolutionary and interventionary violence. These should include improved machinery for community observation and disclosure for civil-war and interventionary settings; improved reporting procedures, clearly applicable to interventionary and counter-interventionary activities; strengthened community peacekeeping machinery; improved community procedures for the prevention of genocide or other gross abuse of human rights; improved procedures and machinery for political settlement of internal conflicts; and more adequate community procedures and standards for the appraisal of self-determination claims. Underlying all such improvements is a need for a more realistic approach to deciding which problems are solely within the domestic jurisdiction of a state and which are genuinely of international concern. The spectacle of the General Assembly treating the carnage in East Pakistan (now Bangladesh) as a matter of domestic jurisdiction, or the Organization of African Unity reacting in a similar fashion to the slaughter of non-combatants in the conflict in Burundi, stands in sharp contrast to the human-rights goals of both organizations.

The laws of war and the rules and structures for regulating the conduct of hostilities have been as—if not more—deficient in responding to revolutionary and interventionary violence as the norms for differentiating permissible from impermissible resort to coercion and the community institutions for collective security. Although nations have been willing to agree to rules

---

[4] *See* Falk, "Introduction," in R. Falk (ed.), *The International Law of Civil War* 1 (1971); Falk, "Civil Strife, Intervention, and Minor Coercion," in R. Falk, *Legal Order in a Violent World* 97–368 (1968); Farer, "Intervention in Civil Wars" and "Harnessing Rogue Elephants," *supra* note 3; Firmage, "Summary and Interpretation," in R. Falk (ed.), *The International Law of Civil War* 405 (1970); Higgins, "Internal War and International Law" in III C. Black & R. Falk (eds.), *The Future of the International Legal Order* 81 (1971); Moore, "The Control of Foreign Intervention," *supra* note 3; Moore, "Intervention: A Monochromatic Term for a Polychromatic Reality," in II R. Falk (ed.), *The Vietnam War and International Law* 1061 (1969), reprinted in J. N. Moore, *Law and the Indo-China War* 83–114 (1972).

and procedures for regulating the conduct of international hostilities, as embodied in the Hague Regulations of 1907[5] and the four Geneva Conventions of 1949,[6] they have been unwilling to agree to a comparable regime for the regulation of purely internal hostilities. The most that has been achieved to date is the enumeration of a few minimum standards for the protection of non-combatants embodied in Article 3 of the Geneva Conventions of 1949. This Article Three coverage is narrow both in scope and applicability, and a more comprehensive regime for the regulation of purely internal conflicts is long overdue. In its absence, conflicts such as the Nigeria–Biafra Civil War, the Pakistan–Bangladesh Civil War, and the recent Burundi conflict assume a savagery which might be moderated with a more completely developed and clearly applicable regime of human rights for settings of internal violence. In addition to the absence of a well-developed regime for internal conflicts, the present laws of war are designed primarily for conventional warfare across international boundaries and are frequently unresponsive to problems of guerrilla warfare and interventionary settings. There are severe problems in applicability of the Conventions to insurgent movements and intervening powers and in regulating the tactics and weapons of modern insurgency and counter-insurgency warfare. Finally, all of the deficiencies of the traditional laws of war, such as the lack of a clear and comprehensive code of air warfare, are felt—if not amplified—in civil war and mixed civil-international settings.

Efforts at arms control have focused in large measure either on the problem of preventing conventional war or, as has largely been the case after World War II, have wrestled with the enormous problems of reducing the risk of war with nuclear weapons or other weapons of mass destruction. In contrast, little progress has been made on measures which would decrease the threat of limited and proxy wars. Proposals illustrative of those which might be considered include machinery for the reporting of military assistance and limitations on the transfer of conventional arms.[7]

The standards and procedures for the ascription of personal responsibility for intentional violation of the major conflict-management norms assimilate all of the limitations of the other strands as applied in revolutionary and interventionary settings. Thus, in revolutionary settings, interna-

[5] Convention Respecting the Laws and Customs of War on Land, Hague Convention No. IV and Annex, Oct. 18, 1907, in II *Treaties, Conventions, Int'l Acts, Protocols and Agreements Between the United States of America and Other Powers, 1776–1909* 2269, 2285 (Malloy ed. 1910).

[6] The Geneva Convention for the Amelioration of the Wounded and the Sick in the Armed Forces in the Field, *T.I.A.S.* No. 3362 (1949); The Geneva Convention for the Amelioration of the Condition of Wounded, Sick, and Shipwrecked Members of Armed Forces at Sea, *T.I.A.S.* No. 3363 (1949); the Geneva Convention Relative to the Treatment of Prisoners of War, *T.I.A.S.* No. 3364 (1949). The Geneva Convention Relative to the Protection of Civilian Persons in Time of War, *T.I.A.S.* No. 3365 (1949).

[7] *See, e.g.*, Bader, "The Proliferation of Conventional Weapons," in III C. Black & R. Falk (eds.), *The Future of the International Legal Order* 210 (1971).

tional law has provided no real standards for the appraisal of personal responsibility other than an occasional hint of culpability for genocidal conduct. Notions of sovereignty and domestic jurisdiction have obscured the community interest in appraisal. And in interventionary settings, the normative weaknesses of the traditional rules have been assimilated in the standards for assessing personal responsibility. That is, criminal responsibility for waging aggressive war depends in interventionary settings on the ability to clearly differentiate permissible from impermissible intervention. Similarly, criminal responsibility for violation of the laws of war depends on the applicability and clarity of the regime regulating the conduct of hostilities as applied in interventionary settings. In addition, the ambiguities of the use of force in interventionary settings and the associated ideological conflict may place unique pressures on national and international institutions concerned with investigation and fact appraisal. Because of its dependent nature as well as its limited practical utility in moderating and policing real conflict situations, it seems likely that this "Nuremberg strand" will make only a modest contribution to the community regulation of revolutionary and interventionary violence.

Although not strictly a strand in the international law of conflict management, the rules and practices within national legal systems concerning the allocation of authority for the use of the armed forces abroad are quite relevant to the control of interventionary activity. Within the United States, the shift from conventional war across national boundaries to more ambiguous limited warfare, covert operations, and counter-intervention, has contributed to the confusion concerning the allocation of authority between Congress and the President. The Constitution gives Congress the power to declare war, and it is reasonably clear that the purpose of this provision was to require congressional participation in the decision to wage foreign wars. It is less clear, however, which of the newer forms of military action amount to "war" in the constitutional sense and which are actions short of war which may be instituted on presidential authority. In recent years, the military actions in Korea, Lebanon, the Dominican Republic, and Indo-China prior to 1964 were instituted solely on presidential authority, at least in the initial decision to commit United States forces. In response to these newer forms, efforts have been made in both houses of Congress to clarify the war powers, particularly as they have been affected by the problems of revolutionary and interventionary violence.[8]

The newer forms of military involvement which have precipitated the

---

[8] See "War Powers Legislation," *Hearings Before the Committee on Foreign Relations of the United States Senate, 92d Cong., 1st Sess.* (Comm. Print. 1971); "Congress, The President, and the War Powers," *Hearings Before the Subcommittee on National Security Policy and Scientific Developments of the Committee on Foreign Affairs of the House of Representatives, 91st Cong. 2d Sess.* (Comm. Print 1970). The 92nd Congress adjourned in October 1972 without reaching agreement on war powers legislation. At this writing, similar legislation is pending before the 93d Congress and seems destined to be a major item of Congressional interest.

reexamination of the war powers have more adequately alerted us to the full range and complexity of the issues. These include decisions concerning future commitments, the stationing of the armed forces abroad, the initiation of hostilities, the conduct of hostilities, and the termination of hostilities. Increasingly, it is recognized that the war powers encompass a process of related decisions and that normative and institutional improvements must be responsive to the whole. And though the focus of recent writings in this area has been on United States constitutional processes, similar issues are presented in any national or multinational decision to use force. In fact, the current impasse concerning the authorization and financing of United Nations peacekeeping forces reflects many of these same issues, particularly authority concerning the conduct and termination of peacekeeping operations. The way in which these issues are resolved, both nationally and internationally, may have a significant effect on the level and character of interventionary activities within the international system.

The adaptation of legal norms and institutions to the challenges presented by revolutionary and interventionary violence can most usefully proceed in a multidisciplinary framework in which lawyers and other social scientists share theory and data in responding to common problems. International relations theorists and political scientists have developed a rich literature on the causes and effects of revolutionary violence, on the systemic conditions for intervention, and on the domestic factors affecting national decisions to intervene. To the extent that legal theory is informed by such insights from neighboring disciplines, it will be correspondingly more policy-responsive. Moreover, law, with its emphasis on normative and institutional development, is only one tool for responding to social problems. Other techniques are equally important for value realization. For example, it may be that a major factor in the continuation of high levels of revolution and intervention is a misperception of the costs and benefits of such policies.[9] That is, some if not most kinds of revolution and intervention may yield few benefits, if any, and even then may be pursued only at enormous costs. If the costs and benefits are more accurately assessed, the levels of violence may decline as decision-makers respond to the new estimates. Similarly, newer behavioral and systemic approaches to the causes of revolution and intervention may point the way toward indicators useful in predicting levels of national or systemic violence or even identify controllable variables which are critical for reducing violence.

Though law is only one tool for social engineering, it is an important tool which should be fully taken into account by national and international decision-makers. International law provides a basis for normative appraisal of actions by reference to long-run community common interest. It also provides a medium of communication, a basis for assessing the probability of international response to national policies, a variety of unique institu-

---

[9] *See* J. Farrell & A. Smith (eds.), *Image and Reality in World Politics* (1967).

tional techniques for conflict management, and a focus on issues not adequately considered by other disciplines. An example of this latter point is the international legal focus on the norms and institutions for the regulation of the conduct of hostilities, an issue largely specialized to international law. But though there are strong reasons why law ought to be taken into account, unfortunately it is not always adequately considered in national security decisions. Under the influence of "realist" perspectives which focus on the deficiencies of control in the international legal system, there has been a tendency, since the onset of the cold war, to play down the usefulness of law. A resulting symptom is that the national security process is poorly structured to take an international legal perspective into account. For example, although at the time of this writing there are over fifty substantive officers on the staff of the National Security Council (NSC), there are no international legal specialists on that staff. In recent years, there have been a variety of thoughtful proposals for strengthening the input of international legal considerations in the national security process, including proposals to place the State Department Legal Adviser on the NSC, and to create a Counselor on National Security Law on the staff of the NSC.[10] The insights and suggestions contained in this volume are reason enough for adopting some such proposals.

THE VOLUME

Law and Civil War in the Modern World is the culminating study of the Civil War Project of the American Society of International Law Panel on the Role of International Law in Civil Wars. The Civil War Project was initiated in 1966, against a background of increased revolutionary and interventionary violence, and had as a principal purpose theoretical inquiry concerning the role of law in civil wars and how law and legal institutions might be made more relevant to the challenge. Earlier studies sponsored by the Panel have included *The Vietnam War and International Law* (Princeton University Press, vols. I–III 1967, 1970, & 1972), edited by Richard A. Falk; *The International Law of Civil War* (The Johns Hopkins Press, 1971), edited by Richard A. Falk; *Civil Strife in Latin America: A Legal History of U.S. Involvement* (The Johns Hopkins Press, 1972), by William Kane; and *The Arab-Israeli Conflict* (The Princeton University Press, vols. I–III 1974 & Abridged Edition, 1974), edited by John Norton Moore. *The Vietnam War and International Law* and *The Arab-Israeli Conflict* bring

---

[10] For a review of the proposals to strengthen the role of international law in the foreign policy process *see* Falk, "Law, Lawyers, and the Conduct of American Foreign Relations," 78 *Yale L.J.* 919 (1969); Moore, "Law and National Security," 51 *Foreign Affairs* 408 (1973); Moore, "The Role of Law in the Management of International Conflict," in J. N. Moore, *Law and the Indo-China War* 8–46 (1972); "New Proposals for Increasing the Role of International Law in Government Decision-Making," 65 *Proc. Am. Soc. Int'l L.* 285 (1971).

together the principal readings and documents on the legal aspects of two of the major world-order issues of our time, both of which have mixed features of internal and international conflict. *The International Law of Civil War* and *Civil Strife in Latin America* volumes provide a series of case studies of the role actually played by international law in selected civil conflicts. *Law and Civil War in the Modern World* builds on these earlier studies and is intended to provide a multidisciplinary and cross-national analysis, focused on theoretical inquiry in the development of an adequate international legal structure for the regulation of revolutionary and interventionary violence. It attempts to probe the assumptions underlying the present law, to suggest the direction and outline of the emerging legal order, and to point the way to a satisfactory general theory for the regulation of intervention.

Part I of *Law and Civil War in the Modern World* focuses on the theoretical underpinnings of an adequate legal theory for the regulation of civil strife and intervention. Chapter 1, by John Norton Moore, explores the intellectual prerequisites of an applied theory, with special attention to the relation between legal and political theory, and provisionally suggests standards for the appraisal of intervention. It is essential that approaches to the regulation of intervention be informed of the intellectual traps which have crippled past efforts, and that they focus on the full range of normative, historical, scientific, and policy tasks requisite for an adequate applied theory. Chapter 2, by Derek W. Bowett, explores the interrelation of the norms of intervention and the Charter structure for the regulation of unauthorized coercion. One of the theoretical difficulties in providing an adequate legal theory for the regulation of intervention has been that the United Nations Charter was responsive principally to the threat of conventional attacks across national boundaries. As a result, there has grown up a separate but interrelated network of standards for assessing the permissibility of intervention which have been termed "the norms of intervention." Frequently the interrelation of the two sets of standards is ignored, and in fact which set is chosen may be critical in normative assessment of a particular world-order issue. Professor Bowett draws on his own extensive work on the United Nations structure for the regulation of coercion to develop a framework for reconciliation of the Charter structure and the norms of intervention.

Part II deals with the relevance of theories of modernization, internal violence, and the international system for the development of norms and institutions for the regulation of intervention. All of the writers in this section are political scientists, historians, or international relations theorists, and their Chapters provide the multidisciplinary background on which efforts at law reform can most usefully proceed. Unlike participants in many other attempts at interdisciplinary collaboration, the authors here demonstrate awareness of the international legal efforts at the regulation of intervention around which the volume is structured and remain sensitive to the relevance and irrelevance of the present state of their theoretical concern for the formulation of a general theory. Chapter 3, by Cyril E. Black, explores the pertinence of theories of modernization to the development of a general theory, drawing on his own pioneering work in the development of theories of modernization. He suggests that the development and modernization of the Third World is likely to be accompanied by repeated civil strife, and that the problem for international law is not to prevent civil wars but to manage them. Chapter 4, by Ted Robert Gurr, focuses on theories of internal violence and counter-violence and their implications for the regulation of coercive intervention. He indicates a variety of ways in which greater scientific knowledge about the causes and conditions of internal violence can assist in achieving postulated goals of both revolutionary and counter-revolutionary actors. In the process, he also suggests an important caveat against overestimation of the predictive ability of present theories of violence and social change. Chapter 5, by John W. Burton, examines the assumptions of traditional international law in which sovereign states are the dominant actors and suggests instead a more fluid systems model which would reflect a complex interaction between clusters of overlapping systems and sub-systems focusing on man rather than solely on his institutions. He then suggests how the altered image relates to problems of civil conflict and the resolution and settlement of conflict. Some of Professor Burton's theoretical assumptions, particularly his emphasis on the realistic description of interpenetrating social processes, share a kinship with newer legal approaches in the United States, particularly the approach cryptically termed the "New Haven approach," utilized by legal scholars influenced by Myres S. McDougal and Harold Lasswell.[11] Chapter 6, by Oran R. Young, explores the principal systemic variables responsible for the present high level of interventionary activity in the international system and their potential for manipulation in the interests of regulating intervention. He concludes that, even if the prospects for manipulating the systemic bases of intervention are not now favorable, it may be possible to achieve some degree of regulation by a focus on the domestic bases of intervention.

Part III deals with the role of domestic factors in interventionary behavior, both from the viewpoint of the political scientist concerned with the identification of internal factors that may underlie interventionary behavior and from the viewpoint of the constitutional lawyer concerned with the structure of constitutional processes for the regulation of the use of the armed forces abroad. In Chapter 7, James N. Rosenau recommends a model of intervention as adaptive behavior, shaped both by internal and external factors. He then explores the internal or domestic factors which

[11] For a brief statement of the "New Haven approach" (more accurately, "policy-oriented jurisprudence") see Lasswell & McDougal, "Criteria for a Theory About Law," 44 *S. Calif. L. Rev.* 362 (1971). *See also* Young, "International Law and Social Science: The Contributions of Myres S. McDougal," 66 *Am. J. Int'l L.* 60 (1972), and McDougal, "International Law and Social Science: A Mild Plea in Avoidance," 60 *Am. J. Int'l L.* 77 (1972).

give rise to intervention, cautioning that a complete theory must also consider the effects of external factors and the interactions between external and internal factors. Chapter 8, by W. Taylor Reveley, III, and Chapter 9, by Lawrence R. Velvel, consider the present constitutional structure in the United States for the control of the use of the armed forces abroad and suggest how the structure might be made more responsive to the problems presented by limited war and participation in internal conflicts. Taylor Reveley takes an overview of the issues in their historical perspective and adopts a detailed framework which specifies the full range of war power issues. Lawrence Velvel focuses on selected problems in constitutional control, particularly the important and neglected problem of the authorizing effect of appropriations measures.

Part IV considers a number of the most important special problems relevant to formulation of a general theory. In Chapter 10, by Ian Brownlie, and Chapter 11, by Richard B. Lillich, two international legal scholars exchange views on whether "humanitarian intervention" undertaken for the protection of human rights can or should be legally permissible, and if so, under what circumstances. Though both scholars share a deep concern for implementation of human rights, they reach different conclusions on the wisdom and permissibility of unilateral humanitarian intervention. Chapter 12, by Michael Reisman, considers the problems posed for international law by the existence of "private armies" or armies not affiliated with recognized states. In doing so he draws on many of the intellectual tools of the "New Haven" school which he helped to shape. Principal recommendations include a careful contextual approach which systematically explores relevant features of the context in which "private armies" function and an adequate focus on the intellectual tasks in decision. Chapter 13, by Edwin Brown Firmage, deals with the history and nature of the "war of national liberation" and its relevance to Third-World settings in Asia, Africa and Latin America. He then suggests, on the basis of this experience, that the factor of "legitimacy," defined in relation to the allegiance of a people to its government rather than by formal criteria, should be used as the criterion for determining the relationship between third parties and states experiencing civil strife. Chapter 14, by Jerome Alan Cohen, and Chapter 15, by William E. Butler, explore Chinese and Soviet theory and attitudes toward intervention. Both studies reveal a deep ambivalence in Chinese and Soviet attitudes toward intervention as well as demonstrate that the state of scholarly analysis of the problem of regulation of intervention is still rather undeveloped in China and the Soviet Union compared with recent efforts in the West. Though a general theory for the regulation of intervention need not accept the official position of particular national actors, to the extent that common ground can be found for the regulation of some types of interventionary activity, the realism of the resulting standards would be greatly enhanced. China and the Soviet Union are singled out for special study because of the relative scarcity of good materials on their attitudes toward intervention, their importance as actors in the international system, and their at least rhetorical support for some kinds of intervention in aid of "national liberation" or "socialist self-determination." It is recognized that there are other important interventionary actors which might also be usefully subjected to similar study, including most prominently the United States, but also including France, Great Britain, India, and Cuba.[12]

Part V focuses on the role of international institutions in responding to the problems posed by internal conflict and intervention. The capabilities of centralized community procedures for responding to problems of internal conflict is a critical factor in assessing the limits of unilateral interventionary competence. Thus it is particularly important to ground a general theory in realistic assessment of the capabilities and potential of existing international institutions. Chapter 16, by Oscar Schachter, deals with the role of the United Nations. He discusses United Nations aims with respect to internal conflicts, the elements in internal strife regarded by the United Nations as warranting involvement, the political and institutional factors that have influenced United Nations responses, and techniques of exercising United Nations influence. He demonstrates that, if the United Nations does not effectively respond to all crises of civil wars and interventions, it nevertheless exercises substantial influence. It also embodies a useful arsenal of techniques for managing such conflicts when the conditions of the international system permit. Chapter 17, Stephen M. Schwebel's essay on "Wars of Liberation—as Fought in U.N. Organs" traces doctrines of wars of liberation from the Goan incident of 1961 through the latest U.N. draft definition of aggression. He shows that, while U.N. resolutions recognize a right of revolution, they leave unresolved the critical questions of whether third States may lawfully assist or intervene in so-called wars of liberation with force of arms. Chapter 18, by Ellen Frey-Wouters, considers the actual and potential role of regional arrangements, such as the Organization of American States and the Organization of African Unity. In the process, she makes specific suggestions for normative and procedural improvements in the role of regional arrangements in dealing with internal conflicts.

Part VI deals with the international legal regime for the regulation of hostilities or what is increasingly coming to be recognized as a regime of human rights for settings of armed conflict. Improvements in these "laws of war" are urgently needed to make a broad human-rights regime clearly applicable to internal conflicts and third-party interventions, to respond to the special problems presented by modern insurgency and counter-insurgency warfare, and to cope with the inadequacies of the traditional rules, such as the lack of a code of air warfare. In Chapter 18, Howard J. Taubenfeld discusses the origins of the international laws of war and efforts to regulate internal conflicts, and describes the extent to which the laws of war were accepted by the combatants in important cases of internal strife

[12] For a provocative study of United States attitudes toward intervention *see* R. Barnet, *Intervention and Revolution* (1968).

and third party intervention. In Chapter 19, Richard R. Baxter explores the applicability of existing conventions regulating the laws of war to different internal-conflict settings and to proposals for making the laws of war more responsive to internal conflicts and external interventions. A major reform suggested is a protocol on internal conflicts which would deal with the problems of applicability and increasing protection for combatants and non-combatants in internal conflict settings. Through the efforts of Professor Baxter and other experts in the laws of war, a preliminary Conference of Government Experts on the International Humanitarian Law Applicable in Armed Conflicts, held in Geneva during May and June of 1972, has considered the possibility of international agreement on such a protocol. A diplomatic conference to consider this and other improvements in the laws of war is currently scheduled for early 1974, under the auspices of the Swiss Federal Council.

Part VII offers comments by a number of members of the Panel on the Role of International Law in Civil Wars. Commentators were invited to briefly comment on chapters which provoked them (or failed to provoke them), gaps in theory, or specific suggestions for the regulation of civil strife and intervention. Some comments, such as Louis B. Sohn's "Guidelines for States and the United Nations," blaze new trails of their own. Professor Sohn deals creatively with the neglected problem of normative standards for appraising what may be "interventionary" behavior of the United Nations (an analysis largely transferable to multilateral interventions in general). Other comments deal provocatively with a critique of individual chapters and an exchange of views on the best normative basis for the regulation of intervention.

Finally, the volume ends with a selected bibliography on "Intervention and Civil War," prepared by Frederick S. Tipson. Though genuinely selective, the bibliography is the most comprehensive on the subject to date. It brings together writings from a variety of disciplines, organized around a framework intended to facilitate the full range of historical, scientific, and prescriptive tasks.

Throughout the volume, an effort has been made to be future-oriented and to stress the changes in the present international legal system which might usefully make law more relevant to the regulation of revolutionary and interventionary violence. Perspectives of the authors vary widely, from the political scientists concerned with developing predictive models for revolution and intervention to the international lawyers concerned with normative appraisal, and among the lawyers, from those concerned primarily with exegesis of existing norms to those concerned primarily with policy appraisal of alternative standards. There are also significant differences among the legal scholars with respect to techniques of fashioning standards for appraisal, some emphasizing the importance of a few clearcut rules if law is to exercise a restraining effect, and others emphasizing the importance of greater contextual differentiation if intervention norms are to be more policy-responsive. All are united, however, in recognizing the importance of the challenge posed to traditional legal structures by revolutionary and interventionary violence and in believing that the challenge can be met.

Editor and Rapporteur:
John Norton Moore

Members of the Panel:

Wolfgang Friedmann, Chairman
Thomas Ehrlich
Richard A. Falk
Tom J. Farer
Edwin Brown Firmage
G. W. Haight
Eliot D. Hawkins

Brunson MacChesney
Myres S. McDougal
Stephen M. Schwebel
Louis B. Sohn
Howard J. Taubenfeld
Lawrence R. Velvel
Burns H. Weston

PART 1 | A FRAMEWORK

Chapter 1 | Toward an Applied Theory for the Regulation of Intervention | *John Norton Moore*

Since World War II, civil wars and mixed civil-international conflicts have replaced the more conventional international wars as the principal form of violence in the international system. Though the *threat* of large-scale nuclear exchange—or even limited nuclear war—must, in view of the enormous destructive potential of modern nuclear weapons, remain the central world-order concern, the principal *realized* violence has resulted from revolution and intervention in civil and mixed civil-international settings. In this respect, the Indo-China War has simply dramatized an already acute global problem, as evidenced by the conflicts in Greece, Palestine, Korea, the Congo (Zaire), Cyprus, Hungary, Lebanon, Cuba, the Sudan, and the Dominican Republic, among many others. Subsequent events, such as the Nigeria–Biafra and Pakistan–Bangladesh Civil Wars and the conflicts in Ceylon (Sri Lanka), Burundi, and Northern Ireland have quashed any illusion that the problem may be temporary.

With increasing realization of the problem there has been a flood of writing on the causes and conditions of revolutionary violence,[1] the systemic causes of intervention,[2] the interventionary activities of the principal actors,[3] the strategies of revolution and counter-revolution,[4] and the legal aspects of the regulation of intervention.[5] But though these legal, political, and his-

[1] *See, e.g.*, T. Gurr, *Why Men Rebel* (1970); C. Johnson, *Revolutionary Change* (1966); C. Leiden & K. Schmitt, *The Politics of Violence: Revolution in the Modern World* (1968); Gottschalk, "Causes of Revolution," 50 *Am. J. Soc.* 1 (1944); Gurr, "Psychological Factors in Civil Violence," 20 *World Politics* 245 (1967); "The Nature of Revolution," *Hearings Before the Senate Committee on Foreign Relations, 90th Cong. 2d Sess.* (1968).

[2] *See, e.g.*, Young, "Intervention and International Systems," 22 *J. Int'l Affairs* 177 (1968).

[3] *See, e.g.*, R. Barnet, *Intervention and Revolution: The United States in the Third World* (1968). For an analysis of the Barnet thesis, *see* Moore, "The Elephant Misperceived: Intervention and American Foreign Policy," in J. Moore, *Law and the Indo-China War* (1972). *See also* W. Kane, *Civil Strife in Latin America: A Legal History of U.S. Involvement* (1972).

There has also been a flood of good case studies on revolutionary and interventionary violence. *See, e.g.*, I–III R. Falk (ed.), *The Vietnam War and International Law* (1967, 1970, 1972); R. Falk (ed.), *The International Law of Civil War* (1971); I–III J. Moore (ed.), *The Arab-Israeli Conflict* (1974).

[4] *See, e.g.*, R. Debray, *Revolution in the Revolution?* (1967) (revolution); R. Thompson, *Defeating Communist Insurgency* (1966) (counter-revolution).

[5] Some of the principal legal contributions to the regulation of intervention are Burke, "The Legal Regulation of Minor International Coercion: A Framework of Inquiry," in R. Stanger (ed.), *Essays on Intervention* 87 (1967); Falk, "Introduction," in R. Falk (ed.), *The International Law of Civil War* 1 (1971); Falk, "Civil Strife, Intervention and Minor Coercion," in R. Falk, *Legal Order in a Violent World*

torical writings have greatly advanced our knowledge of revolutionary and interventionary violence, characteristically they have focused on only bits and pieces of the overall problem. As a result, though writings to date have laid the groundwork for an applied theory for the regulation of intervention, only the rough outline of such a theory has emerged. Continuing progress requires clear focus on the intellectual prerequisites of an applied theory and the systematic performance of all tasks in decision. In the process, it will become evident that further contributions will be required from all disciplines.

I. THE PREREQUISITES OF AN APPLIED THEORY

The theoretical underpinnings which inform individual approaches to problem-solving or even to recognition of a "problem" have a staggering— though often unperceived—potential for clarification or confusion.[6] In this, the regulation of intervention is no exception. At least seven common misperceptions have militated against an adequate applied theory. They are:

1. Confusion between international-legal, national-political, and strategic perspectives for the appraisal of intervention;

2. Inadequate focus on the full range of intellectual tasks in decision, particularly the need for normative clarification;

3. Terminological confusion;

4. Oversimplification of process needs, particularly the need for certainty, in the selection of standards for decision;

5. Exaggeration of the effects of decentralized decision in the international system;

6. Inadequate focus on the interrelation between normative standards for the regulation of intervention and the broader framework for regulation of major coercion;

7. Inadequate focus on appraisal of the conduct and settlement of revolutionary and interventionary hostilities and a corresponding overemphasis on appraisal of the initiation of coercion.

97–368 (1968); Farer, "Harnessing Rogue Elephants: A Short Discourse on Foreign Intervention in Civil Strife," 82 *Harv. L. Rev.* 511 (1969); Farer, "Intervention in Civil Wars: A Modest Proposal," 67 *Colum. L. Rev.* 266 (1967); Firmage, "Summary and Interpretation," in R. Falk (ed.), *The International Law of Civil War* 405 (1971); Friedmann, "Intervention and International Law I," in L. Jaquet (ed.), *Intervention in International Politics* 40 (1971); Friedmann, "Intervention, Civil War and the Role of International Law," 1965 *Proc. Am. Soc'y Int'l L.* 67; Higgins, "Internal War and International Law," in III C. Black & R. Falk (eds.) *The Future of the International Legal Order* 81 (1971); Moore, "The Control of Foreign Intervention in Internal Conflict," 9 *Va. J. Int'l L.* 205 (1969).

Several classics which also consider legal aspects of the control of intervention are L. Miller, *World Order and Local Disorder: The United Nations and Internal Conflicts* (1967); J. Rosenau (ed.), *International Aspects of Civil Strife* (1964); R. Stanger (ed.), *Essays on Intervention* (1964).

  [6] *See generally* A. Kaplan, *The Conduct of Inquiry* (1964).

The first three misperceptions cripple development of an adequate applied theory and they strike legal theorists, historians, and political scientists alike. The last four concern principally the development of normative standards for international legal appraisal—though political scientists and international relations theorists who venture into the area succumb to these misperceptions as readily as the legal theorists who dwell there.

The first need of an applied theory is to achieve clear focus on the variety of perspectives relevant to the appraisal of interventionary action. The principal perspectives and their central concerns are:

> *International-legal*: When is intervention consistent with the common interest of the global community?
>
> *National-political*: When is intervention which is consistent with the global common interest (or perhaps even inconsistent with the global common interest—taking into account the feedback cost of such inconsistency) also consistent with the national interest (or the interest of an intervening international organization)?
>
> *Strategic*: When is intervention likely to be successful in achieving the goals set for the action?

All three perspectives are indispensable in assessing interventionary action. By the nature of his discipline, the international lawyer is principally concerned with the first perspective. That concern, however, should not be taken as an effort to dictate conclusions on or minimize the importance of the second two perspectives—though an international legal theory will also have relevance for national-political and strategic perspectives. Conversely, international lawyers should not be timid in pointing out the importance of an international-legal perspective and in urging that such a perspective be taken into account by national decision makers. Unless foreign policy is to be purely short-term or based on a complete monopoly of power, it must take account of the global common interest. In fact, even if foreign policy were implemented with a complete monopoly of power, we would still want national goals to be informed by moral or "normative" considerations. An international-legal perspective, which focuses on global common interest, is highly relevant to such normative appraisal.[7]

Second, an adequate applied theory must focus on normative clarification as well as on each of the other tasks in decision. Much of the contemporary international relations writing (at least by the "behavioral" wing or "new frontiersmen") focuses on the development of formal theories for prediction, and though aware of the role of values, it eschews normative analysis. The "traditionalist" wing of international relations theory focuses

---

[7] *See* Falk, "Law, Lawyers, and the Conduct of American Foreign Relations," 78 *Yale L. J.* 919 (1969); Moore, "The Role of Law in the Management of International Conflict," in J. Moore, *Law and the Indo-China War* (1972); Moore, "Law and National Security," 51 *Foreign Affairs* 408 (Jan. 1973).

equally narrowly on the description of trends and is only recently developing an adequate awareness of the role of values. A recent influential reader
on research and theory in international politics illustrates this empirical
emphasis of the international relations theorists. In the preface, Professor
James N. Rosenau, himself a "new frontiersman," writes:

> One other criterion of selection [for articles included in the reader]
> needs to be mentioned: aside from the introductory articles presented in
> Part One, each selection had to be ultimately susceptible to empirical veri-
> fication. No materials have been included that analyze the desirability of a
> particular course of action or that espouse the superiority of one set of
> policy goals over another. This is a book that seeks to explore the way
> international politics and foreign policy are or may be. It does not attempt
> to probe the way they ought to be. There is a place, to be sure, for norma-
> tive theory in the study of world politics. One is a citizen as well as a
> student, so that questions of policy and morality can never be avoided.
> Yet, in the belief that the student will perform best as a citizen if the
> distinction between the two roles is clear, this volume is intended for the
> former and not the latter. It is assumed that a greater comprehension of
> why international politics and foreign policy unfold as they do will facilitate
> actions designed to influence how they ought to unfold. We live in troubled
> times, but this fact obligates us to apply our intelligence as well as our good
> will. The individual who feels that the world's problems are too urgent to
> allow for the pursuit of greater comprehension is likely to be neither a
> good student nor an effective citizen.[8]

Similarly, Professor Stanley Hoffmann, writing from an historical-systems
approach, is equally wary of normative analysis:

> Some theoreticians (particularly those concerned with strategy, but also
> some writing on international law or integration) raise the cardinal issue of
> the relation between empirical theory and the so-called policy sciences.
> Research oriented to action requires both an analysis of reality and a
> definite choice of values. Unfortunately, these values are not always made
> as explicit as they should be. The theory may be based on the postulate
> that men should act according to the author's own ideals, or that the for-
> eign policy of the nation for which he writes should adopt as its goal the
> achievement of these ideals—whether the maximization of power according
> to the criterion of greatest efficiency, or the growing integration of the
> Atlantic Community. If, on the other hand, the values are made explicit,
> the orientation of the study raises another problem: were the Author to
> adopt the Prince's values and goals, he would become a professional apolo-
> gist and an official propagandist; were he to start by defining his own values
> but subsequently shift to the study of how they could be achieved by his
> country's leaders and institutions, he might stumble into an even more
> dangerous nationalist perversion, trying to prove that the measures taken

---

[8] Rosenau, "Preface," in J. Rosenau (ed.), *International Politics and Foreign
Policy: A Reader in Research and Theory* xix (Rev. ed. 1969).

by the Prince actually do serve those values or that the triumph of those values would serve the national interest.[9]

And elsewhere he says:

> To advise the Prince presupposes adequate empirical knowledge and a discussion of values. "Policy scientists" tend to skip over the latter and to be premature about the former.[10]

A recent article by Professor Oran R. Young published in the *American Journal of International Law* illustrates, in the course of a direct attack on the principal contemporary policy-oriented approach of Professors Myres S. McDougal and Harold Lasswell, the same pervasive skepticism for policy-oriented theory and a preference for formal predictive theory.[11] Professors Rosenau, Hoffmann, and Young are among the intellectual leaders in international-relations theory and they are properly reacting against the fuzzy blending of unarticulated preferences and anecdotal comparisons which for too long have dominated the writing on international-politics and foreign policy. Moreover, the dangers which they describe in dealing with values are in large measure real. More significant, however, is the danger which they do not describe in eschewing normative clarification. If the *use* of empirical theory inescapably requires linkage with values, how is such linkage to be provided in the absence of a theory which takes account both of values and empirical data? Failure to deal with the normative component of decision is to doom empirical research and formal predictive theory to only anecdotal relevance. Fortunately, we need not choose among the intellectual tasks in decision—all are equally indispensable for an applied theory. These include:

1. Clarification of values [the normative task];

2. Description of past trends [the historical or descriptive task];

3. Analysis of conditioning factors and prediction of future trends [the scientific task];

4. Invention and evaluation of policy alternatives which will maximize preferred values [the policy task].

To be most useful, then, theory *must* encourage clarification of values and formulation of policy as well as the historical and scientific tasks emphasized by contemporary international-relations theorists. It matters little whether

[9] Hoffmann, "Theory and International Relations," in J. Rosenau (ed.), *supra* note 8, at 30, 34.

[10] *Id.* at 37.

[11] Young, "International Law and Social Science: The Contributions of Myres S. McDougal," 66 *Am. J. Int'l L.* 60 (1972). For a more than adequate response *see* McDougal, "International Law and Social Science: A Mild Plea in Avoidance," 66 *Am. J. Int'l L.* 77 (1972).

such a theory is referred to as policy-oriented or as a theory of applied knowledge.

What is helpful for the international-relations theorists concerned with an applied theory, is indispensable for the international-legal theorist. For legal norms exist to guide behavior, and as such they are inescapably normative. Too often, however, legal scholars also focus only on the description of existing legal norms (or more narrowly on analytic exegesis of verbal formulas without reference to community expectations of authority and control). Again, this is not to suggest that the only tasks to be performed by the legal scholars are those of value clarification and policy recommendation. It is certainly highly relevant to describe the existing law. A complete legal theory, however, must relate to all intellectual tasks in decision.[12] Moreover, there is nothing novel or particularly urgent about a restatement of the existing law of non-intervention. Existing certainties and ambiguities in the law are well known and have been repeatedly described.[13] The challenge to the legal theorist is to recommend criteria which *ought* to be adopted as the legal standard for differentiating permissible and impermissible intervention. There is a developing consensus among legal scholars that formulation of adequate criteria will require the following steps:

> 1.   Clarification of the values at stake in the decision to intervene (or to refrain from intervention) by reference to global common interest—not just in vague general terms, but as specifically as possible and with reasons rooted in social consequences;
>
> 2.   Contextual differentiation of claims to intervene—and to conduct and terminate hostilities—by reference to circumstances in which common policies and conditioning factors can be subjected to unitary normative appraisal;
>
> 3.   The development of criteria for appraisal of each category of circumstances that will operationalize efforts to realize the values at stake;
>
> 4.   Continuing retesting and refining of original value choices, contextual differentiations, and criteria for appraisal by reference to empirical data as to the effects on the social process of decisions to intervene or refrain from intervention (and, in the absence of "hard" empirical data, by reference to plausible criticism).

Recognition of the need and importance of adequate normative criteria should not detract from the invention and evaluation of other policy recommendations for realizing preferred values. For example, it is at least as important to strengthen the capability of international institutions to deal with interventionary problems as to develop normative criteria for permissible and impermissible intervention.[14]

[12] *See generally*, Cowan, "Decision Theory in Law, Science, Technology," 17 *Rutgers L. Rev.* 499 (1963); Mayo & Jones, "Legal-Policy Decision Process: Alternative Thinking and the Predictive Function," 33 *Geo. Wash. L. Rev.* 318 (1964).

[13] *See* authorities cited note 5 *supra*.

[14] For a few of the possibilities *see* Moore, *supra* note 5, at 294–314.

A third requirement for an adequate applied theory is to avoid the trap presented by the prevailing terminological confusion. There are at leas four different senses in which the term "intervention" is used in discourse about international relations:

1.   As a synonym for transnational interaction or influence;

2.   As a statement that a particular transnational interaction violates community expectations about permissible international conduct;

3.   As a personal policy judgment that a particular transnational interaction is wrong; and

4.   In one or another specialized sense, as a definition of a problem for study.

Since at least two of these four senses (2 and 3) are highly value-charged, the use of the term "intervention" will inevitably have normative overtones suggesting "wrong" action. Thus to shift between these normative and non-normative meanings can be a potent source for sometimes highly emotional confusion. Moreover, despite these normative overtones, there is an ambivalence common to all national theories of intervention—Soviet, Chinese, American, and other—that some intervention (in the sense of transnational interaction) is justifiable or desirable. The remedy for terminological confusion is to make clear the sense in which the term is being used, to recognize that the principal challenge for the international-legal theorist is to provide standards for separating permissible from impermissible interactions, and to differentiate descriptions of community expectations from personal policy recommendations. It might also be noted that the terminological confusion is largely a reflection of the failure to focus on all of the intellectual tasks in formulating a general theory. That is, senses 1 and 2 are usually employed in performing the historical or descriptive task, sense 3 relates to the value and policy tasks, and sense 4 to the scientific task—though there is some overlap.[15]

A fourth requirement for an applied theory is an understanding of process needs in the selection of standards for decision. A principal "process" need, that is, a need relating to the efficacy of different techniques for articulating criteria for decision, is the need for balance between certainty and predictability on the one hand and policy-responsiveness on the other. This tension between the need for certainty and predictability and the need for policy-responsiveness (that is, between a few definite but necessarily less contextually responsive standards and a greater number of standards sufficiently contextually differentiated as to maximize the values at stake but to increase the difficulty in application) runs through all law. It is particularly acute, however, in a decentralized system, lacking authoritative third-party judgment where the political pressures for non-compliance may

[15] For a discussion of the terminological confusion and each of the four principal senses in which the term "intervention" is used *see* Moore *supra* note 5, at 212–17.

be severe. As such, there is a tendency for international legal writers to overemphasize the need for certainty at the expense of policy-responsiveness. One factor which tends to be neglected in such emphasis is the linkage which the legal realists convincingly demonstrated between a lack of policy responsiveness and a lack of certainty and predictability. Brainerd Currie and other legal scholars have established that, when a standard becomes too non-policy-responsive, decision-makers will simply not apply it, and instead will invoke the host of complimentary principles available in any legal system.[16] Reasonable policy-responsiveness, then, is in the real world a prerequisite for certainty and predictability.

A related issue is whether standards should be phrased in the form of definite rules or whether guidance should be provided by a more open-ended contextual map which seeks to encourage the direct appraisal of the impact of decision on the values at stake without mediation through specific rules. Since rules are necessarily of the "more often than not the values at stake will be promoted by following this rule" variety, an open-ended, completely contextual approach should be more policy-responsive than specific rules—at least if the variety of factual settings is large. Nevertheless, such an approach probably does offer greater ease of manipulation and as a result may lose normative force—at least in the hands of decision-makers unaccustomed to a configurative approach. Professor Richard A. Falk has posed the dilemma starkly:

> In conceiving of the relevance of international law to civil-war situations, it is important to avoid the twin pitfalls of rule-oriented legalism and policy-oriented reductionism. Rule-oriented legalism tends to associate the task of law with the formulation of system-wide categorical rules, perhaps drawn up in a single legal document or convention; such a collection of rules either incorporates contradictory policy objectives or ignores them. In either eventuality, it tends to be irrelevant as a source of specific guidance for governments called upon to act. Policy-oriented reductionism keeps the context "open," specifies a wide number of variable considerations, and calls upon the decisionmakers to act in behalf of world order; the choice of action is left indeterminate, no fixed guidelines are hazarded, and the only imperative is the rhetorical one that a government explain its policy preferences by reference to world-community values. I am proposing an approach intermediate between legalism and reductionism through the identification of critical thresholds, the advocacy of frameworks of guidance, and the emphasis on obligations to provide a public accounting of action undertaken.[17]

[16] See B. Currie, *Selected Essays on the Conflict of Laws* (1963). Currie was awarded the first Order of the Coif Award for Outstanding Legal Scholarship, for his writings demonstrating that a flexible "governmental interest analysis" approach was preferable to a more rigid rule-oriented approach to choice of law problems. For a colorful demonstration of the same point by one of the real giants of legal realism *see* Cohen, "Dialogue on Private Property," 9 *Rutgers L. Rev.* 357, 367 (1954).

[17] Falk, "Introduction," in R. Falk (ed.), *supra* note 5, at 28. *See also* Moore, *supra* note 5, at 253–54, 325.

Though Professor Falk poses the issue starkly, he presents only a caricature of the choices. It is not inevitable that a rule approach will either "incorporate contradictory policy objectives or ignore them." Such an approach may well embody a deliberate choice among contradictory policy objectives. Rather the real issue with a rule approach is whether the contexts to be regulated are sufficiently identified to be the subject of an appropriate number of policy-responsive rules. Similarly, configurative approaches need not display the degree of policy vagueness which Professor Falk ascribes to them.[18] In any event, scholars concerned with guiding decision must provide some criteria for decision, and it is not clear how Professor Falk's recommendation either does so or, if it does, how it differs from the approaches which he decries.[19] In reality, of course, the choice is not either/or. The characteristics of possible standards might be represented on a continuum as:

> *Contextual: Type I* [no rule but clarification of values which are applied directly to different contexts with or without identification of critical contextual features which tend to be usefully policy-responsive]

> *Contextual: Type II* [no rule but identification of critical contextual features or thresholds which may often be policy-responsive]

> *Configurative* [no rule of decision but clarification of basic values at stake and formulation of many rules for guiding decision-makers to features of context which may affect those values and for appraising those features in terms of their significance for the values at stake]

> *Multiple rule* [multiple rules in if x then y form where x represents a policy-responsive feature or features of the real world and y represents a legal consequence]

> *Single rule* [a single rule in if x then y form where x represents a policy-responsive feature or features of the real world and y represents a legal consequence]

There is nothing inconsistent between a policy-oriented approach and selection of any of the above techniques for providing guidance for decision. Indeed, all approaches must at some point be based on clarified values and their relationship to context. The choice of one or another approach will

---

[18] For one thing, the values at stake can be clarified far more precisely than simply referring to "world-community values." A major tenet of a configurative approach is to specify the values at stake with as much specificity as possible. Though observers are free to reject the expressed value preferences, if the values are accepted, an observer should be able to assess the impact of decision with as much reliability as the state of knowledge about the world will permit. Needless to say, rule approaches also suffer from value disagreements and inadequate knowledge about the real world. In a rule approach, however, the value disagreements and lack of knowledge become critical in formulating the rule rather than in assessing compliance.

[19] The emphasis on the obligation "to provide a public accounting of action undertaken" is an important contribution.

depend on the number of claims raising common problems and conditioning factors which are part of the "problem" for regulation, and the degree to which the "problem" and policy-responsive contextual features are sufficiently clarified to place confidence in the policy-responsiveness of the more specific formulas. With respect to a general theory for the regulation of intervention, it seems clear that a single rule approach is not the answer. More than one major claim has been identified: for example claims to take unilateral action for the protection of human rights, claims to counter-intervene to offset impermissible assistance to insurgents, and claims to take multilateral or regional action for a variety of objectives, etc.[20] Though conclusions at this stage must be necessarily tentative, a combination of multiple rule and contextual approaches—with a configurative approach as a back up—probably will be most effective in achieving the required balance between policy-responsiveness and certainty.

A fifth requirement for an adequate applied theory is to avoid the unrealistic despair associated with exaggerated emphasis on the lack of authoritative third-party judgment in the international system and the related normative relativism sometimes associated with the realization that there are contending world-order systems. The international constitutive process is less centralized and far more diffuse than its counterpart domestic constitutive processes. In this more diffuse process, national decision-makers simultaneously serve as claimants and international decision-makers. Nevertheless, national claims are accepted and rejected by the international system, and it is a mistake to despair of the utility of normative standards for appraisal simply because the process for evaluation of claims is diffuse. It is the task of international-legal scholars to encourage appraisal of national claims rather than to shrink from evaluation. Similarly, the recognition that contending political systems assert different values or policies need not be paralyzing. Again, the task of the international-legal scholar is to identify and reinforce community common interest and to reject special interest: in this determination the scholar must take his stand—though doing so candidly for appraisal by others.

A sixth requirement is to relate normative standards for the regulation of intervention with the broader framework for regulation of major coercion.[21] Intervention claims are merely subsets of a broader problem in regulation of coercion in general, a problem which doctrinally includes individual and collective defense, reprisals, protection of nationals, and a host of other claims to employ coercion. As such, normative standards for the regulation of intervention should be compatible with the broader theory for the regulation of coercion in general. If the task is one of describing the law, then surely conclusions concerning the permissibility of particular types of intervention should be related to the structure of the United Nations

---

[20] *See* Moore, *supra* note 5, at 217–19, 254–59.

[21] For an overview of the framework for regulation of major coercion *see* M. McDougal & F. Feliciano, *Law and Minimum World Public Order* (1961).

Charter which constitutes the principal community norm, and to regional and other community norms concerning use of coercion. And if the task is one of recommending a general theory for the regulation of intervention, then resulting recommendations should be compatible with recommendations for the control of coercion in general. Because of the multiplicity and complexity of claims concerning the use of coercion, to date the most useful general theories for differentiation of permissible from impermissible coercion have been the configurative rather than the rule-oriented theories.[22]

Since many of the issues presented in the regulation of interventionary coercion are the same as those presented in the regulation of coercion in general, it may be useful to briefly review a configurative map of the principal features of the process of coercion. For convenience, the process of coercion will be described by reference to a conceptual map of the *participants* interacting in the process, the *perspectives* or identifications, demands and expectations of the participants, the *arenas* in which the participants interact, the *base values* available to the participants for use in achieving their scope values, the *strategies* employed by the participants, the *outcomes* of the process, and the longer-run *effects* for value accumulation and distribution in the broader social process.[23]

FEATURES OF PROCESS OF COERCION OF RECURRING RELEVANCE
FOR NORMATIVE APPRAISAL

FEATURES OF THE PROCESS OF COERCION	GENERALIZED NORMATIVE CONSEQUENCES OF SUCH FEATURES
Participants	
Is coercion unilateral or multilateral (regional-global, institutionalized-noninstitutionalized)?	Wider participation diminishes the likelihood that claims will promote special interests at the expense of community common interest.
Is coercion domestic or international? [claims concerning the scope of the territorial entity for purposes of applying conflict management norms, *i.e.*, the status of cease-fire lines and de facto divided states, etc.]	Minimization of international violence suggests that de facto separate units should be subject to the same conflict management norms as fully de jure states.
May participants act jointly in collective defense? [claims concerning the scope of collective defense]	Prefer claims which confine the scope of violence while permitting effective defense of threatened values.

[22] I would particularly single out the approach of Myres S. McDougal and Florentino P. Feliciano as the most useful to date for delimiting permissible from impermissible coercion. *See* M. McDougal & F. Feliciano, *supra* note 21.

[23] For an explanation of this "phase analysis" technique for the systematic description of context *see* Moore, "Prolegomenon to the Jurisprudence of Myres McDougal and Harold Lasswell," 54 *Va. L. Rev.* 662 (1968).

FEATURES OF THE PROCESS
OF COERCION

GENERALIZED NORMATIVE
CONSEQUENCES OF SUCH
FEATURES

Perspectives

Is coercion used for value extension or value conservation? [the classic problem of peace versus "justice" —"justice," of course, may be on the side of either conservation or extension—the problem is whether extension by force will be prohibited even when it would serve "justice"]*

This feature presents a central tension in the evolution of conflict management norms from just war theories to the UN Charter. The Charter embodies the judgment that unilateral force may not be used for value extension but only in defense of major values. This judgment was not accepted in the "just war" period and is again being challenged in the contemporary international system, particularly with respect to the use of force to promote self-determination and human rights.

Arenas

Is it ever permissible to attack first? [the problem of anticipatory defense]

This feature is useful for suggesting objectives of the contending belligerents but otherwise should not be decisive. An example of a case where this feature is not and should not be decisive is the Six Day War.

When, if ever, is it permissible to expand the locus of conflict to third states? [involvement of neutrals and claims concerning response against the territory of an attacking or assisting state]

Prefer claims which confine the geographic scope of violence while permitting effective defense of threatened values.

Base Values

What level of consequentiality of values may be protected by intense responding coercion?

Permit responding coercion only when required for the protection of major values such as territorial or political integrity—this is one of the senses in which the classic test of proportionality is used.

Strategies

What degree of immediacy of the coercive threat is required before justifying a coercive response? To what extent must alternative strategies for peaceful resolution or multi-

Permit unilateral responding coercion only when immediate resort to coercion is required for the effective defense of threatened values—this embodies several of the

FEATURES OF THE PROCESS
OF COERCION

GENERALIZED NORMATIVE
CONSEQUENCES OF SUCH
FEATURES

lateral response be pursued or unavailable prior to permitting a unilateral coercive response?

Is the degree of coercion employed greater than that necessary for effective conservation of values? [a feature also highly relevant to assessment of the *conduct* of hostilities]

Is coercion overt or covert, *i.e.*, does it constitute direct or indirect aggression? [Doctrinally, this question asks what constitutes an armed attack. More usefully, it asks what scope and intensity of coercion permits coercive response]

Outcomes

Does responding coercion threaten destruction of values disproportionate to the values initially threatened?

To what extent must the contending belligerents be willing to accept community procedures for peaceful settlement of hostilities?

May resources or territory obtained by coercion be retained? [claims concerning the legal effects of duress and the non-recognition of territorial gains obtained by the use of force]

senses in which the classic test of necessity is used.

Permit only minimum force reasonably necessary for the effective defense of values threatened—this is another of the senses in which the classic test of proportionality is applied and might be termed the principal of economy in coercion.

Permit responsive coercion to the extent necessary for the effective defense of threatened values.

Responding coercion should not threaten destruction of values disproportionate to the values initially threatened—this is a third sense in which proportionality is used. The first sense is actually a corollary of this third sense.

Rejection of community procedures for peaceful settlement is highly relevant both in assessing objectives in the use of coercion and in assessing responsibility for the continuation of coercion.

Permit retention of values obtained through coercion only as necessary for effective defense of threatened values.

---

* The factual determination of the answer to this question may in a particular context be the decisive issue for appraisal. If so, the answer should be sought by systematic appraisal of all of the features of the process of coercion. For that purpose the following subset of contextual features should be examined:

Participants—
Is the action unilateral or multilateral?

This conceptual map provides, of course, only the roughest of outlines of a wide variety of claims concerning every feature of the process of coercion.[24] Problems raised by the regulation of intervention will present many of these general claims as well as the specialized claims unique to intervention problems. Resolution of the host of common issues can most usefully proceed by reference to the more general theory.

A seventh requirement is recognition of the importance of appraising the conduct and settlement as well as the initiation of civil and mixed civil-international hostilities. The principal focus of traditional international-legal analysis of intervention has been the appraisal of the permissibility of the initial resort to coercion. This concern has been expanded over the last few years to cover also the conduct of hostilities in civil and civil-international settings.[25] To date there has been little attention given to development of a framework for assessing the obligation to pursue negotiated settlement

---

Perspectives—
What are the objectives of the participants through time *i.e.*, pre-conflict, conflict, and post-conflict phases as determined by verbal and non-verbal indicators?

Arenas—
Where is the fighting taking place?
Which side attacked first?

Base values—
What is the relative size and strength of the contending belligerents including the formal and informal aliiance systems of the contending sides: *i.e.*, Goa is unlikely to attack India, Tibet is unlikely to attack China.
What is the consequentiality of the values threatened?

Strategies—
Is responding coercion necessary and proportional?

Outcomes—
Is the immediate effect of the action value extension or value conservation? If value extension, is it necessary for effective value conservation?
What is the relative willingness of the contending belligerents to accept community procedures for peaceful settlement of disputes?

Effects—
Is the long run effect value extension or value conservation?

[24] *See generally* D. Bowett, *Self-Defence in International Law* (1958); M. McDougal & F. Feliciano, *supra* note 21; J. Stone, *Aggression and World Order* (1958).

[25] Illustrative of the expanded concern are D. Bindschedler-Robert, *A Reconsideration of the Law of Armed Conflicts* (Carnegie Endowment for International Peace 1971). T. Farer, "The Laws of War 25 Years After Nuremberg," *Int'l Conciliation* No. 583 (May 1971); R. Littauer & N. Uphoff (eds.), *The Air War in Indochina* (Rev. ed. 1971); Bond, "Protection of Non-Combatants in Guerrilla Wars," 12 *William & Mary L. Rev.* 787 (1971); De Saussure, "The Laws of Air Warfare: Are There Any?" 23 *Naval War College Review* 35 (1971); Farer, "Humanitarian Law and Armed Conflicts: Toward the Definition of International Armed Conflict," 71 *Col. L. Rev.* 37 (1971); Levie, "Civilian Sanctionaries—An Impractical Proposal," in I *Israel Yearbook On Human Rights* 335 (1971); O'Brien, "The Law of War, Command Responsibility and Vietnam," 60 *Geo. L. J.* 605 (1972); Paust, "After My Lai: The Case for War Crime Jurisdiction Over Civilians in Federal District Courts," 50 *Texas L. Rev.* 6 (1971); Rubin, "Legal Aspects of the My Lai Incident," 49 *Oregon L. Rev.* 260 (1970).

of hostilities or, stated another way, for assessing the responsibility for continued hostilities.[26] Yet it is becoming increasingly clear that an adequate theory of normative assessment of coercion must be rooted in all three strands and must proceed through time. Such a theory might be graphically represented as follows:

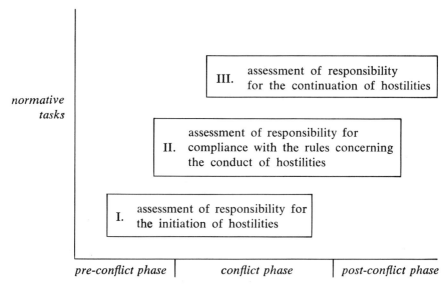

Though each strand calls for detailed criteria for appraisal, the fundamental tenets of each can be summarized in general terms as:

I. Assessment of responsibility for the *initiation of hostilities*—the basic principle is that force should not be used in the international system as a basis of value extension but is permitted only when necessary and proportional to the defense of major values;

II. Assessment of responsibility for compliance with the rules concerning the *conduct of hostilities*—the basic principles are that force should not be used which exceeds that reasonably necessary to defend threatened values (economy in coercion), that non-combatants as such are not permissible targets and that accordingly strategies and weapons employed should differentiate between combatants and non-combatants to the extent possible, and that strategies and weapons employed should not cause unnecessary suffering even among combatants (economy in coercion);

---

[26] *See* Moore, "The Arab-Israeli Conflict and the Obligation to Pursue Peaceful Settlement of International Disputes," 19 *Kansas L. Rev.* 403, 404–7 (1971).

III. Assessment of responsibility for the *continuation of hostilities*—the basic principles are that belligerents should be willing to negotiate in good faith and to terminate conflict on the basis of fundamental Charter norms concerning minimization of violence, self-determination, and human rights.

II. THE APPLICATION OF THEORY:
IN SEARCH OF POLICIES FOR VALUE REALIZATION

Avoidance of the intellectual cobwebs which strew the path to an applied theory is a necessary but, sadly, not a sufficient condition for the development of an adequate theory. Development of such a theory requires the systematic performance of all tasks in decision; the normative, historical, scientific and policy tasks. It would be impossible in a brief introductory chapter to adequately review the good recent literature concerned with each of these tasks. Rather than attempt it, the material which follows will focus on the final policy task, which is the principal concern of applied theory, and will first discuss standards for normative appraisal and then, more briefly, further policies for value realization.

(A) STANDARDS FOR NORMATIVE APPRAISAL

One promising policy for the regulation of intervention is the further refinement of standards for normative appraisal of revolutionary and interventionary violence. This might be termed "international-legal policies for regulation," though in doing so, it should be kept in mind that other disciplines may also share similar concerns. Until some such criteria are provided for determining impermissible or "undesirable" interventions, it will be difficult to develop other policies for controlling intervention. The development of standards for normative appraisal requires clarification of the values at stake, contextual differentiation of interventionary situations and claims made by states concerning such situations, the recommendation of criteria for appraisal of each significant category, and continuing reappraisal of the recommended criteria.

Clarification of Values

Traditional approaches to non-intervention have viewed the protection of national sovereignty as the fundamental underpinning for non-intervention. As a result, such approaches have tended to emphasize invitation by a faction formally recognized as representing the sovereignty of the state. Newer approaches have tended to reject both the value underpinning of the traditional approach and its social consequences, which are seen as creating a Maginot Line for the status quo. In place of the traditional emphasis on sovereignty, there is a developing consensus that the values at stake in interventionary settings should be related to social consequences rather than to outmoded formal criteria, and that there are three principal values at stake in the decision to initiate intervention:

1. The maintenance of world order and the minimization of destructive violence;
2. Self-determination of peoples; and
3. The maintenance of basic human rights.

To this list, a few scholars would add:

4. Promotion of modernization.

Elsewhere I have sought to develop each of these basic community values, and there seems little point in repeating it.[27] It is becoming increasingly evident, however, that much of the disagreement about intervention stems from two sets of value problems. They are, first, uncertainties surrounding the range of claims to self-determination and the merits of each and, second, uncertainties concerning choices among the values at stake, particularly choices between minimization of destructive violence and self-determination of peoples.

In an age in which self-determination has become a slogan of widely disparate political philosophies, it is imperative that its multiple referents be clarified and subjected to appraisal. For purposes of intervention theory, the principal types of self-determination situations (really group-determination or affiliation claims) seem to be as follows: ·

> *Type I*: the control by one nation of another nation's governmental structure or resources. Situations in this category are usually spoken of as colonialism or, in the case of loose control of governmental structures or control of resources other than governmental structures, neo-colonialism. A paradigm example is the Congo (Zaire) prior to independence;

> *Type II*: a society which prevents a particular group within the society from sharing in authority structures or other value institutions of the society. A paradigm example is the system of apartheid in South Africa;

> *Type III*: a people or nation which seeks unification with another nation or peoples of similar ethnic, linguistic, or religious affiliation. A paradigm example would be North Korean claims for unification with South Korea. Some border conflicts may raise similar claims. Jewish claims for the establishment of a Jewish State of Israel are an example of the claim as initially asserted by a people without a nation;

> *Type IV*: an ethnic, religious, or other group within one or more societies that seeks to establish a separate national identity. Paradigm examples are the Bangladesh-Pakistan Civil War and the Nigeria-Biafra Civil War; and

> *Type V*: demands for a particular type of political organization, "socialist," "democratic," or other. A paradigm example is Cuban support for

---

[27] *See* Moore, *supra* note 5, at 246–53.

wars of national liberation in Latin America for the purpose of establishing "socialist" regimes.[28]

In general, self-determination claims receive correspondingly greater international support as one moves from Type V to Type I. There is particularly strong community support for Type I and II self-determination claims and, in fact, as United Nations actions with respect to anti-colonialism and apartheid indicate, there is at least a quasi-acceptance of forceful international assistance for the purpose of achieving self-determination in Type I and II settings despite the general Charter principle of non-use of force in international relations as a modality of value extension. On the other hand, though individual actors may from time to time espouse the use of force to alter a particular form of political organization in neighboring countries (Type V), the claim is generally rejected by the international community. One factor which seems operative in assessing the community response to self-determination claims is the number of states (or their elites) which identify either with the claimants or with the targets. For example, since many African states view themselves as potential targets of Type IV secession claims, they are particularly unsympathetic to such claims. Community attitudes toward self-determination can in some measure be expected to be reflected in community attitudes toward intervention.[29] Thus, as self-determination theory is clarified, non-intervention norms should also become sharper.

A second set of value problems responsible for significant disagreement about intervention is the relationship among the values at stake where they may be competing. In determining the permissibility of unilateral humanitarian intervention for the prevention of gross abuse of human rights, do the dangers posed to self-determination and the maintenance of world order by permitting "humanitarian intervention" outweigh the dangers to human rights by not permitting it? Similarly, should intervention to promote Type I or II self-determination claims be permitted, or does the danger posed to self-determination by self-serving utilization of such an exception plus the risk to the maintenance of world order militate against any such right? These value clashes reflect what is perhaps the central dilemma in intervention theory in the contemporary international system and probably go fur-

---

[28] See generally H. Johnson, Self-Determination Within the Community of Nations (1967); T. Mensah, Self-Determination Under United Nations' Auspices (unpublished J.S.D. dissertation in the Yale Law Library); Emerson, "Self-Determination," 65 Am. J. Int'l L. 459 (1971); Nanda, "Self-Determination in International Law: The Tragic Tale of Two Cities—Islamabad (West Pakistan) and Dacca (East Pakistan)," 66 Am. J. Int'l L. 321 (1972).

[29] The interrelation between the principles of non-intervention and self-determination is readily apparent in the work of the Special Committee on Principles of International Law Concerning Friendly Relations and Co-operation among States in Accordance with the Charter of the United Nations. See Rosenstock, "The Declaration of Principles of International Law Concerning Friendly Relations: A Survey," 65 Am. J. Int'l L. 713 (1971).

ther than any other reason to explain the frequent ambivalence about intervention. In dealing with this problem, it is sometimes possible to narrow what appears to be a value clash by reliance on careful criteria for reducing the risk to other values at stake.

Values at stake in decisions concerning the conduct and settlement of interventionary hostilities are essentially those at stake in any resort to coercion. Interventionary contexts, however, may place greater or lesser pressure on realization of those values than other forms of violence and for this reason require specialized regimes for the conduct and settlement of hostilities.

Contextual Differentiation of Types of Intervention

The second step in the development of standards for the appraisal of intervention is contextual differentiation of similar types of intervention. To be most useful, such differentiation should group situations which are affected by common conditioning factors and raise common policies. Several years ago I suggested the following breakdown of intervention claims:

> Type I Situations—claims not relating to authority structures;
>
> Type II Situations—claims relating to anti-colonial wars;
>
> Type III Situations—claims relating to wars of secession;
>
> Type IV Situations—claims relating to indigenous conflict for the control of internal authority structures;
>
> Type V Situations—claims relating to external initiation of the use of force for the imposition of internal authority structures;
>
> Type VI Situations—claims relating to cold-war divided nation conflicts.[30]

In an analogous recommendation Richard Falk has suggested a five-category breakdown:

> 1. Standard civil war—an internal struggle to gain control of a particular state;
>
> 2. War of hegemony—external coercion to maintain minimum conditions of external hegemony;
>
> 3. War of autonomy—conflict for autonomy from external rule;
>
> 4. War of separation (or subnational autonomy)—conflict for political secession and the establishment of a new state;
>
> 5. War of reunion—conflict for political merger (the opposite of the war of separation).[31]

In view of the conflict in Northern Ireland and the Pakistan–Bangladesh–India War my earlier category I (claims not relating to authority structures) and category VI (claims relating to cold-war divided nation conflicts)

---

[30] Moore, *supra* note 5, at 256–58.
[31] *See* Falk, "Introduction," in R. Falk (ed.), *supra* note 5, at 18–19.

would seem more useful if reformulated. The Indian intervention in Bangladesh had overtones of a humanitarian intervention, yet it was strongly authority-oriented. And though the Northern Ireland conflict is not predominantly a war of unification, it has overtones of such a conflict even though clearly not in a cold-war setting. It also seems helpful to broaden the focus to include claims concerning the conduct and settlement of hostilities as well as claims concerning the initiation of hostilities. Thus a more useful breakdown, complete with sub-categories, would include the following claims:

I. *Initiation of Hostilities*

Type   I—Pre-insurgency assistance
   A. Providing military assistance to a widely recognized government in the absence of internal disorders
   B. Assisting a widely recognized government in controlling non-authority-oriented internal disorders

Type   II—Protection of human rights (particularly against threats to human life)
   A. Using the military instrument for the protection of nationals
   B. Using the military instrument for the protection of non-nationals (humanitarian intervention)
      1. In non-authority-oriented interventions
      2. In authority-oriented interventions

Type   III—Anti-colonial wars
   A. Assisting the colonial power
   B. Assisting the break-away forces
   C. Preventing break-away from the colonial power

Type   IV—Wars of secession
   A. Assisting the federal forces
   B. Assisting the secessionist forces
   C. Justifying counter-assistance by assistance to an opposing faction

Type   V—Indigenous conflict for control of national authority structures
   A. Assisting a widely-recognized government
   B. Assisting an insurgent faction
   C. Assisting any faction in conflicts in which there is no widely recognized government
   D. Justifying counter-assistance by assistance provided to an opposing faction
   E. Restoring orderly processes of self-determination in conflicts involving a breakdown of order

Type   VI—Externally initiated conflict for control of national authority structures
   A. Maintaining or imposing "democratic" or "socialist" regimes

      B. Restoring self-determination denied a particular ethnic, social, or religious group within a society

Type VII—Wars of unification

      A. Imposing unification

      B. Assisting in imposing unification

      C. Assisting in maintaining separation

      D. Justifying counter-assistance by assistance provided to an opposing faction

II. *Conduct of Hostilities*

      A. General applicability of the laws of war to

         1. Government forces

         2. Insurgents

         3. Intervening parties

      B. Applicability of the laws of war to captured combatants as to

         1. Their status

         2. The scope of their protection

      C. Applicability of the laws of war to civilians as to

         1. Their status

         2. The scope of their protection

      D. Permissible tactics and weapons

         1. Tactics

         2. Weapons

         3. Neutrals (relations with neutrals)

III. *Settlement (Termination) of Hostilities*

      A. Procedures for settlement

         1. Willingness to negotiate or accept other procedures for peaceful settlement of disputes

         2. Participants in negotiations

         3. Conduct of negotiations

      B. Content of settlement

         1. Reasonableness of conditions for settlement

         2. Willingness to accept a legally binding settlement

      C. Implementation of settlement and the effect of

         1. Cease-fire regimes

         2. Non-compliance with settlement conditions

         3. International guarantees

It should be emphasized that this is a *tentative* formulation of the relevant issues for the more rational normative appraisal of the process of interventionary coercion.[32] This is particularly true of the formulation of claims concerning the conduct of hostilities and the settlement of hostilities. It is perhaps also worth emphasizing that these classifications are not intended as a slot machine for mechanical solution of intervention problems. Rather they are intended to call attention to the variety of issues in normative appraisal and to serve as a useful technique for identifying like cases

---

[32] For a useful alternative formulation of claims in interventionary settings *see* Higgins, *supra* note 5, at 85–113.

and for formulating standards. Complete exegesis would, of course, call for examination through time of each category of claims.

Standards for Appraisal

The third step in the development of criteria for appraisal is the postulation of recommended standards. Though there is always a danger in premature formulation of standards, the present body of knowledge about civil strife and intervention suggests the utility of efforts to formulate rules and contextual thresholds for appraisal. In fact, timidity in approaching the task of recommending criteria for appraisal is a persistent shortcoming of the literature on civil strife and intervention. It is to be expected that such criteria will be rough at the edges, but it seems likely that a general theory for the regulation of intervention will develop more quickly if efforts are made at providing more specific guidance. In fact, criticisms of earlier formulations have helped greatly in the present restatement.[33] It is in this spirit that the following standards and contextual thresholds are suggested:

Standards Concerning the Initiation of Hostilities

> I. Military assistance to a widely recognized government is permissible prior to insurgency. After insurgency is reached, it is permissible to continue but impermissible to increase the preinsurgency level of assistance. Criteria for determining insurgency, for this purpose of permitting pre-insurgency assistance, include that:
> A. the internal conflict must be authority-oriented, that is, aimed at governmental structures;
> B. the recognized government is obliged to make continuing use of most of its regular military forces against the insurgents, or a substantial segment of its regular military forces have ceased to accept orders; and
> C. the insurgents effectively prevent the recognized government from exercising governmental authority over a significant percentage of the population.

COMMENT: Defense interdependencies suggest that some allowance be made for continuing military assistance programs. The suggested standard would freeze military assistance at pre-insurgency levels once the level of internal conflict becomes sufficiently intense to indicate probable widespread support for the insurgency. One alternative possibility deserving consideration would be to require cessation of all military assistance rather than a freeze on assistance once the insurgency threshold was reached. One difficulty with this is that cessation of assistance can alter the internal balance just as an increase in assistance.

> II. Intervention for the protection of human rights is permissible if it meets the following conditions:

[33] The earlier formulations are set out in Moore, *supra* note 5, at 333–39.

    A. an immediate threat of genocide or other widespread arbitrary deprivation of human life in violation of international law;

    B. an exhaustion of diplomatic and other peaceful techniques for protecting the threatened rights to the extent possible and consistent with protection of the threatened rights;

    C. the unavailability of effective action by an international agency, regional organization, or the United Nations;

    D. a proportional use of force which does not threaten greater destruction of values than the human rights at stake and which does not exceed the minimum force necessary to protect the threatened rights;

    E. the minimal effect on authority structures necessary to protect the threatened rights;

    F. the minimal interference with self-determination necessary to protect the threatened rights;

    G. a prompt disengagement, consistent with the purpose of the action; and

    H. immediate full reporting to the Security Council and any appropriate regional organization and compliance with Security Council and applicable regional directives.

COMMENT: There is continued controversy concerning the permissibility of humanitarian intervention and intervention for the protection of nationals.[34] The suggested standard reflects the judgment that intervention for the protection of fundamental human rights should be permitted if carefully circumscribed. Although it is recognized that legitimating such intervention entails substantial risks, not permitting necessary actions for the prevention of genocide or other major abuse of human rights seems to present a greater risk. Opponents of any such standard should at least endeavor to weigh the risks of permitting such intervention *as carefully delimited by the suggested standard* against the risk of insulating genocidal acts and other fundamental abuse of human rights from effective response. Critical points which bear emphasis are that the standard permits unilateral action only in response to threats of genocide or other widespread arbitrary deprivation of human life in violation of international law, only if diplomatic and other peaceful techniques are unavailable, and only if international agencies (such as the International Committee of the Red Cross), regional organizations, or the United Nations are unable to take effective action. In earlier formulations, I sought to limit permissible intervention for the protection of human rights to interventions which would not significantly affect authority structures.[35] Though still a close case, it now seems to me in the

[34] For a review of the literature and the issues *see* the exchange between Ian Brownlie and Richard B. Lillich in Chapters 10 and 11 of this volume.

[35] My earlier criteria were:

    A. an immediate and extensive threat to fundamental human rights, particularly a threat of widespread loss of human life;

    B. a proportional use of force which does not threaten greater destruction of values than the human rights at stake;

wake of the Bangladesh situation that the earlier formulation may have been too restrictive. The advantage of limiting such interventions to non-authority-oriented actions, however, is that it substantially reduces the risk of using humanitarian intervention as a cover for other aims.

> III. It is impermissible to assist a faction engaged in any type of authority-oriented internal conflict or to use the military instrument in the territory of another state (or zone of a divided state) for the purpose of maintaining or altering authority structures.

COMMENT: This is the basic non-intervention standard which seeks to prevent externally sponsored insurrection and to insulate internal conflict from external intervention. The rule is premised on an assumption that more often than not minimization of violence, self-determination, and human rights will be served by a blanket non-intervention standard. As is suggested by the recent conflict in Ceylon (Sri Lanka), this will not necessarily always be the case. In the Ceylon conflict, a broad spectrum of states including the United States, Britain, India, Pakistan, the United Arab Republic, Yugoslavia, and the Soviet Union provided a low level of military assistance to the widely recognized government of Mrs. Sirimavo Bandaranaike, which ruled with a coalition of socialists and pro-Moscow Communists. The aid was provided to combat an essentially indigenous insurgency instituted largely by ultra-leftist revolutionary students. In view of the national elections shortly before the uprising, in which the Bandaranaike government had been returned to power by a large margin, the insurgents had little claim to represent the people of Ceylon. And in view of the coalition of assisting states and the low level of assistance, the assistance presented little threat of escalating conflict.[36] The Ceylon case suggests that there may be situations in which assistance to a widely recognized government may promote self-determination at little risk to world order. Despite the Ceylon case and others which might be cited, however, it still seems probable that more often than not the basic non-intervention standard is policy-responsive.

> IV. Assistance to a widely recognized government is permissible in response to an armed attack or to offset impermissible assistance to insurgents; if assistance to insurgents or the use of the military instrument constitutes an armed attack it is permissible to reply proportionately against the attacking State.

> C. a minimal effect on authority structures;
> D. a prompt disengagement, consistent with the purpose of the action; and
> E. immediate full reporting to the Security Council and appropriate regional organizations.

Moore, *supra* note 5, at 261–64.

[36] On the Ceylon conflict *see* Morgan, "Intervention by Government Invitation: A Case Study of the Conflict in Ceylon," (unpublished paper in the University of Virginia Law Library).

COMMENT: This standard embodies the right of collective defense, recognized under the United Nations Charter, as well as a related right of counter-intervention in response to impermissible assistance to insurgents. There seems little reason to prohibit assistance to a widely recognized government if impermissible assistance is being supplied to insurgents. It should also be noted that collective defense and counter-intervention tend to become indistinguishable as the level of external assistance to insurgents is increased.

V. Regional peacekeeping is permissible if it meets the following conditions:
   A. Authorization by a regional arrangement acting pursuant to Chapter VIII of the Charter;
   B. A genuine invitation by the widely recognized government, or, if there is none, by a major faction;
   C. Neutrality among factions to the extent compatible with the peace-keeping mission;
   D. Immediate full reporting to the Security Council and compliance with Security Council directives;
   E. An outcome consistent with self-determination. Such an outcome is one based on internationally observed elections in which all factions are allowed freely to participate, which is freely accepted by the major competing factions, or which is endorsed by a competent body of the United Nations.

COMMENT: The greater degree of collective legitimation supplied by regional arrangements suggests a somewhat larger role for regional action than unilateral action. Thus, it seems reasonable to permit regional peace-keeping actions if carefully delimited to ensure that they are genuine peace-keeping actions and not disguised efforts at maintaining or extending hegemony. Under the United Nations Charter, regional arrangements are limited in the use of force not only by the restrictions of Article 2(4), applicable to unilateral action, but also by the article 53 requirement that "no enforcement action" shall be taken without the authorization of the Security Council. Since the suggested criteria limit regional action to that not directed against any government, such action would not constitute "enforcement action" and would be consistent with the Charter.[37]

VI. The General Assembly or Security Council of the United Nations may authorize a peacekeeping action when requested by a widely recognized government.

COMMENT: This standard roughly reflects the existing authority of the General Assembly and the Security Council to authorize a peacekeeping

[37] For a discussion of the normative basis for regional action and the nature of "enforcement action" see Moore, "The Role of Regional Arrangements in the Maintenance of World Order," in III C. Black & R. Falk (eds.), *The Future of the International Legal Order* 122 (1971).

force with the consent of the host government.[38] Such actions are unlikely in the absence of extraordinary consensus that the operation will promote self-determination, human rights, and minimization of violence.

> VII. The Security Council may recommend appropriate measures to restore international peace and security in situations which constitute a threat to the peace, breach of the peace, or act of aggression.

COMMENT: This standard reflects the existing authority of the Security Council under Chapter VII of the Charter. Under this authority, the Security Council can recommend assistance or withdrawal of assistance to one or another faction, or can establish a peacekeeping mission even without the consent of the government concerned.

> VIII. Intervention is permissible if specifically authorized by the Security Council acting within its authority under Chapter VII of the Charter, even though in the absence of such authorization it would be impermissible. Conversely, if the Security Council specifically calls for cessation of a particular intervention, continuation is impermissible even though in the absence of such prohibition it would be permissible.

COMMENT: This standard is a corollary of standard VII. Some recommendations have tended to rely primarily on procedural standards for collective legitimation.[39] Though collective legitimation should neither be uncritically accepted nor be the sole standard, it is certainly a highly relevant feature. In particular, the variety of viewpoints represented on the Security Council and the recognized responsibility of the Council to maintain or restore international peace and security suggest its general competence to authorize and terminate intervention when acting within its area of responsibility under Chapter VII. Moreover, Security Council recommendations, reflecting major power consensus, are not likely to lead to conflict escalation.

An earlier formulation of this rule permitted the same role for the General Assembly as for the Security Council. I am persuaded, however, that in view of the present malapportionment and politicization of the General Assembly, a more cautious approach toward a General Assembly legitimating role is in order.[40] Accordingly, the revised standard takes no

---

[38] *See generally* Sohn, "The Role of the United Nations in Civil Wars," in III R. Falk & S. Mendlovitz (eds.), *The Strategy of World Order* 580 (1966).

[39] *See, e.g.,* R. Barnet, *supra* note 3 at 278–80. Barnet suggests a flat "prohibition on unilateral intervention." According to this standard, only collective interventions by the United Nations would be lawful. Thus, for Barnet, the normative issue turns solely on collective legitimation.

[40] Rosalyn Higgins persuasively demonstrates the shortcomings of both the General Assembly and the Security Council as agencies for normative legitimation. *See* Higgins, *supra* note 5, at 116–18. These shortcomings suggest the naiveté of relying solely on procedural tests for legitimation. They also suggest the need for normative

position on the effect of General Assembly authorization of assistance or request for termination. The narrowing of the earlier formulation also has the virtue of bringing the suggested standard more clearly in line with the generally recognized constitutional limits of the General Assembly and the Security Council, while not barring future developments in General Assembly competence.

Possibly, standards VI-VIII, concerning United Nations authority, should also embody careful guidelines on United Nations action. One guideline, for example, concerning authorization of assistance to insurgents under standard VIII, might be to require specification of specific insurgent movements entitled to receive assistance. One difficulty with blanket authorization of assistance to insurgents is that there is frequently a variety of competing insurgent movements. Blanket authorization then becomes an invitation to ideological competition through selected assistance.

These eight suggested standards for appraisal of interventionary conduct are policy recommendations. They do not represent an effort to describe present international law—though the extent of agreement on particular non-intervention norms and the requirements of the United Nations Charter were relevant features in suggesting what will, hopefully, approximate viable standards.[41] Nevertheless, with the possible exception of standards II, on intervention for the protection of human rights, and V, on regional peacekeeping, all of the suggested standards are strongly supported by present international law. And though controversial, I would urge that standards II and V also point the way to lawful action under the Charter. There is, of course, continuing disagreement whether humanitarian intervention is lawful under the Charter. For reasons which I have developed in full in an earlier article, my own view is that, if carefully circumscribed to ensure genuine promotion of human rights, such actions are presently lawful.[42] Similarly, I would urge that standard V delimits regional peacekeeping action which is now lawful under the Charter.[43] It is difficult to see how such carefully circumscribed regional action is either counter to

---

guidelines to govern collective as well as unilateral action. Nevertheless, collective legitimation is still an important feature in increasing the likelihood of action in the common interest and—if it reflects super-power consensus—in reducing the risk of conflict escalation. For these reasons I would favor a significant authorizing and terminating role for the Security Council when it is acting within its Chapter VII competence. In doing so, I would also urge that the scope of Security Council competence under Chapter VII should be subject to appropriate normative criteria rather than relying solely on a procedural determination by the Council.

[41] The criticisms of Rosalyn Higgins and of my students at the University of Virginia Law School have been particularly helpful in reformulating the earlier standards. *See* Higgins, *supra* note 5, at 119–21. Needless to say, I share Dr. Higgins' judgment, "that it is not beyond our capabilities to evolve guides for behavior to be acted on after a contextual appraisal by the appropriate decision-maker." *Id.* at 117. I expect to continue to reformulate the suggested standards as persuasive reasons for doing so are advanced.

[42] *See* Moore, *supra* note 5, at 261–64.

[43] *See generally* Moore, *supra* note 37.

Article 2(4) of the Charter or, when undertaken with the consent of the widely recognized government, if any, that it would amount to enforcement action requiring prior Security Council authorization under Article 53.

Contextual Thresholds. In addition to the standards suggested above, a number of prudential criteria or contextual thresholds have been identified, which either point the way to increased risk of escalating conflict or to increased concern for self-determination and human rights.[44] Although for one reason or another they do not lend themselves to formulation as normative standards, they do seem useful in providing additional guidance. They concern avoidance of:

1. Intervention in a region or nation committed to an opposing bloc;

2. Participation in tactical operations;

3. Weapons of mass destruction such as nuclear, biological, or lethal and incapacitating chemical weapons;

4. Participation on behalf of a government which is not supported by its people.

COMMENT: These contextual thresholds are useful from all principal perspectives in appraising intervention, the international-legal, the national-political, and the strategic.

Though it seems unwise to create an absolute international-legal standard prohibiting intervention in a region or nation committed to an opposing bloc—a case for humanitarian intervention, for example, might be just as compelling in such a setting and, in any event, such a standard smacks of illegitimate spheres of super-power control—the threat to world order of such cross-bloc interventions would usually be high and suggests at least a "rule of the game" prohibiting such interventions. Even cross-bloc military assistance is risky, as in the case of Soviet military assistance to Cuba. In general, this seems to be a fairly well observed rule of the game, as, for example, United States avoidance of intervention in Hungary and Czechoslovakia.

Professor Tom J. Farer, in several of the most provocative articles to date on the regulation of intervention, has suggested a "flat" prohibition of participation in tactical operations, either openly or through the medium of advisors or volunteers" as a single rule for the regulation of intervention.[45] Under this rule, Farer postulates that all military assistance is permissible, except assistance involving the personnel of the assisting state in combat. This proposal is quite helpful in pointing the way toward the potential for increased escalation, psychological involvement, and increased casualties

---

[44] Professor Falk has suggested this use of "thresholds." *See* Falk, "Introduction," *supra* note 5, at 21–26.

[45] *See* Farer, "Intervention in Civil Wars. . . ," *supra* note 5, at 275. For a critique of the Farer proposal as a single non-intervention standard *see* Moore, *supra* note 5, at 320–27.

and social disintegration which may accompany the commitment of external forces to combat operations. Moreover, as the Nixon doctrine suggests, this rule may be developing as an additional rule of the game for super-power interventions. As a policy-responsive normative standard, however, it seems undesirable, both in permitting a wide variety of activities that would now be regarded as impermissible intervention and, conversely, in overly-broadly prohibiting some forms of intervention, such as counter-intervention to offset impermissible assistance to insurgents and humanitarian intervention, which may sometimes require participation in tactical operations if they are to be effective.

Avoidance of weapons of mass destruction, such as nuclear, biological, or lethal and incapacitating chemical weapons has been a basic rule of the game in interventionary settings. It is generally recognized on all sides that such weapons may have an inordinate impact on civilian populations and may enormously increase the risk of uncontrollable and rapid escalation.

Avoidance of participation on behalf of a government which is not supported by its people has obvious relevance for the promotion of self-determination. In fact, the central tension in adopting a neutral non-intervention norm is that it may sometimes prohibit assistance to a government which *is* supported by its people, as may have been the case in the recent Ceylon (Sri Lanka) conflict, and as may be the case in the continuing conflict in Uruguay. This dilemma has led some scholars to suggest a standard of "legitimacy" based on an approximation of the authority of the government in the eyes of the people. A principal difficulty with such approaches to date is that they have not sufficiently "operationalized" the criteria for determining legitimacy. Until a more sensitive standard based on easily ascertainable criteria for determining legitimacy is developed, it seems preferable to retain a modified neutral non-intervention standard. Nevertheless, legitimacy, measured in terms of support by the people, is at least a useful contextual threshold for appraisal.

Standards Concerning the Conduct of Hostilities. Recommendation of standards concerning the conduct of hostilities would, if complete, require specific recommendations with respect to each of the claims associated with the conduct of hostilities. Short of such complete recommendations, some of the more important needs include the following:

Improvements in the Regime for Implementation of the Laws
of War for Situations of Civil Strife and Intervention
    1.   Improvement in the machinery for appointment and utilization of Protecting Powers;
    2.   Improved education and training in the laws of war;
    3.   Increased fact finding, policing, and sanctioning machinery for enforcing the laws of war;
    4.   Strengthened machinery for settlement of disputes concerning the laws of war; and
    5.   Strengthened national machinery for ensuring and policing national

compliance with the laws of war. For example, introduction of systematic review of law-of-war considerations at a National Security Council level, introduction of systematic appraisal of the lawfulness of new weapons systems, and reexamination of the adequacy of present military and civilian jurisdiction for the prosecution of violations of the laws of war and associated military regulations.

Improvements in the Substantive Regime of the Laws of War
for Situations of Civil Strife and Intervention

1. Agreement on criteria as to conflict of an international character (*i.e.*, agreement on the threshold of applicability of the major regimes governing the conduct of international hostilities);

2. A strengthened regime for conflict not of an international character and agreement on criteria as to its threshold (*i.e.*, a new protocol to the Geneva Conventions of 1949 to deal with conflict not of an international character);

3. A comprehensive code of air warfare governing target selection, weapons, etc.;

4. Broadened protection for captured irregular and guerrilla forces;

5. Strengthened protection for prisoners of war, including a right to repatriation or neutral internment after prolonged (possibly eighteen-months) confinement;

6. Increased protection for the civilian population, for example, by the creation of civilian protection zones as suggested in the Secretary-General's 1969 and 1970 *Reports on Human Rights in Armed Conflicts*; and certainly by revitalization of the principle of the military objective;

7. Increased protection for medical personnel and facilities;

8. Consideration of the special problems in protection of nationals of an assisted state; and

9. Clear recognition of the applicability of basic human rights provisions of the laws of war to insurgent and guerrilla operations as well as to the operations of regular forces.

COMMENT: There are four principal kinds of needs in strengthening the regime for conduct of hostilities in settings of revolutionary and interventionary violence. First, clarification of thresholds of applicability of existing regimes governing the conduct of hostilities, both the threshold of international conflict at the upper end of the scale of violence and the threshold of conflict not of an international character [Article 3 coverage within the 1949 Geneva Conventions] at the lower end of the scale of violence. Second, a more comprehensive regime in both applicability and particularly scope for purely civil wars or revolutionary violence. Third, adaptation of new and existing regimes to problems of insurgency and counter-insurgency warfare and to interventionary settings. This would include the status of insurgents as prisoners of war, the relationship between intervening states and the civilian population of the host state, and a variety of tactics and weapons issues which have recently emerged as central to modern insurgency and counter-insurgency warfare. And fourth, strengthening of new and traditional regimes to overcome weaknesses in the traditional law of war. For example, development of a comprehensive code of air warfare and strengthening of the Protecting Power and other machinery for increased compliance with present Conventions. Following several meetings of government experts on the laws of war during the last few years, it seems hopeful that a strengthened regime may emerge in the next few years which will go far toward meeting many of these conduct of hostilities issues.[46]

Standards Concerning Settlement [Termination] of Hostilities. As tentative standards for appraisal of the obligation to pursue peaceful settlement of hostilities, the following principles of procedure and content are suggested.[47] Standards of procedure are those that concern the modalities by which settlement is reached. Standards of content are those that concern the content of settlement.

Standards of Procedure

1.   The extent to which each belligerent takes the initiative in urging peaceful settlement;

2.   The willingness of the belligerents to negotiate a settlement or at least to negotiate a modality for arriving at settlement: (a) willingness to negotiate at any time without preconditions; (b) willingness to negotiate with all *de facto* belligerents; (c) willingness to negotiate in direct talks; (d) willingness to negotiate with respect to all of the principal issues in dispute;

3.   The willingness of the belligerents to publicly communicate general terms of settlement;

4.   The willingness of the belligerents to suggest specific terms for settlement. Specific suggestions need not always be publicly communicated if public disclosure would inhibit the chances for acceptance;

5.   The willingness of the belligerents to conclude a legally binding settlement, however arrived at, or to agree on a modality for settlement such as arbitration or judicial determination that implies a legally binding outcome.

Standards of Content

1.   The reasonableness of suggested terms for settlement as appraised by reference to fundamental Charter principles including: (a) nonuse of force against the territorial integrity or political independence of any state including: (1) cessation of all belligerent activities and claims of belligerency; (2) nonacquisition of territory (and other values) by force; (3) control of activities of terrorist or paramilitary forces; (4) measures to

---

[46] For a discussion of principal needs and a variety of useful suggestions for improvement in strengthening the regime for the conduct of hostilities in settings of revolutionary and interventionary violence, *see* the authorities collected note 25 *supra*.

[47] These were first suggested in Moore, *supra* note 26, at 404–7.

strengthen peace; (b) self-determination of peoples; (c) respect for fundamental human rights; (d) cooperation for economic and social progress;

    2.   If self-determination is at issue the willingness of the parties to
submit to genuinely free elections;

    3.   The willingness of the parties to accept United Nations recom-
mendations for settlement;

    4.   In situations in which fundamental Charter principles are uncertain
or ambiguous, the willingness of the parties to enter into a compromise
settlement.

COMMENT: Normative appraisal of the permissibility of use of coercion
has traditionally focused on the appraisal of the initiation of hostilities and
the conduct of hostilities. The position on settlement, however, can be as
critical for conflict management as the initiation and conduct of hostilities.
Though it is premature to suggest specific rules for settlement, the suggested standards of content and procedure, taken together, do provide a
useful basis for appraisal of the reasonableness of each belligerent's settlement position. In cases in which violation is particularly blatant, it would
seem reasonable to view continuation of coercion as being as impermissible
as if it were illegally initiated. Though the suggested standards have broader
applicability than simply interventionary settings, the standards concerning
willingness to negotiate with all *de facto* belligerents (whether or not recognized) and willingness to submit to genuinely free elections seem particularly relevant for such settings.

Continuing Reappraisal and Refinement of Standards

The development of adequate standards for appraisal is unlikely to be
the work of any one person. A principal difficulty, however, has been that
theoretical development has not been as cumulative as it should be. Rather,
scholars have tended to approach the task of normative appraisal from a
great diversity of conceptual frameworks. As a result, each new suggestion
receives only minimal critical attention. Happily, there seems to be a developing consensus among many international-legal scholars that an adequate
theory requires explicit postulation of value premises, contextual differentiation of intervention claims, and the recommendation of standards for
decision. International-legal scholars whose work reflects this consensus
include Richard A. Falk, Rosalyn Higgins, and increasingly Tom J. Farer.[48]
Further refinement of an adequate theory calls for continued criticism and
interaction *within a common conceptual framework*. Thus, the statement
of value premises should be subjected to continuing reformulation. Similarly, relevant contextual categories and standards for appraisal should be

---

[48] *See* Falk, Farer & Higgins, *supra* note 5. Richard Falk has identified himself,
Tom Farer, Rosalyn Higgins, John Norton Moore, and Oran Young [as scholars
who] have sought (1) to classify civil-war situations; (2) to clarify claims made
by governments and others in relation to civil war situations; and (3) to recommend policy prescriptions that are intermediate between rules of prohibition and

subjected to continuing scrutiny. In doing so, it is important to encourage *explicit* formulation of alternative standards for appraisal, with supporting reasons as to why the alternative standard is deemed to be more policy responsive. It is also important that continuing reappraisal draw on developments in relevant social science theory, such as recent theories of revolutionary violence and systemic theories of the causes and conditions of intervention.

One of the difficulties in meaningful interdisciplinary work on a theory for the regulation of intervention is that the best theoretical writers in political science and international relations tend to eschew normative analysis (and, frequently, are unfamiliar with the best of the international-legal literature concerned with normative analysis). As a result, developing political science and international-relations theory is rarely applied to the appraisal of the adequacy of suggested standards—even to appraise their adequacy in terms of their own postulated values. It seems likely that, as all disciplines increasingly recognize the importance of all tasks in decision, particularly of the normative as well as of the scientific task, there will be an increasing convergence of interests with predictably good results for an applied theory. The degree of interdisciplinary collaboration represented by the broad range of writers in this volume is a significant step in that direction.

(B) FURTHER POLICIES FOR VALUE REALIZATION

The development of standards for normative appraisal of intervention is a useful if not indispensable policy in realizing the values at stake in interventionary situations. Assessments of legitimacy of actions, particularly as assessments become widely shared and authoritative, can have a significant impact in shaping conduct. Moreover, in the absence of widespread agreement on normative standards, the chances for regulation of intervention by any modality would not seem high. As a result, the development of normative standards deserves the attention it is getting. But development of adequate normative standards is only one policy for realization of the values at stake. It is also important for an adequate applied theory to focus on institutional improvement and the potential for controlling "undesirable" interventions by management of their domestic and systemic causes.

Although the international-legal literature includes an increasing num-

---

rules of discretion—rules, in other words, that authorized limited intervention for limited ends under specific circumstances.

Professor Falk's formulation would be sharpened if he would add that the approach has also included an effort to clarify the values at stake in interventionary decisions. And his point (3) is somewhat puzzling. Presumably any rule (or other normative standard) for the regulation of intervention would "authorize limited intervention for limited ends under specific circumstances." The only alternatives would be to permit or prohibit all intervention. It is hard to follow, then, what is meant by characterizing such standards as neither "rules of prohibition" nor "rules of discretion."

ber of studies on institutional improvements related to the regulation of intervention, the emphasis continues to be on the development of normative standards. Some of the more useful suggestions for institutional improvement, all of which deserve attention, include the following:

1.   Appraisal of the strengths and weaknesses of particular international organizations as agencies for collective legitimation and the exploration of modalities for strengthening such potential (for example, collective recognition and collective determination of the status of particular conflicts);

2.   The improvement of international machinery for observation and disclosure in interventionary settings;[49]

3.   Improvements in arms-control measures concerning the proliferation of conventional armaments (for example, proposals for international reporting of military assistance);[50]

4.   Improvements in regional and global peacekeeping machinery;

5.   Improvements in regional and global machinery for realization of fundamental human rights and for effective response to national and political disasters;

6.   Improvements in regional and global machinery for the holding and observation of elections to determine disputed issues of self-determination;

7.   Development of a capability for predicting revolutionary and interventionary violence based on globally monitored indicators (this is close to being feasible); and, ultimately,

8.   Development of a comprehensive global response system, based on indicators for predicting revolutionary and interventionary violence coupled to community machinery for alleviating the causes of tension, protecting human rights, promoting self-determination, and confining violence.

In addition to suggestions for institutional improvement, there are also interesting possibilities for useful policies resulting from recent advances in the theoretical understanding of revolutionary and interventionary phenomena. One hypothesis for exploration is, are there key domestic or systemic causes of revolution and intervention which might be managed to reduce "undesirable" coercion? Though political theorists working in the area begin to feel uneasy with respect to the possible manipulative potential of such theories, the answer does not seem to lie in eschewing normative analysis or foregoing further development of theory, but rather in recognizing the inevitability of the normative task. Though present theory has not, for the most part, advanced to the point where management of conditioning factors is either feasible or sufficiently certain to predict the consequences, it seems likely that some such factors will emerge as theory is further refined. In fact, present theory is already beginning to focus on a

[49] For a discussion of this suggestion *see* Moore, *supra* note 5, at 304–8.
[50] For a detailed proposal for international reporting of military assistance *see* Moore, *supra* note 5, at 300–304.

variety of domestic variables which may have significant potential both for management and for curtailing undesirable interventions. One such set of variables concerns the procedures by which decisions to intervene are made and how relevant information about the effects of intervention are brought to the focus of national decision-makers. For example, an effort to provide better information to intervening elites as to the realistic costs and benefits of intervention may deter many interventions which would otherwise be mistakenly perceived as advantageous.[51]

CONCLUSION

The past decade has seen great strides in our understanding of revolution and intervention and in efforts at normative appraisal. In the process, the prerequisites of an applied theory for the regulation of intervention are becoming more evident. An adequate applied theory involves awareness, and thus avoidance, of a host of intellectual traps (such as the terminological trap) which have confused efforts at clarification. Even more important, an adequate theory requires performance of all intellectual tasks in decision-making; the normative, historical, scientific, and policy tasks. A principal shortcoming of the work to date on revolution and intervention—whether that of international lawyers, political scientists, or international-relations theorists—is the lack of a commonly accepted framework (incorporating all of the intellectual tasks) for relating individual effort. Though work in the absence of such a framework has been useful, there is a tendency for each discipline to focus on one aspect of the issues, without awareness of and stimulation from the work going on in other disciplines. Political scientists and international-relations theorists have tended to focus either on the development of predictive theories or on description of trends in revolution and intervention. And international lawyers have generally neglected the work in predictive theory—and frequently even in normative clarification—in favoring their predilections for doctrinal exegesis. If theory is ultimately to be useful (that is, applied), it must be rooted in an inter-disciplinary sharing which will take account of all tasks in decision-making. It is futile to attempt an applied theory for the regulation of intervention without appraisal of the values at stake and explicit articulation of value choices for appraisal by others. Similarly, value choices alone can produce only wishful thinking unless grounded in context and scientific knowledge. The task ahead is for international lawyers and international-relations theorists to work together within a common framework for continuing refinement of all aspects of an applied theory. The Chapters which follow are an important step in that collaboration.

[51] *See generally* on problems of misperception in international relations J. Farrell & A. Smith, *Image and Reality in World Politics* (1967).

Chapter 2 | The Interrelation of Theories of Intervention and Self-Defense | *Derek W. Bowett*

The relationship between self-defense and intervention perhaps owes some of its difficulty to the fact that they are both remedial rights which presuppose a breach of some duty: and, if one turns to the relevant duties or prohibitions, it is soon apparent that these are basically two and overlap—the prohibition of Article 2(4) of the United Nations Charter and the prohibition of intervention. The fact that these two prohibitions overlap almost invariably leads to confusion over the relationship of the remedial rights.

The prohibition of Article 2(4) is regarded by some as confined to the use or threat of *armed* force. The prohibition of intervention, at least as defined in General Assembly resolution 2131 (1965) is clearly wider than Article 2(4), whatever the arguments on the extent of the latter. One or both may be relevant in any situation in which a state invokes a right of self-defense or a right of intervention. The fatal error is to assume that where state *A* is in breach of the duty of non-intervention vis-a-vis state *B*, any assistance to *B* by state *C* is to be justified, if at all, as a "right of intervention." It is believed that any attempt to separate the right of self-defense from the "right of intervention" must proceed from a distinction between types of conflict and not from the duties which, being breached, give rise to remedial rights. Turning then to a workable distinction between different types of conflict, it is suggested that there are basically two different types. Many attempts have been made to produce much more sophisticated distinctions, with correspondingly more categories of conflicts,[1] and these attempts have served the useful purpose of emphasizing the varied factual contexts to be found in conflict situations. But it may be doubted whether they have aided the understanding of the proper limits to the remedial rights of self-defense and intervention. On the contrary, so replete are the doctrinal writings with sophistication and distinctions that we are in danger of losing the few basic rules of law which inhibit states in resorting to coercion. And statesmen or "decision-makers" generally may have some justification if they plead that the law is no longer clear.[2]

---

[1] Moore, "The Control of Foreign Intervention in Internal Conflict," 9 *Va. J. Int'l L.* 205 (1969), suggests six types of "situations." R. Falk, *Legal Order in a Violent World* 115 (1968), suggests three, namely rebellion (fully domesticated), insurgency (partially internationalized), and belligerency (fully internationalized). J. Rosenau, *International Aspects of Civil Strife* 287–311 (1964), has an analysis which is beyond this writer's comprehension.

[2] Farer, "Intervention in Civil Wars: A Modest Proposal," 67 *Colum. L. Rev.* 266, (1967), at 273, states: "The central truth of the matter is that today there are no real norms governing intervention by third parties in civil wars." This is a pessimism this writer does not share. The norms may lack precision, but they do exist.

It must be admitted at the outset that state practice is not clear, or certainly not uniform, and what follows in this article is not an exposition of the law into which all state practice neatly falls. But it is believed to be an exposition which is consistent with the few basic rules international society possesses—whether or not all its members always conform—and, moreover, an exposition which accords with the generally-shared values of most members. These are, first and foremost, the need to maintain world peace and minimize resort to coercion not authorized by a competent organ of the world community; second, the need to protect the security and independence of States; third, the need to recognize that states are abstractions and exist to promote human rights, including the right of self-determination of peoples.[3]

The suggested basic distinction is between *International Conflicts* and *Internal Conflicts*: in the first type of conflict, a state is in breach of either Article 2(4) or the duty of non-intervention; in the second type, no state is in breach.

INTERNATIONAL CONFLICTS

Here we presuppose a delict by state *A* which arises from a breach of Article 2(4) or the duty of non-intervention which also constitutes a threat to the security of state *B*. Provided the threat is actual or imminent, leaving *B* no alternative choice of means, *B* may invoke the right of self-defense to justify reasonable and proportionate measures to safeguard its security: this, in essence, is the right of self-defense.[4] In addition, if the situation created by *A*'s breach also constitutes a threat to the security of state *C*, *C* may engage in similar measures to safeguard its security: this, in essence, is the right of collective self-defense, where *B* and *C* act in concert.[5] In this situation, there is no need whatever to confuse the issue by characterizing the measures of either *B* or *C* as a "right of intervention." The difficulties in the way of this simple characterization of the respective positions of the parties involved are partly the result of misconceptions about self-defense. The first misconception is that Article 51 has restricted the right of self-defense to delicts which constitute an actual armed attack.[6] Obviously, if

[3] *Id.*, 271, suggests somewhat different criteria. The above formulation corresponds more closely to that advocated by Friedmann, "Intervention and the Developing Countries" 10 *Va. J. Int'l L.* 205, 208–9 (1970).

[4] D. Bowett, *Self-Defence in International Law*, 269 (1958); W. O'Brien, *The Law of Limited International Conflict* 23–32 (1965), a study by the Institute of World Polity, contains a useful summary of the various views on the meaning of self-defense.

[5] *Id.*, Ch. X, contains this writer's detailed exposition of this controversial concept, and one which is too restrictive for many people.

[6] An able exposition of this mistaken view can be found in I. Brownlie, *International Law and the Use of Force by States*, 265–78 (1963). For more detailed argument rejecting the view, *see* Bowett, *supra* note 5, at 187–93; J. Brierly, *Law of Nations* 417–18 (1963); O'Brien, *supra* note 4, at 23–32, and the many authorities there cited.

one proceeds from this error, one is prevented from characterizing as self-defense any protective measure designed to deal with other forms of delict, including the techniques of subversion, fomenting of civil strife, assistance to armed bands, etc., embraced by the duty of non-intervention. But this is to misunderstand the nature of the traditional right of self-defense and the whole purpose of Article 51 which was to preserve the traditional right.

The second misconception is that the exercise of the right of self-defense can only take the form of armed force. There is, however, no reason why the right of self-defense should not justify whatever measures are proportionate and necessary to deal with the particular threat to security and which would otherwise be illegal. Thus, economic measures inconsistent with treaty obligations, refusal of rights of overflight, the closing of border traffic, expulsion of nationals of the delictual state A, jamming of broadcasts from state A, etc., might all be proper reactions in self-defense in appropriate circumstances.

A somewhat different difficulty is seen in Falk's preference for the use of the notion of "counter-intervention" rather than collective self-defense in situations like Vietnam.[7] He argues, understandably, that the "aggression–self-defense" characterization tends to widen the geographical scope of the conflict (e.g., in the Vietnam conflict, to suggest the reasonableness of attack against the territory of North Vietnam as the "aggressor"), whereas the "intervention–counter-intervention" characterization would tend to restrict hostilities to the area in which the "intervention" occurs (i.e., in the example given, to South Vietnam). And, if one wishes to minimize rather than escalate the conflict, this is desirable. But this only confuses the concepts used and this policy of restraint could equally well be achieved by deciding that, in situations of aggression (breach of Article 2[4]) like Vietnam, a proportionate response in self-defense is best restricted to military action within the victim state. This is essentially a policy decision, not a rule of law, and there is no need to abandon the concept of self-defense to achieve it.

The other difficulty about this simple characterization is that it is still not possible to state with precision what is the content of the obligation to refrain from the use or threat of force (Article 2[4]) or of the obligation of non-intervention. It has to be admitted that the United Nations Committee on Friendly Relations was only able to agree[8] on a very imprecise exposition of the content of Article 2(4). And, though the General Assembly has formulated the duty of non-intervention in resolution 2131 of December

---

[7] Falk, *supra* note 1, at Ch. VII. The Falk thesis may also widen the scope for armed intervention in so far as a state may assert a right of "counter-intervention" in circumstances in which it could not properly claim a right of collective self–defense.

[8] For the text of the Special Committee's Draft Declaration, *see* 7 *U.N. Monthly Chronicle* 62 (June 1970). The Declaration was adopted by acclamation (no state objecting) by the General Assembly on October 24, 1970, in Resolution 2625 (XXV).

21, 1965, by the striking majority of 109 votes to none, with one abstention (the United Kingdom), and in resolution 2625 of October 24, 1970, by acclamation, it must equally be admitted that these resolutions are not a treaty formulation of the duty of non-intervention and therefore no more than evidence of the contemporary view of the duty shared by many States. Moreover, as we shall later see, however wide the terms of these resolutions, they fail to deal squarely with the really controversial questions of whether consent by a recognized government legitimates an otherwise illegitimate intervention, or whether certain interventions—for example, those in support of "liberation movements"—remain outside the prohibition.

But the lack of precision, or agreement, in the formulation of these two paramount obligations is not sufficient reason for rejecting them as irrelevant: to do so would be to jettison the whole basis upon which any hope of retaining a legal restraint on coercion by states can rest. Moreover, the uncertainties surrounding these two obligations do not really affect the question of the relationship between the remedial rights of self-defense and intervention, which is the question to which this essay is directed.

II. INTERNAL CONFLICTS

Internal conflicts are those occurring within a state and in which there is no lawful involvement by another state in the sense of a breach of Article 2(4) or the duty of non-intervention.

In this type of conflict there is, basically, no right of intervention for any outside power and no occasion for any exercise of a right of self-defense. This results from the basic proposition of the equality of states which, in effect, means that the internal politics and internal conflicts within state A are the concern of state A alone and give rise to no right on the part of state B. Whatever the uncertainties about General Assembly resolutions 2131 (1965) and 2625 (1970), it may be seen from their texts that the General Assembly meant to convey the broad principle that internal conflicts within a state are the concern of that state alone.

There are, however, three categories of situations in which some would argue that a "right of intervention" exists,[9] and the argument remains tenable if only because the Assembly resolution failed to deal specifically with these categories.

[9] We reject the traditional distinction between "rebellion" and "insurgency" as meaningless. This distinction used to be thought to justify the proposition that international law imposed no barrier to a state's intervening to assist a Government dealing with rebels, but might do so if the level of insurgency had been reached. The distinction is a veritable quicksand upon which to rest any valid theory of intervention, since it turns upon an entirely subjective recognition of the status of the revolutionary forces.

(i) INTERVENTION BY THE CONSENT OF THE ESTABLISHED OR "INCUMBENT" GOVERNMENT

Here the argument is that consent legitimates what would otherwise be illegitimate. It is believed that, despite the frequency with which it has been invoked by intervening States,[10] it is basically unsound. Its unsoundness stems from the subjectivity of recognition, since an intervening State is free to recognize as the "government" whichever faction in an internal struggle it wishes to support and which will request intervention.[11] It also stems from the inevitable conflict which such a doctrine arouses with the principle of self-determination of peoples, regarded by many states as one of the most fundamental and "peremptory" norms of contemporary international law. And, indeed, once an internal conflict is politically motivated in the sense that the competing factions are in competition for governmental power over the whole or part of the territory—and this is generally the case, since non-political lawlessness and banditry are rare—any outside intervention will prejudice the outcome of the internal struggle and thus impair the right of the people of that state to self-determination. Lastly, the unsoundness of the doctrine of intervention by consent stems from the fact that such intervention frequently induces counter-intervention by some other state, with a consequent escalation of the conflict and greater risk to international peace.

If the doctrine of intervention by consent is to be rejected, as it should be, there yet remains the problem of lack of definition of unlawful intervention. Would this preclude all assistance to the incumbent Government? In principle, assistance which can be used against the rival political forces must be excluded: thus, direct military assistance, the supply of military advisers, weapons, and equipment would be excluded.[12] Other forms of technical or economic assistance which would have no direct bearing on the outcome of the political struggle and which are intended to benefit the state as a continuing entity rather than any particular incumbent government would

[10] Such consent was invoked by the U.K. and U.S. Governments to justify interventions in Jordan and Lebanon in 1958. The "consent" to the U.S. intervention in Santo Domingo in 1965, given by Colonel Benoit, was of doubtful relevance, since the status of the military junta headed by Colonel Benoit was not that of a government. The notion that the intervention of the U.S.S.R. in Czechoslovakia in 1968 was with the consent of either the Czechoslovak government or people is a fiction which presumably even the Soviets cannot believe; for a forthright protest over the invasion, see the Declaration of the National Assembly of Czechoslovakia of August 22, 1968, in *Int'l Leg. Mat.* 1290 (1968).

[11] This, in effect, is what the U.S.S.R. did in intervening in Hungary in 1956. *See* International Commission of Jurists, *The Hungarian Situation and the Rule of Law* (1957).

[12] Farer, *supra* note 2, at 275, argues that the prohibition ought to be restricted to tactical support, either by troops, advisers, or voluneers, and not extended to military equipment or other forms of aid: this, he feels, is consistent with Soviet and Chinese practice and therefore more likely to find acceptance as a principle. Moore, *supra* note 1, at 269, suggests the better solution is to limit all forms of military assistance to the level reached prior to the secession attempt, a solution which seems to this writer dubious if only because it ignores a vital new factor in the problem, namely, the element of self-determination.

not, in principle, be excluded. What of military aid begun before the internal conflict started? Again, in principle, the answer would seem to be that, if it would be unlawful intervention to give such aid when a conflict is in being, such aid should be stopped once the internal conflict has reached a point at which the right of self-determination is in issue.

(ii) INTERVENTION TO ASSIST A STRUGGLE FOR SELF-DETERMINATION

Clearly, many states regard intervention for this purpose as legitimate: it is the avowed purpose of the Liberation Committee of the Organization of African Unity and the basic justification adopted by Arab States in their conflict with Israel. The subjects of self-determination in the two examples given are respectively the African peoples in South Africa, Rhodesia, and Portuguese Africa and the Palestinian people. Not surprisingly, the General Assembly resolution 2151 (1965) contained a deliberately ambiguous paragraph six,[13] which will be construed by many States as excluding intervention for this purpose from the general prohibition.

This category is more difficult than the previous category, if only because whereas one may say that a state's internal politics or political struggles are its own affair (at least if they pose no threat to international peace), one cannot say that the denial by a state of the right of self-determination is its own affair. The development of the right of self-determination has been such that its denial is now, manifestly, the concern of the international society of states and, most states would argue, an international wrong. It is this difference which means that one cannot treat struggles for self-determination as just one other form of internal political struggle in which there may be no intervention by outside powers.

There are nevertheless extreme difficulties in conceding this to be a legitimate category of intervention. First, there is the frequent subjectivity in the decision that self-determination is involved in any particular protest or uprising against governmental authority. The Western Powers tend to regard Soviet occupation of the Baltic states of Estonia, Latvia, and Lithuania as a denial of self-determination. The North Vietnamese certainly regard the Saigon regime and the presence of the United States in Vietnam as a denial of the right of self-determination of the Vietnamese people. The Somali Republic regards the Ethiopian occupation of the Haud and the Ogaden and the Kenyan occupation of the former Northern Frontier Dis-

[13] "All States shall respect the right of self-determination and independence of peoples and nations, to be freely exercised without any foreign pressure, and with absolute respect for human rights and fundamental freedoms. Consequently, all states shall contribute to the complete elimination of racial discrimination and colonialism in all its forms and manifestations." General Assembly resolution 2625 (XXV) of October 24, 1970, further supports this "exception" from the prohibition by the phrase: "In their actions against, and resistance to, such forcible action in pursuit of the exercise of their right to self-determination, such peoples are entitled to seek and to receive support in accordance with the purposes and principles of the Charter." Does this "support" involve armed intervention?

trict of Kenya as denials of the right of self-determination. The position of the Arab States over "occupied Palestine" has already been referred to. These examples could be multiplied many times and they suggest that, as a basis for intervention, support for self-determination is unacceptable so long as the decision that self-determination is denied remains subjective to the would-be intervenor.

One is therefore tempted to suggest that intervention should remain permissible only where the denial of the right of self-determination has been confirmed by a competent organ of the world community—by which is meant the security Council or the General Assembly—and intervention authorized by that organ. If this were to be accepted as the only proper basis upon which intervention in support of self-determination is justified, it would in effect mean that this is not a true category of permissible intervention by states. A more correct categorization would place it under a more comprehensive heading of intervention authorized by competent organs of the United Nations.

(iii) HUMANITARIAN INTERVENTION

Intervention for the protection of the intervening states' own nationals traditionally has been and still is today a part of the customary right of self-defense.[14] Its exercise must be subject to the normal requirements of self-defense, that is to say, there must exist a failure in the territorial state to accord the protection for aliens demanded by international law, there must be an actual or imminent danger requiring urgent action, and the action taken must be proportionate and limited to the necessities of extricating the nationals from the danger.

What becomes more dubious is the assertion of a right of intervention for aliens, based on purely humanitarian grounds, where it seems impossible, in the absence of the link of nationality, to regard this as a species of self-defense:[15] the danger to aliens cannot be conceived as a danger to the state, and the injury to aliens cannot be regarded as a breach of international law[16] vis-à-vis the state wishing to intervene. Thus, for most writers

---

[14] Bowett, *Self-Defence in International Law* (1958), contains a more comprehensive statement of this position. It is shared by Lillich, "Forcible Self-Help by States to Protect Human Rights," 53 *Iowa L. Rev.* 325 (1967), who cites the authors and state practice in support of the proposition. *See also* Moore, *supra* note 1, at 261–64; O'Brien, *supra* note 4, at 29–30.

[15] This is conceded by Lillich, *id.* at 337.

[16] Traditionally, where the territorial state had created a threat to the "human rights" of its own nationals, it might have been said that there was no breach of international law at all. Some states would doubtless still maintain this position, but its validity is now questionable, given the development of the concept of human rights under the U.N. Charter. However, the question whether there is a breach of any other state's right, so as to permit self-defense to be considered, remains and must be answered in the negative. The difficulty is analogous to that facing Ethiopia and Liberia in the South-West Africa Case, (1966) *I.C.J.*, where these two states were denied *locus standi*.

and for most states, forceful intervention based simply on humanitarian grounds and unrelated to a threat to one's own nationals is illegal under the United Nations Charter. Lillich, however, has argued for a more general right of humanitarian intervention on the basis of a right of self-help (as distinct from self-defense), which would not be contrary to Article 2(4), since the intervention would not impair the "territorial integrity or political independence" of any state.[17] This seems to overlook the rejection of precisely this argument when advanced by the United Kingdom in the *Corfu Channel Case*,[18] in relation to Operation Retail, the subsequent minesweeping operation in Albanian territorial waters.

Quite apart from the purely legal question of the compatibility of humanitarian intervention with the provision of Article 2(4) and the general rule of non-intervention, there are policy considerations which suggest that to enlarge the right to protection into a more general right of humanitarian intervention would be to introduce a dangerous exception to these prohibitions.[19] Such intervention will, in the nature of things, be confined to intervention in small states who cannot oppose the intervening forces of a large power. It will be susceptible to use for ulterior motives, as in the past: that is to say, it will be used as a cover for interference in the domestic, internal affairs of the state, notably to influence the outcome of an internal struggle.[20] It may also encourage counter-intervention by other states, with the consequent risk of an escalation of conflict.

For these reasons it is believed that the recognition of a general right of humanitarian intervention is neither legally nor politically acceptable. But in thus excluding state intervention, one does not necessarily exclude the possibility of an intervention authorized by either the Security Council or, possibly, the General Assembly where it can be shown that the situation presents a threat to international peace and security. This would raise quite separate questions which fall outside the scope of the present paper, and it would certainly be this writer's view that an intervention authorized by a competent organ of the United Nations, whilst undoubtedly subject to a test of legality, is *not* subject to the same test as unilateral action by states.

The conclusion therefore emerges that, in relation to unilateral action by states, there is no place in contemporary international law for a right of

[17] Lillich, *supra* note 14, at 336. Moore, *supra* note 1 at 261–64, reaches a similar conclusion.

[18] Corfu Channel Case, (1949) *I.C.J.* 35.

[19] The U.S. landings in Santo Domingo in 1965 are suspect on this ground. Admittedly, though this was a case of protection of nationals, the U.S. did later shift the ground for its justification for the presence of its forces to one of maintaining peace and security in the area at the request of the authorities in Santo Domingo. *See generally* Cabranes, "Human Rights and Non-Intervention in the Inter-American System," 65 *Mich. L. Rev.* 1147 (1967); Lillich, *supra* note 14, at 341–44; Nanda, "The U.S. Action in the 1965 Dominican Crisis: Impact on World Order," 43 *Denver L. Rev.* 439 (1966).

[20] For similar doubts, *see* Bilder, "Rethinking International Human Rights: Some Basic Questions," [1969] *Wisc. L. Rev.* 171, 201.

intervention as opposed to a right of self-defense. Attempts to base action on a right of intervention tend to be attempts to justify action which, under the United Nations Charter, is illegal because, not being permissible self-defense, it is contrary to either Article 2(4) or the principles of non-intervention. This conclusion, which is obviously a restrictive view of permissible coercion by states, becomes completely nullified if, however, one permits too liberal an interpretation of the concept of "collective" self-defense.

THE CONCEPT OF COLLECTIVE SELF-DEFENSE

In the final analysis, all the controversy over this concept seems to be reducible to three basic, alternative meanings:

> (i) If state *A* attacks state *B*, the latter has a right of self-defense and any other state may come to the assistance of state *B* pursuant to the right of collective self-defense.

This is palpable nonsense, since it is an open invitation to states generally to intervene in any conflict between other states, anywhere in the world:[21]

[21] It is nevertheless the basic contention in the "Memorandum of the Department of State on the Legality of United States Participation in the Defense of Viet Nam," March 8, 1965: 5 *Int'l Leg. Mat.* 565 (1965). That Memorandum assumed that, *because* South Vietnam had a right of self-defense, therefore the U.S.A. had a right of collective self-defense. But why? Why not Denmark, or Yugoslavia? Obviously, what was lacking from that Memorandum (apart from factual proof that North Vietnam had attacked South Vietnam first) was the argument that, by reason of the attack, the securiy of the Unied States was endangered. This may well have been the case, but it was not argued at all in that Memorandum.

A further example of this contention is seen in Professor Moore's justification of the U.S./Vietnamese invasion of Cambodia on April 30, 1970, when he argues that "the military occupation of sizeable areas of territory from which Cambodian officials have been ousted certainly constitutes an 'armed attack' within the meaning of Article 51 of the Charter. . . . Cambodia may consequently lawfully request external assistance for its defense"; Moore, "Legal Dimensions of the Decision to Intercede in Cambodia" 65 *Am. J. Int'l L.* 38, 46 (1970). This implies that *any* state might have assisted Cambodia by virtue of the right of collective self-defense. Apart from the defect of principle, the argument is not particularly germane on the facts. Cambodia did *not* request assistance, as Aldrich has explained (*id.* at 76), for the reason that the U.S.A. did not wish to compromise Cambodian neutrality in relation to the Vietnam conflict. Indeed, the whole discussion of collective self-defense in relation to this invasion seems misplaced. This concept is customarily used where the victim and the intervenor are taking collective action. This was not the situation in Cambodia, for the victim, Cambodia, took no action jointly with the U.S.A. The joint action was by the U.S.A. and Vietnam, and could be justified only by reference to a threat to their security, as lawful belligerents, which entitled them out of necessity to invade neutral territory to eliminate a threat to their security posed by the opposing belligerent's use of neutral territory, which the neutral state was powerless to prevent. Much of the disagreement between Falk, *id.* at 1–25, and Friedmann, *id* at 77, on the one hand and Aldrich, *id.* at 76, on the other relates to the question of whether the North Vietnamese activities in Cambodia did present an immediate threat to the security of U.S. and South Vietnamese forces.

it cannot possibly be consistent with a system of collective security (which is what the United Nations Charter attempted to establish) and, specifically, it is quite contrary to the delegation to the Security Council of "primary responsibility" for the maintenance of international peace and security in Article 2(4). It need scarcely be added that, since this so-called right of collective self-defense would be invoked before any reference to the United Nations, and on the basis of a purely unilateral assessment by the intervening state of who is the aggressor, there is a high risk that other states will form a different assessment and intervene on the other side. The result is potential global conflict, all on the basis of a so-called right of collective self-defense. The position is thus virtually indistinguishable from the nineteenth-century system of alliances: states have a right to help their allies.

The basic defect of this meaning of the concept is that it confuses collective self-defense with collective security.[22] With collective self-defense, the right to intervene stems from the threat to the state's own security.[23] If there is no such threat, then the state shares the general interest of state members of the collective security system in maintaining international peace, but this must take the form of participation of collective security action, authorized by the competent organs, and not in unilateral action:[24] otherwise, the result is chaos and complete disintegration of the collective security system.

The argument that the collective security system has already disintegrated is not valid, for two quite different reasons. First, states do not adopt that argument: that is to say, no member of the United Nations has stated that, because of the breakdown of the Security Council, it renounces the Charter limitations imposed upon it and reverts to its traditional, nineteenth-century freedom to fight wars to help allies. Second, it is possible, either in the Security Council or in the General Assembly, to seek a community consensus on whether aggression has been committed and, if so, whether the interests of international peace warrant outside intervention. Such a consensus will tend to emerge, despite the veto and even in the absence of a formal resolution. Moreover, though the argument that aggression must be stopped *immediately* and that delay caused by such consultations of community consensus will be fatal seems plausible in theory, in practice it is apparent that most serious conflicts even today last quite long enough to enable this consultation to be achieved.

(ii)   If state *A* attacks state *B*, the latter has a right of self-defense and any other State may come to the assistance of State *B* pursuant to the

[22] J. Stone, *Legal Controls of International Conflict* 264 (1954).

[23] *See* Friedmann, "Comments on the Articles on the Legality of the United States action in Cambodia," 65 *Am. J. Int'l. L.* 77 (1970), condemning the U.S. action because "it is not an action taken in defense of United States territory or security."

[24] Thus, the Anglo-French invasion of Suez was not supported by the vast majority of states, despite the Anglo-French argument that they had acted in the interests of maintaining international peace in the Middle East.

> right of collective self-defense *where there is a prior treaty commitment or right so to do*

This second alternative is essentially the same as the first, save for the existence of a treaty between the immediate victim and the intervening state. The position is typified by NATO and virtually all the collective self-defense treaties which involve the premise that "an attack on one is an attack against all."[25] The question is why the existence of such a treaty should distinguish this alternative from the first. Clearly, no such treaty can permit a state to escape the Charter limitations on the use of force: Article 103 ensures the primacy of the Charter obligations. In principle, therefore, such a treaty cannot confer a greater right to intervene than a state already possesses by virtue of Article 51. Hence, if we were to envisage a hypothetical situation of a conflict between two Latin-American states, it is difficult to envisage a legitimate intervention by the United Kingdom in collective self-defense, and equally difficult to see how the United Kingdom could acquire such a right to intervene merely by concluding a treaty or an exchange of notes with one of the parties.

This suggests that the treaty cannot be the source of any right of collective self-defense: it may recognize a pre-existing right (and make provision for its effective implementation by way of arrangements for joint command, common use of bases, etc.), but it does not create or add to the existing right. Thus, the existing right must find its basis elsewhere and, it is suggested, that basis lies in a threat to the security of the intervening state. This brings us to the third alternative, which is the alternative preferred by this writer.

> (iii) If state *A* attacks state *B*, the latter has a right of self-defense. And if, in all the circumstances, that attack also creates a threat to the security of another state, that other state has an independent right of self-defense which it may exercise in concert, or collectively, with state *B*.

This notion of collective self-defense is obviously a restrictive one and, readers should note, a minority view[26] commonly rejected by other writers as impractical and contrary to state practice. It nevertheless has the virtue of basing a state's right to self-defense on a threat to that state's own

[25] *See* Article 4 of the North Atlantic Treaty: an attack is defined as an attack on the territory, ships, or aircraft of any Member, anywhere in the North Atlantic Treaty area. An unusual interpretation of collective self-defense, as typified in these treaties, is that it is a form of intervention by consent: *see* Fawcett, "Intervention in International Law: A Study of Some Recent Cases," 103 *Recueil Des Cours* 347, 268 (1961). It is difficult to see why a victim state should be entitled to authorize intervention by other states in an international conflict: that is surely the role of the Security Council.

[26] It was first advanced by this writer in *Self-Defence in International Law*, Ch. 10 (1958), where it is more fully developed. It is to some extent shared by Stone, *supra* note 22, at 245. For criticism of its narrowness, *see* Falk, *supra* note 21, at 12–14; Moore, *supra* note 21, at 55–56; McDougal & Feliciano, *Law and Minimum World Public Order*, 247–53 (1961).

security. Only in this way can collective self-defense be confined so as to be consistent with a system of collective security and to make meaningful the general prohibition on intervention.

The factors which would characterize an attack on one state as, at the same time, a threat to the security of another state are many and varied. They range from considerations of the source and size of the attack to questions of the pre-existing links between the immediate victim of the attack and the would-be intervenor. To return to NATO as an example, a Bulgarian attack on a Greek frontier post involving three Bulgarian infantry companies scarcely looks like an attack on the United States of America, regardless of the magic formula of Article 4 of NATO that an attack on one member is an attack on all. United States' intervention is unthinkable because, at that stage, there is no threat to the security of the United States, and massive response by NATO (as was once contemplated in the Dulles era) would be groundless and, moreover, directly contrary to the requirements of proportionality. In contrast, if we presuppose an attack by eighty-odd divisions of the Warsaw Pact countries on West Germany, with full armour and air support, then the whole of the NATO alliance could realistically treat this as an immediate threat to their own security and react in collective self-defense: the Article 4 formula would correspond to realities. The fact that the NATO countries could treat this threat as a threat common to them all stems from the links established between them: strategic, political, geographical, economic, etc. These links are not so much the result of the Treaty as the reason for it, and they exist independently of the Treaty. The Treaty does no more than afford evidence that the parties are linked by ties which make their security interdependent in certain circumstances. The right to intervene in collective self-defense is dependent upon an affirmative answer to the question: "Is the security of the intervening States in fact threatened?"

This restrictive view of collective self-defense, as stated earlier, is necessary if the prohibition of intervention is to retain any meaning: in other words, a too-liberal interpretation of collective self-defense allows wholesale intervention and makes nonsense of the rule of non-intervention and of the system of collective security.

Two counter-arguments have to be reckoned with. The first is that states' practice does not accord with this view. To this one can reply that the practice of most states in fact, does: the examples of contrary practice are, by reference to states' conduct generally, fortunately rare, and an unlawful intervention must be condemned as unlawful rather than the rules re-moulded to accommodate the inconsistent practice.[27] As suggested above,

---

[27] It is generally true that the writers concerned to redefine the rules or concepts relating to the use of force are predominantly American and much influenced by the need to accommodate U.S. practice. Soviet writers have less difficulty, since they are usually able to ignore any inconsistency between the practice of the U.S.S.R. and the rules of law they propound.

although treaties like NATO can be widely construed so as to be at variance with this restrictive view of collective self-defense, in practice they rarely are so.[28]

The second argument is that, with so restricted a view of collective self-defense, the victim is left unaided and the potential aggressor will be left free to devour his victims one by one. This is a serious criticism and, of course, it is true that a restrictive view of collective self-defense does presuppose an effective system of collective security. But it may be doubted whether, in the face of repeated aggression, the system of collective security is so useless. What is needed by states wishing to check aggression is the support of the community of states in their view that this is aggression and that intervention to check it is desirable in the interests of international peace and security. As suggested above, this can emerge from a consensus within the United Nations, if not through a formal resolution. And the history of the past twenty years suggests that world peace could have been better served if states had awaited the development of such a consensus rather than acted unilaterally by asserting a right to intervene based upon too wide a construction of their right of collective self-defense.

[28] An exception would be the Soviet reliance on the Warsaw Pact in justification for Soviet intervention in Hungary in 1956.

PART II | **THE RELEVANCE OF THEORIES OF MODERNIZATION, INTERNAL VIOLENCE, AND THE INTERNATIONAL SYSTEM**

Chapter 3 | The Relevance of Theories of Modernization for Normative and Institutional Efforts at the Control of Intervention | *Cyril E. Black*

THE PROBLEM

Theories of modernization are concerned with the adaptation of societies in the contemporary era to the impact of the scientific and technological revolution affecting all aspects of human activity at the local, national, and international levels. No human relations remain unchanged in this era of rapid transformation. The unprecedented advancement of knowledge in modern times has enhanced human capabilities in ways that have transformed both levels of achievement and the institutions by means of which these levels can be attained. Relations among states have been affected as much as relations within states.

The intervention of one or more states in the affairs of another state in which a civil war is in progress and the question of normative and institutional efforts at the control of such intervention raise a variety of controversial issues. These include the definition of rebellion, insurgency, and belligerency; the applicability of the international law of war to a civil war; and claims of both governments and insurgents that they are entitled to be treated as belligerents and in the case of insurgents, to be recognized as belligerents. Outside states and international organizations, for their part, may claim on a variety of grounds the right to provide active support either to the government or to insurgents.

Insofar as these are technical questions involving the relevance of the numerous past cases discussed in the treatises and digests of international law to specific contemporary situations, theories of modernization are only indirectly relevant. Those aspects of the law that have been generally accepted by governments reflecting a variety of cultures and ideologies may continue to be respected despite many political changes. Yet law relating to civil war and intervention is particularly vulnerable to political change, for the very process by which the number of sovereign states in the international system has grown from 25 in 1815 to 40 in 1900, and more than 130 in 1970 has been one in which civil wars, frequently marked by intervention, have played a major role.

Theories of modernization are concerned with this process of change, and in particular with the changing norms of interest groups and their political elites in regard to the rights of people to self-government, the nature of the societal changes that lead to major conflicts among interest groups, the relations among states in an era in which the international system of states is being transformed, and the future role of the state itself.

After a brief introduction to the prevalent theories of modernization, we will be concerned with their significance for the understanding of civil war, intervention, and the evolving nature of the state and for normative and institutional efforts at the control of intervention.

THEORIES OF MODERNIZATION

Theories of modernization are concerned with the adaptation of the many diverse societies of the world to the levels of achievement made possible by the scientific and technological revolution. In a broad sense, theories of modernization are simply a contemporary form of generalizations about change that have in recent generations been a main concern of political, economic, and social research. What distinguishes theories of modernization from earlier generalizations about the subject is the world-wide scope of contemporary interest, the recent development of intensive economic and sociological studies, and the beginning of efforts to seek uniformities drawing on the work of several disciplines and on the experience of all countries.

The study of modernization is concerned with the patterns of structural changes that underlie the institutions and ideologies of the diverse societies of the world, which range from relatively primitive to relatively developed. The advancement of knowledge reflected in the scientific and technological revolution that underlies change in modern times is universally valid and available, but the capacity of societies to attain the levels of achievement made possible by this advancement depends both on the adaptability of their institutional heritage and on the ability of their political leaders to understand the nature of the challenges that confront them.

The study of the process of modernization encompasses a considerable variety of approaches which may be summarized in terms of broader and narrower views relating to geographical scope, chronological limits, disciplinary approach, and conceptions of the nature of change.[1]

From a geographical standpoint, the broader view seeks to formulate generalizations based on the entire experience of humankind, while the narrower view limits itself to the study of the less-developed societies. The

---

[1] The following provide a reasonably comprehensive introduction to theories of modernization: O'Connell, "The Concept of Modernization," 64 *South Atlantic Quarterly* 549 (Autumn 1965); S. Eisenstadt, *Modernization: Protest and Change* (1966); I–II M. Levy, Jr., *Modernization and the Structure of Society: A Setting for International Affairs* (1966); M. Weiner (ed.), *Modernization: The Dynamics of Growth* (1966); Huntington, "The Change to Change: Modernization, Development, and Politics," 3 *Comparative Politics* 283 (April 1971; J. Finkle and R. Gable (eds.), *Political Development and Social Change* (2d ed. 1971); and L. Binder *et al.*, *Crises and Sequences in Political Development* (1971). The views of the present writer are set forth in C. Black, *The Dynamics of Modernization: A Study in Comparative History* (1966).

narrower approach tends to assume that the societies that are the most advanced—in effect the West European and the English-speaking—have established an institutional pattern that is inherently "modern" and that the less developed countries must necessarily follow this model. The broader approach is based on the assumption that each society faces the challenge of modernity in terms of its own pattern of institutions and leadership, and that an understanding of the process of modernization must draw on the entire diversity of human experience. This broader approach is therefore interested in the distinctive patterns respresented by the Japanese and Russian experience, and anticipates that the modernization of other societies will reveal an even greater diversity of institutional forms.

In terms of chronological limits, there is general agreement that the scientific and technological revolution began to have a significant political, economic, and social impact in the West in the sixteenth century, although many individual countries in other parts of the world did not undertake the process of modernization until the twentieth century. A "pre-modern" or "traditional" era of several centuries is thus presumed, which represents the level of knowledge and of political, economic, and social institutions of societies before they face the challenge of adopting the relatively rapid changes in function characteristic of the modern era. While there is rather general agreement as to the genesis of this process, there is less agreement as to its future. The broader view tends to see modernization as open-ended, based essentially on the relatively sudden and rapid expansion of the understanding of the human environment that has taken place in recent centuries as compared with the rather slow growth of such knowledge in preceding millennia. Even if this growth in human understanding should at some time return to the relatively modest rate of earlier centuries, all aspects of human activity will continue to change. A narrower chronological view, which tends to limit modernization to the nineteenth and twentieth centuries, sees this process as more or less completed in advanced countries which are considered to be "modern." This view makes vague references to a "post-modern" or "post-industrial" phase, in which attention is focused on social adaptation to an industrial base that is assumed to be completed, but the future is left rather uncertain.

In regard to the disciplinary scope of theories of modernization, one may also discern broad and narrow approaches. The broader approach is multidisciplinary, and tends to see both knowledge and action as a seamless web with respect to which the various disciplines of the humanities and social sciences offer specialized insights without being in any sense mutually exclusive. These disciplines study different aspects of the same phenomena, they contribute essential knowledge, they represent convenient subdivisions for purposes of specialization, but if any one is emphasized too exclusively, it tends to obscure the contributions of the others. The narrower approach sees the process of modernization as limited to the insights of a single discipline. From the standpoint of economic growth, the requirements of industrialization are generally seen as a determining force. And from the standpoint of social mobilization, the main subject of study is the transformation of the institutions through which human beings act. Each of these narrower approaches tends to assume that industrialization is the principal characteristic of the modern era and that political and social institutions must adapt to its requirements.

The broader approach to the process of modernization tends to be impressed by the greatly enhanced capacity afforded by the advancement of knowledge for both the satisfaction of human needs and the destruction of all human achievement. This view of knowledge gives human beings more power over their environment and over each other, and at the same time it confronts them with greater dilemmas in regard to the ends and means for the employment of this power. The narrow approaches, concerned as they are with individual disciplines, tend to see modernization more in terms of development, growth, mobilization, and increasingly complex structures, and have relatively little concern with the potential for destruction inherent in the capacities responsible for this advancement.

Despite these diversities of approach, which are characteristic of a type of inquiry that is still in its first generation, theories of modernization have certain common characteristics that distinguish them from other theories. They are based on a scholarly, scientific approach to the study of developing societies. They recognize the diversity of pre-modern societies, which should be studied on their own terms, and hence the diversity of the institutional processes capable of attaining advanced levels of achievement. They seek to improve the political, economic, and social indicators that permit us to measure the development of societies; and also to determine both the universal characteristics of modernization and the diverse means by which these are implemented. They stress, in particular, the importance of change, and hence the impermanence of human institutions. They also seek to stress the importance of the individual human being, while at the same time recognizing the increasing complexity of the institutional framework within which human life must be organized.

A comprehensive introduction to theories of modernization would have to place these theories in the context of the entire universe of scholarship, theories, and ideologies, and this is clearly not possible in the present essay. One may nevertheless briefly juxtapose theories of modernization to the two predominant current ideological systems: the liberal ideologies characteristic of the West-European and English-speaking societies, and the statist ideologies characteristic of the societies following one or another of the variants of Marxism and Marxism-Leninism. Both of these ideological systems have their origin in the understanding of human affairs represented by the initial flowering of the social sciences in the nineteenth century, and to this extent they have much in common. In the course of a century, however, this level of understanding has come to be ossified in doctrinaire positions that tend to distort the findings of scholarship and to obstruct its further development. Doctrinaire liberalism has come to be narrowly identified with the dominant Western institutions and values, and the heirs of Marxism have focused their attention on the authority of the state. Each of these fixations has tended to limit significantly the adaptability to change of societies under such ideological leadership.

Theories of modernization have been developed from the findings of social science scholarship since World War II, and have played a twofold role. Concerned as they are with the underlying structure of political, economic, and social change, these theories have led in the realm of scholarship to a revision of the assumptions underlying both the liberal and the statist ideological systems. On the other hand, in the realm of policymaking, these theories suggest pragmatic approaches that frequently conflict with the relatively doctrinaire views advanced by the established ideological systems.[2] Theories of modernization are still in their formative period, and practical conclusions drawn from them represent a more diverse and less coherent point of view than those of the established ideologies. There is sufficient common ground in these views, however, to provide the basis for a distinctive approach to problems of civil war and intervention.

Theories of modernization may be distinguished from Western liberal and Marxist-Leninist theories in ways that are significant for one's approach to problems of civil war and intervention. Both the Western liberal and the Marxist-Leninist approaches tend to be ethnocentric, in the sense that they take as their model contemporary Western and Soviet societies respectively. This assumption that one society or group of societies has already found the correct answer to the modern era and that all other societies must follow in their paths prevents them from asking many of the critical questions that must be answered if one is to understand the modern world. These approaches thus take so much for granted, assume that so many of the questions have already been solved, that their contribution to our understanding of the modern era has been limited. Since many of the scholars who write on this subject are either Western liberals or Marxist-Leninists, and many of the others are disciplinary specialists concerned with limited subjects and not interested in the more general problems of change, students of modernization are a relatively small minority among scholars concerned with political, economic, and social change. Even though the boundaries between the various approaches are not sharply drawn, and these have much in common since they are interpreting the same general body of data, theories of modernization have a distinctive approach to questions of civil war, intervention, and international control.

Two characteristics of the many-faceted process of modernization are particularly significant for political development, and hence for civil war in its domestic and international aspects. One is that the advancement of knowledge has led to increased specialization resulting in the need for ever

---

[2] *See* Black, "Theories of Political Development and American Foreign Policy," in G. Lyons (ed.), *The Role of Ideas in American Foreign Policy* (1971).

larger administrative units. In a primitive society, a village of relatively few huts may be virtually self-sufficient. In advanced societies, many aspects of activity overflow national boundaries and some are worldwide in scope. Increasingly, the affairs of one nation are a concern of all others.

The other characteristic of modernization is that the great increase in productivity accompanying it is the result of correspondingly large investments which are normally accumulated by means of the exploitation, to a greater or lesser degree, of the majority by a privileged minority. Whether this exploitation is carried out by a traditional elite adapted to modern conditions or by a revolutionary elite employing state power, the resulting deprivation provides a basis for civil strife in many forms.

These two characteristics of the modern era, the increasing interdependence of individuals and societies and the increasing sense of relative deprivation, are particularly relevant to the problem of intervention in civil wars. These are structural features of the contemporary scene that underlie ideologies and policies.

The sections that follow will adopt what has been described here as the broader approach to modernization. The contribution of such an approach is not to provide answers to the more technical questions of the role of law in civil war and intervention, but rather to describe the changing environment within which these phenomena occur: the relation of civil war to more general processes of change, the changes that values of elites are likely to undergo in regard to intervention, and the changing role of the national and international institutions that are likely to have decisive effect on the implementation of controls. Not the least significant aspect of this inquiry arises from the fact that international law is based primarily on precedents that have occurred during the past century under circumstances that are no longer relevant to contemporary conditions in an era of rapid change.

MODERNIZATION AND CIVIL WAR

Whether one views change in the modern era in terms of an abstract understanding of human beings and their environment or in terms of specific labor-saving machinery that serves to multiply human effort, the effect of the rapid advancement of knowledge has been to change the ways in which human beings have organized their lives. The capacity of human beings to maximize their energies has grown, political authority has been centralized, agriculture and manufacturing, transportation and commerce have been increasingly mechanized, with an accompanying improvement in standards of living; and the social role of human beings has changed from predominantly agricultural and rural to predominantly industrial and urban, with marked alterations in patterns of stratification and rates of mobility.[3]

[3] This and the following sections treat problems of civil war and intervention within the framework suggested in Moore, "The Control of Foreign Intervention in Internal Conflict," 9 *Va. J. Int'l L.* 205 (1969).

The process viewed in terms of any one of these aspects may convey an impression of development and enhancement, but the sum total of the changes inherent in the process of modernization involve all human behavior patterns and are correspondingly unsettling to the identity and security of the individual. While it may be maintained that the political, economic, and social equilibrium has never been fully stable, it is also true that it has never been so subject to change as in the modern era. What from one point of view may appear to be "progress," in terms of the improvements of the potentiality of human effort and consequently in the standard of living, will from another one appear as a threat to established positions. Whether it is a question of landlords versus tenants, or the state versus provincial and municipal authorities, or employers versus employees, or the more privileged at any given point in time versus the less privileged, change in a given equilibrium and especially in cases in which one group improves its status relative to another group is likely to be seen as a threat by the more privileged group. Similarly, all barriers to change, all situations in which individuals may perceive they are not getting a fair share of the goods they produce, all cases in which there is a suspicion that there is taxation without representation are likely to produce feelings of relative deprivation that are liable to trigger an almost visceral impulse to revolt.

Since the modern era is the one in which change in all forms of human activity has been most rapid, it is not surprising that it is also one in which violence has been endemic. It is difficult to find a single country among the 130 or more current members of the international system that was not born in violence and whose development has not been marked by civil strife. This civil strife takes many forms, due in part to the diverse structure of different societies, but the most distinctive forms of strife are related to levels of development.

At the earliest stages in the transition of a society—the traditional era— when the possibility of modern change is first encountered, political leaders of the "old regime" generally have a monopoly of authority and by definition cannot be successfully challenged. Nevertheless, even at this stage, civil strife often breaks out between supporters and opponents of even the limited forms of modernization that may be proposed. The Fronde in France, the Taiping rebellion in China, and the various revolts in Russia from the end of the seventeenth century to the beginning of the nineteenth, may be considered to be of this type. In colonial countries, revolts against the occupying power are also of similar character. At this stage, violence is relatively limited in scope, although it may involve assassinations of political leaders and attempts at coups d'état.

Much more extensive is the type of violence that accompanies a transition from traditional to modernizing leadership. This period normally lasts several decades, and is frequently characterized by a great revolution, such as those in France, Russia, and China, which involve sweeping changes in the symbols of authority as well as in all the major institutions by which the old regimes conducted their affairs. Not all countries pass through such great revolutions, although the liberation of states from colonial control may have similar implications even if they have not normally been accompanied by revolutionary violence of the same scale. At the same time, very few countries have passed through this crisis with as little violence as Japan, and characteristically the struggle between traditional and modernizing leaders has been accompanied by a series of revolts taking different forms over a period of several generations. Even in the case of France, which at the end of the eighteenth century had a revolution generally considered to be among the most radical, subsequent political development alternated between counterrevolution and further political violence in 1815, 1830, 1848, 1851, and 1870–71. In the case of colonial countries, where the metropolitan states may be regarded as the old regimes and the leaders of national liberation movements as the modernizers, the process of national liberation has frequently involved extensive civil strife.

One would think that the capacity of nations for civil war would have exhausted itself in the strife accompanying the transition from old regimes to new, whether or not these had been accompanied by major revolutions, but the subsequent process of transforming countries from a predominantly agrarian to a predominantly industrial way of life, which normally takes place after the initial political revolutions, is also accompanied by extensive violence. Violence in this period generally takes the form of arbitrary methods employed by governments to enforce drastic policies of modernization, and efforts made by interest groups to resist this change. Extensive violence frequently accompanies the emergence to political power of new interest groups such as labor, ethnic minorities, and others. Various forms of social disorganization, such as unemployment and strikes, also engender violence. During this period of economic and social transformation, many individuals and local institutions feel the threat to their security and to their sense of identity accompanying occupational change from a rural to an urban way of life with the attendant destruction of traditions and values. Leaders opposed to modern change may gain sufficient backing in times of trouble to overthrow modern governments in the name of utopias that draw on the ideals of some early period, as did the Nazis and to some extent the fascists in Italy and Spain.[4] Such conflicts may occur well after a country has become predominantly industrialized and advanced relative to most countries of the world.

Few other countries that are most advanced, in contemporary terms, are immune to widespread civil strife. The unprecedented power of the state frequently makes it a particular target for dissatisfied groups in times of unrest, and assassination and urban violence are by no means uncommon. The very extent of social integration tends to magnify resentments such as those arising from unemployment, the integration of ethnic and religious

---

[4] This neglected aspect of modernization is discussed in Turner, "Fascism and Modernization," 24 *World Politics* 547–64 (July 1972).

minorities, etc., that could be handled on a more diffuse basis in less integrated societies. The stability of relatively modern societies depends on the extent to which their formal public institutions are congruent within their political culture, and many countries have developed in ways that have not served to increase their domestic stability over the years.

Civil violence has thus accompanied modernization in virtually all countries and at every stage of development. Although by no means all of the violence could be classified as civil wars in which the question of insurgency or belligerency could be raised, many of them did have such consequences. Indeed, the bulk of traditional international law relevant to this question was evolved in the course of the various civil wars of the nineteenth century in the countries now regarded as advanced.

In considering the implications of this record for the future, theories of modernization offer a different perspective from those of Western liberalism or Marxism-Leninism. Western liberals generally assume that, when countries become independent, they can run their own affairs in an orderly fashion. If the United States, Germany, and China were racked by civil wars in the nineteenth century, it does not follow in the liberal view that Nigeria, Tanzania, or India need undergo internal war in the twentieth century. The Western liberal outlook tends to see development as synchronous, and to believe that the political achievements of the advanced countries can be transmitted to the less advanced just as the latest models of jet engines and steel plants have been transmitted. Civil violence is seen not as organic but as accidental—as fires to be extinguished rather than as rites of passage to be managed.

The Marxist-Leninists, for their part, assume that basic revolutionary transformations are to be anticipated between the stages of feudalism and capitalism, and capitalism and socialism, and also in connection with the national liberation of societies from foreign rule. They do not anticipate revolutions in countries under Marxist-Leninist leadership, however, and normally attribute such strife to the machinations of foreign agents rather than to the types of frustration that have in fact led to civil strife and intervention in communist as well as in other societies. Stressing as they do common—in effect, state—ownership of the means of production, Marxist-Leninists are inclined to believe that societies under their leadership are immune to the types of civil unrest that characterize societies with mixed or predominantly private economies.

The approach implicit in theories of modernization is that rapid change of a fundamental character is organically destabilizing, and that civil violence may occur at any stage of development. Prolonged civil wars are in fact rare in the more advanced countries, but these constitute no more than twenty of the 130 countries that concern us. Most of the others are in the relatively early stages of the type of development that led to violence and upheaval in the nineteenth century in the countries that are considered now to be advanced, and there is no reason to believe that these later developing nations will do any better. Except for Japan, none of the countries of Asia and Africa are likely to achieve by the year 2000, or even a generation or more later, the per capita level of development that the more advanced countries enjoy today, and it is not unreasonable to assume that they will experience a relatively high level of civil violence leading to the types of conflict that raise the problem of intervention.

It is this perspective that theories of modernization offer to those concerned with the international problems raised by civil wars. It would not be difficult, if adequate support for research in this area could be found, to indicate with considerable accuracy the types of situations most likely to lead to civil strife and to suggest the countries and the decades in which such strife is likely to occur in the future. Even without such research, however, it is safe to predict that the types of civil strife known in recent years will continue to be widespread for fifty years or more. To the extent that the further development and proliferation of modern nuclear weapons increases tensions between states, the dangers inherent to the international order in widespread domestic strife will tend to be augmented in the years ahead.

MODERNIZATION AND INTERVENTION

In their approach to intervention, Western liberalism and Marxism-Leninism differ significantly from each other and also from the outcomes that students of modernization are likely to anticipate. The Western liberals are inclined to see intervention in terms of the maintenance of the international order established by the United Nations Charter. From this standpoint, the question of intervention rests on the definition of aggression, and is justified when an aggressor can be clearly identified as a means of punishing the culprit and establishing the tenet of international law that calls for noninterference in the internal affairs of other states. The Marxist-Leninists, for their part, see a relatively clear-cut distinction between wars of national liberation, which are just and in which it is one's duty to intervene in support of the insurgents, and all other forms of internal strife, in which the incumbent government should be supported. Within this general framework, there are significant differences between the Soviet and Chinese views: the latter are much more inclined toward an active policy of intervention, whereas the former are inclined to intervene only in clear-cut cases of insurgency.

Theories of modernization have not yet been adopted as a basis for national policy, and therefore there is no record of a "modernizing" stance to be compared with those of the Western liberals or the Marxist-Leninists. Theories of modernization approach the subject not from the standpoint of state policy, but from that of projecting into the near future the intellectual, political, economic, and social trends that should be taken into account in determining what efforts should be made to control intervention in the years ahead. It is a working theory of this view that all norms based on past precedents, such as those of international law, tend to become outdated even more rapidly in the contemporary era than they did in the past, and that the discussion of measures to be taken in the years ahead should be based on a rigorous consideration of changes likely to occur in the situations under discussion.

The types of change that may be projected in the years ahead on the basis of theories of modernization relate both to the normative and to the institutional aspects of intervention. Throughout the modern era, civil wars and intervention have generally been evaluated in terms of prevailing norms. At a time when most governments adhered to traditional concepts, civil wars such as those associated with the French Revolution were generally regarded as a menace to the security of other states, and these joined forces on frequent occasions in the first half of the nineteenth century to suppress such revolutions whenever they seemed to endanger the security of individual states. As more and more states came under the control of modernizing leaders, however, this view was reversed, and since the peace settlement of 1918, there has been a predominant view that republicanism, national independence, and other values once regarded as radical were in fact normal if not necessarily desirable.

Today, theories of modernization are associated with Western liberalism and Marxism-Leninism as favoring in a general sense modernizing rather than traditional norms. The differences lie in the fact that Western liberalism and Marxism-Leninism are relatively stabilized political views, associated with incumbent governments and strongly influenced by their national interests. They have therefore tended to lose the relatively objective scholarly character that once characterized them, and are not of great value in the evaluation of current and future trends. Theories of modernization, while drawing on the same background and body of experience as the two more political ideologies, are more concerned with political, economic, and social developments that seem likely to take place regardless of the political interests of the major powers. As already noted, these three points of view overlap to a very considerable degree, yet they differ in certain points that are important in the evaluation of intervention.

As concerns the various claims that may be made in regard to intervention, modernization theory is inclined to support the view that certain types of change are normal adaptations of societies to the scientific and technological revolution, and that the states and international organizations that have the power to influence these developments should seek to assist their accomplishment with a minimum of risk to the international community. At very least, it seems likely that influential leaders in many countries and international organizations will tend, in the years ahead, to be guided more than in the past by the conclusions of contemporary social science research rather than by ideologies based on traditional norms.

More specifically, theories of modernization will tend to support the view that reasonably homogeneous and viable societies are more likely to modernize successfully if they are politically independent than if they are under the sovereignty of other states which they may regard as inimical to their interests. There are no doubt many cases where some form of federalism may in the end be better than independence, but even in cases where a dominant government can be of great assistance to such people, the very fact of dominance may counteract such assistance as they are able to give. Under these circumstances, theories of modernization will tend to favor peoples desiring to gain independence or self-government in an anti-colonial war, and to maintain that such benefits as the empires have been able to provide in the past can be provided more effectively through other instrumentalities.

In the case of claims relating to wars of secession, theories of modernization may be able to provide criteria by which to evaluate the extent to which separation or continued unity may be more conducive to the modernization of the peoples concerned. It should be recognized that, in analyzing contemporary situations of this sort, modernization theory is more a blunderbuss than a laser, since the intentions and capacities of secessionist leaders and groups to improve on the policies of an existing government can never be very accurately anticipated. Nevertheless, the attempt will always be made, and one may expect that influential elites in other countries and international organizations will be inclined to evaluate the risks to international security of policies under consideration at least in part in terms of whether a territory desiring to secede will be "better off" alone or if it remains under the existing government.

There are many types of claims in regard to which the insights that theories of modernization may be able to offer are not particularly relevant. These include claims to provide military assistance to governments in the absence of internal disorder as a general matter of international policy, or to assist such governments in controlling rebellions which have not or are not likely to reach a point of insurgency. Even in cases of insurgency, where the control of a central government may be in question, the main trend of modernization theory is likely to lead to the conclusion that the adaptation of individual societies to the scientific and technological revolution is a long and complex process in which differences in policies in rival governments are not likely to be so great as to warrant the risk of a major international conflict. Even in the case of the great revolutions, there is so much continuity between old and new regimes that, after the storm has passed, one may wonder whether the loss of life was justified by the results achieved or, to put it differently, whether similar results could not have been achieved at a lower cost. If one compares the achievements over a long term of governments which have been willing to accept great losses in the lives of their peoples as compared with those that have not, it does not appear that the former have done any better. Japan, for example, is generally regarded as having attained a higher level of per capita achievement than Russia at a relatively much lower human cost.

In the case of claims relating to the external initiation of the use of force, and also claims relating to conflicts between nations divided as a result of a peace settlement in 1945, such as Korea, Vietnam, and Germany, the criteria involved relate primarily to political considerations rather than to those arising from theories of modernization. Objective study by social scientists of the development of societies thus far has not reached sufficiently final conclusions regarding the success of different types of governments and ideologies in guiding the adaptation of societies to the scientific and technological revolution to influence elites in this regard. While the available evidence tends to show that in Europe the "capitalist" countries have generally been more successful than the "communist" countries in promoting economic growth, for example, it is by no means certain whether this success is due to the policies adopted by the contemporary governments or to the less manageable factors of historical development and political culture which make some societies easier to develop than others. There are also cases where individual countries under communist leadership have done better than individual countries under other types of leadership. One may therefore venture the conclusion that, in the wide range of decisions involving intervention in cases of this sort, considerations relating to theories of modernization are not likely to play a significant role as compared to the considerations relating to the preservation of international security.

To the extent that one of the main concerns of theories of modernization is the maximization of effort for the benefit of human welfare, claims concerning the use of military intervention for the protection of human life are likely to be of particular concern. Theories of modernization tend to maintain that a society is most likely to make the best use of knowledge for its welfare under conditions in which every individual can work to full capacity. To the extent that theories of modernization are influential among decision-making elites, they will therefore tend to favor protection of religious, political, and ethnic minorities, and prevention of discrimination against them. The extent to which such action calls for military intervention is a matter to be decided in individual cases by weighing the cost of intervention against the benefits of human rights. All that is maintained here is that theories of modernization will tend to weigh in favor of human rights. A typical example of this type of elite opinion is the creation of the United Nations Committee for the Emancipation of Colonial Peoples, which collects evidence and exerts influence tending to encourage intervention in those cases where it is deemed necessary for the protection of the human rights of the peoples concerned.

MODERNIZATION AND CONTROL OF INTERVENTION

International law is customarily considered to have two subjects: states, defined as entities possessing population and territory administered by governments with a capacity to enter into relations with other states; and other international legal personalities, including international organizations, intergovernmental corporations, and also individuals through the intermediary of international organizations. In effect, international legal personalities gain their status as subjects of international law by the decisions of states, which allocate to international organizations and intergovernmental corporations the authority to perform certain functions on their behalf.

It is interesting to note that, in the traditional view, sovereign states were the only subject of international law, and that the extension of the concept of international legal personality to other subjects is a relatively recent development. It is therefore important to consider the relations of the process of modernization to this development. If there has been a significant extension to the concept of international legal personality from the state to international organizations and intergovernmental corporations, and even under certain special circumstances to individuals, is it not possible that this is the beginning of a trend the conclusion of which will be the transfer of all sovereignty from states to a variety of instruments and international bodies? If this process of transfer of sovereignty from states to other legal personalities should continue, will not international and municipal law tend to merge?

The impact of the scientific and technological revolution on the state has resulted in a dilemma that places it under great strain. Most human activity has been integrated under the auspices of the state, so that, to a greater extent than ever before, each individual tends to look to the state rather than to any other single institution, whether family, local government, or social organization. The continuance of the authority of the state, not to mention its economic stability, is therefore much more important to each citizen than ever before. There is no reason to believe that this trend will not continue, with the effect that each individual will tend to regard the state as vital to individual security.

At the same time, the same processes of specialization and integration that have tended to reallocate centers of organization and decision making from the family to local government and from the local government to the state have also tended to reallocate it from the national to the international level. The dilemma therefore is that as the stability of the state becomes more important to each individual, it becomes less secure because the component elements of human life tend to be moving away from its control toward a variety of international and transnational instrumentalities. The most significant of these instrumentalities are not international government authorities, but international corporations and other organizations that are increasingly developing a life of their own, even though in each country they may operate under national legislation.

One of the important differences between theories of modernization on the one hand and Western liberalism and Marxism-Leninism on the other hand is that the latter have placed great stress on national sovereignty and tend to anticipate that international development will take place through the national states. Western liberals typically see international integration as developing through a world government which will be a parliament of nations just as national parliaments in federal states are parliaments of states. States under Marxist-Leninist leadership likewise emphasize the role of interstate cooperation, and to the extent that they have established international organizations, these have been interstate bodies that in many significant respects do not differ structurally from the interstate bodies created by other types of government.

To the extent that theories of modernization have been concerned with this problem, they have reached somewhat different conclusions. The trends that they have observed are that leadership in international integration is taken not by national states, which are most jealous of their sovereignty and slowest to reallocate it to international bodies, but rather by economic and social institutions. Industry, commerce, and a variety of social organizations are far more likely than national states to base their policies on international and transnational considerations. The trend toward international organizations therefore does not appear to be taking the path of increasing cooperation among states and the assimilation of their sovereignty into international political institutions, but rather through international economic and social activity which takes place to a considerable extent despite state policy. The paths that the peoples of the world appear to be taking toward international integration is therefore not a path of political action, but more of economic and social action. If one may take the federal structure of the United States as an example, for instance, the integration of the country has taken place less through the common action of fifty states allocating their power to the central government than through natural economic and social processes that have led skilled people to migrate to those parts of the country where they can best exercise their capacities. The resulting process is not one of fifty states moving ahead in roughly the same proportion, but rather of three or four major megalopolises attracting skills and resources on the basis of their ability to employ them.

If this analogy, which is true of most other advanced countries, may be projected to the international scale, then the trend of the peoples of the world toward international integration is likely to take place not through the United Nations, but through the accumulation on the part of those peoples best able to modernize. The long-term effects of such a development will thus be not to strengthen the United Nations, but to strengthen those major centers of political, economic, and social development—the United States,

Western Europe, the Soviet Union, and Japan, in current perspective—that have been most successful in adapting their institutions to the requirements of the scientific and technological revolution.

SOME CONCLUSIONS

The most important contribution that theories of modernization can be expected to make to efforts at normative and institutional control of intervention is in providing a more scholarly evaluation of the political, economic, and social realities in the years ahead that should be taken into consideration in making proposals for changes in international law. The danger of forecasting in a period of rapid change is that predictions will rest on assumptions based on past experience that may be inadequate for the purposes of international law. At very least, theories of modernization based on contemporary scholarship in the social sciences are likely to provide a sounder basis for forecasting than projections made by adherents of the currently dominant approaches of Western liberalism or Marxism-Leninism, which rest so largely on doctrinaire conclusions drawn from limited segments of human experience. It will be a decade or even a generation before theories of modernization are generally accepted by policy makers; in the meantime, they represent an approach critical of currently dominant views that should be given serious weight in scholarly discussions of international problems.

One conclusion one may certainly reach is that civil wars broadly defined are a normal, organic part of human experience. The American experience, for example, has included one major civil war and, more recently, civil strife in a variety of forms. In both the nineteenth and twentieth centuries, the question of direct or indirect foreign intervention has been an issue. Most countries have had more experience with civil strife and intervention than the United States. The more developed countries are as prone to civil strife as the less developed countries are, although the conflict seems to take different forms at different stages of development. Attempts to repress civil strife are likely to succeed for only limited periods of time, and the bloodshed and destruction caused by anti-revolutionary wars merely divert revolutions temporarily into different channels. The problem for international law is, therefore, not to prevent civil wars but to manage them.

It is also significant that the normalcy or even the desirability of civil strife will vary greatly with the eye of the viewer. The great powers will normally seek to aid the incumbent governments of their allies and the insurgents in countries regarded as opponents. Policy toward civil strife thus becomes part of the struggle for the balance of power—one of the means by which one alliance system tests its strength against another. Consequently, measures to control intervention should be a constituent part of institutions developed to establish a stable world order. In an age of nuclear weapons, the kinds of gains an alliance system can make by promoting civil strife in an opposing country are likely to be small in comparison with the risks involved. A major challenge of the modern age is the construction of a system of world order within which the unrest within individual countries can run its course without becoming a source or an excuse for international conflict.

Chapter 4 | **The Relevance of Theories of**
Internal Violence for the Control
of Intervention | *Ted Robert Gurr*

My purpose in this chapter is to consider whether theories about the etiology and effects of internal violence have implications for the control of coercive intervention, and if so, what some of them may be. To pose the general question is to invoke myriad subsidiary questions of definition, judgment, and political objectives. I deal with some of these questions in the first section, below, before addressing the more fundamental issue of whether ideally rigorous theories of violence and revolution are more likely to facilitate or inhibit intervention. As will become clear, I think that such theories can have intellectually and morally legitimate uses as part of more general efforts to restrain intervention. The latter part of the essay evaluates some of the specific implications for intervention of two generic types of current theories: the prescriptive and the descriptive. It will be seen that such theories can provide considerable guidance—however contradictory—for those who would intervene. Most of them also imply that in many circumstances coercive intervention is irrelevant or dysfunctional to the objectives of the intervenor.

SOME DEFINITIONS AND ASSUMPTIONS

By "internal violence" I mean concerted, collective uses of destructive force within the polity. The most general and common distinction among types of internal violence distinguishes the violence used by regimes, called *statist violence* here, from the anti-statist and apolitical kinds of violence that here and elsewhere I call *civil violence*. Most prescriptive and empirical theories of violence deal nominally with civil violence: they purport to show how or why violence is organized against the state. Revolution is usually treated in these terms, as are riots, terrorism, guerrilla warfare, and so forth. It is worth pointing out that such concrete events are usually *interactions* between regimes and their opponents, each using violence against the other. The distinction between civil and statist violence is thus often an arbitrary one, and theories which purport to explain events like revolution by reference principally to actions of a regime's opponents are necessarily partial.[1]

[1] This criticism is forcefully made by Terry Nardin, "Theories of Conflict Management" *Peace Research Reviews* (1971), and applies to a number of theories of civil violence and revolution, including my own.

It takes two sides to make riots and revolutions, and it requires a general theory of internal conflict to explain fully their causes, processes, and outcomes.

Some of the theories to be reviewed subsequently deal specifically with revolutionary violence: Che Guevara specifies how to make revolutions, Sir Robert Thompson advises on their suppression, Chalmers Johnson suggests when and why they are attempted. This essay will deal with revolutionary theories and situations more than with any other form of internal conflict—since revolutions attract most interventionist activity. So we should be clear on what is meant by "revolution." Generally, the term signifies massive, abrupt change. My concern here is with *political revolution*, that is, with attempts at massive, abrupt change in political authority structures, accomplished at least partly through violence. Note that the definition includes attempts, which are much more numerous than successes.

There has been much definitional discussion of "intervention."[2] I do not propose to add to it, but instead will adopt Oran Young's definition of intervention as "organized and systematic activities across recognized boundaries aimed at affecting the political authority structures of the target."[3] By this definition, intervention is a subset of a much wider range of transnational interactions including travel, diplomatic representation, trade, espionage, military and economic aid, etc. Interventionist action is distinguished by the motive of its initiator, namely to affect—maintain or alter—regimes. More precisely, it is distinguished by its *primary* motive, since multiple motives can be identified for most transnational actions. I will use a further distinction between coercive and non-coercive intervention also: coercive intervention entails the intervenor's use of punitive sanctions to maintain or alter political authority structures. To illustrate the distinctions, military aid intended primarily to strengthen a regime against foreign attack is not intervention, whereas such aid given primarily to increase its capacity to maintain order in the face of revolutionary threats is interventionist. It is coercive intervention, however, only if it is provided as a direct response to ongoing internal violence. Economic transactions are interventionist, in the sense the word is used here, only when they are established primarily to shore up a weak or threatened regime. Economic transactions also can be used coercively, for example when trade or aid is withdrawn to undermine a regime's popular support, or to pressure it into changing its character.

I hope it is clear that I am not formulating these definitions and distinctions with some clandestine normative purpose in mind. In common usage, "violence" and "intervention" have negative connotations, and when

---

[2] *See*, for example, Rosenau, "The Concept of Intervention," 22 *J. of Int'l Aff.* 165 (Autumn, 1968), and Moore, "The Control of Foreign Intervention in Internal Conflict," 9 *Va. J. Int'l L.* 212 (1969).

[3] Young, "Intervention and International Systems," 22 *J. of Int'l Aff.* 178 (Autumn, 1968).

they are used for purposes deemed worthy, they are likely to be relabeled "force," "self-defense," "support," etc. The definitions I use here are intended to be neutral, to be scrubbed clean of normative baggage, so that they can better be used for analysis. My own normative position is a qualified rejection of coercion and violence as social means and an absolute rejection of them as ends. My rejection of them as means is qualified by the recognition that there are some real and hypothetical circumstances in which greater goods can only be served by coercive means. Some statist violence may be necessary to preserve a generally healthy and satisfying political community; coercive intervention may in exceptional circumstances be advisable in the same cause. Revolutionary violence may sometimes be a people's best, last, and only hope of overthrowing predatory, oppressive rulers; foreign intervention on behalf of such people may similarly be justified. Such qualifications aside, I judge that violence is much too prevalent in most nations' domestic affairs and that coercive intervention is used in international affairs to enormous excess, and moreover that both are often employed with ignorant and self-defeating faith in their efficacy. These judgments necessarily influence my approach to the topic. They should not substantially distort the contingent definitions and analysis.

CAN THEORIES OF INTERNAL VIOLENCE CONTRIBUTE TO THE CONTROL OF INTERVENTION?

It may be only an act of faith that general, theoretical knowledge of internal violence and political revolution will contribute to the control of intervention. Precisely the opposite argument can be made: The more predictable are attempts at political revolutions and their outcomes, the greater the temptation for interventionist elites to manipulate the determining conditions, and hence the greater and more "successful" the number of interventions. There are several rejoinders to this argument. One is that the determinants of revolution and its outcomes, even if precisely understood, may not be manipulable. We shall see subsequently that a number of major variables in extant theories of revolutionary causation are either not manipulable in most situations, or manipulable only at very great cost. A second is that there may be a high degree of indeterminacy in revolutionary causation and consequence. That is, even an optimally precise general theory of internal violence is unlikely to provide predictions of the shape and outcomes of violence with more than moderate probability levels. Interventionist elites may well choose not to intervene if the most precise social-scientific knowledge can only improve the chances of a favorable (to them) outcome from, say, 40:60 against to 50:50. Third, precise theories about internal violence will not necessarily show that military intervention is most likely of success; interventionist policies might be more fruitfully pursued by, say, manipulation of aid, trade, and communication patterns than by military means. Finally, we might anticipate stalemates between equally-knowledgeable and competing interventionist elites, or between an indigenous and an interventionist elite. Armed with equivalent knowledge, each might anticipate the other's moves and countermoves sufficiently well that inaction would be decisively less costly than intervention.

What I have just reviewed are possible objections, not definitive ones, to the thesis that adequate explanatory theories about internal violence may facilitate coercive intervention. They are not definitive because there are no such theories at present; extant theories of statist and civil violence generally, and of political revolution specifically, are largely unvalidated and not operationalized for most contemporary societies. Those limitations alone substantially inhibit their current use for policy purposes. But better theories and better indicators will be devised. No doubt, mathematical simulation models will be developed from them, by which it will be possible to forecast the extent, forms, processes, and outcomes of internal violence in specific countries with considerably more accuracy than is now possible on the basis of intelligence estimates and country-expert judgments.

The ultimate controls on the uses of this kind of social-scientific knowledge are not intrinsic to the theories. Scientific theories of violence and revolution ought to meet criteria of generality, logical consistency, validity, and predictability; the more they are distorted in order to satisfy predetermined judgments of what they *should* predict, or what kinds of actions they *should* support, the worse they are either as theories or as guides to action. Control on the use of such knowledge does not rest primarily with the scientist who formulates the theories, either. The scientist who formulates and mathematicizes such theories has no more than a personal veto over their use. He can at the outset choose whether or not to work on a particular subject in a way that might ultimately facilitate the "wrong kind" of intervention. He also can choose whether or not personally to apply his models to particular situations for the benefit of particular policy makers. But he cannot control or usually even influence the uses others make of his written work.

The most effective controls on the uses of scientific knowledge are those which bear directly on the users. Specifically, undesirable kinds of intervention will only be limited substantially by the general acceptance of normative restraints—both intra- and inter-national—and by the existence of institutionalized procedures in the international community which provide alternatives to and sanctions against undesirable interventions.

I am not denying any role for theories of violence and revolution in limiting intervention. They have several potential functions, but these can be fully effective only in the context of more general normative and institutional support for non-intervention. Three distinct functions are discussed here.

1. *Forecasting the occurrence of major outbreaks of internal violence and revolutionary attempts.* The capacity for making such forecasts is well

within reach. Some of my own quantitative research points in this direction, for example: A few more years of research, applying proven postdictive models of the determinants of "civil strife" to more detailed information and projections of trends in particular countries, would provide just these kinds of forecasts for short-term futures, *i.e.*, one- to five-year spans.[4]

Groups and agencies armed with estimates of "revolutionary probabilities" could as readily use that information to mobilize opposition to intervention as military agencies might use them to calculate intervention. Such estimates could be used to monitor and publicize attempts at intervention in the affected countries. Countries likely to intervene should be readily identifiable, and advance information might be used to help mobilize popular and elite support in them against such action. Institutional mechanisms in the international community for "quarantining" revolutionary situations or for sanctioning intervenors could be brought more quickly into play. Most important of all, in some situations, there would be the possibility that international agencies—and non-interventionist nations—could provide curative help and mediation services to countries on the brink of massive internal violence.

The breakdown of public order and the occurrence of secessions in the Congo in 1960 affords an example. Some such events almost certainly would have been predicted some months in advance, at a high level of probability, by operational versions of several current theories of internal violence. It then might have been possible for a strong United Nations presence to be established to oversee the decolonization process, for political counsel and assistance to be provided by other African states to Congolese officials, and for non-intervention agreements to be worked out among the several nations most likely to intervene. The Nigerian Civil War provides another example. A substantial probability of civil war in Nigeria was inherent in the country's political makeup. The coup d'état in January, 1966, by mostly southern officers, would have registered in any general model of internal violence as a strongly-disposing precipitant to civil war. An immediate mobilization of international machinery to provide mediation then might have deflected the Biafran secession. Even after secession began, the existence of stronger sanctions against intervention could have undermined the confidence of both sides that warfare offered better chances than compromise. It also is likely (writing in January 1974) that the eventual death of Emperor Haile Selassie of Ethiopia will be followed by one or more coups, intensified secessionist rebellion, and an increase in intervention in that country. I am not aware that any international organization is planning for such contingencies.

---

[4] *See* D. A. Hibbs, Jr., *Mass Political Violence: A Cross-National Causal Analysis* (1973); and T. R. Gurr and R. Duvall, "Civil Conflict in the 1960's: A Reciprocal Theoretical System with Parameter Estimates," 6 *Comp. Pol. Studies* 135 (July 1973). At best (or worst) such studies can provide only probability estimates, not precise predictions.

2. *Estimating likely outcomes and consequences of internal violence and revolutionary attempts.* There is some theoretical understanding of the determinants of who "wins" in a revolutionary situation. There is very little scientific competence to explain or forecast the longer-run consequences of internal violence, revolutionary or otherwise, in particular countries. If and when such estimates can be reliably made, the self-interest of interventionist elites probably will more often militate against coercive intervention than is now the case. Much intervention can be regarded as a response to uncertainty: uncertainty about who will "win" a revolutionary confrontation, and uncertainty about the consequences of "winning" for one side or another. Special economic and military assistance to the side favored by an interventionist elite in such circumstances is a way of decreasing the perceived uncertainty—though intervention may in fact increase the unpredictability of outcomes and consequences.

If the immediate outcome of any revolutionary confrontation were more precisely predictable, especially if one side or another was recognized as strongly favored, then intervention would become psychologically and strategically less necessary for those who would intervene on behalf of the "winner" and less attractive for those who would help the "loser." Interventionist elites obviously do now make such judgments, and their interventions sometimes prove decisive: the interventions of the USSR in Hungary, 1956, and of the United States in Guatemala, 1954, are cases in point. The results of many other coercive interventions, however, indicate grossly inadequate advance estimates of the balance of forces between contending parties. Some recent examples are the United States in Cuba, 1961; Communist China in Indonesia, 1965; and Portugal in Guinea, 1970.

More telling arguments against specific coercive interventions probably could be made in light of better understanding of long-range consequences of internal violence. The histories of revolutions and coup d'états in most of Latin America, for example, are powerful evidence that *plus ça change, plus c'est la même chose.* More generally, we should be able to identify a number of general situations and specify a number of countries in which one or another revolutionary outcome is highly unlikely to make much difference in social, political, or economic consequences. The object lesson for the intervenor in such cases should be self-evident: If it doesn't make much difference who wins, why bother intervening? The same principle applies to countries caught up in rapid and disequilibrating change as well as to those which are structurally frozen. Chile and Libya are disparate current examples of countries undergoing massive change, change which will probably—not necessarily—create a succession of "revolutionary situations," each of whose outcomes is likely to be inherently unstable. "Who wins" at a given point may be of short-term importance to an interventionist elite, but if each "winner" is likely to be displaced in turn, then the long-range attractiveness of intervention should lessen.

Erroneous forecasts of revolutionary consequences can also lead interventionist elites to actions that are not merely unnecessary but that ultimately undermine their purposes. This is especially true in the contemporary, polarized world, in which one set of interventionist elites has been ideologically disposed to support almost any kind of revolutionary change, and another set equally disposed to support almost any status quo. Soviet support for the Chinese Communists in the 1930's and 1940's contributed greatly to the Communist victory—which led to the establishment of a powerful, unified, and now unremittingly hostile nation on Russia's longest border. Such a consequence of ideological triumph probably would have been predictable, at a modest level of probability—and seems to have been sensed by at least some Soviet statesmen at the time. The United States for some twenty years opposed and dabbled at intervention in the Mexican revolution: that intervention was not great enough to prevent Mexico's metamorphosis into what is now, from the U.S. point of view, a model of Latin American political stability and economic growth. The official American devotion to anti-Communist nationalism in Southeast Asia has postponed, and probably made impossible, the development of a strong and independent national Communist regime in a unified Vietnam—whereas by almost any initial interventionist claim, such a regime would have been preferable, from the American point of view, to the current chaos in Indo-China. This suggests a third function of empirical revolutionary theory in attempts to control intervention.

3. *Providing better estimates of the consequences of intervention.* A general theory of revolutionary causation might state that revolutionary attempts are a multiple function of specified cultural and social background variables, certain degrees or kinds of change, and the ideological orientations and relative capacities of the contending parties. "Winning" would depend on some specified combinations of these variables favorable to one or the other contender, plus strategies and tactics by which each could take optimum advantage of whatever combinations of conditions they faced. A good theory of this sort would also specify the interaction effects among its variables: How do social change and strategic variables affect the root causes of conflict? To what extent do cultural predispositions and social changes affect what people believe? And so forth. If this kind of validated general theory of revolution was applied to a specific country, a policy analyst could estimate in advance the probable effects of any substantial changes in its variables on revolutionary likelihood and outcome. As part of that function, the analyst could anticipate the internal effects, or lack of effect, of various kinds and degrees of intervention, and could do so with some accuracy.

Interventionist elites do have some kinds of theories of revolutionary causation, often implicit rather than explicit, usually partial, and always unvalidated. Insofar as we know or can infer the content of these "theories," they include only some relevant variables, for example, emphasizing economic conditions and coercive capacities (key variables in the conventional

American model), or organizational tactics and ideological proselytization (two Communist emphases). Such theories seem often wrong or ignorant about "feedback" effects of changes in one variable on other variables. So when interventionist elites act in terms of their partial theories, they often reap quite unintended internal consequences. Economic and technical assistance have long been regarded by some Western elites as desirable means to political stabilization in non-Western nations. Yet such aid frequently has been shown to have such destabilizing effects as increasing population pressures on scarce resources; raising expectations of some groups—the nascent middle classes especially—beyond the possibility of satisfying them; reinforcing the positions of change-resistant elites; creating or exacerbating traditional resistance to modernity; and so on. Military assistance intended principally for the maintenance of internal order has variously facilitated border conflicts among neighboring states, found its way into the hands of opportunistic rebels, obliged poor nations to create modish and costly military establishments, and encouraged many military officers in the belief that they could manage affairs of state better than civilians. Direct military intervention has fruitlessly and bloodily prolonged many revolutionary conflicts and civil wars, generated xenophobic reactions against alien soldiers and their governments, discredited one or both contending parties in the eyes of their supporters, and helped establish or reinforce patterns of chronic elite and institutional instability.

Interventions do not occur in an international vacuum. The actions of one interventionist elite toward an internal conflict usually trigger counter-responses by other interventionist elites and by interested international bodies. The results range from prompt negotiated settlement to escalation into direct military confrontation between sponsors of contending client groups. The international consequences of intervention cannot be forecast by theories of internal violence and revolution; they could and should be evaluated by linked theories that account for different nations' dispositions to intervene, and that specify the probable effects of various strategies of intervention, control, and mediation. Some of the structural and motivational variables relevant to a theory of intervention have been specified by Young.[5] A theory of the processes of major internal conflicts has been developed by Bloomfield and Leiss, who use it and substantial empirical data about post-1945 conflicts to derive "significant elements of a *strategy of conflict control*," which they hope will provide an alternative to "past strategies of 'win' that all too often involved belated, politically costly, and sometimes bloody unilateral military intervention."[6] These kinds of theoretical efforts would interlock with theories of the causes and consequences of internal violence to meet the kinds of functions discussed here. Interventionist elites armed with more reliable estimates of hostile international

[5] Young, *supra* note 3, at 180–84.

[6] L. Bloomfield and A. Leiss, *Controlling Small Wars: A Strategy For the 1970's* (1969), at 7.

responses may be less likely to intervene coercively. And elites that have strategic options which lead predictably toward non-coercive settlements, even if not wholly favorable to their interests, should be more readily dissuaded from coercive interventions.

*   *   *

The gist of the preceding arguments is that validated general theories of internal violence and revolution would increase the predictability of internal conflict situations, outcomes, and consequences. Concurrently, they would make it possible for international actors to anticipate more accurately the internal effects of different kinds of intervention. In this era, such information would almost certainly reduce the number and destructiveness of stupid coercive interventions—those, like Vietnam, which defeat the purposes of some of the intervenors. But it would also identify more clearly situations in which interventionist nations could dabble profitably, and could be used to develop least-cost strategies by which they could do so. In concrete terms, interventionist wars like Vietnam would be less likely, but Guatemalan and Czechoslovakian types of intervention might be more likely. The latter "easy" kinds of intervention are not controllable by the "enlightened self interest" of interventionist elites, but only by whatever normative and institutional constraints exist in the domestic and international environments in which such elites act.

The following sections consider some current, rather than ideal, theories of internal violence and revolution. The question asked is what kinds of general implications they have for making and controlling interventions.

SOME PRESCRIPTIVE THEORIES OF VIOLENCE

Prevailing theories of internal violence and revolution are of two generic types: prescriptive and empirical. Both supposedly stipulate the principal conditions that determine the incidence of violence, its outcome, or both. The prescriptive theories emphasize strategic and tactical factors: they assume the desirability of creating revolution or defeating insurgency and specify when, where, and how to do so. The empirical theories are concerned mainly with identifying the general causes and processes of internal violence. Their primary, nominal objective is to provide a better general understanding of violent conflicts. In some instances, they are stated at such a level of generality that they have few strategic, much less tactical, implications. Almost all their authors have normative commitments to order in preference to disorder, however, and as a consequence they incorporate or conclude with explicit strategic recommendations for forestalling or terminating violence in conflict situations. We will first consider a few prescriptive theories of revolution and insurgency.

Prescriptive theories of revolution, irrespective of their accuracy, have one powerful diagnostic function for those who evaluate international developments: To know which interventionist elites subscribe to which theory is to be able to estimate which countries will intervene in which internal conflicts in what kinds of countries and with what general objectives in mind. Neither the Cuban Communist leaders nor those of China have been reluctant to identify their strategies and tactics for stimulating revolutionary situations and working toward favorable outcomes. Theorists like Guevara, Regis Debray, Mao Tse-tung, and Vo-Nguyen Giap have variously specified what they regarded as revolutionary situations, and what kinds of actions are needed to take advantage of them. Theorists of counterinsurgency like Sir Robert Thompson and Gabriel Bonnet have been equally explicit in specifying the strategies and tactics for responding to such revolutionary situations. The ironic consequence is that the two contending parties in many revolutionary situations, particularly those matching Communist dissidents against a non-Communist regime, know quite well what their opponents are up to. Barring innovations, outcomes ought then to depend on the contenders' respective timing and execution—"ought to" rather than "are likely to," because the theories in vogue may be incorrectly applied to the situation, or intrinsically wrong, or both.

The two prescriptive models of revolution of greatest currency are the Chinese and Cuban models.[7] Both proceed from the Marxist assumption that bourgeois regimes—and by Leninist extension, regimes established under the aegis of imperialist nations—are destined to collapse and to be replaced by some kind of proletarian state. All non-socialist states thus are theoretical candidates for revolution. One condition, explicit or implicit in statements and applications of the two models, narrows somewhat the "revolutionary situations" in which intervention is likely to be attempted. The popular support of rural people is essential: Mao's aphorism that the guerrilla swims like a fish in the sea of the people is one example; Guevara wrote that "full help from the people of the area . . . is an indispensable condition."[8] Beyond this, though, the models share a basic optimism that bourgeois and neocolonial regimes are inherently weak, and that enough revolutionary persistence and experimentation will ultimately undermine them.

Faith in the ultimate success of the Socialist revolution helps explain why the proponents of these theories give relatively less attention to specifying revolutionary preconditions than to strategic and tactical questions. The principal strategic difference between the two theories concerns their rela-

---

[7] The basic writings of what I call the Cuban model are Che Guevara, *Guerrilla Warfare* (1961), and Regis Debray, *Revolution in the Revolution? Armed Struggle and Political Struggle in Latin America* (1967). The Chinese model has more varied sources, among them Mao Tse-tung's *On the Protracted War* and *Selected Works* (especially vol. IV in the 1961 Peking Foreign Language Press edition), and Vo-Nguyen Giap's *People's War, People's Army*. All are available in various translations and editions.

[8] Guevara, *Guerrilla Warfare* 4 (1961).

tive emphasis on Party vs. guerrillas. The Chinese-Communist model stresses the development of a stable and durable organization under strict Party discipline which can engage in protracted conflict, first political and later military, and can absorb many temporary setbacks. The Cuban model gives primacy to the military *foco*, a band of mobile armed fighters who have the flexibility to adapt to the specific conditions in which they operate, and whose organization is "*simultaneously* political and military."[9]

The contingent differences between the models in revolution's developmental stages are great, and have considerably different implications for interventionist strategies based on them. The Chinese model requires first the careful development of Party organization under the leadership of intellectuals, followed by its expansion into mass-based political organization and, if possible, participation in conventional politics. Situational factors determine how the Party then challenges the ruling party or class; pressure for democratic reforms is the more cautious tactic, subversion of existing parties and institutions a bolder one, and both are likely to be followed simultaneously. A shift of emphasis from political to military action is ultimately necessary, on the assumption that no ruling class voluntarily gives up power. Military action begins with highly mobile warfare in rural areas, followed by establishment of a territorial base; both are accompanied by intensive Party organizational activity. If the military phase goes well, the final stage is an assault on the cities.[10] Intervention based on this model will initially involve ideological cultivation of indigenous intellectuals and provision of training and support for Party development. Military support will be provided only much later, if at all.

The Cuban model calls first for the establishment in some favorable rural area of a guerrilla *foco*, a vanguard party and army combined, under unified leadership. The *foco* must first survive and adapt to conditions of guerrilla life, which means among other things developing some degree of acceptance and support from the local people; small, successful strikes against police or military targets may be instrumental in accomplishing this. The guerrillas then expand their military activity, striking the enemy constantly to erode his strength in the areas in which they hope to operate. The third stage is to attack the enemy on his own ground, concentrating on communication lines and bases; finally, the demoralized military will refuse to fight or support the regime, and thus the guerrillas will triumph. Statements of this model sometimes discuss how guerrillas should treat the civilian population (e.g., in Guevara's writings), but give scant attention to political organization. Interventions made in terms of this model are simultaneously ideological and coercive: the object of the intervenor is to find or create a nucleus

[9] Quotation from R. Debray, *Revolution in the Revolution?* 124 (1967). (Italics in original.)

[10] This summary is drawn from Scalapino, "Communism in Asia: Toward a Comparative Analysis," in R. Scalapino (ed.), *The Communist Revolution in Asia: Tactics, Goals, and Achievements* 16–22 (1965).

of guerrillas willing to fight, and to provide them with the requisite training, arms, and supplies.

One inherent weakness of interventions based on these models is that they can be anticipated by indigenous elites and by those inclined to intervene on their behalf. These kinds of revolutionary movements are almost inevitably small and weak at the outset. They can be easily suppressed, or at least neutralized, by regimes that choose to do so—provided that those regimes have a modest degree of competence and legitimacy. In practice, what the revolutionaries must do in such situations is survive as best they can, if they can, in the hope that the ruling elite will lose its nerve or its popular support, or collapse in the face of some other crisis. Moreover, adherence to the models makes the revolutionaries generally if not specifically predictable, which makes it easier for other interventionist elites to formulate and implement strategies of counter-intervention. The suppression of two Cuban-inspired revolutionary movements in Bolivia, in 1967 and 1970, is bitter evidence for Latin revolutionaries of how well their Bolivian and North American opponents read the revolutionary lexicon.

There is not much question that the models are *intrinsically* inadequate, quite aside from the fact that they "telegraph their punch." Empirically, they have few successes to their credit. The Chinese model is a generalization of the Chinese Communist experience, its only non-Chinese success being in Vietnam, 1946–54. Attempted applications in the Philippines, Malaya, and Indonesia have failed outright; other attempts are now stalemated in various ways in South Vietnam, Burma, Thailand, and Laos. At that the Chinese model is more successful than the Cuban, which is a retrospective rationalization of the Cuban revolution that has yet to contribute to a revolutionary win elsewhere in Latin America, despite half-a-dozen attempted applications. The revolutionary answer to this empirical observation is likely to be that repeated attempts are necessary to achieve a few successes. Debray says as much: "The armed revolutionary struggle encounters specific conditions on each continent, in each country, but these are neither 'natural' nor obvious. So true is this that in each case years of sacrifice are necessary in order to discover and acquire an awareness of them."[11] This is an acknowledgment of a wholly unnecessary theoretical weakness. There are any number of relatively sound generalizations about the social, ideological, and political preconditions of revolutionary attempts, not to mention specifications of the kinds of strategies—other than specifically military—that enhance one or another outcome. The failure of the Asian and Latin revolutionary theorists to take these into account, or indeed to do more than generalize from their own singular successes, triply subverts their purposes. It contributes to a high incidence of suicidal revolutionary attempts; provides their opponents many training grounds for developing counter-revolutionary tactics; and serves to discredit not only imperfect

---

[11] Debray, *supra* note 7, at 20.

theories but their advocates and their objectives as well. There is only one dubious gain to offset these devastating liabilities: The possibility that repeated experimentation may find and exploit some unanticipatable combination of pro-revolutionary circumstances.

Since the late 1940's, a considerable body of "counter-insurgency" theory has been developed in Western nations in response to a variety of revolutionary movements and colonial wars of independence. The lack of ability to anticipate such situations on the part of the countries most involved—France, Britain, the United States, and now Portugal—has meant that revolutionary situations were usually ignored until they posed serious security problems. One consequence is that Western counter-insurgency theory is largely military theory: it specifies the kinds of strategies and tactics needed to eliminate armed guerrillas and establish rural security. Such counter-insurgency theories, and the interventionist strategies that have been based on them, tend to be effective in situations like Bolivia, where the principal pro-revolutionary factor is armed guerrilla action, but are demonstrably inadequate in situations like Algeria and Vietnam, in which the revolutionaries have such factors as strong popular and organizational support going for them. The habit of responding to revolutionary situations in military terms, and the availability of tested counter-insurgency tactics, has provided and will probably continue to provide a disposition to intervene on the part of the principal interventionist states in the West, *i.e.*, the United States and France.[12] And Latin American revolutionaries, acting on the basis of inadequate theories of revolutionary causation, will no doubt continue to provide opportunities for successful coercive interventions by the United States, acting through client Latin military establishments.

Not all Western counter-insurgency theories are solely or primarily military. One perceptive exception is Sir Robert Thompson's manual, entitled *Defeating Communist Insurgency*. It outlines a strategy designed to counter the Asian Communist model of revolution, beginning with the obvious premise that "any sensible government should attempt to defeat an insurgent movement during the subversive build-up phase."[13] Five general principles for prevention are stipulated. (1) The government facing an insurgency should be efficient and modernizing. (2) It must function justly, in accord with its own law. (3) It should have an overall plan of coordinated economic, political, social, administrative, and security operations for the country. (4) When faced with the beginnings of insurgency, it should give priority to breaking the insurgents' political organization. (5) If the guerrilla phase begins, the government's first priority is to secure its own base areas.[14] These general principles are operationalized with more specific

---

[12] I refer here to France's repeated and little-publicized coercive interventions in Francophone Africa, *e.g.*, in Cameroun, Gabon, and Chad. Portugal has been engaged in three colonial wars, but these are not interventionist in the present sense.

[13] R. Thompson, *Defeating Communist Insurgency* 50 (1966).

[14] *Id.* at 50–58.

recommendations regarding such matters as the development of consistent legal systems, the use and misuse of military and police forces, development of intelligence networks, use of strategic hamlet systems, etc.

Thompson's theory seems at least as plausible a guide to counter-insurgency as the Chinese model is as a prescription for revolution. On balance, the availability of such a model probably facilitates intervention on behalf of threatened regimes. Its precepts are unquestionably useful to indigenous regimes. They also provide guidance to interventionist elites, in a way that apparently reduces the uncertainty about where and how to intervene. On the other hand, Thompson's model has the virtue of shifting attention away from primary reliance on coercive intervention. The ultimate effects of Thompson's theory on revolutionary outcomes depend partly on its correctness, and there are some grounds for doubting its general applicability. It assumes a "build-up," organizational phase in insurgency, which would not ordinarily occur in Latin Communist attempts at revolution. It shares another flaw with the Communist models of revolution: it is a generalization based principally on one successful case, the suppression of the Malayan insurgency 1948-60, with some supporting evidence from the Philippines, 1948-54. What succeeded in those situations may of course have been due to either general or idiosyncratic factors that Thompson's theory does not take into account. The application of some of Thompson's precepts in South Vietnam—he was an influential advisor to both the South Vietnamese and U.S. governments—also raises doubts, though it is conceded that his proposals seem to have been only partially accepted and poorly implemented. The real irony of Thompson's theory of counterinsurgency rests in its first three general principles. Any regime that is efficient, modernizing, just, and capable of comprehensive planning and administration is unlikely to face a revolutionary threat in the first place, except at foreign instigation. And the only likely source of such foreign intervention currently is a stupid application of one of the Communist models of revolution. So Thompson's theory of counter-insurgency is most likely to be effective in situations of Communist theoretical error. In situations that truly dispose toward revolution, Thompson's first three principles almost by definition do not hold. As a result, his specific counter-insurgency tactics—coercive and otherwise—can be only partly implemented, and insofar as they are implemented they will be likely to contribute to escalation and prolongation of conflict.

SOME EMPIRICAL THEORIES OF VIOLENCE

The prescriptive theories just discussed have been used to justify and guide many interventions. Empirical theories of violence generally have not been so used. The academic language in which they are phrased may have inhibited their policy use. They do not ordinarily draw out the strategic and tactical implications of particular, successful uses of intervention, which makes them seem less immediately relevant to policy makers who want interventionist guidance. Perhaps most important, they have mostly pessimistic implications for interventionists. The determinants they identify of the incidence and outcomes of violence are mostly internal, and few of them seem subject to much external manipulation. Elites who have a predisposition to intervene are probably impatient with such "unverified speculations" which suggest that they have little independent capacity to influence revolutionary outcomes. The implications for intervention of two types of empirical theories are suggested below.

SOCIAL-PSYCHOLOGICAL THEORIES

Some theorists begin with the seemingly self-evident premise that discontent is the root cause of instability and internal violence generally, and revolution specifically. My version of this premise is that the potential for collective violence in a nation or smaller community varies with the intensity and scope (*i.e.*, extent) of socially-induced discontent among its members.[15] The premise is essentially a generalization of the frustration-anger-aggression principle from the individual to the social level. A similar argument is explicit in the theoretical and empirical work of Ivo and Rosalind Feierabend, and of James C. Davies.[16] All these empirical theories elaborate on the basic premise by specifying what kinds of social conditions and processes of change increase social discontent to the threshold of violence. Davies, for example, attributes revolutionary attempts to a "J-curve" pattern of change in value satisfactions. A long-term increase in well-being (of any kind, not necessarily material) generates expectations of continued improvement; any considerable and irremediable downturn in satisfactions generates a "frustration gap" that is likely to have revolutionary consequences. The Feierabends advance theoretical and contemporary empirical evidence that the higher the levels of social and material attainment in a society, the less the violence; *but* that the greater the rate of change toward those conditions, the greater the internal violence, with the principal measured exception of income growth. I identify a number of more specific conditions that either increase expectations or decrease capabilities in ways that generate potential for violent conflict. For example, a group's past rate of change in absolute position and its decline relative to other groups are

[15] More precisely, the argument is that discontent is a psychological drive state which results from "relative deprivation," people's perception that their justifiable expectations are not capable of achievement. See T. Gurr, *Why Men Rebel* (1970), chaps. 2 and 3.

[16] See Feierabend, Feierabend & Nesvold, "Social Change and Political Violence: Cross-National Patterns," in H. Graham and T. Gurr (eds.), *Violence in America: Historical and Comparative Perspectives* (1969), chap. 18; various chapters in I. Feierabend, R. Feierabend & T. Gurr (eds.), *Anger, Violence, and Politics: Theories and Research* (1972); and Davies, "Toward a Theory of Revolution," 27 *Am. Soc. Rev.* 5 (Feb., 1962).

strong positive determinants of its potential for violence. Conversely, the greater the range of alternatives open to its members and the greater the availability of resources in the society, the less is the potential for violence.

These theories also specify various cultural, social-structural, and political factors that channel social discontent into or away from different kinds of internal violence. Here I shall only consider some interventionist implications of the "social discontent" kind of argument. All these theories hold that intense and widely-shared discontent is a necessary precondition for large-scale violence, including major revolutionary movements. This being so, the interventionist elite that wants to foment revolution can either (a) direct its attentions to those countries so characterized, or (b) attempt to generate such discontents. Such strategies require, as a first condition, adequate ways of assessing the full range and severity of social discontents. The Communist fascination with oppressed peasants and workers and the Western obsession with political malcontents as bellwethers of revolutionary discontent is evidence of a fundamental lack of intelligence. Even if this gap were remedied, the ability of any outside agency to manipulate the causes of discontent is dubious. Elsewhere I've suggested ideal strategies for incumbents and revolutionaries who want to manipulate discontent, and quote and comment on them below:

> To minimize the potential for collective violence, these are the kinds of alternatives open to an incumbent elite: first, to minimize change in group value positions, in other words to maintain the status quo in the distribution of social, economic, and political goods. If the elite is committed to progress, or willy nilly caught up in it, the benefits of that progress should be evenly distributed. No group, at least no discontented group, should gain less rapidly than others. If this is impossible discontent can be reduced by increasing the number and scope of value opportunities for the less advantaged groups. . . . The opportunities must have at least some payoff, of course. If they do not, hopes soured have more devastating effects for stability than hopes never pursued.[17]

I submit that these strategies for incumbents are well beyond the capacities of most indigenous elites. Modernized authoritarian elites may be able to so manage social change, and so to some degree may resourceful democratic elites who have unquestioned popular support. But such states are few and pose few revolutionary problems. Interventionist elites which hope to defuse revolutionary change simply are unlikely to have any effective means for providing indigenous elites with these kinds of skills. If the skills are not present, only a very long-term and prescient system of massive assistance can facilitate their development. It may be worth mentioning some of the countries for which the United States has provided substantial social and economic aid with a "stabilizing" objective, though not necessarily the above strategies, in mind: Bolivia, Chile, South Korea, India, Pakistan,

[17] Gurr, *supra* note 15, at 352.

South Vietnam. This is scarcely a roster of triumphs of American aid policy; probably only Korea approximates the goals held by those who formulated the assistance programs.

We can look now to conditions manipulable by revolutionary interventionists:

> If discontent is intense and widespread in a society, revolutionary tasks are simplified; if not, there are means by which it can be increased. Ideological appeals offer the best means. . . . Any relatively disadvantaged group is a potential audience for such appeals. . . . The groups most likely to respond are those that already have been exposed to change and are already discontented with some aspect of their lives. . . . Subordinated urban classes, new migrants to cities, and people on the margins of expanding modern economies make better potential recruits for revolutionary movements than rural peoples still caught in the unchanging web of traditional life. The most effective revolutionary appeals offer means and justifications that are compatible with the discontents and cultural experience of their potential audience.[18]

The tasks of revolutionaries seem somewhat easier. It takes only a modicum of theory and evidence to identify potentially revolutionary groups within a society, and ideological appeals are cheaply articulated. One of the catches is that revolutionary interventionists usually are locked into one ideological frame of reference, which is seldom directly compatible with the situation and attitudes of their audiences. Ideologies have to be "right on" if they are to inflame latent discontents, otherwise their function is limited mainly to reinterpreting and focusing discontents already active. The most serious catch for revolutionary interventionists is that wide and intense discontents, while a necessary precondition for serious revolutionary movements, are far from a sufficient condition. Those who would control revolutionary situations can do so with finality by eliminating severe discontents—if they can. But revolutionaries cannot make revolutions merely by creating such discontents.

This provides a natural transition to consideration of theories of violence that emphasize the causal roles of social and institutional structure and of coercion.

SOCIAL-STRUCTURAL THEORIES

What I call social-structural theories look for "first causes" of violence and revolution in the failure of one or another social mechanism to adapt to some kind of change. Chalmers Johnson's four-variable theory of "revolutionary change" is representative. The first necessary cause of revolution is a disequilibrated social system, one in which either systems of norms and values or the environment change sufficiently so that society's functional

---

[18] *Id.*, pp. 353–54.

requirements can no longer be fulfilled. Leaders faced with this situation may or may not attempt to redress the disequilibrium. If they prove intransigent or unable to do so, they lose legitimacy—the second necessary cause of revolution. They may still continue in power for some time by relying on coercion. The final, sufficient cause of revolution—Johnson calls it an "accelerator"—is the elite's loss of control over the instruments of coercion. The military may be defeated in war, or become increasingly ambitious or disaffected from the rulers; however it happens, recognition that they are disloyal precipitates a popular revolution.[19]

A somewhat different kind of structural emphasis is found in Samuel Huntington's theory of political development and political decay. His interest is the obverse of Johnson's: not what causes revolution, but how a regime can maintain political order in the face of the stresses that accompany substantial change. The crux of his argument is that the processes of social and economic modernization create new kinds of political consciousness and political participation. But modernization simultaneously undermines old patterns of authority and destroys traditional political institutions. Such a situation is inherently unstable, unless modernization is accompanied by, or preferably preceded by, the development of increasingly complex, cohesive, adaptable, and autonomous political organizations that can absorb these "modernized" people and their energies. "The vacuum of power and authority which exists in so many modernizing countries . . . can be filled permanently only by political organization. Either the established elites compete among themselves to organize the masses through the existing political system, or dissident elites organize them to overthrow that system."[20]

My own approach to the social-structural variables is to specify how the balance of institutional support, and the balance of coercive capacities, between a regime and its opponents affect the magnitude and form of political violence. Widespread and intense discontent remains a necessary precondition for internal war—a category that includes revolution—but such wars are likely to begin and persist only if regimes and dissidents have roughly equivalent levels of organizational support and fighting capacity. These relative levels depend partly on sheer numbers of supporters, but even more on such factors as where and how they are organized, their use and misuse of force, degrees of commitment, resources, and so forth. An important background condition favoring dissidents is their geographical concentration in isolated areas, or at least in cohesive groups, where they can protect themselves and maximize any external support that comes their way. A major variable that affects the revolutionary process is the consistency and severity with which the opponents use violence: inconsistent

[19] C. Johnson, *Revolutionary Change* (1966), esp. chap. 5.
[20] S. Huntington, *Political Order in Changing Societies* (1965), at 461. A briefer summary of the argument is Huntington, "Political Development and Political Decay," 17 *World Politics* 356 (April 1965).

violence is highly corrosive of support for the group using it. Another more long-term process variable is the acquisition by dissident groups of their own value-satisfying opportunities and resources. To the extent that they do so, they are likely to shift from combative to more neutral activities. (Other specified combinations of discontent and coercive and institutional balance lead toward turmoil or conspiracy.) [21]

All these three theories have at least some implications for intervention. Johnson's "dysfunction + elite intransigence + accelerator" theory offers perhaps the least. The abstractness of the "dysfunction" thesis offers only the most general guidance to those who might intervene with either revolutionary or status-quo motives; strategies for intensifying or resolving dysfunctions do not seem to be implicit in the argument. External attempts to aid or hinder an elite in dealing with dysfunction can be made, but again nothing in the theory suggests which aid strategies are likely to have what effect. The problem is analogous to the problem of helping indigenous elites deal with revolutionary discontents: Even if accurate diagnoses were available, the problems might well prove intractable. The most obvious focus for intervention in Johnson's theory is the military one. *If* societies with the revolutionary preconditions of severe dysfunction and elite instransigence can be identified, then revolutionary intervenors would be advised to devise tactics that undermine military loyalties to the regime; and status quo intervenors might want to prolong an artificial stability by providing largess for the military. France and the United States regularly use the latter tactic, though not necessarily because they make a Johnson-type diagnosis of the situation. If this were the diagnosis, it would also be recognized that such aid is palliative, not curative. If revolutionary conditions remain, then it is highly likely that at some point the military will loosen their grip—will factionalize, defect from support of intransigent leaders, or themselves come to see necessity in revolutionary solutions. Such an outcome is quite unlikely at any given point in time, hence its attractiveness for status-quo intervention by short-sighted elites; in the long run, if the theory is generally correct and correctly applied, it is highly likely. Briefly, the theory's implication seems to be that coercive status-quo intervention buys only time, not stability.

Huntington's "political organization" argument has quite different implications, specifically for modernizing countries. The revolutionary intervenor who subscribes to the theory would probably be content to work quietly away, developing indigenous support while conventionally-good developmental things like the expansion of education, urban growth, and extension of political participation were underway. It would be in the revolutionary interest to stimulate such development, so long as it seemed likely that the modernizing elite would be unable to establish solid institutional controls over such activity. Interventionist Asian Communist leaders very likely

---

[21] *Why Men Rebel*, chaps. 8–10.

would accept the operational accuracy of the Huntington thesis, adding to it one codicil: a politically-active Party apparatus can and must undermine attempts of bourgeois modernizers to develop the requisite organizational control. Following Huntington's argument again, the Party's own organizational skills would enable it, once in power, to prosecute rapid change without threatening stability. The counter-lessons apply to interventionist elites who want to forestall revolution while modernization is underway. They will want to ensure that thoroughgoing political organizations develop at least as rapidly as, and preferably faster than, socioeconomic mobilization and political participation. Such a policy would presumably require a wide range of political, economic, and social intervention, in contrast to the primary reliance on coercive intervention implied by Johnson's model. The catch—all these theories seem to have catches for those who would intervene—is that many modernizing elites seem to lack the inclination, and even more the skill, to institutionalize. We face a now-familiar problem of theoretical regression: Is the knowledge of Western social scientists and organizers accurate enough that they can prescribe effective organizational means by which non-Westerners can forestall revolution? Probably not. And if not, the Huntington thesis is limited in the aid and comfort it can provide those who want predictably to manage interventions.

The structural level of my theory provides more numerous—not necessarily accurate—and more specific implications for interventions than either of the foregoing theories. The institutional and coercive factors cited in *Why Men Rebel* are both subject to at least some manipulation by revolutionary and status-quo intervenors. Some foci for revolutionary interventions are implicit in the following quotation:

> Unless a regime is very weak, it is incumbent on revolutionaries to organize for group defense and eventual assault. Organization should be flexible enough to adapt to and survive regime repression, broad enough in scope so that it can mobilize large numbers of people for action. . . . Organizational resources should be devoted primarily to coercive means and to agitational activities rather than the satisfaction of the material deprivations of leaders and their followers. Dissident organizations otherwise tend to become ends in themselves. . . . Participation in revolutionary organization should provide sufficient . . . sense of comradeship and shared purpose to ensure the enduring commitment of followers. . . . It must also provide, of course, some minimum of security for its followers; they must feel that they have a fair chance of survival as well as success. The coercive capacities of revolutionaries can be enhanced by subversion or demoralization of regime forces, solicitation of external support, and establishment of isolated base areas among sympathizers. . . .[22]

The success of interventions along these lines is explicitly dependent on the existence of widespread, deep discontents. It is implicitly dependent on the

[22] *Id.* at 354–55.

abilities of the intervenors, and their indigenous clients, to accomplish these kinds of organizational tasks. Some kinds of foreign training can be provided, and so can arms and sometimes military cadres. Only indigenous revolutionaries, though, are likely to know their people well enough to devise and implement successful tactics.

Some strategic implications for coercive status-quo interventions can be seen in this quotation:

> If politicized discontent is relatively mild, the optimum pattern for maintaining coercive control is to minimize the men and resources devoted to internal security, and to apply sanctions with both consistency and leniency. If discontent is severe, consistency of sanctions is even more essential; sanctions applied randomly or inequitably are certain to intensify opposition. The combination of leniency and minimal surveillance will not deter intensely angered men, however. . . . The best strategy then is to maximize surveillance but to maintain a policy of relative leniency. Such a policy is likely . . . to "keep the lid on" long enough so that remedial action can be taken. The courses of remedial action include the judicious distribution of goods and means. . . . They also include the establishment or expansion of effective organizational frameworks in which those goods and opportunities can be put to work, and provision of regular channels for expressing and remedying grievances.[23]

With the exception of a few somewhat unfamiliar ideas about regime coercion, this sounds very much like the conventional statist liberal approach to revolutionary prophylaxis. The intervenor who wants to sponsor such strategies has a familiar set of tools for assisting indigenous security forces, providing developmental and administrative assistance, and so forth. Western nations have been financing these sorts of things for some decades now, and presumably some people are keeping score on the outcomes. My impression is that the most common result is qualified failure: halting social and economic development, chronic political instability and civil violence, but few full-scale revolutionary movements. Reasons for failure are not hard to discern. There are at least four self-evident requirements for predictably-successful statist interventions of this sort: (1) precise knowledge of the determinants and consequences of development and decay, not merely knowledge of revolutionary causation; (2) commitment by both client elites and their foreign supporters to apply that knowledge; (3) substantial popular support for those elites; and (4) substantial internal and external resources. If and when these four conditions coincide, aid and intervention to enhance "political stability" can be rationally justified. Otherwise they are acts of faith, often destructive ones.

[23] *Id.* at 352–53.

CONCLUDING COMMENTS

I've explored only some of the intersections of theories of internal violence and the control of intervention. Interventionist implications of class-conflict theories of violence and of rational, game-playing models could have been considered. I have made only impressionistic and probably superficial reference to the actual incidence and effects of intervention. Despite these limitations, hopefully not because of them, the analysis has led to two kinds of conclusions that require a summary repetition here.

Verified knowledge about violence and about social change generally is too inadequate to make predictable the effects of most revolutionary or statist interventions. It should be possible to anticipate most serious revolutionary attempts and to predict their likely outcomes. We also may know enough to forecast the short-term effect of some specific kinds of interventions in some specific circumstances. But prevailing theories are diverse, and all that ordinarily can be derived from them are general prescriptions, often mutually inconsistent, about what kinds of intervention will achieve what ends. Even if some of these prescriptions are appropriate for specified ends, few are likely to be implemented effectively for want of sufficient operational social knowledge. And even if some are fully implemented, their longer-range consequences are decidedly uncertain. All of these conditions are presumably subject to change. We may become more knowledgeable and act accordingly, or become more ignorantly self-righteous. In the interim, social-scientific knowledge, when and where used to direct or oppose interventions, will probably serve mainly to sanctify decisions made on other grounds.

The sources of control on intervention are not intrinsic to social-scientific theory, but reside in the normative and institutional environment in which interventionist decisions are made. Better understanding of revolution, intervention, social change, etc., should, if used, limit unnecessary and self-defeating interventions. But if it is good theory, it will inevitably help to identify sites and strategies for successful interventions. Lack of confirmed knowledge has not restrained either revolutionary or statist elites from foisting dozens of unmitigated and mitigated interventionist disasters on the people of the third world during the past twenty-five years. The scholars' inclination may be that, in the face of high uncertainty, inaction is preferable to meddling action, especially where many people's lives are at stake. Policy makers, facing ignorance, prefer action's illusion that they are guiding events. Armed with better knowledge, their impulse to action will often be increased. This use of social theory requires controls that the theorist alone cannot provide.

Chapter 5 | The Relevance of Behavioral Theories of the International System | *John W. Burton*

This chapter reflects an image of world society and assumptions and values that are not customary. In particular, they are not those usually held by international lawyers. The attitudes and notions of any writer influence his observations, selection of data, and his arguments. Frequently, especially within any one consolidated discipline and in one culture and ideology, there is no need to restate the more fundamental of these because they are part of an agreed pattern of thought and the accepted framework. But where thinking is altering rapidly and where marked differences appear in approach to a subject, which seems to be this case, basic assumptions must be stated, as they form an essential part of the argument.

1. WHAT APPEAR TO BE TRADITIONAL NOTIONS

Traditional thinking about world affairs by diplomatic historians and political scientists primarily interested in interstate behaviour—and especially legal thinking—reflects an image of world society in which sovereign states are the dominant actors. The image consists of separate entities, each trying to influence or to resist the influence of others, and each prepared to intervene, where possible, in the affairs of others in order to effect influence. The "billiard-ball" model expresses this image: the product of relative size and relative economic and military strength gives a power factor which determines the outcome when any two entities come into contact almost as certainly as, in physics, relative mass-times-velocity determines the resultant when two bodies collide.

A special language has developed in relation to this model. "Intervention" implies intervention by a state authority, or group of state authorities, into the affairs of others; "aggression" and "defense" are interstate concepts. "Power" has a special meaning, implying an ability finally to coerce, again, at a state level. The areas of investigation to which this image of world society draws attention are alliances, threats, wars, diplomatic contacts, interstate institutions. Clear distinctions are assumed to exist between interstate behavior and civil politics, in particular between "international" and "civil" strife.

This image of a world society which is essentially a society of separate state entities and the accompanying concepts and language lead, by implication and perhaps logically, to the invention of certain norms: the right of self-protection of states extending to preemptive actions, the right of states to seek external support in the event of perceived external threat, merging into a right to seek assistance against perceived internal subversion. States being the main actors and separate entities, state authorities have a special role. They have, by implication, some right and even a duty to maintain "law and order" within their territories and to exercise political power to this end. Sometimes the exercise of political power to impose law and order is associated with majority rule, from whence comes a notion of democracy and legality even in cases of severe discrimination against minorities. Legality is also attributed to authorities that represent minority factions, provided they can demonstrate an ability to impose law and order. In support of such norms, attempts have been made to define "aggression" and "intervention" as between states, and to establish interstate institutions through which world society will be without violence within a law-and-order framework. Control of world affairs by majority or powers and "judicial" settlement of disputes, backed by a coercive sanction or force, seem to be the logical idea of such an image of world society.

One further implication needs to be noted. The model is a static one: attention is not drawn to political and social changes and processes of adjustment except to the extent that the model implies resistance to change. Within this image, it was logical for Britain to give assistance to the state authorities of Nigeria against "rebels" of a different tribe. Violence is probably the only way to bring about political and social change within this state-imposed law and order framework.

This billiard-ball model, this image of world society, and the language and norms to which they give rise are an intellectual creation. They do not necessarily relate to the referent world; they relate only to a conception that has been generated. They are in the world-is-flat category, unless and until they have been tested empirically. The problems posed by this image—state aggression, intervention, and other problems—may be intellectually created problems and not those which are necessarily an outcome of the structure of world society or the motivations and needs of those comprising it.

Equally, the practical solutions suggested for these stated problems—alliances, collective security systems, world government, and others—are solutions that are relevant only to a world society of this billiard-ball structure. If the world society does not conform to this image, it would only be accidental if the solutions put forward succeeded in solving the problems.

That a traditionally held image may be a false one is usually difficult to demonstrate even empirically. The world is flat, discipline is the best technique in teaching, punishment is educative, threat deters, are typical of propositions that have been empirically tested with results that challenge but do not always immediately change thought and practice. In practice, our perceptions of reality are our reality, and in political and social relations, behavior tends to create the reality that is perceived. The perception of hostility and aggression, and action to forestall it, creates hostility and aggression. The perception of states as separate entities and significant actors in world society focuses attention on the state system to the exclusion of others. Practice in giving support to state authorities which are under internal threat strengthens the status of states and reinforces the norms of behavior that might otherwise be no more than an intellectual development of one special image of world society.

We are now beginning to open our minds to fundamental challenges because our images and models have not been leading to solutions and not satisfying us intellectually. There is no intellectually satisfying way of fitting into this states-as-actors model the realities of humanitarian intervention, "liberation" movements, steps to encourage such social and political change as would promote human rights and values. Indeed, this traditional model and the whole structure of traditionally-conceived international law would seem to be threatened, once it is admitted that an international concern for such matters of domestic jurisdiction is a significant feature of world society. To argue that this should not be so, that concern for such matters is outside traditional and legal norms, is merely to admit that these norms and reality are in conflict: that our image of world affairs and tested reality are incompatible.

Clearly, the division of world society into national and international is an arbitrary one. Probably it was an obvious division when there were relatively few transactions across state boundaries other than military excursions. State borders then represented marked discontinuities in transactions. But the image remains despite changes in the nature of world society. In many spheres of living today, state boundaries present a formal and not a real discontinuity. Why not an image of world society comprising higher entities, such as common markets, alliance groupings, ethnic units, language and cultural communities, or lower entities, such as local governments? Each has some usefulness according to the questions being asked. Are there today some empirical reasons for taking states as the units and main actors when we seek answers to questions about conditions of peace, adjustments to change, human development, decision making, values, participation, world health, civil violence, and others? The unit we take, the image or model we employ, must be relevant to our inquiries. If we are examining diplomacy, a billiard-ball model would probably be useful, because we would be examining formal relations between state authorities. For some aspects of international law, it may be relevant. But we have to be aware of the limited usefulness of the model. Whichever one we take leads to a set of concepts, notions, attitudes, and practices. Employed outside the limits of the model, they are misleading. World society is perceived by us in ways that fit our model: sometimes its development is influenced by behavior based on the model. Hence we need to take care, and be prepared to throw out a model that does not explain and help solve the problems to which we are directing attention. If the state system were not regarded as significant, then "intervention," "aggression," "international law," the United Nations, and a lot more of our thinking and procedures would become irrelevant. A state system seems to dominate world affairs. This may be due as much to the persistence of our thinking and procedures as it is to the real significance of the state system in world affairs. International lawyers and others who entertain this model may be contributing to the creation of the world society which presents the problems they are attempting to solve! Many other systems also exist. Indeed, there is a sufficient number of significant ones to render much of our billiard-ball thinking at least confused and inappropriate and to make many of our institutions, created on the basis of our billiard-ball image, ineffective and self-defeating. Some concentration on these other systems, especially those that cut across state boundaries, would lead to different images of world society, a different set of concepts and language, and a different type of problem and solution.

Our day-to-day experience in world affairs is that transactions between states, whether measured quantitatively or by assessment of effect on human living, are minimal as compared with transactions between units within the various systems and sub-systems that comprise the totality of world society. The internal dispute in Cyprus, and other conflicts between various interested governments, are usually described as though the actors were the state authorities concerned. Within a United Nations system, based on traditional notions, they are state authorities by definition. But these disputes are not unrelated to linkages within and across national frontiers, be it in Northern Ireland, Rhodesia, South Africa, the United States, Canada, Vietnam, Malaysia, and elsewhere. Israel has linkages wherever there are Jewish communities. There are transactions of religion, ideologies, culture, language, trade unions, and scholars, not to mention trading and communications relationships of which we are more aware. There are non-governmental international functional institutions and governmental institutions which have, because they are functional, only formal connexions with state authorities. Tensions between states are probably minimal as compared with tensions between ethnic, language, religious and other communities that are across and within state boundaries. Forms of "civil" violence are often universal—like student riots, anti-colonialism, anti-feudalism, white v. black, Catholic v. Protestant. Empirically, the state is a relevant unit only in respect to certain formal transactions, not particularly conflictual. Indeed, state transactions are usually the result of a response to other transactions

2. A SYSTEMS IMAGE OF WORLD SOCIETY

Let us try to start with a clean sheet. Our interest is in "civil war" in the modern world, that is, in violence within state boundaries. We know, empirically, that there is a spill-over effect, and that rarely is civil war confined to one area: sympathy and support for the "rebels" and intervention in support of existing authorities are not exceptional. The phenomenon we are examining is one of conflictual political relationships in an area not usually co-terminous with state boundaries. The state is not the appropriate unit of analysis.

There is here an implied assumption which needs to be made explicit. The state remains the appropriate unit of analysis if, in approaching the problem of civil war, we attach a special value to the preservation of the state as a legal entity, over and above any value that we might attach to human rights, perceived injustice, and political and social aspirations of minorities. From a prescriptive point of view, there may be a wish to preserve the status of the state. There is a great deal of room for personal differences here. There are those who value the state and law and order, no matter how maintained, because of the security it can give. There are persons who prefer to conserve rather than contemplate change to an unknown future structure. Then there are those who are prepared to take a risk on future structures that may emerge because they believe existing conditions are unacceptable. My own view is that we should not be prescriptive until analysis is complete, and for this reason I propose to disregard this important problem (while appreciating that this is probably a point of departure for some readers and the reason for disagreements with what follows).

World society comprises a multitude of systems and sub-systems—that is, transactions between units of the same set. One of these systems is that in which state authorities are the units. Others relate to trade, race, religion, ideologies, professions, age groups, health, police, communications, management, unions, and other linkages. The image or model of all these transactions is not unlike a representation of a great number of cobwebs superimposed one on the other. In some cases, the transactions concentrate in such a manner as to depict geographically what we know to be the main centers of modern civilization; in others (for example, in sparsely inhabited areas of the globe), there is little relationship between the world map of physical geography and the world map of systems of transactions.

Clearly, there can be conflict both between systems and within them. This means that there can be conflict between states, and between states and other systems. It is in the nature of systems to seek to preserve themselves, and it is in the nature of evolutionary processes that some systems adapt and alter and some vanish. Conflict between system and system is a part of the on-going process of change within any behavioral organization. It is not necessarily dysfunctional. It can become dysfunctional when, despite a diminution of the social relevance of the system, it is maintained by external support. The external support represents a spread of conflict, and a form of resistance to change and dysfunctional conflict.[1]

This image or model of world society has, like any other, its own set of concepts, its own language, its own set of problems and solutions. What is to be noted is how they differ from the billiard-ball model. For example, whereas the billiard-ball model draws attention to size and power, a systems

[1] I do not restate here what I have had to say about systems, conflict, and dysfunctional conflict in my *Systems, States, Diplomacy and Rules* (1968).

model gives another perspective. There have been many new states created, and civil violence in almost all theatres of the world has demonstrated a felt need for even smaller political units. There is probably no political unit so small as not to be "viable," provided it is incorporated in the expanding world economic system. The argument that Biafra would not be "viable" was a rationalization. Indeed, as political services increase and as popular participation becomes a political need, political units will have to be smaller. The status given to states by traditional thinking and custom is helping to maintain the status quo, and to inhibit what appear to be the political and social needs of world society. There will be many more Biafras and, perhaps, less enthusiasm for external intervention in the future.

To take a more fundamental difference, the legal status of state authorities or any authority in any system is of no concern in a systems model except to the extent that legality is used as a justification for behavior that is a source of conflict. What is of concern is the legitimized status of authorities within any system and, especially, within the state system. It is only recently that the earlier work of Weber and Parsons concerning legitimacy has been developed—and this only because the referent world daily shouts its warnings that what is legal and what is legitimized infrequently coincide. "Legitimacy comes to governments and other institutions of power when their constituents recognize their claim to authority in some principle or source outside them, or when citizens actively and meaningfully participate in the processes of governments . . . its functional validity comes from the concurrence of economic and social forces and needs with political institutions and relationships."[2] Loyalty of people is to values and not to leaders or institutions, and these values are those of the people over whom authority is being exercised. The challenge of this century has been and is to non-legitimized authorities and to institutions that constrain or fail to serve people in their developing goals. Our image of world society must include this reality.

A systems model draws attention to decision-making processes because a study of systems is largely the study of response to the environment. This challenge to non-legitimized authority is not a sudden development and is reflected in the history of decision-making. The notion of legal authority with coercive power was dominant right into the second half of this century at all levels. Scholars spoke of the "power model," which merely indicated the inputs available to decision-makers in terms of resources, skills, and so on, and the outputs of the decision-making process in terms of the allocation of these resources in the pursuit of the various objectives of authorities. It was not until the late forties or early fifties that there was much interest in the decision-making processes as such, that is, in how information is received, classified, stored, and retrieved and how decisions about the use of resources are taken on the basis of the information. It was not until the

[2] Ahmad, "Revolutionary War and Counter-Insurgency," 25 *J. of Int'l Aff.* 1 (1971).

late fifties that there was much interest in feedback from the environment and in how decisions had to be altered because of environmental response— for example, the responses of unions to management decisions. Now attention is being given, in particular situations, to the expression of values. The notions of authority and legitimized authority, which were considered more generally by philosophers and sociologists last century and earlier this century, are to the fore in any serious discussions of contemporary social problems. The appeal to "law and order" and the emotive accusations of anarchy divert attention from the real problem—the lack of legitimization in the authority exercised by governments, local authorities, police, managers, teachers, and parents, all of whom would like to be liberally paternalistic but are nevertheless ready to draw upon whatever coercive powers they have when they fail by persuasion to have their particular values adopted.

Once the mechanical billiard-ball model is discarded, once response of systems to the environment is considered, a range of variables becomes relevant. Important among these is perception and the way in which one actor interprets the behavior and motivations of others. Relating to this are values and the ways in which parties assess the cost of their conflicts in terms of their goals and their perceptions of the responses of others.

We have, then, a complex image of world society, clusters of overlapping systems, focusing on man rather than his institutions and, especially, in relation to conflict, on his values, perceptions, and responses to authority. In the billiard-ball model, a conflict is a "situation," to employ the United Nations terminology, and the parties are the states concerned. But a systems model draws attention to the different issues of interest to the various parties and to the existence of sub-systems that are influential in the outcome. These sub-systems are usually factions within states, each having its links with factions elsewhere. The Middle East "situation" has to be broken down into many conflicts of interest, and treated in this way, and not just as an interaction between states that happen to be members of the United Nations.

Furthermore, an image of world society comprising systems and focusing on values, perceptions, and the options open to actors at all levels leads to the proposition that conflict is not win-lose, fixed sum. The loss of one party is not necessarily the gain of another—which is so frequently the basic notion of power bargaining and judicial settlement. Once values, perception, and costing of options are introduced, there can be—and empirically there always is—the possibility of transference from the perception of a zero-sum conflict into a positive-sum conflict.

Sufficient has been said to indicate that there are concepts and a language which provide an alternative to the traditional concepts and language reflected in so much of legal thinking.[3]

---

[3] A further exposition appears in J. Burton, *Conflict and Communication* (1969).

3. INTERVENTION AND AGGRESSION RECONSIDERED

Now let us see how an altered image of world society leads to different approaches to problems of civil conflict.

Within a systems framework, in which the physical boundaries of states create no more than a formal discontinuity in many cases, intervention and aggression can occur at all levels. In contemporary times, the aggression of state authorities against a community within its legal jurisdiction is widespread and is the source of interstate intervention and even conflict. There is aggression against small groups and the person. The term is not reserved for the state level.

At any level, what is constructive intervention and what is aggression can be determined only by reference to the legitimization status, both of the intervening authority and the authority being affected, in the eyes of those over whom each of these authorities exercises influence. It needs to be noted, and we return to this below, that the legitimacy status must be in respect of the particular act in relation to the particular situation. A seemingly legitimized authority may not be legitimized in respect of one act or policy, and similarly, a seemingly non-legitimized authority may be legitimized in respect of a particular policy. There are, therefore, eight classes of intervention. (1) When a legitimized authority invites the economic or other assistance of another legitimized authority, the resultant intervention is not aggressive either in terms of legal norms or in terms of behavioral relations within a systems framework. Cases of invited aid and disaster relief are examples. (2) There are certain unlikely cases in which the result is indeterminate even by reference to legitimized status. There is the case of a legitimized state seeking the assistance of a non-legitimized authority. It is unlikely for ideological and political reasons. (3) There is the more likely case of a non-legitimized authority seeking the intervention of a legitimized one. This is more likely because of the prevalence of billiard-ball notions and the sense of obligation to assist other state authorities in addition to the ordinary strategic, economic, and other motives. An example was the Biafran case. The Government of Nigeria had a legal status; but in respect of a large proportion of the total society, it did not have a legitimized status. In such cases, investigation usually shows that, in respect of handling of the situation in question, the intervening authority lacks legitimization— this appeared to be the position of the United Kingdom in relation to Nigeria and appears to be the position of the United States in relation to Vietnam. This particular class of intervention turns out in practice to be, therefore, a case of non-legitimized authority being invited to intervene in the affairs of another non-legitimized authority. However, assuming the intervening authority were legitimized, legal norms would not be infringed because the intervention would have been invited; but within a systems framework, there would be aggression by both the intervening state and by the local state authorities against the community which did not accord a legitimized status to those state authorities. (4) The invited intervention of non-legitimized authority to assist another of the same status is more clearly aggressive for the same reasons. So much for the four cases of invited intervention. (5) The uninvited intervention by a legitimized authority into the affairs of another of the same status is unlikely, almost by definition, but would clearly be aggressive. (6) The uninvited intervention by a legitimized state authority or international organization into the "domestic" affairs of an authority that has no evident legitimized status nationally or internationally is likely to infringe some norms of international law, but, in behavioral terms, need not fall into the category of aggressive intervention if the intervention is designed to compensate for the non-legitimized status of that authority. Humanitarian intervention and protection of human rights are examples—but cases of such intervention are hard to find because of traditional inhibitions about "domestic jurisdictions" which are part of billiard-ball thinking. (7) The uninvited intervention by a non-legitimized authority into the affairs of another state the authorities of which have a legitimized status is probably a case of legal aggression and must be regarded as aggressive in a systems framework. (8) This is true also of intervention by a non-legitimized authority into the affairs of another non-legitimized authority.

In summary, the following is the position:

The Intervening Party	The Target Party	
	Legitimized	Non-legitimized
Invited and legitimized	Positive Intervention	Aggression
Invited and non-legitimized	Indeterminate	Aggression
Non-invited and legitimized	Aggression	Could be positive intervention
Non-invited and non-legitimized	Aggression	Aggression

This means that, in practice, intervention by a state in the affairs of another state is aggressive, except in rare cases of disaster relief, except in communal conflicts when the opposing factions all agree to peacekeeping forces or some other form of third party intervention by a legitimized authority, and except in cases in which legitimized authorities intervene in the political affairs of another state to offset the consequences of non-legitimized behavior.

It is often argued by governments and lawyers that world stability would be threatened by constant instability within states: law and order must be maintained. From a behavioral and systems point of view, stability ultimately rests on the legitimization of authority. This in turn depends upon the ability of authorities to adapt to altering values and conditions. The role of the modern state is not the protective one of the past, but one of assisting systems and sub-systems it can influence in making adjustments to changing conditions. In the case of community relations, the state can retain its legitimized status only by ensuring that the communities themselves perceive that their instrumental needs are satisfied by the authorities without discrimination, and by educational, employment, and related policies that avoid communal tensions. The "law-and-order" approach tends to give support to authorities in their discrimination and in economic and social conditions which accentuate communal conflict. Northern Ireland is a good case study. Processes of social and political change stand out as being of central importance in the maintenance of stability, whereas the legal approach tends to emphasize the preservation of existing structures.

4. RESOLUTION AND SETTLEMENT

Let us consider now how to handle conflict within this systems framework of thinking. A key issue is the distinction between settlement, that is, third-party adjudication or determination, and resolution, that is, the resolving of the problem by the parties and hopefully to their mutual satisfaction.

The difference reflects different basic personal assumptions that are subject to empirical verification. The assumption underlying resolution is that conflict of interests is a subjective phenomenon which occurs when conditions exist that prevent accurate assessments of costs and values and consideration of alternative means and goals. If, on the other hand, conflicts were held to be due to aggressiveness or expanionist tendencies, and if power relations determined the nature and structure of society, then the settlement of conflicts could come about only by third-party intervention, enforcement of a settlement, or the defeat of one party by another: each side would endeavor to impose its will on another by negotiating a settlement after defeat, or in circumstances that acknowledge defeat.

There are four components of any process that deals with conflict: the degree of third-party intervention, the degree of participation by the parties, the amount of communication between the parties, and the quality of communication.

In the minds of many, the settlement of conflicts by reference to a judicial body with enforcement powers remains the ideal. But the end result of judicial settlement of important political conflict would probably require coercion because it would not necessarily resolve the conflict to the satisfaction of the parties. There is an absence of participation and communication. At the inter-state level, this process has not been acceptable because no responsible authority will hand over its decision-making powers to a third party, especially when important values are at stake. Similarly, in industry, parties are reluctant to accept judicial settlements, particularly when they are arrived at within a framework of law and order, which seeks to preserve existing institutions. Quasi-judicial procedures, such as nomination by each party of adjudicators, is a compromise which enables at least some participation in the sense that the parties nominate persons to represent their viewpoint. However, there is still an obligation to accept the decision, and the process therefore suffers from the same drawbacks as ordinary judicial settlement. Other forms of settlement have emerged, such as mediation, conciliation, and good offices. The parties participate far more in the sense that the mediator communicates with them and endeavours to find out their viewpoints, but there is effectively no communication between the parties. The end result of this sequence, characterized by less and less coercion and more and more participation and communication, is the direct confrontation of the two parties where there is total participation and communication. This, however, as we know from the Paris peace talks on Vietnam and from direct bargaining between management and unions, merely transfers the conflict from the field or the shop floor to the conference table. The same accusations and counter-accusations and escalation of conflict can be expected, with "deadlock" as the outcome.

It follows that, while participation and direct communication seem more and more to be demanded by parties in conflict, attention to these two features alone does not provide the answer. The quality of communication is a critical factor, and there are good reasons why we should expect this to be so.

The behavior of parties in a conflict is a response to the environment or set of circumstances as perceived by them. Whether it be violent or non-violent behavior, it is, nevertheless, the most appropriate behavior to the party concerned, in the light of the information available and the objectives being sought. It follows that, when parties appear to act aggressively, implying behavior that is likely to be costly in physical and social terms to themselves as well as to others, they are doing so because this appears to them to be the most appropriate response to some perceived threat to their interests and values. The operational factors are knowledge of the environment, selection of goals, choice of means of attaining goals, perception of the motivations and characteristics of opposing parties, and assessments of values and means on the one hand and costs of carrying on conflict on the other hand.

These are all alterable components, that is, they are subjective and as such subject to change. At a given moment, there can be differences of interest between parties that may be termed "objective" differences in the sense that they are irreconcilable, as when two parties seek the same territory or jurisdiction. But it is axiomatic that differences of interest are subjective when values are taken into account. No goal or value is absolute:

there is a limit to which a party will go in sacrificing other goals in order to attain a particular one. Other values have to be preserved: there is a costing process which is a subjective one. Another feature of conflicts of interests that makes them subjective is the perception of the parties. Parties to a conflict have most rigid ideas about the character and motives of their opponents. They have usually experienced many years of conflict, and their selections from past history and their moral judgments justify, confirm, and reinforce their attitudes. To a third party, their images of their opponents appear distorted; no man could so consistently be irrational, immoral, and untrustworthy as one party is perceived to be by the other. That there is distortion is even clearer when it is discovered that each party has the same favorable image of itself and its behavior, and the same unfavorable and treacherous one of the other. Mirror images exist, and each party makes identical accusations about the other on the same kind of evidence.

It is these aspects that determine the quality of communication. Some control of communication is required to ensure that it is effective in the sense that the perceptions of the parties of the motives of each other are accurate, and the costs of pursuing the particular goals are accurately assessed. If two parties in industrial or communal conflict had accurate knowledge and could forecast reliably, they would then settle immediately on the terms on which they would ultimately have to settle, thus avoiding the interim costs. What is required is a situation in which this knowledge can be acquired accurately. This means not merely confrontation of the two parties, but a confrontation effectively controlled by a third party with knowledge about conflict, the way in which it escalates, the patterns that emerge, and any other information that is required to enable the parties accurately to analyze their own particular conflict.

The history of procedures for the peaceful settlement of disputes shows a continuous weakening of the judgment role of the third party as techniques progress from judicial settlement to good offices. While it is difficult to assess relative success, at least without knowing how often various means have been offered and rejected and whether the final outcome led to continuing stable conditions, there is some evidence that the less formal the technique, the greater the range of application, and the greater the success. Whether this be so or not, there is a presumption that each successive process was introduced because of the failure of a previous one in a case similar to the one of current concern, or because existing ones were held to be inappropriate to the case being handled. Techniques for the resolution of conflict apparently must reflect the felt needs of the parties involved. Procedures that imply that the gain of one party is the loss of the other cannot lead to a decision that satisfies all parties. Judicial processes are of this kind. Arbitration and conciliation, and indeed even more informal procedures, likewise postulate that bargains and compromises are desirable and possible. These techniques have failed because their objective is settlement by third parties, or compromises that do not fully satisfy the needs and aspirations of all parties. One objective in handling disputes is to arrive at agreements without recourse to coercion, compromise, or third-party decisions and pressures. What is required are procedures which provide means of transforming what is perceived to be a bargaining or power relationship into a problem-solving one, and of promoting relationships that seek to increase the size of the cake and not merely to argue about its distribution.

Each step in such processes must always be fully under the control of the parties; there must be no fear on the part of the parties that they might be engaged in a set program or procedure which is imposed on them, or might be obligated in advance to accept settlements. It is interesting to note that the United Nations Conference on Trade and Development instituted elaborate procedures of reconciliation where parties could freely discuss differences before placing agreed suggestions to the main body. These procedures are not used, just because there is perceived to be some moral obligation to accept the outcome of consensus viewpoints. Parties need to be in a framework in which there are no commitments, formal or implied, until the point of formal agreement.

The role of the third party comes to be, therefore, crucial. It is a role governed by rules and principles which can now be tabulated, just as most techniques and professional skills can be set down. The role of the third party is not to persuade, and not to be a judge of the reasonableness of argument. It is, nevertheless, an active role. It is to explain conflict, its origins, its escalation, sometimes by reference to other conflicts, sometimes by analytical means, but within the context of a continuing discussion between the parties. It is, by various techniques, to control communication so that misperceptions which parties to a dispute have of each other are exposed, and costs of the conflict in relation to goals sought are accurately assessed. While no bargaining or negotiation takes place in such a problem-solving framework, preconditions of agreement may be established.

The handy name for third-party intervention of this kind is "controlled communication." To participation and communication—which ends in further conflict or stalemate—is added a particular type of control.

In addition to certain rules a third party should observe, his professionalism includes techniques in modeling the conflict, in representing it in diagrams, in breaking it down into components, in demonstrating recurrent patterns at different organizational levels, and generally in supplying whatever is required in an analysis of complex human relations. Decision-making theory, integration theory, the interaction of role and personality, perception problems, scapegoating, identification processes, and many such aspects of total organizational behavior must be drawn upon in ways appropriate to the situation and in ways which are meaningful to the parties involved. For these reasons, the third party needs to be a panel—at least two or three and sometimes more—because no one professional can be fully informed about the theoretical and empirical store of knowledge available and bring to bear upon the situation the appropriate tools at the appropriate time.

There can be controlled communication only between identifiable persons. We have become accustomed to descriptive accounts of conflicts and situations of tension that lump together the parties on each side. The implication is that a solution depends upon agreement between management and unions, or government and rebellious community. But this is misleading. There are many parties and factions involved in every dispute. They are not all equally involved, nor are they concerned with the same issues. The Cyprus case, for instance, was not one dispute. The two communities were in dispute over issues at the down-to-earth level of personal security, political participation, and non-discrimination. But other disputes involved different parties and different issues. There was the dispute between the Greek and Turkish governments, and the issues were their defense requirements and traditional prestige considerations in relation to Cyprus. They might have been purporting to be acting on behalf of and in defense of the communities; but their own negotiations and activities indicated that their interests were not firstly those of the local communities. There was another dispute between the United States of America and the Soviet Union—not mentioned in the Security Council resolution as parties—and the United Kingdom was also interested. The issues relevant to all three were related to global strategy. No compromise or solution could be found by a mediator to satisfy all of these varied interests. Ultimately, if a solution were to be found, face-to-face discussion was required first of all at the level of the communities.

A problem may be the sum total of a series of disputes, and be referred to as such as a historical event; but for purposes of analysis and resolution, each sub-dispute requires separate treatment. It is failure to separate out the parties and issues that gives a problem an appearance of intractability requiring some coercive settlement. It is probable that it is failure to resolve conflicts at the local level that leads to interventions from other levels.

The reasons for the existence of different disputes within the one conflict are now becoming clearer. More recent approaches to the study of international relations have emphasized the degree to which international conflict is a spill-over from internal or communal strife. Parties within a state seek outside assistance, and other states, sometimes with different interests to pursue and frequently without full knowledge of the reasons for the internal conflict or the consequences of their intervention, are usually ready to intervene. Thus the local dispute becomes a matter of international concern.

A general operational proposition is that the starting point in analysis and resolution of conflict is at the systems level of highest transactions. A settlement imposed from other levels could occur as, for example, after defeat of one side. It could even lead to resolution; but only after a sufficiently long period of time, and by procedures that ensured the severance of past transactions and the building of new systems. The systems or transactions concept helps to demonstrate that the resolution of conflict is primarily concerned with reestablishing transactions at local levels.

It cannot be assumed that the issues as perceived by the parties about to start a dispute are those at the source of conflict. Insofar as the origins of conflict are within parties, the issues are likely to be both misstated and confused. There are many reasons why this is so. First, the issues in conflict are not clear to the parties themselves. Second, whatever might be the issues originally, they tend to be pushed into the background as conflict escalates. Fear and threat, denial of participation rights, perceived injustice, disappointment in expectations are the typical origins of conflict behavior: it is the specific causes of these, including misperceptions of the environment, that are the issues in conflict. In industrial relations, all issues are equated with wage demands, and disputes are negotiated in monetary terms. Settlement of these demands does not remove the issues in dispute, and the level of job satisfaction and willingness to work remains virtually unaffected.

Once control is effective, and once there have been developed, with the help of the third party, models which explain important aspects of the conflict to the mutual satisfaction of the parties, the tendency is for discussion to move toward exploration of possible solutions. A first step in this connection is consideration of areas of functional cooperation.

Consideration of functional cooperation occurs in three different contexts. First, there are the areas of investigation relevant to the analysis of the conflict which require cooperation between the parties, perhaps still with the assistance of the third party. In practice, functional cooperation in analyzing a dispute has limited scope because, by the time parties are willing to cooperate, they are more interested in steps to resolve conflict and to prevent its reoccurrence than in an examination of the past, even though this would guide them in taking these steps. Second, there are functional activities required to prevent conflict reoccurring. These inevitably relate to suspected causes of conflict. The third context in which functional cooperation is considered is in the defining of common aims, the finding of alternative means of achieving objectives, and the evolving institutional means of cooperation.

Once parties have arrived at a relationship in which they are prepared to consider alternative goals and alternative means of achieving existing ones, the conflict is virtually resolved. The stage is not yet set, however, for the technically difficult and time-consuming process of detailed planning. It cannot be assumed that the felt needs of the parties, that is, the areas in which they themselves would be willing to cooperate, and the programs they agree to explore reflect the real needs. Felt needs are not necessarily the needs of the system. In the condition of euphoria which accompanies a prospect of the end of conflict, parties tend to consider idealistic schemes which are more related to the personal and political aspirations of leaders than to the realities of the situation. At this stage, the third party has a special role and is required to inject information into what would otherwise be direct negotiations in which information was lacking other than that already available to the parties. The third party is required to play a conservative and even a cynical role to ensure both political realism and an awareness of the problems to be solved. For example, it is at this stage that the danger is greatest of representatives losing touch with the interests they represent.

Assuming that functional cooperation has been promoted and that studies had provided answers to basic questions, the conditions would then have been established for negotiation between the parties, either with or without a third party. At this stage, negotiation is not bargaining; it is discussion of details and administrative planning because the problem has been identified and analyzed in terms of alternative values or options. Functionalism is the inevitable outcome—the political neutralization of areas that are better dealt with by specialists. In Britain, the controversial issue of control of television and broadcasting is overcome by creation of an independent commission. In Northern Ireland, the controversial issue of housing allocation is dealt with the same way. There are few areas not subject to this treatment. A high degree of functionalism offers an alternative to the majority government which is unworkable and irrelevant to the needs of societies that comprise different communities, and where, as is the case in Cyprus, the different communities are so distributed as to make partition costly or impossible.

The reason why some conflicts persist and why advantage is not taken of traditional means of peaceful settlement of disputes may be that these means are not appropriate or relevant to international relations or the particular disputes. There may be a direct connection between political willingness to settle, resolve, or avoid disputes, and methods and opportunities by which this might be done. Parties—states or communities—have usually shown themselves not to be willing to submit disputes to a court. They are not prepared to run the risks of adverse judgments or to be obligated to act in accordance with a verdict. They are more willing to submit to the processes of mediation. In cases in which they are not willing to do so, the question has to be asked, why? The problem may be to find the methods, techniques, or structures in which parties are prepared to cooperate. Willingness to avoid a conflict that is more costly than gains, to resolve rather than just to settle a conflict, is usually present: at least leaders say it is present. If two parties are not prepared to meet face to face or take advantage of mediation, there is, then, some reason that appears to them to be sound: past experience of negotiation, fear of internal repercussions, or others. The inflexibility cannot be changed by exhortation, by appeal to moral responsibilities, and by advocacy of "civilized" methods of resolving conflict. Means have to be found that reduce inflexibility by being relevant to the conditions in which parties operate. It is no defense of traditional methods or of failure of mediation to argue merely that there was an absence of willingness on the part of parties to employ these methods.

5. STRUCTURAL CHANGE

There are influences, such as a universal challenge to non-legitimized authority, relevant to behavior within the particular field. To what extent and in what ways can these wider influences be affected by attempts to resolve conflict at the local level? Putting the same question in another way, can structural change in world society be brought about by dealing with problems within the existing structures and at the level at which conflict occurs?

One difficulty about structural change is that, at some stage or other, everyone wants it, but everyone has different ideas about what is required. Some would like to turn the clock back, others have specific values to be implemented—the issue becomes an ideological one. Revolutionary situations are situations of criticism, revolts against the present, and the outcomes are not necessarily wholly those of anyone's liking and have unforeseen consequences. What structural change is desirable, for example, in Northern Ireland?

If an ideological approach is rejected, what is left is an open-ended process—open-ended in the sense that the final structural outcome might be quite different from any preconceived notion. If the process is guided at all stages even by only the agreed values and goals of those concerned, this surprise result is most likely to be that which most nearly satisfied the common consensus. This is part of the argument, as far as one can judge, of contemporary thinking about "anarchy"—local behavior and decisions create the wider structure. It is a reaction to centralized authority and to ideological solutions that are imposed by central authorities.

It has already been argued that conflict must be resolved at the level of greatest transactions—the shop floor or the two communities in Cyprus. What is evolved at this level has consequences for the wider community, but what is evolved at this level relates to fundamental human values out of which should emerge social institutions. At this level, there is constant change—in values and in relationships. At this level, there is "continuing revolution," to borrow a fashionable concept. And this is as it should be. In industry, no manager should complain if new relationships, new means of handling interactions, and even innovations in work procedures are evolved at this level. Such dynamism can be a manager's dream—and not a nightmare. The way to ensure that such dynamism has results of organizational value is his only problem, and in this matter a third party can frequently be helpful. It is out of these processes that local structural change should take place and, in due course, wider structural changes affecting the wider social environment. Structural and institutional changes imposed from the top, reflecting no more than ideological commitment, are unlikely to be the answer to felt needs or to be acceptable.

There are circumstances in which major structural change is the only means of effecting relatively minor changes. Structures and institutions easily become static, seeking only to preserve themselves. Frequently, within these static structures, there are all manner of anomalies, inefficiencies, and injustices. In industry, differentiations in wages, allocations of labor, established positions, goals, and attitudes tend to become rigid. In communal relations, the same frictions occur. Peaceful change, even by gradual means, is resisted by any whose interests are likely to be prejudiced by change. In these circumstances, it is sometimes necessary and possible to introduce superordinate goals—new objectives of such importance that values attached to the old structure are seen to be expendable. Structural change can be suggested by third parties or imposed from the top. But fierce reactions are likely, especially from minorities that may be adversely affected, and usually by all, even those who may gain. Superordinate goals need to come from those directly concerned.

This is the meeting point between revolutionaries who believe the whole structure of society needs changing by revolt and those who favor peaceful change because of the unforeseen costs of violent change. Structural change is not gradualism; but if promoted at the level of greatest transactions, and in an on-going way, it can be bought about peacefully and by accommodating those who may be adversely affected.

What we all finally seek is the institutionalization of conflict resolution, by one process or another. If judicial procedures are not effective in many cases, then others need to be found. In industrial and social life, the non-judicial resolution of conflict has been functionalized; business firms that undertake inquiries into industrial conflict and family-guidance councils are examples. The techniques are still primitive, but experience is leading to new insights into the nature of conflict and to improved techniques. Such processes have yet to be institutionalized at the level of world society, where they have been inhibited by a widespread insistence on judicial processes. The rule of law is a Western concept and falls short of the needs and interests of society at its present stage; the rule of consensus is an Eastern concept and is open to the influence of ideological and emotional excesses; the rule of sociological analysis avoids the static features of the one and the transitory features of the other.

6. THE EMERGING WORLD SOCIETY

The question before us is what type of world society is likely to be least prone to dysfunctional conflict and to aggression or intervention at the state level.

Kaplan, among others, has examined various types of world society, for example, balance of power and bipolar types.[4] These are types of world society in which states are perceived to be the dominant actors. The type

---

[4] Kaplan, "Intervention in Internal War: Some Systemic Sources," in J. Rosenau (ed.), *International Aspects of Civil Strife* (1964).

of world society which is emerging is of a different order. What we need to consider is what is emerging under technological and behavioral pressures, and how what is emerging can be influenced by an understanding of behavior, values, and processes.

At this point we are thrown back to the original problem of images of world society. If a systems image is more akin to the referent world than the billiard-ball model, then we should anticipate the emergence of more and more, small and smaller political units within a widening economic and cultural interdependence as political services develop and participation demands become effective. The revelant model is a world society of non-aligned political units. The increasing interdependence, promoted by communications and technology in industry, will further accelerate the growth of functional institutions. Functionalism will emerge in world society as a means of dealing with interdependence outside a political framework as it has developed at other system levels.

While there are trends due to largely uncontrollable influences, such as population growth, organizational needs, and technological innovations, there are also areas which are subject to influence, provided there is an adequate understanding of these trends and of behavioral theories. The billiard-ball image and policies based on it, which promote the status of state authorities and inhibit processes of political and social change, confront trends but do not influence them. A systems approach and an examination of systemic needs and of fundamental human values, such as ethnic identity and political participation, leads to quite different policies. Restrictive state interventions that inhibit change, from tariff policies to assistance to non-legitimized authorities, create structures that can exist only within a threat or power system. Constructive interventions, from retraining labor to promoting political and social change of a character that establishes continuing legitimization of authority, create structures that are self-supporting. The processes by which this is achieved and, in particular, processes whereby conflict is transformed from a perceived zero-sum or win-lose relationship into a positive and problem-solving one are probably the key which we seek. In short, the message is, let us help world society to evolve in the direction of flow dictated by human needs and environmental conditions, by assisting change and adjustment to it—not by confronting change with orders to preserve the status quo and with interventions and aggressions in the name of legal norms and law and order.

Chapter 6 | Systemic Bases of
Intervention | *Oran R. Young*

This chapter is concerned with the extent to which, in the international system, intervention by some actors in the internal affairs of others can be explained or understood in terms of the structural and contextual characteristics of the system itself. To this end, it is necessary to begin with a clear definition of intervention. In the present essay, "intervention" refers to organized and systematic activities directed across recognized boundaries and aimed at affecting the political authority structures of the target.[1] Note that this definition (1) requires organized and systematic rather than haphazard or inadvertent activities, (2) refers to actions crossing recognized boundaries in contrast to disputes about the boundaries themselves, and (3) limits the term "intervention" to actions intended to affect the political authority structures of the target.[2] Consequently, the content of the concept "intervention" as employed in this essay varies somewhat from its content in some other usages.[3] Specifically, it should be emphasized that the definition of intervention employed in this essay does not limit intervention to situations involving the occurrence of civil strife within the target. It is no doubt true that systematic interference in the internal affairs of an actor undergoing civil strife will generally constitute intervention in terms of the present definition. But it is easy to imagine the occurrence of intervention in the internal affairs of actors that are not experiencing civil strife.

Two additional introductory remarks are in order at this point. First, intervention is relatively easy to identify in empirical terms in international systems that are composed entirely of distinct territorial units whose boundaries are clearcut and well defined. If these conditions are not present, however, the problems of empirical identification are apt to increase substantially. Thus, systems composed of several distinct types of actor, some of which are not territorially based, generate problems of overlapping and indistinct jurisdictions, which often make it difficult to decide what constitutes intervention. And when the boundaries separating actors are vague or undifferentiated, the extent to which any given action constitutes interven-

---

[1] This definition is discussed at greater length in Young, "Intervention and International Systems," 22 *J. of Int'l Aff.* 177 (1968).

[2] Note that intervention may be directed either toward changing existing political authority structures or toward shoring up existing structures against internal and external forces of change.

[3] For a good review of alternative usages of the concept "intervention" see Moore, "The Control of Foreign Intervention in Internal Conflict," 9 *Va. J. Int'l L.* 209 (1969), *reprinted* in J. N. MOORE, LAW AND THE INDO-CHINA WAR 115 at 119–26 (1972).

tion will obviously be difficult to determine. During the Vietnam war, for example, arguments arose again and again concerning the extent to which the actions of North Vietnam constituted intervention in the internal affairs of South Vietnam or simply belligerent acts in an ongoing civil war. It is important to bear these ambiguities in mind in the present discussion because the contemporary international system is manifestly not composed entirely of distinct territorial units whose boundaries are clearcut and well defined.[4]

Second, this essay focuses on the systemic bases of intervention. Specifically, it is an attempt to see how much leverage can be gained in explaining intervention by reference to the structural and contextual characteristics of the international system in which it occurs. There is no doubt that other factors, such as the internal politics of both the intervenor and the target, are often major determinants of the occurrence and consequences of intervention. Consequently, the perspective adopted in this essay is a highly restricted one, but its very restrictiveness should serve to highlight the relevance of general systemic factors for any attempt to understand the phenomenon of intervention.

A. THE FEASIBILITY OF INTERVENTION

It seems helpful to begin by distinguishing the capacity to intervene in the internal affairs of others from the desire to intervene. Thus, an actor may desire to intervene in the affairs of another, but find it physically impossible to do so. By the same token, an actor may possess the physical capacity to intervene in the internal affairs of others, but lack any interest in doing so. It is the proposition of this section that the structural and contextual characteristics of the prevailing international system will operate to determine the limits of the physical capacity of the actors in the system to intervene in each other's internal affairs. To put this point in different terms, the characteristics of the international system will place significant limits on the range of distinct choices concerning intervention facing the individual actors in the system at any given moment in time.[5]

Consider first an extremely simple (and correspondingly unrealistic) international system exhibiting the following characteristics:

1. The actors in the system are territorially based and homogeneous with respect to basic type. That is, there are no overlapping jurisdictions, and no actor has any claim to authoritative or sovereign control over any other.

---

[4] For an extended discussion of this point *see* Young, "The Actors in World Politics," in J. Rosenau, V. Davis & M. East (eds.), *The Analysis of International Politics: Essays in Honor of Harold and Margaret Sprout* (1971).

[5] In more formal language, these systemic factors will establish the range of alternative strategies with respect to intervention available to the actors in contrast to the utility payoffs associated with these strategies.

2.   The boundaries separating the actors are clearcut and well defined. Thus, there can be no ambiguity as to when a recognized boundary is crossed.

3.   The actors are roughly equal with respect to population, territory, resources, and so forth. In other words, the actors in the system display an essential symmetry.

4.   There are no effective alignments or coalitions in the system.

5.   With respect to military capacity, the defense is distinctly superior to the offense.

6.   All the actors in the system are characterized by internal political viability. Accordingly, while the political regimes of the actors may differ from each other, no actor is in a state of actual or incipient revolution or civil war.

7.   The level of independence or self-sufficiency among the actors in the system is high. Consequently, the ability of the actors to reward or punish each other by manipulating dependencies is not of decisive importance.

Any international system displaying these characteristics can be fairly described as a "no intervention" system. Thus, regardless of the desires or incentives of the actors, it is difficult to see how intervention is feasible in such a system. By conditions 1 and 2, the actors are clearly differentiated, homogeneous with respect to basic type, and identified with clearcut territorial bases. Under the circumstances, the system is one of perfectly horizontal and non-overlapping authority patterns, so that intervention cannot result from any type of hierarchical authority relationships among the actors. Nor can intervention occur as a result of ambiguity concerning the authority structures of the system or the precise boundaries of the authority of the individual actors. All these possibilities are ruled out by the presence of clearcut boundaries in conjunction with a perfectly horizontal system of authority relationships.

By conditions 3, 4, and 5, the actors can be expected to be roughly equal with respect to power and to lack the capacity to gang up on each other. Condition 3 guarantees that intervention will not be made feasible for some actors in the system due to substantial disparities in the putative power of the individual actors.[6] And condition 4 extends this limitation by ruling out the possibility of creating major disparities in power through the formation of alliances or coalitions. Condition 5 gives any actor attempting to resist intervention an asymmetrical advantage over the intervenor. If this condition were absent or reversed, actors of equal putative power might still be able to intervene in the internal affairs of each other successfully because of differences between the offensive activities associated with intervention and the defensive activities required to resist intervention.

Finally, conditions 6 and 7 close out other potential bases of interven-

---

[6] The distinction between putative power and actualized power is developed in K. Knorr, *Military Power and Potential* (1970).

tion. The absence of internal political viability not only reduces the capacity of an actor to mobilize its putative power to resist intervention, it is also apt to create opportunities for intervention by outside actors. Thus, outside actors may find intervention in situations involving civil strife feasible because (1) it can frequently be accomplished in a camouflaged fashion, (2) one or more of the internal factions may actively seek intervention on the part of some external actor, and (3) the incumbent regime of the target is likely to find it difficult to mobilize successfully to resist such intervention. Beyond this, condition 7 indicates that the individual actors in the system are relatively self-sufficient, with the result that the degree to which each actor is dependent upon the others is minimized. Consequently, there is little scope for actors to intervene in the internal affairs of others by manipulating the dependencies of the target in such a way as to generate rewards or punishments linked to specific postures concerning the political authority structure of the target.[7]

What happens if the conditions associated with this idealized "no intervention" system are relaxed? It appears from the discussion of the previous paragraphs that the relaxation of any one of these conditions would open up some scope (in contrast to incentives) for intervention. Thus, there are obvious possibilities for intervention in systems involving hierarchical authority relationships and overlapping jurisdictions. And the introduction of vague or undifferentiated boundaries simply adds to these possibilities. The relaxation of conditions 3 and 4 would make possible intervention arising from disparities of power among the actors in the system. And the relaxation of condition 5 would open up some scope for intervention even among actors characterized by the same order of magnitude of power. The relaxation of condition 6 to permit the existence of actors that are not internally viable in political terms would expand the scope for intervention along the lines suggested in a previous paragraph. Finally, the introduction of a high level of interdependence (or even asymmetrical patterns of dependence) among the actors would increase the capacity of actors to intervene in the affairs of others by manipulating dependencies in such a way as to establish rewards or punishments for specified postures relating to the political authority structures of the target.

How does all this relate to the real world incorporated in the contemporary international system? An examination of the contemporary system suggests that it violates all the conditions of the "no intervention" model. Although the system is still oriented generally toward horizontal authority relationships, non-territorial actors are becoming more important, overlapping jurisdictions are becoming a central problem rather than a manageable by-product of the traditional states system, and ill-defined boundaries are a major feature of relations among territorial actors let alone inter-

---

[7] For a discussion of the manipulation of dependencies which is helpful in this context, *see* J. Thibaut and H. Kelley, *The Social Psychology of Groups* (1959), Ch. 7.

actions involving both territorial and non-territorial actors.[8] Similarly, the contemporary system exhibits qualitative differences among its actors with respect to population, territory, resources, and so forth. Alliances and coalitions are common and influential, even though they may be losing their efficacy as defensive arrangements in the nuclear arena.[9] And the offense is evidently superior to the defense with respect to a number of important levels of military activity in the contemporary world.[10] Beyond this, a lack of internal viability is highly prevalent among the actors in the international system. While this is a self-evident condition among the less developed actors in the system, it appears to be a phenomenon of growing importance even among the advanced actors. Finally, the level of interdependence among the actors in the system is presently relatively high and rising. And while the attractiveness of intervention associated with this condition may be mitigated somewhat by the importance of symmetrical patterns of dependence which give the target of any interventionary effort some ability to fight back through actual or threatened retaliation, the scope for intervention arising from high levels of interdependence can hardly be doubted.[11]

It seems clear, therefore, that the scope for intervention in the contemporary international system is great, and the various conditions that make intervention feasible can be expected to interact with each other in such a way as to produce a wide range of potential channels for intervention. Nevertheless, none of this guarantees that intervention will actually be a widespread occurrence in the contemporary system. This is so because the discussion so far has focused solely on factors determining the feasibility of intervention or the physical capacity of actors to intervene in the internal affairs of others. Accordingly, it is necessary to turn now to a discussion of the payoff structure that actors in the system are likely to attach to interventionary activities.

B. THE UTILITY OF INTERVENTION

The existence of some scope for intervention (as discussed in the previous section) is a necessary but not a sufficient condition for the occurrence of intervention. That is, even when an actor finds intervention in the internal affairs of another feasible, the effective decision-makers of the actor may decide that intervention is not worthwhile. In order to deal with this possi-

[8] For a more extended discussion of these points, *see* Young, *supra*, note 5.

[9] For a discussion of this question, *see* K. Knorr, *On the Uses of Military Power in the Nuclear Age* 152–63 (1966).

[10] This point has been widely discussed in the literature on the role of force in international relations. Note that the conclusion seems relevant to sub-limited warfare as well as nuclear warfare. For an early exploration of this issue *see* B. Brodie, *Strategy in the Missile Age* (1959).

[11] On this issue *see* Young, "Interdependencies in World Politics," 24 *Int'l J.* 726 (1969); and Morse, "The Politics of Interdependence," 23 *Int'l Org.* 311 (1969).

bility, let us assume that whenever intervention is feasible, the actors in the system (through their effective decision-makers) weigh the expected costs against the expected benefits of intervention[12] and that they only opt for intervention when the expected benefits outweigh the expected costs.[13]

To begin with, it is important to note that the benefis and costs of any given intervention will ordinarily stem from several distinct sources. First, some of the benefits and costs will be determined by the structural and contextual characteristics of the prevailing international system. Relationships of this kind are the subject of this section. Second, some of the benefits and costs associated with any given intervention will generally be a function of the internal political processes of the intervenor. To take some commonplace examples, intervention in the internal affairs of another actor may cause severe upheavals in the domestic politics of the intervenor, and the expenditure of scarce resources on intervention may impose significant opportunity costs on the intervenor. Both of these factors have, in fact, been cited frequently as major costs of the American intervention in Vietnam. Third, the internal political processes of the target also operate in most situations to affect the costs and benefits of intervention for the intervenor. Intervention in the affairs of a united target mobilized to resist intervention, for example, will ordinarily be more costly than intervention in the affairs of a target experiencing civil strife in which one of the factions actively seeks the participation of the intervenor.[14]

Any formal analysis of the expected utility of intervention for an actor contemplating intervention in a specific situation, therefore, would have to take account of the costs and benefits of intervention arising from each of these sources and aggregate them in some explicit fashion. Such an analysis is beyond the scope of this essay. Instead, this section seeks to identify, in a preliminary fashion, the principal structural and contextual characteristics of the international system that can be expected to influence the costs and benefits accruing to an intervenor in any given case of intervention.

1. COMPETITIVE INTERVENTION.

Whether a given actor can intervene in the internal affairs of another unilaterally or whether it must expect to face competition in its interventionary activities will often be a major determinant of the expected utility of intervention. And the probability of competitive intervention is, in turn, a func-

[12] For convenience, intervention is conceptualized here as an either–or choice. In real-world situations, actors will often be able to choose among a variety of types or levels of intervention.

[13] This formulation ignores the problem of opportunity costs. In applying this perspective to actual choices involving intervention, however, it would not be difficult to introduce the influence of opportunity costs.

[14] This argument implies a *ceteris paribus* assumption. Thus, it may sometimes be the case that the probability of competitive intervention is greater with respect to an actor experiencing civil strife than with respect to an actor that is not characterized by internal upheavals.

tion of political interactions between the initial intervenor (or prospective intervenor) and all of the other actors in the system.

The precise impact of this factor may vary considerably. Consider first the case of an actor contemplating intervention in the internal affairs of an actor which is not being subjected to intervention by any other actor. Here the prospective intervenor must weigh the potential benefits of intervening unilaterally against the potential costs arising from the fact that intervention on its part may stimulate counter-intervention by one or more others in the affairs of the target. Similar problems arise for an actor contemplating counter-intervention in the affairs of an actor already affected by outside intervention. In such cases, the potential intervenor must expect to face costs arising from the difficulties of achieving its goals under conditions of competitive intervention as well as from the possibility that competitive intervention will lead to escalating commitments on the part of the several intervenors.[15] But these costs may sometimes be outweighed for the prospective intervenor by the expected costs of allowing the political authority structures of the target to be influenced or even changed altogether by the activities of the actor already engaging in interventionary activities with respect to the internal affairs of the target. Under the circumstances, the degree of competitiveness of an interventionary situation may have a major impact on the cost-benefit calculations of prospective intervenors, but it will often be the case that this impact will affect both the costs and the benefits of intervention in complex ways. In more formal terms, competitive intervention introduces two new factors affecting the decision-making of the intervenor. First, the prospect of competition will generally necessitate the use of expected-value calculations in evaluating the utility of intervention. Second, relations between any given intervenor and its competitor(s) will be characterized by strategic interaction. That is, the outcomes for each of the potential intervenors will be contingent upon the actions (or choices) of the others.

2. IDEOLOGICAL POLITICS.

In the present context, the role of ideology can be defined in terms of the value an actor places on making the political authority structures of other actors more like its own as an end in itself or, conversely, preventing the political authority structures of other actors from taking on the character- istics of other actors whose authority structures differ radically from its own.[16] Other things being equal, the greater the value an actor places on

[15] The danger of escalating commitments arising from competitive intervention undoubtedly accounts for a great deal of the scholarly interest in the subject of inter- vention in recent years. The Vietnam case offers a number of clear illustrations of this phenomenon.

[16] The emphasis here is on the idea of making the political authority structures of others more like one's own *as an end in itself*. There may, of course, be any num- ber of instrumental reasons why this may be regarded as a desirable goal.

these goals as ends in themselves, the more it will become involved in interventionary activities. Thus, an actor placing an absolute value on these goals would devote all available resources to intervention in the affairs of others until it would either succeed in converting the political regimes of all other actors to its own model or collapse from exhaustion.[17] Note, however, that an actor placing no value whatsoever on these goals as ends in themselves might still engage in interventionary activities for instrumental reasons.

An international system in which two or more actors place high values on these ideological goals is apt to be particularly characterized by interventionary activities. This is true, in the first instance, because the number of cases in which the cost-benefit calculations of individual actors favor intervention will be relatively high in such systems. In addition, conditions of this kind can be expected to increase the incidence of major competitive interventions. And it seems reasonable to conclude that the likelihood of escalation in situations characterized by competitive intervention will be relatively high in systems where two or more actors place high values on the ideological goals under discussion here.

3. SIDE EFFECTS.

Any given actor in the international system engages in a wide variety of interactions with other actors simultaneously. If these interactions were hermetically sealed from each other, every actor could calculate the costs and benefits of each of its interactions on a discrete basis. Such situations would resemble the relationships described by the concept of "isolated exchange" in economics. But in most cases, and this is certainly true in situations involving intervention, the various interactions in which an actor is involved tend to become linked together and to affect each other. Consequently, an actor contemplating intervention in the internal affairs of another actor must consider not only the costs and benefits of the proposed action in terms of its interaction with the target, but also the probable effects of its intervention on its simultaneous interactions with other actors. A striking feature of the American intervention in Vietnam, for example, has been its impact on the interactions between the United States and a variety of other actors in the international system. These side effects may be either positive or negative. To take some simple examples, other actors may be impressed by an intervenor's actions in such a way that they are more willing to submit to requests of the intervenor directed toward themselves, or they may sympathize with the target and take steps to drive up the costs that the intervenor sustains as a result of its intervention. Side

---

[17] In fact, however, actors are unlikely to place anything like an absolute value on these goals. Perhaps the Soviet Union in the immediate aftermath of the October revolution came as close to this position as any actor in modern history. And it is interesting to note how rapidly the Soviet Union retreated from this position when these goals began to conflict with its domestic needs.

effects, like the degree of competitiveness, therefore, may produce both costs and benefits that an actor must weigh in contemplating the utility of intervention.

4. ITERATIVE EFFECTS.

Just as an actor in the international system engages in many interactions simultaneously, it also participates in a series of interactions with others over time. And the individual interactions in these sequences are apt to affect each other so that it is important to give some thought to the future consequences of actions taken in the curent-time period.[18] Although it is often difficult to predict such future consequences with any precision, it is evident that curent interventionary activities can generate a number of costs and benefits affecting future interactions. Thus, a current intervention may contribute to an actor's reputation either in such a way as to allow it to intervene more cheaply in the future, or in such a way as to raise the costs of future interventions. Similarly, a current intervention may prove beneficial by generating precedents that the intervenor can make use of in subsequent interactions, but it may also prove costly if it contributes to the development of precedents that other actors can utilize to frustrate the interests of the intervenor in the future.

5. TECHNOLOGICAL FACTORS.

Insofar as intervention in the internal affairs of other actors requires *some* capabilities involving transportation, communication, or military technologies, technological resources constitute a necessary condition for the occurrence of intervention. Since it is safe to assume that many (if not all) actors possess at least the minimum technological resources for intervention, however, the technological factors associated with intervention generally raise problems of efficiency rather than feasibility. In this context, there are two distinct issues that are relevant to this discussion of systemic factors affecting the utility of intervention.[19] First, technological advances are generally apt to make any given set of interventionary activities relatively cheaper to execute.[20] Second, if the intervenor and the target exhibit different levels of technological development, the edge in terms of efficiency is likely to go to the more advanced actor. This does not, of course, justify

[18] For a variety of examples of such iterative links, consult T. Schelling, *The Strategy of Conflict* (1960).

[19] On these technological questions, consult Wohlstetter, "Illusions of Distance," 46 *For. Aff.* 242 (1968), and Wohlstetter, "Strength, Interest, and New Technologies," in *The Implications of Military Technology in the 1970's* (Adelphi Paper #46 1968).

[20] This is, of course, a crude generalization. It is possible to imagine interventionary activities based on such things as guerrilla infiltration, for example, that would not be affected much one way or the other by technological advances.

any conclusion to the effect that technologically backward or relatively backward actors will avoid interventionary activities.[21] It does mean that technological advancement and technological superiority can cut down the costs of intervention. Other things being equal, therefore, technologically advanced and superior actors will display a greater propensity to intervene in the affairs of others than actors that do not exhibit these characteristics.

6. SYSTEM-WIDE SANCTIONING PROCEDURES.

In any given international system, the presence of system-wide sanctioning procedures may affect the costs and benefits of intervention substantially. It should not be assumed, however, that this is a simple matter of driving up the costs of intervention to prevent individual actors from engaging in interventionary activities. In fact, the issue is considerably more complex. To begin with, system-wide sanctioning procedures may sometimes be employed to induce actors to intervene rather than to induce them to refrain from intervening. Thus, the United Nations has gone to considerable lengths to stimulate British intervention in Rhodesia since the latter's unilateral declaration of independence in 1965. Next, such procedures may be set up in such a way as to manipulate the incentives associated with intervention to favor intervention in some types of situations while making it less attractive in others, or to channel intervention through some types of institutions (*e.g.*, authorized international organizations) in contrast to others (*e.g.*, nation states acting unilaterally). Then, sanctioning procedures may involve rewards as well as punishments. It is possible, for example, to manipulate the utility of intervention by offering rewards for refraining from intervention (or engaging in intervention) as well as threatening punishments for acts of intervention (or the failure to intervene). Finally, sanctioning procedures may vary widely with respect to institutional format. Thus, sanctioning procedures relevant to intervention may be governed by a formal and centralized institution such as an effective international organization of universal scope.[22] But they may also operate informally and on a decentralized basis as is presently the case with some parts of the system of international law[23] and various internalized norms associated with the "rules of the game" of international politics. As an influence on the utility calculations of actors contemplating interventionary activities, therefore, the sanctioning procedures of the prevailing international system are apt to constitute an influential but complex factor.

[21] Cases may occur, for example, in which relatively backward actors place an extraordinarily high value on the results that can be achieved through intervention. It is sometimes alleged that this position characterizes at least some effective decision-makers in Communist China.

[22] Note that the relevant mechanisms may also be legal, political, or both.

[23] For an interesting discussion of this possibility, *see* Fisher, "Bringing Law to Bear on Governments," 74 *Harv. L. R.* 1130 (1961).

7. WORLD PUBLIC OPINION.

Most actors in the international system place some value on the opinions of attentive publics external to themselves (in contrast to the domestic public), concerning their interventionary activities. Consequently, they can be expected to take this factor into account in calculating the costs and benefits associated with any contemplated act of intervention. But the precise relevance of this factor to specific utility calculations will often be difficult to spell out. The effective decision-makers of different actors are likely to vary with respect to the value they attach to favorable reactions from world public opinion. It is often argued, for example, that there is an important difference between the United States and the Soviet Union in this respect. Some commentators have gone so far as to suggest that democratic governments are always more sensitive to the views of external publics than authoritarian governments. Similarly, the opinion of external publics tends to vary from situation to situation. Thus, many of those who opposed American intervention in Vietnam would like to see systematic American intervention aimed at changing the authority structures of the Union of South Africa. Accordingly, while world public opinion may operate as a cost with respect to some interventionary activities, it may well reduce the costs of intervention in other situations. Moreover, world public opinion is seldom united. The opinion of some external publics may well favor intervention in a given situation, while the opinion of other external publics operates in the opposite direction.[24] Consequently, although it is reasonable to expect actors to consider world public opinion in calculating the costs and benefits of intervention, the impact of this factor will frequently be divided and often prove difficult to estimate with any precision.

The issues discussed in this section do not constitute an exhaustive list of systemic factors affecting the utility of intervention. They are sufficient, however, to yield several practical conclusions. First, even when intervention is feasible in physical terms, it should not be automatically assumed that it will in fact be a widespread phenomenon. It is not difficult to imagine situations in which decision-makers conclude that intervention is too costly even though it is perfectly feasible. Second, calculations concerning the utility of intervention are apt to vary substantially from actor to actor. Asymmetries along this line are virtually bound to occur on the basis of the systemic factors affecting the utility of intervention alone. And the inclusion of various domestic factors affecting the utility of intervention would only reinforce this conclusion. Third, the calculations of any given actor concerning the utility of intervention are apt to vary from situation to situation although they may exhibit some long-term secular trends with the passage of time. As with the previous point, the inclusion of various domestic influ-

---

[24] Both the United States and the Soviet Union have often experienced this phenomenon. And in general, this type of reaction is likely to vary directly with the level of ideological diversity in the international system.

ences affecting the utility of intervention would only reinforce this conclusion.

The previous section argued that the scope for intervention is great in the contemporary international system. Is there an analogous conclusion to be drawn concerning the utility of intervention in the prevailing system? In general, this question is considerably more intricate. It would be necessary to consider the calculations of all the actors in the system with respect to the whole range of factors governing the utility of intervention to reach a general conclusion about the utility of intervention in the contemporary system. It is worth noting here, however, that while intervention occurs with considerable frequency in the contemporary system, it does not occur in many situations in which intervention is perfectly feasible.[25] That is, even though it is not uncommon for actors to conclude that intervention is profitable as well as feasible, there are many situations in which effective decision-makers conclude that the costs of intervention are likely to outweigh the benefits, even though there is no lack of capacity to intervene.

C. THE CONTROL OF INTERVENTION

The notion of eliminating or minimizing intervention in international relations has long been a subject of interest to scholars and publicists. But non-intervention has always remained an elusive concept as well as a difficult objective to achieve in practice.[26] Does the systemic perspective on intervention outlined in this essay yield any interesting conclusions concerning the problems of controlling intervention?[27]

To begin with, the systemic perspective raises questions concerning the desirability of controlling or eliminating intervention. In general, it is not possible to ascribe goals or values to the international system itself, since the system does not display any of the attributes of a purposive actor. Consequently, it makes no sense to discuss whether or not intervention is desirable or undesirable from the point of view of the international system *per se*.

Nevertheless, it is possible to lay down specific criteria relating to various attributes of the system and to consider the impact of intervention in terms of these criteria. Perhaps the most common criterion of this kind

[25] In fact, a little reflection suggests that intervention occurs in only a small proportion of the situations in which it is feasible. This in no way reduces the importance of those cases of intervention which do occur, but it does indicate that the costs of intervention are often both high and appreciated as such by the effective decision-makers of the actors in the international system.

[26] For a variety of perspectives on the concept of non-intervention, *see* I–III R. Falk (ed.), *The Vietnam War and International Law* (1968, 1969, 1972).

[27] The following discussion concentrates on the problems of eliminating or minimizing intervention in all its forms. It would also be possible to deal more specifically with the problems of selective intervention, the institutional framework of intervention, and so forth.

centers on the question of systemic stability, even though it is clear that at least some of the individual actors in the existing international system do not place a positive value (and may even place a negative value) on the stability of the prevailing system.[28] But the relationship between systemic stability and intervention is anything but clearcut. A great many interventionary activities have no significant bearing on the stability of the international system. This is true, for example, of most cases of unilateral intervention. Whatever else one may think about the Soviet interventions in Hungary in 1956 and Czechoslovakia in 1968 and the American intervention in the Dominican Republic in 1965, these interventions did not pose severe threats to the stability of the international system. Moreover, some types of intervention may actually tend to maintain or even improve the stability of the system as a whole. Thus, intervention may sometimes operate to accomplish or facilitate political changes that reduce disruptive forces in the system or to thwart political changes likely to encourage forces interested in making qualitative changes in the system.[29] Consequently, any threats to the stability of the international system arising from interventionary activities must be identified with specific types of intervention such as situations involving highly competitive actions on the part of several outside parties or interventionary interactions that are likely to produce escalation to the level of international warfare among actors that began by intervening in the same target. In fact, a great deal of the modern concern with the problem of intervention has arisen from cases of this kind. Consider in this connection such examples as Spain in the 1930's, the Congo in the 1960's, and Vietnam at the present time.

Under the circumstances, it is clear that the bulk of the interest in non-intervention must stem from the individual actors in the system or from private individuals and publicists rather than from any source that can be described as systemic. But even these potential sources of support for the idea of non-intervention are apt to prove ambiguous. Thus, an actor that favors non-intervention in some situations and emphasizes the doctrine of non-intervention in those cases is apt to face different utility calculations in other cases which lead it to embark on a policy of intervention. There are few (if any) actors in the international system whose utility calculations with respect to intervention are so lopsided that they can unhesitatingly adopt a general policy of non-intervention applicable to all situations. Most

[28] The term "stability" is used here to refer to the avoidance of qualitative changes in any of the essential features of an international system. Note that one can posit the criterion of stability and examine the requirements of systemic stability without becoming an advocate of stability in normative terms. In fact, a knowledge of the requirements of systemic stability is just as important for those who wish to destroy an international system as for those who wish to preserve it.

[29] Note that such interventions will be regarded as conservative or reactionary by those who wish to transform the existing international system into something different. Thus, recent American interventions have sometimes been described as reactionary while recent Soviet interventions (perhaps the role has now been taken over by the Chinese?) have sometimes been regarded as revolutionary.

publicists and individual analysts end up in the same position. That is, their support for intervention in some situations makes it inconsistent for them to argue for a general policy of non-intervention even though they may be radically opposed to intervention by certain actors in some specific situations.[30] One obvious response to this dilemma is to consider the prospects for a policy of selective non-intervention. But this alternative is not ordinarily a workable one, since even when actors are willing to subscribe to the principle of selective non-intervention, their specific lists of permissible and impermissible situations for intervention or types of intervention virtually always exhibit irreducible incompatibilities.[31]

Despite all these problems with the notion of non-intervention, however, suppose that one remains interested in the idea of eliminating or minimizing intervention. What does the systemic perspective on intervention suggest about the prospects for achieving this goal? In the first instance, intervention could be controlled by manipulating or altering the conditions determining its feasibility. That is, eliminating or reducing the physical capacity of the actors in the system to intervene in the internal affairs of others is one obvious technique of controlling intervention itself. The discussion of the feasibility of intervention in an earlier section of this essay, however, suggests that this approach to the control of intervention is not apt to prove efficacious. The scope for intervention is extensive in the contemporary international system, and the conditions underlying this situation are not likely to prove easy to change. Disparities in the population, territory, and resources of the actors, for example, are marked and solidly entrenched, and there is no obvious way of getting rid of the possibility of coalition-building without making radical changes in the system as a whole. Similarly, the lack of internal political viability is a pervasive characteristic among the actors of the contemporary system. And although the obstacles to achieving internal viability in any individual actor may not be insurmountable, there is little likelihood that internal viability will become a general characteristic of the actors in the system in the foreseeable future. Moreover, the level of interdependence among the actors in the system is evidently rising rather than falling, thereby adding to the scope for intervention with the passage of time. In short, the conditions which make intervention feasible in the contemporary system are macro-characteristics of the system itself, which are not apt to change as a consequence of the purposive activities of a few actors even though they may change gradually over time without any purposive impetus.

If it is not possible to control intervention by making it infeasible,

---

[30] Thus, many Americans who are radically opposed to the intervention of the United States in Vietnam are also involved in efforts to precipitate systematic interventionary activities by the United States in the Union of South Africa.

[31] Another alternative is to work toward the channeling of all interventionary activities through certain authorized institutions such as the United Nations. But this alternative would also be affected by the incompatibility of various sets of parochial interests.

another option is to make it less attractive by manipulating the structural and contextual characteristics of the system that affect the utility calculations of the actors with respect to interventionary activities. This may be a somewhat more hopeful course to follow for an actor or an individual interested in eliminating or controlling intervention. Thus, it may not be altogether hopeless to try and reduce the ideological value some actors place on the goal of making the political authority structures of other actors more like their own. It is sometimes suggested that the development of more effective sanctioning procedures in the international system is a hopeful strategy for the control of intervention.[32] Nevertheless, this approach to the control of intervention is also fraught with difficulties. Interventionary activities cannot be prevented from producing side effects and iterative effects, even though it is conceivable that the impact of these effects on specific utility calculations can be altered. The problem of competitive intervention cannot be made to disappear. Continued technological advances and markedly different rates of technological development among the actors of the system must be expected to reduce the putative costs of intervention in at least some situations. And there appears to be as much interest in the contemporary international system in employing system-wide sanctioning procedures to stimulate intervention, at least in some types of situation, as in using such procedures to eliminate or control intervention. Perhaps the most prominent current examples are associated with the efforts of the African states to make use of the United Nations as a mechanism for mobilizing interventionary activities directed toward Rhodesia and the Union of South Africa. But this is a common enough interest throughout the international system. Moreover, the manipulation of most of these systemic factors in the interest of reducing the attractiveness of intervention depends, to a considerable degree, on the difficult task of coordinating the calculations of a number of separate actors. This is so because the exact impact of most of these factors on the utility calculations of the individual actor with respect to intervention will be a function of strategic interaction among a number of actors.

Even if the prospects for manipulating the systemic bases of intervention in the interests of eliminating or minimizing intervention do not seem favorable in the contemporary international system, it is still possible to pursue this goal by focusing on the domestic political processes of the individual actors which affect their calculations concerning the utility of intervention in the internal affairs of others. This strategy for the control of intervention falls outside the scope of this essay, but it is possible to suggest several differences between this strategy of control and the strategy of manipulating the systemic bases of intervention which may make the idea of focusing on domestic political processes relatively attractive for those interested in controlling intervention. First, from the point of view of any

[32] For several substantive discussions of this strategy, *see* the essays in Part V of this volume.

individual interested in controlling intervention, the emphasis on the domestic politics of his own actor brings the problem closer to home. This is likely to make the techniques of driving up the costs of intervention more concrete and familiar and to give the individual a greater chance of deriving a sense of personal efficacy from his activities on behalf of a policy of non-intervention.[33] Second, this orientation reduces the impact of strategic interaction on calculations concerning the utility of intervention. Thus, it may be possible to drive up the costs of intervention for a specific actor by manipulating its domestic political processes, regardless of what the other actors in the system do.[34]

[33] At the same time, this focus exhibits an important drawback. Such efforts are directed primarily at the activities of individual actors, and a reduction in the propensity of any individual actor to intervene in the internal affairs of others does not necessarily imply a reduction in the overall level of intervention in the international system. The lowering of the level of intervention caused by the changes in the behavior of the actor in question may be offset (or more than offset) by related changes in the behavior of other actors that now find it possible to reduce the negative expected value they attach to the danger of competitive intervention.

[34] Note, however, that strategic interaction may still occur at the domestic level among those individuals or groups attempting to influence the utility calculations of the actor with respect to intervention.

PART III | THE RELEVANCE OF DOMESTIC CONSTRAINTS

Chapter 7 | Foreign Intervention as Adaptive Behavior | *James N. Rosenau*

Several years have passed since the present writer, having discovered that the literature on intervention was long on moral judgments and short on analytic insights, pleaded for more self-aware and precise efforts to subject interventionary phenomena to the rigors of scientific inquiry. To condemn or condone national societies when they intervene in each others' affairs, it was argued at that time, may quell one's conscience, but it does not enlarge understanding of interventions. It is on the latter, as much as on the former, that policies designed to maximize control over the incidence of foreign intervention in internal conflict must be founded. Until theory and data are developed that explain when and why nations are likely to resort to intervention as a technique of foreign policy, the argument concluded, there is little reason to believe that hopes for an intervention-free world can be translated into legal and political realities.[1]

Happily, for reasons that have nothing to do with the earlier plea, it need not be reiterated. The essays comprising this volume are but the latest in a series of recent efforts to look more systematically at the sources and dynamics of interventionary phenomena. Much still remains to be done, especially with respect to the generation of appropriate empirical data, but there is now a growing body of analytic insights that ought to serve as a basis for any inquiry into the subject. That is, though far from a theory and even further from an empirically tested set of propositions, a perspective from which to investigate interventions can now be pieced together from the mushrooming literature. It consists of perhaps five main premises. Let us briefly summarize these as a means of specifying the central problem with which this paper is concerned.

---

[1] This plea was first expressed orally at the Conference on Intervention and the Developing States, sponsored by the Princeton International Law Society and held at Princeton, N.J., on November 10–11, 1967. It was later published as "Intervention as a Scientific Concept," 13 *J. Conflict Res.* 149 (June 1969). For contradictory assessments of the reactions to the original plea, see Moore, "The Control of Foreign Intervention in Internal Conflict," 9 *Va. J. Int'l L.* 209, 216–17 (1969); and Rosenau, "The Concept of Intervention," 22 *J. of Int'l Aff.* 165 (1968).

This is a revision of a paper presented at the Annual Meeting of the Midwest Political Science Association (Chicago, April 29, 1971). In preparing it, I have benefited greatly from the assistance of Norah Rosenau. The support of the National Science Foundation through its Grant GS-3117 to the Research Foundation of the Ohio State University is also gratefully acknowledged.

FIVE ORGANIZING PREMISES

Although practice does not always match commitment, the emerging perspective rests, first, on the recognition that the label "intervention" has been attached to a wide variety of phenomena and that a more precise definition is needed if our understanding is to grow. It is tempting to view any attempt by one society to exert influence over another as an intervention, especially in the case of influence attempts that are negatively evaluated. The literature has long suffered from the absence of a clear distinction between interventions and other types of influence attempts. Now, however, analysts seem increasingly inclined to eschew broad definitions and to specify precisely the nature of the phenomena they regard as interventionary.[2] Even those who equate all influence with intervention, moreover, do so self-consciously, trying to indicate what they conceive to be the dynamics of influence.[3] To be sure, few analysts subscribe to the extremely narrow definition used here —that interventions are convention-breaking actions directed by one national society at the authority structure of another[4]—but the most recent inquiries do differentiate between military and economic intervention, most of them confining their attention to the former and using a definition for it similar to Mitchell's notion that intervention consists of "any military action either within or outside the boundaries of a state with a high level of civil strife, which is calculated to affect favorably the situation of one or the other faction in that strife."[5]

A second premise on which recent inquiries rest is that interventions, however defined, result from a convergence of factors, some of which are located in the intervening and others in the intervened nation.[6] An intervention is an action of a single country, but it stems from a multiplicity of sources, not all of which are attributes, aspirations, or needs of the country that undertakes the action. The historic patterns and current tendencies of

[2] Good illustrations of this inclination to establish clear-cut definitional boundaries can be found in Wriggins, "Political Outcomes of Foreign Assistance: Influence, Involvement, or Intervention?" 22 *J. of Int'l Aff.* 217 (1968); U. Schwarz, *Confrontation and Intervention in the Modern World* (1970), ch. 4; Friedmann, "Intervention and International Law I," 25 *Int'l Spectator* 40 (1971); Farer, "Harnessing Rogue Elephants: A Short Discourse on Intervention In Civil Strife," 82 *Harv. L. Rev.* 511 (1969); Moore, "Intervention: A Monochromatic Term for a Polychromatic Reality," in II R. Falk (ed.), *The Vietnam War and International Law*, 1061 (1969).

[3] For example, *see* Baldwin, "Foreign Aid, Intervention, and Influence," 21 *World Politics* 425 (April 1969).

[4] For an elaboration of this formulation, *see* my "Intervention as a Scientific Concept," *supra* note 1, at 160–65.

[5] Mitchell, "Civil Strife and the Involvement of External Parties," 14 *Int'l Stud. Q.* 169 (June 1970). The author adds that "Military action includes the provision of arms, bases, financial aid or credits for arms purchase, instructors, volunteers or regular army units."

[6] For examples in which this premise is made explicit, *see* id., at 170; G. Kelly and C. Brown (eds.), *Struggles in the State: Sources and Patterns of World Revolution* passim (1970); and J. Burton, *Systems, States, Diplomacy, and Rules* 116–18 (1968).

the target society can be as relevant, if not more, to whether or not a decision to intervene in its affairs is made. The United States intervened in the Dominican Republic in 1965 when a Communist take-over was deemed to be imminent, but it did not intervene in Chile in 1970 when a similar event seemed virtually certain. In part this difference might be explained in terms of the fact that the United States was led by different presidents and parties who were confronted with different internal and external conditions. Some part of the differential behavior of the United States, however, can be traced to a variety of differences between the Dominican Republic and Chile, and particularly to the fact that a free and open election in the latter led to the prospect—and later to the advent—of a Marxist regime. In other words, although interventions are actions undertaken by a single actor, they occur in the context of an interaction and can be fully comprehended only if this context is taken into account.

The student of interventionary behavior thus needs to examine *both* the internal and external factors from which the behavior derives and then assess their *relative* potency as causal determinants. Such a premise may seem so obvious as not to require articulation.[7] Yet it has often been ignored in the past, as analysts used imperialism or some other such single cause to explain interventions. Even in this day of multivariate analysis, the temptation to see a single factor as explanatory of interventions continues to be strong. Interventions raise such large moral and strategic questions that the inclination to seek complete understanding by blaming a single leader or the simple logic of geography is difficult to resist. Self-evident as it may be, it is therefore useful to articulate the premise of multiple causality. It is especially important to do so in carrying through the present assignment of exploring "the influence of internal restraints and domestic structure on interventionary conduct."[8] The internal restraints against and pressures toward interventionary behavior are so many and so evident that one can easily forget that external factors are also operative.

A third premise follows from the foregoing, namely, that the internal and external factors from which interventions spring will combine under varying circumstances in different ways for different types of nations. Domestic considerations may be highly relevant in one situation and minimal in another, and the systematic nature of these variations may differ for, say, open and developed societies from that for closed and underdeveloped ones. Lest every intervention be viewed as an unique historic event which can be understood only by reference to the specific historic circumstances in which it occurred, a theory is thus needed that posits different types of

---

[7] For a recent inquiry in which the articulation of this premise is supplemented by an empirical exploration of the relative potency of internal and external factors as sources of foreign policy, *see* Rosenau & Hoggard, "Foreign Policy Behavior in Dyadic Relationships: Testing a Pre-Theoretical Extension" (Paper presented at the Annual Meeting of the International Studies Association, mimeo., March 1971).

[8] In a letter from John Norton Moore, the editor of the volume, to the author.

interplay between internal and external factors and that seeks to explain interventionary behavior in terms of the conditions under which such different types of interplay are likely to occur in different types of nations. The theory employed here, called a theory of "national adaptation," has been developed by the present writer elsewhere.[9] As noted below, the theory specifies four types of internal-external interaction, each of which gives rise to a different probability of interventionary behavior.

A fourth and related premise concerns the interplay between internal and external factors that normally underlies military interventions. While economic and cultural interventions may be linked to a variety of external conditions, military interventions are usually associated with the outbreak or prolongation of civil strife in the target nation. The reason for this association is not difficult to discern. National societies do not resort to military action lightly. For a variety of reasons, they prefer to influence the course of events in other nations through diplomatic or other nonviolent means. They resort to armed intervention only under the most extraordinary circumstances, and civil strife tends to be viewed as an extraordinary circumstance because, unlike nonstrife-ridden events, it raises the possibility that control over the strife-torn society will pass to a new leadership who may pursue radically different policies at home and abroad. Another nation that finds these policies consonant with its own may—as Syria did in Jordan in 1970—resort to military intervention in such a situation in order to facilitate the assumption of power by the new leadership. Contrariwise, if the orientations of the insurgent leadership are contrary to the perceived needs of another nation, then the latter may—as the United States did in the Dominican Republic in 1965—resort to military intervention in order to bolster the existing government and insure the defeat of the insurgents. Developments other than civil strife, on the other hand, do not usually raise the possibility of an abrupt and wholesale change in policy, and thus a nation that intervenes is not likely to resort to the most extreme form of intervention. The probability that military interventions will be associated with civil strife is further increased by the fact that both parties to the strife are likely to seek military support abroad. Consequently, as Modelski has persuasively argued, internal wars tend to become internationalized not only because they involve stakes which attract outside intervention, but also because both the incumbents and insurgents actually invite military intervention.[10] The recognition of these international aspects of internal war has become so widely shared that most recent analyses of intervention are as much about civil strife as about intervention itself.[11]

[9] In particular *see* J. Rosenau, *The Adaptation of National Societies: A Theory of Political System Behavior and Transformation* (1970).

[10] Modelski, "The International Relations of Internal War," in J. Rosenau (ed.), *International Aspects of Civil Strife* 14 (1964).

[11] In addition to Modelski's formulation, *see* Mitchell, *supra* note 5, at 178; G. Kelly & L. Miller, *Internal War and International Systems: Perspectives on Method* (Center for International Affairs, Harvard University, Occasional Paper No. 21,

A fifth premise, central to the emerging perspective toward intervention, can also be discerned in recent work, although it is perhaps less widely shared than the others. This is a view of interventions as allocative decisions for intervening societies, in that some domestic resources are redistributed to foreign purposes if intervention occurs; and, if it does not, either the existing basis for allocating resources is maintained or the possibility of reallocations that favor domestic needs is increased. In other words, as Burton notes, interventions require "value judgments . . . that place the support of some types of governments in distant lands before the satisfaction of pressing domestic demands."[12] Thus, Burton stresses, to comprehend the phenomenon of intervention, "We need to look more closely at value systems that determine distribution of resources between domestic and foreign activities."[13]

DOMESTIC SOURCES OF FOREIGN INTERVENTIONS

All five of these premises underlie the ensuing analysis. Using the narrow definition of intervention cited earlier, we shall first identify what appear to be the more important domestic factors that can give rise to and shape interventionary behavior and then attempt to assess the strength of these factors relative to external ones. Taking into account the premise that the relative potency of internal and external factors may vary for different situations and types of nations, we shall deal with this variability by recourse to the theory of national adaptation, which gives central prominence to the interplay of domestic and foreign factors as the basis of resource allocation decisions. In effect, our theory treats interventions as a form of adaptive behavior and views the likelihood of intervention as a function of whichever of the four basic kinds of adaptive orientations is operative at a particular time.

Identification and assessment of internal variables which may partially account for interventionary behavior is not an easy task. Of the three clusters of variables—individual, governmental, and societal—that have been used as an initial subcategorization of the internal sources of external behavior,[14] only the individual variables can be readily identified through

August 1969); Allison, May, & Yarmolinsky, "Limits to Intervention," 48 *For Aff.* 245 (January 1970); R. Barnet, *Intervention and Revolution: The United States in the Third World* (1968); J. Slater, *Intervention and Negotiation: The United States and the Dominican Revolution* (1970); and Rosenau, "Internal War as an International Event," in J. Rosenau (ed.), *International Aspects of Civil Strife*, 45 (1964).

[12] Burton, *supra* note 6, at 116.

[13] *Id.* at 118.

[14] *Cf.* J. Rosenau, *The Scientific Study of Foreign Policy* (1971), Chs. V, VI, and XII. Here individual variables are conceived to be those unique aspects of a policymaker's background, values, and talents that are not part of his official role requirements and that may vary from one occupant of the position to another. Governmental

historical research. Interventionary decisions are ordinarily made at the highest governmental levels under conditions of extreme haste and secrecy. In order to maximize the military advantages of surprise and to minimize the chances of adverse opinion at home and abroad, interventions are not, unlike most policy decisions in most societies, usually the subject of prior discussion within bureaucracies or among publics. The press accounts and debates that for several weeks accompanied the gathering of refugee forces in Florida before the 1961 intervention in Cuba that was supported by the United States stand out as an exception to the typical pattern of interventionary behavior. More typically, an incident of civil strife abroad which occasions an interventionary decision will erupt abruptly and catch officials by surprise. Even officials of open societies must in these situations act before public discussion can occur and before its results are fed back into the decision-making process. Officials normally do not even have time to consult with the non-governmental elites to whom they usually turn before adopting new departures in policy.

These time constraints on the operation of societal variables are evident in some recently gathered data on the flow of public mail to officials and newspapers in the United States.[15] All the data indicate the large extent to which public reactions to interventionary behavior follow rather than anticipate the launching of an intervention. In the case of the United States intervention in Lebanon in 1958, for example, the White House did not include the situation as a special subcategory in its weekly reports to the President of public mail received until after the intervention had occurred; and even then it appeared as an issue deemed worthy of subcategorization for only one week, whereas mail containing suggestions for a new design of the American flag was separately subcategorized for the entire summer of 1958. Perhaps even more striking are the patterns of mail flow that surrounded the United States intervention in the Dominican Republic in April of 1965. An examination of the monthly tabulations of issue mail received from the public by the Department of State reveals that it did not receive *any* letters about the Dominican Republic between December 1963 (when it received seven) and April 1965 (when it received eleven). No tally was kept of the mail received during May 1965,[16] but 4,567 letters about the Dominican

---

variables are posited as the role requirements that are built into policy-making positions and that may vary from one government to another. Societal variables are viewed as those unique aspects of a society's history, capabilities, institutions, and values that may vary from one society to another. In addition, the framework posits a fourth cluster, systemic variables, that refers to those aspects of the international system that are external to a society; they may vary from one society to another at one point in time or from one era to another for the same society.

[15] For an account of how these data were gathered and processed, *see* J. Rosenau, *The Attentive Public and Foreign Policy: A Theory of Growth and Some New Evidence* 22–47 (Center of International Studies, Princeton University, Research Monograph No. 31, March 1968).

[16] It is interesting to note that this was only one of two months between May 1963 and December 1966 for which data were available that the Department's

situation were received in June of that year, and not until May 1966 did the monthly entries for the Dominican Republic return again to zero.[17] Similarly, the Letters-to-the-Editor Department of *The New York Times* did not receive enough letters about the Dominican Republic to treat it as a subcategory in its daily reports to the publisher of issue mail received for all of 1964 or the first four months of 1965. Only for nine days in May and one of June does the Dominican Republic appear as a special subcategory in the 1965 daily reports.

Stated differently, time and circumstances usually make it possible for only individual variables to operate as the immediate domestic sources of interventions.[18] To identify relevant governmental and societal variables, the analyst must deal with causal factors that are more remote in time and more deeply embedded in complex perceptual phenomena. In effect, he must specify those governmental and societal variables that account for the behavior of the individual officials who make interventionary decisions and then trace the operation of these variables through the subtle and fragmented processes whereby they became part of the perceptions on which the behavior of officialdom is based. Plainly, these are not readily observable processes or subjects that lend themselves to conventional historical research. Yet, the problem is not insurmountable. If a substantial sample of modern interventions were to be compiled and their attributes classified, it would be possible to assess the potency of governmental and societal variables[19] and identify in a preliminary way some of the most potent variables in these clusters. Thus the fact that only individual variables are the immediate determinants of interventionary decisions does not eliminate the task of pursuing the analysis to include those that operate at governmental and societal levels.

Perhaps the best way to identify some of the more important internal factors that may underlie interventionary behavior is by examining the processes through which their potency increases. Four such processes— involving what we shall refer to as empirical recollections, anticipatory perceptions, structural characteristics, and cultural orientations—would appear

---

records did not list any issue-categorized totals of the mail received from the public. Presumably, this omission was due to the coupling of the Dominican intervention and the concurrent intensification of the Vietnam teach-ins. Together the two episodes probably overwhelmed the procedures for classifying and tabulating the mail received. The other missing month was October 1966, a pre-election period that may have had similar consequences for the Department's Office of Public Services.

[17] The monthly totals for July 1965 through May 1966 were 280, 185, 185, 215, 140, 150, 90, 75, and 15.

[18] For an elaboration of this estimate of the relative potency of the internal-variable clusters in the immediate time frame, *see* Rosenau, *supra* note 1, at 165–69.

[19] This could be done by using aggregate data analysis to contrast the interventionary patterns of different kinds of governments and societies under varying conditions. For an admittedly preliminary effort to undertake such an analysis, *see* Sullivan, "International Consequences of Domestic Violence; Cross-National Assessment" (Annual Meeting of the American Political Science Association, Sept. 1969).

to be most relevant. The first is based on the operation of memory. Although in the immediate sense interventions are the result of individual officials responding to external stimuli, these responses can be heavily and systematically influenced by memories of the successes and failures of past interventions. Officials in all societies—be they open or closed, developed or underdeveloped, large or small—are bound to be aware of the rewards and punishments that their predecessors experienced after prior interventions. Quite aside from their recollections of the consequences for public careers, they are bound to have some knowledge of the political, social, and economic costs and benefits of earlier interventions for their society. These costs and benefits may not be recalled or assessed accurately but they may well be the focus of considerable controversy.[20] Nor will past interventions be recollected as having exacted similar costs or provided comparable gains, so that in each new situation the officials can be faced with the question of what historical analogy to draw. As has been observed about the current American scene, "A crucial question about the next few years will certainly be whether a situation does or does not look like another Viet Nam."[21] Whatever the analogy that may be drawn, however, the point is that analogies derived from memory are likely to be drawn and that through them governmental and societal variables can acquire potency.

But what internal costs and benefits are likely to be remembered with such clarity and force that their potency is as great as, if not greater than, the civil strife abroad which occasions the need to consider whether or not to make an interventionary decision? As indicated above, one set of empirical recollections that are likely to be especially strong are those of the subsequent political careers and fortunes of the officials and political parties who did or did not engage in interventionary behavior in the past. Such recollections are likely to be particularly salient in those cases where unsuccessful interventions led to the decline of individual careers or of party influence. A prime motive of officials and parties is to stay in office and thus their memories are likely to be especially elaborate with regard to the price their predecessors paid for interventionary decisions. At least in open systems, therefore, public opinion expressed through elections and other institutionalized means that are susceptible to clear recall can acquire considerable potency as a societal variable. Perhaps the classic demonstration of the role of public opinion in this respect lies in the future, when future American presidents will recall the electoral consequences for Lyndon Johnson and the Democrats in 1968 of their failure to end the intervention in Vietnam. Another illustration, drawn from actual history, is provided by England's Suez intervention in 1956 and the subsequent decline in the fortunes of Prime Minister Eden and the Conservative Party. It seems likely that these

[20] For example, *see* Lowenthal, "The Dominican Intervention in Retrospect," 18 *Public Policy*, 135–49 (Fall 1969).
[21] Allison, May, & Yarmolinsky, *supra* note 11, at 248.

costs were salient memories for Prime Minister Wilson and his Labour Cabinet when they decided not to intervene when Rhodesia declared its independence from England nine years later. Indeed, one analyst suggests that England's recent interventionary decisions can be understood more as a sequence of memories of the past than as a set of reactions to the present: "A 'Suez reflex' doubtless affected Labour ministers over Rhodesia in 1965, just as a 'Munich reflex' affected their predecessors in 1956."[22]

The question arises as to whether, in open systems, these societal-opinion variables operate only as restraints on interventionary behavior or whether there are conditions under which they also operate as stimuli to interventions. The question calls to mind the historical judgment that the 1898 action of the United States in Cuba was due in large part to a "yellow" journalism that inflamed public opinion which, in turn, stimulated an interventionary decision by the government. The aroused public pressure in India that underlay Nehru's decision to enter Goa in 1961 might also be noted. Yet, these are hardly appropriate examples. Not only was the Goa episode more of a conquest than an intervention, but both cases exemplify actions based on memories of the past more than they illustrate decisions based on anticipatory perceptions of the future costs of inaction. One is hard pressed to cite an example of an interventionary decision that was in some part founded on memories of the political gains that flowed from successful interventions in the past. Failure and defeat loom large as a recurrent pattern of history, whereas success and triumph seem in recollections more expressive of the particular circumstances prevailing at the time. Stated differently, the cessation of an individual's political career or the decline of a party's fortunes appears in retrospect to be more clearly linked to unsuccessful interventions than does the reelection of an official or party to interventions that proved successful. Virtually by definition, successful interventions are brief and thus get lost in the welter of history, whereas unsuccessful ones tend to persist and give rise to a vast number of visible ramifications. One reason for this distinction is that successful interventions do not foster explanations and justifications at the time they occur as much as do those that fail. Costs and benefits tend not to get assessed with respect to successes and therefore are not remembered, with the result that there is much less detail on which memory can focus in the case of successful interventions. Doubtless the memories of future American presidents, for example, will be much sharper with respect to the price Lyndon Johnson paid for failure in Vietnam than to the gains he derived from success in the Dominican Republic. In short, societal variables cannot be deemed to acquire nearly as much potency through recollective processes that stimulate interventions as they do through those that constrain such behavior.

The foregoing is not to imply, however, that memories of political costs paid by predecessors operate only on officials and parties of open societies.

[22] H. Thomas, *Suez* 154 (1967).

By definition, societal opinion variables will be less potent in closed polities than in open ones, but this does not mean that governmental and societal variables are necessarily unimportant in closed systems. On the contrary, although evidence is hard to uncover, it seems likely that the career costs of failure are much greater in closed than in open systems. The latter institutionalize the judgment of failure in the electoral process, and the exercise of this judgment may not be scheduled until long after the interventionary decision, by which time the saliency of the unsuccessful intervention may be overshadowed by the many other issues that clamor for attention at election time. In closed societies, on the other hand, judgment is not institutionalized and postponed, so that officials do not have a chance to build up a record that might offset an interventionary failure. Aware that their careers are immediately at stake in interventionary decisions, officials of closed polities thus are even more likely than their counterparts in open systems to proceed cautiously and to be restrained by the memories of how past interventionary failures strengthened opposition factions and perhaps even led to a reshuffling of the leadership and the termination of many political careers.

The political costs paid in the past are not the only way in which societal and governmental variables can acquire potency through the recollections of officials. Presumably the consequences for trade balances, bureaucratic coherence, and societal unity of past interventions can also persist as vivid memories in the present. The operation of such memories as constraints on interventionary behavior may be less manifest in the deliberations and actions of officials, but it seems clear that they will be operative. Surely, for example, future American presidents are going to be aware that the Vietnam episode had a profoundly deleterious effect on the cohesiveness of American society. Lyndon Johnson's fate may be uppermost in their memories, but it is hard to imagine them not being sensitive to the societal disunity and fragmentation that accompanied the deepening involvement in Vietnam.

Important as analogies to the past can be, however, they are not the only channel through which the various governmental and societal variables can acquire potency. A second, closely related and no less crucial channel consists of what can be called the process of "anticipatory perception." Officials not only recollect the past; they also perceive the present; and their perceptions of the current domestic scene and their resulting expectations of the internal consequences of a prospective intervention may supplement or offset their memories. If they perceive the present scene as unchanged since the previous intervention, then the recollective and anticipatory processes are likely to supplement each other. On the other hand, if the prevailing conditions are seen as different from those that obtained in the past, the officials may ignore their memories and estimate the social, political, and economic costs and gains of a prospective intervention through the process of anticipatory perception. To be sure, due to the secrecy and short time for decision that accompany interventions, public sanctions for or against such a venture overseas cannot be expressed through mass protests or opinion polls. But officials do have some sense, accurate or otherwise, of prevailing public mood and the potential tolerance for and antipathy to an interventionary project. At the very least, they anticipate the extent of the protests that would occur if time permitted; and, plainly, through these anticipatory perceptions of political, social, and economic costs and benefits, societal variables may crucially inhibit or foster their readiness to intervene in situations of civil strife abroad. Indeed, one reading of the present mood in the United States interprets societal variables as having become so potent in this regard that through anticipatory perceptions they may well prevent certain kinds of interventions in the foreseeable future: ". . . the price of intervention seems higher than ever. One need only think of the likely public response to another—hypothetical—invasion of the Dominican Republic to sense how far the national attitude has evolved."[23]

In other words, economic conditions change, political alignments alter, and social ties shift, so that officials are unwilling to rely exclusively on the lessons of history provided by their memories. Their estimate of the degree of cohesion among the major groups of their society must be continuously revised, as new developments in national life introduce new bases for conflict and cooperation. The stability of societies, polities, and economies can never be taken for granted. Compiled out of fragile attitudes and based on distant ties, they are dynamic systems that are never far from collapse and that are always susceptible to upheaval. Thus the internal conditions that obtained when earlier interventionary decisions were made may no longer prevail, and the memories of the past may have to be explicitly rejected by officials as they ponder new situations abroad in which interventionary calculations have to be made. Apparently such a rejection occurred, for example, when United States officials considered whether to intervene in Jordan's civil strife in September, 1970. "Because of the change in the internal political situation [of the U.S.] and the international climate," one newspaper noted at the time, "the United States virtually rules out any repetition of the forceful support for pro-Western governments in the Middle East that was undertaken by the Eisenhower Administration . . . in 1958."[24] As indicated above, in 1970 the United States was in too much disarray for the analogy to landing the Marines in Lebanon in 1958 to hold up. The strength of such anticipatory perceptions is revealed even more clearly by the fact that this analogy was drawn and rejected by officials who actually participated in making the decision twelve years earlier.

A third channel through which governmental and societal variables can acquire potency is what might be called "structural characteristics." Here we have in mind those aspects of societal and governmental institutions that

---

[23] Johnson, "The New Generation of Isolationists," 49 *For. Aff.* 146 (Oct. 1970).
[24] *N.Y. Times*, Sept. 17, 1970, at 19 col. 1.

shape the memories and perceptions of officials. Memories and perceptions arise out of experience and are sustained by information; the kinds of prior experience that officials have and the nature of the information they receive are in large part functions of the structure of their societies and governments. For example, the degree to which the past experience of officials includes the development of professional political skills is a structural characteristic that can vary widely among societies. Those that are closed and dominated by one party tend to recruit top officials whose entire background was in politics and whose movement up the policy-making hierarchy could only have occurred through the use of political skills. In many open systems, on the other hand, men with little prior political experience receive appointments to high office. Consequently, where the past recollections and present perceptions of the former derive from first-hand knowledge of the dynamics of international politics and the limits of interventionary behavior, those of the latter may be based on only a secondary acquaintance with the process of balancing political risks and gains. Some analysts consider this structural difference between open and closed systems to be sufficiently important to cite as one reason why the 1956 Soviet intervention in Hungary was so much more skillful and successful than the comparable effort by the United States in Cuba in 1961.[25]

The way in which bureaucracies are organized to provide information and advice is illustrative of another governmental variable to which potency can accrue. Just as the memories and perceptions of officials are shaped by the structural route they traverse to the top of the policy-making hierarchy, so are their recollections and assessments, even the historical analogies regarded by them as relevant, to a large extent dependent on the manner in which the information supplied by their subordinates reconstructs the past and constructs the present. Some advice-giving systems are structured to insure a wide-ranging flow of decisional alternatives, while others are founded on *ad hoc* mechanisms to cope with new situation. Some bureaucracies are insulated against political bias and capable of providing unwanted advice, while others lack the independence for unsolicited recommendations to be made. In some governmental structures, responsibility is widely dispersed and policy is made through inter-agency bargaining and compromise, while in others the policy-making process is marked by a concentration of responsibility and clear lines of authority. That governmental variables such as these can shape the nature of interventionary behavior is poignantly illustrated by the fact that they are the first to be cited in a major attempt to explain the United States's behavior in Vietnam by a former official who was a participant in the decision-making process.[26] Similarly, the concentration-of-responsibility variable has also been cited as a source of the

[25] Z. Brzezinski & S. Huntington, *Political Power: USA/USSR* 384–86 (1964).
[26] T. Hoopes, *The Limits of Intervention* 1–7 (1966).

difference between the Soviet Union's 1956 intervention in Hungary and the United States's 1961 Cuban venture.[27]

Besides empirical recollection, anticipatory perceptions, and structural characteristics, the cultural orientations of officials can also increase the potency of governmental and societal variables. Involved here are the complex processes of political and cultural socialization through which officials become bearers of the general value-orientations of a society. In effect, the behavior of policy-makers can be viewed as expressing societal traditions as well as individual tendencies. Differentiating the latter from the former can be difficult; but, at least at a highly abstract level, it is frequently possible to discern the operation of societal values in official behavior. Certainly, for example, the business-oriented nature of American society and the communist-oriented nature of Russian society are relevant societal variables that found expression, respectively, in the historic tendency of U.S. officials to direct convention-breaking behavior at authority structures in Latin America and the postwar tendency of Soviet officials to engage in the same behavior in Eastern Europe. Burton also suggests the operation of these cultural orientations when he observes that "the United States has those institutions of social privilege, marked inequalities of real income, racial tensions and political unrest, and business-military alliances that have been associated with the types of regimes it has endeavored to support in Asia and Latin America. . . . Equally, the Soviet Union has, and previously had to an even greater degree, those institutions of political repression that have been associated with the types of regimes it has endeavored to support."[28] Brzezinski and Huntington considered similar cultural orientations potent when they note that Soviet ideology facilitates interventionary behavior by providing Soviet leaders "with the necessary assurance that their use of force is justified historically," whereas the liberal traditions of the United States tend to undermine such behavior on the part of U.S. officials because of the "deeply rooted . . . American reluctance to use force."[29] Similarly, Hoffman stresses that the pragmatism which has long dominated American orientations also underlies the ineffective quality of most U.S. interventions. He suggests that the pragmatic strain of the American past leads U.S. officials to prefer to intervene on behalf of existing regimes that represent stability rather than insurgent movements that might eventually create a more desirable status quo.[30] Indeed, Hoffman argues that the quality of U.S. interventions is negatively affected by the pragmatic strain, even when it is not directed at the status quo: on these infrequent occasions,

---

[27] Brzezinski & Huntington, *supra* note 25, at 386–87. For another cogent comparative analysis of how governmental variables can shape the policy-making process in foreign affairs, *see* K. Waltz, *Foreign Policy and Democratic Politics: The American and British Experience* (1967).

[28] Burton, *supra* note 6, at 118–19.

[29] Brzezinski & Huntington, *supra* note 25, at 382–83.

[30] S. Hoffman, *Gulliver's Troubles, or the Setting of American Foreign Policy* 201–2 (1968).

American intervention will be, so to speak, ashamed of itself. Not only will it hide behind the fig-leaf of alleged noninterference, but it will be emasculated by the piecemeal, technical process by which it is undertaken. Once again pragmatism becomes a refuge: expert assistance, administrative advice, and some secret shenanigans express the limit of our daring."[31]

THE INTERACTION OF INTERNAL AND EXTERNAL FACTORS

Although many other types and illustrations of governmental and societal variables could be cited, the foregoing analysis of the four channels through which some of them acquire potency is, hopefully, sufficient to establish the central point that domestic factors can shape interventionary behavior. Notwithstanding our earlier conclusion that individual variables are the only internal variables that operate as immediate sources of interventions, a variety of governmental and societal processes and institutions can be influential if a longer time-frame is used to allow for the unfolding of more complex causal processes.

To conclude that domestic factors can be highly potent, however, is not to say that, in fact, they are. As indicated earlier, in the course of identifying potentially relevant governmental and societal variables, one can easily exaggerate their importance. In enumerating all the ways in which interventionary tendencies can spring from internal sources, one can forget that the goal is to trace the *relative* potency of key variables and that external factors may also be operative and substantially more potent than internal ones.[32] It would not be difficult to restructure the preceding discussion so that it would support the hypothesis that interventions derive from both external and domestic sources. Virtually every one of the examples used in the foregoing analysis could be offset by a contrary illustration in which external or systemic variables are shown to be equally, if not more, powerful. Recollection of how the Vietnam episode rent American society and ended Lyndon Johnson's political career may operate to constrain future American officials, but did not deter President Nixon from undertaking an "incursion" into Cambodia in 1970. That empirical recollections and anticipatory perceptions were operative in the Cambodian decision can be readily demonstrated. In his public speech explaining the decision, the President himself referred to the possibility that it would jeopardize his chances for re-election. But he also analogized to Munich and the possibility of a debacle in Southeast Asia, thus suggesting that the recollections and perceptions relative to the domestic scene were no match for those directed

---

[31] *Id.* at 203–4.

[32] For inquiries that stress the potency of external or systemic sources, *see* Modelski, *supra* note 10; Young, "Intervention and International Systems," 22 *J. of Int'l Aff.* 177–87 (1968).

abroad. The internal consequences of the incursion may not have been accurately anticipated, but at the time they were assessed as less onerous than the external ones. Similarly, if the social structures of the United States is as important a source of American interventionary behavior in Latin America as the quote from Burton above suggests, how could the United States decide not to intervene in Chile after the 1970 election when that country brought a Marxist regime to power? The answer would seem to lie as much in external as in internal sources: "Many officials believe that any United States interference could lead to a civil war in Chile and a surge of anti-United States feelings in Latin America as well as to domestic protest comparable to the demonstrations that followed last spring's incursion into Cambodia."[33]

Contradictory examples need not be confined to the United States. Why did not the ideological and societal variables previously identified as potent sources of the Soviet Union's successful interventions in Hungary and Czechoslovakia give rise to similar behavior when, in the late 1960's, the Rumanian regime adopted a much more independent line in foreign affairs? Presumably again the answer is to be found in the fear of repercussions abroad, in this case in the Communist world. Similarly, just as one source cited above as interpreting England's 1965 decision not to intervene in Rhodesia as, in large part, due to recollections of the domestic consequences of the earlier Suez venture, so another source ascribes critical importance to external variables, citing "military logistics" as "a factor in the British decision not to use military force to terminate the unilateral declaration of independence in Rhodesia."[34]

In short, having shown that interventions can be constrained or fostered by domestic factors, we need to return to our initial premise that both internal and external variables are operative, with sometimes the former and sometimes the latter being more potent. The problem is not that of determining whether one or the other is the prime source of interventionary behavior, but one of developing criteria for anticipating when external and systemic variables and when societal and governmental variables are likely to be more potent. As previously indicated, most analysts agree that interventions are the result of an interaction between circumstances at home and abroad. All the studies cited thus far mention both internal and external factors, but most of them ignore the question of when and how the two sets of factors interact. They concede that the potencies of the internal and external variables fluctuate, giving rise to apparent contradictions, such as the United States intervention in the Dominican Republic and its avoidance of such behavior in Chile five years later; but few analysts seek to resolve the contradictions through a general model that encompasses the fluctuations. Rather, most suggest that the fluctuations stem from unique historical

[33] *N.Y. Times*, Sept. 21, 1970, at 2 col. 2.

[34] Yarmolinsky, "American Foreign Policy and the Decision to Intervene," 22 *J. of Int'l Aff.* 233 (1968).

circumstances and thus one can do little more than enumerate both the internal and external factors and concede that they interact in different ways at different moments in time to produce different interventionary decisions.

This is not the place to develop an elaborate theoretical framework that could account for the contradictions and allow for the derivation of hypotheses to predict when each type of variable will be more potent. However, our theory of national adaptation does lend itself to such a task, and it is perhaps useful to indicate briefly the relevant hypotheses it yields. The theory is still far from complete, and the hypotheses derived here may prove to be unfounded when data appropriate to their testing are gathered, but formulating these hypotheses will at least encourage consideration of the possibility that fluctuations in the strength of internal and external variables stem from systematic sources rather than from unique historical circumstances.

INTERVENTION AS ADAPTIVE BEHAVIOR

Perhaps it seems odd to view interventionary behavior as adaptive. In their common usage, the words "intervention" and "adaptation" would seem to embrace mutually exclusive phenomena. Adaptation suggests peaceful accommodation, whereas intervention implies violent change. In a normative sense, too, the two terms appear contradictory. Interventionary phenomena are normally viewed as undesirable, if not reprehensible, whereas adaptation tends to be, if not prized, at least accepted as necessary to the maintenance of order. If, however, national adaptation is conceived to encompass all the processes by which national societies keep the fluctuations in those of their economic, political, and social structures that are essential to their continued existence within acceptable limits, then interventions become merely one of the multitude of ways by which societies can adapt to their environments. As elaborated elsewhere,[35] national adaptation can be usefully viewed as the persistence of the basic interaction patterns (*i.e.*, essential structures) of a society, within limits acceptable to its members. In this formulation, the essential structures are considered to be constantly fluctuating as new internal and external developments alter existing patterns of conflict and cooperation. If the fluctuations are increasingly unacceptable, then the actions which precipitated them are viewed as maladaptive. On the other hand, if an action or policy helps to reduce the fluctuations of one or another of the society's essential structures, then it is regarded as adaptive behavior. In short, the continuous changes which modern societies undergo are seen as continuously shifting them among

[35] Rosenau, "Foreign Policy as Adaptive Behavior: Some Preliminary Notes for a Theoretical Model," 2 *Comp. Politics* 355–74 (April 1970); and Rosenau, *supra* note 9.

different points on a scale of national adaptation.[36] In treating interventions as a form of adaptive behavior, we thus are not implying that they are necessarily adaptive. They may well undermine essential structures and foster fluctuations which move societies toward maladaptation.

This is not the occasion to assess whether interventions are more likely to be adaptive than maladaptive. That is an empirical question, an adequate answer to which requires more time and data than are available here. Rather, assuming that interventions can be either adaptive or maladaptive, our task here is to identify the combinations of internal and external factors that are likely to lead a society to engage in convention-breaking behavior directed at the authority structure of another society. The adaptation model allows us to do this because it posits societies as pursuing one of four basic types of adaptation at any moment in time, each of which is differentiated from the others by the underlying orientation of publics and officials toward the balance that should be struck between internal needs and wants and environmental demands. The differences between the four orientations have been summarized as follows:

> A society can attempt to keep its essential structures within acceptable limits by making them consistent with the changes and demands emanating from its present environment, giving rise to what we shall call *the politics of acquiescent adaptation*. Second, a society can seek to render its environment consistent with its present structures, thus engaging in what we shall refer to as *the politics of intransigent adaptation*. Third, a society can attempt to shape the demands of its present structures and its present environment to each other (*i.e.*, by seeking to establish a desired equilibrium between them), behavior we shall designate *the politics of promotive adaptation*. Finally, a society can seek to live within the limitations that its present structures and its present environment impose on each other (*i.e.*, by preserving the existing equilibrium between them), giving rise to what we shall call *the politics of preservative adaptation*.[37]

It must be emphasized that these four adaptive orientations are not transitory phenomena that can change each time a new internal or external demand arises. Rather, they consist of deep-seated predispositions whereby societies relate themselves to their environments. New internal and external stimuli are not simply responded to. They must be interpreted in some way, implicitly or explicitly, before a response occurs. Bureaucratic procedures may routinize the responses, but they are neither automatic nor random. They arise out of interpretations in which consideration is given to how the responses may serve to contain the fluctuations in essential structures within

---

[36] There is, of course, the possibility that a society will fail to keep its essential structures within acceptable limits and thus pass beyond the maladaptive extreme of the scale. That is, it will cease to exist. Most modern societies, however, do manage to persist, albeit the fluctuations in the essential structures of many of them tend to occur toward the maladaptive end of the scale.

[37] Rosenau, *supra* note 9, at 4.

acceptable limits. To be sure, the behavior of societies is not always marked by high consistency. Transitory perceptions do affect the extent and nature of their responses to situations and these perceptions may render their behavior in one situation inconsistent with their actions in another. Rhodesia, for example, is willing to engage in trade and tariff negotiations even though it refuses to bargain when the United Nations demands changes in its racial policies. Such inconsistencies, however, do not mean that societies pursue more than one set of adaptive orientations at a time. Our model does not allow for such a possibility, since it refers to an orientation level more basic than the one used to select tactics in immediate situations. Adaptive orientations are those that initially interpret all situations at any moment in time. They operate at such a fundamental level that they underlie the choice of tactics and strategies through which societies respond to daily events at home and abroad. Analogizing to the individual, adaptive orientations are the equivalent of the basic personality traits with which a person interprets and responds to his inner needs and external circumstances.[38] Although the basic orientations of societies are often obscured by apparent inconsistencies in their behavior, on occasion the inconsistencies can also provide a good clue to the type of adaptation to which a society is committed at a particular time. For sometimes the inconsistency results not from transitory perceptions, but from adaptive challenges not previously experienced. When this happens, when a society is faced with basic changes at home or abroad with which it has never been confronted, it must either choose to maintain inconsistent policies or seek to render them consistent. The choice it makes provides an important insight into the basic adaptive orientations that are operative. To recur to the Rhodesian example, that society's readiness to enter trade negotiations was a long-established one, whereas the U.N. demands were a new aspect of its environment that compelled the Rhodesians to fall back on their basic adaptive orientations as a guide in finding a satisfactory balance between internal needs and external demands. Thus they acted in terms of their intransigent predispositions while seeking to render their external environment consistent with their essential structures.

While the four types of adaptation are conceived to involve enduring orientations, allowance is made for the fact that societies can and do undergo transformation from one type of adaptation to another. If the potencies of either internal or external variables substantially increase or decrease, then the citizenry and officials of a society may be inclined to pursue and establish a new kind of balance between essential structures and environmental demands. Our model allows for twelve such transformations, but

---

[38] Indeed, in an analogical sense, there is a close similarity between the psychotic personality and the intransigent society: both insist that their environments conform to the demands derived from their internal structures. Similar analogies could be made between the "other-directed" and "inner-directed" personalities developed in David Riesman's *The Lonely Crowd* (1950) on the one hand and acquiescent and perservative or promotive adaptation on the other.

considers three of these (those involving transformation to preservative adaptation) as much more probable than the other nine. Moreover, adaptive transformations are conceived to require such substantial change in the potency of key variables that it is anticipated they will usually result in the replacement of one set of officials by another set. In the case of the shift from or to acquiescent and intransigent adaptation, a thoroughgoing social revolution or international war may be required.[39]

Before elaborating on the kinds of interventionary behavior that the model projects for each type of adaptation, it should be noted that interventionary decisions can provide important clues to the nature of adaptive phenomena. Virtually by definition, and more than most occasions for decision, interventions involve external circumstances that have not previously been confronted by a society. The choice as to whether or not to intervene in the affairs of another society is thus ordinarily a reliable indicator of the kind of adaptive orientation to which a society is committed at that moment in time. Likewise, changes in the pattern of such decisions through time is equally valuable as an indicator of whether the society has undergone an adaptive transformation. The circumstances abroad which occasion the need for an interventionary decision usually portend such substantial alterations in the potency of external variables that measurable and repeated deviations in the pattern of interventionary behavior through time is likely to reflect an adaptive transformation. Viewed in this way (and as elaborated below), the discrepancy between the United States intervention in the Dominican Republic in 1965 and non-intervention in Chile in 1970 becomes understandable as a reflection of the transformation from promotive to preservative adaptation on the part of the United States.

It is not difficult to derive hypotheses as to which of the four types of adaptation are likely to produce the least and the greatest readiness to resort to interventionary behavior. Societies committed to acquiescent adaptation are so fully prepared to adjust their essential structures to the changes and demands emanating from their environments that sudden developments abroad in which societies otherwise oriented might intervene are not likely even to be seen as occasioning the need for an interventionary decision. Officials may perceive such developments as threatening, but their acquiescent orientation will incline them to respond through internal adjustments rather than through convention-breaking behavior directed at the suddenly altered authority structures abroad. An important exception to this hypothesis actually provides further support for it. Acquiescent societies are likely to engage in interventionary behavior when they are the targets of certain demands to engage in such behavior. If the demands originate in those parts of their environment to which they are acquiescent, then it is highly probable that the demands will be heeded. Thus, for example, East Germany intervened in Czechoslovakia in 1968 not because developments

39 Rosenau, *supra* note 9, at 16–20.

in Czechoslovakia posed a threat to its essential structures, but because it was predisposed to maintain its essential structures through acquiescence to Soviet leadership, which, in this case, insisted that East Germany and its other European satellites participate in the intervention. Such exceptions, however, are rare and, more typically, acquiescent societies can be expected to avoid recourse to interventionary behavior.

Likewise, it seems clear that the greatest readiness to intervene in the affairs of others will exist in societies with intransigent orientations. Unwilling to adjust certain aspects of their essential structures to external demands and thus being committed to rendering their environments compatible with those unnegotiable dimensions of their essential structures, intransigent societies are likely to be ready to intervene in any situation abroad that poses an immediate threat to the unnegotiable aspects of their structures. Israel's posture toward its Arab neighbors is an example in line with this prediction.[40]

As for the interventionary behavior of societies oriented toward promotive and preservative adaptation, it seems clear that these orientations involve neither the extensive readiness of intransigent societies to engage in such action nor the lack of such readiness that characterizes acquiescent societies. Officials of both promotive and preservative societies are committed to either building or maintaining an equilibrium between internal and external demands and thus are unlikely to emulate either their acquiescent counterparts' acceptance of all environmental changes, or their intransigent counterparts' insistence that certain external conditions be altered to meet internal demands. Likewise, it would seem that promotive orientations, arising as they do out of aspirations to tailor external and internal demands to complement one another, are likely to imply a greater readiness to undertake interventions than preservative orientations would imply. The latter do not involve efforts to reshape the equilibrium inherent in the existing demands at home and abroad, so that officials of preservative societies will be more tolerant of sudden changes abroad than will officials of promotive societies. The probability that promotive societies will engage in more interventionary behavior than preservative ones is further increased by the fact that the former are more likely than the latter to receive invitations to intervene in external situations. Given their orientation to promote new arrangements, abroad, officials of promotive societies are more likely than their preservative counterparts to establish extensive contacts with factions in other societies and thus receive interventionary invitations from a wider number of sources.

The hypotheses derived from our model are not confined to the conclusion that acquiescent, preservative, promotive, and intransigent orientations

[40] There is clearcut evidence, for example, that Israel was ready to intervene in Jordan in September 1970, if that country's authority structure had proved unable to survive an insurgent challenge supported by Syrian tanks. *See N.Y. Times*, Oct. 8, 1970, at 1 col. 2.

can, in that order, be arrayed in a lesser-to-greater scale of interventionary predispositions. It also allows us to specify at least a few of the conditions under which the four sets of orientations are likely to lead to convention-breaking behavior directed at the authority structures of other societies. Acquiescent societies are likely to resort to interventionary behavior only if salient societies in their environments demand that they do so, and intransigent societies are likely to intervene in external situations whenever certain of their essential structures are threatened. Identifying the necessary conditions for preservative and promotive societies, on the other hand, is more difficult, since it poses the question of whether one has to know the exact nature of the equilibrium between internal and external demands they are seeking to promote or preserve before one can specify the conditions under which their readiness to resort to interventionary behavior will be triggered. Happily, while such knowledge would obviously be helpful, our model permits us to by-pass the question and identify some of the conditions.

In the case of preservative adaptation, the model posits a society that is so oriented as being limited in the scope of its external behavior. Such societies are ready "to live with" rather than to change the limitations inherent in their environments, and are thus not likely to reallocate resources from internal projects to deal with external circumstances that are geographically remote and not directly linked to their essential structures. Being sensitive to both internal and external demands, a preservative society is unlikely to reallocate resources of the magnitude needed to launch an intervention, except when the changes abroad occur in contiguous or nearby societies. A drastic change in the authority structure of an immediate neighbor can pose a direct threat to essential structures, so that the preservative society may feel impelled to undertake an intervention in order to maintain the existing internal-external equilibrium. Promotive societies, on the other hand, are not so likely to confine their interventionary decisions to contiguous or nearby situations. Since they are oriented toward the creation of a new balance between their essential structures and their external environments, they are much readier to make major reallocations of resources between the domestic and foreign sections and to define geographically distant situations as relevant to the equilibrium they are seeking to promote. Stated differently, officials of promotive societies are exposed to considerably fewer internal demands than their preservative counterparts (*i.e.*, societal variables are much less potent for them),[41] and they are thus more capable of committing resources to distant purposes, with the result that their interventionary behavior is both more frequent and more extensive than that of preservative officials. Furthermore, given the greater readiness of promotive officials to foster new arrangements abroad, their interventionary behavior is likely to be undertaken on behalf of larger purposes and accompanied by more grandiose rhetoric than is the behavior of preservative officials. While

---

[41] The reasons for this difference are developed in Rosenau, *supra* note 9, at 5–16.

the former are likely to justify their actions, for example, in terms of the need to free whole populations or to uphold valued social institutions, the latter are likely to refer to the necessity of protecting their own nationals or of reinstating a particular regime.

These differences between promotive and preservative adaptation go a long way toward explaining the apparent contradiction between the 1965 actions of the United States in the Dominican Republic and its inaction with respect to Chile in 1970, if one assumes—as the present writer does—that the United States underwent a transformation from promotive to preservative adaptation during the 1966–69 period.[42] Chile was perceived as simply too distant and costly in 1970 because by that time the postwar United States orientation to promote a "Free World" had come to an end and had been replaced by a tendency to accommodate internal needs and external circumstances to each other. Since the Dominican Republic is not as geographically remote as Chile, the United States might well intervene in its affairs again if its authority structure should again be seen as bordering on collapse. Such behavior would not be inconsistent with the new preservative orientations, whereas comparable developments in more remote parts of the world would be so.

CONCLUSIONS

Although our model has yielded four basic variations in the relative potency of domestic factors as sources of interventionary behavior, there is one other question that needs to be briefly considered. In order to assess the relevance of domestic factors to the reallocative decisions through which societies undertake interventions, it is also necessary to ask whether the adaptive orientations of these societies are as central as their capabilities. Some might argue that interventions occur only when societies have the wherewithal to implement them[43] and thus that their adaptive orientations are secondary considerations, coming into play only after estimates of relative capability have been made. Such an argument underestimates the strength of adaptive orientations and overestimates the rationality of officials. There is, to be sure, a connection between the type of adaptation a society pursues and its capabilities. It is no accident that acquiescent orientations are likely to be found in small and weak societies located adjacent to large superpowers, that promotive orientations are most likely to be found

---

[42] Elsewhere I argue that the transformation first became manifest in the 1968 New Hampshire primary. The triumph of Senator Eugene McCarthy in that primary election revealed that societal variables had undergone a sharp increase in potency, thus compelling U.S. officials to forego promotive orientations and to develop preservative ones. *See id.* at 15.

[43] For example, Yarmolinsky suggests that "the availability of military force may be the principal practical determinant of a decision to intervene" Yarmolinsky, *supra* note 34.

in modernizing societies or in large superpowers, or that preservative orientations are perhaps most characteristic of developed and open societies.[44] Likewise, it can hardly be disputed that societies are generally not likely to undertake interventions knowing that they lack the strength to be successful. Nevertheless, we would argue that the way in which a society relates internal needs and external demands to each other is not just a matter of rational calculation, but that it springs from orientations toward self-environment ties which include nonrational dimensions, and that consequently adaptive orientations precede capability estimates as much as they are fostered by them. Indeed, it is precisely the discrepancy between adaptive orientations and relative capabilities that accounts for the failure of so many interventions. Frequently intransigent, promotive, and (to a much lesser extent) preservative orientations lead societies to reallocate domestic resources to foreign purposes and engage in interventionary behavior when the reallocated resources are not sufficient to bring about an adaptive solution to the perceived problem.

In sum, our conclusions about the relative potency of domestic factors derived from the adaptation model seem no less relevant when capabilities are taken into account. There do seem to be processes through which and conditions under which the internal needs and aspirations of societies either heighten or constrain their readiness to intervene in each other's affairs. Our analysis suggests that domestic factors may have little or no potency, but it has also highlighted several circumstances in which their potency is considerable.

[44] For an elaboration of the reasons for these associations, *see* Rosenau, *supra* note 9.

Chapter 8 | **Constitutional Aspects of**
United States Participation in Foreign
Internal Conflicts | *W. Taylor Reveley III*

I. AN OLD ISSUE OF NEW IMPORTANCE

American participation in foreign internal conflicts presents no sudden constitutional issue. The intervention issue, however, during the last quarter century has assumed an importance unequaled except in the early decades of our national life. Then, the country was internally divided and drawn into war, first with France and later with Britain, in its attempt to deal with conflicts stemming from the French Revolution. Then as now, questions of participation in foreign civil strife have posed problems vital to our national security, as it may be threatened by both foreign attack and internal dissension.

The reasons for the present transcendence of the issue may be broadly stated. During most of the nineteenth century, three factors in particular—geographical isolation, limited military technology and a viable European balance of power—left the United States with no felt need either to intervene abroad on a significant scale or to develop and maintain a standing capacity for such action.[1] Intervention, when it occurred, tended to be modest in the use of men and resources. It rarely involved the affairs of other states or was thought vital to our national defense and, thus, as a rule, it could easily be abandoned. Even had extensive intervention occurred, the resulting danger would have had finite limits, for geography, military technology, and the prevailing balance of power would have kept conflict within survivable bounds. Finally, the consequences of intervention were limited further by nineteenth-century concepts of international legality and morality. Under prevailing norms, the use of force to protect one's nationals or property, to punish violations of international law, or to order the affairs of politically immature people were not thought unacceptable, thus lessening the legal and political costs of intervention.

Conditions today are radically different. Geographical immunity no longer exists. The world movement of men, ideas, information, and goods has made Americans interdependent with other peoples. This interdependence, coupled with advances in military technology, has led to a belief that our security is intimately tied to that of many other countries and to our pledges to defend them. To maintain the credibility of commitments to

---

[1] Parts of this essay draw heavily on Reveley, "Presidential War-Making: Constitutional Prerogative or Usurpation?," 55 *Va. L. Rev.* 1243 (1969).

defend vital areas, we have often felt compelled to protect friendly regimes in nations of little intrinsic significance. Fear has existed that the loss of one such state could easily lead to the general collapse of others similarly situated. Thus, once begun, it has not been easy to abandon any intervention. This has been particularly the case as evolution in the balance of world power has left the United States as one of two major pillars of a system that operates amid a host of unstable Third-World nations. Further, a vastly heightened American military capacity has provided the President with a potent, flexible means of intervention abroad on a moment's notice, while the existence of nuclear weapons permits no assurance that conflict will remain within survivable limits.

Finally, the political, moral and legal costs of intervention have greatly increased. Growing international respect for self-determination and peace has led to the prohibition of one state's intervention in another state's affairs and to the emphasis on collective control over the armed enforcement of international law, with an accompanying distaste for unilateral police action. Use of force by international disputants, except in self-defense, has been outlawed. Thus, many uses of force that would have been permissible under nineteenth-century standards are unacceptable today. Accordingly, even if contemporary American participation in foreign civil war involves little or no fighting, it still may be costly in terms of its violations of international political sensibilities, law, and morality. These changed conditions, in combination, have made American intervention in the internal strife of other countries a matter of great political and constitutional moment.

II. THE RELEVANCE OF THE CONSTITUTION TO INTERVENTION DECISION-MAKERS

Even granting that intervention posed fundamental problems for a time when the country was young, what relevance can the Constitution, a product of the late eighteenth century, have to intervention dilemmas whose dimensions have changed radically even within the last twenty-five years? Some argue that it has none. American decision-makers, they say, do little more than attempt a constitutional rationalization for their *Realpolitik*. The threshold inquiry here, accordingly, must be the extent to which this charge of irrelevance has substance.

This inquiry has limited validity on three scores. First, the breadth and complexity of the pertinent constitutional provisions make statement of the law difficult. At issue ultimately are the constitutional limits on the adoption of any foreign policy that may lead to intervention in foreign internal strife, and not simply constitutional controls on actual intervention decisions. Participation in foreign civil war generally occurs only *in extremis* to salvage long-standing policies. Thus, a decision to intervene is usually subject to pressures for commitment that could have been avoided or mitigated had a different foreign policy been pursued.

Second, difficulty in defining the law also arises from certain characteristics of the relevant constitutional provisions. They are vague in their allocation of authority over American foreign relations between the President and Congress. Each is granted a line of powers that, in isolation, could support a claim to final authority. Edward S. Corwin has spoken of these grants as "logical incompatibles," noting that "the Constitution, considered only for its affirmative grants of powers capable of affecting the issue, is an invitation to struggle for the privilege of directing American foreign policy."[2] Beyond its complementary grants of power to the President and Congress, the Constitution encourages confusion and struggle by the highly abstract terms of many of its crucial provisions. "The Congress shall have Power . . . [t]o declare War" and "[t]he executive Power shall be vested in a President of the United States of America," for example, leave much to further definition. Finally, the document frequently fails to indicate where the ultimate authority lies on certain basic questions, such as the deployment of American troops or the termination of hostilities.

Third, the relevant provisions govern public affairs that are not conducive to the rule of law. They involve national security, occasionally under conditions that require, or seem to require, speedy or secret action. Power and expediency always have a disproportionately large influence when vital interests are believed to be threatened. This is especially true when decisions must be quickly made, with little time for thought about any but the most pressing considerations, and when the exact contours of any action taken, however unsavory, may be draped in total or partial secrecy. Obedience to law, under such circumstances, is generally viewed as only one among a number of desiderata, many of which may be thought to be more compelling.

How, then, can it be said that the Constitution does affect American participation in foreign internal strife? In short, the breadth and complexity of the pertinent constitutional provisions are not so great, these provisions are not so ambiguous nor the public affairs to which they apply so fearsome that no constitutional expectations have been able to develop and influence the play of power and expediency.

Expectations about the practice required by the pertinent constitutional provisions have influenced both government officials in their intervention decisions and the electorate in judging the legitimacy of these decisions. Since it is extremely difficult to obtain a high level of obedience to legal norms by coercion, the stability of any legal system depends largely upon voluntary obedience to the law. Ours is a stable system. Presidents, like most other members of the American body politic, voluntarily obey its rules. James Buchanan, for example, adhered rigidly to his understanding of the limits of his constitutional powers, going so far as to reject an 1860 Virginia proposal for a conference of the States and an agreement between

---

[2] E. Corwin, *The President: Office and Powers, 1787–1957* 171 (4th rev. ed. 1957).

the Secessionists and the President to abstain from violence, pending its conclusion. Buchanan strongly favored the plan but refused to act, stating:

> Congress, and Congress alone, under the war-making power, can exercise the discretion of agreeing to abstain "from any and all acts calculated to produce a collision of arms" between this and any other government. It would therefore be a usurpation for the Executive to attempt to restrain their hands by an agreement in regard to matters over which he has no constitutional control.[3]

At the other extreme, Franklin Roosevelt believed that he possessed constitutional power to act even in direct opposition to statutory law, if an emergency so warranted, and did so in his activities leading to prewar hostilities with Germany in the Atlantic.

Taking Roosevelt as the primal example when the question concerns the extent of the President's constitutional powers to respond to what he views as a threat to the country, an activist Executive will often find an unusually broad grant of authority. Such presidential findings, however, are not necessarily correct, and they need not be—and frequently have not been—accepted by other persons and groups whose views about the constitutionality of foreign-policy decisions are influential.

Other centers of power, both by what they do and what they might do, can restrain presidential action. Three competing institutions are particularly important: the federal bureaucracy, Congress, and the judiciary. To implement his policies, the President must have the cooperation of the civil and military personnel who actually operate the government machinery. Their cooperation is a fragile thing. Difficult as the bureaucracy may be, however, a greater limit upon presidential authority is Congress. In Richard Neustadt's words, we have "a government of separated institutions *sharing* powers."[4] Unlike parliamentary executives, the President has no ultimate weapons, such as dissolution or excommunication from party ranks, with which to beat reluctant legislators into submission. As a result, an abiding concern of the Executive and his assistants is the likely reaction of Congress to their proposals and actions.

Legislators have a number of tools with which to restrain the President. Through legislation, they can restrict his options, hamstring his policies, and—to an extent—take the policy initiative from him. Strong elements in Congress are presently attempting to reassert by legislation a congressional role in making decisions on intervention. Through the power of the purse, the legislators can similarly limit the President. Although control of the purse has been virtually a non-power in the hands of Cold-War congresses

---

[3] Message to Congress of January 28, 1861, quoted in F. Wormuth, *The Vietnam War: The President versus the Constitution* 12 (April 1968) (Occasional Paper: Center for the Study of Democratic Institutions).

[4] R. Neustadt, *Presidential Power, The Politics of Leadership* 42 (1960).

when funds were sought for the military, present reluctance to embark on major defense spending and criticism of the military establishment suggest that appropriations may emerge anew as a limiting factor. The power of congressional committees to investigate and oversee has proved a powerful instrument for prompting national debate over foreign policy, molding opinion, and thereby influencing presidential action. Legislators can work the political process quietly as well, communicating privately with the President to persuade him that his action is legally or politically ill-advised. Congress can also work in tandem with rebellious elements in the bureaucracy to thwart presidential initiatives. Further, remote though the possibility is, the President must remain aware of the congressional capacity to impeach him or to censure his conduct by resolution, a fate that befell Polk at the hands of a House concerned over the constitutionality of his role in initiating the Mexican War. And, the Senate is constitutionally empowered to advise and consent to presidential treaties and appointments and has devised the power to delay and negate by filibuster.

To date, the courts have served more to enlarge presidential control over foreign affairs than to restrain it. The one opinion directly treating the scope of executive power to use force abroad—an 1860 decision dealing with an 1854 reprisal against a small, stateless town in Central America[5]— took a broad view of the President's constitutional authority. Although given ample opportunity to speak in the Vietnam context, the Supreme Court has refused to consider whether the conflict is unconstitutional for lack of congressional authorization. The possibility remains, nonetheless, that courts, convinced of the unconstitutionality of presidential action, could order the Executive to desist. President Truman's immediate acceptance of the Supreme Court's ruling in the *Steel Seizure* case[6] suggests that a judicial command affecting the use of force abroad would be obeyed by the executive branch, although perhaps not without great political cost to the judiciary and stress upon our constitutional system.

The ultimate restraint upon the President, however, does not come from his own beliefs and abilities or from competing centers of power, but rather from the electorate. A President will fall from grace when his policies seem unwise to the public or when they involve him in activity widely viewed as illegitimate because it transgresses community concepts of legality or morality. Even before an unpopular President is turned out of office, his policies and personnel will have come under attack from other centers of power, emboldened by the Executive's diminished popular standing. Attacks from

---

[5] Durand v. Hollins, 8 F. Cas. 111 (No. 4186) (C.C.S.D.N.Y. 1860).

[6] Youngstown Sheet & Tube Co. v. Sawyer, 343 U.S. 579 (1952). To a significant extent, it is possible to equate a decision such as *Youngstown*, which ordered the return to private management of domestic steel companies seized by executive command, with a hypothetical judicial decision ordering the President to withdraw troops from a foreign internal conflict to which he has unilaterally committed them, unless he obtains immediate congressional authorization for their use. See Reveley, *supra* note 1, at 1277–78 n. 104.

these centers will, in turn, further reduce popular support of the administration, and the President will find it increasingly difficult to govern.

In sum, the process by which the Constitution affects intervention decision-making shares much with the process by which customary international law guides nation states. As a rule, both states and intervention decision-makers appreciate the need to support prevailing norms, and thus voluntarily accept them. Rarely would either, if accused of illegal activity, fail to deny the charge vociferously, adducing legal argument to justify their action. But since the precise demands of constitutional and international rules are often complementary or vague, and since there is little chance of clarification by judicial or legislative action (formal amendment in the case of the Constitution), both nations and intervention participants have latitude in interpreting the relevant provisions. Each tends to define, fill in, and alter the legal contours by a process of claim and concession. If, for example, presidential assertions of authority are acknowledged or acquiesced in by other centers of power and by the electorate, the Executive assumes the power as his constitutional due. Similarly, even unsuccessful claims remain as potential sources of law, especially if they were given more than verbal substance before their rejection. Finally, both intervention decision-makers and nation states have a tendency to take less than ordinary account of law when confronted with crisis, a condition generally accompanying use of force, but each is restrained to a greater or lesser degree by the authoritative expectations of other members of the community, and by the sanctions that they might impose on a violator of their expectations.

III.   CONSTITUTIONAL RULES GOVERNING USE OF FORCE

PROCEDURAL IN NATURE

The limits placed by the Constitution on American use of force abroad are essentially procedural in nature, not substantive. That is, they speak to the *manner* in which use-of-force decisions are to be made and not to their *content*. Accordingly, the relevant constitutional provisions deal with the allocation of power over the conduct of American foreign affairs between the President and Congress, not with the substance of the foreign policies that may be adopted.

Some have suggested that domestic constitutional law may take substantive content from pertinent international constitutional provisions, such as Article 2(4) of the United Nations Charter. At one extreme, the possibility exists that American intervention in violation of international law is per se unconstitutional. A middle reading would place a breach of international law among the factors suggesting domestic unconstitutionality. At the other pole is an analysis that finds no necessary link between domestic and international law. The prevailing American authority supports the second extreme, holding that the constitutionality of American intervention is strictly a matter for domestic law. Thus our participation in foreign internal strife that is illegal under Article 2(4) remains legal under the Constitution so long as the intervention decisions are made in the constitutionally prescribed fashion.[7]

THE CONSTITUTIONAL ISSUES

The constitutional rules governing American use of force, intervention included, apply to decisions that fall into two broad categories: (1) those that risk American involvement in foreign conflict but do not directly place the country in it and (2) those that deal with the actual use of force abroad. Among the former, concern is with (a) commitments to go to war should certain future events occur, (b) the deployment of military forces abroad, and (c) other provocative steps, for example, providing diplomatic or economic aid to a belligerent. As indicated previously, category (1) decisions may generate pressures that virtually ensure subsequent decisions in favor of war. For example, it is usually true that, to limit armed intervention, it is first necessary to restrain the policies out of which a felt need for such intervention arose. Within category (2), concern is with three phases of conflict decision-making: (a) the initial commitment of the military to hostilities, (b) the conduct of the fighting, and (c) the termination of the fighting. The pertinent constitutional issues may be briefly stated:[8]

    I. *Decisions that risk American involvement in foreign conflict*
        A. *Formal commitments to contingent future use of force*
            1. To what extent may the President on his own authority constitutionally commit the country to contingent future use of force?
            2. To what extent may Congress on its own authority constitutionally require or forbid the country's commitment to contingent future use of force?
            3. When, if ever, may a commitment for contingent future use of force, however approved, be self-executing without further authorization at the time of its implementation?

[7] Vietnam makes clear, however, that when American intervention is thought to violate international law, the political opposition to it in this country is heightened, and its domestic opponents strain to find that the decision to intervene was made in a manner illegal under the Constitution. Significantly, also, approval by an international body of American use of force has been thought by some to obviate the need for its approval by Congress. Under this analysis, the Korean War, though never congressionally sanctioned, was constitutional because it was authorized by the United Nations.

[8] Heavy use has been made of Professor John Norton Moore's analysis in *Hearings Before the Subcom. on Nat'l Security Policy and Scientific Developments of the House Comm. on Foreign Affairs*, 91st Cong., 2d Sess. 123, 125 (1971).

B. *Deployment of military forces*
1. To what extent may the President on his own authority constitutionally deploy military forces abroad?
2. To what extent may Congress on its own authority constitutionally require or forbid the deployment of military forces abroad?
C. *Provocative action involving neither formal commitment to contingent future force nor military deployment*
1. To what extent may the President on his own authority constitutionally take steps, primarily of a diplomatic or economic nature, that significantly risk involvement of the country in foreign conflict?
2. To what extent may Congress on its own authority constitutionally require or forbid the taking of steps, primarily of a diplomatic or economic nature, that significantly risk involvement of the country in foreign conflict?

II. *Conflict decisions*
A. *Commitment*
1. To what extent may the President on his own authority constitutionally commit the military to foreign conflict?
2. To what extent may Congress on its own authority constitutionally require or forbid commitment of the military to foreign conflict?
3. What form or forms may congressional authorization of the use of force take?
B. *Conduct of hostilities*
1. To what extent may the President on his own authority constitutionally control the strategic and tactical decisions of duly authorized hostilities?
2. To what extent may Congress on its own authority constitutionally control the strategic and tactical decisions of duly authorized hostilities?
3. To what extent may the President on his own authority constitutionally alter the scope (purpose, place, means, duration) of hostilities from the scope duly authorized?
4. To what extent may Congress on its own authority constitutionally limit the scope of hostilities either at their outset or during their conduct?
C. *Termination of hostilities*
1. To what extent may the President on his own authority constitutionally terminate hostilities?
2. To what extent may Congress on its own authority constitutionally require or forbid the termination of hostilities?
3. What form or forms may congressional termination of hostilities take?

Analysis of most of the issues above is beyond this essay. Emphasis will be on II-A, the commitment aspect of conflict decision-making, specifically as regards the congressional power to declare war. Although United States participation in foreign civil strife may take a variety of forms other than armed intervention, the latter generally has the greatest domestic and international costs. Accordingly, the controls on decisions to commit troops to hostilities form the constitutional bedrock here. Further, in light of the broad prerogative over intervention decisions claimed by Cold-War presidents, the constitutional grant to Congress of the power to declare war is of primary importance, for if there are constitutional limits on presidential authority sua sponte to commit military resources to foreign internal strife, this provision provides them more than any other.[9] An understanding of this congressional power, moreover, sheds significant light on the majority of the other issues in question.

Before focusing on the congressional power to declare war, it will be helpful to sketch the basic pattern of the Framers' language and intent. Against this background, the specific constitutional issues at hand may be more usefully considered.

OVERVIEW OF LANGUAGE AND INTENT

The constitutional provisions on intervention appear in Articles I and II and are of four sorts: grants dealing with foreign affairs as a whole; those concerning specifically the military aspects of foreign affairs; grants of inherent, non-enumerated powers; and provisions providing the President and Congress, respectively, with weapons with which to coerce one another.

In the first category, the President is modestly endowed, at least in terms of formal, stated grants of power. Generally, he holds the executive power of the Government and has the authority to request the executive departments to report to him, as well as the power to nominate men to fill principal offices. He is enjoined to see that federal law is faithfully executed and to inform Congress periodically of the state of the nation and is authorized to present Congress with legislative recommendations. More specifically, the President is empowered to make treaties and diplomatic appointments with the approval of the Senate, and he is commanded to receive foreign diplomats.

---

[9] The Framers also viewed congressional control over the raising and support of the military as a primal check on presidential use of force, whether at home or abroad. See, e.g., The Federalist, No. 26, at 106–07 (C. Beard ed. 1948) (A. Hamilton); id. No. 41, at 177 (J. Madison). But with the establishment of a large, standing military capacity, the assumption of worldwide defense commitments, and widespread belief that presidential use of troops abroad requires bipartisan support in the interests of national security, the power of the purse has become relatively meaningless. In the wake of Vietnam, it is possible that Congress will once again use its control of appropriations as a check on the Executive, although it is unlikely that the President will ever be deprived of the mobile task forces that enable him to intervene abroad on short notice. To use its power over the purse to restrain such action, Congress would have to be willing to refuse funds to support a use of force once begun, or to fund it only at the cost of other programs the President favors.

Congress has more extensive powers in this category. Generally, the legislators hold all the legislative power of the Government, including the power over appropriations, the House having the priviledge of initiating all money bills. More specifically, Congress as a whole controls a wide range of matters with notable transnational impact, especially in an increasingly interdependent world.[10] The Senate, in effect a third branch of government in foreign affairs, has the power to give or withhold consent on treaties and appointments.

In the second, specifically military category, presidential grants again lag behind their congressional counterparts. The Executive is simply named Commander-in-Chief, and given the power to commission officers. His appointment prerogative mentioned previously also comes into play in the military sphere. Congress, on the other hand, has a battery of responsibilities, including, *inter alia*, the power to raise and support the armed forces and the power to declare war.[11]

In the third category, inherent but undefined powers, the President arguably comes into his own. Whereas Article II, Section 1 vests in him "the executive Power," Article I, Section 1 vests in Congress only those "legislative Powers *herein granted*." Moreover, while the legislative article is quite tightly drawn, the executive article, in Corwin's words, "is the most loosely drawn chapter of the Constitution":

> [W]hereas "legislative power" and "judicial power" today denote fairly definable *functions* of government as well as fairly constant *methods* for their discharge, "executive power" is still indefinite as to *function* and retains, particularly when it is exercised by a single individual, much of its

[10] "The Congress shall have Power To lay and collect Taxes, Duties, Imposts and Excises, to pay the Debts . . . ;
To borrow Money on the credit of the United States;
To regulate Commerce with foreign Nations . . . ;
To establish an uniform Rule of Naturalization . . . ;
To coin Money, regulate the Value thereof, and of foreign Coin, and fix the Standard of Weights and Measures; . . .
To establish Post Offices . . . ;
To promote the Progress of Science and useful Arts, by securing for limited Times to Authors and Inventors the exclusive Right to their respective Writings and Discoveries; . . .
To define and punish Piracies and Felonies committed on the high Seas, and Offenses against the Law of Nations. . . ." *U.S. Const.* art. I, § 8.

[11] "The Congress shall have Power To . . . provide for the common Defence . . . ;
To declare War, grant Letters of Marque and Reprisal, and make Rules concerning Captures on Land and Water;
To raise and support Armies . . . ;
To provide and maintain a Navy;
To make Rules for the Government and Regulation of the land and naval Forces;
To provide for organizing, arming, and disciplining the Militia, and for governing such Part of them as may be employed in the Service of the United States . . . ;
To exercise . . . Authority over all Places purchased . . . for the Erection of Forts, Magazines, Arsenals, . . . and other needful Buildings. . . ." *Id.* art. I, § 8.

original plasticity as to *method*. It is consequently the power of government that is the most spontaneously responsive to emergency conditions; conditions, that is, which have not attained enough of stability or recurrency to admit of their being dealt with according to rule.[12]

Thus, the President can make a strong case that, as the holder of the executive power, he possesses residual authority to go beyond his enumerated powers to take whatever steps he deems necessary for the country's security. Congress, to the contrary, confronts a linguistic hurdle. Supreme Court dicta, however, suggest that "herein granted" may not be an insurmountable barrier where foreign affairs are involved.[13] And the "necessary and proper" clause gives congressional powers a measure of elasticity.

In the final, coercive category, Congress regains its textual edge. The President can seek to bend the legislators to his will through the threat of veto and special session, but Congress can virtually destroy him. Impeachment and censure remain remote possibilities, but hostile use or nonuse of legislative power is an ever present mode of persuasion.

Such is the relevant constitutional language. It indicates that both the President and Congress are to have a role in decisions regarding foreign policy, especially those concerned with the use of force. Indeed, so far as the respective grants of power are concerned, the congressional role appears the dominant. But, as noted earlier, the language is often vague, the grants of power are complementary and occasionally fail altogether to speak to vital issues.

Like their language, the intent of the Framers is somewhat ambiguous. The relevant provisions were written only after long discussion and much compromise—processes certain to breed confusion about the exact nature of the end product. As is the case where many views are advanced, and where the drafters do not know from past experience what demands reality will make upon their rules, much that the Framers adopted was left either vague or unsaid, to be prescribed by practice.

The Constitution's foreign affairs provisions were drafted in a context of legislative control of external matters in America,[14] and of executive domination in Britain.[15] The Framers wished to alter the American practice

---

[12] Corwin, *supra* note 2, at 3.

[13] *See* United States v. Curtiss-Wright Export Corp., 299 U.S. 304, 318 (1936).

[14] "Prior to the installation of the Constitution on March 4, 1789, the direction of foreign policy was in the hands of a unicameral legislature which functioned through a Committee of Secret Correspondence (1775–7), a Committee for Foreign Affairs (1777–81), and the Department of Foreign Affairs (1781–9). The last was under a secretary who was responsible to the Congress." R. Leopold, *The Growth of American Foreign Policy* 67 n. 1 (1962).

[15] Madison stated in 1793 that "[t]he power of making treaties and the power of declaring war are *royal prerogatives* in the *British government,* and are accordingly treated as executive prerogatives by British commentators. . . ." *Quoted in* E. Corwin, *The President's Control of Foreign Relations* 21 (1917); *see* James Wilson's comment, I *The Records of the Federal Convention of 1787*, at 65–66 (M. Farrand rev. ed. 1937) [hereinafter cited as *Records*], and Hamilton's analysis in *The Federalist* No. 69, at 295 (C. Beard, ed., 1948) (A. Hamilton).

to profit from executive speed, efficiency and relative isolation from mass opinion,[16] without incurring the often ill-considered and autocratic policies of the largely unchecked British monarch and cabinet. Thus, speed and efficiency, on the one hand, and restraint upon executive prerogative, on the other, appear to have been the basic objectives of the Drafters. Accordingly, they created an Executive independent from Congress, who was at his strongest in external matters. Simultaneously, they placed in Congress powers designed to prevent unilateral control of foreign relations by the President.

COMMITMENT OF AMERICAN FORCES TO COMBAT ABROAD

Intent of the Framers

Initiation of Hostilities.—"The Congress shall have Power to . . . declare War" is not self-defining language. It seems reasonably clear, however, from proposals made and rejected at the Constitutional Convention, from debates there, subsequent statements by the Framers, and from practice in the early years of the Republic that the Drafters intended decisions to initiate the use of force abroad to be made not by the President alone,[17] or by the Senate alone,[18] nor by the President and the Senate together,[19] but rather by the entire Congress, subject to the signature or veto of the President. The Framers recognized the potential costs of foreign conflict and wished to check its unilateral initiation by any single individual or group. Madison expressed this concern early in the Constitutional Convention: "A rupture with other powers is among the greatest of national calamities. It ought therefore to be effectually provided that no part of a nation shall have it in its power to bring them [wars] on the whole."[20]

[16] The Framers seem to have been seriously concerned about the "temporary errors and delusions" of the people, their "passing popular whims" and "public passions." *See The Federalist* No. 49, at 220 (C. Beard, ed. 1948) (J. Madison); *id.* No. 63, at 268 (J. Madison); *id* No. 71, at 303 (A. Hamilton). Thus, they sought a check on mass opinion in a strong President, *id.* No. 71, at 303 (A. Hamilton), and in the Senate's "temperate and respectable body of citizens," *id.* No. 63, at 268 (J. Madison). *See also id.* No. 62, at 263–64 (J. Madison).

[17] Mr. Butler, apparently the only proponent of his view, favored "vesting the power in the President, who will have all the requisite qualities [*e.g.*, dispatch, continuity, unity of office] and will not make war but when the Nation will support it." II *Records* 318.

[18] "Mr. Pinkney opposed the vesting of this power in the Legislature. Its proceedings were too slow. It wd. meet but once a year. The Hs. of Reps. would be too numerous for such deliberations. The Senate would be the best depository, being more acquainted with foreign affairs, and most capable of proper resolutions. If the States are equally represented in Senate, so as to give no advantage to large States, the power will notwithstanding be safe, as the small have their all at stake in such cases as well as the large States. It would be singular for one-authority to make war, and another peace." *Id.* (footnotes omitted).

[19] Hamilton presented a plan in which the Executive was "to make war or peace, with the advice of the senate. . . ." I *Records* 300.

[20] I *Records* 316. Madison was speaking to the possibility that individual states through their "violations of the law of nations & of Treaties" might bring foreign war upon the country as a whole. *Id.* The unfortunate consequences of war were

Objections were made to legislative involvement in use-of-force decisions on the ground that it would result in undue delay.[21] But the approach of Mr. Mason proved more persuasive. He stated that he was "agst. giving the power of war to the Executive, because not [safely] to be trusted with it; or to the Senate because not so constructed as to be entitled to it."[22] Fear seems to have existed that if the President were given the right to initiate hostilities unilaterally, he might unwisely engage the country in ruinous conflict or use the existence of war to raise military forces with which to seize control of the country. Moreover, the Executive, like the Senate, was not directly elected, and thus was thought to lack the moral authority to commit the entire country to so potentially devastating a course. The House of Representatives possessed the legitimacy given by direct election, but, due to its close ties to the general public, was suspected of flighty judgment.[23] Accordingly, the Representatives' passions were to be controlled by involving the Senate and President in conflict decisions. Involvement of the Senate, moreover, would ensure that force could not be initiated abroad unless a majority of the states agreed. In short, an attempt was made to devise a scheme in which use of force would be authorized only after measured deliberation by all elected federal officials, thus avoiding involvement in hostilities where the costs, upon reflection and debate, appeared to outweigh the gains, or where the primary "gains" would be executive aggrandizement or the satiation of popular passion. These checks were designed to increase the likelihood that any conflict, at least at its outset, would be supported by most Americans, thereby lessening the possibility of disastrous internecine struggle within the country over war policy.

Sudden Attack.—The discussion to this point has been of authority to *initiate* the use of force abroad—to take the country from peace to conflict. When, however, hostilities are thrust upon the United States by another power, the Framers apparently intended that there be unilateral presidential response if temporal exigencies do not permit an initial resort to Congress.[24]

---

alluded to by others among the Framers. Mr. Ellsworth, for example, argued that "[i]t shd. be more easy to get out of war, than into it." II *Records* 319. And Mr. Mason was "for clogging rather than facilitating war. . . ." *Id.*

[21] See notes 17 & 18 *supra.*

[22] II *Records* 319.

[23] See note 16 *supra.*

[24] The Framers first proposed to grant Congress the power "to make" war, as opposed to declaring it. In due course, however, "Mr. M[adison] and Mr. Gerry moved to insert '*declare*,' striking out '*make*' war," leaving to the Executive the power to repel sudden attacks." The motion passed, though it had failed upon an earlier vote. *Id.* at 318–19, 313. What precisely those who voted in favor of the change intended is difficult to say in light of existing information, but it does seem clear that the amendment was not even remotely designed to empower the Executive to initiate hostilities. Compare a provision temporarily inserted by the Committee of Style, which stated that "[n]o State, without the consent of the Legislature of the United States shall . . . engage in any war, unless it shall be actually invaded by enemies, or the danger of invasion shall be so imminent, as not to admit of a delay, until the Legislature of the United States can be consulted." II *Records* 577.

Under circumstances of sudden attack, there is no longer a need for check and deliberation: virtually all would agree that force is properly used to repulse assaults on the nation or its citizens. Speedy and effective defense measures are the constitutional objectives given a sudden attack.[25]

The Framers did not delineate what constitutes a thrust of conflict upon the United States. It obviously includes any direct, physical assault upon American territory. The sudden-attack rationale also reasonably supports presidential action to rescue American citizens or military units beset abroad.[26] Moreover, it has generally been agreed that, if a blow is clearly imminent, the Executive need not wait for it to fall.[27] Accordingly, under the sudden-attack proviso, a declaration of war by a foreign power of only paper force would not justify unilateral presidential response, whereas an undeclared but impending nuclear strike at our cities would.

The Framers did not indicate who determines that a sudden attack is underway, but the President logically must be the one to do so.[28] Absent such presidential discretion, the sudden-attack exception to the necessity for prior congressional approval of hostilities would become meaningless, for it assumes the need for an American response before Congress can reasonably be expected to act.[29]

Response to sudden attack, on the other hand, is not synonymous with offensive action against the attacker, though admittedly there is not always

---

[25] Arguably, under such circumstances, ordinary war-making decisional procedures are superseded by an inherent right of the country, as a sovereign state, to protect its territorial integrity against foreign attack. Since the President is generally the citizen most able to galvanize a defensive reaction, he acts. Language in United States v. Curtiss-Wright Export Corp., 299 U.S. 304, 316–18 (1936), lends a measure of judicial support to this contention.

[26] Cf., e.g., In re Neagle, 135 U.S. 1, 63–64 (1890); Slaughter-House Cases, 83 U.S. (16 Wall.) 36, 79 (1873); Durand v. Hollins, 8 F. Cas. 111, 112 (No. 4186) (C.C.S.D.N.Y. 1860).

[27] Congress early provided "that whenever the United States shall be invaded, or be in imminent danger of invasion from any foreign nation or Indian tribe, it shall be lawful for the President . . . to call forth such militia . . . as he may judge necessary to repel such invasion. . . ." Act of February 28, 1795, quoted in Martin v. Mott, 25 U.S. (12 Wheat.) 19, 28–29 (1827) (emphasis added). See also the Committee of Style provision cited in note 24 supra and U.S. Const. art. I § 10.

[28] Cf. Martin v. Mott, 25 U.S. (12 Wheat.) 19, 30 (1827), where, referring to the statute quoted in note 27 supra, Mr. Justice Story stated for the Court that "[w]e are all of opinion, that the authority to decide whether the exigency [invasion or imminent danger of invasion] has arisen, belongs exclusively to the President, and that his decision is conclusive upon all other persons."

[29] Mr. Justice Grier stated in 1863 that

"If a war be made by invasion of a foreign nation, the President is not only authorized but bound to resist force by force. He does not initiate the war, but is bound to accept the challenge without waiting for any special legislative authority. . . .

. . . .

This greatest of civil wars was not gradually developed. . . . [I]t nevertheless sprung forth suddenly. . . . The President was bound to meet it in the shape it presented itself, without waiting for Congress to baptize it with a name; and no name given to it by him or them could change that fact." The Prize Cases, 67 U.S. (2 Black) 635, 668–69 (1863).

a clear line between the offensive and the defensive. Under the Framers' rationale, unilateral use of force by the Executive must stop once it has ended the reality or prospect of immediate physical assault on the country or its citizens, for once the sudden attack has been successfully repulsed, there is no longer temporal necessity for failing to obtain congressional approval of hostilities.[30] Thus, while the nature of the Executive's unilateral defensive measures will depend upon the nature of the enemy thrust, at no time should his response be disproportionate to the assault. Should he be responding to a nuclear attack, presumably there would be little or no distinction between defensive and offensive action; the exchange would likely be terminal for both parties. But should enemy submarines shell coastal cities with conventional ordinance, the President need only clear the coasts of enemy ships; the invasion of the enemy homeland ought to await congressional authorization. Similarly, though the President may resist with all necessary force an attack on Americans abroad, once the attack is repulsed he may not use it as pretext for unrelated offensive action against the enemy. In sum, under the Framers' rationale, the Executive does not receive full wartime powers simply because another state has suddenly attacked this country or its citizens abroad. Rather he is authorized only to make a proportionate response.

Definition of "War."—The problem remains as to when under the declaration-of-war clause the Framers intended that Congress must approve the use of force. As the constitutional provision granting Congress control over letters of marque and reprisal suggests,[31] the Framers understood "war" to be a broad concept. Judging by early practice, it appears that war in the constitutional sense was deemed to arise when the United States decides to engage in any but *de minimis* use of force. The Naval War with France of 1798–1800 involved neither appreciable fighting nor complete rupture of relations between the combatants. It was, however, thought to require and it did receive congressional authorization.

Possible Forms of Congressional Authorization.—The language of the Constitution does not require that Congress act only by formal declaration

---

[30] *See* Reveley, *supra* note 1, at 1287 n. 148.

[31] Wormuth, *supra* note 3, at 6, states:

"Even before the adoption of the Constitution, American law recognized that it was possible to wage war at different levels. In 1782 the Federal Court of Appeals, the prize court established under the Articles of Confederation, observed: 'The writers upon the law of nations, speaking of the different kinds of war, distinguish them into perfect and imperfect: A perfect war is that which destroys the national peace and tranquility, and lays the foundation of every possible act of hostility. The imperfect war is that which does not entirely destroy the public tranquility, but interrupts it only in some particulars, as in the case of reprisals.'

The framers of the Constitution accepted this conception and assigned the power to initiate both perfect and imperfect war to Congress, which was 'To declare war, grant letters of marque and reprisal, and makes rules concerning captures on land and water.'" (Footnote omitted). *Accord*, Little v. Barreme, 6 U.S. (2 Cranch) 170 (1804); Talbot v. Seeman, 5 U.S. (1 Cranch) 1 (1801); Bas v. Tingy, 4 U.S. (4 Dall.) 37 (1800).

of war, nor is there any evidence that the Framers intended a formal declaration to be the only method for congressional approval of the use of force. From the Naval War with France to date, all branches of the federal government, the courts included, have recognized that authorization may take other forms. So long as the chosen method makes possible meaningful participation by both Houses of Congress in the decision to use force, and so long as it permits a clear expression of congressional intent, it satisfies the purposes behind the war-declaration clause. Legislation to increase the size of the armed forces or to appropriate additional money to sustain an already ongoing use of force may be regarded as authorization *if* legislative intent to that effect is made abundantly clear. But this clarity absent, such legislation can not be construed as implied approval, since it may have been adopted for reasons other than to approve hostilities. The Framers did not place a constitutional burden upon Congress to make its views clear or be deemed to have acquiesced, but rather upon the President to obtain legislative approval before he uses force.

Since the Constitution was ratified, there has been widespread and continuing belief that, pursuant to the Framers' language and intent, decisions to use military force abroad must receive congressional approval. Presidents prior to 1900 generally held such expectation themselves and acted accordingly, and twentieth-century Executives before the Cold War frequently gave the concept verbal support, though their conduct often belied their words. Many members of Congress, particularly in the Senate, and most of the general public retain a view that the Constitution requires congressional authorization of decisions to fight. This expectation, however, does not stand unchallenged, although argument in favor of presidential hegemony over use-of-force decisions has, as a rule, not frontally attacked it.

When offered, doctrinal justification for executive control has tended to ignore the constitutional grants to Congress and to read expansively the complementary provisions applicable to the Executive.[32] Thus the President, as enforcer of the law, has been said to have constitutional authority to take whatever steps he believes necessary to implement treaties, international law, and the basic foreign policy objectives of the United States. The President's constitutional role as the country's principal diplomat has been interpreted by some to include control over both the conduct and the shaping of foreign relations. As Commander-in-Chief, the Executive has been deemed to have constitutional authority to do that which he finds necessary for the defense of the nation. The fact that he holds the inchoate executive power has been treated as confirmation of his plenary authority over our relations with other states: if his enumerated powers are found wanting in constitutional weight, his inherent authority as Chief Executive is said to flesh them out as required. Ultimately, the President's various powers are rolled into one ill-defined, mutually supportive bundle and used to justify presidential

[32] *See* Reveley, *supra* note 1, at 158–59 nn.

authority to do virtually "anything, anywhere, that can be done with an army or navy."[33] All, it is argued, because national security demands no less.

There is, then, some uncertainty today about the content of the constitutional law governing the commitment of American troops to hostilities abroad. Expectation that congressional approval is required is rooted in the language and intent of the Framers, and in practice throughout most of our history. Expectations supporting presidential hegemony draw tremendous support from events of the last thirty years. To better evaluate these conflicting views, it is necessary to consider in more detail actual practice regarding the making of conflict decisions, especially those involving intervention.

Practice: Three Stages in the Evolution of the Balance of Power

While Congress and the President have always struggled over the control of foreign policy, presidential hegemony in this area is a recent phenomenon. At the risk of oversimplification, three historical stages may be identified in the evolution of the balance of power between the Executive and the legislators over intervention decisions.[34]

A.

The first stage ran from Independence through the declaration of the Spanish-American War and was generally a time of meaningful, occasionally dominant, congressional decision-making. The legislators debated the issues and took identifiable positions. Presidents, as a rule, sought authorization before intervening. Beyond genuine collaboration between the branches, this period was also characterized by consensus that intervention was generally not in our national interest, except as required to fill out continental boundaries.

So far as Europe was concerned, the nonintervention consensus formed during the late 1700's and early 1800's, when the United States experienced the classic intervention dilemmas of the small state, its primary concerns being to avoid potentially fatal involvement in European internal struggles and to ward off foreign intrigues in American domestic politics designed to force the country to intervene. Congress sounded the first note in its June 12, 1783, resolution that "the true interest of these states requires that they should be as little as possible entangled in the politics and controversies of European nations," a theme taken up by George Washington in his Farewell Address and repeated by Thomas Jefferson in his 1801 Inaugural Address injunction against "entangling alliances."

---

[33] Youngstown Sheet & Tube Co. v. Sawyer, 343 U.S. 579, 641–42 (1952) (Jackson, J., concurring).

[34] The historical material that follows is not footnoted. Authority for it may be found in the references cited in Reveley, *supra* note 1, at 1257–65, especially R. Leopold, *The Growth of American Foreign Policy* (1962).

The nonintervention consensus was severely tested during the world war that began with the beheading of Louis XVI in 1793. Intervention on behalf of the French revolutionaries was not an unappealing prospect for many. The overthrow of the *ancien régime* was immensely popular among large segments of the American public. France had been instrumental in our revolution and remained an ally. Though Paris did not request American military protection for French possessions in the New World, as it had a right to do under the alliance, it did seek to use United States ports for its warships and privateers. George Washington, however, backed by congressional neutrality acts, closed American ports to the warships of all European combatants. Paris, in turn, sought a reversal of American policy by attempting to influence the outcome of the 1796 presidential election, and began to attack American ships on the high seas. Congress retaliated by suspending commerce with France, abrogating the Franco-American alliance, augmenting the armed forces, and by authorizing President Adams to conduct a naval war with the French. Though this conflict was ended by an 1800 treaty, when Congress declared war on Great Britain in 1812 for refusal to respect American neutrality, the senate came within two votes of seeking war on France as well.

Non-intervention in European struggles remained a keystone of American policy throughout the rest of the century. In 1823–24, for example, when a pro-Hellenic block in Congress sought American assistance for the Greek revolutionaries, sponsoring demands to send an agent to Athens, President Monroe and Congress as a whole were unreceptive. Although Congress never voted directly upon the question of intervening in support of the liberal revolutions that struck Europe at mid-century, it intermittently debated the issue during 1848–52, and was never willing to give economic, military or diplomatic aid to the revolutionaries. American aversion to involvement in European affairs was again demonstrated in 1885, when strong congressional opposition blocked final American participation in the General Act of Berlin that, among other things, provided for the neutrality of the Congo should war among the powers break out elsewhere.

Until the United States obtained Asian territory as a result of the Spanish-American War, it had little occasion even to consider significant intervention in Asia, much less in Africa or the Middle East. Police actions were conducted in these areas by the President on his own authority to protect American citizens and their property or to take reprisals against those who had harmed them. These actions, however, were de minimis, and Congress gave them little or no attention. Police actions in Latin America received more scrutiny, with Presidents occasionally refused congressional authorization to use force. In 1837, for example, President Jackson was denied permission by Congress to take military action against Mexico for its refusal to pay claims for damages to American interests harmed on its soil. He was instructed to make another effort at peaceful settlement.

American relations with Latin America during the period in question centered on a desire that European involvement in Latin affairs be minimized but not that it be replaced by American intervention. Latin rebellions against Spain began in 1808, but it was not until 1822 that President Monroe asked the House and Senate to join him in extending recognition to the new South American governments, if they thought it wise, by voting the appropriations needed to make recognition effective. Congress as a whole had previously concurred in presidential reluctance to recognize these states, though Speaker of the House, Henry Clay, was their vigorous proponent. Even in the wake of the Monroe Doctrine, pleas from the new Latin governments for alliance with this country were not favorably received. Indicatively, the question of American participation in an 1826 Congress of American States at Panama prompted fiery debate. That gathering was called primarily to discuss Latin unity, but also to consider the defense of the hemisphere, the possibility of converting the non-colonization principle of the Monroe Doctrine into a multilateral obligation, and the liberation of Cuba and Puerto Rico. During a legislative recess, President Adams informed the Latins that the United States would like to attend and nominated two delegates, subject to Senate confirmation and House funding. Extensive congressional debate ensued, in which several future Presidents voiced opposition to Adams's action: Buchanan accused him of ignoring the principles of Washington's Farewell Address; Van Buren suggested that any alliance could undermine congressional power to declare war; and Polk also was opposed. Nonetheless, the Senate ultimately confirmed the appointments and the House funded them. American participation in the conference was not to be, however, as one delegate died en route and the other failed to arrive before its conclusion.

Congressional reluctance to become involved in Latin strife was demonstrated again in 1848, when a native uprising in Yucatan, a province of Mexico, threatened to exterminate the resident whites. They appealed to the United States, England, and Spain, offering to surrender their sovereignty if necessary to win assistance. President Polk, for humanitarian and strategic reasons, wished to intervene. He requested authorization from Congress. The legislators preferred debate to action, although the Senate Foreign Relations Committee finally reported a bill permitting temporary occupation of the peninsula if necessary. When the bill encountered opposition, the danger of European intervention faded, and the Democratic National Convention approached, the issue died. Similarly, in 1859 during Mexican civil strife, President Buchanan asked for congressional authorization to assume a temporary protectorate over parts of northern Mexico and to establish a line of forts there and, failing that, for approval to send troops over the border to ensure "indemnity for the past and security for the future." He warned that failure to give him such authority could lead to recolonization by European powers. Congress refused authorization. Interventionary efforts by Presidents Pierce and Buchanan throughout the

Mexican internal struggles of 1853–61 were generally blocked by congressional unwillingness to support the executive proposals.

French support of Maximilian in Mexico prompted great public agitation in the Union, leading to a House resolution in April 1864 declaring that "it does not accord with the policy of the United States to acknowledge any monarchical government erected on the ruins of any republican government in America under the auspices of any European Power." The Senate failed to act on all kindred resolutions, however, and the Executive was assiduous—to the ire of the House—in its efforts to avoid American intervention in Mexico pending resolution of our own internal strife. The ten-year Cuban insurrection against Spain, beginning in 1868, also generated much sympathy in this country, including many demands that the rebels be recognized as belligerents and be supplied with men, arms, and money. Again, the House in 1869 formally urged belligerent status for the rebels, but failed to win the support of the Senate and the President. A similar motion in the House in the following year was defeated. Congress as a whole, the Senate in particular, rebuffed an 1869–71 attempt by President Grant to resolve an unstable situation in the Dominican Republic by its annexation.

In contrast to our practice elsewhere, there were instances of significant American intervention on the North American continent during the nineteenth century. President Madison took advantage of an uprising against Spain in the Baton Rouge district in 1810 and occupied the territory west of Mobile over the next three years. He sent an agent into East Florida in the hope of stirring up rebellion against the Spanish authorities—all, it appears, with congressional approval. In January 1811, when fear existed that the British might seize Florida, the President had secretly sought and obtained from Congress authority to occupy temporarily all or part of Florida if such occupation were requested by local officials and if there were the threat of occupation by a European power.

General Andrew Jackson's 1818 military expedition into Florida was blatant intervention, involving the temporary occupation of key towns and the execution of two British citizens while on Spanish soil, but it is not clear whether he acted on President Monroe's orders. The expedition in any event lacked congressional authorization. Nonetheless, a Senate report condemning it was tabled, and a House resolution disapproving the executions was heavily defeated. In a far more significant vote on the same day, the House rejected 112 to 42 a bill prohibiting any future dispatch of American troops into foreign territory without express *prior* congressional approval. Like Jackson's expedition, John C. Fremont's armed exploring mission to California in 1846 lacked congressional authorization, despite its role in the rebellion by American-born settlers in the Sacramento Valley against Mexico. Though it is not clear to what extent Fremont acted on orders from the President, Polk's known desire for rebellion in California and for its incorporation into the Union constituted significant diplomatic interference in Mexican internal strife. Polk's action regarding California, like that concerning the border between Texas and Mexico, was taken unilaterally.

American annexation of the Lone Star Republic in 1845, however, was an instance neither of intervention in Mexico internal struggles nor of unilateral decision-making by the Executive. Popular sympathy for the Texas rebels led to a notably lax discharge of American neutrality laws during the 1835–36 struggle, but it is clear that the revolt would have succeeded even had the laws been stringently enforced. Mexico proved unable to recapture Texas after it won initial independence. The Lone Star Republic had been independent for nine years and had had two annexation requests rejected by the United States before it was in fact incorporated. Only after Congress had voted funds for a diplomatic agent to be appointed when the President deemed it appropriate and after the Senate had voted 23 to 19 that Texan independence should be acknowledged did Jackson nominate a representative in 1837. He had previously noted that recognition could be the equivalent of a declaration of war and indicated that a President should not act without "a previous understanding with that body by whom war can alone be declared." The use in 1845 of a joint resolution rather than a treaty to annex Texas, in order to circumvent the two-thirds requirement in the Senate, was procedurally questionable, but clearly did not indicate a lack of majority support in both houses for the incorporation.

In addition to the previously mentioned Naval War with France of 1798–1800, the era in question included the Barbary Wars of 1801–5 and 1815 and three formally declared foreign conflicts. While these wars did not involve American intervention in foreign internal strife, brief comment on the congressional role in the decisions to fight is helpful as another indication of the relationship between the two branches then prevailing.

The Barbary Wars, though not formally declared, were conducted with specific congressional approval. President Jefferson unilaterally dispatched a naval squadron to the Mediterranean to protect American shipping from attack by Tripoli, but before receiving congressional approval of the First Barbary War, he refused to permit American naval commanders to do more than disarm and release enemy ships guilty of attacks on United States vessels. Accordingly, an act was passed authorizing the President "fully to equip, officer, man and employ such of the armed vessels of the United States" as he found necessary to protect American commerce; to instruct the commanders of these ships to "subdue, seize, and make prize all vessels, goods, and effects, belonging to the Bey of Tripoli, or to his subjects;" to commission privateers, and to take whatever "other acts of precaution or hostility as the state of war will justify." When Algiers in 1815 attacked American shipping, President Madison obtained authorization to use force similar to that given in 1802 against Tripoli. Congress refused the President's request for a formal declaration of war, granting him instead simply approval for limited hostilities.

The decision to enter the War of 1812 was made by Congress after extended debate. Madison made no recommendation in favor of hostilities, though he did marshal a "telling case against England" in his message to Congress of June 1, 1812. The primary impetus to battle seems to have come from a group of "War Hawks" in the legislature. Similarly, McKinley was pushed into war with Spain in 1898 by congressional and popular fervor, though he himself inadvertently heightened passions by sending the *Maine* to Havana. Full congressional authorization was given before the initiation of hostilities. Congress first passed a joint resolution authorizing the President to use armed force if necessary to ensure Cuban independence and Spanish withdrawal from the island, and then followed with a formal declaration of war when Spain recalled its ambassador from Washington and showed no sign of leaving Cuba.

Congress was, on the other hand, presented with a presidential *fait accompli* in 1846. Polk provoked the Mexicans into a conflict which the legislators felt compelled to approve, particularly in light of the colored version of the facts presented by the President. But, within two years, the House of Representatives censured Polk for his part in the initiation of the conflict. By an 85–81 vote the House ruled that the war had been "unnecessarily and unconstitutionally begun by the President of the United States."

B.

The second of the three stages mentioned previously began at the turn of the century and continued into World War II. Close collaboration between the Executive and Congress became the exception, as did presidential deference to congressional views on the use of force abroad. The legislators, nonetheless, remained a strong force in the shaping of foreign policies. Although their influence was often negative, obstructing the efforts of Presidents who saw a need to use American power to defend nascent security interests abroad, American military strength had grown to the point that the Executives had significant capacity for maneuver without prior congressional action.

During the first two decades of the twentieth century, Congress generally chose to watch quietly as the President unilaterally intervened in Latin American internal struggles, presumably because majority sentiment favored militant American hegemony over the area. Presidents enjoyed similar freedom in the Far East, though they exercised it less robustly. The first wholly unauthorized executive intervention of significance, nonetheless, took place in China, during the Boxer Rebellion at the turn of the century. McKinley committed several thousand American troops to the international army that suppressed the Chinese nationalists and rescued western nationals trapped in Peking. The President was accused by a few democrats of usurping congressional power to declare war—to no effect, since Congress had adjourned before the crisis broke and neither party wanted a special session in an election year. To an extent, McKinley is also vulnerable to a charge of unilateral intervention in his suppression of the Aguinaldo-led attempt to win independence for the Philippines during the years 1899–1902. The decision to insist that Spain surrender all of the Philippines to the United States was made by the President alone, and Senate approval of the treaty of peace with Spain did not constitute a clear endorsement of American control of the islands.

During most of the 1920's and 1930's, American force abroad was used sparingly, in part because of a more relaxed approach to the difficulties of the Latin states and in part as a result of a strong popular desire to avoid involvement in the struggles of the world's other great powers. American opinion had been gravely offended by the tawdry aftermath of World War I. The mood of the country showed itself vividly when Japanese bombers deliberately sent an American gunboat, the *Panay*, to the bottom of the Yangtze River on December 12, 1937. Quite unlike the popular reaction to attacks on the *Maine* and on destroyers in the Tonkin Gulf, the *Panay* incident gave immediate and tremendous impetus to a congressional attempt to amend the Constitution to subject war decisions to popular referendum, except in case of invasion.

Congressional devotion to neutrality and to nonintervention in the affairs of other states made intelligent use of American influence difficult during and after the First World War. Wilson's troubles in bringing American power to bear against Germany, however, were minor compared to those experienced by Roosevelt under far more desperate circumstances. The Neutrality Acts of 1935, 1936, and 1937 made no distinction between an aggressor and its victim. Under the acts, Americans, especially the President, were to avoid any dealings which might involve the United States in another war. These laws, and the congressional and popular attitudes which they represented, placed a disastrous limitation on Roosevelt's attempt to use American power and influence to head off the impending crisis.

Both Wilson and Roosevelt, but especially the latter, were forced to resort to deception and flagrant disregard of Congress in use-of-force decisions, because they were unable to rally congressional backing for action essential to national security. Among his major unilateral steps, Roosevelt in 1940 exchanged fifty destroyers for British bases in the Western Atlantic; in 1941 he occupied Greenland and Iceland, ordered the Navy to convoy ships carrying lend-lease supplies to Britain, and on September 11 of that year declared, in effect, that henceforth the United States would wage an air and sea war against the Axis in the Atlantic. Woodrow Wilson in 1917, after Germany's resumption of unrestricted submarine warfare, had armed American merchantmen and instructed them to fire on sight. The President had sought congressional approval but was thwarted by a Senate filibuster. He proceeded nonetheless, though he later admitted that his course was "practically certain" to lead to United States involvement in war. These instances of presidential use of force, while they did not involve intervention in foreign internal strife, provide the major pre-Cold War precedent for presidential domination of intervention decisions today.

C.

The trauma of the Second World War and of the Cold War led to a third stage in which Congress—in penance for its policies during the twenties and thirties and fearful lest its interference harm national security—left direction of foreign affairs largely to the President, with the exception of a period during the early fifties. A "Great Debate" over Truman's authority to send troops to Korea and Western Europe raged for three months in early 1951, culminating in a futile Senate resolution calling for congressional authorization before the dispatch of further troops to fulfill NATO commitments. The attempt under Senator John Bricker's aegis to limit the scope of treaties and the use of executive agreements came to naught in 1954, after Eisenhower made clear his unalterable opposition. The hysteria bred by Senator Joseph McCarthy, playing upon frustration and fears engendered by developments in China, Eastern Europe, and Korea, however, did significantly lessen Truman's freedom of action in foreign affairs during the latter years of his presidency.

Until very recently, the legislators since 1945 have as a rule presented no obstacles when the President wished to use force abroad, or to pursue policies likely to lead to its necessity. The Cold War has enjoyed bipartisan backing, both when the Executive acted wholly without congressional consent and when he had authorization of sorts. The decisions to employ arms off Formosa, in Korea, Lebanon, Cuba, the Dominican Republic, Vietnam, Cambodia, and Laos were essentially the President's, as were the policies that led Washington to feel that force was essential. The Korean War was entered with no prior congressional authorization, and never received even *ex post facto* blessing, perhaps because it was not an unpopular conflict at its inception. Eisenhower was authorized in January 1955 to use force if necessary to defend Formosa and its outlying islands, and in March 1957 to block Communist aggression in the Middle East. A joint congressional resolution adopted in October 1962 authorized President Kennedy to use force if necessary to prevent the spread of communism from Cuba or the development there of an externally supported military capability dangerous to the security of the United States. And President Johnson received in August 1964 a joint resolution providing in part that "the United States is . . . prepared, as the President determines, to take all necessary steps, including the use of armed force, to assist any member or protocol state of the Southeast Asia Collective Defense Treaty requesting assistance in defense of its freedom."

When force was used in Lebanon, in the Atlantic off Cuba during the Missile Crisis, and in Indochina, however, it was unclear to what extent the respective Executives based their action upon prior congressional approval and to what extent upon claims of inherent presidential power. It seems likely that the four presidents would have acted as they did, even without the resolutions. Eisenhower, in fact, did not claim to be acting pursuant to the Middle East Resolution when he intervened in Lebanon in July 1958, presumably because Congress had authorized the use of force only when the attack came from a Communist state. Johnson relied more heavily on the Gulf of Tonkin resolution, since in terms of its language it certainly authorized the war he waged. But the executive interpretation of the Gulf of Tonkin resolution has been bitterly contested as a misreading of congressional intent. The fact that this controversy could arise points to a fundamental characteristic of recent congressional participation in decisions regarding the use of force. With the Gulf of Tonkin resolution as perhaps the most egregious example, the resolutions in question have tended to be blank checks, leaving so much to presidential discretion as to vitiate their impact as anything other than demonstrations of national unity in time of crisis.

Nonetheless, well aware that Congress could at any time end their initiatives by refusing the requisite implementing legislation, Presidents have generally talked with congressional leaders while making policy and informed them before the fact about impending commitments. But Congress has had little part in actually shaping use-of-force policy over the last quarter century. Foreign aid may have been subjected to an annual bloodletting, but not the President's capacity to commit and maintain troops abroad. It is possible that a fourth stage is now developing in public and congressional restiveness over Vietnam. Whether the legislators' growing insistence on participation in use-of-force decisions will survive the end of the present conflict, however, remains to be seen.

Present State of the Law

Against this background of the Framers' language and intent on the one hand and actual practice on the other hand, summary answers to the three commitment questions noted earlier[35] may be attempted. To what extent may the President, on his own authority, constitutionally commit the military to foreign conflict? Language and intent suggest that he may do so on only two occasions: (1) when the hostilities do not amount to "war" and (2) when war has been thrust upon the United States by the sudden attack of another state. War as defined by the Framers in their implementation of the Constitution and by most nineteenth-century practice was a broad concept, covering all hostilities with more than de minimis costs. Further, even though the Framers intended the President to respond on his own motion to sudden attacks when there is no time for prior recourse to Congress, it does not appear that the sudden-attack exception was intended to authorize more than simple defensive measures by the President, pending congressional action on the desirability of continued conflict. Until this century, Presidents in fact rarely used any but de minimis force abroad without congressional approval.

[35] See page 158 *supra*.

Before the two World Wars and since 1945, on the other hand, Presidents have unilaterally involved the country in significant conflict, upon occasion in violation of prior congressional directives. National security has been most often cited as the compelling force behind such executive action. Thus, twentieth-century events, especially those of the last thirty years, suggest that even major foreign wars may be fought by this country solely on presidential authority. In short, expectations rooted in the Framers' language and intent and in pre-twentieth-century practice are presently challenged by the contrary presidential practice of the last generation.

It follows that the constitutional allocation of control between the President and Congress over the use of force is uncertain today. Whether the Constitution will ultimately be deemed to have been amended by usage, and recent presidential assertions of authority thereby legitimized, or whether earlier constitutional expectations prevail, and presidential war-making be abandoned or limited, remains very much in doubt. Should Congress fail in the next generation to reassert its use-of-force voice, it is likely that a new constitutional consensus will form in which there is no requirement of congressional approval of American involvement in hostilities, except when formally declared war is desired. But there may succeed in Congress attempts to vindicate long-standing expectations that the legislators must authorize American war-making. Should this occur, recent presidential practice will be viewed not as an amendment of the Constitution by usage, but rather as a passing imbalance in the allocation of use-of-force power between the President and Congress.

To what extent may Congress on its own authority constitutionally require or forbid the commitment of the military to foreign conflict? As regards the former, the Framers' design no more intended unilateral congressional war-making than it did executive, except perhaps as the legislators might enact a war measure over presidential veto. As a practical matter, however, it would be nearly impossible for Congress to force a reluctant Commander-in-Chief to commit American forces to foreign conflict, unless the legislators choose to impeach and replace him with a more pliant Executive. Though there have been times in our history when Congress urged a President toward the use of force, American troops have rarely if ever engaged in significant foreign hostilities until the incumbent Chief Executive affirmatively approved our involvement. Like its companion issue, the unilateral war-making authority of the President, the constitutionality of congressional war-making without the consent of the President is unsettled, but its ambiguity results from insufficient rather than conflicting precedent.

As regards congressional authority to forbid the use of force, the Framers intended it whenever congressional approval of hostilities is constitutionally required. Presidents in fact have been refused congressional authorization to use force and have desisted on that ground, though they have not sought and been refused in this century. Between 1900 and 1941, however, there did occur a less direct form of legislative prohibition of hostilities: the passage of neutrality acts and the refusal to enact measures necessary to implement fully presidential defense policies. But these legislative impediments to the use of force were often circumvented by the President. Despite the absence of precedent in this century, it seems clear that explicit congressional refusal to authorize hostilities would be thought by most Americans to make unconstitutional our involvement in them. It is not clear, though, that most Americans would regard as unconstitutional a President's attempts to persist in his use-of-force policies in the face of congressional refusal to pass necessary implementing legislation.

What form or forms may congressional authorization take? It appears that no one form was contemplated by the language and intent of the Framers, and a variety of methods have been used since 1789, the formal declaration of war being only one among them. Whatever the form, the clearer its expression of congressional intent regarding the use of force, the greater its capacity to satisfy the objectives of the declaration-of-war clause.

IV. RECOMMENDED RESOLUTION OF THE EXISTING CONSTITUTIONAL UNCERTAINTY

UNDERLYING ASSUMPTIONS

A.

In constitutional interpretation, the ultimate criterion must be the long-term best interests of the country. If the Constitution is to remain functional, its requirements have to move in pace with our changing needs and values. Further, in light of the Constitution's linguistic flexibility, and the difficulty of its formal amendment process, alternation by usage has appropriately become the principal means of modification. Thus, constitutional interpretation need not always track the Framers' intent, and upon occasion even their clear intent must be abandoned without the process of formal amendment.

B.

At the same time, the mantle of constitutionality does not automatically fall on whatever happens to be the situation existing at any given moment. Although the Constitution's interpretation must evolve to meet the differing needs of differing times, the document is not simply a chameleon whose principles are ever in flux. The stability and predictability necessary to law preclude our toleration of any such constitutional chaos. Moreover, the language and intent of the Framers are often clear in broad outline if not in concrete detail, and historically most Americans have been concerned that constitutional requirements endure as they are revealed in the Drafters' language and intent. Much of the controversy surrounding the Vietnam War concerns not simply the merits of the conflict but also the legality of United States involvement, as measured against preexisting constitutional expectations. We want governmental power to be exercised in the prescribed manner, and when conduct is deemed to fall outside the rules, efforts are generally made to bring it back within. Accordingly, recent conduct may not be upheld. Its simple existence is certainly not conclusive of its legality.

C.

In determining whether to persist in a course of action at odds with prevailing expectations, in the hope of thereby creating a new constitutional consensus, a fundamental consideration must be the effect of that persistence on the rule of law. Amendment of the Constitution by usage may appear to the public to be simple disregard of its requirements. Should the public conclude that the government is flaunting the Constitution, though the government may think itself engaged in amendment by usage, popular confidence in and commitment to law will be lessened. Since ours is a system that rests primarily on voluntary obedience of the rules and not on coerced submission to them, popular respect for the rule of law is essential.

Accordingly, it is always in the nation's best interests to avoid unnecessary change in constitutional interpretation, lest a measure of our legal system's strength be cast aside with the old expectations. Absent the necessity of abandoning existing constitutional patterns, the contemporary interpreter would do better to follow them, reshaping and extending them to meet the needs of the times. Though the Framers may not have conceived of the conditions to which one of their provisions now applies, if its underlying principle remains tenable, the principle should be carefully and skillfully preserved.

NATIONAL BEST INTERESTS

Since it is clear that the Framers intended Congress to approve American participation in hostilities and that this intent is still reflected in widespread community expectations, our interest in an unimpared rule of law militates in favor of preserving the Framers' principle unless it has come to be at odds with contemporary realities. The question becomes, then, whether congressional approval of American war-making is compatible with the existing demands of national security. An answer lies in consideration of the forces, historical and institutional, that have lead to the present balance of power between Congress and the President.

Of the historical forces contributing to the existing allocation of the foreign affairs power, the three most important have been the increased pace, complexity, and danger of international events. The presidency enjoys certain institutional advantages that make it a natural focus for governmental power during times of rapid change, complexity, and crisis. These advantages stem largely from the fact that the President, unlike Congress, is one rather than many. As a single man, always on the job, he is able to move secretly when the need arises, and to combine rapid, decisive action with the flexibility in policy demanded by quickly moving developments. His singularity and continuity also facilitate long-range planning. Because he is at the center of an unsurpassed information network and because he is assisted by countless experts, the possibility exists that his decisions will take into account the complexity of the problems faced.

Fault, on the other hand, is readily found with the congressional decision-making process: it often has been uninformed and inexpert, indecisive and inflexible, overly public and too slow, and sometimes it has not been assembled and working when crises arose. Some have suggested that for these reasons Congress is inherently incapable of participating effectively in use-of-force decisions.

Such is not necessarily the case. To the extent that Congress' problem is the nature of its decision-making process, improvement is possible. If the legislators so desire, they can act with reasonable dispatch. Dispatch could be facilitated by the adoption of procedures to overcome the obstacles that now clog congressional debate and decision. It is questionable, however, that great speed is required in most intervention decisions. With the possible exceptions of Korea and the Cuban Missile Crisis, its necessity during the last twenty-five years has been exaggerated. In the Korean situation, moreover, rapid congressional authorization could very probably have been obtained, since Congress was in session. In the Cuban situation, the President's reluctance to involve Congress appears to have been a fear of exposing the nature of the American response before it could be sprung full-blown on the Soviets, rather than a lack of time.

To the extent that the problem of Congress stems from its failure to operate secretly, existing procedures for executive session could be further developed. Inclusion of the legislators in secret decisions is not without precedent. In situations such as the Cuban Missile Crisis, however, where the President believes that the American response must be developed while the government maintains an outward appearance of normality, it would be difficult to involve Congress as a whole without alerting the enemy. But Cuban Missile Crises are rare. The secrecy dilemma usually arises in the context of classified information. Much information that the executive branch now withholds could be safely shared with Congress. Even were such data not available to the legislators, it is questionable that their ability to make most decisions would be materially impaired. Information is frequently deemed secret by the executive branch for reasons other than its inherent nature, and it is probable that the overwhelming bulk of the data needed to make an informed decision on most use-of-force issues can be found in the national press.

Similarly, it is debatable that experts, most of whom are housed in the executive branch, must make the basic decisions regarding use of force.

The determination that participation in foreign internal strife is in our national interest, for example, requires the setting of priorities in light of existing values. It is largely a political decision, and thus arguably less susceptible to resolution by diplomatic and military experts than by politicians, although experts and relevant information are important to ensure that the political decision-makers see and understand the various alternatives and their probable consequences. Information and expertise are already available in the military and foreign relations committees of both houses, and Congress could act to increase the supply of both to be available to it, though cooperation of the executive branch would also be required, particularly regarding access to classified data. Once adequately buttressed by information and experts, Congress would be better prepared to make rapid, wise decisions and to avoid inundation and intimidation by the torrent of data and expert opinions flowing from the President and his people.

A fourth historical force that has served the President more readily than Congress has been the development of communication devices that give government officials immediate access to the electorate. The Chief Executive, as the most active, intelligible branch of government, has been able to exploit the media in an unsurpassed manner, especially on occasions involving the use of force. Though Congress will never be able to compete with the President in so manipulating public opinion, it can improve its present efforts. Unlike the President, Congress seldom works to appear competent to deal with national security problems. Accordingly, the collective image of legislators tends to be one of a parochial and inefficient group, unduly concerned with trivia and self-interest, a projection deadly to popular confidence in congressional capacity in foreign affairs. Since Congress as a whole can do little to improve its image through professional public relations techniques, it must deal with the substance of the problem by demonstrating a willingness and capacity to grapple effectively with the country's use-of-force dilemmas. From that should come requisite coverage in the media.

A fifth force behind presidential aggrandizement has been the democratization of politics in this country, rewarding the branch of government that seems most representative of all the people and thus most concerned with the welfare of the nation. Some have argued that, since the President alone is elected by all the people, he is entitled in foreign affairs to bypass the legislature whenever possible and appeal directly to the public for support. But such a view is compelling only if Congress is in fact an undemocratic body—as it was when malapportioned districts, excessive obeisance to the seniority system, and undue devotion to local, special, and personal interests were at their peak. Reapportionment, a move toward younger, less ossified leadership, and a growing concern with national problems preclude a dismissal of Congress on these grounds today. Although individual congressmen will generally be somewhat more parochial than the President, this is appropriate for men who are the representatives of a part rather than the whole of the national electorate.

There has also been a related fear that only the President has the will-power to make the hard decisions required for a practical foreign policy, and that only he is capable of persuading a reluctant electorate to support them. Congress, out of both a predilection for the status quo and a fear of offending constituents, is said not to represent the true spirit of the nation, and to pose a negative force which the President must overcome. Though admittedly the Executive is often more willing to make hard decisions than Congress, it is probable that a reasonably persuasive President could bring the legislators, as well as the electorate, to support costly but necessary policies. Moreover, to eliminate Congress as a participant in the shaping of foreign policy removes the country's first line of defense against an Executive who is himself incapable of making sound decisions.

A sixth force behind the growth of the presidency has been the election of many men who have worked to enlarge the scope of their powers and responsibilities. It is at this point that serious doubts arise as to the capacity of Congress to reverse the trend toward executive domination in use-of-force decisions. Though the legislators still have the power to force even a reluctant President to consult Congress, a majority of them may well choose not to assert it. Elements among the leadership might oppose for reasons of personal power the changes in the decision-making process that would be required. Some legislators at any time will approve of the President's poli-cies and be unwilling to think in institutional terms. Some perhaps would fear that realistic procedures for congressional involvement in such crucial decisions could not be fashioned. Some will always prefer to avoid having to make such politically explosive decisions, and virtually all would be hard pressed to find the time to make the effort to re-establish and then sustain a congressional voice in foreign policy decisions. The tendency, accordingly, will be for the legislators to make a few noises about executive usurpation without really acting to vindicate their authority.

Should Congress not have the will to reassert itself, a final force behind the President's rise—momentum—will continue to inure solely to his ad-vantage. But should the legislators prove themselves capable of acting, and acting wisely, momentum may serve them also. Successful congressional involvement in any use-of-force decision would lead to greater opportunities for future participation, as public and presidential confidence in Congress grew along with the legislators' confidence in themselves.

In sum, though the present balance of power between the President and Congress over war-making reflects to a degree the demands of national defense, we have more drifted into an era of executive control than we have consciously chosen it as a necessity of our security. The historical and insti-tutional forces noted above have made presidential aggrandizement and congressional recession the paths of least resistance, but these forces do not seem to have created a context in which presidential hegemony is a *sine qua non* of defense. Thus, taking into account the requirements of security, we can redress the balance.

The Extent of Unilateral Executive Authority

A.

The institutional advantages of the President over Congress in dealing with swiftly moving, complex and dangerous times have been noted. Contemporary world conditions necessitate that the country not be denied the benefit of these advantages. Thus the President must retain the discretion that he has recently exercised (a) to commit American forces to hostilities without delay, as in Korea and (b) to commit them to hostilities secretly, as during the Cuban Missile Crisis. Accordingly, the sudden-attack exception must be broadly read to permit unilateral use of force by the President whenever he determines that the need for speed or secrecy precludes prior resort to Congress. By the same token, the President must have authority to act suddenly or secretly in whatever geographical area and for whatever purpose he thinks necessary, if national security is adequately to be protected.

Recent attempts in Congress to delineate legislatively the occasions in which the President may use force on his own authority are ill-advised. It is not possible to list all of the situations in which events now unforeseen may prove such action necessary, nor is it possible to define without notable ambiguity even those occasions now identifiable. The vagueness of any list so enacted would breed confusion and uncertainty, and its incompleteness would virtually guarantee its eventual disregard. Legislation of this sort is the antithesis of the clear and easily enforceable measures that Congress must enact to regain a voice in use-of-force decisions.

B.

Though congressional war powers should not preclude the presidential authority just described, they do properly circumscribe it on three scores. First, the President must never act on his own authority if he might reasonably have gone first to Congress. Second, unilateral executive action must be no more provocative than the situation compels. For example, presidential response to sudden attack must be proportionate to the assault, going no further than necessary to repel it and prevent its immediate recurrence. Were the President to take offensive action unrelated to the attack, he could so embroil the country in conflict that Congress would have little choice but to approve war. Third, the President must as quickly as possible lay the facts of the conflict before Congress with his recommendations for further action. It is then for Congress to authorize or refuse to authorize further hostilities. If the President is unable to obtain the requisite approval, he must end the use of force.

Congress could effectively codify these constitutional limitations on executive war-making. A legislative statement that the President may act unilaterally only when circumstances reasonably preclude prior resort to Congress would make clear that such executive action is an exception to the norm: that the legal presumption is that he must obtain prior approval. Statutory language to this effect would encourage executive restraint and provide other centers of power with a common standard for judging his conduct, and for sanctioning him should he exceed his constitutional authority. Such a "reasonableness" standard, of course, would leave reasonable men in disagreement when the facts are evenly balanced, but it should ensure consensus were a President blatantly to attempt to ignore Congress. Similarly, a legislative statement that unilateral executive action must be as nonprovocative as the circumstances reasonably permit would ensure consensus were a President to seize on a minor enemy attack as justification for a major American offensive.

Further, as is now proposed in Congress, there should be legislation (a) requiring the President to report immediately to the legislators his commitment of American forces to hostilities and (b) facilitating congressional action on the conflict. Such legislation, once duly enacted into law either with the President's signature or over his veto, would leave him little choice but to seek congressional authorization. Equally important, it would squarely face the legislators with conflict issues. Absent such statutory compulsion, it is unlikely that recent practice can be reversed, as it is not credible that the President will voluntarily and consistently subject his use-of-force decisions to the possibility of congressional modification or rejection. Nor is it credible that Congress, when presented with future executive *faits accomplis*, will often move to approve, modify, or reject them unless it has previously established a procedural framework that encourages and facilitates its weighing of the costs and benefits of further conflict.

To these ends, legislation must set a short time in which the President is to turn to Congress, perhaps twenty-four hours after the commitment of troops if Congress is then in session and forty-eight hours if it must be summoned. Should the President have acted on his own authority to achieve secrecy, however, the time of reporting should be left to his discretion, provided it does not extend beyond the point at which the President learns that the enemy knows about the American action. The legislation must also direct the President to present Congress with the pertinent facts: details of the way in which armed force has been used to date and why its commitment could not have awaited congressional authorization, as well as other data essential to informed congressional decision on further hostilities. If this information is classified, the statute should provide for its presentation *in camera*. The legislation, finally, should include procedures to prevent obstruction of the decision-making process within Congress, no matter what the effect of the expediting measures on ordinary committee and leadership prerogatives.

C.

In light of congressional reluctance to act with dispatch in the past, there should also be legislation providing that, after a reasonable period, perhaps thirty days from the time of the Executive's initial report to the legislators, congressional failure to act regarding the conflict would be deemed approval of the presidential course. Similarly, should Congress elect to authorize hostilities, it should be responsible to make clear its intent regarding their nature or be deemed to have left such matters to executive discretion, though no statutory provision to this effect is necessary.

The President cannot claim that congressional silence regarding his use-of-force policies constitutes tacit approval of them if he has never directly submitted those policies to Congress for approval, modification, or rejection. Nor can he rely for authorization purposes on an appropriations act or other legislation unless Congress expressly states that it constitutes approval of hostilities. The constitutional burden is initially upon him unequivocably to seek congressional authorization. But once he has sought that authorization, the constitutional burden must shift to the legislators, either to approve, rewrite, or deny the President's policies, or else be deemed to have agreed to them. National security cannot tolerate a collapse of use-of-force decision-making, and if Congress defaults on its obligations in this regard, the void is appropriately filled by the President. Thus proposals, now in Congress, to terminate automatically any presidential use of force within thirty days after its beginning unless Congress has approved it are unwise. To terminate such an executive act, a majority in both houses ought to oppose it with sufficient conviction to vote it down.

Form of Congressional Authorization

Although formal declarations of war are effective devices for rallying domestic support, for empowering the government to take emergency measures, and for notifying the world that total victory is sought, these declarations are not useful when conflicts are deliberately limited in scope and purpose.[36] A joint resolution is generally the most tenable method of

[36] "There are . . . numerous policy arguments why the formal declaration of war is undesirable under present circumstances. Arguments made include increased danger of misunderstanding of limited objectives, diplomatic embarrassment in recognition of nonrecognized . . . opponents, inhibition of settlement possibilities, the danger of widening the war, and unnecessarily increasing a President's domestic authority. Although each of these arguments has . . . merit, probably the most compelling reason for not using a formal declaration . . . is that there is no reason to do so. As former Secretary of Defense McNamara has pointed out '[T]here has not been a formal declaration of war—anywhere in the world—since World War II.'"
Moore, "The National Executive and the Use of the Armed Forces Abroad," 21 *Naval War College Rev.* 28, 33 (1969) (footnote omitted).

expressing congressional approval of the use of force today. The resolution should be adopted only after the legislators are aware of the crucial facts of the situation and have had reasonable time to consider their implications. The authorization should not, as a rule, be a blank check leaving the objectives, geographical areas, kinds of military activities, and duration of the hostilities to the President's sole discretion. Congress, in short, should make clear in its committee reports, debates, and statutory language the scope of any conflict that it authorizes. To be realistic, however, the resolution must leave the Executive some discretion to respond to changing circumstances. If the legislators wish to delegate full responsibility to the President, that should be their prerogative, although the circumstances in which such delegation would be wise are rare.[37]

When Congressional Authorization is Required

An essential issue remains: the constitutional dividing line between those uses of force that are wholly within executive discretion and those that must be approved by Congress, whether it is consulted before or after the President has committed troops. Obviously, there is no certain dividing line. But if there is to be systematic and meaningful involvement of Congress in conflict decision-making, a certain line has to be drawn. Otherwise the President will not be inescapably notified as to when he must seek congressional approval, and other centers of power will remain in doubt as to when it is necessary and proper for them to insist that he do so. Accordingly, the simpler and clearer the standard, the more likely its success in restoring a congressional voice in use-of-force decisions.

But at the same time that the dividing line must be simple and clear, it must also be responsive to the complex hazards of conflict: on the one hand, the physical and economic costs and diminished legal rights produced by hostilities and, on the other hand, the political and moral costs and potential legal sanctions of using force against another state. Costs of the second sort can be great even if those of the former are minor, for though hostilities may involve little or no fighting, they nonetheless can cost the country dearly if they violate international political sensibilities, law, or morality. Congress should have an opportunity to vote on the merits of incurring costs of either sort.

A two-element standard might suffice. Congressional authorization should be required whenever more than 5,000 men are sent (1) into combat or (2) into the territory of another state without an invitation from its government, whether or not fighting results. The figure 5,000 is ultimately arbitrary, though the necessity to commit more than that number to combat generally indicates the existence of large-scale conflict. Further, presidential

---

[37] The extent to which Congress may constitutionally delegate its war power to the President has been a matter of some controversy in the past. In the wake of *United States v. Curtiss-Wright Export Corp.*, 299 U.S. 304 (1936), however, it seems unlikely that strict anti-delegation rules apply in the foreign context.

authority to use up to 5,000 troops for combat purposes should cover most situations, such as the rescue of American citizens or military units attacked abroad, in which the Executive might legitimately expect no congressional objection to the use of force. The limit of 5,000 admittedly would also enable the President to involve the country significantly in foreign strife that Congress might well oppose, for example, our early commitment in Vietnam. The controls on such commitments, however, should take a form other than the conflict-approval procedures proposed here, lest the viability and solemnity of the latter be debased by too inclusive a coverage.

Such controls could include, for example, congressional insistence on detailed and periodic executive reports about the commitment to the pertinent legislative committees and, when useful, to Congress as a whole; committee investigations into and recommendations regarding the commitment; systematic consultation concerning the commitment between the President and congressional leaders; debate of the commitment on the floor of Congress and passage by either or both houses of resolutions on its merits; the refusal by Congress to pass appropriations or other legislation necessary to support the commitment; and the censure of the President by either or both houses for his actions regarding the commitment. Such steps persistently taken could virtually ensure presidential involvement of Congress in the shaping of all of his conflict policies. Since few Executives are unaware that they are strongest when supported by Congress and hamstrung when opposed, they are likely to bow with grace to congressional insistence on such a decision-making role, unless the legislators blindly advance policies unresponsive to the needs of the times.

As regards element (2) of the standard, the same considerations apply. The dispatch of more than 5,000 troops into the territory of an unwilling state generally indicates the use of force to significantly coerce other governments, with consequent international political, moral, or legal costs. It also often risks the outbreak of large-scale conflict. On the other hand, most such uses of force that would be clearly acceptable to Congress, for instance intervention to evacuate foreigners after the collapse of civil order in a country, would require less than 5,000 men, and any commitments of less than 5,000 that might be unacceptable to Congress are best controlled in other manners. While element (2) of the standard would be difficult to apply when it is unclear whether American forces are unwelcome in the state into which they have been sent, there should be consensus about the crucial situations, those involving a government that explicitly opposes American intervention.

A more fundamental flaw perhaps is that the standard as a whole does not cover situations involving more than 5,000 men in which there is neither dispatch of American forces into combat nor reluctance on the part of the host government to receive them onto its territory, but where their commitment appears significantly to risk war, for example, our 1958 intervention in Lebanon. Any test such as "appears significantly to risk war," however, would be too vague to command immediate consensus on the facts of most cases. Thus it could be too easily ignored to be included among the means to maintain the war-making balance between the President and Congress. It is vital that no standard be adopted that is easily disregarded, lest the habit of obedience to other standards be undermined. Again, congressional participation in decisions such as the Lebanese intervention should come in ways other than the formal conflict-approval procedures under consideration.

Thus, under the statutory scheme proposed above, the President would be required to seek explicit congressional authorization of any use of force unless it involved fewer than 5,000 men or unless his commitment of more than that number entailed neither immediate combat nor entry into the territory of a state against its government's will. An example of presidential use of force acceptable on these counts was the joint 1964 rescue by United States and Belgian troops of 2,000 civilian hostages held by rebellious elements in the Congo. The American forces numbered less than 5,000. They engaged in virtually no fighting and entered the Congo at the invitation of its government. Significantly, also, the American troops never confronted in hostile manner the forces of the Congolese government nor those of a third or *de facto* state operating within its territory. The rescue operation had purely humanitarian objectives, was quickly completed, and, under the circumstances, ran little risk of sparking large-scale conflict.

The above recommendations for a restored balance between the war powers of the President and Congress do not call for a return to 1789. Contemporary realities of national security dictate greater discretion for the President than the Framers thought necessary. But these realities do not require abandonment of the Framers' basic principle: the meaningful involvement of Congress, as well as the President, in the making of use-of-force decisions. Given the procedures outlined above, it remains practical to require legislative approval of American war-making. These procedures are deliberately simple, since it is unlikely that more elaborate schemes could be adopted or, if adopted, that they would work.

CONCLUSION

It is well to be clear that a greater congressional role in use-of-force decision-making would not guarantee less American intervention in foreign internal strife. Congress at times in our history has been more militant than the Executive, and it is doubtful that a majority of Congressmen even of late have been less hawkish than the President. A greater congressional voice, on the other hand, should not significantly heighten the instance of American intervention. It is difficult for Congress to act abroad through a reluctant Executive.

Nor would greater congressional involvement ensure policies that correspond to existing security realities, as the legislators' myopia during the 1920's and 1930's indicated. Nonetheless, it remains probable that legislative involvement in intervention decisions would result in wiser policies. The simple process of articulating and debating goals and strategies—a process inherent in meaningful executive-congressional collaboration— should lead all concerned to a fuller understanding of the interests and alternatives at stake. This, in turn, would help avoid hasty, ill-conceived decisions. Moreover, decisions to use force made by both the President *and* Congress would be less likely to plunge the country into dissension over the merits of the conflict. Finally, congressional approval of American war-making would remain faithful to the language and intent of the Framers, as well as to practice throughout most of our history and to the continuing expectations so produced. Keeping that faith would significantly serve our national interest in maintaining public confidence in the rule of law.

It is sometimes suggested that claims of presidential disregard of constitutional controls on use-of-force decision-making are pointless, since there still exist, within our system, forces that can restrain executive foreign policies. Thus, it is said, leave all to the political process. If the President has usurped congressional powers, he will be struck down in good time. The reality ignored, however, is that peoples' conduct is very much influenced by what they believe they have an obligation to do. Moreover, in so sensitive an area as national security—the area most at issue when questions of intervention arise—the natural tendency will be to leave matters as they stand, since the presidential hegemony of recent years is tenable, if not constitutional. Accordingly, unless Congress believes that it has a constitutional duty to make its voice felt in intervention decisions, unless the President believes that he has a constitutional duty to seek and honor congressional views, and, ultimately, unless the electorate insists on such a relationship between the two branches, presidential control is likely to continue undisturbed, save in those rare instances when executive policies result in lengthy, costly, and seemingly fruitless struggles.

Chapter 9 | Selected Constitutional Issues Arising From Undeclared Wars | *Lawrence R. Velvel*

I. INTRODUCTION

This chapter has a limited purpose: To set down some thoughts on a few of the major constitutional problems which are relevant to undeclared foreign wars. It does not attempt to provide a full-scale review of all the various arguments pertaining to the constitutionality of such wars, nor does it attempt to say everything that might be said about the issues discussed in this chapter.[1]

In writing of the constitutional problems of undeclared foreign wars at this point in time, one must make extensive reference to the American experience in Indo-China. For it is that experience which has stimulated most of the thought given to the constitutional problems of undeclared foreign wars and has provided much of the factual data which constitutional lawyers use in assessing the problems of such wars. Thus, though this chapter has a wider relevance than the Indo-China War, it will draw heavily on it.

II. THE DANGER TO THE SEPARATION OF POWERS

Any war in which the United States is involved brings with it a number of individual constitutional problems. But war also brings with it an overall constitutional problem concerning the balance of American government. At least since the American Civil War, large-scale military efforts have caused a tremendous expansion of Executive power at the expense of power of the other branches. This expansion has certainly occurred in undeclared foreign wars such as the war in Indo-China.

The expansion of Executive power is extremely dangerous because it causes a breakdown in the constitutional structure of separated and balanced powers which prevent hasty, arbitrary, or unwise action by government and insure that the lives and liberties of the citizen will be protected. In the case of Vietnam, the degree of danger arising from the wartime

---

[1] I have lengthily set forth my views on most of these arguments in L. Velvel, *Undeclared War and Civil Disobedience* (Dunellen, 1970); "The Constitution and the War: Some Major Issues," 49 *J. Urban L.* 231 (1971); "The War in Viet Nam: Unconstitutional, Justiciable and Jurisdictionally Attackable," 16 *Kan L. Rev.* 449 (1968), *reprinted in* II R. Falk, (ed.), *The Viet Nam War and International Law* 651 (1969); *Brief of the Constitutional Lawyers' Committee On Undeclared War* in Mass. v. Laird, 400 U.S. 886 (1970), *reproduced at* 17 *Wayne L. J.* 67 (1971).

growth of Executive power was increased because the accretion of Executive power during the Vietnam era came on top of an already existing, thirty year cold-war trend toward Executive hegemony.

A brief listing of a few of the actions taken by, or the powers claimed or exercised by, the Executive during the Indo-China War provides a graphic demonstration of the danger of unwise decision-making and the perils to life and liberty which arise from overweening Executive power. One may start, of course, with the very fact of the war itself. This war is now widely regarded as one of the great disasters of American history. Its toll in human casualties has been enormous; it has contributed to a disastrous inflation and to the urban crisis; its effect on the attitudes and beliefs of young citizens and minority citizens has been patently destructive. And in the eyes of millions of citizens, this tragedy has occurred for no discernible constructive purpose. How, then, did this horror come to take place? It occurred because the Executive branch possessed the vast political power, even if not the constitutional authority, to take this nation into war and to keep it in war for a long period of time. The Executive's power was so great that, as we now know, it made decisions by stealth and secrecy, it could and did get away with duping the Congress, and the Congress was almost totally unable to change the situation in any significant way.

Once the nation was in a war, of course, other actions which also demonstrated the danger of enlarged Executive power followed. For example, the widespread dissent to the war caused the Executive to fear that the nation's security was being undermined by internal subversives, and so the Executive began claiming and exercising the power to wiretap American citizens without a court order whenever it came to believe that such citizens were sufficiently subversive. Also because of its fear of subversion and disorder, the Executive felt compelled to proclaim the rightness of suspending citizens' constitutional rights during the Mayday events. On several occasions, the Executive refused to give Congress information on military contingency plans, military aid plans, the details of private agreements to defend other nations, information on intelligence activities, and the details of the foreign policy views of persons who are highly influential in shaping American foreign policy. The Executive thus left the national legislature without information vital to the legislative process. When information which the Congress and the people should know was published in the Pentagon Papers, the Executive attempted to suppress publication in violation of the First Amendment's ban on prior restraints. Having lost that round, the Executive, by attempting to secure indictments and convictions of those responsible for the release and publication of the Pentagon Papers, now seeks to insure that never again will any non-politician release a secret record of governmental transgressions.[2] Based on the various opinions in the Pen-

[2] Politicians, of course, and high government officials constantly relate secret information in their memoirs.

tagon Papers case, I must say that it looks as if the Executive has an excellent chance of having potential criminal convictions affirmed in this latest effort to insure public and congressional ignorance. (The reader should note that this article was written in 1971. By the time it went to press in 1973, the list of governmental transgressions had been enormously extended by the whole range of vicious practices brought to light in the Watergate affair.)

Finally, it is evident that, in the modern era, large-scale hostilities contribute to serious economic problems: inflation, balance of payments difficulties, and liquidity problems have all been fueled extensively by the war. The Congress' original reaction to much of this, as with the statute[3] which authorized the original wage-and-price freeze announced on August 15, 1971,[4] has been to give the Executive sweeping power to regulate huge sections of the economy. The Executive has exercised this power by dubious means, such as a hasty cabal-like meeting of the President and his advisers over a weekend, and closed sessions of Boards, Commissions, and Councils which produce regulatory edicts that are often arbitrary, discriminatory, and unsupported by viable reasons or even any reasons at all.

Thus I would warn that the greatest constitutional danger stemming from undeclared foreign wars is the aggregate, overall danger to the system of separated and balanced powers. Encompassed in this overall danger are many individual violations of constitutional rights and many individual transgressions against wisdom. This is hardly a new perception: if memory serves, Woodrow Wilson, in speaking with a visitor shortly before taking the nation into World War I, made a statement to the effect that liberty and sense are in great measure the losers when the nation goes to war. But though the perception is hardly new, it should be relearned—as, I believe, was said by Holmes: we occasionally need to be reeducated in the obvious. And in regard to the entire political, social, and economic situation created by the Indo-China War in particular, I would hope that the nation could quickly relearn the ancient lesson of the desirability of having a system of truly balanced powers.

III. THE LIMITS OF THE EXECUTIVE'S POWER TO CARRY ON HOSTILITIES WITHOUT EXPLICIT CONGRESSIONAL AUTHORIZATION

In the preceding section it was no doubt made clear, even if by implication only, that I believe the war in Indo-China is unconstitutional. The framers of the Constitution were familiar with and greatly feared excessive Executive power, including Executive power over the decision to go to war. They

---

[3] Pub. L. No. 91–379, 84 *Stat.* 799, *as amended*, Pub. L. No. 91–558, 84 *Stat.* 1468; Pub. L. No. 92–8, 85 *Stat.* 13, Pub. L. No. 92–15, 85 *Stat.* 38.

[4] Executive Order 11615.

therefore resolved that not the Executive but the Congress should have the power to make the decision on war. The thrust and purpose of the declaration of war clause is thus that, except for his power to repel an immediate attack on American lives, forces, property, or territory when there is no time to consult Congress in advance, the President must obtain prior congressional authorization before he is legally authorized to conduct hostilities.

The scheme envisaged by the framers has the great virtue of being both relatively uncomplicated and contemporaneously wise.[5] Nevertheless, those who disagree with the constitutional plan and seek to thwart it, and also those who in good faith have honest queries about where lines should be drawn under the Constitution, often raise a number of questions pertaining to the legality of the Executive's use of given kinds or amounts of military force in various situations, some of which are hypothetical and some of which have occurred.

The boldest point put forth by Executive lawyers and apologists is that the President has the legal authority to fight prolonged and major wars without authorization from Congress. The President's authority to do so is said to stem from his powers as commander-in-chief and chief executive, from his foreign affairs power, and from his duty to take care that the laws are faithfully executed. Although government lawyers still make in their briefs this bold claim of executive power, their constitution-destroying claim has been soundly rejected by the courts[6] and has been decimated by various authors.

A more interesting question than the one just discussed is whether there are circumstances, short of a major prolonged war, under which the President can carry on military hostilities abroad without prior congressional authorization, even though he is doing more than repelling an immediate attack. For example, would it have been constitutional for the President to have ordered bombing reprisals against North Korean bases in retaliation for the capture of the U.S.S. Pueblo? Could the President land troops in an underdeveloped country—say the Dominican Republic or the Congo— for the purpose of conducting a quick mop-up of some rebels or guerrillas? Or could the President order American forces to take some relatively brief combat actions on behalf of an ally—Israel, for example—that is undergoing an attack or has otherwise become engaged in hostilities? My answer to all of these questions is that it would be unconstitutional for the President to take these actions without prior congressional authorization.

As stressed above, the Constitution was framed to ensure that Congress makes the decision on war. However, not only do military actions such as those described above often constitute acts of war perpetrated without con-

---

[5] See *Undeclared War and Civil Disobedience, supra* note 1, at 12–13, cf. 91–96.
[6] *E.g.,* Berk v. Laird, 429 F.2d 302 (1970); Orlando v. Laird, 317 F. Supp. 1013 (E.D.N.Y. 1970), *aff'd,* 443 F.2d 1039 (2d Cir. 1971), *cert. denied* 92 S. Ct. 94 (1971); Mottola v. Nixon, 318 F. Supp. 538 (1970), *appeal pending,* (9th Cir., No. 26662).

gressional authorization, but either by the process of action and reaction, or by the pressure of continuous engagement, such actions could result, wittingly or unwittingly, in the United States becoming bogged down in heavy and sustained warfare. Bombing North Korean bases, for example, could easily have led to a second front in Asia, and an action against rebels in an underdeveloped country can unexpectedly mire us in a long war—as Vietnam has shown. Thus, if the President can take, without prior congressional authorization, the kinds of military actions described above, then Congress's right to make the decision on war and acts of war will be rendered meaningless for practical purposes, and the President will have the de facto power to ensure that the Constitutional plan for decision-making on war will in effect be thwarted.

This very real fear that the constitutional plan can and will be thwarted, as occurred with the Indo-China War, leads me to reject the entire concept that, aside from repelling an attack, the President can engage in any hostilities whatsoever without securing prior congressional authorization. If the United States is going to run the risk of taking military actions which conceivably can lead to war, then this risk should be run only after a public and congressional airing of its potential dangers and benefits, and only after an explicit congressional decision. Perhaps the ability to make the decision in secret in the Executive branch has some military or political benefits which might be lost under my view, but even if some benefits of secrecy are lost, an explicit congressional decision, which carries with it public discussion and debate, is the choice which our Constitution was framed to require, and it is a choice which is likely to be far and away the more beneficial one in the long run.[7]

Moreover, I would point out one further advantage of the constitutional restrictions on the war-making powers of the President. If congressional authorization is needed for a war, people often ask, then at what point do hostilities become of sufficient magnitude to require such authorization? Is it when the United States has one hundred men fighting, one thousand, ten thousand, etc.? In regard to the Indo-China War, of course, this problem was a red herring designed to circumvent the Constitutional plan under the guise that allegedly insuperable questions of where the line should be drawn would arise if war must be authorized by Congress. Regardless of where one may draw a reasonable line as to when hostilities are of sufficient magnitude to require Congressional authorization, the hostilities in Vietnam long ago exceeded it.

But there are other contexts in which the problem could make more sense, such as reprisals by bombing, quickly suppressing rebels, or allowing military advisers to go into combat with the forces they are advising. How-

---

[7] See *Undeclared War and Civil Disobedience, supra* note 1 at 12–13 91–105; "The Constitution And The War" *supra* note 1, at 271–81.

ever, any serious problems would be obviated under the concept that, except for repelling an immediate attack, the President must obtain congressional authorization before having our forces engage in combat. Under this concept, he cannot order *any* acts of combat, however small in size or short in duration, unless Congress first authorizes him to do so. Thus, rather than giving rise to difficult problems of drawing the line, the constitutional plan is relatively easy to apply.

Another issue is: if Congress *does* explicitly authorize hostilities, what is the scope of that authorization, *i.e.*, what combat acts can the President legally order under Congress' authorization? While this question could suitably be discussed at this point, it shall be deferred to a later section.

There are a few questions pertaining to the President's power to order acts which do not in themselves constitute combat but which could ultimately get the nation involved in some form of hostilities. The first of these concerns the President's alleged power to station troops abroad in allied countries in which there is no expectation that hostilities will occur imminently or even in the near future. There is as yet no definitive answer as to the Executive's constitutional power to station troops in such countries without prior legislative authorization. The constitutional argument for requiring congressional authorization is that, if hostilities ever do break out, the presence of American forces can cause the United States to be dragged into combat. Therefore, Congress should initially determine whether forces should be stationed in a particular country. On the other hand, requiring congressional approval for the stationing of men abroad is not necessarily dispositive as to whether the nation should or will significantly engage in hostilities at a later date. And if congressional approval for stationing forces abroad is not necessarily dispositive as to American participation in later combat, then perhaps it is not all that crucial in the first place to constitutionally require congressional authorization for sending the troops to allied nations during peacetime. On balance, however, I lean to the view that the Constitution should be construed to require congressional authorization, since the presence of American troops in an allied nation *can* cause this country to be dragged into combat, particularly where the troops are serving as a trip wire to ensure significant and extended American participation should a future war break out.

The next question regarding the President's power to order actions which do not constitute combat is whether, without consulting Congress even though there is time to do so, he may send American forces into foreign positions for the purpose of being in place to repel an attack which is expected in the near future against American lives, forces, or property. In my judgment, congressional authorization, which includes an authorization of combat, must be obtained for such a move. For hostilities are expected by hypothesis, and therefore congressional authorization is requisite in order to insure that Congress effectively retains its decision-making power on whether the country should engage in combat. Of course, if there is no time to obtain congressional authorization before moving the forces into position —a situation which should hopefully be rare in these days when Congress can be rapidly assembled—the President can have the forces take up positions while he seeks congressional authorization as soon as possible.

But it should be noted that the President's latitude to move forces into foreign positions to meet an attack when there is no time to consult Congress is limited to doing so where necessary to protect *American* lives, property, or forces. I do not believe the Constitution was intended to give him the power to repel attacks on *other* countries' forces or territories without congressional authorization. Moreover, permitting the President to repel attacks on other nations without legislative authorization would greatly increase the chances that he could get the country mired in hostilities that the Congress does not really want. As an example of how this could occur, suppose a major rebellion was suddenly launched in Spain or Greece, with attacks on those nations' forces, and the President immediately sent American divisions into combat on the side of the governments of those countries. Congress might not wish to authorize combat to defend their right-wing governments, yet might feel forced to do so because our divisions are already in combat. Or even if Congress refused to authorize participation in combat, still it might prove very difficult to withdraw our men before significant hostilities and casualties have occurred. And to the extent combat and casualties occur, Congress' right to decide on hostilities will have been thwarted.

A final problem regarding acts which do not themselves constitute hostilities is the question of which organs of the American government can make commitments under which the country may be obliged to participate in future foreign hostilities on behalf of an ally. In connection with this question, it may be noted preliminarily that a prior commitment to defend country X or country Y is definitely not the same thing as an authorization of war. For example, commitments to defend nations have been made, among other ways, by treaty and by Presidential promises to other countries.[8] But when it comes to deciding whether to carry out those commitments by participating in hostilities at a later date, the Congress must authorize the participation by enacting a proper legislative authorization at the time of the hostilities.[9] The treaty or presidential promise cannot itself authorize the war.

The question of which organs can make military commitments come down to whether such a commitment can be made by the President and Senate acting jointly through a treaty, whether it can be made by having

[8] As will be explained later, I believe that commitments made by the President alone are unconstitutional.

[9] *Undeclared War and Civil Disobedience, supra* note 1, at 21–23.

each house of Congress enact a suitable bill by a mere majority vote in each house (with the congressional passage of the bill being followed, of course, by the President signing the bill),[10] or whether it can be made by the President alone through the use of an Executive agreement or some other device.

To begin with, it would seem that it is permissible for a military commitment to be made by treaty. For the framers appear to have contemplated that treaties would be the vehicle for making important agreements with other nations,[11] and treaties surely are a recognized method of making military commitments. Admittedly, permitting the President and Senate to make a military commitment by treaty detracts from maintaining the full integrity of the constitutional scheme established by the declaration of war clause, which places the war-deciding power not in the President and Senate, but in the Senate and House. For while a prior military commitment is not the same thing as an authorization of war, it can nevertheless be very influential in causing the country to later decide to enter hostilities; and it would thus seem that full consistency with the constitutional plan for deciding on war would require that a prior military commitment which can lead to war be made not by the President and Senate through a treaty, but by the same bodies which have the power to decide to enter war, the Senate and House. But while permitting a military commitment to be made by treaty may be somewhat inconsistent with the declaration of war clause, such inconsistency is the price for having a Constitution which contains one clause giving the war-declaring power to Congress and another clause giving the treaty power to the President and the Senate. Moreover, the practical effect of the inconsistency is mitigated somewhat by two factors. First, as pointed out above, a treaty commitment does not obviate the need for a later authorization of war by both houses of Congress. Second, having the war authorizing power lodged in both the Senate and House is a method of seeking to insure that a war will not lightly be entered into but will instead receive careful consideration and wide approval. Similarly, the constitutional requirement that a treaty be approved not merely by a majority but by two-thirds of the Senators who vote on it helps to insure that a treaty which contains a military commitment that can be influential as to a later war will not be lightly entered into, but will receive careful consideration and wide approval.

The next question is: if one assumes that a commitment cannot be made by the President alone, then must military commitments be made solely by treaty, which requires a two-thirds Senate vote, or can they also be made by a majority vote in each house of Congress, plus, of course, the signature

---

[10] For a discussion of the necessity for presidential signature of a declaration of war, *see id.* at 293–94. In my view, the discussion there applies to any war bill regardless of whether or not it is a formal declaration of war.

[11] This is the clear impression received from reading *The Federalist*, Nos. 64 and 75; and II J. Story, *Commentaries On The Constitution of the United States*, 372–87 (1858).

of the President?[12] The arguments for requiring that commitments must be made by treaty are as follows: A military commitment is a significant agreement with another nation, and the framers of the Constitution appear to have contemplated that significant agreements with other nations should be made by treaty. Then too, the country should be extremely careful about making military commitments which could ultimately lead to war, and the requirement that a treaty must be approved by two-thirds of the Senators who vote on it is a better safeguard in this respect than is a requirement that a commitment be approved by a mere majority in each house of Congress. This idea has much force when one considers the knee jerk militaristic temperament which in the past has been displayed by many legislators: the requirement of an extraordinary two-thirds majority in the Senate for a treaty can help to insure that such a temperament does not prevail in the making of a commitment. Finally, requiring that a military commitment be made by treaty rather than by mere majority vote in each house of Congress comports with the view, expressed in the Federalist papers and by Mr. Justice Story, that the President and Senate would be far better qualified than the House to make important foreign-affairs decisions—a view which was a reason for excluding the House from the treaty power in the first place.[13]

There are also, of course, arguments for saying that a military commitment can be made by a majority vote in each house of Congress. Under the declaration of war clause, a mere majority in each house can make the decision for war itself. Consequently, it seems reasonable to hold that a majority in each house can make a military commitment which, by its very nature, has a less awesome immediate impact than the ultimate decision to go to war. Also, the requirement that there be a majority in *each* house does give some added hope for careful consideration and wide approbation before a commitment is made. Further, if Congress later believes it unwise to enter warfare to carry out the commitment, it can simply refuse to authorize hostilities. And as a practical matter, there is at least a slim possibility that, even if one says it is constitutional for a commitment to be made by a majority in each house, this will not always mean that a mere majority in each house will in fact be sufficient to obtain enactment of a commitment. For if just over one third of the Senators feel strongly enough against the commitment, they can filibuster it to death.

Given the arguments on both sides, it is a close question whether it is constitutionally permissible for a military commitment to be made by a

---

[12] I am speaking here of Congress making a commitment by enacting a bill which is specifically and intentionally directed to this purpose. I am not speaking of Congress making a commitment by enacting a mere appropriations bill—in my view, Congress cannot constitutionally make a military commitment by enacting a mere appropriations bill.

[13] *The Federalist, supra* note 11; II Story, *supra* note 11, at 379, 381–83.

majority vote in each house of Congress. Because the framers appear to have contemplated that treaties should be the vehicle for important agreements with other nations, and because the requirement that a treaty be approved by two-thirds of the Senators who vote on it provides an important safeguard against rash action, I come down on the side of saying that a military commitment must be made by treaty rather than by the action of a mere majority in each house. But one could easily come down on the other side.

Finally, there is the question of whether the President alone can make a military commitment through the use of an Executive agreement or some similar device. Any such commitments are flatly unconstitutional, since they are inconsistent with both the declaration of war clause and the treaty clause. A prior military commitment, while not dispositive as to whether the nation shall later go to war, can be influential in that regard; and permitting the President to make such commitments which can lead to war thus detracts significantly from the full effectiveness of the declaration-of-war clause and from the treaty clause.

Of course the following point might be raised. A military commitment can be made by treaty even though this is somewhat inconsistent with the constitutional plan established by the declaration-of-war clause for the making of the decision on war. And if the President and Senate can make a commitment by treaty, then why should inconsistency with the Constitutional plan for decision-making on war prevent the President alone from making a military commitment through the use of an Executive agreement or some analogous device? The answers to this question seem to be plain. First, there is the fact that, while permitting military commitments to be made by treaty is inconsistent with one constitutional clause, the declaration-of-war clause, permitting such commitments to be made by the President alone is inconsistent with two clauses, the declaration-of-war clause and the treaty clause, and therefore it gives that much more reason not to permit military commitments to be made by Executive agreement.

Second, as pointed out above, given the fact that the Constitution *does* contain a treaty clause as well as a declaration-of-war clause and that it is a recognized function of treaties to be used as a vehicle for making commitments, it is unavoidable to have some inconsistency between the treaty clause and the declaration-of-war clause. But the Constitution contains no clause specifically providing for presidential military commitments or for Executive agreements, and thus it is much easier to adopt rules which avoid inconsistency between these clauses and the declaration-of-war clause. The claim often put forward that the constitutional power to make Executive agreements is an inherent one does not mean that such agreements can be permitted to be inconsistent with specific Constitutional provisions. If the situation were otherwise, it would to some extent be meaningless for *Reid v.*

Covert[14] to have held that Executive agreements cannot violate the Constitution, and Executive agreements could be used to undermine the Constitution.

Finally, one of the factors which helps to mitigate the practical effect of the inconsistency between the treaty and declaration-of-war clauses is absent from Executive agreements and similar devices. An Executive agreement is not approved by two-thirds of the Senate, and thus there is lost this device for insuring that a military commitment which can lead to war will receive careful consideration and will have a high degree of approval before it is entered into. Indeed, under an Executive agreement, or presidential promise, or similar arrangement there is not only a loss of the device of requiring two-thirds approval, but the degree of consideration and approval can be lessened still further by the fact that *no* Senator or Representative need approve the Executive action, which may even be, and often has been, secret.

IV. THE APPROPRIATIONS ARGUMENT

A. GENERAL DISTORTION OF THE CONSTITUTION

I have made clear my view that the expansion of Executive power in our generation poses a great danger to the concept of separated and balanced powers, and that with the exception of repelling an immediate attack, the President cannot conduct hostilities without prior congressional authorization. Now I would like to turn to one of the main legal arguments which the Executive has used to break down the separation of powers and to argue that the war in Indo-China has been constitutionally authorized by Congress. This is the argument that general or special congressional defense appropriations, passed with full knowledge of the existence of the war, have served to authorize the American military effort. Indeed, at the time of this writing, late in 1971, this appropriations argument has probably become the most effective Executive argument as to the legality of the war. For not only have federal courts recently placed great reliance on the appropriations argument,[15] but the Tonkin Gulf Resolution has undergone an unlamented demise[16] and there has been a spreading judicial and public disbelief in Executive arguments based on the President's foreign-relations power, his Commander-in-Chief power, and his power under the Constitution's take-care and chief-executive clauses.[17]

[14] 354 U.S. 1 (1957).

[15] Orlando v. Laird and Berk v. Laird, 443 F.2d 1039 (2d Cir., 1971), *aff'g* 317 F. Supp. 1013 (1970), and 317 F. Supp. 715 (1970), *cert. denied* 92 Sup. Ct. 94 (1971); DaCosta v. Laird, No. 189, *decided* Oct. 1, 1971 (C.C.A.2d), *aff'g* 327 F. Supp. 378. *Contra*, Mottola v. Nixon, 318 F. Supp. 538 (1970), *appeal pending* (9th Cir., No. 26662).

[16] Pub. L. No. 91–672, § 12.

[17] Authorities cited *supra* note 6.

In carrying out the system of separation of powers, the framers of the Constitution very carefully assigned particular powers to each branch and withheld powers from other branches. Congress was assigned lawmaking powers, such as the power to regulate commerce, to establish a post office, to establish rules for immigration, to raise armies, to declare war. To the President was assigned the veto power. Under the appropriations argument, however, this constitutional scheme in effect gets turned completely around. For if the President can take actions which the Constitution reserves to Congress, and if his actions can be legal if Congress later appropriates money for them, then the President in effect has the power to initially make the laws and the Congress in effect has only the power to exercise a subsequent veto by denying appropriations. By standing the Constitution on its head in this way, the appropriations argument makes nonsense of the framers' carefully worked out plan that gave particular powers to Congress and other powers to the President; it destroys the separation of powers concept that no branch should be able to seize powers reserved to another one; and it opens the door to the exercise of arbitrary, hasty, and ill-conceived decision-making.

As described so far, the constitutional inversion is bad enough. But in fact it is yet worse. The Constitution deliberately contemplates a certain amount of difficulty in turning a new policy into law. First, a bill must be passed by each house, with a majority in each house being required. Then, unless he allows it to become law without his signature under Article I's ten-day clause, the bill must be approved by the President. If he vetoes it, it cannot become law unless two-thirds of those voting in each house cast their vote to override the veto. Since legislators are often cautious about enacting new policies, the need to obtain majorities in each house, and to obtain even two-third majorities to override a veto, means that the Constitution envisions placing a significant burden on those who would enact new policies into law. Moreover, in practical terms, the burden on the proponents of a new policy can be increased because of congressional rules and procedures. For example, committee chairmen who are hostile to a new law which is only one provision of a more general bill may succeed in having it struck from the general bill in committee. Hostile committee chairmen often can utilize rules of procedure to keep a new law from being presented as an amendment. And in the Senate, opponents of a new law might filibuster against it.

This process is obviated under the appropriations argument, however. Instead of the legislative burden being on those who would enact a new policy, it is on those who would oppose the policy. For example, the President could establish some new policy, such as seizing industry or drafting men without statutory authority. The burden is then on the opponents of these policies to obtain a majority in each house willing to vote to cut off the appropriations being used to finance the President's action. Such a cut-off would probably be attempted either by a restrictive rider to an appropriations bill which finances the particular Executive agency performing the President's action, or by an entirely separate bill restricting the use of funds. In either event, obtaining a majority in each house to cut off funds would be especially difficult. For once a policy is in operation, and even if it is in operation because of illegal Executive action, Congressmen are substantively very cautious about stopping the on-going policy, they do not wish to take the political risks of stopping it, etc. Moreover, the difficulty of stopping the policy can be compounded because now congressional rules and procedures may work against the opponents of the policy instead of against its proponents. For example, committee chairmen who are hostile to the opponents might keep an independent cut-off bill locked in committee, or might succeed in having a cut-off provision struck from a more general bill, or might prevent the introduction of a floor amendment, or a debate on a floor amendment, or a vote on a floor amendment.

If, despite the various obstacles, the opponents of the President's policy somehow succeed in having a majority in each house vote for a bill cutting off funds, the President might veto the cut-off bill. If the cut-off bill is separate from an appropriations bill, he need have no financial compunction about such a veto. If the cut-off bill is a rider to an important appropriations bill, such as a bill to provide money for an Executive department, he could still veto the whole bill without serious financial compunctions or even compunctions about making the veto stick: the opponents of his act would have to muster a two-thirds majority in each house to override his veto and the exigencies of the situation are such that, if the opponents cannot muster the two-thirds, then Congress will probably have to pass another appropriations bill, *sans* the cut-off, in order to support the particular department involved. Congress cannot, after all, leave the State Department, the Defense Department, etc., without necessary funds. Thus, instead of a policy being put into effect only if 51 percent of the legislators voting in each house approve it in advance, under the appropriations argument it can be put into effect by presidential fiat and will remain in effect unless 51 percent, and ultimately 66⅔ percent of those voting in each house disapprove; and one or both houses may at some point register disapproval without this having any effect, as shall be shown later in regard to American activities in Indo-China.

I simply cannot bring myself to believe that the framers of the Constitution intended to create a structure in which the kinds of inversions and distortions set forth above are even conceivably possible. Their well-known fear of Executive power, their careful enumeration of which powers belong to which branch, their desire that new laws and policies must be approved by majorities and sometimes even by specially high majorities, all cut the other way. Neither can I believe that contemporary Americans, who have made a major mess of their society, are so much smarter or more knowledgeable than the framers as to what is necessary for effective government that we should stand the Constitution on its head in the way described above. Thus the appropriations argument, in my opinion, is nothing more than a vehicle by which Executive apologists would make the President consumingly powerful even if it is necessary to wreck the Constitutional plan in order to do this.

B. THE APPROPRIATIONS ARGUMENT'S DISTORTION
OF THE POWER TO DECLARE WAR

It should be readily evident that the danger of the trend toward Executive hegemony, and the capacity of the appropriations argument to distort the Constitution, are not problems which are limited to war, but are general problems which extend to other areas as well. Yet it would be worthwhile to set out portions of the Indo-China experience as a specific illustration of these general problems. For it is in the case of Indo-China that the problems have reached their zenith; and in future situations of military hostilities, the Executive Branch, given the state of mind which has prevailed in that branch for years, is likely to again assert those military actions which it takes as being constitutionally authorized by congressional appropriations.

One may start by pointing out that it is eminently respectable to believe that had Congress been asked to specifically and intentionally authorize a potentially long and costly war on the Asian continent, it would never have done so. It might not have done so in 1965—indeed, in 1965, even Lyndon Johnson apparently was afraid that it would be difficult to get Congress to specifically and intentionally authorize war.[18] It is terribly dubious that Congress would have specifically and intentionally authorized a three-year continuation of large-scale war in 1968; yet today, in 1971, we are still engaged in heavy fighting. In all probability, Congress would not, in 1971 or 1972, authorize a two- or three-year continuation of the war; yet who can say with certainty that we won't still be engaging in some kind of important combat in 1973 or 1974?

In getting the nation into and keeping it in a war, two Presidents have used various of the factors which have abetted the general trend toward Executive hegemony. Johnson and Nixon have constantly, and with much success, used their access to the mass media to try to brainwash people into believing that what they were doing was right. The military and Executive bureaucracies have in juggernaut fashion spent huge sums prosecuting the war and other huge sums propagandizing for our efforts. The country has been lied to and information has been withheld, *e.g.*, Johnson constantly lied about his intentions in regard to getting into war; the administration lied about peace feelers; it was not until late 1969 that the Congress and the nation found out about the secret war in Laos; our air activities in Cambodia

---

[18] T. White, *The Making of the President 1968* 26 (1969); *also see* T. Hoopes, *The Limits of Intervention* 24–32 (1969).

were misrepresented, etc. Two Presidents have used their influence over their party members to obtain support. At least one major opponent has been purged, Senator Goodell.

And although Congress ultimately placed some restrictions on ground combat in the secondary theatres of Laos, Cambodia, and Thailand, for most or all of the war ordinary Congressmen, even had they desired to do so, were in no procedural position to successfully resist the President's usurpations and derelictions. Seniority rules have put hawks at the head of highly important armed-services[19] and appropriations committees, and the membership of such committees was also hawkish. Bills to cut off funds for the war would have gone to these committees in the House of Representatives and would have been bottled up there. Committee chairmen in the House saw to it that floor procedures were invoked which made it impossible to introduce floor amendments to cut off funds. Committee chairmen and ranking minority members saw to it that time to speak was not fairly apportioned. Military authorization and appropriation bills were treated as "package" or "lumped" bills, which authorized or appropriated money for a great variety of military needs, many of which are essential to military security, such as ships, planes, bases, and military salaries. The costs of the war were not separately earmarked in the bills so as to be separately identifiable; the costs of the war were substantially less than half the monies appropriated for defense; and over 80 percent of the forces for which money was appropriated are not in Indo-China. Thus Congressmen felt obligated to vote for the "package" bills, a situation which was only made worse when "lumped" appropriations bills contained some pork-barrel projects for the Congressman's own districts.[20]

In addition to being in no procedural position to successfully oppose the President, many Congressmen were simply unwilling to oppose him for fear of losing votes in the next election. This kind of cowardly political thinking, which put personal re-election ahead of a critical national problem, was made easier when votes were unrecorded, so that constituents who opposed the war might not know how their legislator voted.

Given the above, it is obvious that, by placing the imprimatur of legality on the undeclared war in Indo-China, the appropriations argument has completed the squaring of the circle—it has completed the process by which the Executive has become hegemonous over Congress in the matter of deciding whether to go to war. In doing so, it distorted the Constitution. For under the appropriations argument, rather than the Congress having had the Constitutional power to make the initial decision on whether we should go to war, on what our objectives should be, on what kind of war we should fight, etc., it is the President who made this decision. Rather than

---

[19] Namely, Senator Stennis in the Senate and Representatives Vinson, Rivers, and Hebert in the House.

[20] The matters discussed in this paragraph are presented in Congressmen's affidavits printed at 117 *Cong. Rec.* 16866–16880.

the President having had solely the power to veto a congressional war bill, it is the Congress that has had a veto power, which it could exercise by denying funds necessary to prosecute the war.

Such a distortion of the Constitution was bad enough in itself, but was made even worse because the appropriations argument subverted the Constitution's plan to make it difficult to go to war. Under the Constitutional plan, if the President desired to have the nation fight a costly six- or seven-year war in Indo-China, he should have obtained the assent of a majority in each house. This doubtlessly would have been extremely hard to do. But under the appropriations argument, the President was able on his own to take the nation into a long war and the burden of obtaining a majority in each house then fell upon those who opposed the war and would cut off funds for it. However, for the procedural and other reasons described above, and for reasons such as a fear that men in combat would be harmed if money were cut-off, it was almost impossible to obtain legislative majorities to cut off funds for ongoing combat activities. The difficulty of obtaining majorities willing to do this was even further compounded because if, despite virtually insuperable obstacles, a majority in each house had been amassed to vote for a cut-off bill, the President could have vetoed it. If the cut-off bill was separate from other legislation, the President need have had no financial compunctions about the veto and two-thirds of those voting in each house would have had to override the veto before the money was cut off. If the cut-off bill was a rider to some general appropriations bill for the Department of Defense, the President could still have vetoed the bill without serious financial compunctions or even serious compunctions about making the veto stick: the opponents would have had to obtain a 66⅔ percent vote in each house in order to override the veto and, if they could not do so, Congress would eventually have felt compelled to enact a new appropriations bill, *sans* a cut off, in order to support the far flung bases and activities of the Department of Defense.

Moreover, we have been and are going to continue to be in the untoward situation where we stay in combat even though one house has at some point voted against it. For example, a 1969 Church-Cooper amendment precluding American combat in Laos and Thailand was passed by the Senate before it found out that we were already engaged in combat activities in Laos, but the Senate later receded in the House-Senate conference and we continued to engage in combat activities in Laos.[21] A second and even more severe example of continuing in war though one house is on record against it is the following: The Senate indicated its distaste for the war by passing the Mansfield amendment to a military appropriations act.[22] The amend-

[21] This is described in *Undeclared War and Civil Disobedience, supra* note 7, at 256–57.

[22] *Authorizing Appropriations For Fiscal Year 1972 For Military Procurement, Research, and Development, and For Anti-Ballistic Missile Construction; and Prescribing Reserve Strength*, Conference Report, 28 (1972). H. Rep. No. 92–618.

ment proclaimed it a national policy that, given certain conditions as to the release of prisoners, there should be negotiations for an immediate cease fire, and there should be phased American withdrawals which would be completed within six months. The House-Senate conference deleted the six months deadline,[23] and the President, in signing the appropriations bill, took pains to make clear that he is going to ignore the Mansfield amendment.[24] Thus, six months after the date of the Senate's original passage of the Mansfield amendment, the nation will be fighting in Indo-China though the Senate is on record as being against this. (It should also be noted that, in 1973, before this book went to press, *both* houses repeatedly voted to immediately cut off funds for the bombing of Cambodia, but the President vetoed a bill which contained the cut-off. The House of Representatives then voted 241 to 173 to override the veto, but this was short of the two-thirds majority required to override. In order to avoid a constitutional, legislative, and fiscal crisis, the President and Congress then entered into a compromise under which funds for the bombing were cut off in a month and a half.)

V. THE FORM OF A CONGRESSIONAL AUTHORIZATION OF WAR

Having said that a war must be authorized by Congress and that appropriations are not a legal method of authorization, the question arises of what is the precise form which congressional authorization must take? Naturally, in keeping with the declaration-of-war clause, Congress could issue a formal declaration of limited or general war. Requiring a formal declaration of limited or general war can serve the valuable purpose of insuring that Congress knows full well that it is authorizing military hostilities and of insuring that Congress in fact *intends* to authorize significant hostilities. As was so dramatically illustrated by the Tonkin Gulf Resolution, when Congress is presented with only a vague and general resolution of support for the President rather than a bill formally declaring war, it may not know that it is being asked to authorize significant and long-lasting hostilities, it may not intend to authorize such hostilities, it may not want them, and it may pass the resolution only because it wishes to announce support for past presidential efforts to ward off attacks and because it hopes that the Resolution will help deter war by deterring the other side from expanding its action. This kind of congressional naiveté, which was fostered in 1964 by the Executive's statements that it wanted no wider war, will be out of the question when Congress is presented with a bill which formally declares

[23] *Id.* at 8, 28–29.
[24] Finney, "Nixon Will Ignore Call By Congress For Vietnam Cuts," *N.Y. Times*, Nov. 18, 1971, at 1, col. 8: Kilpatrick, "President to Ignore Viet Rider," *Wash. Post*, Nov. 18, 1971, at 1, col. 3.

limited or general war. For no Congressman can be innocent of the impact of such a bill.

But there are many who have argued that a congressional authorization of hostilities need not take the form of a formal declaration of limited or general war. The most basic reason for this argument is the notion that a formal declaration would lead to all manner of untoward consequences and that it is historically outmoded anyway. However, it is clear that, even without a formal declaration of war, it is possible to structure an authorization of war in a way that will fully accomplish the purposes of the declaration-of-war clause. An authorization structured in such a way should be regarded as constitutional. For the important thing is not form but substance. When Congress enacts a law pursuant to its power to regulate commerce, we do not require that Congress say "We hereby regulate commerce." In other words, we do not require Congress to use the precise phraseology contained in the Constitution. What is required instead is that Congress enact a law whose substance specifically carries out the purpose of the constitutional phrase giving Congress the power to regulate commerce. So it should be under the declaration-of-war clause. Indeed, so it in fact was early in the country's history, when Congress specifically authorized limited hostilities without using a formal declaration of war.[25]

From earlier portions of this article the reader is aware of my views on the purpose of the declaration-of-war clause. Its purpose is to insure that Congress—both houses of it—has the legal decision-making power on the matter of war. It is Congress that is to decide whether to get into a fight; it is Congress that is to decide whether we can fight on land, on the water, in the air, all of these, or some of these; it is Congress that is to decide the permissible geographical areas of combat and the enemies against whom we can fight; it is Congress that is to decide the political objectives for which we fight; it is Congress that is to decide how big a war we can fight and how long it is permissible to fight.[26] This overall congressional decision-making power stems from the intent of the framers (which has been lengthily dis-

[25] This occurred in regard to hostilities against France, 1 *Stat.* 578, and Tripoli, 2 *Stat.* 129–30, and in regard to projected hostilities against Great Britain, 5 *Stat.* 355.

[26] The President has the power not to fight as big and long a war as is authorized, not to fight in every authorized area, and in general, not to carry the war to the very maximum authorized by Congress. He possesses this power for two reasons. First, tactics and strategy may dictate a smaller effort than the maximum authorized, and, as commander-in-chief, he is chief strategist and tactician. Second, the framers wanted it to be hard to get into war but easy to make peace. II M. Farrand, *Records of the Federal Convention* 319 (1911); M. Pusey, *The Way We Go To War* 45 (1969); II Story, *supra* note 11, at 97. Not extending the war to the maximum authorized can, in keeping with the framers' intent, make it easier to end the war. But note that the President's power not to extend the war to the maximum authorized does not mean he can extend it *beyond* the maximum authorized. Whereas not extending it to the maximum is in keeping with the framers' intent and the logic of the Constitution, extending it beyond the maximum is out of keeping with the framers' intent and the logic of the declaration of war clause.

cussed in prior writings),[27] is contemporaneously wise, and was made eminently clear by John Marshall. In discussing whether it was lawful for an American naval vessel to capture a particular ship during the naval war with France, Marshall said:[28]

> The whole powers of war being, by the constitution of the United States, vested in Congress, the acts of that body can alone be resorted to as our guides in this inquiry. It is not denied, nor in the course of the argument has it been denied, that Congress may authorize general hostilities, in which case the general laws of war apply to our situation; or partial hostilities, in which case the laws of war, so far as they actually apply to our situation, must be noticed.
>
> To determine the real situation of America in regard to France, the acts of Congress are to be inspected.

In order to carry out the purpose of the declaration-of-war clause without issuing a formal declaration of war, Congress can issue a specific, intentional, and discrete authorization of war. In a bill which is independent of other bills (*i.e.*, which is discrete), Congress should specifically say that it is "hereby authorizing" hostilities.[29] It should name the kinds of forces—land, sea, or air—which can be used, and it can place numerical limits on the forces. It should name the enemies against which, and the areas in which, force can be used. It should, within broad general categories, state the kinds of weapons that are usable—*e.g.*, conventional weapons but not atomic or bacteriological ones. It should state the political objectives of the use of force and it can and should place time limits on the use of force. (Even prior formal declarations of unlimited war have stated the kinds of forces that can be used—military, naval, and, in some cases, the militia or privateers. Some prior formal declarations have also expressly pledged all the resources of the nation for the politico-military objective of bringing the conflict to a successful termination.[30] And, of course, prior formal declarations have stated who the enemy was.)[31]

Drafting a specific, intentional and discrete authorizing resolution which meets the criteria set out above would not be at all difficult. For example, suppose Congress wanted to authorize hostilities in Indo-China. The authorizing resolution, which should be independent of any other bill, could read as follows:

> For the purpose of preventing the rise of Communist governments in Indo-China, the President is hereby authorized and directed to use the

---

[27] *See* authorities cited in *supra* note 1.

[28] Talbot v. Seeman, 1 Cranch (5 U.S.) 1, 28 (1801).

[29] This language, or language almost identical to it, has been used in every formal American declaration of war. 55 *Stat.* 795; 55 *Stat.* 796; 55 *Stat.* 797; 40 *Stat.* 1; 30 *Stat.* 364; 9 *Stat.* 9; 2 *Stat.* 755.

[30] 55 *Stat.* 795–97.

[31] *See supra* note 29.

land, sea, and air forces of the United States against the government of North Vietnam, the Viet Cong, the Pathet Lao, and Cambodian Communist insurgents. The American forces shall not exceed 500,000 men, and can be used on the land, in the air, and on the inland and territorial waters, of the Indo-China peninsula. Conventional weapons, but not atomic or bacteriological ones, may be used. This resolution shall expire one year from the date of its enactment.

An authorizing resolution such as this would possess several advantages relating to the way in which it carries out the declaration-of-war clause's purpose of insuring that Congress—both houses of it—is the body which makes the decision on war. When confronted with a resolution such as that above, Congress is going to know that it is being asked to get us into a war. There will be no hornswoggling of the type which occurred when the Tonkin Resolution was passed—nobody is going to be able to tell Congress, and Congress will not believe, that it is merely supporting past actions and deterring a war. Moreover, unless there has been a massive Pearl Harbor-like attack against us, a Congress which knows it is being asked to get us into war is a Congress which is likely to publicly discuss and probe the need for war and the alternatives to it. The probing will be aided and stimulated by wide-spread discussion of the subject in the press. We will not get into war by Executive secrecy and stealth, nor for reasons which cannot bear public scrutiny and have not been critically analyzed. All of this, too, contrasts with the situation at the time of the Tonkin Resolution. Then the decision for war was secretly made by Executive officials and carried out by stealth and chicanery; it was made for reasons which were not critically examined by Congress or the public; and the alternatives to, and possible consequences of, the war were not deeply examined by Congress, the press, or the public. (There are indeed many, apparently including at least one former high administration official, who think that we would not have gotten into the Vietnam mess if, instead of the Executive going to war by stealth and chicanery, the issue had been thoroughly aired in Congress at the time of the Tonkin Resolution.)

The suggested type of authorizing resolution will also insure that we do not have a situation where a President can, of his own accord, take us into a war and continue a war, thereby creating a long-lasting, massive *fait accompli* from which the nation cannot be extricated unless a majority or a two-thirds majority in each house of Congress votes to get out. If an attack occurs, the President cannot proceed to engage in a lengthy war on the theory that he is all the while repelling the attack. Rather, if he wishes to continue or expand fighting once the initial attack is over, he must obtain congressional authorization. If there has been no attack, then he can engage in no hostilities at all prior to obtaining authorization.

A further advantage of the suggested kind of authorization is this: the very fact that it is discrete—is separate from any other bills—will minimize the chance of parliamentary maneuvering designed to force legislators to vote in favor of hostilities even though they do not really wish to. Such trickery *could* occur if an authorization is not required to be discrete, but instead can be attached to other bills.

Yet another advantage of the kind of authorization suggested here is that, by imposing time limits, Congress will retain control of the nation's destiny. When the time period of the authorization is about to expire, Congress can redebate the question of the war, whether the war makes sense, what alternatives there are, and so forth. If Congress wishes to renew the authorization, it can do so. But if it thinks it unwise to continue the war, then it can simply refuse to renew the authorization, thus requiring the Executive to withdraw armed forces from hostilities as rapidly as possible after the authorization of war expires. In this way Congress can cause the war to be ended without having to cut off money to men facing the enemy—which many legislators, with some justification, regard as humanly, politically, and morally impossible. Continuing the appropriations to our men will not make the war legal. Rather it will be illegal because the time period of the specific, intentional, and discrete authorization will have expired without renewal.

The suggested type of authorization will also accomplish the desirable goal of enabling us to know with fair certainty whether particular military actions are authorized. For example, under the sample authorization set out above, which only authorizes fighting on the Indo-China peninsula, we would know that an invasion of Cambodia is authorized, but that an invasion of Communist China is not. Also, by helping to make clear what the Executive cannot do, the suggested type of authorization helps to achieve one of the original goals of the declaration-of-war clause, to wit, that it serve as a check on Executive warmaking.

The suggested type of authorization would not place the President in a tactical or strategic straitjacket, for if he wished to fight in new areas, use more men, use a new generic category of weapons, or what have you, he could come to Congress for an expansion of the authorization. Of course, since he would not be able to do such things *without* first obtaining an expansion of the authorization, the element of surprise might be lost. Under my sample authorization, for example, the President would not be empowered to launch a surprise invasion of Communist China or to suddenly begin using germ warfare against the Viet Cong. However, it strikes me as being all to the good that the President will not be able to take such rash surprise actions. The desirability of avoiding rashness is not only valid in theory, but has been concretely shown by our entire Indo-China experience, starting with the very fact of the war itself and including such particular episodes as the surprise invasion of Cambodia, the secret air war in Laos and later in Cambodia, and the tremendous devastation wrought by our defoliation program.

A final advantage of the suggested type of authorization is concerned with the extent to which it puts a constitutional check on the war-making power. As a matter of constitutional structure, the question of which branch has the constitutional power to decide to go to war is somewhat more complex than most of the debates on the question would indicate. The long debate over the legality of the Indo-China War, including the prior discussion in this article, has largely been centered on whether it is the President or Congress which has the constitutional authority to take this country into war. And it is understandable that the debate was centered on this question. After all, the Executive has repeatedly claimed that the President has the power to take the nation into war; the most it has conceded *arguendo* is that there should be congressional concurrence and cooperation, which in the Executive's view has existed by virtue of appropriations;[32] and it was necessary for opponents of the Executive's claim to take direct issue with it.

The reason why the problem is slightly more complex than deciding whether Congress alone or the President alone has the constitutional power to decide to take the nation into war is that, while the Constitution does indeed give the lawmaking powers to Congress, it gives the veto power to the Executive. Thus, while Congress is the body which has the constitutional power to make the initial legal decision on whether a certain policy shall be enacted into law, if it decides in the affirmative, the President has the constitutional power to subsequently stop the policy from becoming law by vetoing it, and he will succeed unless two-thirds of each house are so committed to the policy that they override his veto. Conversely, if the President desires that a policy become law, Congress has the Constitutional power to prevent this by refusing to enact the policy in the first place. And as it is with laws in general, so it is with a formal declaration of war or a specific, intentional and discrete authorization of war. Congress has the initial power to decide whether we should get into war. If it decides affirmatively, and enacts a war bill, the President has the constitutional power to decide to check Congress by vetoing the war bill, and his veto will stick unless two-thirds of each house vote to override. Conversely, if the President wants war but Congress disagrees, Congress can check the President by refusing to enact a war bill in the first place. So, as a matter of constitutional structure, the requirement of a specific, intentional, and discrete authorization of war insures that both Congress and the President must agree before we get into war. It is thus clear that the kind of congressional-executive concurrence and cooperation which the constitutional structure envisions as being necessary to get into war is not, as the Executive maintains, for the President to take us into war of his own accord and for Congress to later "concur" and "cooperate" by voting for appropriations. It is

---

[32] *Brief for the Defendant Opposing the Motion for Leave to File Complaint,* Massachusetts v. Laird, 400 U.S. 886 (1970); United States v. Sisson, 294 F. Supp. 511 (1970).

rather for Congress to first enact a bill authorizing hostilities and for the President to then sign the bill.

In concluding this section, I would like to turn from discussing specific, intentional, and discrete authorizations of war to a short discussion of formal declarations of war. If Congress formally declares a general and unlimited war against a particular enemy, as it has on past occasions, then there is no point in the declaration containing some of the kinds of limitations discussed above, such as limits on the size or kind of forces, or the permissible areas of combat. (There might, however, be some point in the declaration containing limitations against germ warfare, and there could even be merit in stating our political objectives.) But if Congress were to formally declare only a limited war, then it would be wise for the declaration to contain all the same limitations as those which should go into a specific, intentional, and discrete authorization of hostilities. These limitations will insure that the war is limited in the way Congress intends; will insure that Congress will be the body to decide how big a war can be fought, where it can be fought, against whom it can be fought, the permissible political objectives, etc.; and will accomplish various others of the goals which have been discussed above.

VI. THE PRESIDENT'S POWER AS COMMANDER-IN-CHIEF

The final question with which this chapter shall deal is the extent of the President's authority as commander-in-chief in a war that has been properly authorized by Congress. In such a war, I would expect that ordinarily the commander-in-chief power would not present troublesome problems. Properly construed, the commander-in-chief power gives the President the right to direct the nation's military strategy and tactics in congressionally authorized hostilities,[33] and thus the extent of the President's power would depend in practice on the extent of the authorization of hostilities. This would present no problem were Congress to authorize an all-out-unlimited war as it did in World Wars I and II. In such cases, the wording of and the historical circumstances surrounding the declaration or authorization of war leave no doubt that the President, as commander-in-chief, can use all legal tactics to defeat the enemy on any front. If Congress should enact not an authorization of all-out war but only an authorization of limited hostilities with stated limitations as to the kinds and number of our forces, the enemies

---

[33] Joseph Story makes this clear, and it is also made clear by Hamilton's view that as commander-in-chief the President would be "first general and admiral" of the nation, albeit nothing more than this. II Story, *supra* note 11, at 360–61; *The Federalist Papers*, No. 69; Chayes and Michelman, "Legal Memorandum on the Constitutionality of the Amendment To End The War," in "Congress, The President and the War Powers," Hearings Before the House Subcommittee on National Security Policy and Scientific Developments of the Committee On Foreign Affairs, 91st Cong., 2nd Sess., 369 (Comm. Print 1970).

against whom the war shall be fought, the areas in which fighting can take place, the generic categories of permissible weapons, the political objectives, and the time during which the authorization shall be in force, then here again the commander-in-chief power should not present much of a problem. For the truly major questions regarding the scope and extent of the commander-in-chief's authority to fight the war will be answered by the authorization itself, and enlargements of this authority, or minor questions, can be taken care of by coming back to Congress for further authorization.

What the situation basically comes down to, then, is this: If hostilities have not been properly authorized by Congress, the commander-in-chief power does not give the President any power to engage in war. If a war *has* been properly authorized by Congress, then the extent of the President's authority as commander-in-chief to engage in hostilities should present little problem.

There is, however, one possible *caveat* which in some persons' minds could conceivably complicate the foregoing. Suppose that the Congress authorizes only a limited war, but that during the course of the war the President claims he must expand it beyond the authorized limits of time, force levels, geography, or enemies in order to protect his troops or in order to accomplish political objectives of Congress. And suppose further that the President claims that his expansion does not constitute a new war but is only part of an existing war. (Except for the admittedly critical factors that the war in Indo-China has never been properly authorized in the first place and Nixon is pursuing there his own political objectives rather than those of Congress, the hypothetical given above is similar to some of Nixon's most important claims as to why he is constitutionally justified in staying in Indo-China for as long as he wants, and why he was constitutionally justified in invading Cambodia.)[34]

I do not believe that the President's commander-in-chief power extends to expanding hostilities beyond properly authorized limits on the claim that he is protecting troops, or accomplishing objectives of Congress, or merely carrying out an existing war. The commander-in-chief power is confined to directing the nation's military strategy and tactics within congressionally authorized limits—a measure of confinement which ensures that congressional power to make vital decisions on war will be effective. If the President should expand the war beyond the limits set by Congress, then he is usurping this congressional power. Moreover, rather than protecting our troops, an expansion of a war beyond congressionally imposed limits is likely to result in more of our troops being killed and maimed. Finally, as

---

[34] A statement of Nixon's claim appears in Rehnquist, "The President's Constitutional Authority To Order The Attack On The Cambodian Sanctuaries," in "Congress, The President, and the War Powers," *supra* note 33, at 539; also consider, "Transcript of President's Address To The Nation On Foreign and Domestic Issues," *N.Y. Times*, May 1, 1970, at 2, col. 8; Frankel, "Senate Semantics And New War Rationale," *N.Y. Times*, June 25, 1970, at 3, col. 1.

shown by the situation surrounding the Cambodian invasion,[35] sometimes there can be too many factors, cutting in opposite directions, to make any kind of clear determination as to whether an expansion of hostilities constitutes a new war or part of an existing one.

[35] At least two major arguments can be adduced for saying the Cambodian invasion was part of an existing war. As the Executive has pointed out, the North Vietnamese were using the Cambodian sanctuaries as bases for their participation in the existing war in Vietnam. Second, war, in one form or another, was going on all over Indo-China—in Laos and Cambodia as well as in Vietnam—and all of the hostilities could be said to be related to each other in both political and military terms. In short, even at the time of the Cambodian invasion, there was already an existing war in Indo-China.

On the other hand, there are also several reasons for considering the Cambodian invasion to be a new war. In the first place, the invading troops did cross a national boundary. Secondly, they did so for the purpose of fighting in a nation where Americans are not previously known to have conducted large-scale ground operations. Third, the invaded nation had theretofore been a neutral in the war. Fourth, in many quarters, there is a deep suspicion that the invasion was not mounted solely for the military purpose of protecting American troops, but was also mounted for the political objective of shoring up the newly established Lon Nol government. (Also, there was much presidential talk of accomplishing the political objective of convincing the Russians that President Nixon was sufficiently unpredictable that they should be cautious in the Middle East.)

PART *IV* | **SPECIAL PROBLEMS**

Chapter 10 | **Humanitarian Intervention** | *Ian Brownlie*

1. INTRODUCTION

In the recent literature of the law, proposals have been made to the effect that forcible intervention in human rights situations is lawful and, further, that the present need is to clarify the criteria by which the legitimacy of such action may be judged. My purpose is to subject these proposals to a critique. The critique will relate particularly to the views of Richard Lillich and the Interim Report of the Sub-Committee of the Committee on Human Rights of the International Law Association.[1] The Interim Report was based upon two articles published previously by Lillich.[2]

It is as well if I point out that I share the objectives of the principal Committee in shifting the emphasis from definition to implementation in matters of human rights.[3] Though not a participant in International Law Association (ILA) committees, I have given questions of human rights and their implementation prominence in my published writings.[4] The issue, of course, is to discover the best means of implementation acceptable to the majority of states. While publicists and experts can take the initiative in prompting states to action, they cannot afford to ignore the expectations, attitudes and aptitudes of governments when formulating proposals.

Unless the context clearly requires a different interpretation, "humanitarian intervention" in my usage is the threat or use of armed force by a state, a belligerent community, or an international organization, with the object of protecting human rights. It must be emphasized that this usage begs the question of legality and stresses function or objective. In diplomatic usage, the term "humanitarian intervention" has been used more widely to describe diplomatic intervention *de bene esse* on behalf of non-nationals or on behalf of nationals in matters which are in law within the domestic jurisdiction of the state of their residence or sojourn.

[1] *Report of the Committee on Human Rights*, International Law Association, The Hague Conference (1970), at 8.

[2] Lillich, "Forcible Self-Help by States to Protect Human Rights," 53 *Iowa L. Rev.*, 325 (1967); *id.*, "Intervention to Protect Human Rights," 15 *McGill L.J.*, 205 (1969).

[3] International Law Assoc., *Report of the Fifty-Second Conference* (1966), at XVIII.

[4] Brownlie, "The Individual before Tribunals Exercising International Jurisdiction," 11 *Int'l & Comp. L.Q.* 701 (1962); *id.*, "The Place of the Individual in International Law," 50 *Va. L. Rev.* 435 (1964); *id.* "Eichmann: A Further Comment," [1962] Crim. L.R. 817; *id. Principles of Public International Law* Part IX, at 419–86 (1966); *Basic Documents in International Law*, Part Six at 132–219 (1967); *Basic Documents on Human Rights* (1971).

2. THE LEGAL CONTEXT

It is important to discuss the considerations of policy concerning the use or threat of force to protect human rights. But it is equally important to keep the issues in their proper legal context. Indeed, so far as the reasonable expectations and assumptions of governments are a material factor in resolving issues of policy, law and policy need not stand in opposition one to another.

It is clear to the present writer that a jurist asserting a right of forcible humanitarian intervention has a very heavy burden of proof. Few writers familiar with the modern materials of state practice and legal opinion on the use of force would support such a view. In the first place, it is significant that the very small number of writers cited in support of this view by Lillich[5] include two, McDougal[6] and Reisman,[7] who lean heavily on a flexible and teleological interpretation of treaty texts. Leading modern authorities who either make no mention of humanitarian intervention and whose general position militates against its legality, or expressly deny its existence include Brierly,[8] Castrén,[9] Jessup,[10] Jimenez de Arechaga,[11] Briggs,[12] Schwarzenberger,[13] Goodrich, Hambro, and Simons,[14] Skubiszewski,[15] Friedmann,[16] Waldock,[17] Bishop,[18] Sørensen,[19] and Kelsen.[20] In the lengthy discussions over the years in United Nations bodies of the definition of aggression and the principles of international law concerning international relations and cooperation among states, the variety of opinions canvassed has not revealed even a substantial minority in favor of the

[5] ILA Report, *supra* note 1, at 11–12; Lillich, "Intervention to Protect Human Rights," *supra* note 2.

[6] McDougal, "Authority to Use Force on the High Seas," 20 *Naval War College Rev.* 28–29 (1967). McDougal's interpretation of the U.N. Charter has changed since he and Feliciano published *Law and Minimum World Public Order* (1961).

[7] Reisman, "Memorandum Upon Humanitarian Intervention to Protect the Ibos" (unpublished) 12 (1968).

[8] J. Brierly, *The Law of Nations*, 309–10 (5th ed. 1955), *see also* the 6th ed. by Waldock (1963), at 402.

[9] E. Castrén, *The Present Law of War and Neutrality* 54 (1954).

[10] P. C. Jessup, *A Modern Law of Nations* 157–87 (1956).

[11] Jimenez de Arechaga, *Derecho constitucional de las Naciones Unidas*, 80, 401–2, 407 (1958).

[12] H. Briggs, *The Law of Nations*, 957–64 (2nd ed. 1953).

[13] G. Schwarzenberger, *The Law of Armed Conflict*, 28–58 (1968).

[14] L. Goodrich, E. Hambro, & A. Simons, *Charter of the United Nations*, 43–55 (3rd and rev. ed. 1969).

[15] Skubiszewski, in M. Sørensen (ed.), *Manual of Public International Law*, 739–81 (1968).

[16] W. Friedmann, "General Course," *Recueil des Cours* at 200–214 (internal pagination) (1969–II).

[17] H. Waldock, 106 *Recueil des Cours*, 194–6, 230–46 (1962–II).

[18] W. Bishop, 115 *Recueil des Cours*, 423–41 (1965–II).

[19] M. Sørensen, 101 *Recueil des Cours*, 234–45 (1960–11).

[20] H. Kelsen, *Principles of International Law*, 58–87 (2nd ed., rev. and ed. by Tucker, 1968).

legality of humanitarian intervention.[21] The *Repertory of Practice of United Nations Organs* provides no support; nor does the International Law Commission's Draft Declaration of the Rights and Duties of States.[22] The voluminous materials in Whiteman's *Digest*[23] lack even a passing reference to humanitarian intervention. Counting heads is not, of course, a sound way of resolving issues of principle. However, quite apart from the weight of the opinion of experts cited above, it is the writer's view that these authorities are reporting and reflecting the universal consensus of government opinion and the practice of states since 1945. Their views thus combine both policy in the sense of the reasonable expectations of states and the normative quality of rules based on *consensus*. With due respect to Lillich, it must be said that, if a new view is to be put forward, either it should be based on a much more substantial exposition of the practice, doctrine, and general development of the law relating to the use of force by states or the view should be offered *tout court* as a proposal to change the existing law.

The legal regime created by the United Nations Charter rests on a suspicion of unilateral action by states, coupled with a certain faith in collective action, either as collective self-defense or as action by regional arrangements other than those made for the purpose of collective self-defense but yet permitted under Chapter VIII, or as action *authorized* by the United Nations,[24] or as action by the competent organs by means of United Nations forces. This faith in collective action and dislike of action by individual states is rather contradictory,[25] but that is the scheme of the Charter as established. Apart from self-defense and collective self-defense self-help by states is now illegal. Even those prone to give a broad definition of self-defense do not, in general, support the view that humanitarian intervention is lawful.[26] The minority who would support the legality of intervention to protect the lives of nationals rely significantly on the category of self-defense:[27] and humanitarian intervention is not a form of self-help by definition, whereas self-defense is a legitimate form of self-help. The minority who argue that Article 51 reserves without transformation the right of self-defense in customary law[28] rely on the category of self-defense and

---

[21] *See* occasional references, in Off. Recs., Gen. Ass.: 6th Sess., 6th C'ee, 292nd Meeting, para. 7; 9th Sess., 409th Meeting, para. 23.

[22] "Report to the General Assembly, [1949], *Y.B. Int'l L. Comm'n*, 277, 286.

[23] M. Whiteman, 5 *Digest of International Law*, 230–50, 321–702, 706–873, (1965). The nearest item is the marginal note at 475: "Stanleyville, 1964—rescue operation, humanitarian reasons."

[24] As in the case of the Beira resolution: S.C. Res. 221, 2 U.N. SCOR (1966).

[25] As a friendly critic has pointed out: Bowett, 13 *Int'l & Comp. L.Q.* 1107–8 (1964).

[26] Bowett appears to be the only exception; *see* Bowett, *Self-defence in International Law*, 95, (1958). His view is very much by the way with a minimum of citation of authority.

[27] As Bowett does, principally in the work last cited. *See also* Waldock, 81 *Recueil des Cours*, 455, 466–67, 503 (1952–II).

[28] The argument involves a total failure to examine the nature of the customary law at the material time, namely, in 1945.

do not suggest that the erratic "rights of intervention" variously propounded by pre-1928 writers survive.

The force of the preceding section is this. When Lillich[29] quotes my conclusion that any legal basis for humanitarian intervention is now "extremely tenuous"[30] as a mere opinion, he does not make it clear that this view accords with that of numerous distinguished authorities. Moreover, my view is not an opinion casually thrown out, but is the outcome of a very extensive examination of state practice, especially in the period 1880–1945. Lillich's handling of the literature seems little short of arbitrary when, having referred to Article 2 (paragraphs 4 and 7) of the Charter, he then observes:[31] "Until recently there has been little discussion of whether these provisions prohibit the right to intervene with force to protect one's nationals or to protect nationals of a third State or the State against which the intervention is directed." This ignores a very large literature. In my work, *International Law and the Use of Force by States*, I devote several substantial sections to these issues and provide numerous references. The point is that it is impossible to place any form of intervention in the context of the law without examining the legal regime *as a whole*. Many writers spend little time discussing forcible protection of nationals or humanitarian intervention *as such* because they are commonly regarded as no longer viable categories.

3. STATE PRACTICE

In my own work on the use of force, I place special emphasis on the relevant state practice and diplomatic materials. Indeed, a policy-oriented view, as well as a concern for state practice as such, requires such an emphasis. The ILA Report and Lillich's articles on humanitarian intervention are almost entirely devoid[32] of any serious examination of the practice in the period of "customary international law," apparently pre–1945.[33] Reference is made to Turkish treatment of Christians and Russian treatment of Jews —instances of diplomatic intervention. The other pre–1914 references are to the collective intervention in Greece in 1827 and American action in Cuba in 1898. Both these cases can only be recruited as examples by "ex post factoism." The governments of the time did not use a legal justification

---

[29] ILA Report, *supra* note 1, at 14; Lillich, *supra* note 2 at 346; *id. supra* note 2, at 217.

[30] Brownlie, *International Law and the Use of Force by States*, 298 (1963). In fact, he is quoting my view on forcible protection of nationals. My conclusion on humanitarian intervention appears at 342.

[31] ILA Report, *supra* note 1, at 11–12.

[32] ILA Report, *supra* note 1, at 10–11; Lillich, *supra* note 2, at 332; *id.*, *supra* note 2, at 209.

[33] By a solecism, Lillich assumes an opposition between the U.N. Charter and customary law.

in the case of the Greek insurgency.[34] Jurists classify the intervention in Cuba in 1898 in various ways, and the Joint Resolution of Congress justified the intervention in terms of American interests.[35] An examination of the practice[36] provides one possibly genuine example of altruistic action, namely, the intervention of 1860 in Syria to prevent the recurrence of massacres of Maronite Christians. The only approximation to use of the justification between 1913 and 1945 was in the Proclamation on the German occupation of Bohemia and Moravia, made by Hitler on March 15, 1939. In this, he referred to "assaults on the life and liberty of minorities, and the purpose of disarming Czech troops and terrorist bands threatening the lives of minorities."[37]

The period of the United Nations Charter is totally lacking in practice on the point. However, the ILA Report[38] holds out the Stanleyville operation of 1964 and the initial introduction of troops into the Dominican Republic as instances of permissible intervention to protect human rights. The Stanleyville operation took place with the authorization of the Government of the Congo, which, both legally and otherwise, makes a great deal of difference.[39] The landing of troops in the Dominican Republic in 1965 was without the authorization of the local sovereign. Certainly, on April 30, the United States President stated that the object had been to protect the lives of Americans and nationals of other countries. Of this, two observations are amply justified. First, on the facts, it is very difficult to believe that this was the objective or, at any rate, the principal objective. Secondly, even if that were the objective, it does not provide a legal justification for use of force today. The truth is that one cannot treat all state conduct as "practice." The United States action in the Dominican Republic was an action of national self-interest and was simply illegal. The deputy legal adviser, Leonard Meeker, came close to admitting this when he observed in retrospect: "It will surprise no one here if I say that international law which cannot deal with facts such as these, and in a way that has some hope of setting a troubled nation on the path of peace and reconstruction, is not the kind of law I believe in."[40] The writer's opinion is that a state using force on the territory of another, without the license of the effective government, has a burden of justification to discharge, since it is presumptively a trespasser. On the evidence, the United States had no more title to intervene than did the U.S.S.R. in the similar political circumstances in Czechoslovakia in 1968.

[34] Brownlie, *supra* note 30 at 339.

[35] *Id.* at 46.

[36] *Id.* at 45–46, 339–40.

[37] Woodward and Butler (eds.), IV *Documents on British Foreign Policy 1919–1939*, no. 259 at 257.

[38] ILA Report, *supra* note 1, at 16. *See further* Lillich, *supra* note 2 at 338–44; *id.*, *supra* note 3 at 213–16.

[39] *See* 5 M. Whiteman, *supra* note 23 at 475.

[40] Meeker, 53 *Dept. State Bull.* at 64 (1965), quoted by Lillich in *supra* note 2, at 343.

4. THE ARGUMENTS FOR LEGALITY OF INTERVENTION TO PROTECT HUMAN RIGHTS

My examination so far leads to three conclusions. First, the role of humanitarian intervention, even before the first attempt at regulating resort to war in the League Covenant, was dubious, and the practice probably did not present a constant and uniform usage.[41] Secondly, the practice of the League period cannot be said to assist the somewhat derelict doctrine, although a number of writers, especially prior to the Kellogg-Briand Pact, continued to give it support.[42] Thirdly, the practice in the period of the United Nations Charter is totally inadequate to the task of establishing an interpretation in terms of subsequent conduct of the parties favorable to intervention to protect human rights.

There are two points remaining for consideration. First, how is the "protection of human rights" to be defined? This point will be reserved, partly because the issue of definition is not necessarily identical with the substance of the matter—the existence of the particular legal title to act. Secondly, apart from the subsequent conduct of the parties as a guide to interpretation, what is the proper interpretation of the Charter provisions? The approach to the Charter of the ILA subcommittee is curious to a degree since, in contrast to most lawyers, they place the customary law and the Charter in opposition. For most lawyers the principles of the Charter are the customary law, *i.e.*, general international law, governing use of force by states.[43] This is especially the case after twenty-five years of state practice based upon the Charter.

The ILA subcommittee's[44] remark that the drafters of the Charter "paid no attention to whether these doctrines [of humanitarian intervention] were to survive the Charter" is simply not true. The participating governments took a view of the legal regime as a whole and, because they made no reference to what statesmen would have regarded as a non-issue, it can hardly be said that they were reserving their position on the point.

The ILA subcommittee produced two other points. The first was to cite[45] Professors Reisman and Thomas[46] for the view that intervention which does not impair the "territorial integrity or political independence" of a state is not prohibited by Article 2(4). This argument is used by very few lawyers and has long been discredited. If there is an ambiguity, then, according to ordinary principles of interpretation, one has recourse to the preparatory materials. These make it clear that the phrase "against the territorial integrity" was added at San Francisco at the behest of small states

---

[41] *Asylum* case, [1950] I.C.J. 276–7.
[42] *See* the citations collected in Brownlie, *supra* note 30, at 341.
[43] *See, e.g.*, Lord McNair, *Law of Treaties*, 216–18 (1961).
[44] ILA Report, *supra* note 1, at 11.
[45] *See* ILA Report, *supra* note 1, at 12, and notes 24–28.
[46] A. Thomas & A. Thomas, *Non-Intervention*, 15 (1956).

wanting a stronger guarantee against intervention.[47] Of course, the states taking action within the territory of other states commonly attempt to mitigate their policies by assertions that their motives are limited or even benevolent. The other legal argument in the sub-committee's Report[48] is irrelevant to the present issue. This asserts, correctly, that the United Nations can intervene, if the state violating human rights causes an actual threat to peace.

5. POLICY ISSUES

My own assumption is that, basically, Professor Lillich is intent on making lawyers look afresh at humanitarian intervention and that it is constructive to look at his views on their merits as a legislative proposal. A preliminary point to be made is the unprepossessing character of the historical evidence: the near impossibility of discovering an aptitude of governments in general[49] for carefully moderated, altruistic, and genuine interventions to protect human rights. What follows is concerned with humanitarian intervention *as it would be practiced* on the basis of existing evidence of behavior patterns. Naturally, the moral setting, even in genuine cases, is far from simple. There is a moral and legislative problem of the type raised by euthanasia, itself a form of "humanitarian intervention." Euthanasia is unlawful, but doctors on occasion commit technical breaches of the law, for example, by administering massive drug dosages which accelerate coma and death. It is very generally assumed that legalizing euthanasia would alter the moral climate and produce harmful abuse.

Particularly when considering policy issues, attention should be paid to the actual behavior of states. Reference to the behavior of states before 1920, or 1945, on the premise that in the practice of that time one can find models of humanitarian intervention, involves a failure to see the development of the law as a whole. Before 1945, matters of human rights were, apart from treaty, within the domestic jurisdiction of states. When the League Covenant was drafted, modest Japanese proposals concerning racial and religious discrimination received no support.[50] Guarantees concerning minorities were imposed only on defeated states and new states, such as Poland, as the price of recognition.[51] It is surprising to expect a worthwhile doctrine of intervention to protect human rights at a time when the most

---

[47] In case Professor Lillich considers these matters as not having been explored before, he should look in my book, *International Law and the Use of Force by States* at 265–68, where full documentation is available.

[48] ILA Report, *supra* note 1, at 13.

[49] This is literally a general statement and does not relate to the "imperialistic hypothesis." *Cf.* Lillich, *supra* note 2, at 327, note 15.

[50] *See* McKean, "The Principle of the Equality of Individuals under International Law" (unpublished thesis, Oxford).

[51] *Ibid.*

modest proposals not for implementing but for merely setting of standards were struck down as threats to domestic jurisdiction.

The present writer recognizes that domestic jurisdiction is much less of a shield than it was in 1920 in matters of human rights. The question remains whether state conduct in administering intervention unilaterally has improved since the period before the League and the United Nations. Is it the case that the performance of individual states is and would be better than the centralized enforcement and other measures available to the United Nations? The latter is certainly unreliable, but is the alternative more reliable? I am accused of "throwing the baby out with the bath water" by adopting a cautious attitude to intervention to protect human rights,[52] but my view is that those making novel proposals need to produce more evidence. What is the price *in human terms* of intervention? What were the casualty ratios in the Stanleyville operation in 1964, the Dominican Republic in 1965, and other possible examples? How many were killed in order to "save lives?" To what extent does the typical intervention cause collateral harms by exacerbating a civil war, introducing indiscriminate use of air power in support operations, and so on? Was there a policy of pacification and general involvement, together with extraction of concessions by treaty or otherwise as the price of withdrawal?[53]

Since a part of Lillich's argument is based on the *essence* of state practice, *i.e.*, on what it was really about, aside from the existence of some formal title to intervention, one can also look at the evidence in his way. The *general* picture, as others may see it, is not encouraging. In the years of Stanleyville and the landings in the Dominican Republic, there were far more serious and persistent threats to human rights which were ignored. In 1965, not less than 300,000 persons of Chinese origin were murdered in Indonesia. The facts were well reported in the world press. The regime responsible received massive material support from several governments, including a million-pound-sterling credit from the United Kingdom. The whole field is riven by political expediency and capriciousness. One area of human rights in which there is a strong consensus in the United Nations is racial discrimination and especially the practice of *apartheid*. The United States has shown caution in supporting even mandatory economic sanctions against South Africa through the Security Council.[54] Moreover, human rights is a category which can provide good public relations for national policies. In the Western hemisphere, concern for human rights sharpened considerably after the change of regime in Cuba in 1959.

There are other, more precise, considerations of policy. A major issue, unexplored by the ILA subcommittee, is the whole question of the use of

---

[52] ILA Report, *supra* note 1, at 14.

[53] The realities of the "collective intervention" in China from 1900–1901 are chronicled by F. Grob, *The Relativity of War and Peace*, 64–79 (1949).

[54] It may seem unfair to single out the United States, but Lillich places much emphasis on United States recent practice.

force in community relations. The situation in Ulster, the desegregation issue in the United States, and comparable problems in many countries, cannot be "solved" by a use of force. Community relations can be policed in a crude sense; massacres can be prevented. The wrong kind of intervention and the drawing of police lines, however, may increase alienation, worsen communal relations, and produce new problems. A further point of great importance is the extent to which the position of minorities is hazarded by foreign protection or sponsorship. There is a good deal of literature, ignored by the ILA subcommittee, on the working of the League of Nations machinery for the protection of minorities. Even when the supervision was through international machinery and was not very demanding, it was felt by many commentators that the position of "minority" groups within the state was invidious by reason of their partly externalized status.

6. THE VALUE OF PROTO-LEGAL GUIDELINES

The ILA subcommittee's Report recapitulates[55] five standards formulated by Professor John Norton Moore[56] which can be used in evaluating the legitimacy of a putative humanitarian intervention. They are as follows: "(1) An immediate and extensive threat to fundamental human rights, particularly a threat of widespread loss of human life; (2) A proportional use of force which does not threaten greater destruction of values than the human rights at stake; (3) A minimal effect on authority structures; (4) A prompt disengagement, consistent with the purpose of the action; and (5) Immediate full reporting to the Security Council and appropriate regional organizations." Nanda and Lillich[57] have offered criteria which are similar but include the existence of an invitation by the recognized government and the relative disinterestedness of the intervening state or states. If an invitation to intervene has been made, then the action would be lawful on any view. Apart from that and consistent with my own view of the law, I would regard such criteria as of value, as providing (a) good criteria should humanitarian intervention become a part of the law, and (b) a fine basis for a political plea in mitigation in parliaments, U.N. organs, and regional organizations. My enthanasia parallel applies here: a defense lawyer and a court still need to distinguish the false from the genuine case, as a matter of mitigation.

7. DEFINITION OF INTERVENTION TO PROTECT HUMAN RIGHTS

A subject not taken up by the ILA subcommittee is the isolation of "intervention situations." Obviously, they do not extend to all violations. Profes-

[55] ILA Report, *supra* note 1, at 15.

[56] Moore, "The Control of Foreign Intervention in Internal Conflict," 9 *Va. J. Int'l L.* 205 at 264 (1969).

[57] *See* the ILA Report, *supra* note 1, at 15.

sor Moore refers to "an immediate and extensive threat to fundamental human rights, particularly a widespread loss of human life." Oppenheim (edited by Hersch Lauterpacht)[58] gives apparent approbation to intervention "when a state renders itself guilty of cruelties against and persecution of its nationals in such a way as to deny their fundamental human rights and to shock the conscience of mankind." Since a good number of states qualify in this way every decade, the opportunities for intervention will be very many. It is also the case that only a few powerful states will have a choice of voluntary intervention of this kind. Nearly every legal issue may raise a problem of definition, but few are on this scale. It is significant that governments are commonly more cautious than writers in giving currency to vaguely formulated and easily abused excuses for unilateral action. In the Cuban missile crisis, the United States Department of State avoided reference to the somewhat fugitive concept of anticipatory self-defense[59] and chose to use a justification related to the Organization of American States as a regional arrangement.[60] Various states have neighbors playing host to intermediate-range ballistic missiles, just as they may have neighbors guilty of cruelties which may shock the conscience of mankind. "Realism" in the sphere of policy includes restraint and caution in state policy.

8. HUMANITARIAN INTERVENTION: PERMISSIBLE FORMS

The presentation so far rests on the proposition that unilateral action by a state in the territory of another state on the ground that human rights require protection, or a threat of force against a state for this reason, is unlawful. Nevertheless, action in part concerned with the protection of human rights and the prevention of genocide may be lawful under one of several titles in existing law. Under Chapter VII of the Charter, action may be taken in instances of violations of human rights which give rise to a threat to the peace. Such action may relate to Articles 40 (provisional measures), 41 (economic sanctions), or 42 (military sanctions). Peacekeeping operations, of which the United Nations Force in Cyprus (UNFICYP) is an excellent example,[61] may have a function closely related to preventing communal strife and oppression of minorities.

Regional action under Chapter VIII of the United Nations Charter may extend to threats to the peace of the region generated by violations of human rights. In the crisis in the Dominican Republic in 1965, the United States was anxious to open the umbrella of regional action as quickly as

---

[58] L. Oppenheim, *International Law*, 312–13 (8th ed., H. Lauterpacht ed. 1955).

[59] See L. Henkin, *How Nations Behave*, 227–36, (1968).

[60] Leonard Meeker and others, writing subsequently, did not forbear to rely on anticipatory self-defense, but this was not the stance of the United States Government as such.

[61] UNFICYP is a creation of the Security Council, apparently under Chapter VI of the Charter.

possible. The Security Council has shown itself to be tolerant and, indeed, supine in the face of regional initiatives or acts of political solidarity not easy to reconcile with the clear terms of Article 53 of the United Nations Charter. Regional policies may have little to do with human rights as such; the O.A.U. was concerned by the Nigerian Civil War principally in terms of a fear of secessionist tendencies.

Government invitation, though not without its difficulties,"[62] may provide a legal basis for intervention. Finally, intervention may be lawful, in the sense of "not prohibited" but a part of the competence of states, in areas outside national, *i.e.*, exclusive territorial jurisdiction. Thus intervention may be lawful to prevent atrocities by insurgents, pirates, terrorists, and others not acting on behalf of a state or organization of states, in control of ships, aircraft or spacecraft, on or over the high seas, in space or over Antarctica or areas with a similar regime.[63]

9. CONCLUDING REMARKS

My general position is clear and general recapitulation is unhelpful. But a few points may be made by way of emphasis. The position taken up by Lillich is completely outside the general consensus of state practice and the opinion of experts of various nationalities. In the Sixth Committee of the General Assembly, when Spiropoulos once stated that intervention to prevent genocide against a racially related minority in a neighboring state should be lawful,[64] the reaction from other delegates, including those of Israel, Nationalist China, and Panama, was unfavorable.[65] A development proximate to a concept of humanitarian intervention is the support by some members of the United Nations, including most members of the O.A.U., for the view that intervention against a liberation movement is unlawful and assistance to such a movement is lawful.[66] It is common knowledge that there is no consensus on this as yet in the United Nations.[67]

I am in favor of humanitarian intervention, *i.e.*, effective implementation of human rights, in conditions in which this can occur within the law and when the methods and circumstances of the operation do not lead to results which bear no positive relation to the original objective, even assum-

---

[62] Brownlie, *supra* note 30, at 321–27.

[63] On the seizure of the passenger liner *Santa Maria* in 1961 by Captain Galvao, *see* Green, 37 *Brit. Y.B.I.L.* 496 (1961).

[64] Off. Recs., Gen. Ass., 9th Sess., 6th Committee, 409th Meeting, para. 23.

[65] Off. Recs., Gen. Ass., 9th Sess., 6th Committee, 412th Meeting, para. 35; 417th Meeting, para. 31; 418th Meeting, para. 13.

[66] These large issues were not within the scope of my paper. *Cf.* Judge Ammoun, Separate Opinion, *Barcelona Traction* Case (Second Phase), [1970] *I.C.J.* 304.

[67] But *see* the Report of the Drafting Committee, U.N. Gen. Ass., 1970 Special Committee on Principles of International Law Concerning Friendly Relations and Co-operation among States: item, "The principle of equal rights and self-determination of peoples."

ing it to be genuine. What I find depressing is the absence of evidence that proponents of humanitarian intervention and other very plastic doctrines have spent much time examining state practice in detail.[68] This should be essential for those concerned with policy. In concluding, I would reiterate the conclusion in Tucker's edition of Kelsen's *Principles*:[69]

> In the last analysis, however, criticism of any attempt to restrict the right of self-help, while failing to provide those institutions which would render self-help unnecessary, rests upon a reading of history that can hardly be regarded as self-evident. This interpretation must be that more often than not the individual use of force by States has served the purposes of law and that to restrict States in the measures of self-help they may take must seriously jeopardize the prospect of ever achieving a satisfactory and effective rule of law in international society. Given the circumstances that have always attended the use of force in international society, this criticism is surely questionable. If anything, the history of State relations and of the occasions in which States have allegedly employed force as a legitimate measure of self-help suggest quite the contrary interpretation.[70]

[68] My work on the use of force relates as closely as possible to state practice and diplomatic materials and provides a good many appropriate references. Critics too often quote my conclusions but ignore the evidence very fully presented. *See* Brownlie, *supra* note 30.

[69] H. Kelsen, *supra* note 20, at 87. This passage and its footnote do not appear in the first edition.

[70] The footnote to this passage reads: "A similar conclusion seems equally appropriate with respect to the view that in the relations of states force has more often than not served as an instrument for vindicating the requirements of a 'minimal justice'." *Id.* 87 n.

Chapter 11 | **Humanitarian Intervention:**
A Reply to Ian Brownlie and a Plea for
Constructive Alternatives | *Richard B. Lillich*

The preceding chapter by Ian Brownlie represents another welcome contribution to the current debate on the contemporary relevance of the doctrine of humanitarian intervention.[1] As could be expected of one of the leading advocates of the view that Article 2(4) of the United Nations Charter absolutely prohibits forcible self-help by States, save in cases of individual or collective self-defense against armed attack authorized by Article 51, the distinguished author of *International Law and the Use of Force by States*[2] reaches the categorical conclusion that "unilateral action by a State in the territory of another State on the ground that human rights require protection, or a threat of force against a State for this reason, is unlawful."[3] Somewhat unexpectedly, however, he finds the present writer's criteria for

---

[1] *See* Brownlie, "Humanitarian Intervention," Chapter 10 *supra* [hereinafter cited as Brownlie]. The debate may be said to have begun with the publication of two articles by the present writer, "Forcible Self-Help by States to Protect Human Rights," 53 *Iowa L. Rev.* 325 (1967), and "Intervention to Protect Human Rights," 15 *McGill L.J.* 205 (1969). *See also* Int'l L. Ass'n, "Interim Report of the Sub-Committee on the International Protection of Human Rights by General International Law," in *Report of the Fifty-Fourth Conference* 633 (1970). As Brownlie correctly assumes, "basically, Professor Lillich is intent on making lawyers look afresh at humanitarian intervention. . . ." Brownlie 223. Other writers, especially concerned with human rights deprivations in Rhodesia and Nigeria, have accepted this call. *See, e.g.,* McDougal & Reisman, "Rhodesia and the United Nations: The Lawfulness of International Concern," 62 *Am. J. Int'l L.* 1 (1968), and Reisman, "Humanitarian Intervention to Protect the Ibos" 167, in R. Lillich (ed.), *Humanitarian Intervention and the United Nations* (1973).

[2] I. Brownlie, *International Law and the Use of Force by States* (1963) [hereinafter cited as I. Brownlie].

[3] Brownlie 226. While not unexpected, given the general nature of his views, Brownlie's blanket condemnation of unilateral humanitarian intervention was by no means a certainty. Previously he had not ventured beyond the cautious assertion that "it is extremely doubtful if this form of intervention has survived . . . the general prohibition of resort to force to be found in the United Nations Charter." I. Brownlie, *supra* note 2, at 342. *See also* text accompanying note 6 *infra*. Thus the preceding chapter constitutes a partial clarification as well as a general restatement of his views on the subject.

© The Procedural Aspects of International Law Institute, Inc., 1973. The author prepared this chapter for the research project on Humanitarian Intervention Through the United Nations, established under the terms of a grant from the National Endowment for the Humanities to the above Institute. The NEH grant was made possible by matching grants from the Doherty Foundation and The Fund for Peace, to whom the author also wishes to express his appreciation.

judging the legitimacy of a state's use of forcible self-help for humanitarian purposes of some value, if only "as providing a fine basis for a political plea in mitigation in parliaments, U.N. organs and regional organizations."[4] Indeed, by twice citing a supposed parallel between euthanasia and humanitarian intervention, a parallel one hopes he will develop more fully in his subsequent writings, Brownlie seems to suggest that some such interventions, while technically breaches of Article 2(4), might be condoned, if not actually approved, by the world community.[5]

Any critique of Brownlie's views on this subject, of course, must invoke an aura of *déjà vu*: it has all been said before.[6] Moreover, as Professor Jennings has aptly observed, the "argument cannot be solved by dialectics; it will only finally be resolved by the actual course events take. The matter is not in the hands of the lawyers."[7] In the opinion of the present writer, the actual course events took during 1971 in Bangladesh (formerly East Pakistan) should put an end once and for all to the doctrinal argument that "action in part concerned with the protection of human rights and the prevention of genocide may be lawful" when, and only when, undertaken by international institutions.[8] Surely the abject inability of the United Nations to take effective action to terminate the genocidal conduct and alleviate the mass suffering in Bangladesh necessitates a fundamental reassessment by Brownlie and like-minded authorities of the role of self-help, and especially of humanitarian intervention, in international affairs today. Pending such a reassessment, many of the specific arguments made in the preceding chapter require "prompt, adequate and effective" rebuttal, if only for the record, while Brownlie's general attitude toward humanitarian intervention, including his suggested euthanasia approach, warrants a more extensive critique.

[4] Brownlie 225. *See* text at notes 126–130 *infra*.

[5] *Id.* at 223 & 225.

[6] Most trenchantly, by Stone in his "Book Review," 59 *Am. J. Int'l L.* 396 (1965). For a rejoinder to this critique of his treatise, see Brownlie, "A Reply to Julius Stone," 63 *Am. J. Int'l L.* 795 (1969). Stone's monograph remains the standard work construing Articles 2(4) and 51 to permit a limited right of forcible self-help by states. *See* J. Stone, *Aggression and World Order* 98–101 (1958). Given his present absolute approach to Charter interpretation—*see* text at and accompanying note 3 *supra*—it is noteworthy that in a 1959 review of Stone's book Brownlie did not exhibit the certainty he now displays. "It is of course true that certain rights of intervention *may* have survived in the customary law; and the judgment of the *Corfu Channel* (*Merits*) *Case* on one interpretation permits forcible self-help at least in the enforcement of rights of passage through international straits." Brownlie, "Book Review," 8 *Int'l & Comp. L.Q.* 707, 717 (1959).

[7] Jennings, "General Course on Principles of International Law," 121 *Recueil Des Cours* 325, 584 (1967–II). "The actual direction in which events turn will probably be relatively little affected by legal argument about the 'right' meaning and interpretation of Articles 2(4) and 51. The problem is not one of drafting legal precepts controlling the use of force but one of devising international institutions through which the use of force in international relationships can be legally ordered and controlled on an international instead of a sovereignty basis."

[8] Brownlie 226.

I. PRE-CHARTER PRACTICE

One interested in the doctrine of humanitarian intervention and its contemporary relevance approaches the subject cautiously. On the one hand, some scholars, including a friendly critic of the present writer (and, incidentally, of Brownlie too), consider "that past law relating to humanitarian intervention has little relevance to the present system."[9] On the other hand, numerous authorities, including Brownlie, "place special emphasis on the relevant State practice and diplomatic materials."[10] Rightly noting that "a policy-oriented view, as well as a concern for State practice as such, requires such an emphasis," Dr. Brownlie finds this writer's prior studies "almost wholly devoid of any serious examination of the practice in the period of 'customary international law,' apparently pre-1945."[11] While the present writer admittedly has yet to essay an extensive examination of pre-Charter humanitarian intervention claims,[12] in the words of McDougal and Reisman, responding to a similar indictment by Marshall,[13] "the raw materials for such a survey are readily accessible in many sources."[14] Reiteration of the numerous instances where humanitarian interventions occurred during the nineteenth and early twentieth centuries previously had been considered superfluous.[15]

A cursory perusal of Chapter I ("Humanitarian Intervention") of Dean Ganji's *International Protection of Human Rights*, a standard work not included in Brownlie's references, reveals many cases where interventions occurred for humanitarian purposes. In addition to the intervention of 1860 by Austria, France, Great Britain, Prussia, and Russia in Syria, acknowl-

---

[9] Claydon, "Humanitarian Intervention and International Law, 1 *Queen's Intra. L.J.* 36, 61 (1969).

[10] Brownlie 220.

[11] *Id.* at 220. *But see* Claydon, *supra* note 9, at 56, who refers to the writer's "comprehensive examination of rules relating to humanitarian intervention under customary international law."

[12] Such an examination is now in progress under the grant described in the acknowledgment at the beginning of this chapter.

[13] Marshall, "Comment," 3 *Int'l Lawyer* 435 (1969).

[14] McDougal & Reisman, "*Response*," 3 *Int'l Lawyer* 438, 441 (1969). Note also their mixture of prescience and outrage: "In our contemporary strife-torn world, with Biafra following quickly upon the continuing tragedy of Rhodesia and with perhaps even greater tragedies to come, Professor Marshall's bland demurrer to the entire institution of humanitarian intervention can only merit prompt consignment to complete oblivion." *Id.*

[15] *Accord, id.* at 438: "We had not thought it necessary in a journal for international lawyers to spell out in detail the content of the doctrine of humanitarian intervention or to multiply references to establish its long and continuing authority. A venerable institution of customary international law, reconfirmed at the inception of the modern period by both Grotius and Vattel, humanitarian intervention has been regarded as accepted law by most contemporary international lawyers. The foundation of the doctrine has been the shared concern of the peoples of the world for the minimum conditions of the survival of humanity."

edged somewhat grudgingly by Brownlie as "one possibly genuine example of altruistic action,"[16] Ganji lists the following instances:

1. The intervention of France, Great Britain, and Russia against the Turkish massacres and suppression of the Greeks, which resulted in the independence of Greece in 1830;[17]
2. The peremptory demands of Austria, France, Italy, Prussia, and Russia (during the years 1866–68) on the Ottoman Empire for the institution of positive action leading to the betterment of the lot of the persecuted Christian population of Crete;[18]
3. The Russian intervention against Turkey (1877–78) on the occasion of insurrections resulting from Turkish misrule and from the outrageous persecutions of the Christian populations of Bosnia, Herzegovina, and Bulgaria;[19] and
4. The intervention of Austria, Russia, Great Britain, Italy, and France in Turkey as a result of insurrections and misrule in Macedonia (1903–8).[20]

Moreover, to these cases of humanitarian intervention he adds "many instances of humanitarian protest and representation by one or more states on behalf of the citizens of other states."[21] While, apparently ignoring the implications of his own investigations, Ganji surprisingly concludes that "the doctrine of humanitarian intervention *does not seem* to claim the authority of a customary rule of international law,"[22] he frankly concedes that this view is a minority one by acknowledging that the doctrine "claims the authority of such jurists as Grotius, Vattel, Wheaton, Heiberg, Woolsey, Bluntschli, Westlake, Rougier, Arntz, Winfield, Stowell, Borchard and many others."[23]

Since Brownlie himself once asserted that "[b]y the end of the nineteenth century the majority of publicists admitted that a right of humanitarian intervention (*l'intervention d'humanité*) existed,"[24] citing nine of the above twelve authorities, his complaint that the present writer has failed to examine pre-Charter practice adequately,[25] a failure perhaps excused by the writer's reliance upon the authoritativeness of Brownlie's own treatise, is

---

[16] Brownlie 221.
[17] M. Ganji, *International Protection of Human Rights* 22–24 (1962).
[18] *Id.* at 26–29.
[19] *Id.* at 29–33.
[20] *Id.* at 33–37.
[21] *Id.* at 39. He describes them *id.* at 39–41.
[22] *Id.* at 43 (emphasis added).
[23] *Id.* at 41. "On the other side, as opposed to this school, we find the non-interventionist school which claims the authority of such jurists as Halleck, Angelins Werdenhagen, Kant, Despagnet, Mamiani, and Pradier-Fodere." *Id.* For an excellent annotated bibliography listing the many authorities who recognized the doctrine of humanitarian intervention, see E. Stowell, *Intervention in International Law* 461–540 (1921).
[24] I. Brownlie, *supra* note 2, at 338.
[25] *See* text at note 11 *supra*.

somewhat puzzling. After devoting a single paragraph in his treatise to an examination of state practice, Brownlie does reach the conclusion, repeated in the preceding chapter, that contrary to the views of the above authorities, "no genuine case of humanitarian intervention has occurred, with the possible exception of the occupation of Syria in 1860 and 1861."[26] Yet this lame attempt to discredit the very authorities he otherwise relies upon produces the opposite effect in the reader. True, "[t]he doctrine was inherently vague and its protagonists gave it a variety of forms,"[27] but it was acknowledged by scholars and invoked by governments, and no contemporary reassessment can deprive it retroactively of its pre-Charter impact.[28]

Finally, Brownlie's somewhat ironic allegation that the jurists he cites "have tended to *ex post facto* classification of interventions which were justified without reference to any specific doctrine of humanitarian intervention"[29] cannot go unchallenged. His reference in the preceding chapter to "the collective intervention in Greece in 1827 and American action in Cuba in 1898" as examples of "ex post factoism," moreover, provides a convenient opportunity to refute this charge.[30] In the case of Greece, the Preamble to the London Treaty, which governed the intervention of France, Great Britain, and Russia, specifically records that their objective was to put "an end to the sanguinary struggle," to put "a stop to the effusion of blood. . . ."[31] Motivated "no less by *sentiments of humanity*, than by interests for the tranquility of Europe,"[32] they sought to establish peace between the contending parties. Other motives undoubtedly were at work, but Ganji rightly notes thta they were "not contrary but rather complementary to the humanitarian objects."[33] As for Brownlie's disingenuous assertion that "the Joint Resolution of Congress justified the [Cuban] intervention in terms of American interests,"[34] reference need only be made to its Preamble,

---

[26] I. Brownlie, *supra* note 2, at 340. *See* text at note 16 *supra*.

[27] I. Brownlie, *supra* note 2, at 338. *Accord*, M. McDougal & F. Feliciano, *Law and Minimum World Public Order* 536 (1961), who speak of the "amorphous doctrines on 'humanitarian intervention' . . . ."

[28] Despite the fact that a respected scholar describes it as "highly questionable," Friedmann, "Intervention and International Law I," in L. Jaquet (ed.), *Intervention in International Politics* 40, 59 (1971), the present writer sees no reason to modify an earlier assertion that "the doctrine appears to have been so clearly established under customary international law that only its limits and not its existence is subject to debate." Lillich, "Intervention to Protect Human Rights," *supra* note 1, at 210. Since the preceding sentence makes no attempt to gloss over the uncertain aspects of the doctrine, *see also* text at and accompanying note 27 *supra*, another critic's charge that the present writer has ignored relevant data in order to achieve "greater heights of certianty [sic]" constitutes a classic example of "strawmanship." *See* Claydon, *supra* note 9, at 52.

[29] I. Brownlie, *supra* note 2, at 339.

[30] *See* Brownlie 220.

[31] Treaty Between Great Britain, France and Russia for the Pacification of Greece, July 6, 1827, 14 *Brit. & For. State Papers* 632–33 (1826–27).

[32] *Id.* at 633 (emphasis added).

[33] M. Ganji, *supra* note 17, at 23 n. 49.

[34] Brownlie 221, *citing* I. Brownlie *supra* note 2, at 46.

which recounts "the abhorent conditions which have existed for more than three years in the Island of Cuba . . . [and which] have *shocked the moral sense* of the people of the United States. . . ."[35] While once again other motives for intervention obviously existed, Stowell's characterization of the action by the United States as "[o]ne of the most important instances of humanitarian intervention"[36] easily withstands the charge of "ex post factoism."[37]

Admittedly, the rather loose nineteenth-century rules governing the use of force meant that the various types of forcible self-help, as well as humanitarian intervention, "were not yet clearly differentiated as legal categories."[38] Nevertheless, commentators of the period, clearly innocent of "ex post factoism," quickly perceived the tension between the claims of humanity and the claims of non-intervention and sought to fashion a juridical basis for "[i]nterference on the score of humanity" in extreme circumstances.[39] As far back as 1836, for instance, Wheaton observed that:

> [t]he interference of the Christian powers of Europe in favour of the Greeks, who, after enduring ages of cruel oppression, had shaken off the Ottoman yoke, *affords a further illustration of the principles of international law authorizing such an interference*, not only where the interests and safety of the other powers are immediately affected by the internal transactions of a particular state, but where the general interests of humanity are infringed by the excesses of a barbarous and despotic government.[40]

[35] Preamble to the Joint Resolution of Congress of April 20, 1898, 30 Stat. 738 (1899) (emphasis added). Note the similarity between the emphasized words in the text and the standard description of conditions which sanction humanitarian intervention, *i.e.,* conditions which "shock the conscience of mankind. . . ." 1 L. Oppenheim, *International Law* § 137, at 312 (8th ed. H. Lauterpacht 1955).

[36] E. Stowell, *supra* note 23, at 481.

[37] In addition to the extract from the Preamble to the Joint Resolution of Congress quoted in the text at note 35 *supra*, which contradicts "ex post factoism," see also the first ground for forcible intervention advanced by President McKinley in his Special Message to Congress, namely, "the cause of humanity," the need "to put an end to the barbarities, bloodshed, starvation, and horrible miseries now existing [in Cuba], and which the parties to the conflict are either unable or unwilling to stop or mitigate." 6 J. B. Moore, *Digest of International Law* 219 (1906). Earlier in this message, moreover, the President specifically stated that in recommending intervention he was "following many historical precedents where neighboring states have interfered to check the hopeless sacrifices of life by internecine conflicts beyond their borders. . . ." *Id.*

[38] "In his survey to 1914, which reveals no surprises, Brownlie has perforce to acknowledge that a very wide state liberty of resort to war then existed, that the lines between this and resort to hostile measures short of war, intervention, self-defense, self-preservation and necessity were 'confused.' It would be more correct, of course, to say that, since there was liberty to resort to war, these categories were not yet clearly differentiated as legal categories." Stone, *supra* note 6, at 398–99.

[39] T. Woolsey, *International Law* 73 (3d ed. 1872).

[40] H. Wheaton, *Elements of International Law* 91 (1836). According to Stowell, Wheaton is the first scholar who attempted to establish a juridical basis for humanitarian intervention. *See* E. Stowell, *supra* note 23, at 469.

While the term "interference" persisted in use of some years,[41] Brownlie correctly observes that, after mid-century, writers began to employ the phrase "intervention"—"presumably as a result of increasing appearance of the term in state practice."[42] By 1900, as he points out, a majority of publicists acknowledged the existence of a doctrine called humanitarian intervention.[43] This traditional doctrine obviously should not be "superimposed on the present international legal order without regard to the criteria which formed the basis of past decisions,"[44] but since a careful examination of the criteria invoked in the humanitarian interventions mentioned above reveals so many similarities to contemporary claims to use force for humanitarian objectives, neither should its importance be dismissed out of hand.[45]

II. POST-CHARTER PRACTICE

The practice of states before 1945, to quote Falk, "exhibits many instances in which intervention was prompted by humanitarian considerations that one can condemn only by waving too vigorously the banners of sov-

[41] *See* text at note 39 *supra*.

[42] I. Brownlie, *supra* note 2, at 44. The appearance of the term coincided with the disappearance of Lord Palmerston from the British corridors of power. A recent biographer, describing Palmerston's strong objections to the improper use of language by his clerks in the Foreign Office, relates that "[f]rom time to time he flared up when his subordinates used words which he thought were of foreign origin. He insisted that they write 'interference', not 'intervention', which was a French word." J. Ridley, *Lord Palmerston* 111 (1971). Palmerston apparently maintained his "linguistic patriotism" during debates in the House of Commons as well. "When he said that an MP had talked about 'non-interference', the MP corrected him, and said 'Non-intervention'. 'I will not talk of non-intervention', said Palmerston, 'for it is not an English word'." *Id.* at 156. *See* text at note 24 *supra*.

[43] *Id.*

[44] Claydon, *supra* note 9, at 53.

[45] Professor Westlake's description of one reason why States intervene for humanitarian purposes could have been written with the events of Bangladesh in mind:
"In considering anarchy and misrule as a ground for intervention the view must not be confined to the physical consequences which they may have beyond the limits of the territory in which they rage. . . . The moral effect on the neighbouring population is to be taken into the account. Where these include considerable numbers allied by religion, language or race to the populations suffering from misrule to restrain the former from giving support to the latter in violation of the legal rights of the misruled state may be a task beyond the power of their government, or requiring it to resort to modes of constraint irksome to its subjects, and not necessary for their good order if they were not excited by the spectacle of miseries which they must feel acutely. It is idle to argue in such a case that the duty of the neighbouring peoples is to look on quietly. Laws are made for men and not for creatures of the imagination, and they must not create or tolerate for them situations which are beyond the endurance . . . of the best human nature that at the time and place they can hope to meet with. It would be outside our scope to pass judgment on present or recent cases, but it is by these principles that we must try such interventions as have taken place in Turkey, or as that of the United States in Cuba." J. Westlake, *International Law* 306-7 (1904).

ereignty."[46] The United Nations Charter, framed as World War II drew to a close, revealing the full horrors of Nazi Germany's treatment of the Jews, sought to furl these banners where matters of basic human rights were concerned.[47] While the Charter contains no provision authorizing unilateral or collective humanitarian intervention by States, neither does it specifically abolish the traditional doctrine.[48] Actually, despite Dr. Brownlie's vigorous objection, it warrants reiteration that "[t]he drafters of the Charter, as Dean Huston's study shows, paid no attention to whether these doctrines [of protection of nationals and humanitarian intervention] were to survive the *Charter.* . . ."[49] One therefore may accept as common ground Brownlie's contention "that it is impossible to place any form of intervention in the context of the law without examining the legal regime *as a whole*,"[50] while rejecting his conclusion that the Charter and subsequent practice thereunder absolutely forbids intervention for humanitarian purposes by a state or a group of states.

Examining the United Nations Charter "as a whole," it is apparent that its two major purposes are the maintenance of peace and the protection of human rights. Article 2(4), the Charter provision relevant to both these purposes, prohibits "the threat or use of force against the territorial integrity or political independence of any State, or in any other manner inconsistent with the Purposes of the United Nations." Since humanitarian interventions by states, far from being inconsistent with Charter purposes, actually may further one of the world organization's major objectives in many situations,

[46] R. Falk, *Legal Order in a Violent World* 161 (1968). "The treatment of the Jews by Hitler provides a recent vivid illustration of a situation in which respect for the internal autonomy seems to be less compelling than the impulses which prompt and, in the opinion expressed here, vindicate intervention." *Id.*

[47] *See, e.g.*, U.N. Charter arts. 55 & 56. "The human rights sought to be secured by the Charter are far broader in scope and content than those whose breach would traditionally permit humanitarian intervention." A. Thomas & A. Thomas, *Non-Intervention* 384 (1956).—Note, however, that, according to the Thomases, "it is doubtful if the Charter has made any extension of the general international law right to intervene for humanitarian purposes; as a matter of fact, by prohibiting intervention by force, except collective intervention by the organization in the event the actions constitute a threat to international peace, it has limited the general international law right to intervene for humanitarian purposes." *Id. Compare* text at and accompanying note 48 *infra.*

[48] I. Brownlie 342. *Compare* Reisman, *supra* note 1, at 39: "The advent of the United Nations has not excised this traditional customary right although it has set a structure of normative conditions about it."

[49] Lillich, "Intervention to Protect Human Rights," *supra* note 1, at 210. Brownlie objects to the above statement on the ground that it "is simply not true." Brownlie 222. In his opinion "[t]he participating governments took a view of the legal regime as a whole and, because they made no reference to what statesmen would have regarded as a non-issue, it can hardly be said that they were reserving their position on the point." *Id.* The criticized statement, of course, makes no claim that the drafters reserved their position. It merely describes what occurred at San Francisco, namely, that the drafters did not discuss humanitarian intervention. While Brownlie is entitled to draw whatever legal conclusions he wishes from this failure, so too should other commentators without having their factual observations impugned.

[50] Brownlie 220 (emphasis in original).

such interventions run afoul of Article 2(4) only if they are thought to affect the "territorial integrity" or "political independence" of the state against which they are directed. Brownlie, adopting what one commentator has called "an arid textualist approach,"[51] considers all humanitarian interventions by States to have such an effect and hence to violate the Charter. Taking what Professor Stone has labeled "the extreme view"[52] of Article 2(4), he rejects out-of-hand Stone's argument that what the article prohibits is not all threats or uses of force, but only those actions specifically directed against "the territorial integrity" or "political independence" of a state.[53] "This argument," Brownlie states, "is used by very few lawyers and has long been discredited."[54]

Stone's view is a minority one, admittedly, but, far from being "discredited," it seems to be gaining new recruits annually, at least insofar as humanitarian intervention is concerned. While the present writer agrees with Brownlie that "[c]ounting heads is not, of course, a sound way of resolving issues of principle,"[55] in view of the thirteen authorities Brownlie cites in his attempt to demonstrate that humanitarian intervention by states violates the United Nations Charter, a few contrary authorities should be mentioned here. First and foremost among these scholars is McDougal, who, several years ago, reassessing his earlier position,[56] acknowledged that

> I'm ashamed to confess that at one time I lent my support to the suggestion that article 2(4) and the related articles did preclude the use of self-help less than self-defense. On reflection, I think this was a very grave mistake, that article 2(4) and article 51 must be interpreted differently. . . . In the absence of collective machinery to protect against attack and deprivation, I would suggest that the principle of major purposes requires an interpretation which would honor self-help against prior unlawfulness. The principle of subsequent conduct certainly confirms this. Many states of the world have used force in situations short of the requirements of self-defense to protect their national interests.[57]

In collaboration with Reisman, he subsequently utilized this revised approach to justify non-United Nations intervention to prevent serious human rights deprivations.[58] Brownlie casually dismisses their conclusions on the

[51] Claydon, *supra* note 9, at 57.
[52] J. Stone, *supra* note 6, at 98.
[53] *Id.* at 95.
[54] Brownlie 222.
[55] *Id.* at 219.
[56] *See generally* M. McDougal & F. Feliciano, *Law and Minimum World Public Order* (1961).
[57] McDougal, "Authority to Use Force on the High Seas," 20 *Naval War College Rev.* 19, 28–29 (1967). Note that McDougal recommends reinterpreting both Articles 2(4) and 51. Exclusive reliance upon Article 51 to justify forcible self-help measures would cause problems for authorities like Brownlie, who believe that "humanitarian intervention is not a form of self-help. . . ." Brownlie 219. *See also* Lillich, "Forcible Self-Help to Protect Human Rights," *supra* note 1, at 336–37.
[58] *See* Reisman, note 1 *supra*.

ground that McDougal and Reisman "lean heavily on a flexible and teleological interpretation of treaty texts,"[59] but surely the convincing arguments they marshall, and which Brownlie in large measure chooses to ignore, deserve consideration.

In the first place, it should be noted that the above approach to humanitarian intervention is conditioned upon "the absence of collective machinery" to protect human rights, not upon a preference for unilateral over collective intervention.[60] Effective United Nations action remains everyone's goal. The real issue, which Brownlie largely ignores, and which is made especially poignant by events in Bangladesh, is whether, absent such action in serious human-rights deprivation cases, states today must sit by and do nothing merely because Article 2(4) arguably was intended by its drafters in 1945 to preclude unilateral humanitarian interventions. Doctrinal analysis of Article 2(4), much of it written shortly after the Charter's adoption or based upon attitudes and expectations formed during the immediate post-war period, frequently fails to mention that, to the extent that states consciously relinquished the right to use forcible self-help, they took such action under the assumption that the collective implementation measures envisaged by Chapter VII soon would be available. Yet even staunch supporters of the collective approach, such as Judge Jessup, admitted that unilateral humanitarian interventions might be permissible if the United Nations lacked the capacity to act speedily,[61] while skeptical observers like Stone foresaw more fundamental reasons justifying the doctrine's continued existence.[62]

Reisman, who accepts the Stone thesis that the United Nations Charter

[59] Brownlie 218.

[60] "Clearly international participation in the protection of human rights process is preferable to measures of forcible self-help undertaken by one or more states, whose reasons for acting may or may not accord with the inclusive interests of the world community. Unfortunately, the day when effective international procedures will exist still appears to be far off." Lillich, "Forcible Self-Help to Protect Human Rights," *supra* note 1, at 345 n. 116.

[61] "It would seem that the only possible argument against the substitution of collective measures under the Security Council for individual measures by a single state would be the inability of the international organization to act with the speed requisite to preserve life." P. Jessup, *A Modern Law of Nations* 170 (1949).

[62] "Indeed, whatever view we take of the technical legal question, it is well to pause and consider how it would be if States were committed by Membership in the United Nations to submit in default of collective action, to all kinds of illegality, injustice and inhumanity as long as these do not take the specific form of an 'armed attack' under Article 51. Suppose, for example, that a Great Power decided that the only way it could continue to control a satellite State was to wipe out the satellite's entire population and recolonise the area with 'reliable' people. Suppose the satellite government agreed to this measure and established the necessary mass extermination apparatus for carrying out the plan. Would the rest of the Members of the United Nations be compelled to stand by and watch this operation merely because requisite decision of United Nations organs was blocked, and the operation did not involve an 'armed attack' on any Member of the United Nations?" J. Stone, *supra* note 6, at 99.

does not absolutely rule out forcible self-help,[63] acknowledges that, as a historical interpretation, the contrary view espoused by Brownlie and other writers[64] is "quite accurate."

> From the standpoint of the contemporary needs of the international community however, it is clearly outmoded. Only in the most exceptional cases will the United Nations be capable of functioning as an international enforcer; in the vast majority of cases, the conflicting interests of diverse public order systems will block any action. A rational and contemporary interpretation of the Charter must conclude that article 2(4) suppresses self-help insofar as the organization can assume the role of enforcer. When it cannot, self-help prerogatives revive.[65]

As the above extract reveals—unlike Stone, who speaks in terms of an absolute right to use forcible self-help—Reisman regards the right as conditional. Hence his statement that, given the present status of the United Nations, "self-help prerogatives revive," and his correlative comment elsewhere about "the partial suspension of the full thrust of Article 2(4)."[66]

---

[63] Reisman criticizes the assumption made by exponents of the traditional approach "that self-help is no longer necessary, since an authoritative international organization can provide the police facilities for enforcement of international rights. Historically, this may be the correct interpretation of the Charter in general and article 2(4) in particular. However, subsequent dissension among the great powers in the Security Council has clearly rendered this construction caducous; rigorous adherence to the historical view means that self-help measures are rendered unlawful but no other form of enforcement takes their place." W. Reisman, *Nullity and Revision* 848–49 (1971).

One of the first observers to comment upon the difficulties caused by the traditional approach was Fitzmaurice, "The Foundations of the Authority of International Law and the Problem of Enforcement," 19 *Modern L. Rev.* 1, 5 (1956).

[64] Among the most noted being Quincy Wright, who repeatedly reiterated that any unilateral intervention "is clearly contrary to the United Nations Charter, which seeks to abolish forcible self-help in international relations except in individual or collective self-defense against armed attack, and relegates other law enforcement activities to collective action through the United Nations." Wright, "Espionage and the Doctrine of Non-Intervention in Internal Affairs," in R. Stanger (ed.), *Essays on Espionage and International Law* 3, 8 (1962).

[65] W. Reisman, *supra* note 63, at 850. He adds that "[i]nternational practice appears to substantiate this construction of the Charter," *id.* at 850, citing examples *id.* at 850–51. *See also* text at and accompanying note 86 *infra*.

[66] "The problem can be approached from the standpoint of the contemporary meaning of Charter Article 2(4), an apparently blanket proscription on the unilateral use of force, which had relevance, at least within the paper world of the Charter, when read in conjunction with the implementative programs of Chapter VII of that instrument. Unfortunately, the programs of Chapter VII were never realized. Hence, a continuing strict interpretation of Article 2(4) would be an invitation to lawbreakers who would anticipate a paralysis in the Security Council's decision dynamics; such an anticipation is by no means unrealistic. . . .

A more realistic policy formulation would recognize the present inability of the world community to move to implementation of Chapter VII and would therefore accept the partial suspension of the full thrust of Article 2(4)." Reisman, "Sanctions and Enforcement," in III C. Black & R. Falk (eds.), *The Future of the International Legal Order* 273, 332–33 (1971).

Although both approaches would justify unilateral humanitarian intervention today, Reisman's approach is preferable in that it clearly contemplates the gradual phasing out of the doctrine as the United Nations develops the capacity and the will to act in such situations.

In addition to being conditional, the McDougal-Reisman approach to humanitarian intervention relies upon a major-purposes construction of the Charter, under which the protection of human rights is accorded equal weight with the maintenance of peace. As mentioned above, this construction would permit humanitarian intervention by states despite Article 2(4) when such intervention were consistent with human rights objectives.[67] "A close reading of [Article 2(4)] will indicate that the prohibition is not against the use of coercion per se," Reisman, paraphrasing Stone, has observed, "but rather the use of force for specified unlawful means. . . ."[68] He continues:

> Since a humanitarian intervention seeks neither a territorial change nor a challenge to the political independence of the state involved and is not only not inconsistent with the Purposes of the United Nations but is rather in conformity with the most fundamental peremptory norms of the Charter, it is distortion to argue that it is precluded by Article 2(4). Insofar as it is precipitated by intense human rights deprivations and conforms to the general international legal regulations governing the use of force—economy, timeliness, commensurance, lawfulness of purpose and so on—it represents a vindication of international law, and is, in fact, substitute or functional enforcement.[69]

Although this construction of Article 2(4) has been called an exercise in "doctrinal manipulation" by Farer,[70] it at least merits more examination than it has received from Brownlie.

The latter, who rightly describes the Charter as resting "on a suspicion of unilateral action by States coupled with a certain faith in collective action,"[71] recognizes that such action is "certainly unreliable,"[72] a classic example of British understatement, but adopts a rather fatalistic attitude toward the human-rights deprivations his rigid construction of Article 2(4) tolerates. "This faith in collective action by individual States is rather contradictory," he admits, "but that is the scheme of the Charter as established."[73] Unlike Friedmann, who comes to the same result but finds it "a painful conclusion to reach,"[74] there is little evidence that Brownlie has con-

[67] *See* text at page 238–39 *supra*.
[68] Reisman, *supra* note 1, at 177.
[69] *Id*.
[70] Farer, "Law and War," in III Black & Falk, *supra* note 66, at 15, 55.
[71] Brownlie 219.
[72] *Id*. at 224.
[73] *Id*. at 219.
[74] Friedmann, *supra* note 28, at 56–57: "In the present writer's perspective, it is better to save and strengthen the minimum international order predicated upon the

templated the costs in terms of human life and dignity his construction of the Charter demands.[75] Other authorities, including several cited by Brownlie to support his absolute view of Article 2(4), have made careful cost-benefit analyses and have concluded that Article 2(4) does not constitute an absolute prohibition against all unilateral humanitarian interventions.[76] Among the contemporary commentators taking this position, in addition to McDougal, Reisman, Stone, and the present writer, are the following: Alford,[77] Goldie,[78] Lauterpacht,[79] J. N. Moore,[80] Nanda,[81] Perez-Vera,[82] Röling,[83] Thapa,[84] and Verzijl.[85]

Finally, the McDougal-Reisman approach to humanitarian intervention, conditioned upon the absence of collective action and otherwise consistent

---

coexistence of many states of different structures and persuasions, while working intensively on the strengthening of the many cooperative efforts and institutions that are needed to ensure the survival of mankind, than to sharpen and embitter the many political conflicts of our time by the legitimation of intervention."

[75] While he fails to examine the costs of nonintervention, he is not reluctant to raise questions about the side effects of intervening for humanitarian purposes:

"What is the price *in human terms* of intervention? What were the casualty ratios in the Stanleyville operation in 1964, the Dominican Republic in 1965 and other candidate examples? How many were killed in order to 'save lives'? To what extent does the typical intervention cause collateral harms by exacerbating a civil war, introducing indiscriminate use of air power in support operations and so on? Was there a policy of pacification and general involvement, together with extraction of concessions by treaty or otherwise as the price of withdrawal?" Brownlie 224. These pertinent questions, raised but not explored, reveal the onesidedness of Brownlie's approach.

[76] Several authorities cited by Brownlie actually acknowledge the right of humanitarian intervention,, at least where the intervening state seeks to protect its own nationals. *See* Friedmann, *supra* note 28, at 58; Waldock, "General Course on Public International Law," 106 *Recueil Des Cours* 1, 240–41 (1962–II); and H. Kelsen, *Collective Security Under International Law*, U.S. Naval War College, International Law Studies, 1954, at 62 (1956). It should be noted that, unless one relies exclusively upon Article 51 to justify the protection of nationals, *see, e.g.*, D. Bowett, *Self-Defence in International Law* ch. V (1958), any rationale allowing interventions to protect nationals also authorizes humanitarian interventions generally. *See* text accompanying note 57 *supra*. *Cf.* Farer, *supra* note 70, at 55, who observes censoriously that "[t]he doctrinal effort to combine defense of nationals with intervention for transnational humanitarian purposes is another response to the post-Charter world."

[77] Alford, *Modern Economic Warfare (Law and the Naval Participant)*, U.S. Naval War College, International Law Studies, 1963, at 169–91 (1967).

[78] L. F. E. Goldie, "The Transvaluation of Values in Contemporary International Law," 53 *Iowa L. Rev.* 358, 362 (1967).

[79] *See* 1 L. Oppenheim, note 35 *supra*.

[80] J. N. Moore, "The Control of Foreign Intervention in Internal Conflict," 9 *Va. J. Int'l L.* 205, 261–64 (1969).

[81] Nanda, "The United States' Action in the 1965 Dominican Crisis: Impact on World Order—Part I," 43 *Denver L.J.* 439, 472–79 (1966).

[82] Perez-Vera, "La Protection d'Humanite en Droit International," [1967] *Revue Belge De Droit International* 401, 414–15.

[83] Roling, "On Aggression, On International Criminal Law, On International Criminal Jurisdiction—I," 2 *Nederlands Tijdschrift Voor Internationaal Recht* 167, 176–77 (1955).

[84] Thapa, "Humanitarian Intervention," August, 1968 (unpublished thesis in McGill University Faculty of Law Library).

[85] 1 J. Verzijl, *International Law in Historical Perspective* 243 (1968).

with the major purposes of the Charter, receives substantial support from the conduct of states and the response of the United Nations itself during the post-Charter period. Granted that this pattern of conduct falls far short of a consensus approving the doctrine, neither is it "totally inadequate to the task of establishing an interpretation in terms of subsequent conduct of the parties favourable to intervention to protect human rights."[86] Indeed, only one holding an exceptionally narrow view of international law and relations would conclude, as Brownlie does, that "[t]he period of the United Nations Charter is totally lacking in practice on the point."[87] By ruling arbitrarily that certain state conduct does not constitute practice,[88] and by ignoring completely the implications to be drawn from certain decisions (or non-decisions) of the United Nations during the past decade,[89] he adopts the posture commonly attributed to the ostrich.

Without examining once again the Stanleyville rescue operation, which the present writer already has characterized as a legitimate humanitarian intervention,[90] it is worth considering what that operation and the ensuing

[86] Brownlie 222. For a superb commentary on the importance of examining subsequent conduct, see Engel, *The Interpretation and Modification of the Charter Through the Subsequent Practice of Organs and Members of the United Nations*, December, 1971 (occasional paper of the American Society of International Law). Engel correctly concludes that "the Charter (or any other international constitution) must be interpreted 'in the light of our whole experience and not merely in that of what was said' some twenty-five years ago at San Francisco." *Id*. at 47.

[87] Brownlie 221. His statement that "[t]he voluminous materials in Whiteman's *Digest* lack even a passing reference to humanitarian intervention," *id*. at 219, is now dated. *See* 12 M. Whiteman, *Digest of International Law* 204–15 (1971).

[88] "The truth is that one cannot treat all State conduct as "practice." The United States action in the Dominican Republic was an action of national self-interest and was simply illegal." Brownlie 221. Brownlie does not reveal the criteria he uses to differentiate acceptable practice from illegal conduct. For a policy-oriented view of the Dominican Republic intervention and its contribution to state practice, see Nanda, note 81 *supra*.

[89] With two exceptions, the preceding chapter contains no references to United Nations practice after November 1960, the date Brownlie completed work on the doctorate thesis that became his treatise. I. Brownlie *supra* note 2, at Ch. V. This failure to update research over the past decade certainly lessens the value of Brownlie's subsequent observations on conduct. It is somewhat surprising, moreover, in one who professes despair at "the absence of evidence that proponents of humanitarian intervention and other very plastic doctrines have spent much time examining state practice in detail." Brownlie 228.

[90] Lillich, "Forcible Self-Help to Protect Human Rights," *supra* note 1, at 338–40. *Accord*, Reisman, *supra* note 1, at 26–28. *Cf*. R. Falk, *supra* note 46, at 324–35, who criticizes the operation but apparently does not question its legality. *See also* Farer, "Harnessing Rogue Elephants: A Short Discourse on Foreign Intervention in Civil Strife," 82 *Harv. L. Rev.* 511, 519 (1969), who takes a somewhat similar stance.

It should be noted that Brownlie discounts the precedent value of this humanitarian intervention on the ground that it "took place with the authorization of the Government of the Congo, which, both legally and otherwise, makes a great deal of difference." Brownlie 221. While an invitation to intervene is a factor to be taken into account in weighing the legitimacy of a claimed humanitarian intervention, it does not automatically render such an intervention legal, nor should it be deemed, conceptually, to lift the action out of the humanitarian intervention category *ab initio*. Lillich, *supra*, at 349. Indeed, the problems invitations to intervene generate are so

United Nations debate generated by it reveal about the world community's attitude toward humanitarian intervention claims twenty years after the Charter's enactment.[91] While African accusations in the United Nations against the intervening states—Belgium, Great Britain, and the United States—occasionally bordered on the slanderous, they generally were grounded upon the political rather than the legal aspects of the case. Thus even the Sudanese representative observed that "[i]n normal circumstances, it would be difficult to oppose a rescue operation for humanitarian purposes."[92] The debate does show, as Higgins concludes, that "the international community is reluctant to approve such interventions,"[93] but it also should be noted that, in the vague Resolution finally adopted by the Security Council, "[d]eploring the recent events in [the Democratic Republic of the Congo],"[94] "[t]he concept of humanitarian intervention was not mentioned, and Belgium and the United States received no official condemnation."[95] Indeed, a recent student notewriter suggests that the Resolution constitutes an implied if not an express approval of the operation: "After the Congo debates, the legal principle of Article 2(4) remains, but what that Article means has been altered by political evolution. There is now an unwillingness

---

many that one writer has been moved to remark that "it is irrelevant whether the intervention has been invited or not." Schwartz, "Intervention: The Historical Development II," in L. Jaquet, *supra* note 28, at 29, 32. This observation probably goes too far, but an analysis of a claimed humanitarian intervention that stops once it perceives an invitation does not go far enough.

[91] Here one should recall Claude's advice that the "crucial feature of the United Nations is not its Charter but its members. What the Charter purports to require of the organization is less significant than what its members require it to import: their biases, objectives, rivalries, interests, and concerns." I. Claude, *The Changing United Nations* 52–53 (1967).

[92] 19 U.N. SCOR, 1170th meeting 28 (1964).

[93] Higgins, "Internal War and International Law," in III Black & Falk, *supra* note 66, at 81, 103. She observes generally that "[t]he doctrine is obviously open to abuse, and this writer has suggested elsewhere that it is not to be regarded as compatible with contemporary international law." *Id.* at 102, citing R. Higgins, *The Development of International Law Through the Political Organs of the United Nations* 220 (1963), where the learned author actually reaches a conclusion somewhat at variance with the one she now professes to hold: "It would thus appear to belong to that category of acts which may be generally legal, but which may be deemed impermissible in any given case."

[94] S.C. Res. 199, 19 U.N. SCOR, Supp. Oct.–Dec. 1964, at 328, U.N. Doc. S/6129 (1964) (10–0–1). Farer observes that, "[i]n view of the profusion of 'recent events,' antithetical appreciations of the Resolution's objective were thus expedited." Farer, *supra* note 70, at 55 n. 151.

Ambassador Stevenson, for instance, replying to a suggestion by the Ghanaian representative that the Resolution impliedly condemned the rescue operation, stated: "I think it is quite clear from the statements made during this debate that the overwhelming majority of the members of this Council do not so interpret that paragraph of the resolution. The fact that my delegation has voted for the resolution as amended makes it perfectly clear that we do not so interpret it." 19 U.N. SCOR, 1189th meeting 12 (1964).

[95] Note, "The Congo Crisis 1964: A Case Study in Humanitarian Intervention," 12 *Va. J. Int'l L.* 261, 274 (1972).

on the part of the world community to read Article 2(4) as an absolute prohibition on the use of force in humanitarian intervention."[96]

One must be careful, of course, not to overclarify the outcome of the above decision (or non-decision) of the United Nations. Moreover, other actions of the United Nations, such as the adoption of a broad non-intervention principle in the recently-adopted Declaration on Principles of International Law Concerning Friendly Relations and Co-Operation among States in Accordance with the Charter of the United Nations,[97] cut against the implied approval thesis advanced by the above notewriter. Nevertheless, the fact that neither the Stanleyville rescue operation nor any other claimed humanitarian intervention has been condemned by the United Nations as a violation of Article 2(4), in marked contrast to its repeated condemnation of claims to use forcible self-help by way of reprisals,[98] throws considerable light upon the world community's attitude toward humanitarian interventions today. At the very least, this practice shows that such interventions might be considered condonable in appropriate instances, a view kited by Brownlie that warrants serious study.

III. A PLEA FOR CONSTRUCTIVE ALTERNATIVES

It is common ground between Brownlie and most authorities, including the present writer, that humanitarian interventions by the United Nations are preferable to such interventions by individual states.[99] As he rightly observes, "[u]nder Chapter VII of the Charter, action may be taken in instances of violations of human rights which give rise to a threat to the peace."[100] Moreover, other authorities, such as Ermacora, contend that,

---

[96] *Id.*

[97] G.A. Res. 2625, 25 U.N. GAOR Supp. 28, at 121, 123, U.N. Doc. A/8082 (1970), *reprinted in* 65 *Am. J. Int'l L.* 243, 248 (1971). On the sweeping nature of this stated principle, which occasioned doubts by the United States, *see* Rosenstock, "The Declaration of Principles of International Law Concerning Friendly Relations: A Survey," 65 *id.* 713, 726–29 (1971).

[98] *See, e.g.,* S.C. Res. 188, 19 U.N. SCOR, Supp. April–June 1964, at 9, U.N. Doc. S/5650 (1964) (9–0–2), where the Security Council formally condemned Great Britain for a reprisal against Yemen.

[99] *See* text at and accompanying note 60 *supra.* Reisman, who agrees that "action within the frame of an authorized organization is most preferable," correctly notes that "such action would include direct organizational intervention as well as delegated organizational intervention." Reisman, *supra* note 1, at 188. He adds that "barring organizational action, a collective intervention is preferable to an intervention by a single state." *Id.* Organizational action, of course, may be undertaken when appropriate by regional organizations as well as by the United Nations. *See generally* J. N. Moore, "The Role of Regional Arrangements in the Maintenance of World Order," in III Black & Falk, *supra* note 66, at 122.

[100] Brownlie 226. *See* Ermacora, "Human Rights and Domestic Jurisdiction (Article 2, § 7, of the Charter)," 124 *Recueil Des Cours* 371, 434 (1968–II): "One category of interventions is of special interest in this context, namely the measures under Chapter VII of the Charter. Such measures are *ab initio* outside the scope of the intervention problem, whether they are taken in connection with human rights

under recent United Nations resolutions, gross or consistent patterns of violations of human rights "are no longer essentially within the domestic jurisdiction of States, and therefore the principle of non-intervention is not applicable."[101] Unfortunately, despite the fact that these jurisdictional bases for remedial action by the world organization exist, "[a] model which accords primary competence to the United Nations to intervene for humanitarian purposes does not . . . reflect the present conditions of the [international] system."[102] A combination of the failure to establish a permanent international military force and the existence of the veto power, records Friedmann, has "effectively destroyed the power of the United Nations to act as an organ of enforcement of international law against a potential lawbreaker."[103] He thus reaches the pessimistic conclusion that, like it or not, in the immediate future "the effective power of using military or lesser forms of coercion in international affairs essentially remains with the nation States."[104]

Brownlie, apparently living in what Reisman has dubbed "the paper world of the Charter,"[105] considers humanitarian interventions by the United Nations to be more reliable than such interventions by individual states.[106] It is difficult, if not impossible, to find support for this view in the events of the past decade. In the case of the Stanleyville rescue operation, for example, the United Nations failed to take effective action during a four-month period between the seizure of the hostages and the airdrop by the intervening states.[107] At about the same time, as Brownlie himself points out, "there were far more serious and persistent threats to human rights which were ignored. In 1965, not less than 300,000 persons of Chinese origin were murdered in Indonesia."[108] Yet the United Nations and its

---

questions or not. For Article 2, § 7, expressly refers to measures under Chapter VII and excludes them from the principle of non-intervention. The practice of the United Nations shows that interventions in the field of human rights are admissible in any case if there is a threat to international peace and security."

[101] *Id.* at 436.

[102] Claydon, *supra* note 9, at 60.

[103] Friedmann, "General Course in Public International Law," 127 *Recueil Des Cours* 39, 68–69 (1969–II). *See also* Friedmann, *supra* note 28, at 66:

"As the number and heterogeneity of members has increased, the United Nations has in fact become less and less able to intervene authoritatively, and with the necessary degree of unanimous support, in internal as well as other international conflicts. This is not only due to the absence of a permanent military force and to the increasing difficulty—after the defiance by the U.S.S.R. and France of the Certain Expenses Opinion of the International Court of Justice—to finance ad hoc order forces. A more fundamental reason is the increasing division of the United Nations into antagonistic blocs, which makes it a forum for the confrontation and occasional accommodation of conflicting political and national forces rather than a genuine supranational authority."

[104] Friedmann, *supra* note 103, at 70.

[105] *See* text accompanying note 66 *supra*.

[106] *See* text at notes 71–73 *supra*.

[107] Note, *supra* note 94, at 262–63.

[108] Brownlie 224.

Member States, supporting his observation that "[t]he whole field is riven by political expediency and capriciousness,"[109] did nothing. The dismal failure of the United Nations with respect to Bangladesh is too recent to need recounting. From these instances and others one is compelled to conclude that, at the very least, "the prospects for effective United Nations actions are presently weak."[110] Indeed, without overstatement, they may be said to be almost nonexistent.

Given this bleak outlook, one would have thought that Brownlie and other proponents of the view that humanitarian interventions are permissible only when undertaken by the United Nations would have turned their attention to strengthening its capacity to respond in such situations.[111] At the very least, one would have expected from them a body of literature canvassing the difficulties and suggesting possible solutions to the obvious procedural defects, such as the absence of a standby international expeditionary force and the presence of the veto power, both of which must be remedied before effective and uniform humanitarian interventions by the United Nations can become a reality.[112] One especially would have welcomed serious examination of the conventional wisdom which places collective interventions in a preferred position over unilateral ones.[113] Yet the

---

[109] *Id.*

[110] Claydon, *supra* note 9, at 62.

[111] *See* text accompanying note 7 *supra*. While the criticism that follows focuses upon Brownlie, it applies equally to other authorities taking this view. Thus Schwarz categorically asserts that "the prohibition of intervention by force of arms is stated in contemporary juridical science as a principle without exception. In modern literature and practice, only intervention on behalf of the United Nations or assimilated organizations seems to be admitted as lawful." U. Schwarz, *Confrontation and Intervention in the Modern World* 179 (1970). *Accord,* M. Ganji, *supra* note 17, at 44. Yet these writers offer no recommendations to make United Nations interventions a reality.

[112] Friedmann does remark that "the utmost effort should be devoted to the strengthening of the international institutional procedures, and particularly the authority of the United Nations, with respect to intervention in the affairs of any one country, notably in the case of internal disorders and secession. The weakness of the authority and procedures of the United Nations is today the counterpart of the growing number of unilateral interventions." Friedmann, *supra* note 28, at 57.
Yet he avoids specific recommendations and ends upon a somewhat pessimistic note:
"The collectivization of intervention through the United Nations can become an effective alternative only if and when the nation states will—perhaps as a result of another disaster—come to recognize that the common interests of mankind must prevail over the divisive policies and actions that have brought the world to the brink of disaster." *Id.* at 66. *See also* text at and accompanying notes 103 & 104 *supra.*

[113] *See* R. Falk, *supra* note 46, at 161–62. The present writer has accepted the conventional wisdom for purposes of this chapter. *See* text at and accompanying notes 60 & 99 *supra. But see* Slater, "The Limits of Legitimization in International Organizations: The Organization of American States and the Dominican Crisis," 23 *Int'l Organization* 48, 71 (1969):
" 'International organization,' 'multilateral,' and 'collective action' are all honorific words eliciting favorable connotations, especially among the generally liberal and internationalist elite sectors of public opinion. Thus, behind the frequent exhortations to policymakers to allow international organizations to play a greater role in

writings of Brownlie and like-minded authorities make no mention of these problems.[114] Likewise, they are wholly devoid of constructive alternatives to the admittedly "unreliable" response by the United Nations. Brownlie's message in the preceding chapter, for instance, amounts to no more than a plea to keep the "faith in collective action. . . ."[115]

If, as Falk has remarked, "the renunciation of intervention does not substitute a policy of nonintervention; it involves the development of some form of collective intervention,"[116] then concomitantly the failure to develop effective international machinery to facilitate humanitarian interventions arguably permits a state to intervene unilaterally in appropriate situations.[117] Writing a decade ago, Ronning wisely observed that "it is as useless to outlaw intervention without providing a satisfactory substitute as it was to outlaw war when no satisfactory substitute was available."[118] He also posed the difficult question, which becomes more relevant every year,

> whether refusal to compromise on the principle of absolute non-intervention will not threaten the very principle itself. It can of course continue to be honored in countless declarations and protests, but if it does not square with the hard facts of international politics, that will be the extent of its honor.[119]

---

national policies lies the implicit assumption that collective bodies will exert a moderating, liberalizing, or enlightening influence. But this is not invariably so. . . ." *Accord*, Higgins, *supra* note 93, at 115–18.

Cf. Falk, "Introduction," in R. Falk (ed.), *The International Law of Civil War* 24–25 (1971), who concludes that "[t]he criteria of decision are so elusive and the vagaries of world consensus so pronounced that there is reason to distrust interventions in civil wars, even if they occur under the auspices of international institutions." He observes, however, that "United Nations aloofness may be tested by prolonged civil wars that expose large portions of the civilian population to hardship. Starvation of large numbers in Iboland during the Nigerian Civil War posed such a challenge to the world community. It may be desirable to encourage specific humanitarian procedures whereby claims that are unconnected with the military dimension of the conflict are made on behalf of the international community and, if necessary, enforced against the parties to the civil war. The Red Cross or some ad hoc group could be entrusted with emergency relief operations on behalf of the international community." *Id.* at 26.

[114] *But see* Sassoon, "Violence and Counterviolence in the Middle East: A Legal Analysis," October, 1971 (occasional paper of the American Society of International Law): "A total prohibition of force was premised on certain assumptions: first that the Security Council would have at its disposal military capabilities of compulsion; second that the five permanent members of the Council would have a united purpose; and third that it would objectively and impartially discharge its responsibilities. None of these assumptions is a reality." *Id.* at 61.

[115] *See* text at note 73 *supra*. *See also* Friedmann, *supra* note 28, at 65–66, who argues for "United Nations Intervention as an Alternative to Unilateral Intervention."

[116] R. Falk, *supra* note 46, at 339.

[117] *See* text at notes 60–66 *supra*.

[118] C. Ronning, *Law and Politics in Inter-American Diplomacy* 83 (1963). More recently, Sassoon has asked rhetorically "if self-help can be outlawed without providing a 'functioning' alternative. The answer, given by state practice, is that it cannot." Sassoon, *supra* note 114, at 2.

[119] C. Ronning, note 118 *supra*.

Although Brownlie does not consider this question, events during the past decade reveal a widening "credibility gap" between the absolute non-intervention approach to the Charter which he espouses and the actual practice of states. Indeed, as in the case of armed reprisals, it may be said that the law governing humanitarian intervention "is, because of its divorce from actual practice, rapidly degenerating to a stage where its normative character is in question."[120]

If, as seems to be the case, "a simple prohibition to intervene is unable to cope with the problem of intervention,"[121] then surely, as the present writer noted some years ago, the most important task confronting international lawyers is "to clarify the various criteria by which the legitimacy of a state's use of forcible self-help in human rights situations can be judged."[122] Nanda, taking this approach, has suggested five such criteria: (1) a specific limited purpose; (2) an invitation by the recognized government; (3) a limited duration of the mission; (4) a limited use of coercive measures; and (5) a lack of any other recourse.[123] Occasionally overlapping these criteria but also including several additional ones, the present writer has recommended elsewhere his own five tests by which a unilateral humanitarian intervention should be judged: (1) the immediacy of the violation of human rights; (2) the extent of the violation of human rights; (3) the existence of an invitation by appropriate authorities; (4) the degree of coercive measures employed; and (5) the relative disinterestedness of the state invoking the coercive measures.[124] Moreover, Moore has suggested three further criteria: "a minimal effect on authority structures, a prompt disengagement consistent with the purpose of the action, and immediate full

[120] Bowett, "Reprisals Involving Recourse to Armed Force," 66 *Am. J. Int'l L.* 1, 2 (1972).

[121] Bos, "Intervention and International Law II," in L. Jaquet, *supra* note 28, at 69, 73 (emphasis omitted). *See also id.* at 75:

"It was my purpose to posit that States are no paper tigers, that intervening States are not necessarily scoundrels, but may be driven by great ideals, that their intervention may as well contribute to a final world legal order as those undertaken by international organizations, and that our aim as lawyers should not so much be to throw stones at interveners as to seek the foundations of that order—foundations we cannot hope to produce at our desks, but which are to be assembled from the ideals and practices of our own age."

[122] Lillich, "Intervention to Protect Human Rights," *supra* note 1, at 218.

[123] Nanda, *supra* note 81, at 475.

[124] Lillich, "Forcible Self-Help to Protect Human Rights," *supra* note 1, at 347-51. One writer has complained that "[n]one of Lillich's criteria of legitimacy would enable a decision-maker to determine when humanitarian intervention begins and when it ends." Claydon, *supra* note 9, at 55.

As the above-cited article plainly states, it may begin "only on those rare occasions when the danger to the individuals concerned is imminent and the state whose duty it is to protect them is unable or unwilling to do so," and it must end without a "prolonged presence in the country. . . . Suffice to say that the longer troops remain in another country, the more their presence begins to look like [non-humanitarian] intervention." Lillich, *supra*, at 347, 350. It is hard to be more specific on either point. Further clarification about the commencement and termination of humanitarian interventions may be found in J. N. Moore, *supra* note 80, at 264.

reporting to the Security Council and appropriate regional organizations."[125]

Brownlie, invoking an analogy to euthanasia, the legalizing of which he assumes "would alter the moral climate and procedure harmful abuse,"[126] rejects the above criteria as determinants of legitimacy, but accepts them as

> a fine basis for a political plea in mitigation in parliaments, U.N. organs and regional organizations. My euthanasia parallel applies here: a defence lawyer and a court still need to distinguish the false from the genuine case, as a matter of mitigation.[127]

Thus, following in the footsteps of nineteenth century scholars such as Sir W. Vernon Harcourt[128] and his disciple Lawrence,[129] Brownlie seems to have reached the camp of those authors who, in Stowell's words, "deny the legality of humanitarian intervention in law, but who condone it to a greater or less degree in practice."[130]

Whether one regards humanitarian interventions as legal if they meet the various criteria recommended above, or whether one considers them illegal de jure, yet condonable de facto, if they satisfy the selfsame criteria, seems to the present writer of more jurisprudential than practical importance.[131] Like Falk, who while condemning reprisals nevertheless has worked out a systematic framework for the assessment of claims to use

[125] *Id.* Reisman, whose criteria parallel the ones in the text, concludes that a unilateral humanitarian intervention "would require a showing among other things of overriding necessity, lack of time to seise an authorized international organization of the matter, subsequent seising as soon as possible, compliance with the international law of the use of force and submission to the supervision and appraisal of the appropriate inclusive international organization." Reisman, *supra* note 1, at 39–40.

[126] Considering the policy issues surrounding humanitarian intervention, he concludes that "the moral setting, even in genuine cases, is far from simple. There is a moral and legislative problem of the type raised by euthanasia, itself a form of humanitarian intervention. Euthanasia is unlawful, but doctors on occasion commit technical breaches of the law, for example, by administering massive drug dosages which accelerate coma and death. It is very generally assumed that legalising euthanasia would alter the moral climate and produce harmful abuse." Brownlie 223.

[127] *Id.* at 225.

[128] Writing under the pen name Historicus, he contended that "[i]ntervention is a question rather of policy than of law. It is above and beyond the domain of law, and when wisely and equitably handled by those who have the power to give effect to it, may be the highest policy of justice and humanity." W. Harcourt, *Letters by Historicus on Some Questions of International Law* 14 (1863). In an oft-quoted brace of sentences, he maintained that "[i]t is a high and summary procedure which may sometimes snatch a remedy beyond the reach of law. Nevertheless, it must be admitted that . . . its essence is illegality, and its justification is its success." *Id.* at 41.

[129] Like Sir W. Vernon Harcourt, he considered humanitarian intervention "a high act of policy above and beyond the domain of law." Such an intervention, he added, "is destitute of technical legality, but it may be morally right and even praiseworthy to a high degree." For this reason, international law "will not condemn interventions for such a cause." T. Lawrence, *The Principles of International Law* 129 (4th ed. 1910).

[130] E. Stowell, *supra* note 23, at 59 n. 13. *See* text at notes 4 & 5 *supra.*

[131] *Compare* text accompanying note 74 *supra.*

retaliatory force, Brownlie apparently believes that the above criteria, largely based upon the traditional doctrine of humanitarian intervention, are acceptable illustrations of "a kind of second-order level of legal inquiry that is guided by the more permissive attitudes toward the use of force to uphold national interests that is contained in customary international law."[132] Under this highly sophisticated approach, subsequently adopted and developed by Bowett, numerous criteria are formulated which, when met by a state taking unilateral action, may prevent its running afoul of the United Nations Security Council.[133] The Security's Council's recent resolution which avoids condemning India for its invasion of East Pakistan (now Bangladesh) might be considered an example of this "second-order legality" approach.[134] The parallel to Brownlie's euthanasia analogy is obvious.

If the present writer has not overclarified Brownlie's position, it would appear that, at least as to outcome, there is actually little difference between their views. While this writer prefers a doctrinal approach which forthrightly sanctions unilateral humanitarian interventions when they meet detailed criteria to one which unqualifiedly proscribes such interventions but condones them when compatible with the selfsame criteria, he nevertheless welcomes Brownlie's tentative contribution to the current debate on humanitarian intervention. Hopefully, in his subsequent writings, Brownlie will give serious consideration not only to refining the above criteria, for whatever purposes they may be of use, but also to establishing procedures under which humanitarian interventions through the United Nations someday may take place. Both Reisman's Protocol of Procedure for Humanitarian Intervention[135] and Senator Edward Kennedy's proposal for an

---

[132] Falk, "The Beirut Raid and the International Law of Retaliation," 63 *Am. J. Int'l L.* 415, 430 n. 39 (1969).

[133] Bowett, *supra* note 120, at 26–28.

[134] S.C. Res. 307, 26 U.N. SCOR, Oct.–Dec. 1971, at xx, U.N. Doc. S/RES/307 (1971) (13–0–2). To the extent that India's invasion was authority-oriented, justifying is upon grounds of unilateral humanitarian intervention becomes more difficult. *See* Schwarz, *supra* note 90, at 31, 32. *Cf.* J. N. Moore, *supra* note 80, at 264: "If the protection of human rights requires the overthrow of authority structures, it would seem best to require the United Nations authorization as a prerequisite for action. To allow unilateral action in such cases would be to permit all manner of self-serving claims for the overthrow of authority structures."

On the other hand, arguments can be advanced that unilateral humanitarian interventions to terminate genocidal conduct should be permissible even when they cause a state's authority structure to be altered or overthrown. Certainly the great nineteenth-century humanitarian interventions, like the one which produced an independent Greece, were authority-oriented. *See* text at note 17 *supra.* Moreover, such interventions may be the only way to save literally thousands of lives. Paraphrasing policy-science terminology, one might state an acceptable approach as follows: "The use of force by one or more states to reestablish minimum public order in another state is permissible, despite the fact that it involves more than minimal interference with the latter's authority structures, if the invocation of force causing such interference is consistent with and in support of liberal humanitarian policies on which rests enlightened community order." Such an approach would justify India's action.

[135] Reisman, *supra* note 1, at 195.

Emergency Relief Force[136] may be too ambitious for today's fragmented world community, but these and other innovative recommendations[137] certainly deserve more attention than they have received to date.[138] Granted that most international lawyers have been remiss in their failure to address such procedural problems,[139] Brownlie and other authorities critical of unilateral humanitarian intervention have a special obligation to respond to this plea for constructive alternatives.[140]

[136] *N.Y. Times*, Feb. 9, 1969, at 1, col. 4. *See also* his recent proposal of a United Nations Emergency Service (UNES). Kennedy, "International Humanitarian Assistance: Proposals for Action," 12 *Va. J. Int'l L.* 299 (1972).

[137] One of the most imaginative recommendations has come not from an international lawyer but from former General Gavin, who has proposed a multinational sky cavalry force, immediately available to the United Nations, to engage in peacekeeping and rescue and relief operations. *N.Y. Times*, April 15, 1971, at 43, col. 1.

[138] Without mentioning Reisman's proposed protocol, Dr. Younger has remarked that "I do not believe that any universal code governing intervention could at present be devised which would as yet secure . . . acceptance; nor is there any international authority capable of enforcing such a code upon unwilling members." Younger, "Intervention: The Historical Development I," in L. Jaquet, *supra* note 28, at 12, 27. While the chances of obtaining agreement to a substantive code governing intervention are remote, a protocol establishing procedures for humanitarian interventions may be within the realm of possibility. It is being studied under the grant described in the acknowledgment at the beginning of this chapter.

[139] Obviously, these problems raise numerous substantive issues, *see* text accompanying note 138 *supra*, the most important one being what human rights deprivations should trigger humanitarian interventions. The criterion suggested by Moore is "an immediate and extensive threat to fundamental human rights, particularly a threat of widespread loss of human life. . . ." J. N. Moore, *supra* note 80, at 264. *See also* Lillich, "Forcible Self-Help to Protect Human Rights," *supra* note 1, at 348–49. At the present stage of the world community's development, the only consensus may be that "massacres can be prevented." Brownlie, 225.

[140] The present writer is specially interested in the current views of the former Attorney-General of Pakistan, Syed S. Pirzada, who in 1970 strongly criticized the doctrine of intervention by states on humanitarian grounds, stating that such "interventions, if any, should be made by the United Nations or its various organs." *Int'l L. Ass'n, Report of the Fifty-Fourth Conference, supra* note 1, at 620. Attacking this writer's Interim Report, he righteously proclaimed "that Pakistan's stand on human rights has been unequivocal in every forum. Whenever an occasion has arisen it has reaffirmed its faith in fundamental rights for the dignity of every human person. Pakistan has incorporated the fundamental rights in its Constitution. Discrimination based on race, sex, language or religion does not exist in Pakistan." *Id.* at 621.

Chapter 12 | Private Armies in a Global War System: Prologue to Decision | Michael Reisman

> The law of the state often tries to obstruct the coercive means of other consociations . . . But the state is not always successful. There are groups stronger than the state in this respect . . . This conflict between the means of coercion of the various corporate groups is as old as the law itself. In the past it has not always ended with the triumph of the coercive means of the political body, and even today this has not always been the outcome.[1]
>
> MAX WEBER

An army is a corps of people, sharing loyalty to a common symbol, skilled in the manual of arms, and operating within a command structure one of whose manifest functions is to direct corps members or "soldiers" in the purposive exercise of violence.[2] Given the pivotal position of effective power

[1] Max Weber, *On Law in Economy and Society* 18–19 (Rheinstein, ed., 1967).

[2] The functional definition of the term "army" is intended to sever it from the popular contemporary connotation according to which an army must be associated with a territorial entity; the absence of such an association, it follows, renders the "army" unlawful, in degrees varying with the context. Fortunately, this view is becoming obsolete among students of social control who are increasingly sensitive to the eufunctional role of private armies in maintaining order in large, complex systems. *See*, for example, J. Kakauk and S. Wildhorn, *Private Police in the United States* (Rand, 1971). Unfortunately, there has been no systematic effort to clarify norms in this area or to consider dysfunctions.

As understood here, an army is a group of people which may include men, women, and children, with identifications focused on some common symbol. The symbol need not be territorial, and it need not be exclusive in monopolizing the identifications of its members. Thus, where the group itself is the symbol, intensity of identification may be increased by conscious breaches of the morality system of a more inclusive group to which members feel some association but from which they feel they are irreparably barred because of their "blutkit" or "blood-cement" which ties them to the lesser group. *See* Alexander, "War Crimes and their Motivation," 39 *J. of American Institute of Crim. L.* 298 (1948), and *cf.* B. Lewis, *The Assassins: A Radical Sect in Islam* (1968).—On the other hand, a mob is excluded from this

This article is a tentative formulation of parts of a more general study, now in progress, of international law in a global war system. It has benefitted from the advice and criticisms of my colleagues in the World Public Order Program at the Yale Law School: Myres S. McDougal, Harold D. Lasswell, Lung-chu Chen, and Arie E. David. Professors M. Libontati of Temple University School of Law and R. Lempert of the University of Michigan School of Law read an early draft and made many helpful suggestions. Professors J. Goldstein and Jay Katz of Yale Law School read a later draft and made many useful comments. Professors Donald Black, Albert Reiss, and Stanton Wheeler of the Department of Sociology at Yale University were generous in research suggestions. I am particularly indebted to Mr. Jerrold Guben, of the Russell Sage Program at Yale Law School, for numerous research cues in a literature of which his knowledge is quite unparalleled. James Malysiak, Yale Law School, 1973, was helpful in research and criticism. A somewhat different version appeared in 14 *Va. J. Int'l L.* 1 (1973).

in almost all societies of which there is record, it is no surprise that elites who have asserted a monopoly of authority have sought as well the exclusive prerogative of maintaining armies.[3] Characteristic of the myth of the contemporary nation-state is its claim for monopoly over the exercise of violence. Were there a rough conformity between state theory and practice, one could expect to count about as many armies in the world as there are

---

definition in that it lacks sufficient organization over time and its members lack a sufficient identification with a persisting symbol. A mob may become a private army, not because of a refinement in skills of violence, but because of the evolution or imposition of organization and the clarification of a group symbol system. This may have been the case with the Boxer Bands, though different theories regarding their origin and transformation have been suggested: *see* C. Tan, *The Boxer Catastrophe*, 33*ff.* (1955). But for a different construction of the social organization of mobs, *see* E. Cannetti, *Crowds and Power* (1962); *but cf.* G. Rudé, *The Crowd in the French Revolution* (1959), especially at 234 *et seq.*, who distinguishes the crowd as a composite actor from a mob or a mass. For detailed confirmation of Rudé's conception and a rejection of Le Bon's theory, *see* L. Richards, *"Gentlemen of Property and Standing": Anti-Abolition Mobs in Jacksonian America*, 82–130 (1970).

A private army, as understood here, involves duration over time, but not necessarily continuous temporal sequence. A gang which assembles for specific "jobs," religious assassins as discussed in Lewis *supra*, a religious sect which convenes at certain phases of the moon for ritual violence, ethnic armies which form in lulls of the agricultural cycle and cross borders to kill and pillage other groups, social bandits in Hobsbawm's sense of the term (E. Hobsbawm, *Bandits* [1969]), policemen who assemble sporadically to perform extralegal functions, and a political group which meets weekly or monthly to drill are examples of private armies.

I deem the component of command structure important because it distinguishes a composite social actor with temporal duration and a capacity for purposive action from more random conglomerations of individuals exercising violence. Command structure need not imply hierarchical organization nor need it require institutionalized roles or "offices"; nonetheless, these are rather usual indicators.

While armies, as all social processes, perform multiple manifest and latent functions, the distinctive skill of any army is its expertise in the use of violence. Violence refers to levels of coercion deemed extraordinarily high in the social settings in which deployed. The term is strictly designative and does not purport to connote whether the violence in question is lawful or unlawful or whether its agents are authorized by some inclusive community process. Purposive violence refers to high coercion used to attenuate the choices of targets and to influence their behavior in desired ways. Hence it can include terror or acts of random violence which are used, rationally or not, for manifest political purposes. For discussion of indices of violence *see* S. Levy's "A One Hundred Fifty Year Study of Political Violence in the United States," in H. Graham & T. Gurr, *The History of Violence in America* 84, 86–87 (1969).

[3] Probably the earliest intellectual discussion of this claim is Socrates' monologue *Crito*, more satisfying rhetorically than substantively. Throughout the Middle Ages, certain strata symbolized their social preeminence by the wearing of weapons, which they deemed a matter of right; thus Nietzsche argued that the elite was the group which demanded authoritative power for itself. F. Nietzche, *On the Genealogy of Morals* 57 (Kaufman trans., 1969). The counter-myth, as Pareto noted, was complementary: "Theories designed to justify the use of force by the governed are almost always combined with theories condemning the use of force by the public authority." 4 V. Pareto, *The Mind and Society* 1527 (Bongiorno and Livingstone trans., 1935).

The modern trend toward centralizing the apparatus of violence probably begins with Charles VII of France, and though a process which has never been perfected, its symbolic apogée seems to have been reached some two centuries later. Whenever social formations could effectively range themselves against the central authority, they usually sought and received an authorization for arms. Thus, the English Bill of

nation-states. In fact, the equation seems in perpetual imbalance.[4] In certain circumstances, the number of effective fighting units not affiliated with the governmental apparatus of recognized states can grow even larger. I will refer to such units as "private armies." The private army is a fact of international life. How does international law respond to it?

Rights of 1689 was a response to the claims brought by the Protestants after they were forcibly disarmed by James II. Subsequently, this was ideologized as a buttress of freedom against centralized tyranny and was incorporated, in the United States, into the Second Amendment to the Bill of Rights: for an interesting construction, see L. Emery, "The Constitutional Right to Keep and Bear Arms," 28 *Harv. L. Rev.* 473 (1915). There seems to be little doubt that there is a trend away from an ideology of an individual right of arms, but counter-trends are present. In any case, these do not seem to affect the formation of private armies and brigades.

[4] I have found no comprehensive studies or surveys of the number and location of effective fighting units about the globe without regard to their association with some formal state apparatus. Security agencies may have compiled detailed trend and factor studies of private armies within the United States, but with the exception of the recent Rand Study (*supra* note 2), systematic surveys are not available. The "Congressional Investigation of the Pinkertons" in 1892 is now of historical interest: H. R. Rep. No. 2447, 52nd Cong. 2d Sess., 1892. Another rather detailed study is found in the Holmstead Hearings on "Violation of Free Speech and Rights of Labor," *Report of the Committee on Education and Labor pursuant to S. Res. 266, 74th Congress, A Resolution to Investigate Violations of the Right of Free Speech and Assembly and Interference with the Right of Labor to Organize and Bargain Collectively* (1939). See especially, *id.* P. I, at 7–10; P. II, "Private Police Systems"; and P. III, "Industrial Munitions."

The papers collected in Gurr & Graham, *supra*, are indispensable. An impression of contemporary trends may be gained from the most cursory survey of magazines serving the police industry. They contain advertisements which are slanted in whole or in part to private police forces: organized private armies within plants, housing projects, universities, and security specialists within corporations, as well as entrepreneurial police forces, operating nationally and/or regionally and available to customers at fixed rates. On the early development of a private police force, *see* G. Howson, *Thief Taker General: The Rise and Fall of Jonathan Wild* (1970); R. M. Brown, *The South Carolina Regulators* (1963). On private armies retained by railroads and extractive industries in the eastern United States, *see* J. P. Shalloo, *Private Police: with special reference to Pennsylvania* (1933) and *see* the excellent bibliography there. *See also* A. Bimba, *The Molly Maguires* (1932) and W. Brohl, *The Molly Maguires* (1964). For a general survey, R. M. Brown, "Historical Patterns of Violence in America" in Graham & Gurr, *supra*, at 45. It seems that much of the elite personnel of many private armies in the United States is recruited from former members of public armies, such as the armed forces, local police, and the FBI. Detailed studies on the collaborative and competitive relationships between these private and public armies is urgent for the purposes of policy and scholarship. (After this writing, volumes 3 and 4 of the RAND study appeared, dealing in part with this problem.) For a recent survey of urban armies, see Marx and Archer, "The Urban Vigilante," *Psychology Today*, Jan. 1973, at 45.

In addition to these private armies, there are quasi-secret groups of ethnic, racial, and political-interest orientation, whose activities may include the refinement and application of violence: On secret societies, *see* Tan, *supra*, and E. Hobsbawm, *Primitive Rebels* (1959). Some journalistic surveys of current secret groups qualifying as private armies are found in J. H. Jones, *The Minutemen* (1968) and D. Chalmers, *Hooded Americanism* (1965). On vigilantes, *see* "The American Vigilante Movement" in Graham & Gurr, *supra*, at 218. For a general account of the rise and activities of the Klan, as well as its political interventions, *see*, W. Randel, *The Ku Klux Klan: A Century of Infamy* (1965). *See also* C. Alexander, *The Ku Klux Klan in the*

PRIVATE ARMIES AND TRADITIONAL PRESCRIPTIONS

The traditional corpus of international law comprised express and tacit communications between the effective elites of territorial communities about the practices which ought to be reciprocated among themselves. Precisely because of the reciprocal character of the arrangements, there was a high degree of deference to the fundamental postulates of their system: the

---

South West (1965); D. Whitehead, *Attack on Terror: The FBI against the Ku Klux Klan in Mississippi* (1970). For a survey of American radical activist groups, *see* E. Newman (ed.), *The Hate Reader* (1964). For a survey of urban groups, some of which may be characterized as private armies, *see* R. Poston, *The Gang and the Establishment* (1971).

Poston touches on the interesting and apparently not uncommon phenomenon of armies alternating between private and public functions and armies which are private but which are coopted for public uses. Some structural explanations of this phenomenon are essayed in Wolf & Hansen, "Caudillo Politics: A Structural Analysis," 9 *Cont. Stud. Soc. & His.* 168 (1967). Some descriptions are found in R. Quirk, *The Mexican Revolution* (1960). The converse also occurs; where strata become polarized and the police cease to be a mediating force, one group will coopt the public police or garrison for what are, in effect, private functions, a sequence which occurred in labor wars in the United States and which occurs, in a sense, in every case in which graft or petty payoffs are made to a policeman. *See*, for example, A. Niederhoffer, *Behind the Shield: The Police in Urban Society* 69*ff*. (1969).

Private armies in other regions and countries are rarely studied as such, but a rich scientific literature does examine and theorize on aspects of the subject. Among the more specific studies, *see* on China, J. Spence, *To Change China: Western Advisers in China 1620–1960*, 57–92 (1969), J. Ch'en, *Yaan Shi-K'ai* (1961); and on warlordism, J. Sheridan, *Chinese Warlord: The Career of Feng Yu-hsiang* (1966), and *cf*. Wolf and Hansen, *supra*; on Spain, G. Brenan, *The Spanish Labyrinth* (2nd ed., 1967); S. Payne, *Falange* (1961); on Ialy, 4 Pareto, *supra*; on Germany, R. Waite, *Vanguard of Nazism: The Free Corps Movement in Postwar Germany 1918–1923* (1952), H. Hohne, *The Order of the Death's Head* 51–75 (Barry trans., 1970); on Mexico, J. Womack, *Zapata* (1968) and R. Quirk, *supra*; useful material on Japanese feudalism and the formation of fighting groups is found in A. Craig, *Chōshū in the Meiji Restoration* (1961); J. Hall, *Government and Local Power in Japan, 500–1700* (1966); on Russia, J. Blum, *Lord and Peasant in Russia* 551*ff*. (1961); R. Mousnier, *Peasant Uprisings in Seventeenth-Century France, Russia and China* (Pearce trans., 1967); R. Pipes, *The Formation of the Soviet Union: Communism and Nationalism 1917–1923* (1964); on France, C. Tilly, *The Vendée* (1964); some pertinent material on Brazil can be found in E. da Cunha, *Rebellion in the Backlands* (Putnam trans., 1944).

Many journalistic and contemporary history books provide valuable glimpses into the distribution of violence specialization in different sectors. *See*, for example, R. Gott, *Guerrilla Movements in Latin America* (1971); L. Pye, *Guerrilla Communism in Malaya* (1956); B. Crozier, *South East Asia in Turmoil* 135*ff*. (1965). On private armies in Vietnam, *see* D. Duncanson, *Government and Revolution in Vietnam* 220*ff*. (1968).

Diplomatic correspondence provides a rich store of data about and official responses to private armies. Not surprisingly, virtually every volume of *Foreign Relations of the United States* from 1905 to 1950 includes many references to private armies. In a number of instances, the discussions are fairly detailed. Thus communiqués from Mexico in 1913 included many evaluations of private armies: 1913 *Foreign Rel. U.S.* 721*ff*. (1920). Communiqués from China in 1919 and 1929 detailed the different private armies involved in conflict: 1919 *Foreign Rel. U.S.* 271, 331 (1934); 1929 *Foreign Rel. U.S.* vol. II, 117 (1943). In many situations, private armies

territorial integrity and political power base of each elite group. The vigor of this trend is indicated by the prominent position given to these principles in the Charter of the United Nations.[5] The symmetry and formalism of traditional law is nowhere better reflected than in the rule derived from this general principle regarding a state's responsibility for "private" military incursions from its territory into another state. In brief, each state was responsible for all activity within its borders, and if military action emanated from its boundaries into the territory of another state, it remained liable to that other state for the actual and constructive violations of the other's sovereignty.[6] The other state enjoyed not only the right of claim on the diplomatic level, but, in exigent circumstances, the prerogative of unilaterally coercive actions in abatement.[7]

---

seem not to have been viewed as pathologies. Thus, the U.S. chargé in Vienna reported to the Department of State in 1934 that "Dollfuss' greatest weakness as a dictator is that he has no army of his own." 1934 *Foreign Rel. U.S.*, vol. II, 18 (1951).

Some insights into the private armies of the Charter Companies can be gained from A. Hickman, *Men Who Made Rhodesia: A Register of Those Who Served in the British South Africa Company's Police* (1960).

In addition to these manifestly politically oriented private armies, it is not uncommon in certain regions to find villages, tribes, and religious sects which are armed and have a secondary or residual command structure which can be mobilized at certain times. Is the proliferation and degree of organization of such armies, as Pareto suggested, inversely proportional to the general or sectoral effectiveness of the central government? *See* Tan, *supra* at 29.

For data on international mercenary forces, *see* A. Mockler, *The Mercenaries* (1969); J. Le Bailly, *Une Poignée de Mercenaires* (1967); J. Larteguy, *The Guerrillas* (1969).

[5] Thus, Article 2(4) presents as a fundamental principle that "All Members shall refrain in their international relations from the threat or use of force against the territorial integrity or political independence of any state, or in any other manner inconsistent with the Purposes of the United Nations." In context, of course, the perpetuation of a certain territorial allocation may actually maximize instability and increase the probability of wars. For some discussion of this point in regard to the Charter regime, *see* Chen and Reisman, "Who Owns Taiwan: A Search for International Title," 81 *Yale L. J.* 599 (1972).

[6] 2 J. B. Moore, *International Law Digest* 428–32; 1 Lauterpacht-Oppenheim's *International Law* 338*ff.* For judicial dicta *see* Trail Smelter, 3 *UNRIAA* 1905; Corfu Channel, [1949] *I.C.J. Reports* 18.

[7] The clearest policy statements are afforded by the diplomatic correspondence surrounding the Amelia Island case. One McGregor and a private force, characterized by the United States as buccaneers but self-characterized as part of the forces of the insurgent colonies of Buenos Aires and Venezuela, preyed on the commerce of the United States and of Spain from a base on Amelia Island, situated at the mouth of St. Mary's river and at that time under Spanish sovereignty. President Monroe sent naval vessels to evict the private army and to destroy their vessels and fortifications. The diplomatic correspondence, available in 2 J. B. Moore, *Digest of International Law* 406–8, indicates a rather general acceptance of the act, though protests were lodged by Spain and a representative of Venezuela, New Granada, and Mexico. Secretary of State Adams communicated to the French minister that "When an island is occupied by a nest of pirates, harassing the commerce of the United States, they may be pursued and driven from it, by authority of the United States, even though such island were nominally under the jurisdiction of Spain, Spain not exercising over it any control." *Id.* at 408. The actual facts of the Amelia Island case do complicate its precedential value, although subsequent doctrinalists have not troubled to review them.

The basic policy here is not only, as has often been assumed, self-defense, but also international collaboration in the prohibition of the use of force by entities not associated with or operating under delegation from a nation-state. For convenience, this interlocking obligation and right will be referred to here as the "private-army rule." If the rule's result conforms to its theory, a degree of national and international stability is supposedly secured by the mobilization of international authority against all agents of political change who wish ultimately to resort to force; the rule, in short, seeks to sustain those aspects of the status quo deemed essential by territorial elites.

The artificiality of the private-army rule and its underlying conception and the difficulties of applying it systematically and efficiently were apparent in the milieu in which it originated. It is even more glaringly inappropriate in a successive era in which there is a much richer diversity of authorized participants in the processes of international law, between many of whom there are deep ideological divisions. New international policies (many of them highly peremptory), which test the authority and legitimacy of national action, cut directly across the elite claims which formerly derived from the traditional rule. The precedent of United Nations action in Rhodesia simply codified diverse trends in the Charter, in United Nations' practice, and in customary international law. The Rhodesian case confirmed that international law's prerequisites for the status and privileges of statehood extend well beyond effective control by the local territorial elite; the prerequisites now include, to some extent, establishing an expectation of present and probable future conformity with minimum standards of human rights.[8] If we keep in mind that legitimate statehood is not acquired at some moment, thereafter existing in perpetuity, but is a varying function of the attitudes of all other participants in the world effective power process, it is

---

For one thing, Spain had been exercising no control over the island, and her entire title may have been questionable. *See generally,* Chen and Reisman, *supra* note 5. Indeed, by 1821, some three years after the incident, the United States was asserting a "possessory title" against Spain (*id.* at 408). Furthermore, President Monroe, in 1818, in the course of explaining the United States' action, introduced other considerations he deemed relevant: the national composition of the private army was quite different from the territorial entities which it claimed to represent, the private army had asserted claims to Florida, it had commissioned privateers, and its treatment of contraband and slaves had been of "the most odious and dangerous character." 2 Richardson, *Messages* 23; 2 Moore, *supra* at 408. *See also* Wright, "Territorial Propinquity," 12 *Am. J. Int'l L.* 519 (1918). Other instances which have been used to support this aspect of the private-army rule are the Caroline case of 1837 (2 Moore at 409 and *see* 1 Lauterpacht-Oppenheim, *supra* at 300*ff.*), and the Mexican interventions (2 Moore, 420*ff.*). In a number of instances, there have been bilateral agreements between governments regarding the elimination of private armies. *See* Wright, *supra* at 533.

    [8] Res. 2022 (XX), Nov. 5, 1965; Res. 2024 (XX), Nov. 11, 1965; Res. 217 (1965), Nov. 20, 1965; Res. 221 (1966), April 9, 1966; Res. 232 (1966), Dec. 16, 1966. SCOR 253–29 May 1968; SCOR 277–18 March 1970; SCOR 288–17 Nov. 1970; GAOR 2138 (1966 or 1967); GAOR 2151 (1966 or 1967); GAOR 2379 (1968); GAOR 2262 (XXII), 3 Nov. 1967; GAOR 2383 (1968); GAOR 2508 (1969); GAOR 2652 (1970).

clear that the Rhodesian precedent provides us with a continuing criterion for evaluating the legitimate exercise of state power.

Since the promulgation of *Pancha Shila*,[9] the traditional private-army rule seems to have been explicitly rejected by Communist states in association with a number of nations in the Third World. In fact, their counter-rule that wars of "national liberation" are lawful under international law[10] is only a replication of the private-army phenomenon, clothed in a new array of symbols. A war of "national liberation" is simply a war. One side (and perhaps all contending groups) chooses to cosmeticize its exercises of violence as acts aimed at culminating in "national liberation." "National liberation" and "legitimate" or "constitutional government" often lose sharp factual reference and become complementary symbols invoked to justify the responses of official elites from contending world public-order systems toward budding or blooming violence in third states. Whatever the traditional rule of international law may be, private armies become instruments of policy for larger states. This is not to imply that all participants in local wars are equally wicked, that their proffered programs are equally shams behind which power is sought, or that neutrality (were it possible) is the appropriate course for third states. The point is that words such as "national liberation" or "legitimate constitutional government" must be tested in present and projected contexts: considering all the features of the context, what will the success of one side or another mean to members of the community involved, to their region, to the world? Will the success of either side lead to a greater approximation of human dignity?

The private-army rule encounters many other difficulties. The nation-state system which establishes international law lives, perforce, with the fact of revolution. Indeed, dicta in leading international judgments recognize a right of revolution.[11] Since, in an interdependent world, the complex of events involved in an insurrectionary process regularly transcends national borders,[12] the private-army rule, as stated, becomes an international confirmation of effective power; a private army is unlawful if it is not winning. In this respect, the rule provides no guidelines for decision.

When the logical rigor of the nation-state theory cracks under the stress of political reality, one of the first casualties is the private-army rule. A significant number of the nominal states of the world do not exercise anything approaching plenary power within their borders; they are treated as

[9] First enunciated in the Sino-Indian Agreement of April 29, 1954, and reiterated in the joint statement of Chou En-lai and Nehru of June 28, 1954. For a discussion of the Soviet development of the Principles of Coexistence, *see* E. McWhinney, *Peaceful Coexistence and Soviet-Western International Law* (1964).

[10] *See generally*, T. Wolfe, *Soviet Strategy at the Cross-roads*, especially at 289 *et seq.* (1964); J. Gilbert, *Arms for the Third World: Soviet Military Aid Diplomacy* 111 *et seq.* (1969).

[11] *See*, for example, Chief Justice Taft's statement in Tinoco, 18 *Am. J. Int'l L.* 147 (1924).

[12] Interdependence and its relevance to localized acts of violence are discussed in detail *infra* at 283–84.

nation-states because of the tacit or express agreement or the coincidental disinterest of the effective global elites. At times, private armies operate from within the borders of these states. If the private-army rule of international law were strictly applied and reprisals were undertaken, these nominal states might crumble. Hence, there are strong and effective claims for the suspension of the rule in certain circumstances.[13] When this occurs, the private army's activities cannot even be appraised, much less regulated. A regional license for disorder is spawned.

In the future, the private-army rule will probably provide an even less useful focus, with ever slacker guidelines for decision. As the nation-state system cedes to an international system with a richer diversity of effective participants often bound by much tighter links of interdependence, the use of military force by non-state entities will probably increase. Because of interdependence, violence enacted within a single state will increasingly have impacts—psychological and material—on people in other territorial communities. More and more private armies will become international problems.[14]

These problems will present themselves to official and private actors. For the official, the appropriate response would seem patent: private armies are processors of violence which have not secured the overt approval of the political institutions of states or of those territorial elites who have arrogated control of the symbols of political legitimacy. But for individuals committed to a world order of human dignity, private armies present a particularly cruel dilemma. Private armies are disruptive while order seems necessarily instrumental to the realization of many other values. And there is, particularly among lawyers, an almost instinctive deference to the authority of political institutions in other communities, which is stimulated by transference, professional ideology, and the hope of reciprocity. Moreover, violence itself seems inimical to the very notion of human dignity.

Yet insistence on non-violence and deference to all established institutions in a global system with many injustices can be tantamount to confirmation and reinforcement of those injustices. In certain circumstances, violence may be the last appeal or the first expressed demand of a group or unorganized stratum for some human dignity. In this century, for example, the process of decolonization would not have been likely without the threat or use of force. And, of course, the discovery of a new private army

---

[13] *See*, for example, Falk, "The Beirut Raid and the International Law of Retaliation," 63 *Am. J. Int'l L.* 415 (1969). Consider also Professor Farer's comment on U.N. reaction to the raid: "The United Nations membership may have been influenced by the conviction that the fragility of the Arab governments precluded them from asserting fully effective controls over Palestinian guerrillas and hence they should not be held fully responsible for guerrilla activities." T. Farer, "Law and War," III C. Black & R. Falk (eds.), *The Future of the International Legal Order* 70 (1971).

[14] For authoritative intimations of degree of interdependence as the criterion for international jurisdiction, *see* Tunis-Morocco Nationality Decrees, *P.C.I.J.* Ser. B, No. 4, at 7.

is often nothing more than the refinement of an attention focus: violence in the observed sector may have been an ongoing process, or the private army may be responding to violence and not initiating it. Although we almost instinctively characterize a private army as "disruptive," it may, in fact, be a force for order in a community system of anarchy or stabilized disorder.[15] It is precisely because of the discrepancy and resultant tension between vital commitments to policies of human dignity and commitments with self-investments to institutions which are supposed to implement those policies that private armies require critical personal moral decisions.

PRIVATE ARMIES IN A GLOBAL WAR SYSTEM

Systems have their own logical coherence and internal consistency. Because so much of international law is a component of the nation-state system, the private-army rule in international law is not surprisingly a defense of the nation-state. The rule prescribes that only the nation-state may legitimately employ violence. Thus it seeks to reinforce the claimed monopoly of the use of violence by nation-state elites in order to sustain the formal legal structure of the international system as one of nation-states. Although the justification for the asserted monopoly is that it will maximize the security of the most inclusive community, the actual aggregate effect of the claim to and partial monopoly of coercion is the maintenance of a global war system. The system perpetuates itself through a complex of social and psychological factors which must now be explored.

For our present purposes, we may designate interactions as a system whenever the behavior and subjectivities of participants are self-sustained by expectations that the interactive pattern is the best one available despite costs and partial dysfunctions; the politically relevant members of the system, through self-imposed demands and expectations, continue to operate in roles that support the system and to insist that others play coordinate roles.[16] A system need not be enthusiastically supported by its members. Indeed, many may have great reservations about its operations and may insist upon certain structural or personnel changes.[17] What renders it a

[15] Wolf & Hansen, *supra* note 4, at 168.

[16] There is, of course, no dearth of proffered definitions of social systems. For present purposes, Parsons's is useful and concise. "System is the concept that refers both to a complex of interdependencies between parts, components and processes that involve discernible regularities of relationship, and to a similar type of interdependency between such a complex and its surrounding environment." Parsons, "Social Systems," 15 *Int'l Ency. Soc. Sci.* 458 (1968).

[17] Many complaints are aimed at the personnel rather than at the system itself. Perhaps Mosca was being overly droll when he observed that "In all barbarous countries populations may be dissatisfied with their leaders but ordinarily they neither conceive of better political systems nor desire any." G. Mosca, *The Ruling Class* 97 (Kohr trans., 1939). The integrative role of participant dissenters cannot be overemphasized. Many political scientists have observed the disparity between the invocation of a decision process and the final results of the process. It seems clear that

system is the minimal support given to it regularly if not habitually. By war system we refer to a social system conditioned by high expectations of violence, experiencing enough violence, directly or vicariously, to sustain that expectation, and incorporating within its myth and folklore a cosmology of war.[18]

Anthropological studies provide numerous examples of war systems. Consider the Jibaro Indians of Eastern Ecuador:

> The wars, the blood feuds within the tribes, and the wars of extermination between the different tribes are continuous, being nourished by their superstitious belief in witchcraft. These wars are the greatest curse of the Jibaros and are felt to be so even by themselves, at least so far as the feuds within the tribes are concerned. On the other hand, the wars are to such a degree one with their whole life and essence that only powerful pressure from outside or radical change of their whole character and moral views could make them abstain from them.[19]

Evans-Pritchard reports that the "social relationship" of the Nilotic tribes of the Southern Sudan "is one of hostility and its expression is in warfare."

> The Dinka people are the immemorial enemies of the Nuer. . . . Almost always the Nuer have been the aggressors, and raiding of the Dinka is conceived by them to be a normal state of affairs and a duty, for they have a myth, like that of Esau and Jacob, which explains it and justifies it.[20]

---

promotion, agitation, and invocation perform, among other things, the function of catharsis within social systems. Hence dissent, and especially institutionalized dissent, can be socially integrative, despite a characteristic anti-social or anti-elite rhetoric. In contrast, participant dissenters who work "from within" may perform different integrative and homeostatic functions. The mid-elite or elite participant, who is capable of expressing some dissatisfaction with systemic dysfunctions but still believes that the overall social arrangement is beneficial, has achieved a high degree of sophisticated perception of the dynamics and interrelating details of the system of which he is a member. Hence, in addition to personal and sub-group catharsis, his dissent is systemically "constructive" and he is more effective in stabilizing the system over time. *But cf.* Marcuse, "Repressive Tolerance," in R. Wolff, B. Moore & H. Marcuse, *A Critique of Pure Tolerance* 81 (1965).

[18] The theory of a war system has been developed in different ways by a number of writers. The most comprehensive and influential exposition is found in Lasswell, "The Garrison State and Specialists on Violence," in H. Lasswell, *The Analysis of Political Behavior* (1947). *See also* H. Lasswell, *World Politics and Personal Insecurity* (1935). A related theory, most persuasively propounded but without Lasswell's emphasis on psychopersonal dimensions, is found in R. Falk, *This Endangered Planet* (1971). The term has also been used in regard to power politics alone. *See,* for example, B. Cochran, *The War System* (1965). *See also* J. Lasley, *The War System and You* (1965). An eerie and brilliant fictional anticipation is found in Emmanuel Goldstein's "Theory and Practice of Oligarchical Collectivism" in G. Orwell, *1984* 185, 187 (1949).

[19] Karsten, "Blood Revenge and War Among the Jibaro Indians of Eastern Ecuador," in P. Bohannan (ed.), *War and Warfare: Studies in the Anthropology of Conflict* 304 (1967).

[20] E. Evans-Pritchard, *The Nuer* 125 (1940).

Cultural and religious factors and a geopolitical situation may interstimulate to establish and maintain a war system. West Pakistan, for example, has been described as a culture saturated with a war system mentality.

> An unspoken martial creed dominates the lives of Pakistanis. Conscription has rarely been needed for it is a holy duty to fight for the Islamic Republic of Pakistan. The army dominates life everywhere. The leading daily newspaper is named Jang, which means "war" in Urdu.[21]

War systems may also be conditioned by economic[22] and perhaps even by environmental factors. Thus, Rappaport suggests that, within one cultural setting, the ritual sacrifice of animals was aimed at regaining an ecological balance and that notional contents of ritual messages were actualy concerned with this rather than with transempirical matters.[23] War systems may also be supported by the value demands of one group within a society, even though a large part of the cost of that war will be borne by another group within that same society. Where, for example, intergroup conflict is an avenue through which poor but enterprising youths may acquire property, wives, or prestige and power within the tribe, they may insist on the continuation of group conflict, even though older, enfranchised tribal members who will be the targets of inevitable retaliations from attacked tribes stand to lose in continuing conflict. This fascinating infragroup dialectic has been observed among the Blackfeet Indians,[24] but it is not difficult to marshal many examples closer in time and space. Specialists in violence have a similar interest in the continuation of those conditions which make their skills indispensable to the group which they serve or wish to serve. Thus the military caste and proto-military groups and movements may promote the virtues of the spartan life, of struggle, and of the mystique of the purifying effect of battle.[25] Individual personalities appropriate to a war system may be recruited as well as shaped by culturally designated civic inculcators.[26]

---

[21] Browne, "For the West Pakistanis, War is' Closer to Home," *N.Y. Times,* December 10, 1971, p. 16, col. 7–8.

[22] *See generally* H. Engelbrecht & F. Hanighen, *Merchants of Death: A Study of the International Armament Industry* (1934); C. Thayer, *The War Business* (1969); E. Sutherland, *White Collar Crime* (1949); E. Janeway, *The Economics of Crisis: War, Politics and the Dollar* (1968).

[23] R. Rappaport, *Pigs for the Ancestors: Ritual in the Ecology of a New Guinea People* (1967).

[24] Ewers, *The Blackfeet,* Ch. 7 (1958).

[25] For one aspect, consider General Moltke: "Eternal peace is a dream, and not even a good dream, for war is a part of God's world ordinance. In war, the noblest virtues flourish that otherwise would slumber and decay—courage and renunciation, the sense of duty and of sacrifice, even to the giving of one's life. The experience of war stays with a man, and steels him all his life." Cited in H. Foertsch, *The Art of Modern Warfare* (Knauth, trans., 1940), at 3, and see other mystical statements of this order, collected at 3–5. *See also* E. King, *The Death of the Military: A Pre-Mortem* 53*ff.* (1972).

[26] *See,* for example, "The Military Public Relations Network," in H. Yarmolinsky (ed.), *The Military Establishment* 194 (1971); and particularly, "Ideological Education of the Military and the Public," *id.* at 222. A number of interesting facts and

The notion of a war system is, of course, an ideal type.[27] Actual systems have a number of dimensions, some simultaneous, some sequential and some contingent. For our purposes, a system is a war system when the war myth is a fundamental though not always manifest feature and is retained and supported through time by effective participants.

The myth complex of a war system is sustained by a pervasive anxiety for personal and group security. The apprehension of severe injury to the self-system is a primary human experience.[28] I am not concerned here with whether it is myogenic, an aspect of foetal experience, a result of birth trauma, or the sudden stimulus overload caused by the initial impact of the post-parturitive environment on an as-yet neurologically unorganized system, a result of the deprivation of focal needs of the infant, such as the breast, a later experience caused perhaps by the baffling and frightening disparity between the child's expectations and those systematized as the adult world, or an acculturated experience. Anxiety is not, in itself, a psychopathological phenomenon. The primary experience of anxiety or fear is crucial for individual survival insofar as it alerts the self-system to aspects of the environment which do threaten it with injury or destruction. Indeed, from a strict Freudian perspective, anxiety may be hypothesized as the instinctual counterpart or complementary of aggression. Anxiety acquires interest as a political pathology when fear for the survival of that cluster of nuclear and extended selves which comprise the individual personality either exceeds the environmental threat, or when it generates or contributes to such threat, becoming a crucial aspect of group experience used for political organization.[29]

---

attitudes were revealed in "Military Cold War Education and Speech Review Politics," *Hearings before the Special Preparedness Subcommittee, Committee on Armed Services, U.S. Senate, 87th Cong., 2d Sess.*, 1962, Pt. 4, at 1815*ff*. On the other hand, some studies have concluded that formal acculturation in the military was a minor variable in the formation of what Janowitz has called the "absolute viewpoint." M. Janowitz, *The Professional Soldier—A Social and Political Portrait* 267 (1960), and *see infra* at notes 27 and 28. Thus Dr. Abrahamsson found that among the three factors leading to homogeneity in the military—selection and self-selection, upward cooptation, and indoctrination—the third factor seemed to be the least decisive. Abrahamsson, "Military Professionalization and Estimates on the Probability of War," in Van Doorn (ed.), *Military Profession and Military Regimes: Commitment and Conflict* (1969).

[27] *See* Weber, "The Pure Types of Legitimate Authority," in S. Eisenstadt (ed.), *Max Weber on Charisma and Institution Building* 46 (1968).

[28] Anxiety is used here in the psychological rather than philosophical sense; no reference is intended to existential anxiety as Kierkegaard developed it, for example, in his *Concept of Dread. See generally* S. Freud, *The Problem of Anxiety* and K. Horney, *Our Inner Conflicts* (1945). A study of particular relevance to the possibilities of manipulation of anxiety for political purposes is S. Schacter, *The Psychology of Affiliation: Experimental Studies of the Sources of Gregariousness* (1959).

[29] A detailed theory of the politics of affiliative anxiety goes beyond the bounds of this essay. In particular, certain instinctual issues, e.g., Thanatos, cannot be explored. It should, nonetheless, be obvious that many contextual features as well as residual group experiences influence the level of anxiety in any setting and its amenability to political organization. Some anxiety aspects of group experience which

The political symbolization of anxiety is the threat of war and aggression by others upon the nuclear and extended self. Within the syntax of this symbol system, the conclusion that one must fight wars to maintain security is a simple geometric proof. The political solution involves the maintenance of violence specialists, prepared, at any time, to fight for the group. The specialists increase security by deterring wars; is it not obvious that, if a group is to minimize the possibility of wars without sacrificing security, it must be *prepared* to fight wars? Will not preparation deter aggressors?[30] But the presence of violence specialists increases insecurity as well as security, for by their constant and constructive presence, the specialists continue to signal the causes for anxiety and to stimulate other groups to mobilize in defense against them. The result of the interaction of all of these factors is a constant process of mobilization of the population under the supervision of security experts, anxiety managers, and specialists in violence. Their promise is security, but the inevitable result is the reinforcement of personal and group insecurity,[31] for the preparations by one group

---

influence current political trends have been briefly explored in Reisman, "Diplomatic Alternatives in the Middle East: From Obsolescent Goals to a New Program," *Approaches to Peace in the Middle East, Hearings Before the Subcommittee on the Near East, Committee on Foreign Affairs,* House of Rep., 92nd Cong., 2nd Sess. (1972). The later Freud's theory of the aggressive instinct provides an important hypothesis. The relation of individual ego development and intergroup conflict is explored in some detail in Reisman, "Responses to Discrimination and Genocide: The Convention on the Elimination of Racial Discrimination," 1 *Denver J. Int'l L. and Policy* 29 (1971). It is there hypothesized that this relationship demarks group identities as a fundamental experience of the self and, in appropriate contexts, facilitates the operation of affiliative anxiety.

[30] Janowitz has stated the point felicitously in his distinction between "absolute" and "pragmatic" types in the military: "officers with an 'absolute' viewpoint are more prone than are the 'pragmatic' ones to believe in the likelihood of major atomic warfare. Thus, belief in the inevitability of war becomes transformed into a political matter, with strong ideological overtones. As an issue of doctrine, it is posed: Must the United States be limited in its strategy to the principle that the enemy will be permitted to strike the first blow?" M. Janowitz, *The Professional Soldier—a Social and Political Portrait* 267 (1960). *See also* A. Vagt, *A History of Militarism, Civilian and Military* (1937) *passim.* Professor Huntington suggests that professionalism leads to an occupational distortion of overestimating threats initially as a means of maximizing security, but ultimately as an autonomous distortion of reality: "Consequently, at times he will see threats to the security of the state where actually no threats exist." S. Huntington, *The Soldier and the State—The Theory and Politics of Civil–Military Relations* 66 (1964). Working with Swedish data, Abrahamsson concluded that military professionalization resulted in a "trained incapacity" for realistic appraisal of the effect that peace and international tension reduction would have on national defense. Abrahamsson, "The Ideology of an Elite—Conservatism and National Insecurity," in van Doorn (ed.), *Armed Forces and Society—Sociological Essays* 71 (1968). In a subsequent study, the same investigator concluded that recruitment and cooptation were the primary causes for this occupational distortion. *Idem.,* "Military Professionalization and Estimates on the Probability of War," in van Doorn (ed.), *Military Profession and Military Regimes* 35 (1969). *But see* "Nuclear Equilibrium" and "Worst Case Planning," in Yarmolinsky, *supra,* note 26, at 99.

[31] Stekel, in his massive study of obsession neurotics, noted the relation and ultimately the continuing dynamic between a war system and psycho-personal organization. With certain statistical generalizations, he observed, after the First World War,

will always be the signal for other groups to begin to prepare them-selves.[32]

The manipulation of anxiety is, of course, a standard technique of social control, used politically, theologically, and educationally to secure from a target certain preferred patterns of behavior. The term "anxiety manager" refers to a functional role specialized to making the lay members of a com-munity sufficiently aware of the challenges to group security from within and without so that these members can be mobilized for self-protection. Such purposive generation of anxiety in the public interest follows a fairly conventional sequence: security managers are "uniquely" and "profession-ally" aware of dangers to group integrity, the maintenance of which is their

---

an enormous increase in compulsive neuroses and concluded that the condition "be-longs to those destructive social phenomena which we have come to know in the most varying and frightening forms as 'post-war diseases'. . . . "The state of war has exerted a pressure on peoples such as has never before been observed in history. Free will and personal freedom were entirely suppressed in favor of the community; there were restrictions everywhere; the fact of militarism transformed the life instinct into the 'duty to die for the Fatherland.' Whoever was forced to put on a uniform, was faced with the conflict between life instinct and the fear of social contempt (and social punishment)."

The conflict was temporarily stabilized, for many, by the development of a com-pulsion, in this case a hate compulsion; indeed, "the analysis of compulsives always reveals the importance of hatred in the structure of the compulsive system."

Note the incompatibility of this compulsion with the group's ethical code. "The war turned hate into a virtue, although the universal religion of charity had branded it as evil. The church found a way out and we were again permitted to hate without scruples, as long as the object of our hate was presented as the enemy of the father-land. But this hatred, which had risen from the depth of cultural suppression could not easily be reconverted into love, when the war was over. He who has learned to hate, has also come to know the pleasure of hating." W. Stekel, *Compulsion and Doubt* 609–10 (Gutheil trans., 1949, Universal Library Edition, 1962.) *Cf.*, on initiation into an army, Hollingshead, "Adjustment to Military Life," 51 *Am. J. Soc.* 439 (1946). For inquiry into different emotional dislocations apparently generated by induction, *see* Abrams, "Armed Forces and Society: Problems of Alienation," in J. Wolffe and J. Erickson, *The Armed Services and Society: Alienation, Management and Integration* at 24.

[32] Once a war system is functioning, many other value specialists acquire a vested interest in it. For general discussion and early citations, *see* E. Sutherland's classic *White Collar Crime* 164*ff.* (1949). Among the contemporary studies, *see* H. Magdoff, *The Age of Imperialism* (1969); C. Thayer, *The War Business: The International Trade in Armaments* (1969); V. Perlo, *Militarism and Industry* (1963); F. Cook, *The Warfare State* (1962); S. Melman, *Disarmament: Its Politics and Economics* (1962). The Marxist view that capitalism produces a surplus of value which cannot be ab-sorbed and hence must be destroyed in a war system which is a necessary concomitant to capitalism has not been established empirically; in the light of the anthropological data collected above it would appear to be a simplistic formula which cannot explain war systems in pre-capitalist and non-capitalist cultures. Some doubt about the validity of the Marxist view in regard to capitalist systems is raised in Lieberson, "An Em-pirical Study of Military-Industrial Linkages," 76 *Am. J. Soc.* 562 (1971); *but cf.* Stevenson, "American Capitalism and Militarism: A Critique of Lieberson," 77 *Am. J. Soc.* 134 (1972).

Gratifications and indulgences other than wealth may also flow to certain participants within a war system. Once the system is internalized, for example, tremendous returns in rectitude may accrue to all who participate directly or vicariously in self-sacrifice for the group.

primary concern, but group members are not sufficiently aware of such dangers to contribute the time and resources deemed necessary for minimum group security. Hence anxiety managers, by a variety of communicative techniques, make the danger phenomenally real to the general public—in the short run by the graphic presentation of the danger, in the longer run by acculturation to the general state of anxiety characteristic of a war system.

The security manager's original assessment of danger to the group may be self-serving, but it can also be concluded in good faith within his own frame of reference and yet be deemed utterly unrealistic by a disengaged observer. The discrepancy here is a product of occupational ideology. The security manager commences with an assumption of threat to group survival or group integrity which may derive from professional ideology, psychopersonal factors which initially moved him to self-recruit to security management, or both. This assumption is thereafter bloated by the "rational" projective device of "worst-case planning." Hence the social ideology of his occupation as well as personal factors will always move the security manager to have and present a most ominous picture of threats to group security. It is the function of the anxiety manager to transform this occupational ideology into a general cultural ideology.

A number of conditions seem to account for the increase of anxiety management. The transition from comparatively small professional and mercenary armies to the *levée en masse* in the eighteenth century required new techniques for mobilizing vast numbers of individuals; the development of new patterns of identification with a national symbol and then indications of threatened attack and destruction of that symbol were one economic way of attaining this objective. Indeed, mass society itself may require high degrees of civic mobilization for rapid and startling changes in collective behavior.[33] The extraordinary advance of warfare technology is another factor: the spiral of obsolescence and renewal of technological warfare requires greater investments and increased lead time. The security specialist working within this time-frame realizes that a possible danger twenty years hence can only be averted if vast resources are invested *now*. Popular support can only be mobilized, *now*, however, by exaggerating the immediacy and magnitude of the danger *now*. Hence the anxiety manager must develop intensified, almost neurotic public conceptions of a non-existent danger. Senator Vandenburg is reported to have told President Truman that if Tru-

---

[33] See, for example, Haas, "Social Change and National Aggressiveness, 1900–1960" in J. D. Singer (ed.), *Quantitative International Politics* (1968). For an extraordinarily suggestive, speculative essay on the relationship between mass society, the biological and psychological bases of anxiety and violence level, see Wiegele, "Toward a Psychophysiological Variable in Conflict Theory," 1 *Experimental Study of Politics* 51 (1971). For a rather general historical treatment of civic mobilization in national crisis, see J. Williams, *The Other Battleground: The Home Front, Britain, France, Germany 1914–1918* (1972).

man wanted public support for "containment," he would have to "scare hell out of the American people."[34]

The degree of unreality and misperception may be initially exaggerated because the security specialist operates on the basis of "worst-case" planning, which requires contingency preparations for the worst conceivable cases. The mobilization of popular support for such contingencies involves skewering the popular conceptions of insecurity far from reality. When, as we shall see, this takes place in a system of states in which counterparts constantly look at one another for hints of intentions, the mobilization becomes a self-fulfilling prophecy, and the war system grinds on.

Note that the anxiety manager need not perceive himself as exploiting the public; he may believe the danger exists and that his role is educational. Indeed, danger may exist, and the communication may, in fact, be educational. On the other hand, the alleged crisis may be falsified and a sense of panic generated in a group in order to move group members to displace onto the anxiety manager or another symbolic figure. Thus the medicine man or healer may gain the obedience of a group by persuading members that magical powers under his exclusive control which are capable of warding off or curing disease will operate only if group members behave in ways prescribed by him. An aggravating technique may involve exaggerating the likelihood of incidence of the disease, its horrors, or even the inevitability of the disease if his prescriptions are not followed. A promised health program or political campaign against a dreaded disease may provide the same bounties for a political leader.

Much of international relations can only be understood in terms of a war system. The rhetoric of peace is more than neutralized by the symmetrical prominence of the military in competing governments. The manifest drive is for security, in a system which is structured for insecurity. Note the crucial infrastructural aspect of nation-states themselves in such a system. The allocation of power is, of course, an inescapable concern, but one of the functions of a system of nation-states, indeed one of its inevitable features, is perpetuation of insecurity through such artifacts as the "balance" or "imbalance" of power.[35] The expectation of violence, manufactured and maintained, is communicated to citizens who in turn displace their magnified anxiety onto national symbols.[36] This, in turn, maximizes the power of

---

[34] S. E. Ambrose, *Rise to Globalism* 151 (1971).

[35] This is not the place to investigate the curious infiltrations into social theory of metaphors drawn from the physical sciences. Whatever meaning "balance" may have had in contemporary physics, it is obviously a highly ambiguous semantic instrument for social process. Because the components of power remain undefined, the balance is perpetually insecure. Of course, for states which practiced "balance of power" politics, the term served as a scientistic figleaf for covering naked power interventions into the relations of other nations to secure value allocations in favor of the intervening state.

[36] The vast public relations and media network which is regularly deployed to shape and maintain certain public attitudes has been discussed and cited *supra*. In addition, a large number of para- and postgraduate military organizations play sec-

incumbent national elites. The core of international law, as we have seen, has comprised express and tacit communications between various territorial elites about the minimum reciprocal deferences demanded for the bases of power of each. Precisely because the private army challenges this base, the traditional private-army rule prescribes that there may be no private armies. The principle of national liberation is no exception to this general rule, for the significant word is "national." Wars of national liberation, at least to the present time, have not sought to supplant the nation-state, but only to seize control of it. The most vigorous proponents of national liberation have been among the most vocal supporters of sovereignty.

The authoritative prohibition of private armies in traditional international law must not be misunderstood. Private armies are unlawful, but precisely because they perform such a crucial function for the global war system, they receive selective support from different national elites. While a war system requires a culture of parochialism, self-sacrifice, and the paraphernalia of wars, it does not require wars. Rather, it requires a pervasive *expectation* of impending violence in order to sustain and magnify personal insecurity. Small wars can be nourished as a neat means of keeping this expectation alive.[37] Because many private armies are limited in ambition and scope to a single national arena, they are an extremely useful and comparatively safe way of achieving this effect. At the same time, by providing a focus for "confrontations" of the greater powers and regional

---

ondary roles as opinion leaders and policers. For a discussion of eight major personnel complexes which perform these functions, *see* "The Military Public Relations Network" in Yarmolinsky, *supra* note 26, at 194, 206. Intensive transference phenomena are generated in all mundane civic situations in which the symbols and totems of the inclusive group are approvingly displayed. Thus the flag in the church and in the sports arena provides signals for general tacit support for the elites who are the official guardians of these symbols. And not surprisingly, teachers, clergymen, and sportsmen may integrate into their messages the crisis of the inclusive group and the comfort which can be taken in its brave protectors. Much of this mass mobilization is, of course, endemic to industrial and technological societies, which require highly organized and standardized mass production and consumption behavior and hence use techniques which regularly shape and sustain the self-systems of individual group members so that they can be instantly deployed in patterns of behavior deemed socially desirable.

[37] Media provide fantastic opportunities for political elites to generate maximum anxiety from small wars which may have no connection with their own constituency. The naive view that repeated graphic presentations of violence in Vietnam, Biafra, or Bengal will make an audience "realize" the full horror of war and hence never engage in or wage wars operates on the curious assumption that the heroic efforts of political and military leaders restrain awful popular drives for wars. Actually, the presentation of such violence may well exacerbate latent anxieties in many community members. Vicarious participation in violence may provide some gratifications, but it is a complex communication which also stimulates the conclusion that "this is real" and could happen to the viewer should his defenses ever lapse. The net result may be a gain for the violence specialist and the anxiety manager. Graphic presentations of domestic violence may be put to the same use.

hegemonies, a deep sense of personal and group insecurity is sustained.[38] Thus the war system continues, promising minimum individual and group security through the instrumentality of nation-states, but based upon and fostering personal and group insecurity.

The viciousness of a war system is circular as well, for even those who concede its horror and absurdity perceive that what may have begun as or become a neurotic anxiety for security has, in part, generated and, in part, reinforced a situation in which the sense of insecurity can be quite accurate and rational. Many of the environments which man inhabits are inimical. In international politics, there is, indeed, a very real enemy, with very real operations-plans. One is driven to support counter-measures of defense even as one realizes that these measures may themselves increase aggregate anxiety, reinforce the enemy's hostility, and maximize insecurity. Strict pacifism is viewed within the war system as a denial of reality, as irrational and socially irresponsible. It "plays into the hands of the enemy." "Rational" pacifism, in contrast, expresses itself in demands for arms control, efforts at reciprocal disarmament which maintains appropriate arms "levels" or "balances," prescription of principles of the inviolability of states, and establishment of security organizations, whose avowed aims are the maintenance of "the territorial integrity and political independence of member states." Given the pervasive expectation of violence, however, it becomes imprudent to trust these organizations overly; states hedge by retaining their own forces, with "balances" and authoritative restraints, and the juggernaut continues.[39] Paradoxically, rational pacificism reinforces the war system.

Private armies acquire a unique systemic dimension in a war system, but they are not an exclusive function of a war system, produced by it for its own purposes. As we shall see, many types of social and personality conditions generate private brigades. Official and private observers have no diffi-

[38] While it would be easy to impute responsibility for these events to "wicked" individuals, to do so would be to miss the real point. The sustained determinant of behavior here is the aggregate system and its systemic roles. Individual anxiety managers do, of course, maximize anxiety in order to aggrandize personal power and, where possible, should be made responsible for this. Yet, given a war system, someone will always hazard such a gambit.

[39] A stunning example of this phenomenon is found in the U.S.–U.S.S.R. Strategic Arms Limitations or "Salt" negotiations. In 1971, a Brookings study forecast that, if a pact could be concluded, "the U.S. would probably increase spending on intelligence collection and research and development as a hedge against Soviet cheating or a possible breakdown of the agreement." The prediction proved entirely too modest. After a set of agreements were reached in May, 1972 (30 *Cong. Q. Weekly Rep.* No. 23 [June 3, 1972] at 1256, 1258, 1259, 1261), anticipated pressure from more anxious domestic political forces was to be deflected by a Department of Defense initiative of its own. Thus, the inevitably anonymous Pentagon official was quoted as saying "To quiet the thunder from the right, it becomes your patriotic duty to do everything that isn't prohibited by the treaty. That's what happened in 1964 after the limited test-ban agreement: We had more tests than before." Levine, "A Grain of Salt: U.S.–Soviet Arms Pact May be More a Symbol than Effective Rein," *Wall Street J.*, May 26, 1972, p. 1, col. 8.

culty in indicating those areas about the globe where conditions are ripe or overripe for local violence. If a rapid transformation of the world arena from a war to a peace system were possible, these same areas would continue to be flammable until the social disorders had been cured. Then the significance of a denotation of violence would not be its threat of escalation, but rather its indication of some social pathology and its invocation for social reconstruction.[40]

If transnational decision-making were restricted to official elites, suggestions for a different approach to the problem of private armies would not be practicable. Most official elites—incumbent and aspiring—are committed to the continuation of a system which they see as palpably maximizing their own interests; like many others, they have internalized a system which they manage. Bureaucracy, of course, generates its own infrainstitutional political dynamic, and aspiring elites can be expected to formulate a new program of symbols as a counter-ideology to mobilize support and aid in taking over. Where fundamental challenges to the global system promise political dividends, they will be symbolically adopted—until bureaucratic power has been secured. More effective and perhaps more lasting changes in decision-making must come from unofficial sectors of society: from media, private opinion leaders, universities, intellectuals, members of the clergy, and so on. That these extra-individual officials can play a role in the formulation, application, and revision of policy has been demonstrated in the past few years.[41] Since they are increasingly being confronted with claims to international authority, they urgently require a new set of goals and a framework for locating events.

CLAIMS TO INTERNATIONAL AUTHORITY

The complexities of the private army require transnational significance when a claim is made on other participants in the world system to respond, in some way, to the extant or probable consequences of acts in a particular case. A claim need not be formulated as a "legal" petition nor need it be consciously lodged by a self-perceived claimant. We may speak of a claim when events "demand" the attention of decision-makers.[42] Consider, for

[40] For discussion, see infra at 278 ff.

[41] For brief discussion of the role of civic initiatives in international law, see Reisman, "Polaroid Power: Taxing Business for Human Rights," 4 For. Pol., 101, 107–10 (1971); idem., "Sanctions and Enforcement," in III Black & Falk (eds.), supra note 13, 273, 310ff. (1971); idem, "Making International Humanitarian Law Effective: The Case of Civic Enforcement," in J. Paxman & E. Boggs (eds.), The United Nations: A Reassessment 30–38 (1973). On the potentials of the intellectual, see K. Mannheim, Ideology and Utopia 136ff. (Wirth, Shells trans., 1936); but for discussion of institutional influences, see H. Wilensky, Intellectuals in Labor Unions (1950).

[42] The emphasis on unformulated claims is critical to the analysis which follows, for, as Dean Pound observed, it permits the observer to apply policies and perspectives of authority to any flow of behavior. The degree of formulation of claims varies with

example, an unaffiliated army operating in state A which habitually crosses the border of state B to escape capture, to replenish arms, to rest, and so on. The border area of state B may be an uninhabited desert; the officials of state A may have pressing diplomatic reasons for not crossing into B in "hot pursuit," for not protesting the de facto sanctuary afforded by B and even for ignoring the regular crossing. We consider these crossings a claim because they demand attention and hence activate *some* response; however disposed, the response implements and perhaps creates international policy.[43]

The procedures for lodging claims in institutionalized processes have a compelling fascination for the technically oriented lawyer. Without minimizing the circumstantial importance of these procedures, our concern is with substantive claims. Our conception of outcomes of the process of claim is an independent inference of the fairly stable perspectives and operations created or sustained by the interaction of claimants and decision-makers. In a case, for example, where representatives of a private army in state X seek discussion in the General Assembly, but where the effective elites of the Assembly bar such matters from the agenda, we are not concerned with the procedural refinements adduced by lawyers. Rather, we seek to identify the actual outcome, in context, of dismissing the request for inscription on the agenda. The decision may be tantamount to a refusal to view the private army or selected aspects of it as a matter of world public order, leaving it instead to civic order regulation. Or it may be tantamount to shunting the case off to a more restrictive arena: for example, a cabal of the powers or a regional organization. Or it may, by accelerating certain tendencies, be an

---

the type of arena. "In organized arenas, claims are clearly formulated. In arenas of a low degree of organization, in contrast, subjectivities are often modulated by indirect communication. It is the investigator who must infer claims from behavior and formulate them verbally. This exercise necessarily requires an examination of events in the most comprehensive context and the use of inference devices not conventionally employed by the law." M. Reisman, *Nullity and Revision: The Review and Enforcement of International Judgments and Awards* 145 (1971).

[43] The massive international legal literature on the precipitating events which sanction outside participation in fairly localized violence is not directly relevant to the thesis developed here. In a state of global simultaneity, a process of interinfluence inevitably links outsiders with the more direct participants in violence; modulations of outsiders' behavior cannot but influence the outcomes of the localized violence. Hence there is only futility in identifying situations which outsiders ought not to influence; the critical question is *how* they ought to influence. As to the precipitating events themselves, my thesis, developed in detail below, is that they are only one element in a decision regarding how to respond to some local violence; of much greater importance is the question of the probable consequences in terms of all community goals of not intervening and/or of intervening in any of a number of ways. Law's responsibility is the amelioration of the future, not the integrity of the past. Hence in each case, the challenge to a creative international law is the invention of a program of response which maximizes all community values. *See generally* Moore, "The Control of Foreign Intervention in Internal Conflict," 9 *Va. J. Int'l L.* 206 (1969); *but cf.* Farer, "Intervention in Civil Wars: A Modest Proposal," in I R. Falk (ed.), *The Vietnam War and International Law* 509 (1968).

intended decision in the guise of a non-decision.[44] If, for example, the private army in state X is certain to be destroyed unless it secures help from or through General Assembly discussion, the Assembly's refusal to undertake the issue is an unequivocal verdict and sentence.

The briefest scheme of the process of claim includes claimants, their perspectives, the varied situations in which claims are lodged, and the strategic modalities by which claims are lodged. The aggregate outcomes of claims would set out the contours of the constitutive process and public order features of private armies. While we cannot, within the limits of this essay, consider these features in detail, a number of observations are crucial. Consider them in regard to the phases of the process of claim.

CLAIMANTS

Some claims are raised directly by the private army or its representatives or by local groups, elite and rank-and-file, directly affected by the activities of the private army and/or the counterforce against it. In other circumstances, officials of external states or of international agencies may lodge claims on their own behalf or on that of direct participants. Despite the rigid prohibition in traditional international law, it is becoming increasingly more common for third states to champion the private army or its target, as the case may be, and to designate themselves claimants for their particular protégés. Private organizations and individuals may also be claimants. Corporations with operations or aspirations in the arena of belligerency may turn to their own governments for some action which the corporations deem favorable to their own objectives. Such lobbying is a claim, often of critical magnitude. Civic-action groups may press national or international officials for some decision affecting the private army in question. All of these demands can be considered claims to authority in that they invoke decision-makers to respond on the basis of asserted community policies.

PERSPECTIVES

The perspectives of claimants—their identifications, demands, and expectations—vary in many ways, accounting, in part, for the conflicts which precipitate claims. But these perspectives converge in the process of claim in that, at some level of consciousness, they are appealing to a more inclusive authority system. Hence the mere process of claim is a reinforcement of authority for both claimants and decision-makers. The act of claim is a crucial social event for law.

SITUATIONS

Claims may be lodged in highly formal decision situations (for example, organs of the United Nations or international or national tribunals) or they

[44] *Id*. at 625 *ff*.

may be inferred from diffuse behavior in extremely unorganized situations (for example, the border-crossing problem which we considered earlier). In most sectors of international law, the vast majority of claims take place in the diplomatic setting, through bilateral inter-elite communications. Situations have great influence on the form and content of a claim, and the investigator may require entirely different sets of tools for identifying claims in different situations.

STRATEGIES

Claims may be communicated to elite groups (diplomatic communication) or they may be directed to broad audiences, via radio, TV, leaflets, and so on (ideologic communication). The communications may be attended by actual or threatened force (military strategy) or with promises of economic indulgence or deprivation (economic strategy). Most claims will integrate, in varying ways, all of these components. Many claims seek, of course, by the excessive use of coercion, to render themselves into unilateral decisions.

SPECIFIC CLAIMS

The claims made by private armies and/or others affected by them are most economically grouped in terms of claims regarding participation, perspectives, the establishment of institutions and the access to established arenas, value support or deprivation, and the use of certain instruments of policy. Let us consider briefly each of these groups of claims.

1. *Claims for Participation.* Because the interpersonal attribution of status has value consequences, a large number of claims are lodged regarding eligibility for and the preferred attributes of participation. A private army may claim the status of an "entity," as a belligerent, a state, a guerrilla army, and so on; others may insist on characterizing the same groups as bandits, brigands, terrorists, pirates, etc. The legal incidents which attach to such characterizations can be critical features of the subsequent context. Claims for the participation of outsiders generally invoke such complementary norms as "international concern" or "domestic jurisdiction" and may also seek to establish preferential patterns in regional and global participation. Many participatory claims may be lodged after the fact. In a subsequent claim for compensation, for example, the association of the deprivor with a state may impart a degree of immunity from claim.[45]

2. *Claims Regarding Perspectives.* An entire category of claims relate to the perspective patterns of contending parties. Major demands may be made regarding the identification or disidentification of participants with certain public order systems. Claims may also insist upon explicit revelation of the sought public order system for which violence is being used.

[45] *See*, for example, Johnstone v. Pedlar [1921] 2 *A.C.* 262.

3. *Claims Regarding Situations.* Private armies and their supporters may insist upon the establishment of an entirely new power arena within their area of operations or, alternately, may assert that they exercise violence in order to bring about selective changes; opponents claim support for the continuation of established situations. Where outsiders condition support for one side or another on certain situational innovations or retentions, a pattern of authoritative demand may be discernible.[46] Claimants will also seek access to a variety of institutionalized processes, as a means of maximizing their interests. The right of access to general international organizations and functional agencies will be contested; on a different plane, claimants may seek access to nation-states, the use and recognition of passports, and so on.

4. *Claims Regarding Bases of Power.* In any interactive system, participants regularly claim protection for certain base values which they believe crucial to their security and, at the same time, turn to others for additional values which may be used as power bases. Hence the claims considered here relate to every single value which may be of some use in securing or regaining power. For many of the value claims, there have been complex prescriptions of the world community; arms, for example, are purportedly limited in diffusion by both international policy as well as national licensing procedures.[47]

5. *Claims Regarding Modalities.* Participants in private-army situations make and are subjected to claims (by outsiders as well as by their own counterparts) as to the appropriate modalities and targets of violence. Thus claims to use or refrain from using terror, ideological compulsion techniques, economic deprivatory techniques, ecologically degenerative strategies, etc., will be lodged. Closely connected with these claims will be the identification of legitimate targets of coercive modalities.[48]

THE INTERNATIONAL RESPONSE: THE WORLD CONSTITUTIVE PROCESS

An earlier study explored the complex processes of authoritative decision in the world community.[49] Many different individuals and groups participate in international decisions in direct and indirect forms, and many different decision arenas may have contributed to the culminating value

---

[46] One can assume, for example, that the institution of conditional recognition is used quite widely: recognition is bartered for certain assurances about future behavior.

[47] *See* Bader, "The Proliferation of Conventional Weapons," in III Black & Falk (eds.), *supra* note 13, at 210; L. Frank, *The Arms Trade in International Relations* (1969).

[48] Reisman, "Sanctions and Enforcement," *supra* note 38, at 309–10.

[49] McDougal, Lasswell & Reisman, "The World Constitutive Process of Authoritative Decision," I Black & Falk, *supra* note 13, at 73.

allocations and comparatively stable expectations which an observer would characterize as a decision. In major security cases, international organizations seem to be playing an increasingly rhetorical role. The nation-state agencies and individual official roles active in international decisions are many and complex. The traditional focus of the international scholar has been on those agencies or roles formally specialized to international decisions: legal adviser's offices in Foreign Ministries or the Department of State. What these agencies do becomes, by definition, international law. But because these institutions are the very guardians of the system of myths which I have described, their formal response to private army claims is almost always negative. A realistic scholarly focus would include all those agencies and roles, overt *and* covert, actually making private army decisions; their responses are not always uniform. Thus, the Foreign Office of State X may support the government of State Y in its internal difficulties, while a covert security agency of X may be supporting a private army in Y, challenging the government. Indeed, in the intricacies of international politics, the covert agency may, in varying degree, be supporting both government Y and private army Y!

Although officials of nation-states often appear to be the nominal decision-makers in cases of private armies, they themselves may be responding to the influence of business units, pressure groups, religious groups, media elites, or a vast inchoate constituency which has been partially mobilized for specific purposes.[50] Since these secondary groups may, themselves, be formed, operated, or influenced by external actors, a process which seems to affect a number of large nation-states may extend itself again across national boundaries. With such a complex and extraordinarily flexible decision process, the appropriate question is not who has been a functional decision-maker in the past, but rather how can those individuals disposed to playing a role in the international authority process maximize their own effectiveness.[51]

The perspectives of decision-makers introduce other complexities. There are, of course, enormous diversities in the extant and contingent identifications of individual decision-makers with the territorial and non-territorial communities about the globe. Two particularly relevant dimensions of identifications are (1) the extent to which decision-makers develop *inclusive*

[50] For useful documentation, bibliography, and hypotheses, *see* Sumida, "Transnational Movement and Economic Structures," in IV Black & Falk, *supra* note 13, at 524.

[51] There is an enormous literature on the question of who, if anyone, ought to participate in localized violence. *See generally* Moore, "The Role of Regional Arrangements in the Maintenance of World Order," III Black & Falk, *supra* note 13, at 122; Firmage, "The Role of International Law in Regulating Foreign Participation in Internal Conflicts," in R. Falk (ed.), *The International Law of Civil War* 405 *et seq.* (1971); and *see also* the useful introductory essay by Falk, *id.* at 1–28. A most useful survey of sources is offered in the copious notes in Higgins, "Internal War and International Law," III Black & Falk, *supra* note 13, at 81.

identifications and (2) the extent to which they are dis-identified with the contemporary state system. The conjunction of these two patterns of identification is an index of how decision-makers may try to exploit private-army instances in order to transform the dynamics of a global war system into a peace system. Demand and expectation patterns will follow these general contours.

The range of decision situations for private-army cases is extremely broad. A tourist excursion, a border police station, a national court or the lower level of a national agency, an international tribunal or an international organization may provide the setting or a setting in a sequence of arenas of private-army decision. In any circumstance in which a claim, as the term has been defined here, is lodged, a functional decision situation is generated. Hence a vast array of citizens may find themselves transformed into decision-makers.

In different circumstances, those who perform decision functions may draw on any value as a power base. Official elites may base themselves primarily on effective power, but this, in itself, frequently serves to attract many other values. Thus Tönnies spoke of institutional charisma:[52] where community members have been conditioned to respect and "look up" to their leaders, official power *per se* comes to import enlightenment, skill, respect, and rectitude; these potential bases can make non-official participants more effective in transnational decision processes. The most critical value available to non-official participants is enlightenment. Without it one is unable to break the conditioned interpersonal cycle of deference to official elites in the Tönnies' or *fait accompli* phenomenon; nor can one identify the neurotic dimensions of security anxieties and the role they play in a war system. In many strata, enlightenment, respect, and rectitude attributes represent great bases for influence. In some circumstances, skill in agitation and mass mobilization may promise a high degree of effectiveness.

By strategies we mean the timed sequence of events in which values are deployed to secure certain outcomes. In a complex, unorganized arena, not all strategy programs involve the use of language and the formalities of institutionalized and ritualized decision; military and economic strategies may be used without a commentary. The media and interpretation specialists, located in counterpart political institutions, will later attribute significance to these strategies, thereby reinforcing the prescriptive complementarities we have noted previously. On the other hand, the deployment of values accompanied by communications to either elites (diplomatic) or large audiences (ideologic) may attempt to couple events with an authentic interpretation of them.

---

[52] F. Tönnies, *Community and Association* (Loomis, trans., 1955). The Tönnies' hypothesis is supported by subsequent research. *See* F. Greenstein, *Children and Politics* 29 (rev'd ed. 1969). For the general phenomenon, *see* Paul, "Impressions of Personality, Authoritarianism, and the *Fait Accompli* Effect," *J. Abnormal and Soc. Psych.* 53 (1956).

Inferences by observers and participants about fairly stable expectations of authority and value allocation comprise the outcomes of these complex decision processes. We may distinguish constitutive and public order outcomes as well as outcomes which are decision functions of the process. Private-army decisions can be usefully considered "constitutive" when, in addition to their nominal impact on a particular private army, they significantly reinforce or change the fundamental international process of authoritative decision as it pertains to private-army cases. A decision by the General Assembly, for example, permitting representatives of a private army to address the Assembly or one of its subsidiary bodies once that private-army question had been inscribed on the agenda would involve an enormous constitutive change. Similarly, a hard-fought decision to continue to bar private-army representatives could also be considered constitutive in that it reinforced a particularly important aspect of the world constitutive process. Though every decision has a constitutive dimension in that it has some effect on the global process, we reserve the characterization "constitutive" to those decisions with significant impact on the process which establishes and maintains the fundamental institutions of decision.[53]

Every decision, constitutive or otherwise, has public order impacts, for it affects expectations and practices involving allocation of all values. Indeed, concern with the immediate public order effects of an impending decision is what motivates the participants to act. A decision aiding or impeding a particular private army can thus be gaged in terms of its effects on power allocations, wealth production and distribution, skill, enlightenment, respect and so on.

A decision is a complex of activities, beginning with the provision of intelligence data on through to the appraisal of the social effects of a flow of decisions. In systematic breakdown, we distinguish intelligence gathering, the promotion of policy, the prescription of policy as authoritative, the invocation of decision-makers upon alleged deviations of behavior from prescriptions, application of prescriptions to such behavior, the termination of prescriptions and finally the appraisal of the aggregate performance of the decision process for certain or for all sectors.[54] Policy preferences may be projected for each of these decision functions and performance indices can be developed by comparison of policy and trends. Such an investigation is beyond the scope of the present essay, but its implications for the private-army problem must be noted. For example, a flow of accurate intelligence is required for rational decision; yet there is comparatively little data on private armies and it is delivered sporadically and usually only after the situation has become critical.

---

[53] McDougal, Lasswell, & Reisman, *supra* note 46.
[54] *Id.* at 131 ff.

THE CONDITIONS FOR PRIVATE ARMIES

The conditions which account for the appearance of private armies are many and complex. Certain individuals recruit themselves to the specialty of violence for personal reasons; many may fulfill deep personal needs by serving in anti-establishment rather than establishment brigades. Millenarist or antinomian drives may play a role.[55] Others may be attracted to the intimacy and security of life in a corps. Within limitations, the military life offers a range of legitimate forms of self-expression, from monastic self-repression to suicidal vainglory.[56] And there are, perhaps, biological "bonding" drives or instincts which act to bring certain individuals together.[57] In some cultures, the warrior mode is an accepted, if not honorable calling;[58] at certain periods in history, it has been considered the most honorable.[59] Even where it is generally denigrated, it may, as a distinct subculture, generate its own respect and rectitude system.[60]

Many structural features which may account for the rise of private armies remain to be explored. It is, as yet, unclear whether large-scale or small-scale societies are more likely to produce private armies[61] or what effect centralized as opposed to decentralized systems have on the emergence or duration of private armies.[62] Certainly Hobsbawm's theory of the social bandit as primarily an agrarian phenomenon[63] has been challenged by the emergence of an "urban guerrilla."[64] The corollary hypothesis of the

[55] N. Cohn, *The Pursuit of the Millenium* 149 ff. (1957).

[56] On the military as a multivalue social system, *see* C. Coates & R. Pellegrin, *Military Sociology: A Study of American Military Institutions and Military Life* 153 ff. (1965); S. Stouffer et al., *The American Soldier* (1949); M. Janowitz, *The Professional Soldier* 44 (1960); and *see generally* L. Festinger, *A Theory of Cognitive Dissonance* (1957).

[57] D. Morris, *The Naked Ape* (1967); L. Tiger, *Men in Groups* (1969).

[58] "Banditry of expropriated peasants, in countries such as China, Spain, and many others, is not regarded as a dishonest but rather as a praise-worthy and heroic occupation." F. Borkenau, *World Communism: A History of the Communist International* 325 (1962). For a general discussion of social banditry, *see* E. Hobsbawm, *Bandits* (1969). *But see* G. Alroy, *The Involvement of Peasants in Internal Wars* (1966).

[59] Thus the right to bear arms was long restricted to the nobility. Cf. N. Timasheff, *The Sociology of Law* 11 (1939).

[60] *See*, for example, D. Maurer, *The Whiz Mob* (1964), for an instructive picture of the generation of a fairly autonomous respect dynamic in a sub-culture characterized by the dominant culture as criminal. On internal military responses to negative characterizations by the more general culture, *see* Rosser, "American Civil-Military Relations in the 1980's," 24 *Naval War Coll. Rev.* 6 (1972).

[61] *See generally* Stinchcombe, "Social Structure and Organization," in J. March (ed.), *Handbook of Organizations* 142 (1965) and especially 153 ff.

[62] Chinese experience suggests that a weak center and poor communications encourage military regionalism. J. Sheridan, *Chinese Warlord: The Career of Feng Yu-hsiang* (1966). For other relevant hypotheses, *see* E. Luttwak, *Coup d'Etat* 25–52 (1968).

[63] Hobsbawm, *supra*, note 3.

[64] M. Oppenheimer, *The Urban Guerrilla* 41 ff. (1969).

likelihood of private armies in sparse as opposed to dense population areas and rural as opposed to urban settings must now be reexamined. Nor are there more than unverified hypotheses regarding the effect of different patterns of formal social organizations or types of stratification on the emergence of private armies.[65] The general assumption that private armies are a product of deteriorating government seems oversimplified. Pareto had assumed that

> Whenever the influence of public authority declines, little states grow up within the state, little societies within society. So, whenever judicial process fails, private or group justice replaces it, and *vice versa*.[66]

A more plausible hypothesis would be that private armies will form in circumstances in which identity groups believe that their interests can be maximized by the use of purposive violence. The effectiveness of group processes will be only one consideration in such an assessment.

Many of these points are considered in Wolf's and Hansen's structural analysis of *caudillo* politics, a dynamic and nonetheless strangely stable system of multiple private armies characterized by

> the repeated emergence of armed patron-client sets, cemented by personal ties of dominance and submission, and by a common desire to obtain wealth by force of arms; . . . the lack of institutionalized means for succession to offices; . . . the use of violence in political competition; and . . . the repeated failures of incumbent leaders to guarantee their tenure as chieftains.[67]

Caudillaje, as Wolf and Hansen show, is a response to a unique set of economic and social variables which in turn conditions alliance patterns, personal values, and sexual and other relationships.[68] It arises, they believe, from "the inability of any socio-economic class to monopolize sufficiently

---

[65] Of some contemporary significance is the possible division of urban and rural environments as a cause of conflict in which private armies proliferate. *See* C. Tilly, *The Vendée*, 16–37, 340 (1964).

[66] IV V. Pareto, *The Mind and Society* 1519 (Bongiorno and Livingstone, trans. 1935). Nor need the absence of indigenous community institutions for legitimate violence lead necessarily to the growth of private armies. A high degree of homogeneity among the population may lead, instead, to the growth of an institution of "popular justice": *see*, for example, A. W. Lintott, *Violence in Republican Rome* 6–21 (1968).

[67] Wolf & Hansen, "Caudillo Politics: A Structural Analysis," 9 *Cont. Stud. Soc. Hist.* 168–69 (1967).

[68] Another study of different institutionalized techniques of power seizure and change in Hispanic America—including *caudillaje, machetismo, cuartelazo, golpe de estado, revolución, imposición,* and *continuismo*—concluded that all of these power changes were conditioned by Hispanic culture. "Hispanic culture tends everywhere in Latin America to dominate in the power sense; . . . the institutions of Hispanic culture such as the family, church, army, educational institutions, and economic systems, are essentially authoritarian in nature, hence, conditioning the individual to more frequent acceptance of processes of dictatorship, including violence, than processes of political democracy." Stokes, "Violence as a Power Factor in Latin-American Politics," 5 *West. Pol. Q.* 445, 467 (1952).

both wealth and power in order to organize a centralized political apparatus."[69]

If the private armies of the *caudillaje* are a product of an anarchic system whose continuation elites believe to be in their preferred interest, other private-army situations may in fact be centrally organized and planned. In the Spanish colonial empire, for example, as in earlier feudal arrangements, public order was to be maintained by the garrisons of individual nobles or *padrones*. Thus, in Mexico, "the viceroy and the military authorities found it convenient that a militia leader be at one and the same time the landlord of the men who served under his command."[70] In certain circumstances in the United States, private police and even gangs have performed comparable public functions in collaboration with the official police.[71] In all such situations, a degree of order is purchased at the price of an ever present possibility of challenges to the nominal center by tolerated power clusters on the peripheries. Probabilities of *putsch* or revolution at the center as opposed to secession would seem to be governed by variables such as degree of centralization and decentralization, degree of integration of the population, geographical scope, status and power of competing peripheral power clusters, and the potential for autarkic existence of putative seceding components. Presumably, the system would continue to be one of private armies when the variables "balanced out" so that respective private army elites felt they optimized their interests in a continuation of that political system rather than in a resolution through a central *putsch* or a secession.

Many private armies are generated in situations of rebellion, and serious studies of the phenomenon must perforce incorporate the vast scientific literature on the sociology and psychology of rebellion.[72] Actual case studies emphasize the interdependence of many complex factors. Consider the cross-cultural historical studies of the intense peasant revolts in many countries in Europe and Asia in the 17th century.[73] A century of inter-state wars required larger standing armies, which raised the tax load and necessity for popular material contributions appreciably; this aroused resistance from the peasantry which in turn called forth increased coercion in tax-collecting measures. In the same period, atmospheric calamities caused bad harvests, shortages and epidemics. Bad weather, cold winters, and cold and wet summers seem to have been extraordinarily frequent in the 17th century.[74] The general result was widespread impoverishment. Against this background,

---

[69] *Id.* at 177.

[70] E. Wolf, *The Mexican Bajio in the 18th Century* (Middle American Research Institute Publication, No. 17) 177, 192, quoted in Wolf & Hansen, *supra* note 63.

[71] *See* II Kakalik & Wildhorn, *supra* note 2.

[72] For hypotheses and comprehensive bibliography, *see* T. Gurr, *Why Men Rebel* (1970), and *see also* H. Graham & T. Gurr (eds.), *Violence in America: Historical and Comparative Perspectives* (1969).

[73] *See*, in this regard, Mousnier, *supra*, note 4. Comparisons are drawn at 305 ff.

[74] *Id.* at 314–15. Compare E. Thompson, *The Making of the English Working Class*, especially 472 ff. (1963); E. Hobsbawm & G. Rudé, *Captain Swing* 195 ff. (1969).

some of the revolts were stimulated by aristocrats as instruments for secur-ing power among themselves. Some may have been influenced by new patterns of stratification. Others may have been begun by unpaid soldiers or, as in Russia, by a nobility which felt oppressed by the innovative police methods of the Czar. Subtle geographical factors may also have played a role.

Revolts, of course, need not lead to the continuation of durable private armies. Conversely, situations short of revolt may produce an abundance of private brigades. In periods of rapid social change abounding in social dis-continuities and the disintegration of traditional social units, private bri-gades may provide tight frameworks for identification, livelihood, the exchange of affection, the exercise of skills, and the achievement of self-respect.[75] They also offer plentiful opportunities for discharging rage and frustration. Where these private armies project rather comprehensive sym-bol systems, it is probable that they provide a great personal experience for formerly pre-political individuals, who, for the first time, find an oppor-tunity to identify with an inclusive group beyond the nuclear family, or a kin-group of real or fictitious consanguinity. This factor may be par-ticularly important when kin-groups are disintegrating.[76] Unfortunately, we have no descriptions or accounts of the exhilaration of being a member of a peasant army in a great revolution.[77] Yet it is not difficult to imagine why this focus for new loyalty proves more successful than do the conven-tional symbols of the nation-state. Thus, for many societies, the private

[75] For a detailed exploration of the psychological and social conditions which may have facilitated the growth of private armies in Weimar Germany, see R. Waite, *Vanguard of Nazism: The Free Corps Movement in Postwar Germany 1918–1923* 18–32 (1952), and especially the psychoanalytic suggestions concerning the formation of youth movements in these circumstances. It was part of Hitler's genius to manipu-late such violence-oriented groups in order to acquire official power. Once he had control, these same groups became impediments to the systematic exercise of power; hence they were eliminated in the "Blood Purge." Hitler himself provided an extraor-dinary explanation of why the Free Corps elite had to be purged: "[They are] perma-nent revolutionaries who in 1918 had been shaken in their former relation to the state and uprooted, and had thereby lost all inner contact with the human social order. Men who have no respect for any authority . . . men who found their profession of faith in nihilism . . . moral degenerates . . . constant conspirators incapable of any real cooperation, ready to oppose any order, filled with hatred against all authority, their restless and excited minds find satisfaction only in incessant intellectual and conspiratorial activity aimed at the destruction of all existing institutions. . . . These pathological enemies of the state are the enemies of all authority. . . ." (Quoted in Waite at 280–81.)

The conditions of growth of popular violence in contemporary modernizing states are graphically presented in S. Aiyar, *The Politics of Mass Violence in India* (1967).

[76] Lewis observes, in regard to the Assassins, that "In the atomized and insecure society of the later Caliphates, men sought comfort and assurance in new and stronger forms of associations." B. Lewis, *The Assassins: A Radical Sect in Islam* 128 (1968). Since modernization is usually accompanied by the distintegration of traditional units of social organization, one can hypothesize an increase in the number of private armies as part of a more general phenomenon of an increase in crime.

[77] But see J. Deniefe, *A Personal Narrative of the Irish Revolutionary Brother-hood* (1906, 1969).

army may prove to be a successful transitional form for the politicization of crucial cadres drawn from pre- and sub-political groups and for their gradual integration into a community akin to the nation-state. Insofar as large numbers of people languish in forms of pre-political thralldom, a condition for the emergence of private armies continues. Indeed, the demands and protests which seem to be part of the structural transformations from traditional to modern society may themselves generate private armies.[78]

The private armies which are most challenging to international policy and decision are those with a significant degree of popular support, whose manifest objective is the creation of a new or separate territorial community. This problem, misnamed for historical reasons "self-determination," refers to a much broader phenomenon: the continuous demands of individuals to express themselves in group identities and to seek lawful modes for group expression and protection.[79] The process of "consociation," as Weber called it,[80] need not be violent; in a preferred social order, it would be a persuasive, rational process. It may become violent for a number of reasons. Self-selected "revolutionary" elites may exploit violence as a means for forging new, intense, and comparatively inclusive identifications among a people.[81] Incumbent elites who feel challenged by a pressing counter-elite may resort to violence for personal or cultural reasons. Not a few elite groups in the twentieth century have evidenced the manner, intelligence, and/or goals of thugs.

But a more pervasive condition for the emergence of private armies in self-determination situations may be found in the fundamental international legal system itself. The basis of this system is a reciprocal respect among territorial elites for the territorial integrity of each community, the most critical base of power of these elites. A private army, no matter what its popular base, is viewed as alien and hostile to the system and is resisted. And precisely because the private army is a signal for political and personal anxiety, elites can always count on a large degree of popular support for

---

[78] S. Eisenstadt, *Modernization: Protest and Change* (1966), and *cf.* Tully, *supra* note 61.

[79] Note that the principle of self-determination is complementary to principles of inviolability and continuity of state organization. The reason why such a potentially destructive doctrine or a functional equivalent is retained by established national institutions is that virtually all extant states were created by extra-constitutional, if not violent, means. Because a claim to rule on the basis of naked power alone is a concurrent invitation for others with power to aspire to rule, enfranchised elites require an authority myth. Hence self-determination or something similar provides doctrinal legitimization for the existence of a state. Any myth, if accepted, can perform such a function: e.g., divine right, social contract, dux bellorum, volksgeist, and ritualized group trauma; the current doctrine of self-determination springs from a natural-law source and has been expanded by revolutions since the eighteenth century. Of course, once the doctrine has served its purpose, it must be deactivated. Hence it is distinguished and deemed to refer only to certain circumstances, for example, colonial situations.

[80] Weber, *supra* note 1.

[81] *See supra* note 2.

their own program against it. Because the international system does not provide for the orderly emergence of new communities, the process of consociation is perforce violent; aspiring elites of would-be communities know full well that they must win all or lose all. International agreement against private armies does not, as we have seen, avoid or obviate the problem, for decision-makers located at different points in interlocking national and international systems are presented with and must respond to private army claims. The result is muddled policy, disorder, and value waste.

PROJECTIONS

The conditions for the emergence of private armies are sufficiently rich and varied to assure the presence of private armies in any number of constructive futures. A construct of a world of garrison states[82] might retard the tendency of human beings to develop identification systems on the basis of interaction patterns. The complete control of communications, the increasingly adroit management of anxiety, wide use of truth serums and psychopharmaceuticals, the use of neuro-surgery on "deviants" and a variety of other techniques in the increasingly sophisticated arsenal of technological social control might reduce rank-and-file and mid-elite strata to automatons; it would not, however, prevent the emergence, within the elite, of a counter-elite which would itself use the techniques of mind control to turn the populace against the incumbents.[83] In another construct, nuclear or nonnuclear war might destroy the state system and the greater part of the social infrastructure of large segments of the globe. Thereafter, private armies without territorial identifications, ambitions, or inhibitions would roam desolate stretches. In such a construct, the policy problems which we have discussed in this essay will have scant occurrence.

If the state system, as currently organized, is projected into the indefinite future, the phenomenon of private armies may be expected to multiply, for individuals in a process of consociation will have recourse only to skill in arms and violence for formation and maintenance of group processes. If the current social and economic structures continue throughout most of the world, claims of private armies may continue to demand attention of decision-makers. They need not lead to major confrontations, but may be manipulated by elites in such manner that they maintain a high expectation of violence and thus reinforce a global war system. Support of private armies and local wars, with the constant threat of intervention, will then become a primary strategy of elites for the maintenance of the war system. As it has in the past, the globe will be divisible into civic zones, in which the level of intercommunal violence is comparatively low, and war zones in

[82] Lasswell, *supra* note 18.
[83] On mass conversion, *see* Sargent, *Battle for the Mind: A Physiology of Conversion and Brainwashing* (1957) and the bibliography there.

which the practice and expectation of violence is high.[84] Private armies of different and shifting affiliations may roam more or less at will.

It is not improbable that current social and economic structures throughout the world will change radically in the imaginable future. A decisive lowering of the cost per unit of energy, coupled with the further development of technology, may weaken the social fibers of geographical interdependence which have been woven to assure ready access to raw materials and markets; many "resources" will then be artificially rendered from available environmental resources.[85] Coupled with this development is the probable change in social value systems and the obsolescence of the need for external markets. Thus, the net result may be sets of communities about the globe which are less outward-looking, less interdependent and, hence, less concerned about private armies and violence in other communities. In this construct, the phenomenon of private armies might continue in diverse settings, but it would not be the occasion for claims on and decision responses by other national and international decision-makers. On the other hand, the drama of private armies might be retained by elites as a means of maintaining the anxieties of a war system and thereby maximizing their own power.

The most desirable of future constructs, that of a world-order of human dignity, envisages a rational regional organization of the world, based on the maximum shaping and widest sharing of all values. Within these regions, there will be networks of differential value structures, ranging in scope and institutionalization according to the goal values of the community. Thus, a wealth community based on economic criteria will be overlapped by a variety of power arenas, structured on different principles. In this system, the process of consociation will proceed persuasively rather than coercively, as decision-makers arrange and adjust the various territorial groupings to take account of the changing identities and demands of individuals. With the general expectation of reasonable responses to claims, the claims themselves will cease to be strident demands for "independence" but rather for various degrees of prescriptive competence for specific value sectors. Private armies, where they occur, will no longer be connected to the process of consociation and will be subjected to the appropriate criminal rather than political sanction.

ALTERNATIVES FOR THE FUTURE

The reasons for the appearance of private armies are, as we have seen, multiple. Within the projectible future, it is realistic to expect many more

---

[84] For the distinction between civic zones and zones of terror, *see* E. Walter, *Terror and Resistance: A Study of Political Violence* (1969).

[85] *See generally* Basiok, "The Import of Technology in the Next Decades," 14 *Orbis* 17 (1970); *id.* "Technology and World Power," 200 *Headline Series* No. 200 (1970).

private armies to come into or to continue in operation in any particular sector because of conjunctions of external and internal stimuli. These armies and those affected by them may lodge claims on the international level. The inclusive authority system of the world, fragmentary as it is, does project a rule for private armies. But because of the complexity of the events presented to decision-makers in private army problems, there can never be a single, simple answer. The event complexes from which the specific question springs are always unique as is the world context in which they occur. In many cases, the traditional private army rule cannot be applied; in the minority of cases in which it might be applicable, the results may well be dysfunctional. Lawyers too often overlook the painfully obvious fact that though the events which precipitate decisions come from the past, decisions themselves are future-oriented; the test of their quality is not whether they conform to the past, but rather whether they structure processes and value allocations in the near and distant future in preferred ways.

A contemporary focus on the traditional private army problem in international law would address itself to the problem of official and unofficial decision-makers at many different junctures of transnational interaction, who are obliged to respond, in a direct or ancillary fashion, to events involving the activities of armies not affiliated with an established nation-state. Formulated in these terms, it is readily seen that the private-army question is simply a part of the much broader phenomenon of the establishment and maintenance of authorized participants in international law. The problem of private armies, like the problems of recognition and self-determination, touches on aspects of the more inclusive conception. Indeed, the attenuation of focus of each of these subconceptions by inhibiting rational decision may accelerate the formation of private armies.

Decision-makers faced with any of these questions require a way of locating the particular events to which they are obliged to respond in a broader social and constitutive process, to understand what dynamic conditions have given rise to a particular private army, to clarify the policies and goals of the global, regional, and national communities concerned, to relate the probable consequences of different decision options open to them to preferences for social and constitutive processes, and, finally, to develop a rich and flexible range of strategies for dealing with these problems with an eye to the immediate and to longer-range effects. The challenge is not merely to suppress violence, for violence is a ubiquitous feature of social processes and a characteristic of law. The challenge instead is to respond creatively to violence in ways which use it to lever toward an improved world-order.

A complete acquittal of these requirements goes beyond the scope of the present essay. For the moment, I intend to deal only with the problem of goals and decisional principles which might better orient the contemporary decision specialist with regard to the private-army problem and to the improvement of those aspects of the constitutive process most pertinent to it. Here, as elsewhere, goal clarification is critical. The free individual recognizes and accepts the inevitable element of choice in every decision which he observes or in which he participates. Hence he projects (and invites others to project) explicitly those social goals he recommends and for which he assumes responsibility. The goals that follow, from the most general to the most specific, are such recommendations.

THE GOAL OF HUMAN DIGNITY

Because all of social reality is a vast interlocking manifold, single events have varying systemic implications. Hence the necessity arises for clarifying an extensive general goal for which all more specific goals can be considered instrumental and against which all available choices may be evaluated. The most fundamental recommended goal is that of a public order of human dignity in which all values are abundantly produced and widely shared.[86] The innate worth of each individual human being is postulated; the test of public power is the extent to which it provides the conditions for optimal self-realization. There are no formal preferred institutional structures for human dignity, since contexts change and varying structures are required to mediate between community goals and environmental conditions. Yet enough peremptory demands continue through time to provide some profile of preferred public order systems. First, social and political structures must provide a high expectation of minimum order within the prevailing context of effective power; anxiety for personal and group integrity can be minimized only when the comprehensive world decision structures take account of the potential for anxiety stimulation of component parts. Second, structures must enable the maximum sharing of power and other values among participants. Third, structures must facilitate the high production and dispersion of all other value components of human dignity, not only within the putative territorial community but in the more inclusive communities of which it is a part.

I. PRELIMINARY PROCEDURES

1. THE PRINCIPLE OF PRELIMINARY SELF-OBSERVATION

The projection of explicit goals imports the formulation of a program of goal-oriented or "rational" behavior. Weber's definition of rational action continues to recommend itself as a concise description:

---

[86] For a brilliant integration of the many international prescriptions for human dignity, *see* McDougal, Lasswell, & Chen, "Human Rights and World Public Order: A Framework for Policy-Oriented Inquiry," 63 *Am. J. Int'l L.* 237 (1969).

A man's action is purposively rational if he considers the goals, the means, and the side effects, and weighs rationally means against goals, goals against side effects and also various possible goals against each other.[87]

The crucial agency of goal choice as well as formulation of instrumental programs for goal realization, is the individual's self-system. Hence the need for a set of procedural principles for on-going self-observation in order to increase the probability of making instrumental choices likely to realize the major goal and in order to minimize choices which *seem* to be rationally related to manifest goals but which are, in fact, responses dictated by cultural conditioning, group identification, and the residue of psychopersonal experience.[88] This is not the place to consider factors such as phylogeny, neurotic rigidity, parochial and sub-group conditioning or institutional stereotyping, or the available techniques for neutralizing their distortions, but a number of specific factors should be noted. For individuals with certain types of crisis exposure, the mere fact that "violence" is being used by groups unaffiliated with the state may push them to extremes of response. For psychopersonal reasons, challenges in another arena to authority may be summarily rejected or supported without regard to the merits of the activities or the consequences of the response. A leader of one of the contending groups may be identified at a level of consciousness with an imago. Subtle identifications such as "we" soldiers against those non-professionals may operate.[89] Religious or cultural conditioning may push the decision-maker to extreme perceptions of good and evil or right and wrong. Seemingly inconsequential geographical features may become subtle signals of past associations. Thus, "North" versus "South" may recall the American Civil War to some decision-makers. Deep ambivalences about racial prejudice may paralyze some potential decision-makers from responding to

[87] M. Weber, *The Theory of Social and Economic Organization* (Parsons trans., 1947).

[88] All ego autonomy from instinctual drives as well as environmental stimuli is, of course, relative and in many circumstances tenuous. The discussion here is not intended to imply that I have or that there is a way of achieving perfect "rationality," but rather to emphasize the prevalence of the problem for decision-makers and appraisers, to propose the potential for its minimization if not neutralization, and to suggest a range of procedures which may be available in many situations of choice. To paraphrase Freud's famous apothegm, "Where id was, there shall ego be," I suggest that we demand of ourselves and of others that the ego component displace the id component in those situations of decision or choice-making in which other human beings are affected in proportion to the number of others affected and the magnitude of the effects. *See generally* Hartmann, "On Rational and Irrational Action," in Hartmann, *Essays on Ego Psychology* 37 (1964), and Rapaport, "The Autonomy of the Ego," in Gill (ed.), *The Collected Papers of David Rapaport* 357 (1967) and "The Theory of Ego Autonomy," *id.* at 722.

[89] G. Draper, *The Legal Classification of Belligerent Individuals* 5–9 (1970), cited in Farer, "The Laws of War Twenty Five Years After Nuremberg," 583 *Int'l Concil.* 36–37 (1971). On the intellectual susceptibility to self-imposed blinders, *see* O'Brien, "Politics and the Morality of Scholarship," in C. O'Brien & W. Vanech (eds.), *Power and Consciousness* 33 (1969).

events between racial groups. Which factors prove critical will depend on the psychopersonal and psychocultural history of each individual.

Conditioned responses (as opposed to rational responses) do not appear as such; they are invariably decked out in the paraphernalia of crypto-rationality accompanied by invocation of selective legalisms, culled from the rich body of complementary norm-sets in law systems. They often take the form of dissociation: "This matter doesn't concern me (us)"; "domestic jurisdiction"; the "obligations of neutrality"; an "inability to be effective." Through use of any number of techniques of self-exploration, the individual decision-maker may recognize that a certain choice toward which he is tending is conditioned by different residues of past experience. The important point is to recognize the relevance of this self-scrutiny as a recurring decisional task. Once it is grasped, every situation may be used simultaneously as a means of auto-exploration as well as extra-exploration.[90]

2. THE PRINCIPLE OF CONTEXTUALITY

Systematic contextual approaches to sectors of the social process are necessary to the law, not because they are intellectually elegant, but because they are the only way of rendering the law an effective instrument in a complex and manifold social process.

The traditional and, unfortunately, contemporary approach of international law to violence involves severing it from its context and characterizing it as delictual *per se* without regard to its genesis or to the probable consequences of the jurist's characterization.[91] If such an approach were recommended in domestic criminal law, it would be dismissed as utterly primeval, for many criminal lawyers are moving to the realization that social control requires focusing on the causes of deviations from norms and the projected effects of what the decision-maker may do as well as on the symptomatic deviation itself.[92]

Rational decision will require examining, within the limits of time and economy, every feature of the present and projected contexts. Anecdotalism will be avoided only if a systematic map of the social process is employed. Contextuality may disabuse the decision-maker of certain notions which he entertains and, from the outset, force him to a wider range of considerations and alternatives. Consider, for example, the ubiquity of violence. A legalistic approach will tend to identify as violence only those coercive activities of groups not affiliated with the nation-state, or more generally, not used to maintain or further the interest of the particular group with which the observer identifies.[93] A contextual approach, in contrast, will permit the

---

[90] A praxis of self-scrutiny is developed in Reisman & Shapiro, "Goal Clarification" (forthcoming).

[91] H. Kelsen, *General Theory of Law and State* 21, 50 *et seq.* (1961).

[92] R. Arens & H. Lasswell, *In Defense of Public Order* (1961).

[93] IV V. Pareto, *The Mind and Society* (1935).

observer to inventory *all* the violence in a society or a sector thereof without regard to the putative "legality" of its agency.

The principle of contextuality has a number of ramifications for private armies: the assessment of pre-arena events; the principle of conditional recognition; the principle of contextual location; and the principle of post-arena events. Each of these will be considered as a separate principle.

Assessment of Pre-Arena Events

Contextuality implies not only a lateral extension of focus (as well as a focus on the self-system examining the process), but also an extension in time. The focus of law is traditionally initiated by a conflict. But a plenary contextual focus involves a comprehensive consideration of the complex of events which preceded the eruption of conflict and which, in different ways, may continue to condition the conflict. On the rhetorical level, of course, advocates and decision-makers always assert that they have systematically assessed the pre-arena events. Closer examination shows that this is usually a pleonastic device. The phase analysis—a technique which will be developed in some detail in the following pages—is a useful way of organizing data from social process, for it permits detailed examination of particular factors without ever losing the sense of their integrity and variability with the broader context.

The Principle of Conditional Recognition

The animating commitment to value preferences rather than to specific institutions means that a policy test must be applied, not only to the private army in question, but equally to those incumbent elites or entire institutional arrangements which it is seeking to supplant. Although this principle challenges the entrenched position of the nation-states in international law, it conforms to an older tradition oriented toward the individual; even in the heyday of state sovereignty, international law allowed for such exceptional remedies as humanitarian intervention.

The recommended principle of conditional recognition in private-army cases is less a matter of derivation from monistic doctrine than a dispassionate acceptance of the actual dynamics of recognition. In any interactive process, participants' attitudes, and the behavior thereby shaped, are critical components in the multivalue bases of power of any other participant vis-a-vis whom they are directed. Thus an elite group is a "government" not only because of the effective control it disposes (or fails to dispose) in some sector, but also because other internal and external participants choose to view it as a government and to act accordingly: to give it all the crucial perquisites which make the status of government worth seeking. Although conceptions of linear causality should generally be avoided in the complexities of social interaction, there are certainly circumstances in which observers can note that a particular elite group has authoritative power because other participants have chosen to recognize it as so seised.

Conditional recognition thus requires that the contending private army as well as the incumbent government (which it either seeks to displace or from which it seeks territorial separation) be equalized for purposes of analysis. The observer, in short, assesses two "private" armies. Indeed, to assume that one must support an extant government simply because it is the extant government begs the juridical questions of the private army and imposes an answer by definition.

The Principle of Contextual Location

Suspending recognition is preliminary to a contextual examination of the conflict; past trends as well as probable future sequences are considered by use of a general phase analysis which seeks to comprehend a dynamic social process in terms of who is involved in it (participants), what are the psychological components which animate the participants (perspectives), where and under what circumstances do the participants interact (situations), what values do different participants draw on in order to inter-influence (bases of power), and how do they manipulate these values (strategies) and with what outcomes. Each phase stimulates a number of critical questions.

Participants. Are the nominal antagonists the real parties? Are they proxies for outside groups, such as states, transnational political orders, classes or castes, or international wealth groups? Would support for one or another of these groups (or failure to support—a decision in the guise of a non-decision) lead to a secure termination of hostilities, continuation of hostilities or the stimulation of new forms of hostilities? In many places in the world class, caste, or racial, ethnic, linguistic, or tribal groups are the fundamental social units; while the replacement of one of these groups with another may resolve a particular conflict in conformity with broader community goals, it may also kindle ancient hostilities between that group and other social stratifications. The result may be the stimulation of a sequence of private-army problems, the deterioration of local public order, and a world-wide increase in the expectation of violence.

Are the nominal antagonists representative of the population at large? Are they simply feuding "first families" or oligarchic groups enacting closet dramas against the backdrop of an inert, prepolitical population? Would supporting one or the other of the contenders increase the politicization of the population or increase effective power sharing? Questions such as these require *independent* investigations. Whatever the case may be, contenders may be expected to incorporate contemporary legitimization symbols. In war, all sides recruit Peace, God, the Muses, the Masses, Liberty, and other modish symbols.

Perspectives. What are the perspectives which animate the different participants or the significant non-participants? Specifically, what are their demands, identifications or expectations? Each of these components stimulates a number of questions.

Identifications. Identifications tend to condition the entire attention focus of an individual and to stimulate demands on the self. As such they are critical components of social interaction. Some of the more critical questions regarding identification patterns of elites and rank-and-file in private armies are:

1. Intensity of Identification with a Territorial Community: To what extent do the elite and rank-and-file of a private army identify with an existing or projected territorial community, the establishment, control, or maintenance of which is the ostensible justification for their exercises of violence? Although doctrine and formula insist that an army as such is the exclusive apparatus of the state, a corps of violence specialists need not identify itself with any significant intensity with the symbols of a nation-state. In this respect the "private" army may be the garrison of a state as well as a guerrilla band which ranges itself against the state.

Before the ascendancy of mercantile classes vouchsafed the imprint of their interests on developing international law, private armies were the primary intergroup actors for extended periods; the code of honor of knights and soldiers provided a normative framework for much of their interaction;[94] it is not improbable that modern mercenary groups manifest some of the same shared code of arms and honor. In these historical cases, a territorial link was not significant. But significant changes in community structure, resource use, and interdependence have made territory more important. In contemporary conflict, it is critical to distinguish bandits and outlaws from private groups exercising violence with some degree of terri-torial ambition or defense of group integrity. Past decision has, for the most part, drawn such a line, but it has usually done so for advocative rather than scientific designative purposes. The presence of minimal identifications does not, of course, automatically render the activities of a private army lawful; many other factors in extant and projected contexts must be considered. While territorial intentions do not automatically legitimate, their absence in a private-army program may signal some concern, for some degree of stable social organization would seem to be the *sine qua non* of value production and minimum human dignity in the contemporary interdependent world.[95]

2. Inclusivity of Identification with a Territorial Community: To what extent do those private armies associated with a present or a projected terri-torial community identify with all members of that community? To what extent do they identify with a single class, stratum, or ethnic or linguistic group? Inclusivity of identifications generates the presumption that the success of the private army will minimize subsequent internal conflict. Exclusivity of identification promises to generate counter-private armies,

[94] A. Bozeman, *Politics and Culture in International History* 399–401 (1960); Draper, in Farer, *supra* note 84.

[95] Chen & Reisman, *supra* note 5, at 5–6. Nonetheless, groups organized for vio-lence might contribute to certain types of preferred social change. Here, as elsewhere, evaluations must be contextual and goal-oriented.

civil, racial or ethnic war, and possibly genocide or classicide. The identification symbols of private armies oriented to territorial control regularly characterize themselves as the most inclusive; this is often a strategy of mobilizing the widest possible support for such groups. Hence, actual identifications must be examined with scrupulous care by means of an investigation of the full flow of perspectives *and* operations of the armies concerned. The converse of these questions must also be posed: are the activities of the private army supported by individuals who share an identification pattern? Is the identification territorially inclusive or exclusive, i.e., does it allow for the addition of all other members of the community over which the private army would exercise control or does it exclude individuals and groups?

3.   Intensity of Identification with Regional and Global Communities: In an intensely interdependent world, the effects of many critical events diffuse through regional and global communities, affecting larger numbers of people and, as a result, bringing into play more inclusive policies. The exercise of violence in order to consolidate a nation-state, for example, may not be an exclusive or "domestic" consideration. Consider the implications for transnational security. Since the change of personnel or of myth of state may influence that polity's future membership in latent war or peace communities, the elites of other states will become involved. They will inquire into the identifications of the private army with a system of regional order and with an actual or preferred system of world-order. A number of questions become relevant. To what extent are the identifications of the private army regionally endogamous or exogamous? To what extent do they conform to the principles of the Charter and the Universal Declaration of Human Rights?[96]

Demands. The phase analysis of the pre-arena or precipitating events of the private-army phenomenon provides data on the intensity and distribution of demand in the relevant, affected population. The appropriate questions concern not only the demands of those associated with the private army or armies, but also the demands of those associated with incumbent groups as well as the demands of those sectors of the population who identify with none of the contenders. Investigations of demands should go beyond the rather simple questions of separation from or displacement of an established elite and should consider systematically actual as well as contingent value demands. What are the demands of groups A, B, and C regarding power, wealth, enlightenment, respect, or rectitude? The difficult job of unraveling demand structures may pay off handsomely in pointing to hitherto unseen possibilities for integrative programs and stable political alliances between groups which had been quite hostile to each other. Contingent demands refer to latent potentialities for new and different value

[96] McDougal & Reisman, "Rhodesia and the United Nations: The Lawfulness of International Concern," 62 *Am. J. Int'l L.* 1 (1968).

demands which can be stimulated by some external agency. Contingency explorations extend the range of strategies available to decision-makers faced with private-army problems.

Human beings who associate to apply violence may be pursuing all values. Manifest objectives may range from the more obvious such as *power* and *wealth*, to *well-being*, the delight in physical prowess, being "in shape"; the pleasure of exercising the unique *skills* of violence; the desire to win *respect* from peers; *rectitude*, the waging of holy wars as well as wars of vengeance, or the sheer ecstasy of killing. Latent functions, to borrow Merton's phrase, may extend to almost every organizing procedure of a particular community. Thus, in some societies, young men go to war in order to prove their manhood, to achieve a mystical adult identity, to win wives, horses, and other property, or to find outlets from repressive institutions in their home societies. Insofar as the brigade environment becomes the primary, even nuclear, society for soldiers, all other values may become manifest and latent objectives, in varying degree. Whether the army we are considering is private or is associated with a recognized nation-state, any aggregate of soldiers will probably be pursuing all values, though the predominant objectives may vary from soldier to soldier.

It is obviously of critical importance to identify the full range of value demands of private armies, manifest and latent. Only with a sense of these demands can one proceed to gauge the ramifications of the continued operation and success of these groups. Consider a number of value demands. While all private armies are primary participants in the power process, not all such groups demand access to or a major share in authoritative power. For example, brigands, a functional term which can include generals of official armies as well as the bandits they sometimes pursue, may perceive their interests in the continuation of a dominant culture from which they periodically pilfer. In this respect, their demands condemn them to the position of a parasitic sub-culture. On the other hand, politically motivated bank robbers, who steal in order to finance political operations, may demand not access to the wealth process, but radical change in the entire social process. Where the primary value demand of members of a private army is virocratic respect, the group demand is not for the termination of a war system, but rather for its continual operation.

Because of these complex interrelations, the demand structures of personalities can be most efficiently examined through systematic inquiry into each value category. The aggregate of all value demands provides a profile of a preferred public order system. This, in itself, becomes a major factor in decision response. The following questions are relevant.

1. What are the preferred public order demands of the private army for the territorial community over which it seeks control? Do these demands amount to a radical change of the extant public order? Change in certain public-order sectors only? Retention of the existing public order system?

2. What are the regional public-order demands of the private army?

3. What are the global public-order demands of the private army?

As in any heterogeneous group, there may be a number of competing public-order demands put forward by different internal participants. What will prove to be the dominant, operational-demand pattern may depend in significant part on the purposive or unintentional deeds and words of external participants. Demand studies may, then, open the way for demand shaping.

Expectations. What are the world views, the complex of matter-of-fact expectations about the past and the future which are entertained by the different participants in a private-army situation? To what extent will alternative courses of decision change those expectations in desirable or undesirable ways? Obviously, presuppositions and cultural postulates, which are held so deeply that participants themselves are unaware of them or deem them to be phenomenal rather than cultural, affect the entire frame of reference of participants; they determine the options which participants will perceive, the perspectives which they will attribute to adversaries and allies, the events which will dominate their focus and those which will escape perception. Expectations about authority, how it is formed and how it is changed and terminated, will be critical considerations for decision. A subgroup which operates on the basis of the charismatic authority of a leader, for example, will require an entirely different set of responses if it is to be transformed into something compatible with other goals, while members of a subgroup in a *caudillo* system may shift allegiance to a larger group if the newer leader manifests in higher degree the preferred qualities of *caudillaje*. In each case, different conceptions about authority import different dynamics of establishment and change of group decision structures. Strata which operate with a world-view holding gloomy prospects for effective human change in power and environmental processes may be almost unmobilizable until these expectations have been changed. Because the private-army situation is almost always cross-cultural, involving groups shaped by decisively different experiences, careful examination of expectation patterns will be critical, both for understanding conflict and for formulating alternatives.

Situations. Private armies become matters of pressing "international concern," not simply because claims are lodged about them, but also because the elites of a global system internationalize them. Certain wars will remain matters of local, sporadic violence because of the comparative geographic isolation of the arena and the low technological capacity of the participants. Where conflict occurs in a strategically located sector or where participants have a technological capacity which, if exercised, will upset tacit international restraints, an otherwise local conflict internationalizes itself by mobilizing the attention of larger states. Hence the first situational question: Without regard to other values at stake, will a recommendation of comparative inaction increase the localization of a private-army conflict or, alternatively, will a recommendation of some action decrease the internationalization of the conflict? Any number of strategies may be employed to achieve these results. Whether a conflict should be domesticated or internationalized is, of course, determined by the assessment of impact on broader goals of world-order and human dignity.

Private armies operate in military arenas. Is it possible to shift the focus of conflict, in part if not in entirety, to a comparatively civic arena? Is it possible to change a private-army conflict to a non-violent political conflict? The formation of a coalition between contenders, for example, can change the structure of a conflict situation; though the private armies may remain intact, a new group of functionaries acquires a strong vested interest in the maintenance of a civic rather than military arena. A consideration of perhaps greater importance is the extent to which outsiders are, by their intervention, transforming an arena of comparatively low violence to one of higher violence.

Situational features may provide important insights into the perspectives of participants. Choices of arenas of belligerency in which there are many civilians, for example, might indicate low propensities for according minimal human dignity in other political situations.

Bases of Power. The focus is on values—power, wealth, enlightenment, skill, well-being, affection, respect, and rectitude—which are or can be deployed (a) in a continuing or escalating conflict; (b) in projected constructs of different futures, military and civic.

What values are contending parties capable of drawing on? What values are available in the arena of conflict but are not being mobilized by either side? Most important, what values might become available if a military arena could be converted to a non-military arena? Assessments of bases of power are, of course, critical tasks; a crucial consideration of all outsiders is the probable winner or loser or the probabilities for stalemate. Without regard to the merits, probable losers just do not receive ready support from internal as well as external participants.

The point of emphasis in value assessments is comprehensiveness and contextuality; all values must be considered, and they must be evaluated in both extant as well as projected contexts. Mere arithmetical computations are to be eschewed. In particular, the intangible values which military inventories do not include must be studied; patterns of affection, loyalty, respect, and rectitude are the sweat and sinew without which no value combination can work effectively.

Strategies. How do immediate participants choose to deploy their values? Is there evidence of a cultural bias or a personal predilection for the use of coercive or of persuasive strategies? Are there indications of a desire or willingness to limit violence, when used, within the normative bounds of the so-called laws of humane warfare? Strategy choices by participants are indications not only of how they will proceed in a military arena, but also how they will behave should they succeed and acquire power in civic arenas. The choice of the technique of terrorism, for example, may imply cavalier disregard for human value or a comparative ease in derogating from verbal commitments to human dignity in crisis situations.[97] A preference for mechanized weapons, for instance, may indicate a facility for dehumanizing targets. Conclusions such as these must, of course, be derived contextually. A demonstrated preference for non-coercive strategies will not necessarily win the support of others. On the contrary, realistic interappraisals of effective elites about the globe may construe a willingness to use violence as an indicator of sufficient "toughness," "guts," and determination to run a state.

Contextual Projections

To what extent can observers discern the probable outcomes of a private-army case, assuming that they and those with whom they identify do nothing? What do these outcomes mean, in terms of *all* values, for (1) the individuals in the community in which the private army operates; (2) the surrounding communities; (3) the encompassing region; (4) the world constitutive process? Observers associated with large powers are prone to a hubris which arrogates the entire world as the property of the symbol to which they give allegiance; hence the instinctive formulation of projection is: What happens if *we* win? What happens if *we* lose? Without considering for the moment the moral defectiveness of such egocentricity, it is plain that it is an exceedingly inefficient way of essaying projections of probable futures. Whatever composite entity "we" may refer to, it will always be only one participant in the future, and it will always be dependent on others whose interests must be accommodated.

PROCEDURES FOR DECISION

We have now considered a number of procedures preparatory to choice, which permit the observer or decision-maker to focus on the self as the instrument of perception and choice and on the manifold social process which precipitates and provides targets for decision. While these procedures are, of course, continuous, they are conjoined at some point with the overt formulation of possible responses aimed at the selective influence of events. Many of the substantive goals of these responses have been adverted to in the previous pages; most generally, we have urged responses which secure a degree of self-policing minimum order and, at the same time, approximate or move toward an improved world-order of human dignity. We have noted

[97] On the other hand, what one belligerent characterizes as terror may be characterized as lawful by the observer. One must be wary of characterizations of criminality in intergroup behavior. The lawfulness of any violence, it would seem, must always be tested contextually.

as well the unique nexus between private armies and the effective international law of a war system; hence there is a coordinate goal of responses which minimize the political stimuli of personal and group anxiety and contribute toward changing a war system to a peace system. In the following pages we consider procedural principles relevant to the formulation of responses to the private-army problem.

CONTEXTUALITY IN THE FORMATION AND APPRAISAL OF RESPONSES

From the contextual viewpoint, the test of effectiveness of the military strategy is not the degree to which a military objective has been secured, nor is the test of the effectiveness of an economic strategy the extent to which an economic objective has been attained. Whatever specific program of techniques is settled on, the only realistic evaluation of its success is in terms of all the value consequences which it precipitated as compared to all the value consequences which alternative, rejected strategy programs might have precipitated, each assessed in terms of the full range of goals projected. Thus, contextual evaluation may shift the outcome of a military engagement from the center of attention to a comparatively trivial position; even where a specific outcome retains significance, it must always share consideration with the other consequences of action. Specifically, what are the effects of a planned response on the extant political structures of the country or countries to be affected, and what are the effects on the civic orders in these communities? Will the response reinforce these structures or initiate or accelerate their dissolution? Will changes or reinforcements increase or decrease approximation to human dignity? Will they change a military arena to a civic arena? What are the effects of the planned response on the physical environment? For example, if an optimum ecological balance is one which homeostatically discriminates in favor of the human species, does the planned response move toward or away from such a balance? What are the effects of a planned response on regional systems? On the global system? On the inclusive constitutive process?

The components of every program must be considered in context. Yet some strategies may, in the broader configuration of events, predictably accelerate certain trends; this consequence should be considered and, where possible, neutralized. In a war system, for example, the use of the military strategy raises the expectation of violence and increases anxiety; thus violence reinforces rather than weakens the total system. Insofar as one's goals include minimization of a war system, strategies which reinforce it should be eschewed or should be accompanied by symbols which reduce these undesirable consequences.

AUTHORITY: CONFORMITY AND CONFORMATION

In pluralistic communities, norms are expressed in complementarities. The function of authoritative decision is to seek accommodation of complementary interests in a manner most consonant with the common interests of the entire community. Hence, the sonorous assertion that decisions should take account of or conform to the law are of scant help to decision-makers, for the "law," in any specific case, is always expressed in complementary norms which prohibit and permit. Virtually every private-army case is subjected to the dualism of traditional international law of "domestic jurisdiction" and "international concern." But no situation can self-characterize as one or the other of these alternatives. A choice must be made. The delineation of claims precipitated by the private-army phenomenon shows that even a preponderantly "domestic" army case may initiate a transnational process of claim for some values. The problem is further complicated by the fact that a private-army case may involve a *per se* challenge to the system of formal international authority; it may, for example, be the vanguard of a competing world-order system which seeks radically different socio-political arrangements about the globe. In short, the invocation of one of these complementaries conceals a complex decision about the location of competence for that particular case.

Do not minimize the role of authority in transnational behavior; expectations of what is substantively and procedurally right, shared by politically relevant strata about the world, are critical components and inescapable products of behavior. Response options and priorities which an official inventories in a specific case have been influenced, in part, by what was done and aggregately evaluated in the past. The choices which that official makes in the instant case will contribute to perspectives of what is appropriately lawful behavior in the future and will provide the authority environment within which that same official and those with whom he identifies must later operate. Thus the role of international law or, more broadly, authority in decisions involves both conformity with expectations derived from the past as well as a conformation of authority perspectives for the future. "What is this day supported by precedent," counseled Tactius, "will hereafter become a precedent."[98] Processes of conformity and conformation provide enormous possibilities for disjunction, as decision-makers select, under the press of events, what they deem most worthwhile from the past and project it into radically new contexts in the future.

It would seem obvious that alternate responses to private armies should seek to adhere to those peremptory norms of international law which avatar basic principles of human dignity.[99] Norms concerned with fundamental good faith in agreements, minimization of deprivation, or humane constraints on the use of violence derive from periods earlier than the contemporary war system and should be consciously chosen to condition all

[98] Tacitus, *Annals* XI, 24.

[99] Article 53, Vienna Convention on Treaties, U.N. Doc. A/Conf. 39/27 (May 23, 1969). *See also* Schwelb, "Some Aspects of International Jus Cogens" 61 *Am. J. Int'l L.* 946 (1967). *But cf.* G. Schwarzenberger, *International Law and Order* 27 ff. (1971).

present behavior; norms such as these are unquestionable components of a world order of human dignity. But not every putative authority prescription should receive automatic deference. Every legacy of the past must be reevaluated in present and projected contexts to determine the extent to which it contributes, if at all, to the common interests of the world community. This does not mean that a norm which is no longer fully expressive of the common interest may be simply and automatically abrogated in word and deed; the termination of prescriptions is itself a complex process and every termination must weigh the extent to which it erodes or strengthens overall expectations of authority.[100]

In addition to selections from the past, current responses to private-army questions must also consider the prescriptive effects which they themselves will engender: the authority environment which they will create for the future. To what extent will a particular response to a private-army problem, for all its short-range advantages, create authority expectations which are inimical to common interests? There is no need for elaborating the dire expectations which are regularly generated by many short-term "effective" strategies.

PREFERENCES FOR PERSUASIVE RESPONSES

It was not chance that decreed that strategy and bargaining theory would provide a bureaucratic *lingua franca*. Among the presuppositions of this theory are an environment of conflict and a segmented, linear conception of time, each component of which is discretely resolved by a win or a loss. Both of these presuppositions are social misperceptions. There are sectors of conflict as well as sectors of cooperation in world social process, and participants themselves play the major role in deciding whether to conflict or to cooperate. The flow of social process is continuous and characterizations of "segments" in which one has won or lost are usually pathetically short-sighted human projections, quickly washed away by ceaseless change. Yet each of these perceptions is critical to the operation of a war system. Each provides for continuous conflict, rather than attempts to transform it, and a regular scoring whose only meaning is justification for and continuation of the system. The use of an idiom derived from strategy and bargaining theory tends to predispose decision-makers and appraisers to coercive strategies by the automatic definition of the other as an "adversary" whom one, in a unilateral rather than reciprocating system, "deters" or "influences." The emphasis is on ingenuity in the formulation of coercive rather than persuasive responses, and the other party is an object whose behavior, but not whose perspectives, remains of chief concern.

The point is not that coercion can be dismissed from social order, but

---

[100] McDougal, Lasswell & Reisman, "The World Constitutive Process of Authoritative Decision," in I C. Black and & R. Falk (eds.), *The Future of the International Legal Order* 73, 149 (1969).

rather that it unnecessarily becomes the characteristic pattern, the paradigm of thinking and creating, raising the aggregate expectation of violence and stunting creativity in the development of alternative strategic methods. The contrast can be sharpened by reference to a theory of persuasion, which seeks to secure changes in the behavior of others by appeals to their interests, rather than by the threat of deprivations upon deviation. Persuasion is directed at perspectives. It seeks to establish an ascendant identity among the latent competing identities or selves in the persuadee, to demonstrate that the proposed program is in accord with the real demands of the persuadee and to refine the persuadee's range of expectations so that he himself can test the aggregate consequences of alternative courses of action available to him. Persuasion involves different interactions which can influence the persuader as well as the persuadee.

If responses to the private-army problem seek to minimize violence and to transform a war system to a peace system, it is obvious that emphasis must be shifted to persuasive rather than coercive responses; the expectation of coercion generates that anxiety which is fundamental to a war system. Hence decision responses must aim at changing perspectives through selective communications rather than by simply securing a degree of conformity in behavior. The shift to persuasion is more than strategic: it imports, as well, creating new types of solutions.

PREFERENCES FOR INTEGRATIVE SOLUTIONS

Integrative solutions are ones in which conflicting interests are accommodated in innovated processes of value shaping and sharing in such a manner that contenders must merge the realization of their separate interests; hence they acquire a shared interest in the continuation of the new process and self-police. Integrative solutions are preceded by an independent focus more comprehensive than that forwarded (as an instrument of conflict) by the adversaries themselves; these solutions activate and incorporate contingent elements of the broader situation which participants themselves had not introduced. Thus, they involve not only a reconsideration of strategic devices, but new considerations of goals; as such they are highly reciprocal in all sequences of their formulation and implementation. A preference for persuasion tends to orient decision-makers toward a search for integrative solutions.[101]

THE PRINCIPLE OF TEMPORAL EXTENSION

Decision-makers, we have noted, characterize events in terms of decisive moments in which they either "win" or "lose." The anticipation of such a moment permits them to mobilize their own self systems as well as vast

---

[101] See M. Follett, *Creative Experience* (1924).

numbers of people, maximizing control by keeping all in an intense state of anxiety. Of course, the decisive moment is regularly moved into the future until it is ultimately mythologized as an Armageddon. At this point, anxiety and mobilization are perpetuated in two intertwining trends: toward great wins and toward avoiding The Great Loss. One of the many problems of this frame of reference is that it tends to bloat the importance of every single response to an event, such as a private army, increasing thereby focus, anxiety response and the entire arena of conflict.

Without minimizing the importance of human choices and responses to events, there must be a sensible degree of temporal humility. Whatever is done, there will always be a moment afterwards; in composite decision processes, there are no final decisions, for every decision involves a response, a review, and—through time and changing context—an emendation.[102] If a private army wins a battle, there may still be another. If a government falls, a new one will arise and exchanges may be initiated or continued with it. *Ad infinitum.* A lesson in the exposure to crisis is that crises are succeeded in time; recognition of this feature can diminish the intensity of crisis and increase the rationality of decision response.

THE PRINCIPLE OF REALISM

In his examination of authority and control, Augustine observed with appropriately delicate implication, that a bandit is a little king and a king can be a big bandit.[103] A private army may not seek to become a responsible community structure, but the actions of others can urge it in this direction. It is appropriately pious to defer to the established authoritative institutions of a community. But where those institutions cannot secure an effective control base, the realistic alternative may not be to seek to increase that base. It may be more realistic, more economic and, in the long run, perhaps more humane, to stand aside until new institutional patterns have emerged and then to seek to influence them. An outsider, it should be remembered, is one who influences; an insider is one who participates directly.

THE LEGAL SCHOLAR'S CONTRIBUTION

Private armies involve violence and change, factors which both attract and repel. To many, the mere application of unauthorized violence is frightening; for many of these, the use of "authorized" violence is not. Others may be attracted by the exercise of violence without regard to its manifest objective, for it provides some form of ultimate testing, ultimate realization, risk

---

[102] *See* Reisman, *supra* note 39, Ch. 1.

[103] Augustine, IV *De Civitate Dei*, 4; and *see* Aquinas, II *Summa Theologica*, 2, Q. 66, Art, 8, Reply 3.

or self-destruction. The prospect of change arouses comparable variations in reaction: those who identify with an order may feel threatened by the claim for change, even though change itself might represent a net benefit for them. Those who have rejected an extant system of order will view the prospect of change with delight and anticipation. Most people who are informed of private armies receive their information through the mediation of elites who can be expected to put that construction on it which is most favorable to their interests.

Private armies cannot, as we have seen, simply be terminated. Because they involve purposive or incidental change, decision-makers who are presented with them as problems should use them, insofar as possible, for the purpose of changing a war system and maximizing the conditions of human dignity. There are a number of contributions which international legal scholars can make to the improvement of the policy process as it pertains to the private-army problem. These relate to standpoint, to focus on social process, to goals for constitutive process, and to the systematic performance of certain intellectual tasks which are requisite to rational decision.

1. Standpoint: As a member of a small, interactive, and thoroughly global profession which has been committed since Grotius to the refinement of the legal process as an instrument for clarifying and implementing the common interests of the world community, the international lawyer has both a unique opportunity and professional necessity to maintain a standpoint distinct from that of the participants in the world social process. From such a standpoint, private-army cases can be seen in most comprehensive context, and optimum international responses, derived from the basic goals of the world community, can be fashioned and recommended. Equally important, the perceptions available from such a vantage point may be transmitted to active opinion leaders in different communities and through such diffusion provide a more realistic and contextual perspective on private armies.

2. Focus: From the vantage point of an observer committed to the common interests of the world community, a plenary focus on the world social process and on patterns of effective power as well as processes of authoritative decision can be developed and used for locating private-army problems in the broader flow of world affairs. Realism of perception is increased as is the likelihood of fashioning responses which approximate more closely all relevant social goals. The transmission of such a focus to official and private decision-makers may thus contribute to the rationality of decision.

3. Constitutive Goals: Private-army decisions can reinforce or change the world constitutive process; hence it is important to impress upon official decision-makers as well as on their public appraisers the constitutive dimensions and opportunities available in private-army decisions. If such decisions are to improve, revisions are urgently required with regard to all the decision functions of the constitutive process: intelligence, promotion, prescription, invocation, application, termination, and appraisal. International lawyers are well placed to clarify the appropriate policies which ought to guide each of these decision functions in order to use the constitutive process as an instrument for changing a war system to a peace system.

4. Fundamental Intellectual Tasks of Decision: It is difficult to imagine rational purposive action which does not perform five intellectual tasks: goal clarification, trend study, factor analysis, projection, and the invention of alternatives. The international lawyer is particularly sensitive to these tasks, since they are the crux of explicitly systematic and creative legal operations. Whether the lawyer is serving an institutional process from within or appraising its activities from without, the insistence on the performance of these tasks can only help to improve the effectiveness and explicit rationality of private-army as, indeed, of all decisions.

Each of these operations draws on the enlightenment and skill which are the peculiar prerogative of the international legal scholar. Through diffusion, each may contribute somewhat to an improved international response to private armies. That response can never be a single rule, for there is no simple pat answer to the idiosyncratic problems raised in each case. Yet there must be a response. In light of the recent revelations of the pathological aspects of the use of official power in a number of private-army situations, there is a tendency to assume that any use of power destroys both applier and target; hence the best course might appear to be persistent self-inhibition and disengagement. Unfortunately, power is a ubiquitous aspect of social process and the prime characteristic of political processes; the decision not to apply what is at one's own disposal can never vouchsafe that the arena will remain civic and non-belligerent. Realistic ingenuity involves the use of power economically in order to establish a world order of human dignity. Thus, the recurrence of private armies may provide a challenge and an opportunity.

Chapter 13 | **The "War of National Liberation"**
and the Third World | *Edwin Brown Firmage*

> . . . under all circumstances War is to be regarded not as an independent
> thing, but as a political instrument; and it is only by taking this point of
> view that we can avoid finding ourselves in opposition to all military his-
> tory. . . . Now, the first, the grandest, and most decisive act of judgment
> which the Statesman and General exercises is rightly to understand . . . the
> War in which he engages and not to take it for something, or to wish to
> make of it something, which by the nature of its relations it is impossible
> for it to be. This is, therefore, the first, the most comprehensive, of all
> strategic questions.
>
> KARL VON CLAUSEWITZ (1780–1831), *On War*

The so-called "war of national liberation"[1] has developed a mystique and
an aura of almost deterministic and inevitable, ultimate success. This
impression has been created by Mao Tse-tung's defeat of the Kuomintang
in 1949, our traumatic experience in Vietnam and, to a lesser extent, to
the ease with which Castro accomplished his revolution in Cuba. This essay
will examine the history and the nature of this concept of warfare compared and contrasted with the nature of politically motivated internal
violence in Asia, Africa, and Latin America, that part of the world described
by Lin Piao in his famous speech, "Long Live the Victory of People's War,"
as constituting the natural areas for successfully waging "wars of national
liberation." Lastly, some conclusions will be suggested leading toward
the formation of policy and the development of law in relation to internal
war.

I. THE WORLD SCENE

Revolutionary activity, like all other political modalities today, has been
affected by world-wide phenomena not directly linked to "national liberation" movements. First in importance has been the scope and rapidity of
technological change. While the profound impact of technology upon

---

[1] The terms "national liberation" and "wars of national liberation" will be used
in reference to violence associated with the communist formulation of their doctrine
of internal war. The term should not be used in a generic sense with reference to all
wars stemming from nationalist movements not associated with Marxist ideology. *See*
Quade, "The U.S. and Wars of National Liberation," I R. Falk (ed.), *The Vietnam
War and International Law* 102, 104 (1968).

political forms is nothing new,[2] the rate of change has been so rapid and pervasive as to now justify the use of the term "revolution." (While recognizing the semantic confusion which might result from the use of the term in connection with an essay on liberation movements, there simply is no other word to describe such overwhelming technological change.) The technological revolution has had a greater influence upon all political forms, including revolutionary movements, than any other single factor. Prior to World War II, a complete technological change occurred approximately within the time separating major world conflicts, i.e., 1870–1914, 1919–1939. After World War II, this tempo of technological change has occurred every five years and is now thought to occur every four years.[3] The impact of this phenomenon upon political, economic, and military institutions can hardly be overestimated.

Most direct and obvious but not necessarily most important is the effect of such change upon weaponry and consequently upon war. For the first time man possesses weapons capable of such complete destruction that human life upon the planet may be threatened with extinction. While it has been asserted at least since the development of the cross-bow that certain weapons would end war, the real effect of weapons technology upon war has been to alter its nature. The threat of nuclear war has produced sufficient restraint upon war-makers that the level of violence has been sub-nuclear since the end of World War II. In addition, formal wars between major states have been few due in part to the ever-present danger of conventional world war escalating to a nuclear level. Internal war—from palace coup and more sustained civil strife with mass support aimed at dominating the institutions of government to civil war designed to accomplish radical changes in the social structure—has been the dominant form of political violence in our time. Since "rational" premediated war is not the only kind of war instigation (nuclear war by accident, by miscalculation, or by madmen cannot be excluded from possibility) we are not assured that this will be so in the future; but with some "luck" it is most likely to continue to be the primary type of political violence. The hot phases of the Cold War—from Greece to Korea to Vietnam[4]—have been fought within these boundaries. Within whatever

---

[2] For example, the social and military structure of medieval society was radically changed by the invention of the stirrup. For an analysis of this and the technological developments which affected that society, see L. White, Jr., Medieval Technology and Social Change (1970).

[3] For projections of this phenomenon into the future, cf., H. Kahn & A. Weiner, The Year 2000 (1967); H. Kahn, On Thermonuclear War (1961); E. Jantsch, Technological Forecasting in Perspective (1967); Bell, "The Year 2000—The Trajectory of an Idea," Daedalus (Summer 1967).

[4] The tragic characterization of violence in Vietnam as being part of the post-World War II hegemonial jousting for position between the super-powers analogous to violence in Greece and Korea, was perhaps the seminal mistake committed by the Truman and Eisenhower administrations and dogmatically accepted by each succeeding administration to the present. By the time of the Nixon administration, our characterization of violence in Vietnam as being a test of strength between Chinese

delimitations reason places upon man's activities, the advent of nuclear weapons assures the continuation of the age of the guerrilla.

While the technological developments in weaponry have at the same time potentially expanded the destructive potential of war and to the present served as a powerful deterrent to major and formal war between states, modern weaponry and the nature of guerrilla war have combined to destroy the seventeenth and eighteenth centuries concept of limited war.[5] Today, the term "limited war" usually is used to indicate war limited in geography, weapons employed, and participants (with the use of surrogate states or other entities standing in for their respective major state champions) but relatively unlimited in terms of the classical distinction between combatants and non-combatants. The selective use of terror against representatives of the incumbent regime has become a regular feature of guerrilla war; the relatively unrestricted use of weapons of mass destruction (beneath the nuclear threshold) against civilian populations supposedly providing some degree of aid to guerrilla forces has also become common.

The horror of modern war has stripped it of whatever romantic covering it once enjoyed. This has been reflected in a legal regime which has once again attempted to place restrictions upon the competence of states to wage war and upon its conduct. Prior to this century, the law had ceased its earlier efforts to proscribe war.[6] It is no longer fashionable

---

and Russian Communism on the one hand and the "Free World" on the other hand had resulted in some indeterminable degree of self-fulfillment. World history—and certainly United States history—would have been dramatically different had the anti-colonial revolution in Vietnam been recognized for what it was—the last death throes of the French colonial empire—and analogized, for purposes of U.S. policy, to post-World War II violence in Indonesia rather than to events in Greece and Korea.

[5] "The seventeenth and eighteenth centuries in Western Europe found a world in which force, as a relation of states, was not carried to the point where its use meant the total destruction of the states themselves. In the dynastic struggle for power, war as an instrument of national policy found no logic in the destruction of conquered peoples. The acquisition of control of the riches they could produce was the very subject matter of war. Hence, war did not commit the total civilian population to the total destruction of others and of itself as well. Travel, commerce, and intercourse still persisted among the populations of the warring states. It remained for the French revolution and Napoleon to transform the character of land warfare, for England to transform the character of sea warfare, for the great powers of World War I and II to create the methodology of air warfare, and for nuclear warfare to threaten the total extinction of organized societies." K. Carlston, *Law and Organization in World Society* 195–96 (1962).

[6] "The outstanding feature of the last half century is the decisive change from a Legal regime of indifference to the occasion for war, in which it was regarded primarily as a duel, a means of settling a private difference, to a Legal regime in which Law placed substantial limitations on the competence of states to resort to force." I. Brownlie, *International Law and the Use of Force By States* 424 (1963); *cf.* Francis Bacon, who reflected his seventeenth century world when he glorified foreign war as doing for a state what exercise does for the body: "a foreign war is like the heat of exercise, and serveth to keep the body in health; for in a slothful peace both courages will effeminate and manners corrupt." W. Ballis, *The Legal Position of War: Changes in its Practice and Theory From Plato to Vattel* 75 (1937).

to glorify war as a means of civilization or colonization. While some ascribe this in part to the civilizing effects of a changed regime of law[7] it is more likely that the law—like the fashionability of war—is more basically a reflection of the perception of war altered by its modern nature, in turn changed by the present technology of weaponry.

Other aspects of a changed technology, including developments in travel and communication, have had at least as great an impact upon the frequency and the nature of war as have technological changes in weaponry. Increasing civil strife has occurred as "people with rising expectations and undiminished birth rates found that the progress they heard about on transistor radios and saw in the persons of foreign travelers could not be achieved in the form they wanted it or with the speed they demanded."[8] The pressure toward modernization has become one of the few most powerful movements and concepts of our time. Whether this can be accomplished by peaceful means and within a framework of democratic government[9] is one of the major issues confronting the international system.

Ours is an age of tension caused in part by the irrationality of a condition in which the component parts of the state system maintain a near monopoly on the levers of power, both economic and military, and assert the right to unilateral decision as to their use, while no longer possessing the power to assure the safety or, in fact, the continuation of the society within its bounds. Problems exist, from war prevention to atmospheric pollution, which have little if any relation to the territorial boundaries which divide the states.

In turn, this has led to a still nascent development of international organization which has begun to affect the decentralized, horizontal state system by providing some limited degree of centralization and vertical elements.

While the development of monster weapons has ironically lowered the upper limits of "permissible" warfare (for a time at least), zealous dogmatism—possessed by communist and capitalist states alike and not matched since the wars of religion devastated Europe—has led to the degradation of the impediment which enlightened self-interest used to provide against the use of war as an instrument of politics. A further result of this dogmatic zeal has been some attrition in that rule within the "rules of the game" of the state system that warfare, once started, would only be carried out insofar as benefitted the pragmatic self-interests of the states; the most basic application of this rule is that it is not in the interests of the states players of the "game of nations" that any player be completely

---

[7] R. Osgood & R. Tucker, *Force, Order and Justice* (1967).

[8] Firmage, "International Law and the Response of the United States to Internal War," in II R. Falk (ed.), *The Vietnam War and International Law* 89, 90 (1969).

[9] *Cf.* R. Heilbroner, "Counterrevolutionary America," *Commentary* (April, 1967); I R. Falk & C. Black, *The Future of the International Legal Order* 22 (1969).

extinguished.[10] The ideological coloration which has clouded the identification of self-interest on the part of the two superpowers has been so intense that it has sometimes appeared that the major impediment to a war to the death, similar to that waged by Rome against Carthage, was the realization that in such a war the use of nuclear weapons would insure to both combatants the fate of Carthage. It is far from certain, over the long run, whether the fear of nuclear conflict will continue to dominate the gut instincts of dogmatism.

Finally, another "ism" has been a more powerful determinant of the nature of political violence in the Third World than either capitalism or communism: for it has been nationalism—not communism, idealism, altruism, capitalism, or democracy—which has destroyed the remaining fabric of nineteenth-century colonialism. Some colonial powers heeded the injunction attributed to Edmund Burke, "not the least of the arts of diplomacy is to grant graciously what one no longer has the power to withhold," and acquiesced to the inevitable without violence. Others learned the hard way.[11] The most anguishing dilemmas were posed for leaders of the major states of the West when the "forces of nationalism and communism were merged to some indeterminate degree in opposition to 'legitimate' Western-oriented governments."[12] Such a mixture forced a choice between two normally compatible principles of United States foreign policy, namely, support for new nations against their former colonial masters even when this meant opposing a NATO ally (*e.g.*, U.S. support of Indonesia against the Netherlands), and opposition to the exportation of Communism by the use of military force. When these two principles were in seeming conflict, as in Vietnam, the course of American foreign policy was determined by such characterization and by the subsequent decision as to which element—anticolonialism or violent Communism—appeared to be the dominant ideology within a particular nationalist movement.

[10] *Cf.* Kaplan, "Balance of Power, Bipolarity and Other Models of International Systems," 51 *Am. Pol. Sci. Rev.* 684 (1957); M. Copeland, *The Game of Nations* (1969).

[11] "We cannot possibly stop this series of revolutions of rising expectations. We cannot even do a great deal to hasten them over their crisis periods, to allay their violence, to guide their course toward true democracy. But we—our leaders, supported by a public opinion educated to a certain amount of patience—can do something better than we have done with, for example, the Chinese and the Cuban revolutions. We cannot intervene to crush a revolution we do not like, as the Russians did in Hungary; but we can avoid mistakes like the Bay of Pigs. We cannot, as a Toynbee would like us to, put ourselves at the head of such revolutions. But we can avoid our present policy of belling with the hounds of the awakened multitudes, and especially the awakened intellectuals, of Asia and Africa and running with the hares of the old effendi or possessing classes. For one thing, the odds are overwhelming that these particular hares will be caught—and then we shall be in a very bad position." C. Brinton, *The Anatomy of Revolution* 271 (rev. ed. 1965).

[12] Firmage, *supra* note 8, at 90.

II. THE "WAR OF NATIONAL LIBERATION"—
A HISTORICAL PERSPECTIVE

DEFINITION

The term "war of national liberation" is here used to denote violence associated with the Communist formulation and implementation of doctrine of internal war.[13] The term has been variously used by Soviet jurists and apologists to justify war in three situations: first, in defense of the homeland; second, to liberate a people from capitalism; and third, to accomplish the separation of a colony from governance by a colonial power.[14] It is currently used by Marxists most often in the third sense. Understandably, Westerners have tended to consider the doctrine as little more than a subterfuge for any sustained act of political violence designed to further either Marxist dogmatic belief in world domination or Russian or Chinese nationalistic geopolitics.[15] While there is substantial truth in this view, this point, considered alone, distracts attention from the profoundly more important prerequisites to successful "national liberation," as seen by Mao Tse-tung and Lin Piao.[16] While any number of Communist writings—particularly those of Lenin and Trotsky—could be pointed at to defend a definition of "war of national liberation" so sweeping that virtually any

---

[13] See supra note 1.

[14] G. Ginsburgs, "Wars of National Liberation and the Modern Law of Nations—The Soviet Thesis," 29 Law and Contemp. Prob. 910 (1964).

[15] E.g., "What is a 'war of national liberation'? It is, in essence, any war which furthers the Communist world revolution—what in broader terms, the Communists have long referred to as a 'just' war. The term 'war of national liberation' is used not only to denote armed insurrection by people still under colonial rule—there are not many of those left outside the communist world. It is used to denote any effort led by Communists to overthrow by force any non-Communist government." Dean Rusk, "The Control of Force in International Relations," in I Falk (ed.), The Vietnam War and International Law 338 (1968).

"It would serve no good purpose to dwell at greater length on the detailed vagaries of the Soviet campaign in praise of 'just' wars. Anything so subjective and, one may add, so contingent on political whim, simply does not lend itself to meaningful analysis." Ginsburgs, supra note 14.

" 'War of national liberation' has become, then, one of those accordion-like terms which can be given either a strict or broad construction. Even states which have achieved independence by the most innocuous and pacific means may qualify as members of the anti-imperialist camp so long as they express the correct attitudes toward U.S. Imperialism. A fortiori, Peking is likely to apply the term 'war of national liberation' to almost any revolution or rebellion anywhere in the third world on the assumption that any violent disturbance can only propel the Chinese wave of the future and weaken the United States." B. Schwartz, Communism and China: Ideology in Flux 191, (1968).

"If the idea of 'liberation' extends eventually to any movement directed against a nonsocialist order, as it apparently does, then this is a far-reaching justification for active participation in internal wars." R. Falk, Legal Order in a Violent World 144 (1968).

[16] See discussion infra.

violence committed by Communists upon non-Communists could be included and hence justified[17]—unless leaders in the West actually put more trust in the dogmatic prophecies of the early Marxists than do present-day leaders in China and Russia (and we often react to their words as if we do)—it is submitted that we should be paying more attention to actions of the two Communist superstates and to those words which seem to be designed as a blueprint for implementation.[18] The express pre-conditions placed upon the instigation of a "war of national liberation" and the meticulous specificity of its strategy can then be emphasized. It is only in this manner that the prerequisites to direct third-party participation (as opposed to cheers from the sidelines) can be understood.

Since the official Soviet textbook on international law[19] and almost all Communist commentators, with perhaps more appropriateness than they realize, have linked the Marxist doctrine of "wars of national liberation" with the heavily theological doctrine of "just war," it is necessary to trace briefly the history of that concept.

THE "JUST WAR"

Elements of the concept of "just war" can be found both in primitive society[20] and in ancient Greece.[21] For Plato and Aristotle, war was a natural

[17] *E.g.*, "Socialists, without ceasing to be Socialists, cannot oppose any kind of war. In the first place, Socialists never have and never could oppose revolutionary wars. . . . In the second place, civil wars are also wars. He who accepts the class struggle cannot fail to recognize civil wars which under any class society represent the natural, and under certain conditions, inevitable continuation of the development and aggravation of class struggle. . . . In the third place, socialism, victorious in one country, does not exclude forthwith all wars in general. On the contrary, it presupposes them. The development of capitalism proceeds highly unevenly in various countries. This cannot be otherwise under the conditions of commodity production. From this follows the unavoidable conclusion: Socialism cannot win simultaneously *in all* countries. It will win initially in one or several countries, while the remainder will remain for some time, either bourgeois or pre-bourgeois. This should result not only in frictions, but also in the direct striving of the bourgeois of other countries to smash the victorious proletariat of the socialist state. In such cases, a war on our part would be lawful and just. This would be a war for socialism, for liberation of other peoples from the bourgeoisie. Engels was completely right when in his letter to Kautsky of September 12, 1882, he directly recognized the possibility of 'defense wars' by *already victorious* socialism. He had in mind exactly the defense of the victorious proletariat against the bourgeoisie of other countries." V. Lenin, "Military Program of Proletarian Revolution," written in 1916, as quoted in S. Possony (ed.), *Lenin Reader* 488–90 (1966).

[18] *E.g.*, Lin Piao's famous speech given in 1965, "In Commemoration of the Twentieth Anniversary of Victory in the Chinese People's War of Resistance Against Japan: Long Live the Victory of People's War." *See* the analysis *infra*.

[19] *International Law: A Textbook for Use in Law Schools* 402 (Moscow: Foreign Languages Publishing House [no date]).

[20] "The idea that war is an illegal act, a delict, if it is not a sanction, that is, a reaction against a delict, is by no means an achievement of modern civilization. It is to be found under the most primitive conditions. It is expressed even in the relationship between hostile groups within primitive society. In his article "Primitive Law," Radcliffe-Brown writes: 'The waging of war is in some communities, as among the

part of politics and was justified when directed against those who disputed the power of the state to govern[22] or when its object was the attainment of peace.[23] While Cicero was also concerned that the objective of war was always the accomplishment of peace, ancient Rome, not surprisingly, was concerned more with constitutional formalities of war's initiation than with its objectives.[24] However, both Greece and Rome based the conclu-

---

Australian hordes, normally an act of retaliation, carried out by one group against another that is held responsible for an injury suffered, and the procedure is regulated by a recognized body of customs, which is equivalent to the international law of modern nations.' In general, this is typical of wars among primitive peoples. Since international law is primitive law, it is quite understandable that the principles of *bellum justum* have been conserved in this legal order." H. Kelsen, *Principles of International Law* 29–30 (Rev. ed. 1966).

[21] "The idea of just war is also encountered in the inter-state law of the ancient Greeks. 'No war was undertaken without the belligerents alleging a definite cause considered by them as a valid and sufficient justification therefore.' " Kelsen, *ibid.*, quoting Phillipson.

[22] "And so, in one point of view, the art of war is a natural art of acquisition, for the art of acquisition includes hunting, an art which we ought to practice against wild beasts and against men who, though intended by nature to be governed, will not submit; for war of such a kind is naturally just." Aristotle, *Politics*, (Jowett transl.) 9 *Great Books of the Western World* 449–50 (1952).

[23] *Nicomachean Ethics*, Book X. Chs. VI, XVII; *Politics*, Ch. VII as quoted by von Elbe, "The Evolution of the Concept of Just War in International Law," 33 *Am. J. Int'l L.* 665, 666 (1939).

[24] "While Greek thought on the problem of war produced but a loosely-stated set of political and philosophical ideas, the Romans, in their *ius belli ac pacis* and the writings of historians and philosophers, evolved a body of rules that were destined deeply to influence the growth of the European concept of war. A distinction is made between the institution of war as an element of the *ratio naturalis* or natural world order, and individual wars. The former is accepted as part of the unwritten laws of nature which men may not alter; recourse to arms in a given case, however, may be had only for an injury suffered and after the refusal of the wrongdoer to atone for it. Before hostilities are commenced a collegium of priests, the fetials, determines whether the required conditions for going to war exist. The fetial procedure originated in the belief—common to all peoples of antiquity and even traceable to modern times—that battles are decided by providential interference and that victory is a gift of the gods who thereby legitimatize the conquests made in war. Hence scrupulous precautions were taken to assure beyond doubt that a war was agreeable with deity. A war commenced in accordance with the rules of the fetial proceedings was 'justum,' which means legally correct, and at the same time 'pium,' *viz.*, sanctioned by religion and, consequently, could be expected to receive divine blessings." Von Elbe, *supra* note 23, at 667–68.

The Roman approach was in terms of formal legality. A *justum bellum* was a war commenced in accordance with the positive law with the approval of the college of *fetiales*, the view of the majority of writers being that the *fetiales* were not concerned with the intrinsic justice of the war but only with the correct observance of formalities. The War must also be *pium*, in accordance with religious sanctions and the express or implied commands of the gods. And yet the historians of the Roman world frequently discuss the sufficiency of the motives for particular wars and Cicero was of the opinion that no war was just unless entered upon after an official demand for satisfaction had been submitted or warning given and a formal declaration made. The formal concept of just war and the attempts of Roman writers to give it a moral content were to have a decisive influence on the later scholastics who were always concerned with the Roman sources on any topic." I Brownlie, *International Law and the Use of Force by States* 4 (1963).

sion as to the justness of a war in part upon a distinction between groups against which it was waged: war with the barbarians might constitute a positive virtue, while war among themselves must be justified upon other grounds.

The early Christian Church consistently condemned war under any circumstances, and Christians refused to participate in war regardless of its purpose until after 170 A.D.;[25] after the Church had come to be an integral part of the Empire, the pressures from barbarian tribes caused Augustine to break with early Christian pacifism[26] and chart a course of development[27] of the concept of "just war" which was to survive in international law[28] until Westphalia and in Roman Catholic doctrine to the present.[29] For Saint Augustine, wars could justly be fought only under constituted authority, as an act of necessity, to redress wrongs, with the restoration of peace as its objective. Augustine turned attention from Roman formality to Christian substance, however affected by the exigencies of the age.[30]

[25] Epstein, *The Catholic Tradition of the Law of Nations* 35 (1935); Brownlie, *supra* note 24, at 5; Ballis, *supra* note 5 at 41.

[26] *Id.*

[27] "Augustine is credited with having at first molded it [the Christian concept of just war] into the form of a scientific system. At the time he entered his ecclesiastic career the Christian character of the Empire was of very recent date and the deep impression among the early Christians by that change was still unabated. [The Empire had come to represent a system of universal peace.] . . . Theologically, the institution of war is explained as a means of punishment which God inflicts upon the sinful world; it appears as a sort of 'police action taken by the Sovereign Judge to restore order and to lead people back to the obedience of the law.' However, wars that must be suffered because they are ordained by Providence are to be distinguished from those which, lacking that character, are to be avoided. By what criterion can it be determined that a war falls within the permissible ones? The answer is that a war must be 'just' in the substantive sense of the term. Just are those '*quae ulcisuntur injurias,*' i.e., which are waged to redress a wrong suffered. Thus, wars must always be preceded by an injury; those waged for personal motives, like territorial aggrandizement, as practiced by the Romans for many centuries, are '*grande latrocinium.*' The injury may consist either in the neglect of a state to suppress crimes committed by its subjects, or in attacks upon the rights of others. Consequently, the just war, as a procedure for the repression of wrongs, is either a punitive action or in the nature of a civil suit for damages. Punishment and the measure of damages are determined by the purpose of the just war; its aim is not primarily victory, but the establishment of peace, viz., a state of '*tranquillitas ordinis*' or ordered harmony where all things have their allotted place." Von Elbe, *supra* note 23, at 667–68.

[28] Brownlie, *supra* note 24 at 14–15.

[29] "Augustine's tenets have remained the basis of the Catholic teaching on peace and war up to the present time. Principally they are religio-philosophical. In no way did they lay down legal rules. Nevertheless, they were bound to have repercussions in the legal arena. The centuries following the collapse of the Roman Empire were unfavorable to the development of legal theory, but legal implications of the Augustinian conception were brought to light in the earliest part of the *Corpus Juris Canonica*, the *Decretum Gratiani* (1150), a work of the Benedictine monk, Gratian." A. Nussbaum, "Just War—A Legal Concept?," 42 *Mich. L. Rev.* 453, 455–56 (1943).

[30] Augustine seems to have been a pacifist in the tradition of early Christianity during the first years following his conversion. However, Africa, his birthplace, was about to be invaded by the Vandals when the Roman commander in Africa, Boniface,

Throughout the Middle Ages, the justness of a war was determined not only by its origination and motivation, but also by the identity of the participants. The early distinction between Roman and barbarian was transformed into one between Christian and infidel, or between the faithful and the unfaithful in Islamic thought.[31] While Saint Thomas[32] elaborated upon the teachings of Augustine, little was added to the doctrine of "just war" until Machiavelli[33] began a trend toward secularization by his declaration (based upon state practice rather than by an appeal to the scriptures, the early Fathers, or the Scholastics) that any war was just which was necessary, and necessity was determined by the preservation of the state. Although men such as the Dominican friar and professor at Salamanca, Franciscus de Victoria,[34] maintained a foot in both camps of church and state, Gentili and Grotius formalized a secular and legal structure for the doctrine which was soon to be considered by Vattel to constitute a natural order of morality rather than positive law. After Westphalia, the period until 1815 is characterized by the relegation of the concept of "just war"

---

sorrowing for his dead wife, considered leaving the military for the ministry. Augustine wrote Boniface to dissuade him: "The monks indeed occupy a higher place before God, but you should not aspire to their blessedness before the proper time. . . . The monks will pray for you against your visible enemies. You must fight for them against the barbarians, their visible foes." As quoted by Edvard Hambro, "International Law and the Judaeo-Christian Tradition," an address delivered by the President of the General Assembly of the United Nations before the Fourth Annual Convocation on World Justice and Peace, Seton Hall University, November 5, 1970.

[31] "During the period since the seventh century the religion of Islam had appeared and spread rapidly. As with Christianity the religious doctrine contained guidance on lawful reasons for resort to war by its adherents, such reasons including defense, punishment for apostasy, and action against non-Moslems. Byzantium also had a concept of holy war which may have been derived from the Islamic concept of *Jihad*, a war against the unfaithful." Brownlie, *supra* note 24 at 5–6.

[32] "In order for a war to be just, three things are necessary. First the authority of the sovereign by those who command the war is to be waged. For it is not the business of a private person to declare war, because he can seek redress of his rights from the tribunal of his superior. . . .

Secondly, a just cause is required, namely that those who are attacked should be attacked because they deserve it on account of some fault. . . .

Thirdly, it is necessary that the belligerents should have a right intention, so that they intend the advancement of good, or the avoidance of evil. Saint Thomas Aquinas, *Summa Theologica*, Great Books of the Western World 578.

The scholastics and canonists who followed Aquinas elaborated upon the doctrine and stressed that justice demanded the restoration of peace. *See* von Elbe, *supra* note 23 at 669–70.

[33] N. Machiavelli, *The Prince*, Great Books of the Western World 36.

[34] *See* the description of de Victoria's teachings as stated by von Elbe: "Each state, *viz.*, a community 'which is complete in itself,' has the right to declare war; it is an essential element of its sovereignty. It may, however, be exercised only in cases where an adequate cause justifies forcible actions with their accompanying horrors and devastations. The answer as to what constitutes such cause is first stated in negative terms: Neither the difference of religion, nor the expansion of empire or the promotion of the personal glory of the ruler may justify resort to war. The positive concept adopts Augustinian ideas. 'There is a single and only cause for commencing a war, namely, a wrong received.'" Von Elbe, *supra* note 23 at 674–76.

to morality and propaganda, as positivism turned the law toward the customary practice of states rather than Christian dogma.[35]

In perspective, there is one dominating similarity between the traditional doctrine of the "just war" and its Marxist version, and that similarity is one which in reality is but a specific example of a more general and common observation: that Communism has at least as much in common with religion as with either politics or economics. The Communist doctrine holds that the "just" nature of war, or its "defensive" character, is determined not by who attacked whom, but rather by the identity of the participants as socialist or non-socialist, Communistic or capitalistic, and colonial people or colonizers. This is comparable to the distinction which the classical "just war" doctrine made at different times between Roman and barbarian, Christian and infidel, or the faithful and the unfaithful. It is based upon the same necessity of the dominating influence of a dogma of exclusivity over a more rational toleration of diversity. However, one may well question the extent to which this dogmatic article of faith actually affects Chinese or Soviet policy in regard to extending tangible aid to revolutionizing forces in other states. The factors which affect this decision are the important points for the policy-maker. These will be analyzed in later parts of this essay.

EARLY MARXIST WRITING AND EXPERIENCE

Marx and Engels were not basically concerned with the "just" nature of wars, as described by earlier jurists, philosophers, and churchmen. Rather, the two great theoreticians of Communism, influenced by Hegel,[36] considered wars to be "progressive" or "reactionary," depending on their impact upon the materialist course of history.[37] Both were concerned, however, with the wars of liberation of the nineteenth century. Marx wrote that:

> A people resolved to be independent should not be satisfied with conventional methods of warfare. Riots, revolt, and guerrilla tactics are the ways by which a small nation can overcome a large one. It is the only way a weak army can resist a large, well-trained army. The Spaniards demon-

[35] Brownlie, *supra* note 24 at 14–15; J. Stone, *Aggression and World Order*, (1958); R. W. Tucker, *The Just War*, (1960).

[36] ". . . another just-war notion had appeared in the Hegelian philosophy, but it was different in character. According to Hegel, the *Weltgeist* manifests itself through history, which Hegel considers as the embodiment of reason. The outcome of historical struggles, therefore, reveals ex post facto which nation was right in the philosophical sense. Like St. Augustine, Hegel is not concerned with the military decision of a war in itself, momentous though it may be, but with historical evolution in its broader aspects and hence with developments which, by their very indefiniteness if not for other reasons, escape the application of juristic methods." Nussbaum, *supra* note 29 at 475–76.

[37] See F. Engels, *The Peasant War in Germany* (1850; 1966).

strated this in 1807–1812, and the Hungarians did the same thing more recently.[38]

Lenin the revolutionary, while in agreement with Marx the theoretician that the internal economic contradictions within capitalism would lead to its demise in every country, was disposed to hasten the inevitable by direct intervention in the political system. He had a Clausewitzian perception of war as part of politics, to be used expressly for the accomplishment of political goals,[39] coupled with a dogmatic belief in the inevitability and hence the "rightness" of the class struggle[40] and consequently the justice of any war designed to further the cause of the proletariat.[41] A war's "justness" was not determined by which side started it or by a common-sense identification of an "aggressor." Rather, any war fought to further the eventual demise of capitalism was a "defensive" war. Wars fought before the era of capitalism were "just," if they hastened the advent of capitalism, in that the natural process of evolutionary development and decay was thereby furthered. During World War I, he reflected upon past wars and projected into the future:

> The epoch of 1789–1871 left deep traces and revolutionary memories. Before feudalism, absolutism and alien oppression were overthrown, the development of the proletarian struggle for Socialism was out of the question. When speaking of the legitimacy of 'defensive' war in relation to the wars of *such* an epoch, Socialists always had in mind precisely these objects, which amounted to revolution against medievalism and serfdom. By 'defensive' war Socialists always meant a '*just*' war in this sense (W. Liebnecht once expressed himself precisely in this way). Only in this sense have Socialists regarded, and now regard, wars 'for the defense of the fatherland,' or 'defensive' wars, as legitimate, progressive and just. For example, if tomorrow, Morocco were to declare war on France, India on England, Persia or China on Russia, and so forth, those would be 'just,' 'defensive' wars, *irrespective* of who attacked first; and every Socialist would sympa-

---

[38] As quoted by H. Chambre, *From Karl Marx to Mao Tse-tung* 215–16. (1963).

[39] "Applied to wars, the main thesis of dialetics . . . is that '*war is simply the continuation of politics by other* (i.e. violent) *means.*' This formula belongs to Clausewitz, one of the greatest writers on the history of war, whose ideas were fertilized by Hegel. And this was always the standpoint of Marx and Engels, who regarded *every* war as the *continuation* of the politics of the given interested powers—and the *various* classes within these countries—at a given time." V. I. Lenin, *The Collapse of the Second International*, June, 1915, as quoted in Possony, *supra* note 17 at 488.

[40] "In this question (as also in views on 'partiotism') it is not the offensive or defensive character of the war, but the interests of the class struggle of the proletariat, or rather, the interests of the international movement of the proletariat that represent the only possible point of view from which the question of the attitude of Social Democracy toward a given phenomenon in international relations can be considered and solved."—V. I. Lenin, *Militant Militarism and the Antimilitarist Tactics of Social Democracy*, August, 1908, as quoted in Possony, *supra* note 17 at 487.

[41] *See* note 17 *supra*.

thize with the victory of the oppressed, dependent, unequal states against the oppressing, slave-owning, predatory 'great' powers.[42]

Lenin's *What Is To Be Done?* is the classic formulation of the doctrine of revolution from above and represents a departure from the determinism of Marx.

It was Stalin, however, who linked directly the concept of "just war" with Marxist doctrine and then proceeded to outline the nature and the necessity of what would today be termed the "war of national liberation." After the Fifth Congress of the Communist International in 1924, Stalin, as the self-proclaimed ideological successor of Lenin, announced the necessity of an alliance between the liberation movements in the colonies and the struggles of the proletariat in Europe:

> Leninism has proved . . . that the national question can be solved only in connection with and on the basis of the proletarian revolution and that the road to victory of the revolution in the West lies through the revolutionary alliance with the liberation movements of the colonies, and dependent countries against imperialism. . . . Leninism . . . recognizes the existence of revolutionary capacities in the national liberation movements of the oppressed countries, and the possibility of using these for overthrowing the common enemy, for overthrowing imperialism.[43]

Ideas central to "wars of national liberation" came out of the experiences of the Russian and Chinese revolutions. These very different revolutions contained some common or somewhat similar elements which influenced the doctrine and the practice of later "liberation movements." It is possible here only to note the most important of these elements and provide reference to essays treating them separately.

First, contrary to the early and basic writings of Marx and Engels, the role of the peasants was found to be essential to the success of the Russian revolution[44] and the overwhelmingly dominant feature of the Chinese Communist revolution.[45] This revelation became apparent in part at least to Mao long before the final decade of the forty-odd years of the Chinese revolution; his recognition of this fact in 1925 led to perhaps the second[46] most important document in communist revolutionary literature subsequent to the writings of Marx and Engels.[47]

Second, while mass support from various nationalist bourgeois ele-

---

[42] V. I. Lenin, *What is to be Done?* (1902) (1969).

[43] Stalin, *The Foundations of Leninism*, 1924, as quoted in F. Schatten, *Communism in Africa* 63 (1966).

[44] Leon Trotsky, *The History of the Russian Revolution* (1932), particularly chapter three, dealing with the proletariat and the peasantry.

[45] C. Johnson, *Peasant Nationalism and Communist Power* (1962).

[46] Lenin's *What is to be Done?* must be rated first. *See supra* note 42.

[47] Mao Tse-tung, *Report on an Investigation of the Peasant Movement in Hunan, March 1927*, 1 *The Selected Works of Mao Tse-tung* (1965).

ments was sought and accomplished in both revolutions, the role of the intelligentsia[48] proved to be crucial to the success of both as might be expected in any "engineered" revolution from above.[49]

Third, perhaps of most importance to the Western policy-maker today and essential to a conclusion of this essay, the Chinese Communist revolutionaries built particularly upon an emerging nationalist consciousness and exploited it to their own ends. It is the Chinese revolution, not so much the Russian, that is looked to as a prototype of "national liberation" by Marxist revolutionary elements in the Third World. Chalmers Johnson has shown that the rise to power of both the Chinese and the Yugoslav Communist Parties was made possible dominantly by the fact that both were able effectively to make the nationalist cause their own after powerful nationalistic forces were unleashed within those states as a consequence of Japanese and German invasion.[50] Prior to the invasions, both parties had been relatively impotent in their attempts to foster and lead revolutionary movements. The Bolsheviks were able to use World War I as an outside factor somewhat comparable to the role of the Japanese invasion of China in the Chinese Communist revolution. But the result in China was a powerful development of national consciousness which was brilliantly exploited by Mao in a way that has no direct counterpart in the Russian revolution.

CURRENT WRITING AND EXPERIENCE—RUSSIA AND CHINA

Whatever the correct proportionality of influence which dogma and national self-interest may have upon Soviet and Chinese policies regarding "wars of national liberation," current state action and policy declarations by political leaders and theoreticians more accurately forecast what those policies may be.

The words and the actions of the Soviet Union on the issue of nationalism are in brutal contrast. The most recently famous official Soviet statement on "wars of national liberation" is contained in a speech delivered by Khrushchev on January 6, 1961, in which such movements were not only declared to be "just wars" but "sacred" in that through them colonial peoples would achieve nationhood. Two points should be noted, however. First, Mr. Khrushchev was vague regarding any commitment of tangible economic or military aid to such endeavors. Third-party participation was left deliberately open. Second, he clearly used the term "national liberation" in reference to Third World colonial revolt. He did not put forward a program of centralized world conquest. Soviet publicists have

---

[48] Malia, "What is the Intelligentsia?," 89 *Daedalus* (Summer 1960); Schwartz, "The Intelligentsia in Communist China," 89 *Daedalus* (Summer 1960).

[49] Lenin, *supra* note 42.

[50] Johnson, *supra* note 45.

consistently followed this interpretation.[51] Official government statements made in 1971 confirm the strong support of the Soviet Union for "wars of national liberation."[52]

Insofar as actions speak louder than words, the behavior of the Soviet Union at home and abroad reveals the extent of its support for nationalism, as distinguished from its position regarding "wars of national liberation." In 1956 the Soviet Union invaded Hungary and put down what the United Nations General Assembly termed a "spontaneous national uprising."[53] In 1968 Czechoslovakia was invaded over the announced opposition of its government, which was forcibly deposed. This was followed by the pronouncement of the so-called Brezhnev doctrine of limited sovereignty[54] under which it was declared that Communist countries' sovereignty is limited to the extent that armed intervention by the Soviet Union and other socialist countries would be precipitated and justified whenever, in the judgment of the Soviet Union, Marxist principles of social development were threatened by internal or international forces. The position of the Soviet Union regarding its domestic nationalities, the concern for which is thought by some to have been one factor leading to the invasion of Czechoslovakia[55] may be seen by examining the policy of deportation of national groups.[56]

In summation: the Soviet Union has maintained its strong moral support for "wars of national liberation" in the Third World, with the question of tangible support being left deliberately vague and probably dependent upon the desirability and feasibility of maintaining a successful effort, as determined from the point of view of the Soviet Union. Current

[51] ". . . refusal to oppressed peoples of the rights to make use of national-liberation war as an extreme and temporary measure in response to the forcible attempt to hold them back in a position of colonial dependency and imperialistic oppression runs counter to established, universally recognized principles and norms of international law. With fire and sword the western powers seized and kept 'their' colonies. But aggression and annexation cannot remain unpunished. . . . Refusal of the necessity of punishment for aggression and annexation means the recognition of lawlessness in international relations." M. Tuzmukhamedov, as quoted by Ginsburgs, *supra* note 14 at 928.

[52] *C.f.*, the testimony of Robert Conquest, Hearing before the Subcommittee on National Security and International Operations of the Committee on Government Operations, U.S. Senate, 92d Cong. 1st Sess., April 30, 1971. In speaking about the recent Party Congress, Conquest said: "A terrific ecomium to their military power was followed by very strong emphasis on support for national liberation movements everywhere. . . ."

[53] A/3546, Feb. 20, 1957; A/3592, June 12, 1957; A/2849, July 14, 1958.

[54] For an analysis of the so-called "Brezhnev doctrine" and the reaction of Communist parties around the world, *see* Firmage, "Summary and Interpretation," in Falk (ed.), *The International Law of Civil War* 405, 419 (1971).

[55] *E.g.*, the testimony of Robert Conquest, note 52 *supra*. It is thought by some specialists that the example of a nationalistic government allowing internal liberalization, occurring so close to the Ukraine—long a seedbed of nationalism—was the spectre which more than any other single factor precipitated the Soviet intrusion into Czechoslovakia.

[56] R. Conquest, *The Nation Killers* (1970).

Soviet writing has limited almost exclusively the use of the term "wars of national liberation" to colonial revolution in the Third World. No general doctrine of world revolution has been defended recently under that rubric. The Soviet attitude toward nationalism has not changed the older Russian desire to achieve hegemony over Eastern-European states; potentially autonomous internal nationalistic forces in that region will be eliminated with whatever level of violence is necessary to accomplish that end.

It has been the Chinese revolution, however, along with the writings of its leader and the dominant Marxist theoretician and revolutionary leader after Lenin, Mao Tse-tung, which have most influenced the forms of "wars of national liberation" in the Third World. The origin of the Chinese revolution is difficult to date. The imperial government showed its fissures increasingly from the time of the Opium War of 1840 (Mao seems to date the revolution from this time)[57] and the Manchu dynasty fell in 1911. The Kuomintang was founded in 1913 under the leadership of Sun Yat-sen and began the movement toward centralized national control. After the death of Sun Yat-sen, a battle ensued between Chiang Kai-shek and Mao, which was to last over twenty years and culminated in the expulsion of the Kuomintang from the mainland. After suffering shattering early defeats during this civil war, Mao retreated in 1934 and 1935 from Southern China to the remote northwest, in the famous Long March of over 6,000 miles, to the caves at Yenan. There he analyzed the nature of his strengths and weaknesses and developed a theory of warfare based upon the dogma outlined by Lenin at the Second Comintern Congress in 1920 and, more importantly, upon Mao's own experience in fighting against a Kuomintang which held the cities and controlled the bureaucracy, the army, and the main routes of transportation. Mao perceived the political weakness of the Kuomintang, which had few political roots in the countryside, in a nation in which 85 per cent of the people were rural peasants. Breaking with orthodox Marxism, Mao built a revolutionary structure based upon the peasants and designed to encircle the cities from the countryside for a protracted war of attrition. The application of his formula of "the enemy advances, we retreat; the enemy halts, we harass; the enemy tires, we attack; the enemy retreats, we pursue" was followed in years of guerrilla warfare which eventually culminated in the defeat of the Kuomintang.

The Japanese invasion was essential to Mao's triumph, both in its shattering effect upon Chiang's position and also in the opportunity it afforded Mao to capture the nationalist banner and thereby rally the peasants to the support of the Communist Party. (It is the absence of the equivalent of this element that has been at least one powerful factor limiting the success of Mao's model in the Third World.)

The impact of this experience pervades virtually all of Mao's writings. It is without question the dominant influence upon current Marxist

[57] Mao Tse-tung, "The Chinese Revolution and the Chinese Communist Party, December 1939," 2 Selected Works (1961).

theories[58] of the "war of national liberation." The primary teachings of Mao and of the late Lin Piao, Minister of National Defense and until recently Mao's heir apparent, seem to be more completely dominated by this event than by all other factors combined.

While Mao accepts traditional Marxist ideas of class struggle,[59] the necessity of revolution[60] and a Leninist belief in "just wars,"[61] his writing is pervaded by a dominating nationalism[62] which sits uneasily alongside traditional Marxist thinking regarding the international aspect of class-consciousness and identification. But this nationalism may well be the key to his revolutionary success.

One of the most important current documents setting out Maoist thinking on the nature of internal violence and "wars of national liberation" is the speech of Lin Piao, delivered in 1965 on the occasion of the twentieth

[58] "Marx, Engels, Lenin, Trotsky and Stalin agreed on the historical necessity of war as a concomitant of revolution. Hence all at one time or another expressed an interest in the special problems of a people's war. Their studies, however, were not systematized within an ideological framework, as are those of Mao." E. Katzenbach, Jr., & G. Hanrahan, "The Revolutionary Strategy of Mao Tse-tung," F. Osanka (ed.), *Modern Guerrilla Warfare* (1962).

[59] "Mao Tse-tung fully subscribes to the Marxist view that history must be looked upon as a mirror reflecting class activity. 'Dialectically' considered, classes and class struggle form the fundamental motive force of historical development. The social sphere can be understood only in terms of class: 'Classes struggle, some classes triumph, others are eliminated. Such is history, such is the history of civilization for thousands of years.' Revolutions are developmental processes whereby social classes overthrow one another. The unfolding of revolution is determined by fluctuations in class contradictions and the shifting of class forces." M. Rejai (ed.) (in part quoting Mao), in *Mao Tse-tung on Revolution and War* xvii (1970).

[60] "The seizure of power by armed force, the settlement of the issue by war, is the central task and the highest form of revolution. This Marxist-Leninist principle of revolution holds good universally, for China and for all other countries." Mao Tse-tung, "Problems of War and Strategy," 1 *Selected Works* 219–30 (1964).

[61] "There is the old adage 'In the Spring and Autumn Era there were no righteous wars.' This is even truer of imperialism today, for it is only the oppressed nations and the oppressed classes that can wage just wars. All wars anywhere in the world in which people rise up to fight their oppressors are just struggles. . . . All just wars support each other, while all unjust wars should be turned into just wars—this is the Leninist line." Mao Tse-tung, "On Tactics Against Japanese Imperialism," (December 1935), 1 *Selected Works* 170–71 (1964);

". . . all wars in history may be divided into two kinds according to their nature: just wars and unjust wars. For instance, the Great War in Europe some twenty years ago was an unjust imperialist war. . . . But historically there have been revolutionary wars, e.g., in France, Russia, and present-day Spain. In such wars the government does not fear popular disapproval, because the people are most willing to wage this kind of war . . . the government rests upon the people's voluntary support." "Interview with the British Journalist James Bertram," (October 1937) 2 *ibid.* at 57–58.

"The only just wars are non-predatory wars, wars of liberation. Communists will in no circumstances support any predatory war. They will, however, bravely step forward to support every just and nonpredatory war for liberation, and they stand in the forefront of the struggle. . . ." "Interview with a *New China Daily* Correspondent on the New International Situation," (September 1939) 2 *ibid.* at 265–66.

[62] *See, e.g.,* "The Chinese Revolution and the Chinese Communist Party," 2 *ibid. See also* S. Schram, "Mao: The Man and His Doctrines," *Problems of Communism* (October 1966).

anniversary of the "victory of the Chinese People's war of resistance against Japan,"[63] "Long live the Victory of People's War."[64]

The non-Marxist reliance on nationalism is emphasized at the beginning:

> History shows that when confronted by ruthless imperialist aggression, a Communist Party must hold aloft the national banner and, using the weapon of the united front, rally around itself the masses and the patriotic and anti-imperialist people who form more than 90 per cent of a country's population, so as to mobilize all positive factors, unite with all the forces that can be united and isolate to the maximum the common enemy of the whole nation. If we abandon the national banner, adopt a line of "closed-doorism" and thus isolate ourselves, it is out of the question to exercise leadership and develop the people's revolutionary cause, and this in reality amounts to helping the enemy and bringing defeat on ourselves.[65]

The overwhelming lesson learned by Mao in his fight with Chiang, when the Kuomintang appeared to have all the advantages, was that war was a political event and the eventual outcome would be determined by that fact. In internal war, winning battles, taking geographical positions, or, one might add, "body count" is important only to the degree that it affects the political alienation or identification of the people.[66] The very organization of the army is built upon this principle:

> The essence of Comrade Mao Tse-tung's theory of army building is that in building a people's army prominence must be given to politics, i.e., the army must first and foremost be built on a political basis. Politics is the commander, politics is the soul of everything. Political work is the life-line of our army. True, a people's army must pay attention to the constant improvement of its weapons and equipment and its military technique, but in its fighting it does not rely purely on weapons and technique, it relies mainly on politics, on the proletarian revolutionary consciousness and courage of the commanders and fighters, on the support and backing of the masses.[67]

Lin Piao described the work done in the countryside by the "people's army" in what American military men once called in Vietnam the "other war" or rural pacification. To Lin Piao and Mao, it has always been the only war— the political war. In language which reflects the insight which

---

[63] Peking translation.

[64] A copy of the Peking translation of this speech may be found in B. Mazlish, et al. (eds.), *Revolution: A Reader* 357–73 (1971); *See also* "Long Live the Victory of the People's War." *Peking Review*, September 3, 1965.

[65] *Id.*

[66] Mao said that "because guerrilla warfare basically derives from the masses and is supported by them, it can neither exist nor flourish if it separates itself from their sympathies or cooperation." S. Griffith, *Mao Tse-tung on Guerrilla Warfare* 44 (1961).

[67] "Long Live the Victory of People's War," *supra* note 64.

has been so tragically lacking in our involvement in Vietnam, Lin Piao says:

> In other words, you rely on modern weapons and we rely on highly conscious revolutionary people; you give full play to your superiority and we give full play to ours; you have your way of fighting and we have ours.[68]

To maintain mass militancy and to avoid bureaucratic ossification, Mao developed the "mass line" of cadre recruitment from local villages, to be continually followed by interaction between the villagers and the military leadership. This assures that peasant grievances are continually before the leadership, there formulated into broad policy and, theoretically at least, taught back to the masses. This continual interchange leads supposedly to constant purification of doctrine and is Mao's answer to the question of how to involve the people in the decision-making processes of the military and the political institutions.[69] It has been suggested that the recent Cultural Revolution was another attempt by Mao to avoid the Stalinist petrifaction of the revolution through bureaucratization.[70]

The much heralded invitation to the Third World to follow the Maoist model of rural-based, protracted guerrilla warfare of attrition, waged against urban-dominated governments, is an important part of this speech. However, Western analysts seem to have been so transfixed by this spectre, that the really important point made by Lin Piao has been ignored. *And that is that he clearly announced this form of war to be, of necessity by its very nature, a "do it yourself" effort.* This point is sufficiently important—and substantially overlooked—to be shouted in italics. Lin Piao, in commentary which both accurately reflected the nature of the Chinese civil war *and at the same time constituted a cautious and conservative though dogmatic pronouncement of a foreign policy which was not wildly expansionary, said:*

> The peoples of the world invariably support each other in their struggles against imperialism and its lackeys. Those countries which have won victory are duty-bound to support and aid the peoples who have not yet done so. Nevertheless, foreign aid can only play a supplementary role.
>
> In order to make a revolution and to fight a people's war and be victorious, it is imperative to adhere to the policy of self-reliance, rely on the strength of the masses in one's own country and prepare to carry on the fight independently even when all material aid from outside is cut off. If

---

[68] *Id.*

[69] *See* Mao Tse-tung, "On the Mass Line," in S. Schram, *The Political Thought of Mao Tse-tung* 317 (rev. ed. 1969); J. Grey & P. Cavendish, *Chinese Communism in Crisis: Maoism and the Cultural Revolution* (1968).

[70] For a listing of writings on the Cultural Revolution and the development of the proposition that its main objective was the avoidance of bureaucratic ossification, see Pfeffer, "Mao Tse-tung and the Cultural Revolution," in N. Miller & R. Aya (eds.), *National Liberation: Revolution in the Third World* (1971).

one does not operate by one's own efforts, does not independently ponder and solve the problems of the revolution in one's own country and does not rely on the strength of the masses, but leans wholly on foreign aid—even though this be aid from socialist countries which persist in revolution—no victory can be won, or be consolidated even if it is won.[71]

He commented at a later point upon the primary role of the local populace and the limited role of third parties:

Of course, every revolution in a country stems from the demands of its own people. Only when the people in a country are awakened, mobilized, organized and armed can they overthrow the reactionary rule of imperialism and its lackeys through struggle; their role cannot be replaced or taken over by any people from outside. In this sense, revolution cannot be imported. But this does not exclude mutual sympathy and support on the part of revolutionary peoples in their struggles against the imperialists and their lackeys. Our support and aid to other revolutionary peoples serves precisely to help their self-reliant struggle.[72]

One cannot avoid a comparison between this policy and that employed by the United States in Vietnam. The lack of a strong national base for the government of South Vietnam is painfully evident and has been since the early sixties. This fact alone should have at the very beginning determined a different policy for the United States toward Vietnam. The commitment of several hundred thousand men in the mid-sixties was confirmation of the lack of national identification with the Saigon government by a significant part of the population and, at the same time, insured that whatever incipient nationalism and initiative did exist would have difficulty surviving. Full realization of the necessity of forming broad alliances which brought in as much of the spectrum of political and social thought as possible in order to wage political and military war with the National Liberation Front was thus kept from government leaders in Saigon until that time, in the late sixties and early seventies, at which it was in all probability too late. Whatever the chances of forming a broadly based national movement in the forties, fifties, and early sixties—and they were probably not very good then, given the dominance of Ho Chi Minh in Vietnamese nationalist development to that time—the chances were incomparably worse by the time that "Vietnamization" became official policy in early 1968. By that time, the sheer size of the U.S. presence inadvertently had politically emasculated whatever local leadership there was. It may be doubted that political eunuchs will be able to compete with the NLF and Viet Cong cadres who have been immersed in political indoctrination and who fully understand the teachings of Lenin, Mao, Lin Piao, and Ho Chi Minh that warfare is intensely and completely a political event.

[71] "Long Live the Victory of People's War." *supra* note 64.
[72] *Id.*

III. "WARS OF NATIONAL LIBERATION" AND THE NATURE OF INTERNAL VIOLENCE IN THE THIRD WORLD

A survey of politically motivated internal violence[73] in Asia, Africa, and Latin America leads to several conclusions which will be stated prior to a more detailed examination. First, this type of violence has been increasing within the Third World at least during the past two decades.[74] Second, the three regions of the Third World, so-called, have very little in common, either in the nature of their internal violence or in its causation.[75] Third, there have been attempts to foster Maoist-styled rural-based "national liberation" movements in all three regions, with no success (subsequent to Castro) in Latin America, indeterminate success in those areas of Africa still troubled with the presence of the last remnants of traditional colonialism, and no success elsewhere—but with substantial success in Southeast Asia, particularly in Vietnam. Fourth, in Latin America at least, urban-based insurgency would seem to pose a more substantial threat to incumbent governments. Fifth, overwhelming social, political, and economic problems within the Third World insure that politically motivated internal violence both of an organized and a spontaneous or anomic nature will continue at a high level. Sixth, Marxists of various persuasions, domestic and foreign, will react to this condition;

---

[73] Douglas Bwy has divided internal violence into two major categories: first, the spontaneous, disorganized, anomic sort of turmoil; second, internal war of a planned and organized nature. Although this essay deals mainly with the latter, violence of the first category can have or take a political coloration and hence cannot be excluded from consideration. *See* Bwy, "Dimensions of Social Conflict in Latin America," in L. Masotti & D. Bowen (eds.), *Riots and Rebellion: Civil Violence in the Urban Community* (1968).

Other classifications of internal violence should be noted. Harry Eckstein has distinguished between unorganized and spontaneous riots; coups d'état by elites against elites, political revolution aimed at accomplishing constitutional change; social revolution aimed at accomplishing social, economic, and constitutional change; and finally, war of independence designed to accomplish sovereign control for a previously dependent territory. Eckstein, "On the Etiology of Internal Wars," in Mazlish *et al.*, *supra* note 64. Lasswell and Kaplan divide internal wars into palace revolutions, political revolutions, and social revolutions. H. Lasswell & H. Kaplan, *Power and Society* (1950). George Blanksten divides internal war into "real" revolutions, "near" revolutions, and non-constitutional changes in government. Blanksten, "Revolutions," in H. Davis (ed.), *Government and Politics in Latin America* (1958). James Rosenau divides internal war into three major types: first, personal wars; second, authority wars; and finally, structural wars. Rosenau, *"Internal War as an International Event,"* in J. Rosenau (ed.), *International Aspects of Civil Strife* (1964). Chalmers Johnson has suggested six types of internal war: (1) jacquerie; (2) millenarian rebellion; (3) anarchistic rebellion; (4) Jacobin Communist revolution; (5) conspiratorial coup d'état; and (6) militarized mass insurrection. C. Johnson, *Revolution and the Social System*, Hoover Institution Studies 3 (1964). See Stone, "Theories of Revolution," in 18 *World Politics* (January, 1966).

[74] S. Huntington, *Political Order in Changing Societies* (1968).

[75] Fatouros, "Participation of the 'New' States in the International Legal Order of the Future," in I R. Falk & C. Black, *supra* note 8, at 357.

some will attempt genuine though radical reform, while others will attempt to exploit conditions in order to accomplish their own goals which may have little or no relationship to social conditions within the state. Seventh, these conditions in the Third World should produce various degrees of concern (as motivated by reasons of national security) to the United States, depending in part upon the location of the state experiencing civil strife, the nature of the incumbent government, the nature and motivation of the insurgents, and the degree—if any—of foreign involvement in the insurgency. Eighth, in the vast majority of cases there will be little if anything that any third party, including the United States, can do to affect the outcome of the domestic strife. Ninth, in those cases in which the United States might have some interest in intervention—whether on behalf of the incumbent or the insurgent faction—a condition precedent to success would be the legitimacy[76] of the regime on whose behalf the intervention was attempted. Finally, the avoidance, control, and direction of internal violence rests dominantly upon the institutions within the state.

Manfred Halpern has written that "peasants do not make revolutions."[77] They are likely to make rebellions, according to Halpern, but this will further revolutionary aims only if the peasants are aided by other groups. Insurgencies and rebellions usually result in a consolidation of the social order rather than in a radical change, either by a substitution of leadership followed by consolidation after a successful rebellion or by failure, followed by increased repression by the incumbent regime. Halpern argues that there have been no peasant revolutions in Africa, and very few peasant rebellions. Those peasant rebellions which have occurred have been aimed, with few exceptions, at the preservation of the tribal, ethnic, or religious status quo. And the exceptions to this rule (the African rebellion against Arab rule on Zanzibar, the Hutu rebellion against the Tutsi in Rwanda, and the Muslim rebellion against the French in Algeria) were rebellions against alien influences.

The closest thing to a Maoist modelled "war of national liberation" in Africa is the intermittent guerrilla conflict being waged against Portugese control in Mozambique, Angola, and Portuguese Guinea. And there tribalism, poverty, indifference, and disorganization—along with stiff Portugese resistance—have prevented success. The Angolan Communist Party (PCA) was started in 1955. Early in 1956, the PCA founded PLUA (Partido da Luta Dos Africanos de Angola), a national front organization. However, the organization recognized by the Organization

---

[76] The term "legitimacy" is not used here in its "legal" or constitutional sense but rather as the political scientist or sociologist would use it in reference to the allegiance of a people toward its government as being the most appropriate for the society. See discussion *infra*.

[77] Halpern, "There Are No Peasant Revolutionaries," 25 *J. of Int'l Aff.* 159 (Nov. 1, 1971), review of R. Rotberg & A. Mazrui, *Protest and Power in Black Africa* (1970).

of African Unity[78] as constituting the recognized rebel government is Movimento Popular de Libertacao de Angola (MPLA), founded by young Marxists in the PCA and others who are non-Marxists.[79] The secret police have decimated the leadership of MPLA, and its remnants have gone into exile following the inability of the organization to extend its influence beyond its urban origins. In February, 1960, MPLA established its headquarters in Conakry, the capital of the then newly independent Republic of Guinea. It has, with little success, attempted to unite all exiled nationalist groups into a common front. Regional and tribal divisions and hostilities have prevented unity.

Eastern Angolan guerrilla activity is conducted by a separate organization, UNITA (National Union for the Total Independence of Angola). Another rural-based organization exists in the province of Malange and is almost exclusively limited to the Mbundu.[80] In Northern Angola another organization, UPNA (Uniao das Populacoes do Norte de Angola) has as its goal a separate state built around the Bakongo tribe.[81]

Portuguese intransigence toward moderate reform, aimed at an eventually independent Portuguese Guinea, led to the creation of PAIGE (Partido do Independencia de Guinee Cabo Verde) in August, 1956.[82] Any hope of peaceful settlement was destroyed by the massacre at the port of Bissau in August, 1959, when fifty dock workers were shot by Portuguese authorities in order to break a strike.[83] PAIGE is active in rural Portuguese Guinea and is aided by the neighboring states of Senegal and Guinea.[84]

"National liberation" activity in Mozambique has met with even less success than in the other Portuguese territories. Portuguese prepartion, based upon experience in Guinea and Angola, was more effective. Zones were cleared adjacent to the Northern frontier, rural populations were moved to "secure" areas, and airstrips and roads were built for the military in the pattern which has come to be typical of counterinsurgency techniques.[85] Tribalism has affected FRELIMO even more than the other insurgent groups. Its major bases are in Tanzania, which fact has obliged them to recruit dominantly from local Makonde and Nyanja tribes. Larger and more important tribes to the south, particularly the Makua, have resisted FRELIMO. The Portuguese have recruited the Makua into de-

---

[78] 15 *Africa Digest* 44–45 (May 14, 1969).

[79] J. Marcum, 1 *The Angolan Revolution* 30–35 (1969).

[80] *Id.* at 47.

[81] *Id.* at 62.

[82] Davidson, "The Liberation Struggle in Angola and 'Portuguese' Guinea," 10 *African Q.* 26 (1970).

[83] *Id.* at 28.

[84] Zartman, "Guinea: The Quiet War Goes On," 12 *Africa Report* 67 (1967).

[85] Martelli, "Conflict in Portuguese Africa," D. Abshire and M. Samuels (ed.), *Portuguese Africa* 420 (1969). Dodson, "Dynamics of Insurgency in Mozambique," 12 *Africa Report* 52 (1967).

fensive forces and have exploited tribal enmities whenever it suited their purposes.[86]

FRELIMO has received substantial aid from the U.S.S.R., Yugoslavia, Czechoslovakia, and Bulgaria.[87] It is reported, however, that China has given only nominal support to FRELIMO, through the Tanzanian government, and has given no support to PAIGE and MPLA.[88] The Soviets have provided substantial military training and have supplied most of the automatic weapons and small artillery used by PAIGE and MPLA.[89] Tanzania has provided the sites for training and refuge with instructors, reportedly from Eastern Europe, Algeria, Cuba, and China. By the end of 1967, the rebels were reportedly in possession of mortars, bazookas, and notably, the AK 47 assault rifle and a new rocket launcher, both of Chinese manufacture.[90]

The objective of such a low level of military activity on the part of these insurgent groups is not, of course, military victory, but rather carrying on a protracted war of attrition against the Portuguese until the cost in lives and money becomes greater than the Portuguese metropolitan population will bear. While immediate success would not appear likely, some form of national autonomy would seem to be inevitable. Whether the technique of "wars of national liberation," as applied by these groups, will hasten the process of national independence is difficult to determine. The combination of rural support led by an intellectual elite and aided by an urban proletariat, considered by Mao and Lin Piao to be essential to ultimate success, has not materialized. Regional, rural-urban, ethnic, and tribal differences have so far proven to be insurmountable obstacles.

The overwhelming preponderance of internal violence of a political nature throughout the rest of Africa has resulted not from local or foreign Communist activity but rather from tribal wars, religious hostility, regionalism, and coups by military forces. Military governments which have deposed civilian governments now govern over 100 million people in Africa—a third of the continent's population.[91] An army mutiny in Mali in 1968 toppled the government of Modigo Keita;[92] Nkruma was deposed in Ghana in 1966;[93] Dahomey has experienced a series of military governments each following the other with coups;[94] Togo has suffered the same

[86] Martelli, *supra* at 423.
[87] *Id.*
[88] Basil Davidson, "The Seed of Midwinter," *Atlas* 23 (Jan. 1971), *reprinted from New Statesman* (London).
[89] *Id.*
[90] Martelli, *supra* note 85 at 424.
[91] *N.Y. Times*, Feb. 7, 1971, at 2, cols. 3–6.
[92] 15 *Africa Digest* 8 (Jan. 19, 1969).
[93] *Id.* at 24, (March 8, 1969).
[94] *Id.*, vol. 7 at 102 (Oct. 8–Nov. 30, 1959); vol. 11 at 85 (Nov. 15, 1963); vol. 15 at 21 (Jan. 7, 1968).

experience[95] as has Sierra Leone.[96] The tragic Nigerian Civil War in which an estimated two million people died was preceded by a military coup which replaced the civilian regime.[97] Uganda followed the same pattern as the army chief, Major-General Idi Amin, ousted President Milton Obote.[98]

More or less traditional guerrilla warfare and terrorism have marked the sporadic battle between the government of Kenya and the Shifta, an armed band of Somalis living in Northern Kenya. Kenya protested to the U.S.S.R. for allegedly providing military aid to Somalia and from that government to the Shifta.[99] Ethiopia faced a similar struggle with Somalia over control of Eritrea in Northern Ethiopia. The Eritrean Liberation Front (ELF) has mounted a small-scale guerrilla effort in an attempt to free its predominantly Muslim people from Ethiopian rule. The ELF has had the aid of several Arab states.[100] Sudan and Chad have been faced with guerilla warfare and terrorism based upon the same factors, but from opposite positions of governmental incumbency. In Sudan, the Arab North has enjoyed a virtual monopoly on governmental institutions and has consequently faced an increasingly hostile Black African South. Egyptian and Soviet "advisers" to the Northern government at Khartoum have helped the incumbent government prosecute its civil war.[101] (The ranking in Soviet foreign policy between Black Africa and the Arab Middle East is clearly revealed.) French troops have supported the Black African government of Chad against the Arab Muslim North.[102]

Internal political violence in Asia has been dominated by the wars in Southeast Asia. A voluminous literature exists, and no purpose would be served by reviewing it. It is sufficient to note that the classic situation there existed for a successful "war of national liberation." A colonial power, the French, had insured through a century of colonial rule that the vital element of nationalism could be used by whatever native forces op-

---

[95] Id., vol. 10 at 147 (Jan. 16, 1963), and vol. 14 at 173 (March 18, 1963) cover iii (Jan. 21, 1967).

[96] Id., vol. 14 at 123 (May 20, 1967).

[97] Id., vol. 14 at 41 (Sept. 19, 1966).

[98] N.Y. Times, supra n. 91.

[99] 14 Africa Digest 30, 73 (Sept. 19, 1966; Jan. 21, 1967).

[100] Lewis, "Ethiopia: The Quickening Pulse," 54 Current History 79 (1968); Grundy, "Nationalism and Separatism in East Africa," 54 Current History 92 (1968).

[101] O. Albino, The Sudan: A Southern Viewpoint (1970); M. Beshir, The Southern Sudan: Background to Conflict 55 (1968); Time, Mar. 1, 1971 at 30; 20 Atlas 35 (No. 4, April 1971); N.Y. Times, Jan. 5, 1971 at 6 col. 1.

[102] 14 Africa Digest 100 (March 10, 1967); 15 Africa Digest 90 (Sept. 11, 1969).

See generally, R. Rotberg & A. Mazrui supra note 77. J. M. Lee, African Armies and Civil Order (1969).

For views professing to see many more elements of social revolution throughout Africa than indicated in this essay, see Frey-Wouters, "The Prospects for Regionalism in World Affairs," I R. Falk & C. Black supra note 75. James, "Colonialism and National Liberation in Africa: The Gold Coast Revolution," Miller & Aya supra note 70.

posed them. The demography of the area—prior to forced population changes in the American period—was almost exactly the same as pre-1949 China, 85 percent rural. The French and their successors had little political influence in the countryside. After 1949, at least, a friendly state could offer aid and sanctuary to guerrilla forces. And most important of all, sufficient support for a revolutionary force existed in the countryside to provide the friendly environment so essential to the guerrilla—for food, sanctuary, recruits, and intelligence.

Mao's influence on Ho, Giap, Truong Chinh, and others who played dominant roles in the Vietnam War is unquestioned.[103] Under Ho Chi Minh, the Viet Minh waged a classically successful "war of national liberation" against the French in essentially the same fashion as Mao had done against Chiang. The losers held control of the cities (the French held Hanoi and all the major cities of the North as well as the South to the very end), the governmental bureaucracy, the army, and the major lines of communication between the cities. The losers won almost all of the pitched battles until the final stage of Mao's three-part battle plan; by such criteria as "body count," the French won every engagement, including Dien Bien Phu. All the Viet Minh won was the war. Mao's doctrine of seeking victory by concentrating on the "center" of the colonial regime, that is, the metropolitan polity rather than the colonial military regime, was successful in that political disillusionment in France with the war eventually made it impossible to continue. Finally, Mendes-France was chosen Premier upon his promise to end hostilities in Indo-China within thirty days.

While the United States entered the war, from its point of view, not as the colonial successor to the French but rather as an ally of an anti-Communist government, the colonial history of Vietnam and the politically rootless, artificial nature of the South Vietnamese government made it all but impossible to effectively make the nationalist cause our own. And if that could not be accomplished, the regime in Saigon would survive only so long as the United States military presence was there to insure its survival.[104] That presence would soon become as politically impossible for

---

[103] *See* B. Fall, *The Two Viet-Nams* 98, 99, 112–14 (2d rev. ed., 1967). H. Salisbury, *Behind the Lines—Hanoi* 180 (1967). F. Trager, *Why Vietnam?* 206.

[104] An observation written in 1966 and published the next year would seem to have been fulfilled: ". . . no political figure or group has emerged who could serve as the nucleus of a government with which the people in the countryside could identify. No real political support in the countryside exists in favor of a man or a government, even though considerable opposition does exist toward the Communist North. This situation is dangerously close to that experienced by Chiang in pre-1949 China, when he had impressive military forces, some political support in the cities, but few political roots in the countryside. And as in China, the vast majority of the people of South Viet-Nam do not live in the cities. Diem was a legitimate nationalist and no one questioned the depth of his anti-Communism. Attempts to picture him as a French or an American puppet are completely erroneous. And no one since has had the stature or the background of fighting the nationalist fight against colonial powers. The southern equivalent of Ho is painfully absent. Without a man around whom the country can unite and with whom the people can identify, the chances of the forma-

the Americans as it has been for the French, while a protracted war of attrition finally took its toll. Both the Americans and the French fought on the erroneous assumption that they were opposing an insurgency and so adopted the techniques of counter-insurgency. In fact they were facing a nationalist revolution, albeit Communist-led. The end of such a war was inevitable, with only the timing in doubt.

On November 1, 1964, the "Thailand Independence Movement" was formally announced with backing from Peking and Hanoi.[105] While the fate of Laos and Cambodia are probably inexorably linked to that of Vietnam, there is good reason to believe that the validity of the "domino theory" may well stop there. Thailand has no colonial history to cripple the nationalistic legitimacy of its government. Insurgents may well discover that they are the aliens in such a war. The techniques of insurgency —terrorism, political assassination, ambush—can only work when the targets are viewed by the populace as somehow illegitimate. Village leaders appointed by Saigon often had little popular support from the villagers. But the traditional leaders in Thailand are not counterparts. All-out invasion of Thailand by North Vietnam could probably conquer the country, but insurgency alone might well fail.

Elsewhere in Asia, the Burmese Civil War (1948–51) saw an unsuccessful Communist attempt to gain power;[106] but colonialism is not an issue now, and while any incumbent government may well be faced with traditional and sporadic guerrilla harassment, the facts are not such that any classic "war of national liberation," riding the issue of nationalism against an illegitimate incumbent government, can accomplish power by a cheap shot.

In April of 1971, Ceylon experienced a brief and bloody rebellion by the militant Marxist People's Liberation Front. Conditions were such in Ceylon that some form of insurgency would seem to have a chance of success. Unemployment was high, the economy of the country had been steadily declining under inept socialist leadership, which had succeeded in bartering away much of its rubber crop to China in order to support a welfare scheme that would be difficult for much richer states to bear. Part of this system led directly to the insurgency. Free education from primary school through the university had assured the country of thousands of unemployed young students, unable to find work in a sick economy. The

---

tion of a stable government with true political power are slim. And without such a government the chances of successful American counter-intervention are equally slight. We would be faced with the choice of perpetual presence or the rapid evaporation of a politically rootless non-Communist government in the South."—Firmage, "International Law and the Response of the United States to 'Internal war,' " in II R. Falk (ed.), *The Vietnam War and International Law* 89, 107 (Princeton, N.J.: Princeton University Press, 1969), *reprinted from* 1967 *Utah L. Rev.* 517.

[105] For documentation on the formation of the "Thailand Independence Movement" *see id.* at 97, n. 35.

[106] F. Trager, *Burma: From Kingdom to Republic* 101 (1966).

People's Liberation Front ('Che Guevarists') was built dominantly upon this group. The PLF began regular attacks upon government installations and police stations, but evidently had not taken the painstaking local organizational efforts that Mao and Lin Piao had found to be essential; the swiftness with which the government was able to decimate the PLF would indicate that the intellectuals had little support among either peasants or urban workers. Although the demography of Ceylon is almost exactly that of China and Vietnam, with 85 percent of the people living in the countryside (the government had little support outside the cities), the rebels evidently had no sanctuary or refuge and were swiftly defeated.[107]

The post-war Communist insurgency in Malaya was centered among a minority of the Chinese population, which was in turn a minority within a state dominated by the Malayan ethnic majority. The heavy reliance upon terrorism by the insurgents at once violated a basic tenet of Maoist guerrilla warfare and alienated the people who viewed the objects of the violence to be representatives of a legitimate government. It has been estimated that the insurgent forces never numbered over 5,000 at one time.[108] The factor of national legitimacy quite clearly remained with the incumbent government, representing the dominant ethnic group, throughout. No parallel to Vietnam ever really existed, despite attempts by American planners there to emulate the successful counter-insurgency techniques used in Malaya. (A point made earlier deserves repeating: techniques of counter-insurgency will not be successful in combatting a national revolution, aimed at overthrowing the remnants of a colonial system.)

The devastating civil war between what was then East and West Pakistan had its roots in the cultural and ethnic differences between the dominant western wing, which identified with the Islamic peoples to the west, and the smaller and darker East Pakistanis, whose origins seem to be from South and Southeast Asia. The Punjabis of the West long dominated the Bengalis of the East, though East Pakistan had a population of 72 million to 58 million in the West. There was no Marxist element within the causation of civil war in Pakistan, and hence no "war of national liberation," with its Marxist denotation, existed. However, the nascent movement toward Bengali autonomy was powerfully advanced by the brutality and the devastation of the war waged by the West, which had an almost complete control of the army, against the East. A *Times* reporter observed this change:

---

[107] N.Y. *Times*, April 8, 1971, at 2, col. 1; April 10, 1971 at 1, col. 2; April 1, 1971, sec. E, at 4, col. 3; April 11, 1971, at 9, col. 1; April 14, 1971, at 10, col. 1; April 15, 1971, at 1 col. 5.

[108] E. Ballance, *Malaya: The Communist Insurgent War, 1948–60* at 101 (1966). *See also* R. Clutterbuck, *The Long Long War* (1966); D. Hall, *A History of South-East Asia* (1968).

Only a few months ago, people in East Pakistan would complain to visiting journalists of the "dirty and arrogant Hindus." Now they say, "Hindu, Moslem, that does not count any more. We are all Bengalis." The enemy now is "Punjabi," the most commonly used name for the West Pakistanis.[109]

As a consequence of this disastrous civil war, the West Pakistanis may find themselves involved in a protracted guerrilla war against a nationalist Bengali force which would have the support of the local population and an adjacent sanctuary in India for receiving arms, training, and refuge. For West Pakistan, without the population of the East, could no longer pose a threat to India nor contest rights to Kashmir. West Pakistan would become, in effect, a Middle Eastern state without ties to the subcontinent.[110]

The Hukbalhap (Huk) movement in the Philippines originated in the agrarian unrest of central Luzon and was in part contemporaneous with the last years of the Communist Chinese revolution and therefore was not patterned after it. The Huks officially came into being in 1942, with two goals: first, opposition to the Japanese occupation, and second, social and economic reform. Although its leadership eventually came to be Communist-dominated, its origin was more broadly based and there was never any evidence of external direction. In its time of greatest strength, it was able to attract elements of organized labor, students, and intellectuals as well as its dominant peasant base, but it was never able to maintain its influence outside the geographic area of its origin in central Luzon, where social conditions were worst. Like the Chinese Communists, it was only with the advent of World War II and the Japanese invasion that the Communists in central Luzon were able to exert real influence. The critical difference in this respect between the Huks and the Chinese Communists (or the Viet Minh), however, was that at no time "could the Huks claim to be the chief and most effective nationalist anti-colonial group in the same way that the Viet-Minh were able to do in Vietnam."[111] While corruption and severe inequality were prominent parts of the social and political structure in the Philippines, the national structure of the government fit within the traditional society and maintained its legitimacy in the minds of the dominant majority of the people. The Huk rebellion was finished as an organized threat to the government by the mid-1950's.[112]

In Indonesia, a nationalist revolution against Dutch colonial control was triggered by their defeat by the Japanese during World War II, followed

[109] Vincent, "We are All Bengalis . . . ," *N.Y. Times*, April 11, 1971, Sec. E., at 3, col. 2.

[110] *N.Y. Times*, March 28, 1971, at 3, col. 2; Lelyveld, "Pakistan Born of a Shaky Abstraction," *N.Y. Times*, April 7, 1971, at 3, col. 1; *N.Y. Times*, April 14, at 1, col. 2. [This paragraph was written in early 1971, prior to the decisive military intervention of India and the establishment of the separate state of Bangla Desh.]

[111] M. Osbourne, *Region of Revolt* 83 (1970).

[112] For the background of the Huk rebellion, *see* Fifield, "The Hukbalhap Today," 20 *Far Eastern Survey* 13, (1951); Osbourne, *supra* note 111.

by Japanese occupation of Indonesia. The legitimacy of Dutch governance could not be recouped after the war, despite the efforts of the Netherlands to reestablish colonial government. A classic example of nationalist revolution against colonial rule followed the attempts of the Dutch to regain their pre-war position. A combination of constant guerrilla warfare, supported by the local populace, and intermittant large-scale battles occurred between the Republican and Dutch forces. With the perspective afforded by the tragedy of Vietnam, it is clear that a major and perhaps protracted Cold War confrontation was avoided in that both the Soviet Union and the United States correctly characterized this battle as a nationalist, anti-colonial revolution which could eventually end in only one way. United Nations fact-finding played an important part in insuring that such a characterization took place. The first report of the Consular Commission[113] made it clear that the war was a nationalistic guerrilla war fought primarily without front lines, in which the Republican Indonesian forces enjoyed the support of virtually all educated Indonesians.[114]

An attempted coup in 1965 by the Communist Party of Indonesia (CPI) against the leadership of the Indonesian army, in which six generals were murdered, resulted in a successful counter-coup by the army, followed by a short but savage slaughter of Communists and non-Communists alike, in which the leadership of the CPI was eliminated together with much of its mass base. The antipathy between the army and the CPI dated from 1948, when the army successfully aborted an attempted Communist coup during the Republic's revolutionary war against the Dutch.[115]

Four generalizations may be made about the nature of recent politically motivated internal violence in Latin America. First, the tradition of the coup d'état remains. These usually bloodless events occurred with regularity throughout much of Latin America, while actual political and economic control remained in the hands of tiny elites and real social change most usually had nothing to do with these so-called "revolutions."[116] Second, a rash of romantic "revolutions," based in the countryside and supposedly following the examples and teachings of Mao, Che Guevara, and Castro, but actually violating major principles within the teachings as well as example of Mao and Lin Piao, occurred in the mid-sixties in Ecuador, Paraguay, the Dominican Republic, Brazil, Bolivia, Argentina, Peru,

---

[113] S/586, Oct. 14, 1947.

[114] On the role of the United Nations fact-finding mission during the Indonesian crisis, *see* Firmage, "Fact-Finding in the Resolution of International Disputes: From the Hague Peace Conference to the United Nations," 1971 *Utah L. Rev.* 461.

General histories of the Indonesian revolutionary war may be found in G. Kahin, *Nationalism and Revolution in Indonesia* (1966); R. Shaplen, *Time Out of Hand* (1969); and Osbourne, *supra* note 111.

[115] A. Brackman, *Indonesia: The Gestapo Affair* (1969).

[116] Stone, "Theories of Revolution," 18 *World Politics* 159 (Jan. 1966); Bwy, *supra* note 72.

Guatemala, and in other Latin American states.[117] They all failed. Third, urban guerrilla terrorism is presently being conducted by various Marxist-oriented groups in many Latin American states without any more visible effects upon their political and social structures than was accomplished by the earlier efforts in the countryside.[118] However, the massive demographic shift from rural to urban areas, coupled with rising incomes and a softening of class structures (elements now commonly identified as factors' in revolution, contrary to the myth of revolutions rising out of abject poverty)[119] may yet lead to successful urban-based revolutions. Fourth, a point obviously related to the last but of broader sweep: social and economic conditions of sufficient gravity exist in many Latin American states that the possibility of real social revolutions cannot be dismissed.

A fifth generalization should be noted, not related directly to violence but most surely of importance to the concept of revolution. Eldon Kenworthy has observed that if the term "revolution" is possessed of any inherent meaning and is not used only to refer to armed insurrection, then some forms of revolution which no one would have foreseen have been occurring in Latin America.[120] A military government in Peru[121] maintained an anti-Communist position and yet nationalized U.S. firms and instituted sweeping land reform; Roman Catholic clergy have taken positions of leadership in movements working toward radical social reform in Argentina, Brazil, and Columbia; a Marxist government has peacefully come into power in Chile. These events should give pause to any dogmatic prophecy

---

[117] For accounts of the various reasons for the total failure of rural guerrilla activity, *see* L. Vega, *Guerrillas in Latin America: The Technique of the Counter-State* (1969); Landsberger & Hewitt, "Ten Sources of Weakness and Cleavage in Latin America Peasant Movements," in R. Stavenhagen (ed.), *Agrarian Problems and Peasant Movements in Latin America* (1970); Goldenberg, "The Cuban Revolution: An Analysis," in *Problems of Communism* (Sept.–Oct. 1963); Gall, "The Legacy of Che Guevara," 44 *Commentary* 31 (December 1967); Gude, "Political Violence in Venezuela: 1958–64," in J. Davies (ed.) *When Men Revolt—And Why* (1971); and Glick, "Isolating the Guerrilla: Some Latin American Examples," 12 *Orbis* 873 (Fall 1968).

[118] Kenworthy, "Latin American Revolutionary Theory: is it Back to the Paris Commune?," 25 *J. Int'l. Affairs* 164 (No. 1, 1971); Gall, *supra* note 117.

[119] M. Olson, Jr. "Rapid Growth as a Destablizing Force," in J. Davies, *supra* note 117.

[120] Kenworthy, *supra* note 118.

[121] The Alvardo regime confiscated foreign-owned oil companies and instituted massive land reform. Through November 1970 the government had expropriated 3.25 million hectares. After crushing the rural-based guerrillas in 1965 and 1966, the army became convinced that only by massive distribution of land could revolution with mass support be avoided. At that time, 0.8 percent of the land-holders owned 83 percent of the arable land. With the substantial accomplishment of this goal the military government "widely regarded abroad as a progressive military dictatorship that could promote rather than retard social change, also enjoyed broad-based support at home." The military government had drawn support from such diverse elements as the Communist-dominated labor movement, the Roman Catholic Church, the nationalist middle class, and the peasants. Grayson, Jr. "Peru's Military Populism," 60 *Current History* 71 (Feb. 1971).

which presumes to identify iron-clad laws by which all social change must occur.

Che Guevara and Regis Debray maintained that Latin America provided the ideal ingredients for revolution based in the countryside.[122] Guevara died in Bolivia,[123] and movements based upon this model died also throughout most of Latin America in the middle sixties. The pattern was the same in most situations: a small cadre of intellectuals, holed up in rural areas, not so much to attract peasant support—something that almost never occurred—but rather to avoid the increasingly effective counter-insurgency efforts of the armies.[124] No significant support developed from the peasants, from urban workers, or from the military. The army decimated the rural guerrilla bands.

Repeatedly, the rural-based revolutionaries violated the principles of Mao and even their own writings. They had taught that revolutions could not be exported, but yet in several cases the cadres were almost all composed of foreigners. The hard work of organizational preparation, advocated by Mao and Lin Piao, was ignored. Most importantly, prerequisites to success not within the control of the revolutionaries were not present. The nationalist cause was most often preempted by an incumbent government that has been accepted as legitimate by the populace. No alien entity existed (comparable to the French in Indo-China and Algeria, or the Japanese in Indonesia and China) with which to tar the incumbent government or generate a wave of nationalistic feeling which could in some way be directed against the government.

In Bolivia, the country considered by Regis Debray[125] to be most suitable of all for Castro-style rural-based revolution, the guerrillas were decisively defeated in 1967.[126] No peasant support had developed.[127] Urban terrorism in the form of bombings and kidnappings have occurred subsequently but without visible effect upon the government.[128]

Political violence in Venezuela has stemmed in part from its dynamic growth and the dislocations caused by the population movement which has transformed the country from a rural state with one of the lowest per capita incomes in Latin America to a dominantly urban community with

---

[122] "Che" Guevara, "Notes for the Study of the Ideology of the Cuban Revolution," 1 *Studies on the Left* (1960); "Socialism and Man in Cuba," in R. Bonachea & N. Valkes (eds.), *Selected Works of Ernesto Guevara* (1969); Debray, "Castroism: The Long March in Latin America," *Les Temps Modernes* (Jan. 1965).

[123] *See* Gall, *supra* note 117.

[124] *See* W. Barber & C. N. Rönning, *Internal Security and Military Power* (1966).

[125] Debray, *supra* note 122.

[126] Gall, *supra* note 117 at 34.

[127] Che Guevara noted peasant apathy in a diary entry: "The inhabitants of this region are as impenetrable as rocks. You speak to them, but in the deepness of their eyes you note they do not believe you." *Id.* at 31. *See also* de la Souchere, "Bolivia: Why Guevara Failed," 15 *Dissent* 420 (Sept.–Oct. 1968).

[128] 5 *Latin American Digest* 7 (Oct. 1970).

one of the highest per capita incomes in the area.[129] Violence has taken three major forms during the past decade. In the early sixties, various left-wing groups attempted to force a confrontation with the government by the technique of urban violence. After the 1963 elections, a number of these groups attempted the Guevara-Debray model of rural-based guerrilla activity and were decisively defeated by the military in 1965. Betancourt was successful in defeating several right-wing attempts to accomplish military *coups*, and at the same time crushed left-wing efforts to foment mass revolution.[130]

The dominance of domestic factors which determined success or failure of the counter-insurgency efforts in Venezuela are representative of the nature of internal violence generally. The peripheral nature of third-party influence upon the outcome of internal violence is seen throughout the Latin American experience of the last decade. The study of violence in Venezuela by Edward Gude is particularly acute, and his conclusion is relevant especially to those interested in the relationship between legal norms and internal violence:

> The dynamics of this particular case of political violence can be examined largely in the context of the extent to which the government was able to carry out its operations in such a way that they were perceived as legitimate by the significant sectors in the society. By undertaking major moves in response to major insurgent acts, the government was able to maintain a sense of legitimacy. Contributing to this was the largely successful attempt to stay within the legal code. The insurgents, on the other hand, continually committed acts that were considered illegitimate. They were unable to shift the focus to the illegitimacy of governmental acts and legitimacy of their own. This is the crux of the success of Betancourt and the failure of the insurgents.[131]

The apparent failure of the Castro-Guevara-Debray model of rural-based guerrillas has led increasingly to acts of urban terrorism in an effort to induce over-reaction by the government, obtain popular support for the rebel cause, and thus provide a base of mass support for a popular uprising. The model has changed from the revolution that brought down the Batista government (which is increasingly being recognized as having been an easy target for revolution) to the very nearly successful urban revolt in the Dominican Republic in 1965. There, without American intervention, the Constitutionalists would likely have been successful in unseating the right-wing government.[132] Political murder and other acts of

---

[129] Ahumada, "A Diagnosis of Venezuela's Problems," R. Fagen & W. Cornelius, Jr. (eds.), *Political Power in Latin America: Seven Confrontations* 49–50 (1970).

[130] Gude, "The Pattern and Dynamics of Violence," in Fagen and Cornelius, *supra* note 129, at 72–74.

[131] Gude, "Political Violence in Venezuela, "*supra* note 117.

[132] Goodsell, "Balaguer's Dominican Republic," 53 *Current History* 298, 300 (Nov. 1967).

terrorism have continued from that time. While now typical acts of left-wing terrorism have occurred, including kidnapping and bombings, the dominant violence would seem to be coming from right-wing groups aimed at crippling the leadership of the PRD and the pro-Peking Movimiento Popular Dominicano together with purging by political murder soldiers and police who sided with the Constitutionalists during the brief revolt.[133]

Perhaps the largest and best-financed organization of urban guerrillas now operating in the hemisphere is the Uruguayan Tupamaros. This group was organized in 1966 following the failure of rural-based guerrilla activities. They have a strategy common to other urban organizations of bank robberies to finance their operations, bombings and other acts of terrorism to dramatize their activities, and political kidnappings designed to embarrass the government and force governmental over-reaction and a consequent loss of legitimacy and popular support by the people. This group kidnapped Dan Mitrione, the American adviser to the Urguayan police, in 1970 and took four hostages in 1971, including the British ambassador.[134]

One other aspect of Latin American political violence should be noted. That is the increasing semi-official right-wing violence directed without visible distinction against both reformers working through the system and revolutionaries seeking to bring it down. Guatemala has the worst record of any Latin American state. The left-wing guerrilla movements (there are two major units, the MR 13 of Yon Sosa and the National Liberation Army of Cesar Montes)[135] have followed the usual Latin American pattern of defeat in the countryside, followed by a return to urban terrorism. But by far more deaths and destruction have been accomplished in recent years by the right-wing terrorist organization, the "White Hand," a creature of the Movimento de Liberación Nacional, a semi-official organization enjoying close connections with the Guatemalan army. The arms of the "White Hand" are allegedly supplied by the army, which in turn receives them from the American military aid program. This organization, according to *The Economist*, has been responsible for more deaths in several months' activity than resulted from several years of left-wing guerrilla activity. Victims range from students, intellectuals, and labor leaders to peasants suspected of some left-wing affiliation.[136]

---

[133] *Latin America* 148–49 (May 9, 1969).

[134] Kenwothy, *supra* note 118; *N.Y. Times*, July 7, 1971, at 6c, cols. 3–8.

[135] Vega, "The Myth of the Guerrilla," 15 *Dissent* 210 (May–June 1968).

[136] "The Last Revolution," *The Economist* (Jan. 14, 1967), as quoted in Gall, "The Legacy of Che Guevara," *supra* note 117, at 41.

"During the past 18 months . . . (Right-wing groups) have assassinated more than 2,800 intellectuals, students, labor leaders, and peasants who have in any way tried to organize and combat the ills of Guatemalan society. The 'Mano Blanca' (White Hand) itself admits that not more than one in ten of these is probably a Communist." Excerpt from an article written by Father Thomas Melville in *The National Catholic Reporter*, Jan. 31, 1968, and *reprinted* in E. Galeano, *Guatemala, Occupied Country* (1968).

A form of political violence unique in its indiscriminate savagery and the number of its victims is the Colombian "la violencia." It evidently began over two decades ago, when Conservative President Laureano Gomez led a campaign to eliminate the Liberal Party by directing the police to murder members of the Liberal Party and destroy crops (especially coffee trees) in rural Liberal areas. The Liberals reciprocated, and from that time the savage warfare between the parties has taken several hundred thousand lives. Communist attempts to control or direct "la violencia" have been "remarkably unsuccessful."[137]

Latin American internal political violence has been largely unsuccessful in affecting incumbent governments. The Guevara-Debray model of guerrilla warfare, waged from bases in the countryside, has failed. Government response to this and to the more recent urban guerrilla activity would indicate that governments willing to accomplish social reform and sufficiently tough to lead effective counter-insurgency action can deal with internal violence with a minimum of outside aid.

IV. CONCLUSIONS: LAW AND POLICY

> Take heed how you involve yourself in new enterprises or engagements; for once in, you are forced to go on. Whence it results that men are often found labouring through tasks which being embarked in they cannot withdraw from, though had they foreseen a tenth part of their difficulty they would have gone a thousand miles to avoid them. This rule holds most of all in feuds, factions, and wars, before taking part in which, or in anything of a like nature, no amount of careful and cautious consideration will be excessive.
>
> FRANCESCO GUICCIARDINI (1492–1540), *Ricordi*

The "war of national liberation" has not proven to be a magical formula for successful revolution in the Third World. Wars or insurgencies patterned, however loosely, upon the model propounded by Mao and Lin Piao have not succeeded in Africa or Latin America. In fairness, it must be noted that the ease with which Castro was able to overthrow a corrupt government which had lost the support of the middle class and the army probably distorted the perspective of those who attempted unsuccessfully to repeat the process by following the leadership and the teachings of Guevara and Debray. Romantic Latin notions of revolution did violence to the teachings of Mao. The important point, however, is that in the two instances where classic "wars of national liberation" have succeeded—in China and in Vietnam—both Communist organizations promulgating revolution, the Chinese Communist Party and the Viet Minh, were able to capture a surging nationalist sentiment which they did note create. The failure of their

---

[137] Bailey, "*La Violencia in Colombia*," 9 *J. of Inter-Amer. Stud.* 561, 569 (1967).

opponents to become dominantly identified with the nationalist cause was both a cause and a result of their loss of legitimacy (used, again, in the sense of political allegiance, or the identification by the populace of the congruence of the political structure with the society or culture)[138] and their consequent inability to defeat their opponents.

It is of critical importance to observe at this point that there is very little which is natural—let alone inevitable—about the Communist capture of the nationalist cause. The injection of nationalism into the concept of the "war of national liberation" came from Mao, not Marx or Lenin, and was a product of Mao's intense nationalism rather than his Communist ideology. In fact, the element of nationalism fits uncomfortably within Marxist doctrine and is representative of Mao's background and his pragmatism rather than his dogmatism.[139]

In both the Chinese and the Vietnamese revolutions Communist forces were aided in the struggle against their opponents by invasions by the Japanese. In the case of China, this not only helped isolate Chiang by keeping him in virtual exile from the people, but also provided the stimulus for the growth of the nationalist movement which followed the invasion. In the case of Vietnam, the Japanese invasion destroyed the framework of the French colonial system and again provided an impetus to the nationalist spirit.

The point of this for policy is that these factors are not repeatable simply by the work of a revolutionary force, but demand the falling into place of certain historical factors which no one can manipulate. If these factors are indeed prerequisite to successful "wars of national liberation," or even if they are only major factors to the success of such wars, then that form of violent ideological struggle is a rarity, more to be observed with interest than to be feared.

The fall of the ancient Chinese imperial system of government in 1911 was an event of profound consequence and causation much too complex for evaluation here. But the triumph of Mao over Chiang in the culmination of at least one phase of that ongoing revolution is easier to comprehend. The difficulty, if not the impossibility, of a colonial system (or its heirs) to survive in an age and an area of burgeoning nationalism is even easier to predict. Both include conditions seemingly precedent to success: either invasion or a colonial system (or both) giving rise to growing nationalism and the weakening of the opponent; the loss of legitimacy by an opponent unable to identify itself with the nationalist cause; and most often the use of the military instrument by the opponent in such a manner as to demon-

---

[138] C. Johnson, *Peasant Nationalism and Communist Power, supra* note 44; John T. McAlister, Jr., and Paul Mus have noted that peasants have been consistently "unwilling to accept the legitimacy of pro-French and pro-American urban-based governments. . . ." *The Vietnamese and Their Revolution* 26–27 (1970).

[139] *See* Mao Tse-tung, "The Chinese Revolution and the Chinese Communist Party, 2 *Selected Works, supra* note 57; Schram, "Mao: The Man and His Doctrine," *Problems of Communism* (Sept.–Oct. 1966); E. Snow, *Red Star Over China* 129–55 (rev. ed. 1968).

strate its lack of recognition of the basically political nature of the struggle to attain or maintain legitimacy.

Several points pertinent to policy and law follow from this analysis. First, the fact that successful "wars of national liberation" may be relatively unique phenomena not easily repeatable does not lead to the conclusion that internal war is not likely to continue to be the major type of political violence of our time; for it is most likely, assuming that we are fortunate enough to avoid nuclear devastation, that internal strife will continue to be the major form of political violence. (This distinction should be obvious, but will be made explicit anyway.)

Next, factors present in this analysis of the strengths and weaknesses of "wars of national liberation" lead to conclusions relevant to law and policy toward internal war generally:

It is of critical importance and prerequisite to correct decisions upon all issues which follow that an accurate categorization of the identity of the antagonists and the nature of their struggle be accomplished before intervention or counter-intervention is considered. The contrast between our policy toward the post-war Indonesian-Dutch hostilities and the Vietnamese-French conflict from 1945 through 1954 highlights this point. Both were colonial wars of separation, fought by nationalist forces against colonial powers. Our policy toward the Republic of Indonesia should have been our policy toward Vietnam from the immediate post-war period to the present. While the anti-colonial element in both wars was obvious from the beginning, the presence of other factors in Vietnam—the Communist leadership of the nationalist cause, the aggressive designs which Ho Chi Minh apparently had upon other parts of Southeast Asia, and the division of Vietnam in some ways parallel to what had happened in Korea and Germany—led some to characterize that war as being dominantly a Cold War confrontation and to react accordingly.[140] It is now recognized that, while those elements were present in the Vietnamese struggle, the dominating element was anti-colonialism; so it would remain regardless of the non-colonial motivation of the United States. As the successors to the French, arrayed against the forces which had fought the nationalist fight against the French, the Japanese, and then again the French, we were still in opposition to the dominant nationalist segment of the nation whatever our actual motivation might have been. That Ho was a dedicated Communist is unquestioned. The analogy to Cold War divided states, however, is strained.[141] *Vietnam was not divided on the basis of the settlement procedures of World War II, as were Korea and Germany. Rather, Vietnam was temporarily divided on the basis of an interim settlement of a later colonial war between the Viet Minh and the French.* The decision to take up that battle when the

---

[140] *See, e.g.,* Firmage, "International Law and the Response of the United States to 'Internal War,' " *supra* note 104.

[141] Moore, "The Control of Foreign Intervention in Internal Conflict," 9 *Va. J. Int'l Law* 292 (1969).

French disengaged was, whether we so intended it or not, the continuation of a colonial war against the dominant forces of nationalism. It was an unmitigated disaster, and should never have been undertaken. For the first time, the twin principles of our post-war foreign policy—opposition to the spread of Communism by violence and support for emerging nationalism —were at cross-purposes. The dominant forces of nationalism were Communist-led and appeared to have aggressive intentions against their neighbors. We, therefore, categorized the conflict as a Cold War struggle but, while that element was surely present, the dominating factor was actually anti-colonialism. This erroneous categorization, made in 1945–46 and again in 1954 and continued through the early 1970's, at least, determined the nature of our response.

It would be hoped that national and international fact-finding procedures (international as occurred in the case of Indonesia)[142] would provide decision-makers with data sufficiently accurate to enable correct categorization to take place. Prior to the release of the "Pentagon Papers," it seemed that there had been a critical gap in intelligence which had led to this disastrous mis-categorization. It would now appear, however, that the CIA and other intelligence-gathering organizations, along with experts from the Department of State, had correctly informed the decision-makers of the overwhelming popularity of Ho Chi Minh and the lack of political support enjoyed by any potential opponent; moreover, this information was had by administrations at least from President Eisenhower's to the present. This presents difficulties which cannot be completely overcome by institutional reforms aimed at providing improved fact-finding techniques for the makers of policy.

Related directly to the last point but not entirely subsumed within it (violence associated with the process of decolonization has perhaps been the primary type of civil strife which has involved the element of nationalism; it is not the only setting in which such an element has been or could be present), nationalism has proven to be the most sturdy ideology of the post-war era. Surely it was the element of nationalism within those successful "wars of national liberation" that determined their outcome. It has been nationalism—not communism or capitalism—which has proven to be the dominant ideology within many internal wars. (This is not in conflict with the position of those who argue that modernization has been the major stimulus and source of internal tumult; modernization as a process and nationalism as an ideology have most often gone together.) It therefore behooves a third party to be on the right side of that issue if indeed any position must be taken between sides in an internal struggle.

What has been said regarding the concepts of anti-colonialism and nationalism bears upon the establishment of norms designed to guide the policy of a third party toward factions within a state experiencing civil strife.

---

[142] Firmage, *supra* note 114.

In a particular situation, at least, anti-colonialism is a component part of the larger concept of nationalism. So also nationalism may be considered to be but one element in a still larger concept having to do with the entire cultural fabric of a society. If a political scientist or a sociologist were to use a term which would describe a condition of cultural and political harmony between a society and its institutions of government that term would be "legitimacy." Unfortunately, its "legal" meaning has to do with the (constitutional) means by which a government attains power.[143] But the broader and deeper meaning of legitimacy, as used by the political scientist or the sociologist, cuts to the center of those norms governing the relationship between states and particularly those rules relating to intervention.

As used in this essay, legitimacy does not refer to the old constitutional meaning with reference to the acquisition of power by formally orthodox or proper means. Nor does it mean precisely what Max Weber and most political scientists since Weber have referred to, though that is closer to my use of the term. Weber's meaning stressed the opinions of people and the ability of a society's institutions to harmonize with those opinions sufficient to govern. This connotes an emphasis upon manipulative techniques that will somehow "create" authority by means of propaganda, resulting in the acquiescence of the people. The meaning used here, rather, demands sufficient affinity between the people and the institutions of government, based upon the pre-existence of a cultural harmony between them, that allegiance naturally results without the use of coercion.[144]

The relationship between legitimacy and governmental stability is increasingly becoming apparent through the research of political scientists, sociologists and psychologists. Lipset has argued, based upon his research, that legitimacy is the single most important factor in determining (and forecasting) the political stability of a regime;[145] Bwy in his studies of Latin American violence has demonstrated that organized violence (guerrilla war, internal war—as opposed to anomic or spontaneous violence) has an exceptionally strong correlation with the populace's perception of the legitimacy of the political system;[146] Gude has confirmed this in his more restricted study of political violence in Venezuela;[147] the Feierabends' pioneering studies used both the more conventional aggregate data (number of telephones, number of doctors, gross national product, per capita income, number of radios and newspapers—compared with the number of

[143] Cf., Falk, *Legal Order in a Violent World, supra* note 15, at 142–43.

[144] Lipset has defined legitimacy as the capacity of a political system to advance and sustain the belief that existing political institutions were the most appropriate ones for the community. Lipset, "Some Social Requisites of Democracy: Economic Development and Political Legitimacy," 53 *Am. Pol. Sci. Rev.* 69, 86 (March 1959).

[145] *Id.*

[146] Bwy, *supra* note 73; "Political Instability in Latin America: The Cross-Cultural Test of a Consul Model," 3 *Latin American Research Rev.* (Spring 1968).

[147] Gude, "Political Violence in Venezuela: 1958–1964," in J. Davies (ed.), *supra* note 117.

riots, strikes, coups, and civil wars) and new psychological units (based upon the aspiration-frustration-aggression hypotheses of John Dollard and others). They not only tended to confirm the other studies regarding systemic frustration and disenchantment and consequent organized civil strife, but in the process demonstrated exciting new techniques by which the relative legitimacy of a regime could be measured.[148]

Another sophisticated means of measuring frustration and degrees of allegiance toward a government (and consequently forecasting the likelihood and the intensity of civil strife) is the Self-Anchoring Striving Scale of Cantril and Kilpatrick.[149] The aspirations and frustrations of an individual are determined as the individual places himself upon a "ladder" indicating his position relative to other citizens. At the same time, the individual similarly evaluates his government. The results are used as a measure of governmental legitimacy as seen by the citizen. Ted Gurr has also departed from the conventional aggregate indices and has developed psychological units to predict the nature and magnitude of domestic political violence.[150] One particular study indicated that a group of states had less political violence than might have been expected on the basis of aggregate characteristics indicating relative deprivation which they shared with other states experiencing substantially more civil strife. The factor common to the group with less civil strife was a high degree of allegiance toward the government. Gurr's data suggested that "the proposed relationship of legitimacy as an intervening variable is linear: the greater is regime legitimacy at a given level of deprivation, the less the magnitude of consequent strife."[151] Research conducted by David Schwartz combined more traditional sociological units of analysis with psychological variables in a study which described more accurately the phenomenon observed by many students of revolution from Brinton[152] and Edwards[153] to Hopper[154] as a common preliminary to domestic political violence: the withdrawal by the individual from the political process; diminution of numbers voting; an increasing focus on self; a reduction in the scope of loyalties; a sense of public purposelessness; or as Hopper put it, "the milling process."[155] Schwartz has developed criteria to

---

[148] Feierabend, "Aggressive Behaviors Within Polities, 1948–1962, A Cross-National Study," 10 *J. of Conflict Resolution* 249 (Sept. 1966). For a study using traditional aggregate data to develop a theory of revolutionary causation, *see* Tanter & Midlarsky, "A Theory of Revolution," 11 *J. of Conflict Resolution* 264 (Sept. 1967).

[149] Cantril & Kilpatrick, "Self-Anchoring Scaling: A Measure of Individuals' Unique Reality Worlds," 16 *J. of Indiv. Psychol.* 158 (Nov. 1960).

[150] T. Gurr, *Why Men Rebel* (1970); and "A Causal Model of Civil Strife: A Comparative Analysis Using New Indices," 62 *Am. Pol. Sci. Rev.* 1104 (Dec. 1968).

[151] "A Causal Model. . . ." *supra* note 150 at 1107.

[152] C. Brinton, *The Anatomy of Revolution* (rev. ed. 1965).

[153] L. Edwards, *The National History of Revolution* (1926).

[154] Hopper, "The Revolutionary Process," 28 *Social Forces* 270 (March 1950).

[155] *Id.* at 271.

determine and measure this process as a means of gauging the relative legitimacy of a regime as seen by the people.[156]

The traditional rule governing the relationship between third parties and a state experiencing civil strife is that aid may be extended to a widely recognized incumbent, but must be denied to the insurgents at least until the status of belligerency has been attained.[157] A traditionally minority position throughout has maintained that the proper role for third parties toward states experiencing civil strife was one of neutrality.[158] The majority rule favoring the incumbents has been widely attacked[159] primarily on the basis that many governments today, particularly among "new" or "developing" states in the Third World, lack both the complete cultural and political identity with their people to be considered legitimate and also (and to some extent as a consequence) lack the power that in the past has also distinguished incumbents from insurgents. And it is in the Third World where the pressures of modernization and emerging nationalism have resulted in the highest level of civil strife. The factor of legitimacy must somehow be a part of whatever new rule finally emerges as the successor to the traditional norms governing the relationship between third parties and a state experiencing civil strife.

It might be suggested that the criterion of legitimacy rather than incumbency should be used to determine the proper relationship between third parties and states experiencing civil strife. (Indeed, some formulations of the traditional rule use this language;[160] but the meaning of " 'legitimate' government" as used in such a statement of the traditional rule referred to the means by which that government had assumed power and not to the

---

[156] D. Schwartz, "A Theory of Revolutionary Behavior," in J. Davies (ed.), *supra* note 117, at 109. The alienation of the intellectual and other elites constitutes a critically important part in the process of general political alienation preceding revolution. *See* Rustow, "The Study of Elites: Who's Who, When and How," in Mazlish, *et al.* (eds.), *supra* note 64; T. Bottomore, *Elites and Society* (1965); H. Lasswell & D. Lerner (eds.), *World Revolutionary Elites: Studies in Coercive Ideological Movements* (1965); Malia, "What is the Intelligentsia," 89 *Daedalus* (Summer 1960).

[157] L. Oppenheim, *International Law* § 298, at 660 (7th ed. 1952).

[158] C. Hyde, *Principles of International Law* 131–32 (7th ed., 1930); T. Lawrence, *Principles of International Law* (7th ed., 1930). For an analysis of the majority and minority interpretations *see* Firmage, "Summary and Interpretation," in *The International Law of Civil War*, *supra* note 54 at 405–6.

[159] Farer, "Intervention in Civil Wars: A Modest Proposal," in I R. Falk (ed.), *The Vietnam War and International Law* 509 (1969). 514–15; Falk, "International Law and the United States Role in the Viet Nam War," *id.* at 362; Friedmann, "Law and Politics in the Vietnamese War: A Comment," *id.* at 776, 782.

[160] "There is no rule of international law which forbids the government of one state from rendering assistance to the established legitimate government of another state with a view of [sic] enabling it to suppress an insurrection against its authority. Whether it shall render such aid is entirely a matter of policy or expediency and raises no question of right or duty under international law. If assistance is rendered to the legitimate government it is not a case of unlawful intervention as is the giving of assistance to rebels who are arrayed against its authority." Gardner, as quoted by I. Brownlie, *International Law and the Use of Force by States* 321 (1963).

allegiance of the people toward the government. The trend has been toward use of the term "incumbent" without any reference to legitimacy.) Under this formulation of the rule, a third party would not be prohibited from extending aid to a legitimate government experiencing civil strife at least until hostilities reached that stage, without the benefit of third party support of the insurgents, that the legitimacy of the government could no longer be assumed. The effect of this norm would be to invoke the traditional minority rule, stressing neutrality toward all states experiencing civil strife whose governments could not be considered legitimate regardless of the status of the group (insurgents, rebels, belligerents) opposing the incumbent government and regardless of the level of hostilities (insurgency, rebellion, belligerency). The traditional majority and minority rules would thereby be combined into one.

The effect of such a rule would be to protect from outside interference those states whose societies have not yet developed a harmony between their institutions of government and their cultures sufficient to produce general domestic tranquility. This would include some new nations and some ancient cultures now experiencing great abrasion between traditional governing elites and a people increasingly cut loose from the value structures which supported those elites. Intervention within these states, whether in the name of Communism, anti-Communism, capitalism, or modernization, reveals a form of neo-colonialism which assumes a position of superiority sufficient to determine the best form of economics or polity for the target state. Whatever the complete meaning of self-determination, it must include the right to make such decisions free from third-party intervention, by the development of whatever norms and systems of governance which seem most consistent with its own society.

One strength of such a rule would be that it would be supportive of what policy planners in both Communist and non-Communist countries should consider to be the long-range self-interest of their states. Comment has been made about the degree to which the strategy of Mao Tse-tung and Lin Piao has stressed the necessity of self-sufficiency and the prerequisite of good prospects for success on the part of any group attempting a "war of national liberation." In other words, aid would not be extended to any group, unless it was facing an incumbent government that had at least begun the process of a loss of legitimacy, whether that be called allegiance or the Mandate of Heaven. And from the vantage point of a government considering intervention on behalf of an incumbent government facing internal strife, a central criterion (surely after the experience of Vietnam) would have to be the level of allegiance, support, and cultural affinity which existed between that government and the people. Intervention or counter-intervention would not be expected to have a sufficient chance for success unless the entity on whose behalf intervention was contemplated could be considered legitimate.

The arguments against such a formulation of a new rule are probably sufficiently persuasive to prohibit its acceptance. As long as each state possesses unilateral power to determine legitimacy, the international community is still not assured that order would result.[161] (This criticism of the suggested rule is in reality more accurately a commentary on the horizontal and uncentralized nature of the international system; the various institutions within the individual states control most aspects of the international system.)[162] In addition, the suggested rule lacks the simplicity and the value-free objectivity of Farar's proposed prohibition of any aid within a tactical zone of combat to any participant within a state experiencing civil strife.[163] The main argument in favor of substituting legitimacy in place of incumbency as the criterion which determines the rights and duties of third parties in relation to parties involved in civil strife is simply that it brings into the open those factors which a potential intervenor must pragmatically consider—the relative stability of the incumbent regime, the cultural and political affinity between the regime and the society, the allegiance of the people toward the government. By so doing, the rule tends to protect those societies from alien intervention which have not yet developed a government in sufficient cultural harmony with the society to produce uncoerced allegiance and thereby prevent endemic civil strife.

It should be noted that this concept of legitimacy does not require democratic government as a prerequisite. Many societies, including African and American Indian cultures, have had governments which have been authoritarian and hierarchically organized, but have been in harmony with the tradition and the culture of the people and have consequently enjoyed a high degree of allegiance.

Whether the element of legitimacy is used as a substitute for incumbency in fashioning a new rule, or is injected in norms proposed by Falk and Farer as a threshold requirement,[164] or is utilized in some other way, it must be a major factor in the determination by third parties to intervene in civil strife. The result should be a greater degree of freedom from outside interference, for Third World states particularly. Admittedly, the placement of a burden upon a potential intervenor of determining the governmental legitimacy of the "host" state is the placement of a burden hard to be met. The techniques of the social sciences are still rudimentary. To abide by such a norm would severely limit intervention in civil strife. So much the better.

[161] R. Falk, *Legal Order in a Violent World* 142–46 (1968).

[162] ". . . it is not international law but municipal or state law which controls the greater part of action in the international system, and that it is not the international legal process but the national legal process which resolves the major part of conflict arising in the operation of the international system. Although action may possess an international character in that it transcends state boundaries, it is nevertheless segmentalized under the territorial sovereignty and authority of the several states in which it takes place." K. Carlston, *Law and Organization in World Society* 162 (1962).

[163] Farer, *supra* note 160.

[164] Falk, *supra* note 160.

The immediate post-war foreign policy of the United States, characterized by the term "containment," was appropriate for the time even though possibly too much oriented toward a military rather than a political and economic implementation as one of its creators has indicated.[165] This policy was sound in its application to that most important of areas where it was meant to be applied—Europe—revisionist historians writing in reaction to Vietnam to the contrary notwithstanding.[166]

That sound policy was distorted and misused by our country in reaction to the so-called "loss of China." Significantly, then, it was our relationship to a government engaged in a civil war that it lost which provided the political background for the misapplication of correct policies for Europe into settings most inappropriate. The "loss of China" in 1949 provided the fuel for the infamous McCarthy period of poisoned politics, in which political presidential campaigns were waged with pledges to "stop Communism" in Asia as we had done in Europe. The period of the mid-1950's saw the transplantation of European alliance structures into the quicksand of Asian politics—alliances most often designed to combat "indirect aggression" and other forms of domestic political violence. We demonstrated a singular inability to correctly categorize internal violence and reacted almost always as if it were orchestrated by a single alien Communist source. While cases of such foreign-directed Communist subversion undoubtedly did exist, we characterized the anticolonial revolution in Vietnam, which admittedly was intermixed with Northern aggression and was Communist-led, as if it were a simple Cold War confrontation on the model of states (Korea and Germany) divided by the circumstances of the end of World War II. We similarly characterized the Christian-Muslim clash in Lebanon and the urban revolution against a political and military elite in the Dominican Republic as if both were Communist plots from abroad.

In a word, we have been very successful in that part of the world of most importance to the United States—Europe—and we have been singularly unsuccessful in our analyses of civil strife in the Third World. The tragedy of Vietnam may well turn our priorities back to those areas of highest priority for the United States—Europe, Japan, and, for reasons of geographical proximity, Latin America—not to the exclusion of our concern for other areas, but rather to an understanding that policies designed to prevent overt aggression in Europe are most inappropriate when juxtaposed against domestic political violence in the Third World.

[165] G. Kennan, *Memoirs: 1925–1950* at 354–67 (1967).
[166] *E.g.*, one of the best, G. Alperovitz, *Cold War Essays* (1970).

Chapter 14 | China and Intervention:
Theory and Practice | *Jerome Alan Cohen*

As a Chinese proverb says: 'Do not do unto others what you yourself do not desire.' We are against outside interference; how could we want to interfere in the internal affairs of others?"

CHOU EN-LAI[1]

We must give active support to the national independence liberation movement in countries in Asia, Africa and Latin America as well as to the peace movement and to just struggles in all countries throughout the world."

MAO TSE-TUNG[2]

Now that the entry of the People's Republic of China (PRC) into the world community is almost complete, both diplomats and students of international relations have become aware of the importance of ascertaining Peking's views of international law.[3] One of the most fundamental principles of international law is the duty of states to refrain from unlawful intervention in the affairs of other states. In the United Nations, where it now represents China, the PRC will increasingly be called upon to give concrete meaning to the abstractions of the Charter such as Article 2(4)'s prohibition of "the threat or use of force against the territorial integrity or political indepen-

[1] "Text of Premier Chou En-lai's Supplementary Speech at Asian-African Conference," *NCNA* (English), Bandung (April 19, 1955); in *SCMP* 1031: 5–8 (April 21, 1955).

[2] Mao Tse-tung, Report to the Eighth National Congress of the Chinese Communist Party, 1956, in *FKHP* 4: 3 (1956).

[3] This interest is beginning to be reflected in legal literature. *See* J. A. Cohen (ed.), *China's Practice of International Law: Some Case Studies* (1972); Hungdah Chiu, *The People's Republic of China and the Law of Treaties* (1972); Hungdah Chiu and Shao-chuan Leng (eds.), *Law in Chinese Foreign Policy: Communist China and Selected Problems of International Law* (1972); J. C. Hsiung, *Law and Policy in China's Foreign Relations* (1972); L. T. Lee, *China and International Agreements: A Study of Compliance* (1969); D. Johnston and Hungdah Chiu, *Agreements of the People's Republic of China, 1949–1967: A Calendar* (1968); and J. A. Cohen and Hungdah Chiu, *People's China and International Law: A Documentary Study* (Princeton, N.J.: Princeton University Press, 1974).

This article has appeared in 121 *U. Pa. L. Rev.* 471 (1973).
I am grateful to my colleagues Hungdah Chiu and R. Randle Edwards, Research Associates at Harvard Law School, for their valuable suggestions and assistance.

The following abbreviations are used in this chapter:

NCNA	New China News Agency (Peking)
SCMP	Survey of the China Mainland Press, U.S. Consulate-General, Hong Kong.
FKHP	Chung-hua jen-min kung-ho-kuo fa-kuei hui-pien [Collected Laws and Decrees of the People's Republic of China]
CFYC	Cheng-fa yen-chiu [Political-Legal Research] (Peking)
PR	*Peking Review (Peking)*
People's Daily	*Jen-min jih-pao* (Peking)
FBIS	Foreign Broadcast Information Service (U.S. Government)

dence of any state" and Article 2(7)'s prohibition of UN intervention "in matters which are essentially within the domestic jurisdiction of any state." Also, in establishing bilateral diplomatic relations with many states since 1970, the PRC has promised on a reciprocal basis to respect the principle of non-intervention as well as the related principles of mutual respect for sovereignty and territorial integrity, mutual non-aggression, equality and mutual benefit, and peaceful coexistence.[4] And the landmark Shanghai Communique, presumably the first step toward the normalization of relations between the PRC and the United States, pledges Peking and Washington to non-intervention and the other four principles that comprise the famous "five principles of peaceful coexistence."[5]

"Intervention" is, of course, a murky concept. That states influence each other in many ways and to many degrees is a fact of life. But the difficulty has been to determine which of the many forms and degrees of factual intervention may be said to constitute intervention in the legal sense. When using the term "intervention" care must be exercised to distinguish between factual intervention and the legal conclusion that a particular intervention violates authoritative community expectations about permissible international conduct.[6] In this essay, unless the context indicates otherwise, the term is used in the legal sense.

Unfortunately, the legal concept itself is a slippery vehicle. As many writers have pointed out, neither states nor jurists have succeeded in endowing it with an agreed-upon content, and state practice has only added to the confusion.[7] A traditional definition preferred by many publicists confines the term to dictatorial interference by a state in the internal or external affairs of another state, usually involving a threat or use of military force.[8] Although writers and states generally agree that such interference normally violates state sovereignty and international law, in practice states have frequently failed to refrain from intervention even in this limited sense, not to mention coercive interactions of an economic or ideological nature. This has spurred the search for exceptions to the rule of nonintervention. As one authoritative appraisal has summarized the scholarly situation:

> There has been little agreement as to the special circumstances which, exceptionally, may justify intervention. Among such circumstances sug-

---

[4] *See, e.g.,* "Text of the Chinese-Japanese Accord Signed by Chou and Tanaka," *N.Y. Times,* Sept. 30, 1972, at 12. For discussion of these principles, which the PRC has popularized as the "five principles of peaceful coexistence," see Part II of this essay.

[5] *See* "Text of US-Chinese Communique," *N.Y. Times,* Feb. 28, 1972, at 16.

[6] *See* J. N. Moore, "The Control of Foreign Intervention in Internal Conflict," *Va. J. of Int.L.* 9: 205, 212 *et seq.* (1969), for a review of the authorities and analysis of the terminological and legal uncertainties.

[7] *See, e.g.,* Thomas and Thomas, *Non-Intervention* 67 (1956).

[8] *See, e.g., id.* at 68; Brierly, *Law of Nations* 402 (6th ed. Waldock, 1963); 1 Oppenheim, *International Law* 305 (8th ed. Lauterpacht, 1955); 1 Hyde, *International Law Chiefly as Interpreted and Applied by the United States* 245–47 (2nd ed. rev. 1955).

gested by various writers have been invitation or consent by the state concerned, threats to the safety of nationals of the intervening state, previous or threatened unlawful interventions by the other state, chronic disregard by a state of its international obligations, the needs of self-defense or self-preservation of the intervening state, and collective decision to put an end to inhumane treatment by a government of all or some of its own nationals (humanitarian intervention). The legal sufficiency of most of these categories of circumstances as justification for intervention has been challenged by other writers. The legality of extending armed assistance to a government at its request against its domestic opponents remains highly controversial and may not be regarded as "intervention" under some definitions. The right of intervention in exceptional circumstances, if it ever existed, has been further restricted by the prohibitions on the threat or use of force contained in the United Nations Charter. It is generally conceded, however, that collective intervention pursuant to the Charter is lawful.[9]

The law-making activities of the United Nations have done little to clarify the situation. For example, on the one hand, the General Assembly has condemned not only armed intervention but also "all other forms of interference or attempted threats against the personality of the State or against its political, economic and cultural elements" and has refused to recognize "for any reason whatever" the existence of special circumstances that would justify exceptions to this broad, vague declaration;[10] on the other hand, other Assembly resolutions have recommended that all states provide "moral and material assistance" to insurgent movements that seek to liberate from colonialism the peoples of African territories under Portuguese administration and of South-West Africa.[11] The behavior of individual states has often been characterized by a similar ambivalence toward intervention.[12]

What is the PRC's understanding of "intervention"? How has it applied the concept? Does Peking's practice square with its theory? How does the Chinese record compare with that of other states? To what extent does it reflect autochthonous Chinese experience? What have PRC scholars and ideologists written on the subject? In sum, what is Peking's endorsement of the principle of non-intervention likely to be worth?

This introductory essay surveys these important but seldom treated questions of new China's attitude toward international law. After first sketching some historical background, it will examine the concept of intervention articulated in PRC legal literature, and applications of the concept by the government, press and scholars of China, Peking's view regarding

[9] W. Friedmann, O. J. Lissitzyn, and R. C. Pugh, *International Law: Cases and Materials* 971 (1969).

[10] "Declaration on the Inadmissibility of Intervention Into the Domestic Affairs of States," Dec. 21, 1965, G.A. Res. 2131, 20 U.N. GAOR, Supp. 14 (A/6014), at 11–12.

[11] See the resolutions quoted and discussed in Moore, note 6, at 267.

[12] *See id.*, at 243–46.

the applicability of non-intervention to relations among socialist states, and its efforts to reconcile its advocacy of non-intervention with its attempts to influence events in other countries through a variety of means including support for selected "wars of national liberation."

I. HISTORICAL BACKGROUND

Chinese leaders have been concerned with the rules governing interventions in internal affairs almost since the beginning of recorded time. From the eighth to the third centuries B.C., during the latter part of China's pre-imperial history, there existed in the present north-central part of China a number of feudal states which, although nominally vassals of the Chou dynasty, largely functioned as independent entities. These feudal states developed a rough system of commonly-accepted norms, institutions, and processes for the conduct of their relations. Some aspects of that system, like certain aspects of the system that regulated the interaction of the city-states of ancient Greece, bear a striking similarity to the international law that emerged from the multi-state system of fifteenth- and sixteenth-century Europe. The rules relating to intervention provide a case in point.

In pre-imperial China it was generally accepted that each of the feudal states had a right to manage its own affairs and had a corresponding duty not to interfere in the affairs of other feudal states. Nevertheless, this general principle was frequently honored in the breach, and there developed a variety of rationalizations of departures from the norm. Strong, self-righteous leaders who were attracted to intervention as a means of seeking various ends purported to find justification in prevailing ethical doctrines that preached the desirability of the less worthy submitting to the virtuous. Moreover, exceptions to the rule of non-intervention came to be recognized during China's pre-imperial era. The most obvious of these authorized intervention if necessary to the selfpreservation of the intervening state. Another frequently-invoked exception permitted intervention against a ruler who oppressed his own people. Also popular was the claim that intervention was a necessary sanction against a feudal state that had failed to carry out its obligations under a treaty. And in many instances one feudal state used military means to install a friendly sovereign on the throne of a neighbor.[13]

The establishment of the Chinese empire and its gradual expansion over a vast land mass and population required continuing attention to the manner in which China would deal with neighboring peoples who were not under its direct control. Throughout most of two millennia from the founding of the empire in 221 B.C. until the onslaught of Western military expeditions in the nineteenth century, the Chinese emperor served as overlord of what came to be known as the tribute system. This was a rather loose

[13] This paragraph is based on Te-hsu Ch'eng, "International Law in Early China (1122–249 B.C.)," *Chinese Social and Political Science Review* 11: 44–46 (1927).

hierarchy of tributary peoples in which status was relative to the degree of acceptance of Confucian cultural, ethical, political, and social norms and of China's writing system and agricultural practices. An elaborate series of rituals governed contacts between the "Son of Heaven" in the Chinese capital and lesser rulers. These lesser rulers acquired legitimacy, at least in Chinese eyes, only after investiture by the Chinese emperor and periodically sent emissaries to pay tribute to him and to receive magnanimous gifts from him in return. The hierarchical organization and protocol of the Sinocentric East Asian community were designed to acknowledge not only the pre-eminent power of China, whose name means "Central Realm," but also its moral superiority as the embodiment of virtues deserving of universal application.[14]

Underlying the imperial tribute system was the theory that China could "intervene whenever and wherever she judged it necessary because the Chinese emperor was responsible for all the peoples under Heaven and because their rulers were viewed as his appointed representatives."[15] This normally latent right of intervention was occasionally exercised. For example, in 1788 China sent a military expedition to Vietnam to restore to the throne the Lê family, who, until a recent rebellion, had been loyal tributaries of the empire for over a century. A scholarly analysis has concluded:

> The relationship was not between two equal states. There was no doubt in anyone's mind that China was the superior and the tributary state the inferior. The Vietnamese Kings clearly realized that they had to acknowledge China's suzerainty and become tributaries in order to avoid active intervention by China in their internal affairs. . . . It was in the interest of the Vietnamese Kings to surrender part of their sovereignty in return for the assurance that in case of rebellion they would be protected by China and that in time of internal peace they would not be conquered and directly administered by China.[16]

In the nineteenth century, Western force rudely awakened China to the fact that, beyond the tributary peoples of East Asia, lay powerful nation-states with a profoundly different view of society, government and international relations. A series of wars humiliated China and shattered its millennial isolation. The Western "barbarians" were bent on opening up China and compelling it to participate in the Western state system. The onerous and comprehensve restraints that they, and later their emulators—

---

[14] *See e.g.*, J. K. Fairbank (ed.), *The Chinese World Order* (Cambridge, Mass.: Harvard University Press, 1968), especially the editor's "A Preliminary Framework." For general historical perspective, *see* Reischauer and Fairbank, *East Asia, The Great Tradition* (1960); and Fairbank, Reischauer, and Craig, *East Asia, The Modern Transformation* (1965).

[15] Truong Buu Lam, "Intervention Versus Tribute In Sino-Vietnamese Relations, 1788–1790," in Fairbank, *supra* note 14, at 165, 179.

[16] *Ibid.*, at 178.

the Japanese—imposed upon China transformed that proud and long powerful country into a semi-colony. Besides losing substantial portions of its territory, as well as control over its tributary states, China was made to suffer an elaborate structure of extraterritorial privileges, inequitable tariff restrictions, "leased territories," foreign concessions and settlements, foreign armed forces and foreign railway, postal, customs, wireless, and other administrative networks.[17]

In reaction to this unhappy experience, modern Chinese patriots of all political persuasions have sought to liberate their country from foreign domination in order, in the words of Sun Yat-sen, "to obtain the rights of a civilized state" and "to place China in a respectable place in international society."[18] In these circumstances they have understandably taken an active interest in the rules of intervention that the world community purports to apply. Prior to its ouster from the United Nations in 1971, the Republic of China on Taiwan participated in both multilateral and bilateral efforts to strengthen support for the principle of non-intervention.[19]

The leaders of the People's Republic of China have been so sensitive to the history of foreign domination that they have manifested an almost obsessive concern with vindicating and preserving national sovereignty.[20] Actually, although its ranks have recently been decimated by internecine strife and the ravages of time, it is still true that to the present Chinese Communist elite—and especially to Mao Tse-tung, Chou En-lai and other senior leaders—foreign domination is not "history" but the reality with which they have had to struggle continuously for a half-century, first as revolutionaries and later as rulers.

For example, Communist victory in the civil conflict that was renewed shortly after the end of World War II only briefly terminated American military aid to the overthrown Nationalist government. When the Korean conflict broke out, the United States resumed military aid to Chiang Kai-shek's remnant forces on Taiwan, used the Seventh Fleet to prevent Communist reintegration of the island with the China mainland, and subsequently concluded a military alliance with the Nationalists that continues to this day.[21] Taiwan has not been the P.R.C.'s sole experience with

[17] See, e.g., W. L. Tung, China and the Foreign Powers (New York, N.Y.: Oceana Publications, 1970).

[18] Important Documents Relating to China's Revolution, 1912 67–68 (Shanghai: The Commercial Press, 1912).

[19] See, e.g., its support for the "Declaration on the Inadvisability of Intervention, etc.," note 10, in UNGA, 20th sess., Official Records, First Committee, 1398th meeting, Dec. 6, 1965, at 267; and Article 5 of the R.O.C.–U.S.S.R. Treaty of Friendship and Alliance, concluded Aug. 14, 1945. R.O.C. Ministry of Foreign Affairs (ed.), Treaties between the Republic of China and Foreign States (1927–1945) 506 (Taipei: Commercial Press 1958).

[20] See, e.g., J. A. Cohen, "Chinese Attitudes Toward International Law—and Our Own," in Cohen (ed.), Contemporary Chinese Law: Research Problems and Perspectives (Cambridge, Mass.: Harvard University Press, 1970), 282, 284–85.

[21] See, e.g., J. A. Cohen, "Recognizing China," Foreign Affairs 50.1: 30, 35–36 (Oct. 1971).

foreign interference. Peking bitterly resented the covert efforts of other governments to support the 1959 revolt in Tibet as well as their overt condemnation of China for suppressing it.[22] Peking also appeared to interpret American participation in the Korean conflict as ultimately directed toward intervention in China.[23] And it has had to protect itself against the perennial problem of foreign-sponsored espionage and sabotage.[24]

Nor has bourgeois imperialism been Peking's only source of concern. Even in the ostensibly friendly days of the early 1950's, the P.R.C. had to apply considerable and persistent pressures against the Soviet Union in order to liquidate certain naval bases and economic concessions that the U.S.S.R. sought to retain in China and to eliminate Soviet interference in affairs of the Chinese Communist Party and government.[25] And during the past decade Peking has accused Moscow of seeking to stir up rebellion among minority nationalities who live on the Chinese side of the Sino-Soviet border, of continuing its interference in Chinese politics, of engaging in overt acts of aggression against Chinese territory, and of planning to turn China into another Czechoslovakia.[26]

II. ESPOUSAL OF NON-INTERVENTION

This abiding preoccupation with foreign intervention has led the Chinese Government to endorse the principle of non-intervention in international law. Indeed, "mutual non-interference in each other's internal affairs" became the third of Peking's "five principles of peaceful coexistence," a corollary to "mutual respect for each other's territorial integrity and sovereignty," "mutual non-aggression," "equality and mutual benefit," and "peaceful coexistence."[27] Almost one year after the Sino-Indian agreement of 1954 articulated the "five principles," they were elaborated into ten principles by the Asian-African Conference that was held in Bandung. The Joint Communique issued by the P.R.C. and twenty-eight other states not only called for "abstention from intervention or interference in the internal affairs of another country," but also urged "abstention by any country from

[22] See, e.g., text at notes 35–38; also H. C. Hinton, *Communist China in World Politics* 285–89 (Boston: Houghton Mifflin, 1966).

[23] For authoritative interpretation of these events, see Tsou, *America's Failure in China, 1941–1950,* ch. 13 (1963); and Whiting, *China Crosses the Yalu,* ch. 8 (1960).

[24] See, e.g., "Judgment of Military Tribunal on U.S. Spies in the Arnold-Baumer Espionage Case," translated in *PC* (Supp.), no. 24: 3–5 (Dec. 16, 1954); "Judgment of Military Tribunal on U.S. Spies in the Downey-Fecteau Case," translated in *id.,* at 6–8. See also J. A. Cohen, "Chinese Law and Sino-American Trade," in Eckstein (ed.), *China Trade Prospects and U.S. Policy* 144–47 (1971).

[25] See, e.g., Hsiung, note 3, at 54–55.

[26] See text at note 69; and see, e.g., Lin Piao, note 106, at 27–29.

[27] See the "Agreement between India and China on Trade and Intercourse between Tibet Region of China and India, April 29, 1954," English text in *United Nations Treaty Series* 299: 70 (1958).

exerting pressures on other countries" and "refraining from acts or threats of aggression or the use of force against the territorial integrity or political independence of any country." The Joint Communique pledged "Respect for the right of each nation to defend itself singly or collectively, in conformity with the Charter of the United Nations," but it declared that collective defense arrangements should not "serve the particular interests of any of the big powers."[28] With a number of Afro-Asian states the P.R.C. subsequently concluded bilateral friendship treaties that explicitly incorporated the "five principles," and some treaties also referred to the "ten principles" laid down at Bandung.[29]

Although the quantity of scholarship on international law produced in the P.R.C. has not rivalled the substantial body of literature developed in the Soviet Union, a number of Chinese essays have dealt with intervention. A few have discussed the subject in an overall way, while others have focussed on specific incidents.

In elucidating the meaning of "peaceful coexistence" shortly after the Bandung conference, Professor Chou Keng-sheng, one of China's leading legal commentators, acknowledged that the principle of non-intervention is part of the traditional fabric of international law and stated that Article 2(7) of the United Nations Charter reinforces that principle.[30] Following the lead of Soviet scholars, who exercised major influence over Chinese writing on international law in the 1950's, Professor Chou inveighed against taking a formal, mechanical view of what constitutes intervention. He cited Stalin for the proposition that intervention can take many forms— military, economic and subversive. Sometimes, he noted, intervention parades in the garb of "non-intervention," as in the case of the British, French and other Western powers' "indirect aggression" through refusal to interfere in the Spanish Civil War, thereby allegedly causing the overthrow of the Republican Government. More recently, he maintained, the Western imperialists, out of ostensible respect for the principle of non-interference in internal affairs, wrongfully refused to submit for discussion at the U.N. "questions of racial conflict and national self-determination which obviously possess international importance." As examples of such distortions of the U.N. Charter, he mentioned the questions of the Union of South Africa's treatment of its Indian population and France's control of Algeria.[31]

---

[28] "Joint Communique of Bandung Conference," *NCNA*—English, Bandung (April 24, 1955), in *SCMP* 1033: 11–17 (April 24, 1955).

[29] *See, e.g.*, "Treaty of Friendship between the People's Republic of China and the Republic of Ghana, August 18, 1961," English text in Chung-hua jen-min kung-ho-kuo wai-chiao-pu-pien [Ministry of Foreign Affairs of the P.R.C., ed.], *Chung-hua jen-min kung-ho-kuo yu-hao t'iao-yüeh chi* [Collection of Friendship Treaties Concluded by the P.R.C.] 63 (Peking 1965).

[30] Article 2(7) of the U.N. Charter provides in part: "Nothing contained in the present Charter shall authorize the United Nations to intervene in matters which are essentially within the domestic jurisdiction of any state . . ."

[31] Chou Keng-sheng, "The Principle of Peaceful Coexistence from the Viewpoint of International Law," *CFYC* 6: 37, 41 (1955).

In a comprehensive article written in 1960, after the UN General Assembly had condemned China's suppression of the 1959 revolt in Tibet, scholar Yi Hsin did not bemoan the U.N.'s failure to act in cases of racial discrimination and suppression of self-determination. Along the lines set forth in Soviet scholarship, he analyzed the historical evolution of the rule of non-intervention, and classified and criticized the exceptions to which bourgeous international law has subjected it. Among these he included resort to intervention in the guise of non-intervention. Yet what he emphasized was the great extent to which imperialism interfered in internal affairs when it should not have, rather than the extent to which it failed to act when it should have.

By way of illustration, Yi referred to many concrete cases, using China's experience wherever possible. For example, he stated:

> The people of our country have personally experienced the intervention and aggression of imperialist countries on the pretext of protecting their nationals, and there are indeed too many cases to enumerate. During the period of the Chinese Revolution, when the Northern Expedition Forces captured Nanking in 1927, in order to obstruct the Chinese Revolution through the use of arms, the English, American and other imperialists ordered their warships to shell Nanking on the ground that their nationals and consulates were "encroached upon and harmed by rioters." As a result, more than two thousand Chinese soldiers and civilians were wounded or killed and the loss of houses and property was considerable. Immediately afterwards, the United States, England, Japan, France, and Italy further discussed plans for sending troops to intervene and lodged an ultimatum with the National Government in Wuhan, demanding the prosecution of criminals, apology, and indemnity and making other unreasonable demands. In 1928, when the Northern Expedition Forces entered Tsinan, Japan even declared that in order to "protect Japan's rights and interests" it was sending troops to Shantung. On May 3, Japan massacred more than three thousand Chinese soldiers and civilians and cruelly murdered the Chinese special diplomatic commissioner, Ts'ai Kung-shih."[32]

With respect to intervention in order to quell revolution that threatens imperialist interests in a country, Yi claimed that the United States had "illegally occupied our territory, Taiwan, by force of arms . . . on the pretext of a 'collective self-defense.' "[33] To demonstrate intervention in the interest of maintaining "the balance of power," he recalled how Russia, Germany and France forced Japan to return the Liaotung peninsula to China in 1895 and how in 1899 the United States demanded an "open door" policy in China.[34]

[32] Yi Hsin, "What Does Bourgeois International Law Explain About the Question of Intervention," *Kuo-chi wen-t'i yen-chiu* (Research on International Problems) 4: 47, 49 (1960).

[33] *Ibid.*, 50.

[34] *Ibid.*

To illustrate the "class character" of the "humanitarian intervention" practiced by the imperialist states, Yi Hsin referred to the then recent concern over Tibet.

> The term 'humanity' professed in bourgeois international law means bourgeois humanity. Imperialism considers as inhumane those countries in which the proletariat has political power and establishes a dictatorship over the reactionary forces. It considers as "inhumane" the punishment and suppression imposed by the people of a country upon conspiratorial elements who engage in rebellion and subversive activities supported by imperialism. . . . When a country adopts certain progressive measures in internal affairs which reflect the demands of the people but which are unfavorable to the minority, the originally privileged class, imperialism also considers it "inhumane." In all these cases, imperialism considers it permissible to intervene. Moreover, in order to achieve its object, which cannot be publicly announced, imperialism can even fabricate the pretext of 'humanitarianism' in order to intervene. The Chinese suppression of the rebellion of the upper stratum of the Tibetan reactionary clique supported by reactionaries of foreign countries, and the democratic reform of the Tibet region, enabling the liberation of a million or more Tibetan compatriots from the dark and cruel serf system, brought a shout from imperialism, which calumniated the measures as "violations of human rights" and "genocide." Obviously, behind all the shouting is an eager conspiracy of intervention.[35]

According to Yi Hsin, the General Assembly's "so-called resolution on 'the Tibet question' " was the product of American manipulation of the principles of non-intervention embodied in Article 2(7) of the U.N. Charter. He lashed out against bourgeois jurists who "follow their master and do their best to bark like dogs who hear sounds and see shadows."[36] He maintained that Lauterpacht's *Oppenheim*, for example, had sought to argue that since "human rights and fundamental freedoms" have become a persistent feature of the Charter they may have ceased to be a matter which is essentially within the domestic jurisdiction of States."[37] And, he claimed other scholars had put themselves in the service of organizations such as "the so-called 'International Commission of Jurists,' " which had issued a report on the Tibet question that was "full of rumors and slander for the purpose of fabricating an international legal basis for intervention. . . ."[38]

[35] *Ibid.*
[36] *Ibid.*, 51.
[37] 1 *Oppenheim International Law* 280 (7th ed. Lauterpacht, 1948), as quoted in Yi Hsin, note 32, at 51.
[38] *Ibid.*, 50–51.

III. ILLUSTRATIVE APPLICATIONS OF THE PRINCIPLE

Like their Soviet counterparts, most Chinese writers have been reluctant to engage in close analysis of the complex issues implicit in the law of intervention.[39] They too have preferred to discuss specific incidents after the fact rather than to develop a rationale for principled decision-making that might constrict their government's freedom of action or produce an embarrassing and personally hazardous disagreement between scholar and government. This became clear by the late 1950's, as a brief comparison of Chinese views on the cases of Hungary and Lebanon suggests.

Following the lead of the P.R.C. and the official voice of the Chinese Communist Party, the *People's Daily*, Chinese specialists in international law supported the Soviet Union's military suppression of the 1956 Hungarian revolution on the ground that the U.S.S.R. had acted at the request of the lawful Hungarian government. As Ch'en T'i-ch'iang, one of the most prominent scholars, put it: "Acts of intervention in a state with the consent of the government of that state cannot be considered (illegal) intervention."[40] Other scholars shared this rationale.[41] Two years later, however, after the P.R.C. condemned the entry of American forces into Lebanon as "armed intervention in the Lebanon's internal affairs,"[42] Chinese scholars dutifully agreed, despite the fact that the President of Lebanon had requested the entry of American forces. Citing Khrushchev as authority, Professor Chou Keng-sheng, who was frequently called upon to justify the Chinese Government's position on international legal questions,[43] handled the problem this way:

> The traitorous government of Chamoun, opposed by the people of Lebanon, had to appeal to a foreign state to dispatch forces to maintain its shaky rule and therefore it obviously cannot be considered as a government

[39] For the views of Soviet writers, *see, e.g.*, W. Butler, "Soviet Attitudes Toward Intervention," in this volume.

[40] Ch'en T'i-ch'iang, "The Hungarian Incident and the Principle of Non-Intervention," *Kuang-ming jih-pao* [Enlightenment Daily], April 5, 1957, p. 1. *Compare* "Refuting the Loud Western Outcry over the 'Hungarian Issue,'" Editorial, *People's Daily*, Nov. 14, 1956 at 1.

[41] *See* Sun Nan, "What is the Principle of Non-Intervention in Other Nations' Internal Affairs?", *Shih-chieh chih-shih* [World Knowledge] 23: 13 (Dec. 5, 1956), translated in *Extracts From China Mainland Magazine* [hereafter *ECMM*] 74: 1–3 (March 18, 1957); and Tien Pao-shen, "Is the Dispatch of [the] Soviet Army to Hungary an 'Intervention' in Other Nations' Internal Affairs?," *Shih-shih shou-tee* [Current Events Handbook] 2: 23 (Jan. 21, 1957) translated in *ECMM* 76: 1–3 (April 1, 1957).

[42] "The Chinese Government Demands Withdrawal of U.S. Forces from Lebanon, Withdrawal of British Forces from Jordan," *PR* 1.21: 7 (July 22, 1958).

[43] *See* J. A. Cohen and Shao-chuan Leng, "The Sino-Indian Dispute Over the Internment and Detention of Chinese Nationals," in Cohen (ed.), *China's Practice of International Law: Some Case Studies* 268, 289, *et seq.* (Cambridge, Mass.: Harvard University Press, 1972).

representing the Lebanese people. . . . As a matter of fact, the speaker of the Lebanese Parliament had called on the United Nations to request the United States to withdraw its forces; this was, on behalf of the Lebanese people, a repudiation of Chamoun's appeal. Moreover, Chamoun's appeal itself is illegal, because to invite the colonialists to engage in armed intervention in the internal affairs of a state is to betray the independence of that state.[44]

Indeed, in dealing with the Hungarian case, the People's Daily, unlike the scholars who discussed the case, had taken care to emphasize that Soviet actions were "entirely just" not only because they had been taken "in conformity with the Warsaw Treaty, and at the request of the Hungarian Government to assist in restoring order, but also because that request coincided with the genuine desires of the Hungarian people." The revolt in Hungary had not been a "spontaneous mass action, but one imposed on the Hungarian people by a gang of conspirators instigated by the United States and other Western countries."[45]

Thus, when foreign troops enter another state at the request of the government of that state in order to assist in restoring order, Peking's opinion of the legality of this action turns upon whether, in its view, "that request coincides with the genuine desires of the . . . people." This, of course, permits the P.R.C. to decide the legal question on the basis of political expediency, and that is precisely what it has continued to do. In 1969, for example, it condemned the "clique" of Prime Minister Thanom of Thailand—"merely a bunch of lackeys fed by U.S. imperialism"— for "saying that the U.S. aggressor forces had been invited by it to 'help' cope with the revolutionary forces of Thailand."[46] Similarly the P.R.C. has condemned as aggression the actions of American combat forces in Vietnam at the request of the Republic of Vietnam.[47]

Between the Hungarian and Lebanese cases, of course, Chairman Mao had launched one of his periodic major domestic campaigns against intellectuals—the "anti-rightist" movement of 1957, after which a number of scholars of international law ceased publication.[48] Interestingly for our purposes a principal reason offered for the purge of scholar Ch'en T'i-ch'iang

[44] Chou Keng-sheng, "Don't Allow American and British Aggressors to Intervene in the Internal Affairs of Other States," *CFYC* 4: 3–4 (1958).

[45] *People's Daily* editorial, note 40. It should be noted that the United States claimed that the insurrection which had occurred in Lebanon some two months prior to President Chamoun's request for American military forces had been encouraged and strongly supported by Egypt, Syria, and the Soviet Union. *See, e.g.,* 5 Whiteman, *International Law* 826–27, 1169–70 (1965).

[46] *See* the anonymous but authoritative article by Commentator, "The Face of a Traitor," *People's Daily,* Jan. 25, 1969, at 6; translated in *PR* 12.8: 14 (Feb. 21, 1969).

[47] *See* text at note 84.

[48] For analysis of the implications of the "anti-rightist" movement for legal scholarship and the administration of justice in China, *see* J. A. Cohen, *The Criminal Process in the People's Republic of China, 1949–1963: An Introduction* 14–17 (Cambridge, Mass.: Harvard University Press, 1968).

was his failure to assert that the legality of intervention by invitation rests upon whether the invitation "coincides with the genuine desires of the . . . people." Ch'en was accused of having adopted an "anti-Party, anti-socialist position" because his justification of Soviet actions in the Hungarian "incident" had been uncritically broad. He had endorsed the traditional view of most scholars and statesmen that if, during a civil war, a foreign state responds to a widely-recognized government's request for military assistance against the insurgents, the action of the foreign state is legal even though the government has ruled in a manner contrary to the interests of its people.[49] Obviously, he had written, such foreign aid could provoke the anger of the people; nevertheless, even if the revolutionary forces succeeded in establishing a new government, the foreign state could not be deemed legally accountable for its action. It would only have earned the political ill-will of the new government.[50]

Ch'en's critics pointed out the implications of his view for China's civil war. They argued:

> Ch'en T'i-ch'iang is supporting the following proposition: American imperialism does not bear legal responsibility for aiding the Chiang Kai-shek clique in fighting the civil war and in suppressing the revolutionary movement of the Chinese people. There is simply ill will on the part of the Chinese people. In other words, from Ch'en T'i-ch'iang's point of view, such acts by American imperialism do not violate international law.[51]

Obviously, they concluded, American imperialism had committed illegal intervention in China "and only those rightists who breathe out of imperialism's nostrils would say that it cannot result in legal responsibility and simply results in political ill-will."[52]

Ch'en's other publications do not portray a man who consciously sought to "breathe out of imperialism's nostrils." Indeed, he frequently articulated the legal bases for the P.R.C.'s protests against imperialist attempts to intervene in Chinese affairs. Early in 1956, for example, a Nationalist Chinese jet fighter plane that had been harassing the mainland landed in Hong Kong after having been pursued by Communist Chinese air defense forces. The P.R.C. demanded that the United Kingdom, which recognized it as the sole government of China and which did not recognize a state of belligerency in China, detain both plane and pilot. When the British permitted the pilot to return to Taiwan and were preparing to release the plane as well, the P.R.C. Foreign Ministry lodged a protest, and Ch'en T'i-ch'iang swiftly supported

---

[49] For discussion of both the traditional view and the developing minority view that in a civil conflict foreign assistance to both sides should be prohibited, *see* Moore, note 6, at 245–46, 272 *et seq.*

[50] *See* Ch'en T'i-ch'iang, note 40.

[51] Ho Wu-shuang and Ma Chün, "A Criticism of the Reactionary Viewpoint of Ch'en T'i-ch'iang on the Science of International Law," *CFYC* 6: 35, 38 (1957).

[52] *Ibid.*, 38.

his government in an article that appeared in the People's Daily. Drawing upon Lauterpacht's *Oppenheim*,[53] the draft convention adopted by the Institute of International Law in 1900,[54] and especially the 1928 Havana "Convention on the Duties and Rights of States in the Event of Civil Strife,"[55] he claimed that the British government had violated its "obligation not to allow the area under its administration to be turned into a base to conduct hostile activities against the government of a foreign country with which it is at peace."[56] Ch'en maintained that by allowing pilot and plane to return to Taiwan, Britain was permitting renewal of their hostile activities against China, and this constituted an international delinquency.

Actually, Ch'en's fall from grace appears to have been caused not so much by his specific views on intervention as by his general outlook. He apparently spoke frankly in the spring of 1957 during the movement to "Let a hundred flowers bloom, let a hundred schools contend," when Chairman Mao induced many intellectuals to help "rectify" the Party by offering criticisms.[57] During this brief period of free speech, Ch'en, who, until his subsequent dismissal as a "rightist," served as head of the Division of International Law of the Institute of International Relations of the Chinese Academy of Sciences, was said to have "even proposed the reactionary view of the necessity of studying Anglo-American law."[58] Ch'en had been educated at the University of London and in 1951 had published his doctoral dissertation on the law of recognition under the auspices of the London Institute of World Affairs.[59] This professional training seems to have led him astray in new China, for during the "anti-rightist" movement he was attacked as one of "the old international law jurists, who still adhere to the purely legalistic viewpoint" that fails to recognize that international law is simply a legal instrument in the service of country, socialism and peace, to be used when useful but discarded when disadvantageous.[60]

---

[53] *See* note 37.

[54] "Droits et devoirs des puissances étrangères et leurs ressortissants, au cas de mouvement insurrectionnel, envers les gouvernements établis et reconnus qui sont aux prises avec l'insurrection." Sept. 8, 1900, in *Annuaire de L'institut de droit international* 18: 181 (1900).

[55] U.S. Treaty Series, no. 814; 46 Stat. 2749.

[56] Ch'en T'i-ch'iang, "We Cannot Allow Hong Kong to Be Used As A Base for Hostile Activities Against the Mainland," *People's Daily*, March 19, 1956, p. 3.

[57] *See* Cohen, note 48, at 14.

[58] Lin Hsin, "On the Systems of International Law After the Second World War," *Chiao-hsüeh yü yen-chiu* [Teaching and Research] 1: 34, 38 (1958).

[59] T.C. Ch'en, *The International Law of Recognition* (London: Stevens and Son; New York: Praeger, 1951).

[60] Chu Li-lu, "Refute Ch'en T'i-ch'iang's Absurd Theory Concerning International Law," *People's Daily*, Sept. 18, 1957, at 3. For details of the similar attack on scholars of domestic law during the anti-rightist movement, *see* J. A. Cohen, "The Chinese Communist Party and 'Judicial Independence': 1949–1959," *Harv. L. Rev.* 82.5: 967, 989–93 (March 1969).

IV. "SOCIAL INTERNATIONALISM," NON-INTERVENTION AND THE SINO-SOVIET SPLIT

In the mid-1950's, in an effort to gain greater equality in China's relations with the Soviet Union, the P.R.C. attempted to modify the doctrine of "socialist internationalism," often called "proletarian internationalism," which Stalin had developed as a rationale for maintaining Soviet primacy over and interference in other Communist states.[61] Peking sought to obtain a Soviet admission that the "five principles of peaceful coexistence" were applicable not only to relations between socialist states and non-socialist states but also to relations between socialist states themselves. The high point of this effort came with the Soviet Declaration of October 30, 1956, that the policy of peaceful coexistence "finds its most profound and consistent expression in the mutual relations between the socialist countries" and that "the Soviet Government is ready to discuss, together with the governments of other socialist states, measures . . . to remove the possibilities of violating the principle of national sovereignty and . . . equality."[62] The P.R.C. promptly announced that the Soviet Declaration, which had been stimulated by the unfavorable reaction to the initial use of Soviet troops against the Hungarian revolt, was "of great importance in correcting errors in mutual relations between the socialist countries and in strengthening unity among them."[63] When the U.S.S.R. brutally suppressed that revolt shortly thereafter, Chinese writers claimed that this did not violate the Declaration because "the action of the Soviet Army was entirely in the interest of the Hungarians,"[64] being designed "to assist Hungary in safe-guarding democratic rights, the fruit of socialist construction and the people's lives and security, in accordance with the spirit of solidarity and cooperation between brother countries."[65]

The P.R.C. subsequently ceased insisting that the "five principles of peaceful coexistence" be made applicable to relations within the Soviet bloc, but it continued to seek a redefinition of "socialist internationalism" that would not violate the national independence and equality of other socialist countries.[66] This doctrine, as vague as "peaceful coexistence," was said to have a distinctive content that described the superior standards that were supposed to prevail in relations between socialist states. The

[61] For an excellent account of this intricate, unobtrusive effort, see Hsiung, note 3, at 49–61.

[62] "Declaration of the U.S.S.R. On the Foundation for the Development and Further Strengthening of Friendship and Cooperation Between the Soviet Union and Other Socialist States, October 30, 1956," Soviet News 3502: 1–2 (London, Oct. 31, 1956).

[63] "Statement by the Government of the People's Republic of China on the Declaration by the Government of the Soviet Union on October 30, 1956, November 1, 1956," in People's China 22: Supp. 1–2 (Nov. 16, 1956).

[64] Sun Nan, note 41.

[65] Tien Pao-shen, note 41.

[66] See Hsiung, note 3, at 62.

standards sought by Peking called not only for the full equality of socialist states but also for the comradely mutual assistance that was said to be the hallmark of the socialist bloc.[67] By the early 1960's, however, with Sino-Soviet unity virtually at an end, the P.R.C. obviously realized that the generality of the principles of socialist internationalism continued to permit the U.S.S.R. to manipulate them to achieve its own national objectives within the socialist camp and that "mistakes" and "neglect" of the principle of equality among nations were likely to persist unless measures were taken to specify a code of conduct for the socialist countries.

In 1962, for example, before the Sino-Soviet dispute reached the level of open polemics, the then Vice-Premier and Foreign Minister Ch'en Yi implicitly lectured the U.S.S.R. on "the common principles guiding the mutual relations between socialist countries," principles which "are entirely different from those adopted by the imperialist countries." A socialist country, he said at the Bulgarian Embassy in Peking, does not engage in subversive activities, does not try to impose its will on other countries, does not use economic aid to disguise intervention, does not indefinitely maintain military bases and troops abroad, does not enmesh other countries in military pacts that get others to pull its chestnuts out of the fire, does not undermine the peace and neutrality of other countries, and does not suppress national liberation movements.[68] In the circumstances of the time, it did not require much imagination on the part of Bulgaria and other socialist states to question whether the Soviet Union measured up to these standards of proletarian internationalism.

Shortly after Ch'en Yi's speech, Sino-Soviet relations deteriorated to the point that each side abandoned veiled references in favor of more specific indictments. China's leaders charged their Soviet counterparts with having "arbitrarily infringed the sovereignty of fraternal countries, interfered in their internal affairs, carried on subversive activities, and striven in every way to control fraternal countries." The Soviet elite, it was claimed, sought to turn fraternal countries into economic appendages and constantly brought political, economic, and military pressure to bear on them. Drawing particularly on the experiences of Albania and China, the Chinese accused their erstwhile elder brothers of openly attempting to overthrow the leadership of other fraternal countries. "Such measures which gravely worsen state relations are rare even between capitalist countries," they said.[69]

The Soviet invasion of Czechoslovakia in 1968 evoked the shrillest Chinese condemnations. The Chinese press heaped scorn upon the attempts of Soviet spokesmen to devise a "socialist," "internationalist" fig-leaf that

[67] *Id.*, at 57–64.

[68] "Guiding Principles for Relations between Socialist Countries," *PR* 5.37: 11 (Sept. 14, 1962).

[69] Editorial Departments of *People's Daily* and *Red Flag*, "The Leaders of the CPSU Are the Greatest Splitters of Our Times," *People's Daily*, Feb. 4, 1964, at 1–4; trans. in *PR* 7.6: 9–10 (Feb. 9, 1964).

would "legalize" their government's action, which was branded as both aggression and intervention. The theory that "historical development" had made it appropriate to turn "national dictatorship" into "international dictatorship" in order to "protect the [socialist] community" was dismissed as a cloak for "revisionist social-imperialist aggression" and "rapacious expansionist ambitions."[70] The related theory that "the interests of the community" represent "the highest sovereignty" and must be put above the sovereignty of the individual member-states, which is "limited," was charterized as "gangster logic."[71] The theory that "the Soviet Union . . . as a major world power . . . cannot passively regard events that, though they might be territorially remote, nevertheless have a bearing on our security and the security of our friends" was rejected as merely a refurbished version of the other fallacies.[72] The U.S.S.R. was also accused of reformulating its definition of "aggression" so that armed encroachment on countries with the same social system would not be regarded as aggression but as action in defense of the system.[73]

What the U.S.S.R. had done, the Chinese claimed, was to ape the imperialist governments by seeking to conceal its illegal interference in the affairs of other countries amid "professions of humanity, justice, and virtue."[74] "U.S. imperialism invented the so-called 'free world community' and Soviet revisionism followed suit by concocting the so-called 'community of socialist countries.' "[75] Chinese writers overlooked any similarity between Soviet activities in Czechoslovakia and Soviet suppression of the Hungarian revolt, which the Chinese had deemed consistent "with the spirit of solidarity and cooperation between brother countries."[76]

V. CHINA'S INTERESTS ABROAD AND NON-INTERVENTION

What has thus far been said may lead the reader to believe that China has been almost entirely concerned with forging the principle of non-inter-

[70] Kung Chun-ping, "The Theory of 'International Dictatorship' Is A Gangster Theory of Social-Imperialism," *PR* 12.20: 4–5 (May 16, 1969).

[71] "Theories of 'Limited Sovereignty' and 'International Dictatorship' Are Soviet Revisionist Social-Imperialist Gangster Theories," *PR* 12.13: 23–25 (March 28, 1969).

[72] Chien Yen, "Tear Off the Wrappings From Soviet Revisionists' Theory of Responsibility for Security," *PR* 12.36: 20–22 (March 9, 1969).

[73] Wang Chao-tsai, "Tear Off the Wrappings From the Soviet Revisionists' 'Definition of Aggression,' " *PR* 12.22: 13–15 (May 30, 1969).

[74] Chien Yen, note 72.

[75] Chi Hsiang-yang, "Smash the New Tsars' Theory of Limited Sovereignty," *PR* 12.21: 20–22 (May 23, 1969). Some American students of international law have also noted the similarities in Soviet and American deeds and words. *See, e.g.,* Friedmann, Lissitzyn and Pugh, note 9, at 1007.

[76] Recall text at notes 40 to 50 and at notes 64 and 65. The cases of Hungary and Czechoslovakia might have been distinguished on the ground that in the latter case the Soviet Union failed to provide convincing evidence that the existing government had requested the assistance of Soviet forces. *Cf.* Friedmann, Lissitzyn, and Pugh, note 9, at 1004.

vention into a defensive shield for fending off the depredations of all types of imperialism and that its only effort to legitimize interference in the affairs of other countries was thrust upon it in the 1950's because of its embarrassing alliance with the Soviet Union. Actually, of course, this is far from a complete picture of China's position. Although the P.R.C., like previous Chinese regimes, has been primarily preoccupied with problems at home, nevertheless it has been deeply committed to influencing events abroad through a wide range of actions that have inevitably raised questions about its view of the law of intervention. The P.R.C.'s enthusiastic participation in U.N. condemnations of the South African and Rhodesian governments for abuses against their respective peoples, despite Peking's earlier protests that U.N. condemnation of P.R.C. conduct in Tibet constituted intervention in China's domestic affairs,[77] is only a recent illustration of this commitment.[78]

On some occasions Peking has explicitly sought to reconcile its attempts to influence events abroad with the principle of non-intervention. For example, in 1959 China refused to accept the Indonesian Foreign Minister's protest against the activities of Chinese diplomats and consuls to protect overseas Chinese nationals against the discriminatory measures adopted by the Indonesian Government. The P.R.C. claimed that it had always encouraged overseas Chinese to abide by the laws of Indonesia and had never interfered in internal affairs, but that it was obligated to protect the rights of the overseas Chinese and that the execution of this obligation "can in no way be interpreted as agitation to incite overseas Chinese to defy the orders of the local government. . . ."[79]

At the very height of the Cultural Revolution the P.R.C. repeatedly tried to pressure Switzerland into putting an end to the activities on Swiss soil of refugee "Tibetan bandits." Far from expressing concern that this might be construed as intervention in Swiss affairs, Peking actually claimed that Swiss toleration of a "Tibetan Institute" constituted "a gross interven-

---

[77] See, e.g., text at notes 35 and 36.

[78] For example, soon after the arrival of the first P.R.C. delegation to the U.N., Ambassador Huang Hua, China's permanent representative at the U.N., stated "that the question of Southern Rhodesia involved the basic interests of five million people of Zimbabwe. It involved the basic interests of the African people and African countries. In accordance with the decisions of the United Nations and the Charter, the United Nations and the Security Council were entitled to discuss, to intervene, to judge and to make decisions on that question." Meeting of the Security Council, Dec. 30, 1971, reported in *UN Monthly Chronicle* 9.1: 56, 82 (1972). See also *id.* 9.8: 10, 14 (1972). The *Peking Review* reported that at the plenary meeting of the U.N. General Assembly of November 29, 1971, the Assembly, with Chinese support, adopted nine resolutions condemning the apartheid policy of the South African regime. "China at the UN," *PR* 14.50: 24 (Dec. 10, 1971).

[79] "Foreign Minister Ch'en Yi's Letter of December 24 to Indonesian Foreign Minister," *NCNA*-English, Peking (Dec. 25, 1959), in *SCMP* 2167: 47–49 (Dec. 31, 1959). The letter did not distinguish between the P.R.C.'s right to protect overseas Chinese who are also Indonesian nationals and its right to protect overseas Chinese who are not.

tion in the internal affairs of China." The Chinese Government rationalized its charge by pointing out that

> "the Tibetan traitorous clique of [the] Dalai [Lama] which has fled China is the enemy of the Tibetan and other nationalities of China. With the support of imperialism, revisionism and reaction, it is trying to accumulate its forces abroad and look for an opportunity to re-establish the reactionary domination of the serf-owners overthrown by the Tibetan people and to subject again the liberated Tibetan people who are leading a happy life to dark and inhuman serfdom."[80]

Unlike the United States and the Soviet Union, on only a few occasions has China sought to influence events by sending troops abroad. The Korean conflict brought the P.R.C. its first involvement in international warfare. Probably out of deference to the principle of non-intervention, it maintained the fiction that it did not officially participate, but merely permitted Chinese soldiers to "volunteer" for service in Korea. Nevertheless, Peking was careful to argue that the entry into the conflict of the "Chinese People's Volunteers was an act of self-defense taken only after the Chinese had witnessed Taiwan fall prey to aggression and the flames of the United States war of aggression against Korea leap towards it" as American forces advanced towards the Sino-Korean frontier. In these circumstances, stated the chief P.R.C. delegate to the U.N. Security Council meetings of late 1950, there was "no reason whatever to prevent voluntary departure for Korea to participate, under the command of the Government of the Korean People's Democratic Republic. . . ."[81] This was "action not only to assist a neighbor, but to protect our own country."[82]

Chinese forces withdrew from Korea in 1958, five years after an armistice was signed, and early in 1965, Chairman Mao proudly affirmed that China had no troops outside its own frontiers. He said that:

> "China's armies would not go beyond her borders to fight. . . . Fighting beyond one's own borders was criminal. Why should the Chinese do that? The Vietnamese could cope with their situation."
>
> ". . . China gave support to revolutionary movements but not by sending troops. Of course, whenever a liberation struggle existed China would publish statements and call demonstrations to support it. It was precisely that which vexed the imperialists."[83]

---

[80] "Foreign Ministry Protest to Swiss Government," NCNA—English (Aug. 17, 1967), in FBIS 160/67: BBB 1–2 (Aug. 17, 1967).

[81] U.N. Doc. (S/PV. 527), Nov. 28, 1950, p. 96.

[82] "Wu Hsiu-ch'uan's Speech Regarding the American Aggression on China, Dec. 16, 1950"; Chinese text in Chung-hua jen-min kung-ho-kuo tui-wai kuan-hsi wen-chien chi [Collection of Documents Relating to the Foreign Relations of the People's Republic of China] 1949–50, 1: 219–37 (1957).

[83] Edgar Snow, "Interview with Mao," New Republic 152: 17, 22 (Feb. 27, 1965).

Shortly afterward, however, the United States began to carry out air strikes against North Vietnam. The Chinese Government promptly declared that this constituted a flagrant violation of the Geneva agreements of 1954 relating to Indo-China, that therefore "the Democratic Republic of Vietnam has gained the right of action to fight against U.S. aggression, and all the other countries upholding the Geneva Agreements have gained the right of action to assist the Democratic Republic of Vietnam in its fight against aggression." Ominously, the statement went on to note that China had adhered to the Final Declaration of the 1954 Geneva Conference, that the Chinese and Vietnamese are "the closest of brothers," that aggression against the D.R.V. "means aggression against China," and that the Chinese people "will definitely not stand idly by."[84] Following the introduction of large-scale American combat forces in Vietnam, China sent from 30,000 to 50,000 regular members of the People's Liberation Army to North Vietnam, where, with the consent of the D.R.V., they engaged in construction work and manned anti-aircraft defenses until their reported withdrawal in 1969.[85] Chinese troops were subsequently reported to be building roads in Laotian territory controlled by the Pathet Lao, in accordance with an old cooperation agreement between Laos and China.[86]

VI. SUPPORT FOR WARS OF NATIONAL LIBERATION

As noted above,[87] Chairman Mao has stated that what vexes "the imperialists" is not the dispatch of Chinese troops abroad, but China's support for "liberation struggles." With the deepening of the Sino-Soviet split in the 1960's, Peking increasingly sought to portray "Mao Tse-Tung's thought" as the beacon that illumines the revolutionary road of the oppressed peoples of the world. On the 50th anniversary of the Bolshevik revolution, the principal Chinese Communist journals asserted that the "center of world revolution" had shifted from Moscow to Peking.[88]

The strategy of waging revolutionary warfare that Chairman Mao has offered the colonial and semi-colonial countries of Asia, Africa, and Latin America is known as "people's war." Based on supposedly universal elements in the Chinese Communist Party's own experience in attaining power, "people's war, as articulated in Lin Piao's famous elaboration, calls for: leadership by a revolutionary Communist party that analyzes conditions and

[84] "China is Well Prepared to Assist D.R.V. Against U.S. Aggression," Chinese Government Statement, Feb. 9, 1965, *PR* 8.7: 6–7 (Feb. 12, 1965).

[85] A. S. Whiting, "How We Almost Went to War with China," *Look Magazine*, April 29, 1969 at 76, 77; Hsiung, note 3 at 300.

[86] "Laos Acknowledges Presence of China Troops," *N.Y. Times*, Dec. 15, 1969 at 2.

[87] *See* text at note 83.

[88] Charles Mohr, "Peking Says Mao is Today's Lenin." *N.Y. Times*, Nov. 7, 1967 at 10

makes policy according to Marxist-Leninist precepts; mobilization by the party of the broad masses in a "united front" policy that supports protracted war against imperialism, feudalism and bureaucratic capitalism; reliance upon the peasantry and establishment of rural bases under party leadership; creation of a party-led army that is imbued with "proletarian revolutionary consciousness and courage" and actively seeks the support of the masses; resort to Mao's strategy and tactics for gradually moving from mass mobilization and guerrilla warfare to mobile and even positional warfare as the revolution progresses; and adherence to a policy of self-reliance which recognizes that "revolution or people's war in any country is the business of the masses in that country and should be carried out primarily by their own efforts; there is no other way."[89]

In the statement quoted above,[90] Chairman Mao gave the impression that China's support for liberation struggles consists of publishing statements and calling demonstrations in China. Although Lin Piao agreed that no revolution can be exported, he claimed that, unlike "the Khrushchev revisionists," the Chinese "invariably" fulfill their "internationalist duty" to give the revolutionary wars of oppressed nations and people's "firm support and active aid."[91] Huang Hua, China's permanent representative at the U.N., recently said that China offers political, moral and physical aid to African liberation movements.[92] No Chinese leader has spelled out the scope and nature of this aid.

The Chinese Communists have not tried to conceal their ideological and psychological support for foreign revolutionaries, including non-Communist revolutionaries. In addition to continuously issuing militant propaganda that advocates revolution against oppression everywhere, the Chinese have on many occasions implicitly or explicitly endorsed revolution in specific countries and have sometimes endorsed particular revolutionary organizations. Implicit endorsement has taken the form of reprinting policy statements of foreign revolutionary movements in the Chinese press, reporting news of their activities, or publishing maps that designate certain countries as sites of liberation struggles. Explicit endorsement has consisted of statements by Chairman Mao, other leaders or the Communist Party itself.[93]

Peking has sought to export this ideological and psychological support to selected countries by disseminating translations of the works of Chairman Mao and other leaders, local language periodicals and radio broadcasts and symbols of revolution such as Mao badges. It has also attempted to influence local media and to use cultural exchange as a propaganda instru-

[89] Lin Piao, "Long Live the Victory of People's War," *PR* 8.36: 9 *et seq.* (Sept. 3, 1965). For discussion of the Mao-Lin theory, *see* P. Van Ness, *Revolution and China's Foreign Policy* (Berkeley, Los Angeles, and London: 1970), at 50–73, and the sources there cited.

[90] *See* text at note 83.

[91] Lin Piao, note 89.

[92] "Chinese Envoy," *Japan Times* (Kyodo-Reuter dispatch from Khartoum), Feb. 8, 1972, at 4.

[93] *See* the excellent discussion in Van Ness, note 89, especially at 81–88.

ment. China's public support has included playing host to representatives of foreign revolutionary organizations. It has even allowed some of these to establish permanent diplomatic-type missions in Peking, such as the Office of the Palestine Liberation Organization and the South Vietnamese N.F.L. Mission.[94] The latter, after the Provisional Revolutionary Government of the Republic of South Vietnam was proclaimed, was declared to be the official embassy of the new government.[95] And since 1970 the P.R.C. has permitted Prince Sihanouk to operate his Cambodian government-in-exile from Peking.[96]

The P.R.C.'s military and economic support for wars of national liberation has generally been covert. The Chinese have apparently shipped arms, ammunition and other military supplies to a variety of movements. They reportedly have given military training and advice to certain prospective revolutionaries, both in China and abroad, and have financed the organization and maintenance of some revolutionary groups. Following the successful precedent of its aid to the Vietminh, China has provided sanctuary to guerrilla forces acting in selected countries on its periphery, and it has permitted a number of insurgent organizations in neighboring Southeast Asian countries to operate radio stations from Chinese soil. Several governments in Asia and Africa have also alleged that Peking has abetted political assassination and engaged in political bribery.[97]

Yet most observers agree that, apart from rhetoric, the level of Chinese support for revolutionary activities abroad has in fact been quite low and that the degree of success attained has been even lower.[98] China is a poor, vast, developing country that is beset by the political, economic, social, and administrative problems confronting all developing countries and thus has limited resources to allocate to foreign liberation struggles. Beyond that, however, even in promising situations in geographically contiguous countries, China has frequently failed to give even verbal support to local revolutionary groups. Prior to the Cultural Revolution, China refrained from endorsing wars of national liberation in Third World countries with which it had established diplomatic relations; only governments that re-

---

[94] Hsiung, note 3, at 221.

[95] *See* Van Ness, note 89, at 130.

[96] *See* text at notes 113 to 116.

[97] For an illustrative account of the range of P.R.C. efforts to support wars of national liberation, see Jerome Alan Cohen and Hungdah Chiu, *People's China and International Law: A Documentary Study*, note 3, at 181–201. For a useful case study, see J. J. Zasloff, *The Role of the Sanctuary in Insurgency: Communist China's Support To The Vietminh, 1946–1954* (Santa Monica, California: Rand Corporation, 1967).

[98] *See, e.g.,* Thomas W. Robinson, "Peking's Revolutionary Strategy In The Developing World: The Failures of Success," *The Annals of the American Academy of Political and Social Science*, 386: 64–77 (Nov. 1969); A. S. Whiting, "The Use of Force in Foreign Policy by the People's Republic of China," in *id.* (July 1972); Van Ness, note 89, at 157–252; Hsiung, note 3, at 288, 292–93; and Deirdre Mead Ryan, "The Decline of the 'Armed Struggle' Tactic In Chinese Foreign Policy," *Current Scene* 10, no. 12 (Dec. 1972).

buffed Peking's overtures became possible targets for Chinese-sponsored revolution. It was a government's foreign policy, rather than the nature of its rule at home that determined the P.R.C.'s behavior toward it.[99]

Largely for reasons of domestic politics, during the early years of the Cultural Retvolution (1966–67) China's leaders sought to make P.R.C. foreign policy adhere more closely to Maoist revolutionary theory, although their material aid to revolution did not match their revolutionary rhetoric. As the Cultural Revolution subsided, however, the P.R.C. gradually began to revert to the foreign politics of national interest that it had previously practiced. China's 1971 support of the feudal, militaristic government of Pakistan, rather than the war of liberation waged by the oppressed people of Bangla Desh, made this transparent to the world.[100]

VII. RECONCILING NON-INTERVENTION WITH WARS OF NATIONAL LIBERATION

To the extent that Peking does support liberation struggles, the question arises as to how its fulfillment of this "internationalist duty" can be consistent with the principle of non-intervention that it has espoused. Both the U.S.S.R. and the United States also have attempted to subvert existing governments, but to differing degrees they have been more reluctant than China to acknowledge their support for violent political change and to confront the question openly. For example, because of its felt inability to offer legal justification for its overt efforts to overthrow the Castro regime in Cuba in 1961 and the Arbenz regime in Guatemala in 1954, the United States attempted to act covertly in those cases.[101] Although the Soviet Union like China, provides support to selected wars of national liberation, Moscow was slower than Peking publicly to advocate it, and only after the downfall of Khrushchev and the bruising polemic with Peking over the meaning of peaceful coexistence did Soviet publicists begin explicitly to claim that such aid does not violate modern international law.[102]

Yet in their capacity as government officials China's leaders too have generally avoided publicly facing up to this basic problem of international law. Because of this, it has been possible for political scientists to write

[99] Van Ness, note 89, at 166–97.

[100] An article in the *Peking Review* charged that "the so-called 'Bangla Desh' is simply a plot of the Indian government to interfere in the internal affairs of Pakistan . . ." *PR* 14.50: 13 (Dec. 10, 1971). For years India had charged that Pakistan had been allowing Chinese military experts to train and arm Indian rebels on East Pakistani soil. *See, e.g.*, "Reports Say Mizo Rebels Asking Chinese Aid," Information Service of India—English, Delhi, Aug. 20, 1967; printed in *FBIS* 162/67: P 1 (Aug. 21, 1967).

[101] For an account of U.S. efforts to subvert "undesirable governments," including those of Cuba and Guatemala, *see*, generally, Richard J. Barnet, *Intervention and Revolution* (1963) and, especially, 17, 229–36. Regarding "the Bay of Pigs," *see, e.g.*, Hilsman, *To Move A Nation* (1967) 30–34.

[102] *See* Hsiung, note 3, at 53, 68.

excellent studies of Peking's support for wars of national liberation without ever explicitly dealing with the legal aspects.[103] Nevertheless, in their capacity as Chinese Communist Party officials engaged in bitter debate with the Communist Party of the Soviet Union,[104] China's leaders have devoted a great deal of attention to reconciling their aid to wars of national liberation with their endorsement of the principles of peaceful coexistence. Indeed, Khrushchev's sensitivity to the contradiction seemingly inherent in supporting both revolution and non-intervention drew heavy Chinese fire. For example, Chinese ideologists charged in a major editorial attack in late 1963 that "he regards the anti-imperialist struggles of the socialist countries and of the people of the world as incompatible with the policy of peaceful coexistence." Khrushchev was sacrificing "the proleterian internationalist task of helping the revolutionary struggles of the oppressed peoples and nations" upon the altar of peaceful coexistence, they maintained. The true view of peaceful coexistence, a concept which they claimed to favor, is that "intrinsically" imperialism is unwilling to accept it, and insists on committing aggression and suppressing oppressed peoples; therefore, they stated, the socialist countries, together with the people of all other countries, must wage "a tit-for-tat struggle against imperialism."[105]

Thus the argument maintained in this editorial and a series of Party documents[106] was that socialist states should apply peaceful coexistence including the principle of non-intervention, in their relations with non-socialist states except when dealing with imperialist states. Because the latter do not respect the rule of non-intervention and the other principles of peaceful coexistence but suppress oppressed peoples, according to this theory, the socialist states are free to, indeed are obligated to, go to the defense of the oppressed peoples by supporting liberation struggles. It is this "tit-for-tat" collective self-defense theory that the Chinese rely on to demonstrate that there is no inconsistency in a state's striving for peaceful coexistence while simultaneously supporting revolution.

A prominent Chinese legal scholar bolstered the theory of Party ideologists by applying it to concrete cases. Responding to Secretary of State Dean Rusk's speech at the annual meeting of the American Society of Inter-

---

[103] *See* generally Van Ness, note 89; and Robinson, note 98.

[104] *See* John Gittings, *Survey of the Sino-Soviet Dispute* (1968) for a review of the 1963–67 polemics.

[105] Editorial Departments of *People's Daily* and *Red Flag*, "Peaceful Coexistence—Two Diametrically Opposed Policies," *People's Daily*, Dec. 12, 1963 at 1–4; trans. in *PR* 6.51: 6, 9–14 (Dec. 20, 1963).

[106] *See* especially the "Chinese Communist Party Central Committee Comment on the Letter of March 30, 1963, from the Central Committee of the Communist Party of the Soviet Union," June 14, 1963, reproduced in *Kuan-yü Kuo-chi Kung-ch'an chu-yi yün-tung tsung-lu-hsien te chien-yi ho yu-kuan wen-chien* [Comments on the General Line of the International Communist Movement and Related Documents] (Peking: People's Publishing House, 1963), at 33; and Lin Piao, "Report to the Ninth National Congress of the Communist Party of China," April 1, 1969; English translation in *PR* 12 (Special Issue): 28 (April 28, 1969).

national Law in 1965,[107] Fu Chu rejected the argument that the theory and practice of wars of national liberation undermine international law and that support for such wars constitutes aggression. Liberation struggles, he wrote, are "wars of national self-defense conducted by colonized or semi-colonized states or nations to preserve their own sovereignty, independence, unity, and territorial integrity." Because they are waged against imperialist aggression, they are "just wars and are fully consistent with modern international law." Indeed, as in the case of Vietnam, they represent "an important contribution to the preservation and development of international law." Fu Chu sought to button up his case by invoking American history:

> ". . . the American war of independence against England in the eighteenth century received strong support and aid from foreign states. Frenchmen and many (other) Europeans even organized voluntary forces to assist the American people in resisting English colonialists. According to Rusk's 'international law,' French people and people of other countries aiding the American war of independence at that time not only committed aggression against America but also threatened and committed aggression against England. What an absurd conclusion this is. The American people will never agree with Rusk's absurd theory."[108]

Despite the efforts of Chinese ideologists and publicists to justify the position that state assistance to foreign wars of national liberation does not violate the rule of non-intervention, the state practice of the P.R.C. reflects awareness of the fact that most of the world community's member states remain unpersuaded. Rather than officially, explicitly, and consistently maintain its minority position in both practice and theory, the Chinese Government has often employed a variety of tactics to avoid the problem created by its challenge to accepted international legal principles.

We have already seen that the P.R.C., like other intervening states, generally seeks to conceal the scope and nature of its military and economic aid to revolutionary movements. This has been done in obvious deference to the principle of non-intervention. For example, when in 1964 Kwame Nkrumah permitted Chinese guerrilla warfare instructors to enter Ghana for the purpose of training nationals of other African states in the arts of revolutionary warfare, the Chinese embassy insisted upon secrecy; according to a report published by the post-Nkrumah government, the embassy had said secrecy was necessary "in view of the delicate nature of the instructors' assignment in Ghana and also in view of the various allegations by the imperialists that China was encouraging subversion in certain countries."[109]

[107] See *Proceedings of the American Society of International Law* (1965), at 247–55.

[108] Fu Chu, "Rusk's 'International Law' Cannot Conceal the Crime of Aggression Against Vietnam by American Imperialism," *CFYC* 2: 8–11 (1965).

[109] Ghana Ministry of Information, *Nkrumah's Subversion in Africa* (Accra-Tema, Ghana: n.d.), at 7–8.

It is interesting to note how the P.R.C. handled the post-Nkrumah government's charges that the training of saboteurs in Ghana constituted intervention in the affairs of other African states. Peking responded only to the extent that it was possible to offer a plausible justification for the presence of the instructors under traditional international law. It dismissed the essential charges as "absurd slander" and stated:

> As is well known, the military as well as the economic and technical experts sent by the Chinese Government to work in Ghana were dispatched at the request of the Government of the Republic of Ghana and in pursuance of the relevant agreements signed by the two countries. They always worked in accordance with the arrangements made by the Ghanaian Government. They are beyond reproach. No one can succeed in distorting all these facts.[110]

The P.R.C. has frequently sought to resolve the tension inherent in supporting both revolution and non-intervention by resort to such techniques. In 1966, for example, it rejected Indian protests against Chinese radio broadcasts, asserting:

> It is entirely within China's sovereign rights for the Chinese frontier guards stationing (sic) at Natu La on the Chinese-Sikkim boundary to make broadcasts on Chinese territory advocating the friendship between the Chinese and Indian peoples and setting forth the truth about the Sino-Indian boundary question, and no foreigner has any right to interfere in this.[111]

The Foreign Ministry denied Indian charges that the broadcasts had called upon the Indian Army to revolt against its government. Thus, as in the Ghanaian case, the P.R.C. attempted to impose a pattern upon the facts that made it possible to defend its actions in accepted international legal terms. Similarly, when in 1971 Uganda claimed that Chinese Communist instructors had participated in guerrilla warfare that had been launched against Uganda from Tanzania, the Chinese Charge d'Affaires branded the charges an utterly groundless fabrication that gravely undermined relations between China and Uganda.[112]

The recent case of Cambodia illustrates the P.R.C.'s resort to the device

[110] "Chinese Embassy in Ghana Refutes Ghana's Slander" (*NCNA*-English, Peking, March 19, 1966) in *SCMP* no. 3663 (March 23, 1966), at 23.

[111] "Chinese Foreign Ministry Refutes Indian Government's Slanders," *PR* 9.39: 36 (Sept. 23, 1966).

[112] "Chinese Charge d'Affaires a.i. in Uganda Lodges Protest," *PR* 14.31: 29 (July 30, 1971). It is difficult, of course, for academic observers and the public to determine which of the many charges of Chinese intervention are well-grounded. In Africa, for example, "Peking was implicated in several insurgencies and attempted coups, as in Ruanda, Niger, Cameroon, and Zaire, which gained the Chinese a reputation for insurgency." Ryan, note 98 at 9. Yet this hardly means that all such accusations, including Uganda's, are necessarily factual.

of seeking to legitimize support to insurgents by taking advantage of the discretion which individual states enjoy in deciding whether and when to recognize the insurgents as the legitimate government.[113] In 1970 Prince Sihanouk claimed that, following the military coup that deposed him, the P.R.C. granted him a loan to finance his Peking-based government-in-exile and free weapons and transport facilities for the fight that his supporters have been waging in Cambodia. The Prince quoted Chairman Mao as having said: "We are not arms traffickers. We cannot sell you weapons. We can give them to you. As for transport, that's also free."[114] Sihanouk subsequently signed an agreement with the P.R.C. for providing free military aid to his regime.[115] These obviously authorized revelations represent an exception to the usual Chinese practice—designed to insulate Peking from charges of international delinquency—of attempting to conceal the extension of military and economic aid to specific liberation struggles and denying accusations of having extended such aid. It should be noted, however, that the P.R.C. had continued to recognize Sihanouk as the chief of the Cambodian state and that the Prince made his announcements only after the Chinese Government had formally recognized "The Royal Government of National Union Under the Leadership of the National United Front of Kampuchea" as the legal successor to the previous government of Cambodia.[116] Thus China was aiding what it claimed to be the legitimate government at the latter's request, bringing the case, at least to Peking's satisfaction, within the traditional, if controversial, ambit of international law and state practice.[117]

One of the more tongue-in-cheek Chinese rejoinders to an accusation of intervention was made shortly after the Bandung Conference of 1955. At the conference, the Prime Minister of Ceylon had proposed that the P.R.C. call upon the Communist parties in Asian and African states to disband. The *People's Daily* responded: "By demanding that China call on Communist parties in the region to disband, the Ceylonese Prime Minister—who had voiced opposition to every form of outside interference—was inviting China to interfere in Ceylon's internal affairs." It stated that "[w]hen there are people in a country who believe in Communism, a Communist party will appear. This is an internal question of the country concerned."[118] This

---

[113] For a discussion of this device, *see* Wolfgang Friedmann, *The Changing Structure of International Law*, 265–66 (1964).

[114] "Sihanouk Says China Finances His Regime," *N.Y. Times*, June 7, 1970, at 3.

[115] "Government of P.R.C. and Royal Government of National Union of Cambodia Sign in Peking Agreement on Providing Gratuitous Military Aid by China to Cambodia," *NCNA*-English, Peking, Aug. 17, 1970, in *SCMP* 4726: 79 (Aug. 26, 1970).

[116] "Chinese Government Formally Recognizes Royal Government of National Union of Cambodia," *PR* 13.20: 14 (May 14, 1970); "Sihanouk in Peking, Still Termed Chief of State," *N.Y. Times*, March 20, 1970, at 14.

[117] Recall the text at note 9. For discussion of China's premature recognition of the revolutionary Algerian regime, *see* Hsiung, note 3, at 220–21.

[118] "Peiping Won't Ask Reds Outside China to Quit," *N.Y. Times*, April 25, 1965, at 7.

expressed solicitude for the principle of non-intervention must have been wryly received by those states in which the Chinese Communist Party had been offering propaganda, indoctrination, military training, supplies and other support to local Communist parties that were bent upon revolution.[119]

Peking's public endorsements of particular revolutionary movements have generally reflected tacit formal deference to the principle of non-intervention. None of the techniques of implicit endorsement—reprinting the policy statements of foreign revolutionary groups, issuing news reports about their activities or publishing maps that designate countries as sites of ongoing struggles—implicates the P.R.C. officially. Moreover, the leading study of the subject points out:

> ". . . explicit endorsements usually are made in the name of either the Chinese people or the Chinese Communist Party. The Chinese government, as such, does not customarily endorse revolutions, since its formal activities with regard to foreign affairs are generally limited to relations with other governments, rather than with mass organizations or political parties."[120]

It should be noted that, since early 1959, even an endorsement by Mao Tse-tung has not constituted official support for revolution abroad, for at that time Mao gave up his post as head of state and has subsequently served only as chairman of the Party and as a deputy to the National People's Congress. Perhaps significantly, although many of the highest-ranking Chinese officials, as well as publicists, have frequently proclaimed the P.R.C.'s adherence to "the five principles of peaceful coexistence," and the state has bound itself to their observance on many occasions, Chairman Mao himself seldom appears to have advocated non-intervention. Often when he has referred to the principles of equality, mutual benefit and mutual respect for territorial integrity and sovereignty, he has been silent about non-intervention. At times, he has even coupled advocacy of the other principles with vague but broad exhortations to give active support to liberation struggles.[121] Mao's statements contrast in their emphasis with those of the highest Soviet officials, such as Khrushchev, who have frequently endorsed non-intervention.

If in practice the P.R.C. were consistently to take the position that state assistance to foreign wars of national liberation does not violate the principle of non-intervention, it might spare itself the tasks of concealing its military and economic support for liberation struggles; of denying that it

[119] See, for example, the summary of the complex relationship between the Chinese Communist Party and the Malayan Communist Party in the years 1949–54 in S. Fitzgerald, *China and the Overseas Chinese* (1972) 89–98. See also Harold Hinton, *Communist China in World Politics* (1966) 403–4; and Ryan, note 98, at 2–7.

[120] Van Ness, note 89, at 86–87, which also discusses exceptions.

[121] See, e.g., note 2. For one of Mao's relatively rare endorsements of all five of the principles of peaceful coexistence, see "Mao-tse-tung tüng-chih-te chiang-hua" (Comrade Mao Tse-tung's Talk), *People's Daily*, Nov. 7, 1957, at 1–2.

has extended this covert support; of structuring much of its public support for such struggles in ways that diminish the involvement of the government, as distinguished from the press, the Party, and the people; and of justifying in terms of traditional international law the support that the Chinese Government has publicly provided. Yet the P.R.C. has thus far failed to adopt this straightforward, if highly controversial position, apparently because it recognizes that this position is unacceptable to most states and because it needs their cooperation not only in respecting the rule of non-intervention vis-à-vis China but also in pursuing many positive goals.

CONCLUSION

As a result of this introductory survey, one wonders to what extent contemporary Chinese theory and practice relating to intervention are significantly different from what they were 2,500 years ago. Today's Chinese elite, like that of the feudal states of the pre-imperial era, endorses the general rule of non-intervention and adheres to it when convenient. Yet, like their Chou dynasty ancestors, the Chinese Communists find it politically expedient frequently to depart from the norm, they have developed ethical doctrines that preach the desirability of such departures, and they have articulated with the aid of their scholars, specific legal rationalizations for most of those departures. Some of these contemporary rationalizations, such as those that justify intervention in self-defense or in behalf of the oppressed people of another state, had actual counterparts in ancient China. Nevertheless, despite the broad similarities and despite the fact that China's pre-imperial experience may in the nineteenth century have helped a historically conscious elite to understand the multi-state system of the West, that ancient Chinese experience does not seem to have influenced the attitudes reflect not only China's current position as a nation-state but also P.R.C. view of intervention. Nor does the record suggest that the imperial Chinese tribute system has had a significant impact upon Peking's position.

This is not to say that historical and cultural factors have played no role in shaping contemporary Chinese attitudes towards intervention. These the breakdown of the imperial tribute system and the consequent century of foreign domination. That in turn led to a preoccupation with China's defense, the adoption of a Marxist-Leninist world-outlook, the development of a successful revolutionary organization in semi-colonial conditions, and the specific importation of the Soviet intellectual apparatus of international law. From all these materials, China's new leaders have fashioned their own distinctive view of intervention. That view offers a sometimes distorted but often devastating attack upon the hypocrisy of the Western powers and, more recently, the U.S.S.R. in formulating and applying the rules of the game.

Yet, at least for the present period, when it is unable to gain broad international acceptance of its legal justification of state support for foreign wars of national liberation, the P.R.C. has itself proved no stranger to hypocrisy. It has not been candid about its military and economic aid to many liberation struggles. Despite its professed concern for the control of intervention, the norms that it has articulated are not susceptible of objective application. Nor has Peking shown interest in strengthening international institutions to which China and other states might surrender their present unilateral fact-finding and norm-applying powers in intervention-type situations.

What the P.R.C. has done is to demonstrate its ability to play the dangerous game of intervention in international politics with the same facility as the other major players. It can tailor the facts and manipulate the rules to rationalize, at least to its own satisfaction, whatever position seems to be in the immediate interest of the Chinese state. When foreign military forces are introduced to help restore order at the request of the existing government, Peking can brand the action legitimate or illegitimate, according to its own perception of "the genuine desires" of the people. If it is a question of U.N. condemnation of regimes that engage in racial discrimination and suppress national self-determination, the P.R.C. has no difficulty finding that Article 2(7) of the Charter does not bar U.N. action in behalf of the people of South Africa but precludes it in behalf of the people of Tibet. China can lecture Britain about its obligation not to allow Hong Kong to become a base for hostile activities, while simultaneusly offering sanctuary and support to guerrilla movements that threaten neighboring states. Despite its repeated pledges not to emulate the super-powers, the P.R.C. has learned the fundamental lesson of super-power international law—it all depends on whose ox is gored.

Should one be depressed by this? Things could be worse. China's situation is changing in ways that are not devoid of hope for international progress. In his classic reformulation of the Maoist revolutionary credo, Lin Piao stated:

> It is sheer day-dreaming for anyone to think that, since our revolution has been victorious, our national construction is forging ahead, our national wealth is increasing and our living conditions are improving, we too will lose our revolutionary fighting will, abandon the cause of world revolution and discard Marxism-Leninism and proletarian internationalism.[122]

But Lin Piao is no longer the heir apparent, and China now enjoys moderate leadership—for how long, we cannot predict.

China's current moderation is likely to be encouraged by a number of factors. Prior to the Cultural Revolution, it should be recalled, the P.R.C., like imperial China vis-à-vis its tributaries, did not intervene in the affairs of regimes that accepted its legitimacy. The impetus behind Peking's sup-

---

[122] Lin Piao, note 89.

port for wars of national liberation has been its anti-status quo orientation, and that in turn has derived in important part from the refusal of the United States and its satellites to recognize the P.R.C.'s legitimacy. Now, however, Peking has achieved its rightful place in the U.N. and is completing the process of establishing bilateral diplomatic relations with other states. This emergence from the twilight of the world community should nourish the modest degree of sensitivity that the P.R.C. has already shown to charges of intervention, particularly when made by "Third World" states. It should also increase the benefits that can accrue to Peking from satisfactory inter-course with other governments rather than with groups that strive to over-throw them.[123]

Both before and after the Cultural Revolution, Peking demonstrated that the interests of the Chinese state normally take precedence over the interests of world revolution. Peking's number one goal, apart from main-taining the regime in power, is the reintegration of Taiwan into China and the preservation of China's territorial integrity. The moral that Bangla Desh must have driven home to the Chinese leaders is that the doctrine of libera-tion struggle may frustrate the attainment of that goal. In the months before Bangla Desh was established, the favorite Chinese slogan was: "Countries want independence, nations want liberation and the people want revolu-tion."[124] The Chinese Nationalist government on Taiwan may prevent the people there from hearing this slogan, but its implications have un-doubtedly not been lost upon their kinsmen and supporters abroad, espe-cially after the precedent set by Bangla Desh. The people on Taiwan—and for that matter, the people of Tibet and other peripheral areas of China—can also invoke the historical example of the American war of independence in an effort to justify breaking away from China with foreign support. This

---

[123] After these words were written, the author read the recent article by Ryan, *supra* note 98, which describes the "new order of priorities" that since the end of the Cultural Revolution has led the P.R.C. to diminish its tangible support of revolu-tionary organizations. Ryan's summary (p. 2) is worth quoting:

"China's leaders, spurred by the sudden respectability and larger opportunities of membership in the United Nations, sought status, prestige and, above all, influence in the international arena—goals more likely to be achieved by courting the 'inde-pendent and sovereign states' . . . than by fomenting 'people's revolutionary armed struggles.'

The Maoists continue to call for world revolution, but in a different framework. Peking has muted the 'armed struggle' line in many areas, at least temporarily, to gain sympathy and support for its policy objectives. The Chinese Communist Party has not abandoned its claim to be the source of inspiration, repository of the true Marxist faith and most suitable model for the revolutionary forces of the world, nor has it ceased to provide verbal encouragement and round-the-clock exhortation via its extensive propaganda machinery to 'revolutionary masses' outside China. Radio Peking, the New China News Agency (*NCNA*) and the Foreign Languages Press operate full tilt, but their output is designed more to secure immediate psychological and ideological benefits for China than to bring down non-Communist governments. Practically speaking, Chinese support for armed struggle by revolutionary groups has dwindled to what one observer has called 'a few selected insurgencies.' "

[124] *See, e.g.,* "Speech by Ch'iao Kuan-hua, Chairman of Delegation of People's Republic of China," Nov. 15, 1971, in *PR* 14.47: 5, 6 (Nov. 19, 1971).

situation may give the P.R.C., which has always been deeply concerned about its security, tangible incentive to reconsider the balance of advantage with respect to intervention in a swiftly changing, uncertain international environment.

Perhaps the P.R.C.'s entry into the U.N. will offer a way for Peking persuasively to reconcile support for selected foreign insurgencies with its proclaimed devotion to non-intervention. As had already been noted, in recent years the U.N. General Assembly has adopted a number of resolutions recommending that all states extend "moral and material assistance" to insurgent movements that seek to liberate the peoples of the white-dominated regimes of southern Africa;[125] and, following its entry into the U.N., the P.R.C. has enthusiastically joined in similar Assembly efforts.[126] Interestingly, in recent years also, the P.R.C. has ceased publicly to support armed struggle in African states that are ruled by black regimes and has confined at least its public support for revolution in Africa to the areas of white rule.[127] This suggests the possibility, as China continues its current policy of mobilizing the middle-sized and smaller states against the super-powers, that not only in Africa but also on other continents the Assembly might authorize aiding those selective insurgencies that Peking wishes to foster. If this should prove to be the case, because of such collective legitimation, the actions taken pursuant to the resolutions would presumably not constitute illegal intervention. By limiting its support for liberation struggles to those approved by the Assembly, China would thus be able to maintain its Maoist revolutionary credentials and to seek desired changes in selected countries while still not alienating most members of the world community.

Is it unrealistic to foresee such a turn of events? Much may depend on whether the super powers, which have engaged in intervention on a scale never approached by the P.R.C., indicate a readiness to undertake a cooperative effort to curb intervention from all quarters, including their own. To an extent that we often fail to appreciate, Chinese attitudes toward international law represent reactions to the behavior of other states rather than initiatives. Until convinced that the other great powers are prepared to take the rules more seriously than in the past, the P.R.C. too will continue to regard international law as an instrument of policy to be used when useful, to be adapted when desirable, and to be ignored when necessary.

[125] For example, recall text and note at note 11.
[126] For example, recall text and note at note 78.
[127] *See* Ryan, note 98, at 8–9.

Chapter 15 | Soviet Attitudes Toward
Intervention | *William E. Butler*

Soviet attitudes toward the international legal rules governing "intervention" (*interventsiia*) or "interference" (*vmeshatel'stvo*)[1] in the affairs of another state are the product of much more than the present international situation. To be sure, the Soviet leadership shares many of the concerns of its Western counterparts about the frequency of internal political violence abroad, the incidence of genocide, the averting of a nuclear holocaust, and the desirability of avoiding situations which could create a direct confrontation of the major powers, although its perceptions of and reactions to such events may, and frequently do, differ from our own. But other considerations, which are for the most part unique to the Soviet Union, have distinguished the Soviet approach to intervention from that of other states. Salient among these factors are: (1) Marxist-Leninist perceptions and explanations of the sources of change in the international system; (2) early experience with foreign intervention during the Russian Civil War and the subsequent isolation of the Soviet Union in the international community; (3) ideological and material support for revolutionary movements abroad, including assistance to "wars of national liberation"; (4) the respective roles of party and state agencies in relations with foreign entities; (5) the doctrine of socialist internationalism; and (6) attitudes toward the "interventionist" activities of international organizations.

The specific impact of each factor upon the formation of Soviet views has varied. Some, such as the international legal principles of socialist internationalism, have emerged only recently. Others—for example, ideology—have exerted a continuously important but less tangible influence. Some played a prominent role historically, only to disappear and subsequently re-emerge. Thus, foreign intervention in the Civil War, undoubtedly a traumatic though much exaggerated event for the new Soviet leadership, was later invoked ritualistically during the cold war as a harbinger of history repeating itself. As we shall see, each of these factors has left an indelible imprint upon contemporary Soviet attitudes.

---

[1] *Interventsiia* generally connotes a forced intrusion; *vmeshatel'stvo*, somewhat broader in meaning, embraces any kind of "mixing" or "meddling" in another's business. Soviet jurists often use both terms interchangeably, as does the present writer. It is worth noting, however, that *vmeshatel'stvo* is the most commonly used term in Soviet legal media, so Soviet concepts of "interference," which always have been more inclusive than the western notion of "intervention," have a linguistic basis for that distinction. The Russian expression for the principle of non-intervention is *printsip nevmeshatel'stva*, translated herein literally as the "principle of non-interference." Materials in this essay quoted directly from the Russian preserve the linguistic choice of intervention or interference as it appeared in the original text.

HISTORICAL ORIGINS OF THE PRINCIPLE OF NON-INTERFERENCE IN SOVIET DOCTRINE

NON-INTERFERENCE IN THE RELATIONS OF BOURGEOIS STATES

Soviet international lawyers virtually never acknowledge that under certain circumstances a right of intervention may exist in international law. In their view, expressed with particular vigor in the post-1945 era, not only does such a "right" not exist, but there is a legal principle which holds categorically that states may not interfere in the internal affairs of other states (and, later, peoples).

Although Soviet interpretations of the historical origins of the principle of non-interference differ in minor detail and emphasis, Soviet jurists generally agree upon the most significant milestones in the development of the principle.[2]

Non-interference as a principle of state relations is said to date from the French Revolution. However, the French bourgeoisie, having proclaimed the principle in an effort to thwart intervention by monarchist powers, was prepared to support it only to the extent of suppressing feudalism, *i.e.*, of protecting its own political gains. There were other limitations upon the principle as well. Interference at this time was understood to mean armed intervention, and the principle was in any event not applicable to non-European peoples.

The Monroe Doctrine is described as a "cruel hoax." Though couched in terms of non-interference, Soviet jurists believe that the Doctrine in essence gave the United States a free hand in relations with Latin America, under the guise of excluding the European powers.[3] The remainder of the nineteenth century is depicted as a period of two conflicting trends. Developments such as the Calvo and Drago doctrines were seen as positive steps, symptomatic of the desire of both small states and of the bourgeoisie in some larger countries to ameliorate interference in internal affairs "as part of the competition for markets." At the same time, the bourgeoisie of the large capitalist states invoked the principle of non-interference to take advantage of their adversaries.

---

[2] On the origins of non-interference as a principle of international law, *see* F. Kozhevnikov, *Sovetskoe gosudarstvo i mezhdunarodnoe pravo* 106 (1948); Piradov & Starushenko, "Printsip nevmeshatel'stva v sovremennom mezhdunarodnom prave," *Sovetskii ezhegodnik mezhdunarodnogo prava 1958* 230–51 (1959); II V. Chkhikvadze *et al.* (eds.), *Kurs mezhdunarodnogo prava v shesti tomakh* 161–71 (1967); and Piradov's account in F. Kozhevnikov (ed.), *Sovetskoe gosudarstvo i mezhdunarodnoe pravo* 89–109 (1967).

[3] "[T]he principle of non-interference was taken over by the North American bourgeoisie in a form other than it had been formulated by the progressive bourgeoisie in the French Revolution of 1789. The very idea of non-interference of any state in the internal affairs of any other state was distorted and was interpreted by the USA in the interests of the important bourgeoisie." II Chkhikvadze (ed.), *supra* note 2, at 166.

These conflicting tendencies, it is argued, explain how and why the international legal doctrine of non-interference developed as it did in the pre-1917 period. "Official science" of international law in capitalist states on the whole endorsed the principle that interference in the affairs of other states was inadmissible. However, interference was regarded as lawful if it occurred in areas beyond the pale of the civilized world, at the request or with the consent of the victim state, pursuant to an international treaty or agreement, or under conditions which justified self-help. These exceptions are viewed as having been essentially self-serving, and indeed this whole interpretation of events and doctrines assumes that non-intervention came into being, developed, and was modified and manipulated by classes seeking their own aggrandizement.

NON-INTERFERENCE AND THE REVOLUTION

The first Soviet monographs on public international law were produced in the mid-NEP period, long after any prospect of the Bolshevik Revolution sweeping spontaneously across Europe had disappeared. There were, in fact, only three general studies published by Soviet jurists in the inter-war years, two by Korovin and one by Pashukanis, and their respective dates of appearance demarcate the beginning and end of a distinct period in Soviet attitudes toward intervention.

When Korovin wrote, sufficient time had elapsed for Allied intervention in the Russian Civil War to be placed in perspective, yet the possibility of revolutionary intervention by the Soviet government, theoretically at least, had not been abandoned. The essence of intervention, he said, "consists of one state attempting to place its state power in the place of another in order to achieve that legal effect which the latter state power can not or does not wish to exercise."[4] If the local state authority "offers armed resistance" against attempts to intervene, then the conflict was said to have been transformed into an "ordinary war."

The distinction in traditional international law between inadmissible and admissible types of intervention Korovin dismissed as having "no legal or actual significance" because, he said, international coercion is applied in one or another form either for reasons of domestic policy or on the supposition that the adversary lacked the capacity to resist. Law, in his view, did not enter the equation at all. Korovin saw the legal theories of the early twentieth century that condemned all forms of intervention as the natural concomitant of "laissez-faire" economic and political liberalism propagated in the interests of British mercantilism.

Intervention, therefore, was not, in Korovin's view, to be condemned out of hand. Foreign intervention in Russia was merely a manifestation of the class struggle on an international scale; it was to be deplored only because it was repressive and regressive:

[4] E. Korovin, *Mezhdunarodnoe pravo perekhodnogo vremeni* 58 (1923).

Intervention, which in well-known conditions may become the greatest instrument of progress, a surgical intervention facilitating the pangs of childbirth of a new world, in the hands of the Entente powers was a synonym of deepest repression, a senseless attempt to stay the wheel of history and to retard the growth and movement of social forces, and an attempt of the dying to keep a hold on the living.[5]

That Soviet Russia was not opposed to intervention in principle, Korovin wrote, was shown by the systematic support it gave to revolutionaries in the Baltic and Caucasian regions.

By 1926, Korovin had begun to soften his appraisal of intervention. "Scientific theory," he acknowledged, distinguished among diplomatic and armed, officious and official, individual and collective, and open and concealed forms of intervention.[6] But he refused to draw any practical conclusions from such distinctions and remained uncompromising in his belief in the legal absurdity of separating "admissible" from inadmissible types of intervention. He found it "curious" that under "completely different historical preconditions (the possibility of direct intervention of a contracting party for class and sometimes for historical reasons) the obligation of non-interference figures in many treaties of Soviet Russia with bourgeois states."[7]

Soviet domestic and foreign policy had undergone considerable change by 1935. The U.S.S.R. had embarked upon a far-reaching program of planned industrialization and collectivized agriculture, had broken the last vestiges of economic isolation imposed by western governments, had joined the League of Nations, and had entered into an extensive network of collective security arrangements and non-aggression pacts. But Pashukanis's treatment of intervention differed from Korovin's only in minor, albeit interesting, detail.

Korovin's definition of intervention was accepted *in toto* by Pashukanis. But the latter insisted that "authoritative" or "coercive" intervention had to be distinguished from "advice" and "friendly instructions," conceding that this differentiation was "highly conditional" and that intervention had occurred in the guise of advice, mediation, and good offices.[8] Considerable space was devoted to treaties concluded by the U.S.S.R. whose provisions forbade interference in the internal affairs of the contracting parties.[9] Unlike Korovin, Pashukanis expressed no amazement that the Soviet government should assume such obligations. Of particular interest, though, is

---

[5] *Id.* at 59.

[6] E. Korovin, *Sovremennoe mezhdunarodnoe publichnoe pravo* 47 (1926).

[7] *Id.* at 52.

[8] E. Pashukanis, *Ocherki po mezhdunarodnomu pravu* 103 (1935). Chapter 6 of this volume was entitled "Intervention" (*interventsiia*).

[9] None of these agreements, however, purported to define "interference." For a detailed list of the agreements, *see* K. Baginian, *Narushenie imperialisticheskimi gosudarstvami printsipa nevmeshatel'stva* 21–33 (1954).

Pashukanis's criticism of intervention by invitation. This principle, he noted, had been invoked by Germany when extending aid in 1871 to suppress the Paris Commune, and again in 1920 to justify using French occupation forces in the Ruhr to put down a workers' uprising.

Pashukanis also addressed the problem of Soviet state responsibility for the "interventionist" activities of the Communist International and Communist parties abroad. This issue has been a perpetual irritant in Soviet relations with the west, most especially with the United States.[10] Communist movements abroad, he declared, were indigenous. To make the Soviet government responsible for the utterances of the Communist International would be "as illogical as making the Belgian government responsible for the utterances of the Second International," which was situated in Brussels. He further denied that "ideas," despite their enormous impact, could be a form of interference: "[T]he influence of ideas, whose force we cannot deny, may not be relegated to one of the types of intervention, for it lacks the constituent elements of authoritative state interference."[11]

NON-INTERFERENCE AS A DEFENSE AGAINST MILITARISM

Pashukanis's views on intervention by invitation and his emphasis upon Soviet treaty practice did constitute some departure from Korovin's original position of 1924, but it was not sufficient to meet Soviet alarm over growing militarism in Germany, Italy, and Japan. Korovin was attacked severely by Vyshinskii for his concept of intervention (Pashukanis already had been liquidated):

> The fact that a monograph, in which attempts are made to give a legal basis or even a legal justification of the plundering policy of the intervenors—attempts completely inadmissible for a Soviet specialist in international affairs or even for a Soviet scholar in general—has been recommended, although decades ago, in Soviet literature as a textbook for Soviet institutions of higher learning does not change essentially the circumstances of the situation.[12]

Though conceived on the eve of World War II in order to forestall any attempt by an adversary to invoke earlier Soviet doctrine on intervention

[10] For the assurances given by the Soviet government coincident with the establishment of diplomatic relations between the United States and the U.S.S.R. in a Note of November 16, 1933, *see* I G. Hackworth, *Digest of International Law* 304–05 (1940). The United States felt these assurances were violated at the outset. It is doubtful, however, that a movement can ever be persuaded to surrender its revolutionary ethos under conditions such as these.

[11] Pashukanis, *supra* note 8, at 113.

[12] Vyshinskii, "Osnovnye zadachi nauki sovetskogo sotsialisticheskogo prava," 4 *Sovetskoe gosudarstvo* 37–38 (1938). Some of the reasons for Soviet apprehensions on this question are set forth in Arzhanov, "Shpionazh, diversiia, interventsiia kak sistema vneshnikh otnoshenii fashistskoi diktatury (na primere Germanii)," 1 *Sovetskoe gosudarstvo* 181–93 (1938).

against Soviet interests, Vyshinskii's uncompromising attitude toward interference *per se* dominated Soviet legal doctrine and Soviet foreign policy throughout the Cold War period. It continues to this day to be an important tenet in Soviet approaches to the question.

In 1948 Kozhevnikov seized upon the Truman Doctrine and the Marshall Plan as new manifestations of an interventionist policy directed against the U.S.S.R. Quoting Vyshinskii's attack on Korovin, he contended that foreign intervention in the Russian Civil War and a League of Nations resolution calling for settlement of the Georgian question were violations of the "most elementary principles of international law."[13] This latter point was chiefly of symbolic significance. It meant that Soviet doctrine henceforth would treat international law as a defense against interference and as a protection against improper and illegal behavior, instead of a neutral and sometimes irrelevant factor in a community of predatory states.

Kozhevnikov also broadened the doctrinal scope of the principle of non-interference to embrace both the internal *and external* affairs of the Soviet state. M. I. Lazarev, writing in the 1951 international law textbook, accepted this same definition and declared that the principle of non-interference had become a fundamental norm of international law. Considerable attention was given, as was the custom in this period, to Stalin's genius in discovering that interference may take either open or concealed forms.[14] Interference in any form "would be a flagrant violation of the principle of sovereignty and international cooperation and under such conditions can not have progressive significance."[15]

Soviet doctrinal positions with regard to interference became less dogmatic after the death of Stalin, but they were complicated and confused by the draft definition of aggression which the Soviet government submitted in 1953 to the Special Committee created by the U. N. General Assembly to define aggression.[16] This definition was maintained as a negotiating position by the Soviet Union for the ensuing sixteen years. It differed from earlier and later Soviet views in that it linked so-called indirect (encouraging subversive activity, inciting civil war or a coup d'etat in another state), economic (economic pressure or blockade), and ideological (war

[13] Kozhevnikov, *supra* note 2, at 110 (1948). It is significant that Kozhevnikov treated non-interference as a *doctrine* and not as a principle of international law. The chapter was entitled "The Doctrine of Non-Interference."

[14] Stalin's views on non-interference are discussed in detail in Korostarenko, "Printsip nevmeshatel'stva v mezhdunarodnom prave (o vyskazyvaniiakh I. V. Stalina)," 9 *Uchenye zapiski akademii obshchestvennykh nauk pri Tsk VPK(b)* 72–88 (1950).

[15] E. Korovin (ed.), *Mezhdunarodnoe pravo* 197 (1951). The author added that "capitalist encirclement is the basic fact determining the international position of the Soviet Union."

[16] A Russian text of the Soviet draft appears in V. Sobakin (comp.), *Sovremennoe mezhdunarodnoe pravo; sbornik dokumentov* 592 (1964). Two jurists writing in 1958 treated the Soviet draft under the rubric of non-interference. *See* Piradov and Starushenko, *supra* note 2, at 230–51.

propaganda, furthering facist, racist, or extreme nationalist views, etc.) forms of aggression with the more or less traditional notions of armed attack. Most jurists, including those in the Soviet Union, previously had regarded such actions as possibly falling within the category of interference in the internal affairs of another state.

The first international law textbook published in the post-Stalinist period equivocated among traditional notions of interference, the revised definition of aggression, and the view that interference embraced both the internal and external affairs of states.[17] The section on interference was entitled "The Principle of Non-Interference in the Internal and External Affairs of States," but the emphasis was almost exclusively on internal affairs. With regard to external affairs, the author merely noted that Russian actions taken against Turkey in 1878 to prevent the destruction of the Armenian minority population "never could be considered intervention."[18] This is perhaps the closest approximation of an endorsement of humanitarian intervention which is to be found in contemporary Soviet international legal literature; there is, however, no indication of the view being widely shared by other Soviet jurists.

Lisovskii confined his references to Stalin's utterances on intervention to those of the 1930's; however, he maintained that the "theory of admissible intervention was reactionary and incompatible with international law." At the same time, he observed that in the *practice* of imperialist states distinctions were drawn between economic, military, and legal intervention. In fact, judging by the examples offered, these distinctions seemed to reside in Soviet perceptions of interference. Economic intervention included dumping and the "creation of economic privileges"; examples of military intervention were German-Italian actions in Spain (1936), Anglo-American activities in Greece (1947), and American interference in Korea. A case of legal intervention was said to have occurred on February 16, 1918, when the diplomatic corps in Petrograd collectively protested against the Soviet decree annulling state obligations. Another instance of legal interference frequently cited in Soviet media was the enactment of the Mutual Security Act by the United States Congress in 1951.

Definitions of the principle of non-interference advanced by other Soviet jurists after 1955 have been essentially of two types. One type emphasized the object against which interference was directed. Tunkin, for example, wrote: "The principle of non-interference means that no state may interfere authoritatively in affairs within the domestic jurisdiction of another state."[19] K. A. Baginian defined the principle somewhat differently: "Non-interference of one state in the internal affairs of another means the

---

[17] V. Lisovskii, *Mezhdunarodnoe pravo* 89–94 (1955).
[18] *Id.* at 89.
[19] G. Tunkin, *Osnovy sovremennogo mezhdunarodnogo prava* 29 (1956).

inadmissibility of one state's dictating its will to another state; *i.e.*, actions directed against the independence of other states."[20]

Other jurists stress the form of interference. Levin declared that the principle of non-interference meant the "inadmissibility of intervention in any form whatsoever: military, diplomatic, economic, as well as rendering support in any form to forces waging a struggle on the territory of a foreign state to overthrow the government of the latter."[21]

The general discussion of non-interference in Soviet international legal textbooks from 1956 to 1970 is sufficiently similar in approach that it may be treated as a collective unit.[22] By 1957, references to interference in *external* affairs had largely disappeared in Soviet legal media. The inclusion of the principle of non-interference among the legal principles of peaceful co-existence and the great emphasis in the late 1950's and early 1960's upon the elimination of colonialism led many Soviet jurists to abandon the view that the principle of non-interference was derived from the principle of the sovereignty of the state as a subject of international law. Some went so far as to suggest that its derivation lay in the principle of the sovereign equality of states and *peoples*,[23] finding confirmation of their view in the 1960 United Nations General Assembly Declaration on the Granting of Independence to Colonial Countries and Peoples.[24]

Most jurists preferred to give cases or examples of interference by imperialist powers rather than to classify interference by "type." Among those listed in various publications were: Italian intervention in Abyssinia, the attempts of some states to dispute Egypt's right to nationalize the Suez Canal, British actions in Oman (1957), the United Nations resolution on the Hungarian question, British and American actions in Jordan and Lebanon respectively (1958), and United States involvement in the Dominican Republic (1965) and Vietnam.

Taken as a whole, Soviet doctrinal literature evidences a striking reluctance to approach analytically the intricate and very difficult substantive issues that interference raises for international law and order. The several interpretations of the principle of non-interference in Soviet doctrine over the years are illustrative in a general way of the tension between early commitments to support revolutionary change and subsequent concern over Soviet vulnerability to foreign intervention. At either extreme, the attitudes

[20] K. Baginian, *Bor''ba Sovetskogo Soiuza protiv agressii* 97 (1955).

[21] D. Levin, *Osnovnye problemy sovremennogo mezhdunarodnogo prava* 228 (1958). For another definition of this type *see* G. Sharmazanashvili, *Pravo mira* (1961).

[22] *See* F. Kozhevnikov (ed.), *Mezhdunarodnoe pravo* (1957); D. Levin and G. Kaliuzhnaia (eds.), *Mezhdunarodnoe pravo* (1960; 2nd ed., 1964); F. Kozhevnikov (ed.), *Uchebnyi kurs mezhdunarodnogo prava* (1964; 2nd ed., 1966); V. Lisovskii, *Mezhdunarodnoe pravo* (1961 and 1970 editions); L. Modzhorian and N. Blatova (eds.), *Mezhdunarodnoe pravo* (1970).

[23] *See* Kozhevnikov, *Uchebnyi kurs, supra* note 22, at 74.

[24] G. A. Res. 1514 (XV), 14 Dec. 1960. 15 *U.N. GAOR* Supp. 16, at 66, *U.N. Doc.* A/4684 (1961).

of Soviet jurists toward interference have been influenced primarily by the interests and experiences of the Soviet state. Discussions of interference are incident-oriented. It suffices merely to name a particular international event, and the reader is left to supply the constituent elements of the delict.

If this is an accurate characterization of doctrinal attitudes, it should not be supposed that Soviet jurists believe their interpretations of the principle of non-interference are any more ethnocentric than those of foreign jurists. In explaining the origin, development, and application of non-interference in terms of class interests rather than traditional national interests in military, economic, and political power, Soviet jurists are convinced that the "bourgeoisie" have themselves always manipulated concepts of interference to serve their own ends. At the very worst, Soviet jurists see their approach as the mirror image of their non-socialist counterparts.

This also helps to explain why Soviet doctrine has not been preoccupied with delimiting admissible and inadmissible forms of interference. If interference *per se* is deemed to be unlawful, there is little point in discussing whether it ever may be lawful. There nevertheless remains the question: what specific acts, in the Soviet view, constitute interference in the internal affairs of another state? Recently, some Soviet jurists, inspired by the United Nations General Assembly's adoption of the 1960 Declaration and of the 1965 Declaration on the Inadmissibility of Intervention in the Domestic Affairs of States and the Protection of their Independence and Sovereignty,[25] have endeavored to approach this question in a more systematic and sophisticated manner.

INTERFERENCE DISTINGUISHED FROM AGGRESSION

Soviet jurists are distressed by the "gradation" approach espoused by many Western jurists; *i.e.*, by the idea that international relationships have become so complex that interference is merely a question of degree. In their view, such an approach inevitably leads to a discussion about admissible and inadmissible forms of intervention.[26] Nevertheless, it is recognized that "all measures of political and economic influence of one state upon another" are not unlawful. The task of the Soviet science of international law, according to D. B. Levin, is "to develop criteria for distinguishing lawful from unlawful uses of such influence."[27]

---

[25] G. A. Res. 2131 (XX), 21 Dec. 1965, *reprinted in* 5 *Int'l Leg. Mat.* 374 (1966).

[26] "This position legalizes intervention and serves to justify imperialist interventionist policies." Komarova, "O printsipe nevmeshatel'stva," 6 *Sovetskoe gosudarstvo i pravo* 130 (1967).

[27] *See* "XI ezhegodnoe sobranie sovetskoi assotsiatsii mezhdunarodnogo prava," *Sovetskii ezhegodnik mezhdunarodnogo prava 1968* 356 (1969).

Professor Levin's approach is illuminated in his recent book, *Mezhdunarodnoe pravo i sokhranenie mira* (1971), where he eschews distinctions between aggression and interference. The key point, in his view, is that there are two categories of un-

The 1965 Declaration is said to have confirmed non-interference once and for all as a principle of international law. There remains, however, some difference of opinion over the legal effect of the 1965 Declaration. The Soviet representative on the International Law Commission has pronounced the Declaration to be legally binding, stressing that no state voted against it.[28] Another Soviet jurist, noting that the Declaration did not undertake to define "interference," commented upon its importance for the *theory* of international law, primarily because the principles of non-interference and of self-determination were expressly linked in the Declaration.[29]

Drawing upon the general language of the 1965 Declaration, Komarova has attempted to define the actions proscribed by the principle of non-interference.[30] Her list included: (1) actions directed against the existing political, economic, or social system of any state, or attempts to impose another regime on a state, provided that the peoples of the said state approve of the existing system; (2) actions taken by states, groups of states, or international organizations which, although unconnected with attempts to change a social system or political regime in a state, nonetheless represent a threat or use of force for any purposes incompatible with the principles of the United Nations; (3) actions directed against the self-determination of peoples; (4) subversive actions against another state or interference in a civil war in such state; (5) economic, political, or military pressure by one state upon another for the purpose of obstructing the latter in exercising its sovereign rights in domestic or foreign policy; (6) threats to break diplomatic relations if one state extends recognition to another or the conditioning of the continuance of relations upon the receipt of special privileges; (7) attempts to obstruct the free exploitation of natural resources; (8) raising obstacles to domestic legislative activity or administration of justice.

---

lawful use of force. The first, the unlawful use of armed force, encompasses aggressive war, armed intervention, armed aggressive actions, the introduction of armed forces into the territory of a foreign state and retention thereon for the purpose of interfering in its internal affairs, pacific blockade, and the support of armed groups and detachments of mercenaries for the purpose of intruding upon the territory of another state. The second category embraces the unlawful use of economic or political force, and Levin urges that international lawyers ought to develop criteria for distinguishing among uses of political and economic force directed against the territorial integrity or political independence of a state and those which are a normal feature of international intercourse.

[28] N. Ushakov, *Nevmeshatel'stvo vo vnutrennie dela gosudarstv* 115 (1971). Ushakov claims that the Declaration falls within that category of U.N. resolution which confirms or interprets a provision of the Charter or of international law. Such resolutions "go beyond the limits of ordinary recommendations and acquire binding force for members of the United Nations." *Id.*

[29] Komarova, *supra* note 26, at 132. *Also see* V. Israelian (ed.), *Sovetskii soiuz i organizatsiia ob"edinennykh natsii (1961–1965 gg.)* 240 (1968), where it is claimed merely that the Declaration "created a broad legal basis for intensifying the struggle" against imperialist interference.

[30] Komarova, "Poniatie i formy vmeshatel'stva po sovremennomu mezhdunarodnomu pravu," 14 *Uchenye zapiski vsesoiuznogo iuridicheskogo zaochnogo instituta* 143 (1968).

Komarova's analysis of non-interference came at a moment when Soviet jurists were contemplating a new approach to the definition of aggression. It will be recalled that the draft definition submitted by the Soviet government in 1953 added indirect, economic, and ideological forms of aggression to the traditional concept of armed aggression. At the eleventh meeting of the Soviet Association of International Law, held from January 31 to February 2, 1968, there was considerable discussion about the interrelationship between the concepts of aggression and intervention; the majority of those whose views were published seemed to favor separating armed attack from less tangible forms of intervention, at least for definitional purposes.[31]

The proposed separation of aggression from other types of intervention evidently reflected thinking in official quarters, for in July 1968 the Soviet member of the Special Committee on the Question of Defining Aggression supported a decision to give priority to defining armed aggression.[32] A new Soviet draft definition, submitted to the Special Committee in February 1969, omitted any reference to ideological or economic "aggression."[33]

"ADMISSIBLE" INTERFERENCE IN THE INTERNAL AFFAIRS OF STATES IN SOVIET DOCTRINE AND PRACTICE

We have discussed above the historical development of Soviet attitudes toward interference in international law and the kinds of actions or specific incidents which Soviet jurists or the Soviet government consider to constitute unlawful intervention. The examples cited in Soviet legal writing are but a small sample of numerous instances in diplomatic practice where the Soviet Union has objected to interventionist activity on the part of other states.[34] Despite the fact that Soviet jurists would take strong exception to the heading of this subsection, it is clear that the Soviet government does recognize the validity of interference under international law in certain circumstances. Moreover, there are a substantial number of qualifications placed upon the principle of non-interference which, in the Western view, do in fact permit or even encourage intervention, although under a Soviet

---

[31] See note 27 supra.

[32] See Chkhikvadze and Bogdanov, "Definition of Aggression—An Important Instrument in the Struggle for Peace," 7 International Affairs (Moscow) 27–32 (1969).

[33] U.N. Doc. A/AC.134/L.12., reprinted in 8 Int'l Leg. Mat. 661 (1969). The 1970 Report of the U.N. Special Committee on the Question of Defining Aggression said agreement had been reached to delete "indirect" aggression from a proposed draft definition of armed aggression, presumably because of the impossibility of finding an acceptable definition in the near future.

[34] The indexes of the published series of documents of Soviet foreign policy contain numerous references to intervention. See Dokumenty vneshnei politiki SSSR, whose first 14 volumes cover the period 1917–34; also Vneshniaia politika sovetskogo soiuza, published under slightly varying titles for the period 1941–50, and Vneshniaia politika sovetskogo soiuza; sbornik dokumentov, covering 1961 to date.

interpretation such actions would be deemed to be consistent with, or in furtherance of, other principles of international law.

INTERVENTION BY INVITATION OR CONSENT

The sovereign right of states to grant or withhold consent to the actions of other states or even to the acceptance of certain principles of customary international law has been a basic tenet of Soviet jurisprudence since the earliest days of the Soviet regime. It follows that a state may invite, or consent to the request of, another state to take actions which, if imposed, would be deemed interference in internal affairs. In justifying the use of Soviet forces in the 1956 Hungarian revolution, Soviet jurists relied heavily upon "the Hungarian government's request" for aid.[35] The same theory was pursued initially to explain the movement of some Warsaw Pact forces into Czechoslovakia in August 1968.[36] But under Soviet doctrine, such consent or invitation must be given freely, without pressure, and it must reflect the true will of the people of a given state.[37] In the view of Soviet jurists, agreements to establish foreign military bases and the request by South Vietnam for American military assistance are examples of consent given by unrepresentative governments under undue pressure.[38]

ASSISTANCE TO PEOPLES STRUGGLING FOR THE RIGHT TO SELF-DETERMINATION

The extent to which a "nation" or a "people" may be a subject of or entitled to the protection of international law has been a controversial subject in Soviet legal media for many years.[39] There is, however, nearly universal agreement among Soviet jurists that the right to self-determination is a generally-recognized principle of international law, especially since the adoption of the 1960 Declaration by the U.N. General Assembly. Consequently, a state granting assistance to such peoples is acting in accord with international law, and its actions in no way, in the Soviet view, can be

[35] See Korovin, "Jungle Law Versus the Law of Nations," 1 New Times 17 (1957).

[36] See the TASS Statement issued on the date some Warsaw Pact forces moved into Czechoslovakia. Reprinted in 7 Int'l Leg. Mat. 1283 (1968).

[37] See Komarova, supra note 30, at 140.

[38] See M. Lazarev, Imperialisticheskie voennye bazy na chuzhikh territoriiakh i mezhdunarodnoe pravo (1963); F. Kozhevnikov & V. Menzhinskii, Agressiia SShA vo V'etname i mezhdunarodnoe pravo (1967).

[39] Some Soviet jurists would require the "nation" or "people" to possess some state-like attributes, whereas others argue that any cohesive and distinct social unit possesses a "national sovereignty" with the right to self-determination. There is an enormous literature in Russian on the subject. Cf. L. Modzhorian, Sub"ekty mezhdunarodnogo prava (1958); R. Tuzmukhamedov, Natsional'nyi suverenitet (1963); G. Ignatenko, Ot kolonial'nogo rezhima k natsional'noi gosudarstvennosti (1966); G. Starushenko, Natsiia i gosudarstvo v osvobozhdaiushchikhsia stranakh (1967).

regarded as unlawful interference in internal affairs.[40] On the other hand, "armed actions or repressive measures of any nature whatever directed against the independence of peoples" are "flagrant interference" in their internal affairs.[41]

ACTIVITIES OF COMMUNIST PARTIES

The dominant Western impression of the international communist movement since 1917 has been that of a highly disciplined but small group of revolutionaries dedicated to the violent overthrow of legitimate democratic governments through the conspiratorial export of revolution. The Communist Party of the Soviet Union is viewed as the source of moral, financial, and political support for communist groups abroad, and, the U.S.S.R. being a single-party state, the Soviet government is considered to be legally responsible for the Party's activities.

The emergence of national communist-party states and indigenous movements clearly independent from the U.S.S.R., along with the dissolution of the Comintern and Cominform, have dissipated both the extent of Muscovite control over and Western concern about a "monolithic" communist movement. Nevertheless, Soviet jurists go to some lengths to stress that communist groups abroad are independent of the Soviet Union and that their activities cannot be regarded as interference in internal affairs:

> The principles of socialist internationalism, which certain political figures and scholars of the West attempt to give as evidence of "subversive communist activity," in no way contravene principles of contemporary international law. They are an expression of the unity of purposes and views of the working people of all countries in their struggle against imperialism. But this unity is predetermined by class interests and the consciousness of the working masses of various states. The community of interests of the working people of different countries existed long before the rise of the first socialist state. Therefore, it is completely absurd to hold the socialist states guilty for the fact that the working class of capitalist countries is struggling for its rights and for the unity of the working people of the entire world.[42]

In taking this view, Soviet jurists distinguish "ideological struggle" from "subversive activity." The latter is said to comprise such overt activities as

[40] "Since colonialism and racism have been prohibited by international law, and since progressive public opinion recognizes the legality and justness of liberation wars which peoples wage for liberation from colonial oppression, then armed aid and armed cooperation such as, in a particular case, the sale of weapons to a people struggling against colonial domination, is admissible from the viewpoint of international law." Komarova, *supra* note 30, at 150.

[41] Komarova, "Printsip nevmeshatel'stva i narody Afriki," 16 *Uchenye zapiski instituta mezhdunarodynykh otnoshenii* 40–41 (1963); *also see* Ginsburgs, " 'Wars of National Liberation' and the Modern Law of Nations—The Soviet Thesis," 29 *Law & Contemp. Prob.* 910 (1964).

[42] F. Kozhevnikov, *Sovetskoe gosudarstvo i mezhdunarodnoe pravo* 104 (1967).

the training of groups or an individual on the territory of one state for the purpose of penetrating the territory of another in order to subvert its system, conduct terrorist activity or give material or other support to rebel groups there, and overthrow the government or destroy the political and social system of that country.[43]

This definition of subversive activity requires either a physical penetration by a person or persons across a state frontier to carry out such objectives or the carrying out of preparatory activities with the immediate purpose of committing such a penetration. It would seem that financial or other assistance to indigenous groups, including Communist parties, would not fall within this prohibition, unless perhaps such groups were in open rebellion.

ENACTMENT OF LEGISLATION WHICH CONTRAVENES INTERNATIONAL LAW

In the ordinary course of events, Soviet jurists strongly defend the supremacy of states in matters of domestic jurisdiction. It has been argued, however, that laws which are not in accordance with traditional principles of democracy, such as "racist or fascist legislation, laws contravening generally recognized principles of international law, norms of international law, or international obligations assumed by a state," or "laws creating a privileged regime for aliens," may be condemned or criticized without breaching the principle of non-interference.[44]

PRINCIPLES OF SOCIALIST INTERNATIONALISM

In the aftermath of events in Czechoslovakia during 1968, an article in *Pravda* developed an essentially new rationale for the military measures taken to remove the then government of Czechoslovakia. Those who criticized these measures as violations of international law were guilty of espousing an "abstract, non-class approach to the question of sovereignty and of the right of nations to self-determination." The peoples of socialist countries and Communist Parties were free to choose their own way so long as "none of these decisions should damage socialism in their country or the fundamental interests of other socialist countries, or the whole working class movement. . . ."[45]

This statement of principle is now in the process of being assimilated into Soviet international legal doctrine. Known as the principle of socialist (or proletarian) internationalism, the basic content of the principle as applied among socialist states is defined as the construction of socialism

[43] Komarova, *supra* note 30, at 148.
[44] *Id.* at 158.
[45] "Sovereignty and the International Duties of Socialist Countries," *Pravda*, September 25, 1968; *reprinted in* 7 *Int'l Leg. Mat.* 1323 (1968).

and communism and the defense of the gains of socialism in the course of the struggle between the socialist and capitalist systems.[46]

The author of a leading Soviet treatise on international legal theory has stipulated that socialist internationalism affects certain subordinate principles which have become socialist international legal norms and which together comprise a new unified system of international legal principles of socialist internationalism.[47] The subordinate principles listed by Tunkin are:

> (1) respect for the sovereignty of socialist states, on the basis of which peoples exercise the right to self-determination; (2) non-interference in the internal affairs of other states, which reflects respect for the national peculiarities and expectations of each people; (3) full equality of socialist states, which reflects the Marxist-Leninist thesis of the equality of nations and of workers' parties.[48]

The subordinate clauses attached to each of the principles are in fact qualifications of a "class" nature sufficient to differentiate each principle from those operative in general international law. In their socialist form, such principles are said to embrace the obligation of ensuring that such rights may be exercised; for example, "the socialist principle of respect for sovereignty obliges socialist states not only to respect the sovereignty of other socialist states, but also to defend socialist sovereignty in accordance with the demands of proletarian internationalism."[49] In Tunkin's opinion, the Czechoslovak events of 1968 were "in full accord with the principle of proletarian internationalism."[50]

The doctrinal sweep of the legal principles of socialist internationalism is a broad one. To those who would protest that international legal principles permitting intervention to protect the gains of socialism would be in derogation of *jus cogens*, Tunkin responds that these principles are of local applicability and of a higher "quality" than general international law.[51] He

[46] *See* Butler, "'Socialist International Law' or 'Socialist Principles of International Relations'," 65 *Am. J. Int'l L.* 796 (1971).

[47] G. Tunkin, *Teoriia mezhdunarodnogo prava* 503 (1970).

[48] Tunkin, "V. I. Lenin i printsipy otnoshenii mezhdu sotsialisticheskimi gosudarstvami," *Sovetskii ezhegodnik mezhdunarodnogo prava 1969* 25 (1970).

[49] *Id.* at 27. Some Soviet jurists treat this obligation as a separate "principle of mutual assistance." *See* Modzhorian and Blatova, *supra* note 22, at 92.

[50] Tunkin, *supra* note 48, at 27.

[51] *Id.* at 28. It has been suggested that the formulation of the principles of socialist internationalism was discussed in bilateral Soviet-American talks and perhaps implicitly revised or attenuated in paragraph eleven of the Basic Principles of Mutual Relations between the United States and the U.S.S.R.: "The U.S.A. and the U.S.S.R. make no claim for themselves and would not recognize the claims of anyone else to any special rights or advantages in world affairs. They recognize the sovereign equality of all states." Paragraph three further stipulates that both countries ". . . will seek to promote conditions in which all countries will live in peace and security and will not be subject to outside interference in their internal affairs." The text of the Basic Principles is reproduced in 66 *Am. J. Int'l L.* 920–22 (1972). For a skeptical reaction to the efficacy of the Declaration in this respect, see S. Schwebel, "The Brezhnev Doctrine Repealed and Peaceful Co-Existence Enacted," 66 *Am. J. Int'l L.* 816–19 (1972).

suggests that the legal principles of socialist internationalism are compatible with, indeed may represent the ultimate stage of, *jus cogens* in this sphere.

Tunkin's exposition of the doctrine raises innumerable practical and theoretical difficulties for Western and socialist jurists alike. From the standpoint of non-interference, however, the doctrine on its face gives wide discretion for one socialist power to determine unilaterally, or in conjunction with others, when another socialist country's policies have exceeded permissible bounds. The "subjects" of socialist internationalism,[52] the procedure for warning an offending state, the "gains" of socialism, the "expectations" of peoples in socialist countries—all are left vague, undefined, but each is a critical element in judging whether a particular socialist state has transgressed.

INTERNATIONAL ORGANIZATIONS AND NON-INTERFERENCE

International organizations are treated with considerable circumspection in Soviet legal media. For a long time, Soviet jurists debated whether or not such organizations had international legal personality, and to this day there remains a small minority of Soviet scholars who deny that international organizations may be independent subjects of international law.[53] The League of Nations, notwithstanding Soviet membership in its twilight years, continues to be depicted as a "capitalist" organization whose Statute "legalized" interference in the internal affairs of states, most especially the Soviet Union.[54] It is noteworthy in this connection that the definitions of "interference" contained in so many Soviet international law textbooks refer only to actions of one *state* relating to the internal affairs of another; such definitions seemingly exclude international organizations acting in their own right.[55]

That international organizations may act in derogation of the principle of non-interference, however, has long been recognized in Soviet doctrine and practice, and Soviet jurists hold distinctive views about the meaning and scope of Article 2(7) of the United Nations Charter.

The learning and practice which have grown up around Article 2(7) are beyond the scope of this inquiry.[56] Three general observations about the

[52] Tunkin describes proletarian internationalism as a *moral* and *political* principle of the international workers' movement with regard to the People's Republic of China, thereby suggesting there is no mutual legal obligation to assist the Chinese people against their wayward leaders. *Id.*

[53] Modzhorian, *supra* note 39, at 30–41. V. Shurshalov, *Mezhdunarodnye pravootnosheniia* 58–76 (1971).

[54] *See* Ushakov, *supra* note 28, at 28–37.

[55] Komarova, *supra* note 30, at 143, does mention international organizations, but Modzhorian and Blatova adhere to the standard definition of interference in their 1970 textbook, *supra* note 22.

[56] For a convenient summary, *see* L. Goodrich, E. Hambro, and A. Simons, *Charter of the United Nations: Commentary and Documents* 60–72 (3d ed., 1969).

Soviet approach to this provision of the Charter are, however, germane. First, even though Article 2(7) "formally" relates only to the rights and duties of the Organization itself, Soviet jurists contend that this provision nonetheless enshrines the principle of non-interference as a norm regulating relations among states, thereby rejecting the view that if such a principle of international law is to be found in the Charter, it must be derived from Article 2(4).[57] Ushakov claims that it would be contrary to elementary logic "if the United Nations in the person of its organs were bound to refrain strictly in its activity from any interference in affairs relating to the domestic jurisdiction of any state, whereas its members would be free to carry on such interference or, at least, would not be bound by such a duty."[58]

Second, while conceding that the concept of domestic jurisdiction is undefinable, the Soviet government on numerous occasions has taken the view that the placing of certain issues on the agenda or their discussion in United Nations bodies was a violation of Article 2(7).[59] The uprising in Hungary during 1956 and the events in Czechoslovakia of 1948 and 1968 are but two examples. Korovin wrote with regard to Hungary:

> The counter-revolutionary plot in Hungary and its suppression by the workers' and peasants' government, the composition of the Hungarian government, its relations with the government of the Soviet Union, the question of elections in Hungary—these all are beyond any manner of doubt matters of a domestic order, which the Charter removes from the jurisdiction of the United Nations. That bringing them up there was a flagrant violation of the Charter is something that requires no great legal erudition to realize.[60]

Third, certain issues such as colonialism and racial discrimination fall, in the Soviet view and that of most other states, outside the purview of Article 2(7). If a question has been the subject of any international treaty, one Soviet jurist has argued, it is excluded "unconditionally" from the domestic jurisdiction of either state-party.[61] South African treatment of its Indian population is deemed an international question because it was discussed at Empire conferences in 1917, 1921, 1924, and 1926. Portuguese policies in Angola, being connected with the right to self-determination under the 1960 Declaration, similarly are regarded as beyond Portuguese domestic jurisdiction.[62] The Soviet Union has been a strong advocate of

---

[57] II V. Chkhikvadze *et al.* (eds.), *supra* note 2, at 196–97 (1967).

[58] Ushakov, *supra* note 28, at 48.

[59] *See* Loeber, "The Soviet Concept of 'Domestic Jurisdiction'," 3/4 *International Recht und Diplomatie* 165–90 (1961). Komarova regarded the sending of United Nations representatives to South Vietnam "in order to observe falsified elections" as a case of collective intervention. Komarova, *supra* note 30, at 137.

[60] Korovin, *supra* note 35, at 16. *Also see* Baginian, "Printsip nevmeshatel'stva i Ustav OON," 6 *Sovetskoe gosudarstvo i pravo* 62–70 (1957).

[61] Komarova, *supra* note 26, at 45.

[62] *Id.*

more resolute measures by the United Nations to combat apartheid and colonialism in general.[63]

CONCLUSION

In certain broad aspects, Soviet and Western attitudes toward intervention possess a startling symmetry in points of common cause and of divergence. There is mutual concern to contain levels of violence, to avoid direct confrontations, and to reduce the human costs of unleashed nationalist passions. One even begins to see modest signs in the relations of the superpowers that, whatever disposition of a conflicting interest may be made between them, "third powers" should not intrude to the disadvantage of both. The two sides also share an intensely deep suspicion of one another's motives in seeking to define intervention or to subject intervention to "objective" institutional controls. Both sides acknowledge in one way or another that interference may be necessary and lawful under certain circumstances. Both sides have indulged, and probably will do so again, in unilateral intervention to support hegemonical interests within their respective spheres of influence. Moreover, there is general agreement that the present state of the law respecting intervention is much too equivocal for states to be held to highly explicit rules of conduct.

At this point, the symmetry begins to disappear. Ideological preconceptions and Soviet experiences during the past half-century have encouraged the Soviet Union to support absolute prohibitions against interference of any kind (Soviet doctrine in the 1920's lagged decidedly behind Soviet practice of that period). The terms "interference" and "intervention" seem to have acquired a completely normative connotation in the Russian language, whereas Western jurists use them both descriptively and normatively. Marxism-Leninism postulated an antagonistic outside world, bent upon destroying the Revolution. The notion of genuine interrelationships among states, accompanied by a certain degree of inevitable mutual "influence" and "pressure," conceptually at least, has been resisted strongly in Soviet circles. Antipathy toward Soviet ideals and the comparatively weak international position of the U.S.S.R. until the nuclear stalemate of the mid-1950's did oblige the Soviet government to cope with "interference" of various kinds.

At the same time, the mission to support proletarian movements abroad and a deep conviction in the inevitability and justness of their cause have led the Soviet legal community to urge, officially and unofficially, that assistance to wars of national liberation or analogous situations does not fall within the scope of intervention, is not illegal, and actually is undertaken pursuant to other norms of international law. Both of these strains in Soviet

[63] For an appraisal of the work of the Special Committee on the Principles of Friendly Relations and Cooperation Among States in this connection, *see* Ushakov, *supra* note 28, at 124–48.

commitment and experience are to be seen in the approaches of Soviet jurists to the task of defining the principle of non-interference, where the ultimate realization of non-interference is linked with the attainment of revolutionary socialism abroad and the preservation of socialism within the bloc.

These considerations have placed severe inhibitions on the kinds of questions Soviet jurists ask when writing about interference. There is no concrete elucidation in Soviet juristic writing of the scope or limits of the rules applicable to interference in its infinite shades and varieties, and such matters as the rules to be applied during civil strife, the respective positions of the recognized and unrecognized governments, the right of counter-intervention, the legal remedies and sanctions for intervention, etc., have not been treated at all. Of the gaps remaining in Soviet jurisprudence, this surely is one of the largest and most important, and one hopes that it will not be left open indefinitely.

PART V | THE ROLE OF
INTERNATIONAL INSTITUTIONS

Chapter 16 | The United Nations and Internal Conflict | Oscar Schachter

The United Nations has been involved, from almost its very outset, in internal conflicts, notwithstanding the Charter provision of Article 2(7), which excludes United Nations "intervention" in matters "essentially within the domestic jurisdiction of any state." Such internal conflicts, which may be defined as conflicts within a state involving violence between nationals of the same state,[1] have become matters of United Nations concern for various reasons, most commonly because of involvement of foreign states or groups with a consequential risk of endangering international peace. Other grounds for United Nations concern have also been manifest, in particular the strong pressures of the great majority of states to end colonialism and racism and, in some situations, the humanitarian interest in alleviating massive suffering.

It is no more than a tautology to say that involvement of the United Nations in internal conflicts means that such conflicts are of international concern, but it is a somewhat different proposition to assert that this signifies that Article 2(7) no longer has any application to the situation. The Charter does not state or imply that a complex situation such as an internal conflict must be placed in either one of two mutually exclusive categories:

---

[1] Since this chapter is addressed to the role of the United Nations, it is concerned with the internal conflicts that have been brought to the Organization. Our definition extends, therefore, beyond the traditional international law categories of insurgency and belligerency. It would, for example, include cases of rebellion which fall short of insurgency (that is, which do not involve organized military forces under an authority purporting to have the characteristics of a government). However, acts of banditry or other conventional criminal behavior (though possibly of concern to the United Nations as a problem of social deviance) will not be germane to our theme. The chapter will give some consideration to United Nations actions in respect of non-violent internal conflicts, whenever such actions appear to be illustrative of what might be done generally in regard to domestic strife (as, for example, in the use of plebiscites when conflicting claims are made to governmental authority).

For general discussion of the relevance of international law to internal conflict, see E. Castrén, *Civil War* (1966); Dhokalia, "Civil Wars and International Law," *Indian J. Int'l L.* 219 (1971); R. Falk, *Legal Order in a Violent World* (1968); Falk, "Janus Tormented: The International Law of Internal War," in J. Rosenau (ed.), *International Aspects of Civil Strife* (1964); Farer, "Harnessing Rogue Elephants: A Short Discourse on Foreign Intervention in Civil Strife," 82 *Harv. L. Rev.* 511 (1969); Friedmann, "Intervention, Civil War and the Role of International Law," 1965 *Proc. Am. Soc. Int'l L.* 67, 69; in III C. Black & R. Falk (eds.), *The Future of the International Legal Order* (1971); Moore, "The Control of Foreign Intervention in Internal Conflict," 9 *Va. J. Int'l L.* 205 (1968); Pinto, "Les règles de droit international concernant la guerre civile," 114 *Recueil Des Cours* (1945); J. Siotis, *Le Droit De La Guerre Et Les Conflicts Armes d'un Caractère Non-International* (1958); Sohn, "The Role of the United Nations in Civil Wars," 1963 *Proc. Am. Soc. Int'l L.* 208.

international concern or domestic jurisdiction. A United Nations organ may reasonably conclude that some degree of involvement on its part is called for but at the same time recognize that the internal conflict involves issues that should be left to the people of that State to determine.

The fact that Article 2(7) contains no specific criteria for determining what is to be deemed essentially domestic or what constitutes intervention has of course given the United Nations organs wide latitude in applying those concepts to particular cases.[2] But this has not meant that the problem of determining domestic jurisdiction has been eliminated or that it has been solved by labeling situations of international concern. For even when that finding has been made or implied, it has remained necessary for the United Nations body to distinguish between those matters which, as a matter of principle, should be left to the national political processes and those which should be handled by the international Organization. And since the organs concerned have been composed of governments, their decisions have often been "political" in the commonly understood sense. They have been a product of coalitions built on national and bloc interests, influenced by a variety of considerations which range from immediate expediency to long-range strategy and which reflect diverse judgments as to benefits and costs of the proposed actions. Notwithstanding these political factors, the governments have considered it necessary to justify their positions in terms of the Charter, and in doing so they have expressed or implied criteria for drawing the line between the area where United Nations intervention is permissible and the reserved domain. The criteria which emerge in the context of particular cases may be regarded, at least provisionally, as normative in their intent and effect. They tend to crystallize the expectations of governments as to what is permissible and impermissible and thus give significance to precedent and practice. Yet it must be borne in mind that such criteria are the product of political processes and that as a rule they reflect a particular combination of circumstances not likely to be repeated. Therefore, what has worked in one case may prove of limited applicability in even a similar case. Although United Nations experience shows that political bodies can readily "distinguish away" past interpretations, it is also evident that precedents do become established and that governments, like individuals, find it easier to justify their behavior by pointing to previous cases. One cannot ignore the expectations that may have been generated by such precedents even while recognizing that national self-interest will normally be foremost in the calculations of the governments concerned.

In the present chapter, we will not discuss these precedents case by case, useful as such case studies might be. We will rather endeavor to examine the principal features of United Nations decisions during the first twenty-

[2] See R. Higgins, *The Development of International Law Through the Political Organs of the United Nations* (1965), at 64–130; M. Rajan, *The United Nations and Domestic Jurisdiction* (1958); I *U.N. Repertory of Practice of United Nations Organs* (1955), on Article 2 (7), at 55–159.

five years, as seen particularly from the standpoint of the international official concerned primarily with the aims of the Organization and the effectiveness of its collective decisions. It is hoped that the account that follows will provide a comprehensive yet succinct summary of United Nations experience which will throw new light on the actual and potential capabilities of the Organization to deal with domestic conflicts of international concern.

I. THE DIVERSITY OF UNITED NATIONS AIMS RELEVANT TO INTERNAL CONFLICT

After some twenty-five years of United Nations rhetoric, one is tempted to pass quickly over a restatement of its major purposes. They have so often been solemnly reiterated and reformulated, so commonly employed to justify opposing points of view, and so frequently abandoned in practice that they appear more as a litany than as significant goals. Yet it would be profoundly misleading to examine the behavior of the Organization and its member states without clearly identifying its principal aims.

That there are such identifiable aims is evidenced by their inclusion in the Charter (and, in some cases, their formulation in declaratory resolutions) and, more convincingly, by the support they receive in actual cases and controversies—whether or not they are treated as legally binding (by virtue of their inclusion as norms in the Charter or in Customary Law). That they are United Nations aims depends on the extent to which they receive confirmation and support by the collective bodies (again, not merely in words but by commitment of resources), and in this sense their reality is continuously tested. They will often diverge in priorities from purely national goals, but we can assume that collective decisions of United Nations bodies will tend to give effect to those policies which the majority of states perceive as part of their national aims and interests and which also (one needs to add) do not unduly sacrifice other national interests. (Although this observation seems almost self-evident, it needs to be tested in particular cases, since it does not always follow that state behavior in an international organ coincides with the perception of national interests in other contexts.) Still, we can conclude that the decisive element in giving reality to a stated purpose of the United Nations is the fact that the perceived interests of the majority of states, and especially of those states directly concerned, coincide with that purpose.

It has long been apparent that the diverse purposes of the United Nations will often clash with each other. In respect of most internal conflicts, some goals will point to United Nations involvement, others to the contrary. The Charter does not prescribe a hierarchy of purposes or priorities for their application. It would not be wrong to say that the maintenance of international peace is the primary purpose (for it is stated first in the

Charter), but there is no authoritative rule or pattern of practice which declares that peace must invariably be given priority over other major purposes. Several examples from United Nations experience attest to the contrary. A case can be made for giving priority to "sovereign equality," since the Charter is premised on the system of sovereign states, but this basic premise must be qualified by the powers granted the United Nations, in particular the Security Council, and by the special position of the Permanent Members.

The absence of any definitive hierarchy of purposes means in practice that diverse aims can be advanced and that, in the actual choice of priorities, the varying circumstances of particular cases can be taken into account. This avoids or at least counteracts an inflexible legalism in determining which policies should be given precedence. Specific policies can be developed more readily by weighing various purposes, each worthy of consideration, in relation to costs and risks to other values. It can be argued that this leaves the choice too widely open and that almost any action or inaction can find its justification in one or another of the United Nations aims. Granting this, the question remains whether the remedy is to be sought by imposing an order of priorities on major goals or by developing of guidelines and rules of conduct to fit specific situations. Although setting up a hierarchy of goals has an attractive simplicity, the rigidity it would establish would be so far removed from the complex international world that it would hardly be likely to receive adherence in words or in practice. Even the attempt to impose guidelines or rules for relatively well-defined specific situations involves choices among competing values which states are reluctant to make in advance or to abide by in practice.

We shall comment briefly on the United Nations goals which have been most pertinent to its actions in respect of internal conflicts. They are:

1. Maintenance of international peace and security;
2. Maintenance of national sovereignty and independence;
3. Territorial integrity of member states;
4. Self-determination;
5. Promotion and protection of fundamental human rights;
6. Alleviation of massive suffering;
7. Economic and social development of the less developed countries.

1. MAINTENANCE OF INTERNATIONAL PEACE AND SECURITY

It is apparent, on the face of it, that the maintenance of international peace and security, the primary objective of the United Nations, wide as it is, does not include the elimination of internal conflicts per se. This was abundantly clear to the draftsmen of the Charter and has remained so to the member states. The idea that the Charter embodies a policy of "minimum order" (which has been said to include the "minimization of destruction within a contested entity")[3] goes beyond the stated purpose and in fact finds little support in the practice of the Organization. It can be argued that violence of any kind runs counter to human rights, especially the right to life, but this line of reasoning moves the matter outside of the scope of international peace and involves other values. There seems little reason to obscure the distinction between international and internal peace by introducing a still more general notion of minimum order or a general aim of "persuasion over coercion." On the contrary, there is an advantage in retaining the basic Charter distinction so that an appropriate criterion can be applied to cases of internal conflict. Not all internal strife risks endangering international peace, and there are obvious reasons to maintain the distinction in law and politics.

Similarly, the goal of keeping the international peace need not be converted into the more diffuse policy of persuasion rather than coercion. One might make a case for the latter as an element of human rights (though this is by no means self-evident and may require qualification), but it is clear enough that persuasion is not the only peaceful means of resolving international conflicts. Article 33 of the Charter includes procedures of settlement that involve elements beyond persuasion.

None of these observations is intended to suggest that the purpose of maintaining international peace should be construed narrowly. The Charter gives it wide scope by following it with the corollary "to that end: to take effective collective measures for the prevention and removal of threats to the peace. . . ." From its very beginnings, the United Nations has considered it appropriate to take collective measures to prevent and remove threats to the peace which were judged to exist in a domestic situation.[4] Invariably the issue was whether the internal situation involved danger of a breach of international peace—not whether the internal situation involved violence and coercion.

It may be worth noting that the term "international" in this context applies to breach of peace or a threat to the peace involving two or more countries, however localized. Frontier incidents and territorial incursions, even of short duration, have been legitimate subjects for United Nations consideration. Obviously, not all are on the same level of concern. The avoidance of great-power conflict and especially of nuclear warfare has had a priority and an urgency ahead of all other aims. When such conflict has been threatened by internal strife, there has been an intensification of purpose and effort. In contrast, the avoidance of conflict among smaller powers that are members of a regional group has generally been accorded lesser

[3] Moore, *supra* note 1, especially at 252–53. For a general discussion of the principle of minimum order, *see* M. McDougal & F. Feliciano, *Law and Minimum World Public Order* 121–60 (1961).

[4] *See* Report of the Sub-Committee on the Spanish Question, May 31, 1946: I *U.N. SCOR*, Special Supp. *See also* I *U.N. Repertory of Practice of United Nations Organs* (1955), on Article 2 (7), at paras. 12–40, 231–53.

priority, in part because of the assumption that this could be dealt with more expeditiously in the smaller, more homogeneous regional community.

2. MAINTENANCE OF NATIONAL SOVEREIGNTY AND INDEPENDENCE

The goal of maintenance of national sovereignty and independence, expressed in various principles of the Charter, reflects the widely shared conviction of virtually all member governments that, in the present international system of independent states, external coercion should not be used to determine or to manipulate domestic events such as, for example, the choice or the character of the governments of national states. On the whole, such coercion is regarded as inimical whether it emanates from another state, from a non-governmental source, or from an international organization, although there may be important reasons for differentiating these sources. Implicit also in the concept of national independence is that states should be free to decide on their domestic political, economic, and social arrangements without interference by other states or by international bodies, except as authorized by international law and agreement. Still another corollary of sovereignty is exclusive control of the territory of the state and the related principle of territorial inviolability. Thus, protection of these generally recognized attributes of sovereignty is an element in the accepted aims of the United Nations.

3. TERRITORIAL INTEGRITY OF MEMBER STATES

The Charter expresses the objective of territorial integrity of member states in a qualified form in Article 2(4), which prohibits the use or threat of external force against the territorial integrity of any state. But, irrespective of Article 2(4), it is apparent that most, if not all, members of the United Nations regard maintenance of territorial integrity and national unity of states as a major common purpose, implicit in the Charter (it is expressed, for example, in the well-known resolution 1514 [XV]).[5] This is not to say that they will necessarily accord this purpose a priority over other goals; however, it has special prominence in those internal conflicts which involve a threat or risk of secession.

4. SELF-DETERMINATION

Within the United Nations, *self-determination* has been regarded pre-eminently as the right of the peoples in the overseas colonies to become

---

[5] G.A. Res. 1514 (XV), "Declaration on the granting of independence to colonial countries and peoples," Dec. 14, 1960: 15 *U.N. GAOR*, Supp. 16, at 66. This resolution contains the following provision on territorial integrity: "6. Any attempt aimed at the partial or total disruption of the national unity and the territorial integrity of a country is incompatible with the purposes and principles of the Charter of the United Nations."

independent or to achieve self-government.[6] It has also been expressed as a goal in respect of claims by a majority of indigenous inhabitants against rule by a minority of another race, as, for example, in Rhodesia. Apart from these widely accepted meanings, some states (possibly only a minority of United Nations members) hold that the principle of self-determination applies to "all peoples" and that this includes ethnic communities or "nations" under "alien subjugation," irrespective of their colonial status or "overseas" separation.[7] Although this broad principle has rarely been advanced in specific cases to support claims of ethnic communities (in the Wilsonian tradition), it has received support in world public opinion when an ethnic community has been subject to severe deprivation. A notable recent example was the approval expressed by some governments of the claims advanced by the Bengalis of East Pakistan for an independent state of Bangladesh.[8] But whatever its semantic connotation, *self-determination*, as presently used in the United Nations, has not generally been construed as embracing internal democracy in the sense of representative government, though the ideal that a government must "represent the whole people" of a territory is affirmed, albeit indirectly, in the 1970 Declaration of Principles of International Law concerning Friendly Relations.[9] It has also been observed that self-determination has been considered generally to involve a single act of choice and that when a choice was made it was considered that self-determination was fulfilled once and for all.[10]

[6] Emerson, "Self-determination," 65 *Am. J. Int'l L.* 459 (1971). *See also* Moore, *supra* note 1; V. Van Dyke, *Human Rights, The United States and World Community* Ch. 5 (1970).

[7] *See* Nawaz, "Bangla Desh and International Law," *Indian J. Int'l L.* 251 (1971). For references *see* 3 *U.N. Repertory of Practice of United Nations Organs* (1955), Article 55, note 479. *See also* section on self-determination in G.A. Res. 2625 (XXV), Oct. 24, 1970, "Declaration on Principles of International Law concerning Friendly Relations and Co-operation among States in accordance with the Charter of the United Nations:" 25 *U.N. GAOR*, Supp. 28, at 121.

[8] Statements by representatives of India and U.S.S.R. at the 203rd plenary meeting of the 26th Sess. of the General Assembly, Dec. 7, 1971: U.N. Doc. A/PV 2003, at 73, 74, 77, 79, 81, 176–80, 181, 183 and at the 1613th meeting of the Security Council, Dec. 13, 1971: U.N. Doc. S/PV. 1613, at 83–85, 86. For other views on the right of self-determination in East Pakistan, *see* U.N. Doc. A/PV. 2003, at 22, 57, 103, 118, 151.

[9] The seventh paragraph of the section on the Principle of Equal Rights and Self-Determination in G.A. Res. 2625 (XXV), *supra* note 7, says that nothing in that principle authorizes the dismemberment of a state "possessed of a government representing the whole people belonging to the territory without distinction as to race, creed or colour." It has been suggested that this saving clause in the Declaration must also be read in the light of the state's duty to promote respect for human rights and therefore it can have a wider significance than appears to be the case on first reading. *See* Rosenstock, "The Declaration of Principles of International Law concerning Friendly Relations: A Survey," 65 *Am. J. Int'l L.* 713, 732 (1971).

[10] This appears equally true of self-determination in the post-World War I Wilsonian sense as well as of contemporary decolonization. *See* Emerson, *supra* note 6, at 463. Roger Fisher has challenged this limitation: "Self-determination is not a single choice to be made in a single day," 1968 *Proc. Am. Soc. Int'l L.* 166.

5. PROMOTION AND PROTECTION OF FUNDAMENTAL HUMAN RIGHTS

Internal conflicts which have received attention in the international forum have involved, more frequently than not, charges of large-scale violations of basic human rights and the claim that involvement by the United Nations was needed to protect human rights. While it is undeniable that the promotion and protection of human rights is an aim of the United Nations, it is an aim that in the understanding of most member states is to be pursued through general recommendatory resolutions or international conventions of a lawmaking character. Interventionist "action" by the Organization to redress violations of human rights has not been regarded as legitimate except in the case of large-scale racial discrimination or presumably the threat of genocide.[11]

6. ALLEVIATION OF MASSIVE SUFFERING

Unlike the foregoing objectives, alleviation of massive suffering does not expressly appear as a purpose or principle of the Charter, though in some cases it may be regarded as an aspect of basic human rights, more particularly the "right to life" or protection against genocide. It has its own justification, however, and is supported by a general consensus that the international community should seek to alleviate mass distress among victims of civil strife, at least through providing material supplies and technical services.[12]

7. ECONOMIC AND SOCIAL DEVELOPMENT OF THE LESS DEVELOPED COUNTRIES

While the aim toward economic and social development of the less developed countries normally has not been regarded as directly relevant to internal conflict (and therefore rarely enters into the debates concerned with such conflicts), it clearly has a bearing on United Nations action to prevent or ameliorate such conflict when economic and social tensions are contributing factors. As a corollary, the point may be made that the nature and direction of United Nations involvement in internal conflict should be

[11] For references to action against *Apartheid*, *see* resolutions cited in note 23 below. For views justifying intervention on grounds of threat of genocide, *see* discussion on East Pakistan at the 2003rd plenary meeting of the General Assembly, 7 Dec. 1971: U.N. Doc. A/PV. 2003, at 72, 74, 79, 151, 180–81.

[12] *See e.g.*, in the Nigerian case, statement by the representative of Tanzania at the 1695th plenary meeting of the 23rd Sess. of the General Assembly, 15 Oct. 1968: U.N. Doc. A/PV. 1695, at 22, and Report by Secretary-General's Representative to Nigeria on humanitarian activities, 26 Jan. 1970: U.N. Press Release SG/1740; in the East Pakistan case, Texts of Messages Exchanged between Secretary-General and President of Pakistan, 12 May 1971: U.N. Press Release SG/SM/1474; Appeals made by Secretary-General, U Thant, for assistance to refugees from East Pakistan, 19 May 1971: 8 *U.N. Mon. Chron.* 49 (June 1971); 16 June 1971: 8 *U.N. Mon. Chron.* 26 (July 1971).

influenced by a policy of furthering the development of the country. This policy has been implemented on a limited scale in some cases by United Nations measures to rehabilitate the economic and social fabric of a strife-torn country and by encouragement of national action that would further development. A more directly political approach is apparent in suggestions that the international community should be guided in its action by a "principle of modernizing legitimacy, that is legitimacy measured by the capacity of the contending groups to develop the consciousness, creativity, institutionalized power and justice necessary for coping with the revolution of modernization."[13] In effect this "principle" would call for a judgment by the international organization as to which among the contending internal groups would more effectively support such "modernization" goals as democratic institutions, industrialization, wider access to education, and more efficient management of the state apparatus. The fact that its application would raise obvious difficulties for an international institution that includes various social systems and ideologies does not mean that it may not influence the positions of individual states in their policies toward contending groups.

II. THE ELEMENTS IN INTERNAL STRIFE REGARDED BY THE UNITED NATIONS AS WARRANTING UNITED NATIONS INVOLVEMENT

The preceding discussion cautions us against undue simplification of the issues of policy that are raised when internal conflicts become of international concern. Virtually every case involves a multiplicity of goals, and the maximization of one objective will generally conflict with the maximization of another. Governments have no calculus to resolve what appear to be conflicting imperatives, though they realize that from a rational standpoint they must sacrifice some ends to attain others. Moreover, in the actual situations there are always unforeseen and unintended consequences; an action that seems rational in the short run may turn out to be a miscalculation in the long run. These considerations indicate why, from the standpoint of a member government, it may not be easy to determine the policy consideration governing its decision.

On the other hand, from the standpoint of an observer who takes an overview of the line of decisions by the United Nations, it is not difficult to place the cases in well-recognized categories, each such category being defined by the factual element that most justified United Nations involvement. We shall therefore categorize the cases of United Nations involvement in domestic conflicts under five headings, namely:

---

[13] Boals, "The Relevance of International Law to the Internal War in Yemen," in R. Falk (ed.), *The International Law of Civil War* 303, 342 (1971). *See also* Halpern, "A Redefinition of the Revolutionary Situation," 23 *J. Int'l Aff.* 54–75 (1969). But *cf.* Moore, *supra* note 1, at 331–32.

1. Internal conflicts involving charges of external aggression or subversion;
2. Conflicts characterized by breakdown of domestic law and order with consequential danger of external intervention;
3. Anti-colonial conflicts;
4. Conflicts arising from racism;
5. Internal strife involving massive suffering of non-combatants.

Each of these headings may be said to point to a type of internal conflict that is regarded by the international community as of sufficient international concern to warrant some degree of United Nations action. But as we have already cautioned, these categories should not be taken as the sole or decisive determinants of governmental decisions.

1. INTERNAL CONFLICTS INVOLVING CHARGES OF EXTERNAL AGGRESSION OR SUBVERSION

From the earliest days of the United Nations, the principal organs have regarded it as legitimate to deal with internal strife involving charges of external aggression or subversion. The conflicts within Greece (1946–47), Guatemala (1954), Lebanon (1958), Hungary (1959), Laos (1959), Yemen (1963–64), and Vietnam all fall within this category; however, the charges of external involvement were denied or justified by those accused.

In most of these cases the United Nations political organs not only discussed the charges but also established some machinery for inquiry and observation. Commissions of investigation were employed in respect of the situations in Greece, Hungary, and Laos, and observation groups were sent by the Security Council to Lebanon and Yemen.[14] In the Guatemalan case the Security Council did not reach a decision and in effect left the case to the regional organization, the Organization of American States (O.A.S.).[15] The Vietnam conflict was placed on the Security Council agenda at the request of the United States (in early 1966), but no action was taken by the Council. The General Assembly did send a fact-finding commission to investigate alleged violations of human rights in 1963,[16] and the Secretary-General made a number of public statements in which he proposed steps to create an atmosphere conducive to negotiation and termination of the hostilities.[17]

[14] United Nations Special Committee on the Balkans (UNSCOB); Special Committee on the Problem of Hungary; Security Council Sub-Committee (Laos); United Nations Observation Group in Lebanon (UNOGIL); United Nations Observation Mission in Yemen (UNYOM).

[15] See discussion at the Security Council, at the 675th meeting, 20 June 1954, and 676th meeting, 25 June 1954: 9 U.N. SCOR, 675th and 676th meetings.

[16] See the Report of the United Nations Fact-Finding Mission to South Viet-Nam, 7 Dec. 1963: 18 U.N. GAOR, Annexes, agenda item 77, U.N. Doc. A/5630.

[17] For U Thant's statements on Viet-Nam, see 4 U.N. Mon. Chron. 57 (June 1967); 4 U.N. Mon. Chron. 24 (Oct. 1967); especially 7 U.N. Mon. Chron. 98 (Aug.–Sept. 1970); 8 U.N. Chron. 30 (Feb. 1971); 8 U.N. Mon. Chron. 80 (June 1971).

2. CONFLICTS CHARACTERIZED BY BREAKDOWN OF DOMESTIC LAW AND ORDER WITH CONSEQUENTIAL DANGER OF EXTERNAL INTERVENTION

The two principal internal conflict situations involving the United Nations in large peacekeeping operations—the Congo (1960–65) and Cyprus (from 1964 on)—fall within the category of conflicts involving breakdown of domestic law and order with consequential danger of external intervention. One can also include the relatively short period of strife in the Dominican Republic in 1965. All three cases could also be classified under the heading of conflicts involving charges of external aggression and subversion, since in each such charges were made and were actually a significant element in the determinations that the situations were likely to endanger international peace and security. What distinguishes the Congo, Cyprus, and the Dominican Republic from "indirect" aggression cases, such as Greece, Lebanon, and Yemen (which, of course, also involved some internal disorder), is that in the former cases the central governmental authority broke down and there was large-scale civil violence by opposing communal or political groups. While the participants and their supporters (at least on one side) asserted that external forces were responsible for the governmental breakdown, observers would largely agree that domestic strife and related internal factors were the principal reasons for the weakness of central authority.[18] The danger to international peace could reasonably be regarded as arising from external responses to the domestic conflict rather than as cases of "indirect" aggression fomented from without. It is in this sense that the Congo and Cyprus cases are appropriately treated as different from the "proxy wars" or subversion cases within category 1. The Dominican Republic situation of 1965 also seems to fit the "local breakdown" type rather than the external aggression category.[19]

There is no need here to review the well-documented histories of these three cases. It is worth noting, however, that, in the important cases of the Congo and Cyprus, action by the United Nations was instituted not only with the consent of the territorial governments but on their initiative, and

[18] For the question of Congo, *see* Annual Report of the Secretary-General on the Work of the Organization, 1960–1961: 16 *U.N. GAOR*, Supp. 1, Ch. I; *ibid.*, 1961–1962: 17 *U.N. GAOR*, Supp. 1, Ch. I. *See also* C. Hoskyns, *The Congo Since Independence* (1965); McNemar, "The Post-independence War in the Congo," in Falk, *supra* note 13. For the question of Cyprus, *see* Annual Report of the Secretary-General on the Work of the Organization, 1963–1964: 19 *U.N. GAOR*, Supp. 1, Ch. II-19; *ibid.*, 1964–1965: 20 *U.N. GAOR*, Supp. 1, Ch. II. *See also* J. Stegenga, *The United Nations Force in Cyprus* (1968).

[19] Slater, "The Limits of Legitimization in International Organizations: The Organization of American States and the Dominican Crisis," 23 *Int'l Org.* 48 (1969); L. Miller, *World Order and Local Disorder: The United Nations and Internal Conflicts* (1967), at 149; Annual Report of the Secretary-General on the Work of the Organization, 1964–1965: 20 *U.N. GAOR*, Supp. 1, Ch. III-Q; *id.*, 1965–1966: 21 *U.N. GAOR*, Supp. 1, Ch. III-H.

in both cases the United Nations was asked to, and in fact did, provide large-scale peacekeeping forces to prevent a recurrence of violence and to assist in maintaining domestic order. Alongside such domestic policing activities, the U.N. Forces took action to cut off arms supply and other clandestine aid to contending groups. Steps were also taken to encourage political solutions based on a policy of national unity and territorial integrity. It was generally understood that these peacekeeping activities were emergency action or holding operations, for, as U Thant put it, "the United Nations cannot permanently protect the Congo or any other country from the internal tensions and disturbances created by its own organic growth toward unity and nationhood."[20]

Two other major internal conflicts involving secession—in Nigeria and Pakistan—resulted in different assessments by United Nations members. The civil war in Nigeria, like all civil wars, brought external partisanship and support by foreign governments for the secessionist movement. However, such external involvement was not seen as a sufficient danger to international peace to bring about any action by the United Nations beyond humanitarian assistance by the Secretary-General.[21] No doubt the expectation that the federal government of Nigeria would defeat the Biafran secessionists was a factor in limiting the external threat. During the several years of warfare, not even a single member state proposed that the situation be placed on the agenda of the Security Council or of the General Assembly.[22]

In the Pakistan Civil War, it quickly became evident that a threat of international war—between Pakistan and India—resulted from the political and psychological impact on India of the conflict in East Bengal. That danger, though emphasized by the Secretary-General as well as by the world press, did not result in any resolutions in the United Nations until the threat turned into an actual breach of the peace and the civil war into an international war.[23]

3. ANTI-COLONIAL CONFLICTS

In the first few years of the United Nations, it was vigorously contended by the colonial powers with support by some other members that anti-colonial conflicts were essentially domestic and therefore beyond United Nations competence unless Chapter VII of the U.N. Charter were to be applied. This line was rejected by the majority, beginning with Indonesia, and in

[20] Report of the Secretary-General on the withdrawal of the United Nations Force in the Congo and on other aspects of the United Nations Operation, 29 June 1964: 19 *U.N. SCOR*, Supp. April–June 1964, U.N. Doc. S/5784, at 259.

[21] B. Andemicael, *Peaceful Settlement Among African States—Roles of the United Nations and the Organization of African Unity* (A UNITAR Study, 1972), at Pt. D, § 3.

[22] *Id.*

[23] *See* G.A. Res. 2793 (XXVI), 7 Dec. 1971; Security Council Res. 307 (1971), 21 Dec. 1971.

due course it has been abandoned by nearly all of the former colonial powers as well.[24] A series of resolutions by the General Assembly culminating in the "Declaration on the Granting of Independence to Colonial Countries and Peoples" of 1960 (Res. 1514 [XV]) marked the commitment of the Organization to bring colonialism to an end. For the most part this commitment has been expressed in resolutions condemning the remaining colonial powers and calling for action. In recent years there has been a shift to missions of inquiry, which produced reports of colonial behavior by states which were then condemned by the General Assembly and by the Security Council. We shall indicate below in Section IV what other means have been employed recently in anti-colonial conflicts.

4. CONFLICTS ARISING FROM RACISM

A fourth category is needed to cover the situations in South Africa and Rhodesia. Although they have not involved armed hostilities on a scale large enough to constitute civil wars, the opposition to the governments in both countries and the governmental counter-measures have resulted in sufficiently intense and widespread strife as to constitute "internal conflicts" relevant to the present survey. As perceived by a large majority of United Nations members, the conflicts are between the white minority and the black majority, which has been excluded from effective participation in government and deprived of basic rights and freedoms.[25] In contrast to its role in the kinds of internal conflicts described above, in the South African and Rhodesian cases the United Nations has taken sides in an explicit and vigorous manner. The policies and legislation of the two governments have been strongly condemned, there has been a series of resolutions demanding basic changes. Moreover, in recent years such demands have been formulated in peremptory language and have been asserted as obligatory on the basis of the Charter of the United Nations. The member states and the international organization itself have adopted a variety of sanctions on the basis of resolutions of the General Assembly and the Security Council (these will be referred to below in part IV). As in the case of the other internal conflicts dealt with, the United Nations organs have found that both

---

[24] See, e.g., Case No. 17, The Indonesian Question: I U.N. Repertory of Practice of United Nations Organs (1955), at paras. 273–308.

[25] For the situation in South Africa, see resolutions on Apartheid adopted at the General Assembly and at the Security Council, more recently: G.A. Res. 2671 (XXV), 8 Dec. 1970: 25 U.N. GAOR, Supp. 28, at 31; G.A. Res. 2764 (XXVI), 9 Nov. 1971; G.A. Res. 2775 (XXVI), 29 Nov. 1971; S.C. Res. 190 (1964), 9 June 1964, 191 (1964), 18 June 1964: 19 U.N. Resolutions and Decisions of the Security Council (1964), at 12, 13. For the situation in Southern Rhodesia, see resolutions adopted at the General Assembly and at the Security Council, more recently: G.A. Res. 2652 (XXV), 3 Dec. 1970: 25 U.N. GAOR, Supp. 28, at 6; G.A. Res. 2765 (XXVI), 16 Nov. 1971; G.A. Res. 2796 (XXVI), 10 Dec. 1971; S.C. Res. 277 (1970), 18 March 1970, 288 (1970), 17 Nov. 1970: 25 U.N. Resolutions and Decisions of the Security Council (1970), at 5, 7.

the South African and the Rhodesian cases are likely to endanger international peace; indeed they have gone beyond this in the sense of the Charter and have stressed in recent years that both situations involve a "threat" to the peace. (We need here to distinguish between the two cases as well as between the two organs.) The Security Council has made a Chapter VII finding based on threat to the peace in respect of Rhodesia and has adopted economic sanctions under Article 41.[26] However, the Security Council resolutions on South African apartheid have been taken under Chapter VI and in the Charter sense they are not mandatory.[27] The General Assembly has made findings of threat to the peace in both cases and has called on states and on the Security Council to take various sanctions against the governments. The finding that large-scale discrimination in these southern African countries threatened international peace rested, in large measure, on the conclusion that the racist and authoritarian practices were of legitimate concern to other African countries and that they might therefore provoke military action from without.[28] Though this has been strongly questioned by some as low in probability and as a pretext to demand sanctions, the Security Council and the General Assembly have continued by large majorities to incorporate the finding of a threat to the peace in their resolutions demanding the abrogation of the discriminatory policies of the two governments.

5. INTERNAL STRIFE INVOLVING MASSIVE SUFFERING OF NON-COMBATANTS

We have already referred to the civil wars in Nigeria and Pakistan. In both cases the internal conflict brought about suffering of non-combatants on a massive scale and, as a consequence, the United Nations and its associated agencies undertook relief activities while avoiding political involvement. (However, in regard to Pakistan, political involvement occurred as a result of the conflict with India in late 1971.)[29] In both cases the activities of the United Nations were carried out by or under the direction of the Secretary-General, and they involved in substantial measure the various agencies engaged in humanitarian work, in particular UNICEF, the High Commissioner for Refugees, the World Food Programme, and the World Health Organization. In the case of the Nigerian Civil War, the Secretary-General appointed a special representative to report on needs and to assist in relief and humanitarian tasks.[30] The consent of the Nigerian government was

[26] *See* resolutions of the Security Council adopted on Southern Rhodesia, *supra* note 25; Reports of the Security Council to the General Assembly, 1965–1970: 21–25 *U.N. GAOR*, Supp. 2.

[27] *See* resolutions of the Security Council adopted on *Apartheid*, *supra* note 25.

[28] McDougal & Reisman, "Rhodesia and the United Nations: The Lawfulness of International Concern," 62 *Am. J. Int'l L.* 1–19 (1968).

[29] *See supra* notes 8 and 23.

[30] *See* Introduction to the Annual Report of the Secretary-General on the Work of the Organization, Sept. 1968: 23 *U.N. GAOR*, Supp. 1A, paras. 199–204.

obtained for activities on both sides of the areas of hostility. In respect of East Pakistan, the Secretary-General designated the office of the High Commissioner for Refugees as the clearinghouse for assistance to Pakistani refugees in India, and appointed a mission for relief of the population of East Pakistan. The humanitarian relief efforts in East Pakistan were first offered by the Secretary-General to the President of Pakistan, and arrangements were then worked out in consultations between the Secretary-General's representatives and the Pakistani government. It was made clear that the humanitarian activities did not involve "peacekeeping" or "observers" for purposes of reporting on the conflict.[31] However, a separate submission by the Secretary-General was made to the President of the Security Council, suggesting that the Security Council might consider the East Pakistani hostilities as a potential threat to peace and security and that it should play a "more forthright role to mitigate the human tragedy which has taken place."[32] No action was taken by the Council at the time; the matter was only taken up after open warfare broke out between India and Pakistan.[33]

III. POLITICAL AND INSTITUTIONAL FACTORS THAT HAVE INFLUENCED UNITED NATIONS RESPONSES

In the previous section we indicated five categories of internal conflict that have led to action by United Nations organs, defining each category by that element in the situation which was seen by most member governments as the essential basis for international concern and United Nations involvement. Obviously, these elements are not the sole bases for United Nations decisions in regard to internal conflict. Whether or not the United Nations will take action, as well as the nature and scope of such action, will be determined by a variety of considerations that condition the behavior of the individual member states and the collective body. Any attempt to summarize these considerations would require far-reaching inquiry into the particular cases and into the determinants of foreign policy of the principal actors, a task clearly beyond the scope of this chapter. However, it is feasible to identify the considerations which are perceived by observers and participants as most clearly and directly influencing U.N. decisions about involvement:

1. The interest and position of the great powers;
2. Nationalism of the new states and of the "developing" countries;
3. The place of the regional organizations;

---

[31] For Secretary-General's statement on Pakistan, *see* 8 *U.N. Mon. Chron.* 56 (Aug.–Sept. 1971).

[32] *Id.* at 59.

[33] *See* notes 9 and 23 *supra*.

4. The constitutional and financial requirements of the United Nations;
5. Legal considerations;
6. Attitudes with respect to revolutionary movements and human rights.

1. THE INTEREST AND POSITION OF THE GREAT POWERS

That the great powers, particularly the United States and the Soviet Union, exercise a major and often decisive role in United Nations decision-making is sufficiently evident, but it may be useful to underline two aspects which are of particular relevance to internal conflicts. The first relates to the difference in zones of influence—in particular, the difference between those areas in which one or the other of the great powers exercises a measure of control or influence that is widely accepted by the international community (although sometimes contested) and the "Third World," in which a special role or security interest of the great powers is not claimed, or, if claimed, is not accepted by the other states concerned. It is principally in this area, outside the direct zone of influence of the two super-powers (and characterized by instability and fragility of governmental authority), that United Nations involvement has taken place in situations of internal strife.[34] Such involvement has been undertaken with the support (in varying degree) of the great powers and of the great majority of members. In contrast, the resistance of the great powers to U.N. intervention in states within their areas of "security interest" or in states closely allied with them has almost entirely barred significant U.N. action, though not debate or admonitory resolutions.

Another aspect of great-powers influence relates to the interest and, to some degree, to the commitment of the major powers to ideological objectives and to support of political and social systems which conform to such objectives. Although this aspect tends to be minimized in the statements of the major powers (and in fact may have diminished as an operative factor), there remains continuing evidence that these major powers tend to exercise their influence in respect of internal conflicts to further their basic ideological objectives or, at least, to prevent opposing elements from attaining power.[35] Carried into the arena of the United Nations, this has the effect

[34] See Introduction to the Annual Report of the Secretary-General on the Work of the Organization, 1959–1960: 15 *U.N. GAOR*, Supp. 1A, Ch. III; M. Kaplan & N. Katzenbach, *The Political Foundations of International Law* (1961), at 56–80, 341–54; E. McWhinney, *Peaceful Coexistence and Soviet-Western International Law* (1964).

[35] See Friedmann, "Intervention, Civil War and the Role of International Law," in I R. Falk (ed.), *The Vietnam War and International Law* (1968), at 151–59. See also statements by J.F. Kennedy and L. Brezhnev, quoted in Firmage, "Summary and Interpretation," in R. Falk, *supra* note 13, at 418–19; by President L.B. Johnson, in regard to Dominican case: 52 *Dep't State Bull.* 742–47 (1965); by Ambassador A. Stevenson, at the 1196th meeting of the Security Council, 3 May 1965: U.N. Doc. S/PV. 1196, at 16; by representatives of the U.S.S.R., in regard to Czechoslovakian

of bringing the internal political and social issues which are involved in internal strife to the forefront of consideration in international decision-making. Attainment of non-interference in internal political decisions—to which all give verbal deference—is complicated by divergent assessments of "non-interference" and by vigilance in checking or counteracting support by one side of its favored local elite group. There are obvious repercussions on the international machinery, as well as on the extent to which the United Nations influences domestic constitutional and political processes.

2. NATIONALISM OF THE NEW STATES AND OF THE DEVELOPING COUNTRIES

We observed at the beginning of this chapter that "sovereignty" or "national independence" constitutes a primary objective of the Charter and of the majority of United Nations members. In the present context, we would note that United Nations responses to internal conflict have reflected in various ways the sentiment and concerns of countries of the Third World in regard to their national independence, evident especially in the broad acceptance of the existing territorial integrity and national unity of member states. Demands for secession by regional or minority groups are virtually certain to be opposed by the great majority, even though the boundaries of the state in question are somewhat arbitrarily fixed by the former colonial power. It is clear enough that the threat of secession, though perhaps only faint at present, hangs over a great many of the new states, and that they regard it as of the highest importance to reinforce the existing state boundaries irrespective of the claims of separatist groups.[36]

Nationalist attitudes also manifest themselves in an emphasis on the consent of the territorial sovereign as a continuing requirement for any

---

case in 1968, in particular, Foreign Minister Gromyko, at the 1679th plenary meeting of the General Assembly, 3 Oct. 1968: U.N. Doc. A/PV. 1679, at 30–31, and Ambassador J. Malik, at the 1441st meeting of the Security Council, 21 Aug. 1968: U.N. Doc. S/PV. 1441, at 48–50. R. Falk has concluded that "no general framework of restraint is likely to operate successfully within 'spheres of influence' or, as I have called them, special zones of acknowledged unilateral prerogative." "Introduction," in R. Falk, *supra* note 13, at 19.

[36] At a press conference on Jan. 4, 1970, Secretary-General U Thant stated: "So, as far as the question of secession of a particular section of a Member State is concerned, the United Nations' attitude is unequivocal. As an international organization, the United Nations has never accepted and does not accept and I do not believe it will ever accept the principle of secession of a part of its [sic] Member State": 7 *U.N. Mon. Chron.* 36 (Feb. 1970). Also the Organization of African Unity, in a resolution approved by acclamation, declared that "all Member States pledge themselves to respect the borders existing on the achievement of national independence": O.A.U. Assembly Resolution AHG/res. 16 (I), 17021 July 1964. For conflicting views on issue of "secession" and dismemberment in a concrete setting, *see* debates on the question of East Pakistan at the Security Council, 2, 5 and 6 Dec. 1971: U.N. Docs. S/PV. 1606, S/PV. 1607, S/PV. 1608.

international action by independent states.[37] Such consent is held to be indispensable, irrespective of the danger to international peace (except of course where sanctions are taken, as in the cases of South Africa and Rhodesia). On the practical level this takes the form of insistence that international officials be acceptable to the host state and that specific functions and activities meet the host state's approval.

3. THE PLACE OF THE REGIONAL ORGANIZATIONS

In several of the cases of internal conflict brought before the United Nations the issue most explicitly discussed has been whether the case should be taken up by the United Nations or whether it should be retained by a regional organization. Regional bodies have dealt with some cases of civil conflict not formally brought to United Nations organs.

The controversial cases most extensively debated within the United Nations, concerned two situations involving both the Organization of American States and the Security Council—namely, the Guatemalan case of 1954 and the Dominican Republic of 1965. In the Guatemalan case, the government brought to the Security Council charges of external support for right-wing rebels by the United States and other countries, but the United States pressed for prior consideration by the O.A.S. (while the U.S.S.R. urged priority by the Council) and the Council, by its lack of decision, in the end left the matter to the regional body.[38] The Dominican Republic situation of 1965 revealed a similar difference btween the U.S. and Soviet positions as to the role of the O.A.S. but the Security Council adopted a resolution for a cease-fire and for a U.N. mission headed by a representative of the Secretary-General.[39] At the same time, the O.A.S. had a peace mission, and both missions sought to achieve a cease-fire. A controversial issue as to the necessity under Article 53 of Security Council authorization for an O.A.S. peace force (which was charged by the U.S.S.R. and others with intervention against the anti-government forces) did not produce a Council resolution, the big powers sharply diverging and the rest of the Council divided.[40] Central to this issue and to other aspects of the Dominican case were charges that the O.A.S. was dominated by the United States and was therefore not in a position to deal impartially and effectively with a conflict in which the United States had intervened on one side.[41]

[37] P. Manin, *L'Organisation Des Nations Unies et Le Maintien de la Paix, Le Respect Du Consentement De L'Etat* (1971).

[38] See Report of the Security Council to the General Assembly, 1953–1954: 9 *U.N. GAOR*, Supp. 2, Ch. 4.

[39] See Report of the Security Council to the General Assembly, 1964–1965: 20 *U.N. GAOR*, Supp. 2, Ch. 8-H; S.C. res. 203 (1965), 15 May 1965: 20 *U.N. Resolutions and Decisions of the Security Council* (1965), at 10.

[40] See Report of the Security Council to the General Assembly 1964–1965: 20 *U.N. GAOR*, Supp. 2, Ch. 8-S.

[41] See J. Slater, *supra* note 19, and Nanda, "The United States' Action in the 1965 Dominican Crisis," 43 *Denver L. Rev.* 439–79 (1966), 44 *Denver L. Rev.* 225–

The situation was substantially different from African conflicts. Prevailing sentiment favored priority for the Organization of African Unity (O.A.U.) in dealing with the settlement and diminution of armed conflict. In the large-scale civil war in Nigeria, the O.A.U. assumed a diplomatic role, seeking a peaceful solution without departing from the objective of national unity and territorial integrity.[42] The Secretary-General of the United Nations encouraged the O.A.U. in its mediatory role, while he took steps to provide relief in the areas of conflict.[43] No formal action was ever taken by any state to place the Nigerian Civil War on the agenda of the General Assembly or of the Security Council.[44]

In December 1964, the Security Council considered situations involving internal disorder in the Congo (and rescue operations by Belgium with support of the United States in Stanleyville), and the resolution adopted unanimously endorsed the principle that the O.A.U. had responsibility to seek solutions in situations affecting peace and security in Africa.[45] The O.A.U. was requested to keep the Council informed and the U.N. Secretary-General was also asked to follow the situation and report to the Council.

Other examples in respect of African situations can be cited as conforming to the policy "try O.A.U. first," while recognizing that the Secretary-General of the United Nations should have an observational and reporting function as he considers appropriate.[46]

In addition to the cases handled by the O.A.S. and the O.A.U., there have been several other regional bodies concerned with internal conflicts and in some cases playing an important role in their elimination. In some of these cases, as in the O.A.S., the role of a major power was the predominant feature and that major power objected to involvement of the United Nations, although not always with sufficient support to preclude discussion in the United Nations.[47] In the Cyprus case, efforts to settle the conflict through NATO did not succeed and United Nations peacekeeping forces

---

74 (1967). For an interesting analysis of the role of regional organizations in regard to world order, *see* Moore, "The Role of Regional Arrangements in the Maintenance of World Order," in III Black & Falk, *supra* note 1, at 122.

[42] O.A.U. Assembly resolution AHG/res. 51 (IV), 11–14 Sept. 1967; *id.*, AHG/res. 54 (IV), 13–16 Sept. 1968. See also B. Andemicael, *supra* note 21.

[43] *See* Introduction to the Annual Report of the Secretary-General on the Work of the Organization, Sept. 1968: 23 *U.N. GAOR*, Supp. 1A, paras. 201–3.

[44] At a press conference on April 17, 1969, the United Nations Secretary-General expressed the view that any attempt by a Member State to bring the Nigerian question before the Security Council or the General Assembly would not succeed because of the knowledge that the Organization of African Unity was against the inscription of this question on the agenda of these organs: 6 *U.N. Mon. Chron.* 79 (May 1969). *See also* 5 *U.N. Mon. Chron.* 49 (Oct. 1968); 6 *U.N. Mon. Chron.* 46 (Oct. 1969).

[45] *See* S.C. Res. 199 (1964), 30 Dec. 1964: 19 *U.N. Resolutions and Decisions of the Security Council* (1964), at 18.

[46] *See* B. Andemicael, *supra* note 21, Pt. F, § 1.

[47] Wood & Morales, "Latin America and the United Nations," in N. Padelford & L. Goodrich (eds.), *The United Nations in the Balance: Accomplishments and Prospects* (1965).

and conciliation were used.[48] In regard to the Czechoslovakian situation of 1968, the U.N. Security Council discussed the complaint of the Government of Czechoslovakia, but a resolution was vetoed, and no further action was taken.[49] That case is an example of the point made above, regarding the zone of influence of a great power.

4. THE CONSTITUTIONAL AND FINANCIAL REQUIREMENTS OF THE UNITED NATIONS

For the present purposes, it should be sufficient to indicate briefly some of the considerations under this broad heading which have affected United Nations actions.

In keeping with the Charter provision affirming the primary responsibility of the Security Council for matters of international peace and security, most cases of internal conflict have been referred to the Security Council whether for purposes of investigation, peaceful settlement, or peacekeeping. One consequence has been the need for unanimity of the permanent members and, related to that, the formulation of action to reflect the views of all elements represented in the Council.

The requirement of consent of the territorial state (except for cases of enforcement action under Chapter VII) has been applied to all U.N. involvement in internal strife.[50] This has profoundly affected the decision as to involvement and the actions taken to carry out the decision.

The role of the Secretary-General in serving as a channel of communication, in providing information, and in serving as an instrument of conciliation and good offices has been a significant element in U.N. action. The question of his leadership in the command and control of peacekeeping forces has been controversial, which has limited, but not precluded, authorization of such forces.[51]

The requirement of substantial financial support for large-scale U.N. action, particularly peacekeeping, has served to restrain action and to render agreed action uncertain. Although this requirement has been linked to the constitutional controversy about the role of the Security Council, it also reflects the pressures on member states to avoid large-scale expenditures for international purposes, especially when they are determined by a majority of states rather than by the principal contributing governments.[52]

[48] For an account of efforts under the NATO auspices, *see* P. Windsor, *Nato and the Cyprus Crisis* (Inst. for Strategic Studies, Adelphi paper 14, 1964). For U.N. history, *see* L. Miller, *supra* note 19, 116–48.

[49] *See* Report of the Security Council to the General Assembly, 1968–1969: 24 *U.N. GAOR*, Supp. 2, Ch. 3.

[50] For a comprehensive treatment of the requirement of consent, *see* P. Manin, *supra* note 37.

[51] *See* Annual Report of the Secretary-General on the Work of the Organization, 1969–1970: 25 *U.N. GAOR*, Supp. 1, Ch. III; *ibid.*, 1970–1971: 26 *U.N. GAOR*, Supp. 1, Ch. III. *See also Report of the Special Committee on Peace-keeping Operations*, 1 Oct. 1970: U.N. Doc. A/8081; *id.*, 3 Dec. 1971: U.N. Doc. A/8550.

[52] *See* J. Stoessinger, *Financing the United Nations System* (1964).

5. LEGAL CONSIDERATIONS

One cannot exclude from the various factors affecting governmental decisions on U.N. involvement the legal concepts and principles generally accepted by U.N. members. Even though the actions of governments may be assumed to be motivated by considerations of political self-interest, the decisions need to be justified in terms of generally accepted juridical conceptions and precedents compatible with those conceptions. Despite divergencies on many issues, there are some well-established principles and rules as to what is permissible and what is not in respect of United Nations involvement, and these inevitably influence governments' expectations.

The question of the permissibility of United Nations involvement has already been touched on in our introductory remarks and indirectly in our discussion of U.N. purposes and the criteria for determining that an internal conflict is not within the reserved domain of domestic jurisdiction. A restatement in more precise juridical terms may be appropriate at this point.

Article 2(7) prohibits "intervention" but not all actions or decisions of the United Nations in regard to domestic matters. Merely discussion by a U.N. organ of an internal matter or placement of a case or situation on the agenda of an organ is not considered "intervention" (in this sense).[53] Nor is the adoption by a U.N. organ of a resolution addressed to all members or all states on a matter which is regarded as within the domestic jurisdiction of a state.[54]

On the other hand, the meaning of "intervention" cannot be restricted to "forcible" interference by the United Nations (albeit that view has been taken by some scholars). Such "forcible" intervention may be taken only as enforcement measures under Chapter VII of the Charter, yet it is precisely those enforcement measures which are excepted from the prohibition of Article 2(7). Obviously, the exception cannot be coterminous with the application of the rule. Accordingly, the concept of intervention must be extended to acts of the United Nations which fall short of enforcement action. As commonly construed, "intervention," for the purposes of Article 2(7), would occur if an organ passed a recommendatory resolution addressed to a particular state (or identifiable group of states), urging that state to change its policy in a matter regarded as domestic. To see this clearly, we should recall that United Nations organs do adopt a large number of resolutions recommending that states adopt measures or policies relating to matters that are regarded as internal. Examples range from matters of social defense (treatment of criminals, for example) to economic policy, such as measures relating to full employment and domestic savings.

[53] L. Goodrich, E. Hambro *and* A. Simons, *Charter of the United Nations* 67 (3rd ed. 1969); R. Higgins, *supra* note 2, at 69–70.

[54] Resolution of the Institut de Droit International, 29 April 1954, "concernant la determination du domaine reserve et ses effets," Article 5, *Annuaire de L'Institut de Droit International* (1954), at 192.

As long as these recommendations are general, they raise no question of intervention. If they were to single out a particular state and urge that state to adopt the recommended policy, it can be maintained that the resolution would be "intervention" within the meaning of Article 2(7). This appears to be a widely-held opinion of governments and scholars.[55]

It must be remembered that the "intervention" issue arises only if the matter is held to be domestic. If it is not, then the restriction of Article 2(7) does not apply. As our previous discussion indicated, the practice of United Nations organs has been consonant with the conclusion that at least three types of internal conflict are not to be regarded as essentially domestic: (1) conflicts which appear to endanger international peace and security, (2) conflicts between the peoples of a non-self-governing territory and the administering power, and (3) conflicts involving a large-scale deprivation of basic human rights of a distinct racial, ethnic, or national group within the country. In addition, it has been maintained that a situation is no longer essentially domestic when international obligations, whether in treaty or customary law, have been violated.[56]

If the internal conflicts involved any of these situations, they would no longer be regarded as essentially domestic matters, and in principle there would be no barrier to intervention. Does this then mean that any measure of intervention is permitted? It would be difficult to go that far, for other legal principles of the Charter remain applicable. On the basis of practice and attitudes, it can be said that, when an internal conflict is no longer an essentially domestic matter, the competent U.N. organ may intervene by: (1) making recommendations to the government involved, to other parties to the conflict, and to third states; (2) offering the parties good offices or other pacific means of settlement; (3) with the consent of the government of the state concerned, placing observers or peacekeeping police forces on the territory of the state; (4) providing assistance of a humanitarian character in agreement with the government; and (5) adopting enforcement measures (or provisional measures) under Chapter VII when the organ considers that the situation involves a threat to or a breach of the peace or an act of aggression.

Are there legal restrictions on the United Nations in regard to the exercise of the measures just mentioned? In principle, the answer is clear enough. The U.N. organs are bound by the Charter, especially by the purposes and principles of Articles 1 and 2. Thus, the above list of permissible types of intervention is not intended to suggest that the Charter permits

---

[55] I *U.N. Repertory of Practice of United Nations Organs* (1955), on Article 2 (7), paras. 358–62. *See also* A. Ross, *Constitution of the United Nations* 127 (1950); Q. Wright, *International Law and the United Nations* (1960).

[56] I *U.N. Repertory of Practice of United Nations Organs* (1955), on Article 2 (7), paras. 391–406. In the advisory opinion on *The Interpretation of Peace Treaties*, the International Court of Justice declared that a question involving the terms of a treaty cannot be considered as essentially within the domestic jurisdiction of a state: [1950] I.C.J. 601.

carte blanche in these situations. It would, for example, be highly dubious from a legal standpoint for a United Nations body to employ force or use other kinds of pressure—even with the consent of the de jure government—to deprive the people of a state of their political independence. Thus, it can be maintained that the invitation or agreement of an established government cannot legitimize the use of U.N. personnel to suppress an insurrection by the people (or a large section of the people), at least in cases where that insurrection has not received substantial foreign assistance. Nor would it seem to be proper for U.N. agents (whether national officials or international personnel) to use other pressures to bring about the victory of one faction or another in an internal conflict or to determine the internal policies of that state. One might formulate the underlying policy in the terms of the first principle of Article 2—namely, that the Organization is based on the principle of sovereign equality of all members. This may be reinforced by other basic concepts of the Charter which support the political independence of states and the basic human rights of the people. An intervention by or under the aegis of the United Nations which is aimed at, or has the effect of, depriving the people of a country from freely choosing their government or adopting their constitutional, economic, and social arrangements should be regarded as incompatible with the basic tenets of the Charter.[57] The fact that a de jure government has requested or has agreed to such intervention does not make it less so.

6. ATTITUDES WITH RESPECT TO REVOLUTIONARY MOVEMENTS
AND HUMAN RIGHTS

It is clear that many, if not most, of the internal conflicts that have come before the United Nations or that are likely to arise in the future involve demands for far-reaching changes in the existing political structure, in the governing elites, and in the economic and social system. Others are more specifically focused on human rights issues, such as opposition to race discrimination, colonialism, or other forms of alien rule. Sympathies for these objectives or the contrary obviously influence the decisions of the individual governments and the collective actions of U.N. organs. The large number of member states which formerly were colonial areas and the even larger number of non-white members give a high priority to U.N. action against colonialism (or what is considered neo-colonialism) and race discrimination. Such U.N. action is consequently directed against the authorities in power (as in South Africa and Rhodesia).

On the other hand, the divergence in views about revolutionary demands —evident among the third-world states as well as between East and West— results in a tendency toward a more restrained and nonpartisan approach to

[57] See G.A. Res. 2625 (XXV), supra note 9, in particular sections on "The principle of sovereign equality of States" and "The principle of equal rights and self-determination of peoples."

domestic conflicts involving social and class antagonism. This tendency is further enforced by the necessity for agreement by the major powers, which often have opposing views on the internal conflict. What they share is an interest in preventing the internationalization of domestic strife, with its danger of escalation and widespread hostilities on a large scale. Their fear of total war tends to counteract the ideological pull toward military involvement in local wars, and it provides in propitious circumstances (though not always) a basis for an "uncommitted" role by the United Nations.

IV. WAYS AND MEANS OF EXERCISING UNITED NATIONS INFLUENCE IN INTERNAL CONFLICTS

Our discussion up to now has touched on several of the types of U.N. involvement in situations of domestic strife. However, a more comprehensive and explicit examination is needed for an adequate understanding of the actual and potential role of the Organization. The attention given to the more dramatic actions, such as providing peacekeeping forces and economic boycotts, is understandable, but it tends to obscure the range and flexibility of collective action that can be taken by the United Nations or under its aegis. In particular, there is a tendency (perhaps more characteristic of academic observers than of participants) to overlook or minimize processes which involve more subtle and indirect forms of persuasion rather than assertions of authority and displays of force. The latter are more controversial and in that sense more interesting; they also lend themselves more easily to description and evaluation. But in the present state of international affairs, they may be less significant and effective than the relatively non-controversial instrumentalities available to the United Nations. One should bear in mind that the diverse ways and means of U.N. action are not generally exclusive but rather complementary and often interrelated. Moreover, their efficacy in particular cases is not easily determined, for their specific effect is but one element among the many which influence the behavior and attitudes of the parties. To apply to them criteria of effectiveness based on their direct and ascertainable impact (such as one might do with municipal judicial decisions) would be entirely inappropriate and misleading in many instances. The fact that ratings cannot be bestowed on the basis of past experience should not imply that they have not played a significant role or that they may not be used effectively in the future.

We shall distinguish and comment on ten different ways and means for the United Nations to play a role in those internal conflicts which have been determined to be of international concern:

1. Public debate and the expression of international concern;
2. Quiet diplomacy, good offices, and conciliation;
3. Inquiry and reporting;
4. Assistance in ascertaining the "will of the people";

5. On-the-spot observation and surveillance;
6. Consensual peacekeeping and policing;
7. Economic assistance and technical cooperation;
8. Determination of governments entitled to representation in the United Nations;
9. Sanctions and enforcement measures;
10. The elaboration of norms and criteria of conduct.

1. PUBLIC DEBATE AND THE EXPRESSION OF INTERNATIONAL CONCERN

However one may minimize the effect of debate in the United Nations, it is apparent that bringing an internal conflict before the United Nations is generally regarded as a step of great consequence by the participants directly concerned. In fact, the record indicates that the most bitterly-fought issue in many cases was whether the case should be placed on the agenda of the General Assembly or of the Security Council, along with the related questions as to the scope and nature of the discussion.[58] Even when a case is not formally placed on the agenda, discussions of the conflict in, say, the general debates of the Assembly or as a preliminary issue of competence are often regarded by participants as important ways of influencing the parties directly or indirectly. The fact that discussion is taken seriously is not, of course, proof that the results are always important or that they are always productive of restraint and moderation. A propaganda debate may only harden positions and exacerbate emotions. A multiplicity of views or sharp divergencies may weaken a sense of international concern.

On the other hand, it is often apparent that the principal tendency in the debates is to assert a strong international interest in restraint and moderation on the part of the contending groups. This is evidenced in the resolutions urging the parties to seek a solution or to abstain from hostilities and also stressing the necessity for abstention by foreign states or groups. Whether or not the international concern is expressed in debate only or in resolutions as well, it can be assumed that its expression will to some degree affect the perceptions of national policy-makers, who will be interested as a rule in the attitudes of other governments as to the legitimacy and propriety of an action; strong support for one side or a movement for impartial conciliation by a number of states will almost certainly influence the positions of others in the same direction. Moreover, experience has shown that what is said in the U.N. forums may enter into domestic political discussion, within both the state where the conflict exists and other states which may be indirectly concerned. This is perhaps especially significant when it brings to the forefront criticisms of national policy that would otherwise be absent

---

[58] Examples of controversies on the propriety of United Nations discussion range from the early cases concerning Greece and Indonesia, through those of Guatemala, Algeria, and Hungary (in the 1950's) to the more recent conflicts in Nigeria, Vietnam, and Pakistan.

or subdued within a state. This may contribute to basic changes in attitudes of influential groups or individuals who normally would not question the line of their own or another government. Even when there seems to be no immediate impact, one may discern at times a transformation of governmental attitudes over a period of time that seems to take account of the earlier criticism. The fact that this cannot be conclusively demonstrated is not sufficient reason to dismiss it. One of the striking characteristics of our time has been the way in which powerful governments and those less powerful have suddenly changed their positions on major foreign policy issues. What seemed completely impossible one day became inevitable the next; and at least in some cases the change appeared consonant with the criticism expressed in the United Nations forums.[59]

2. QUIET DIPLOMACY, GOOD OFFICES, AND CONCILIATION

The use of quiet diplomacy to ameliorate the effects of internal conflict or to promote settlement has been a feature of most of the cases that have come before the United Nations. The provision of Article 2(7) that nothing in the Charter shall require a member to submit domestic matters to settlement under the Charter has not precluded attempts at settlement of some internal disputes. For, even apart from the question of whether such disputes were "essentially" domestic (a doubtful inference where international peace was regarded as likely to be endangered), the procedures for settlement in those cases were premised on the voluntary agreement of the governments concerned. By giving its consent to such procedures, even if only implicitly, the government directly concerned recognized the legitimacy of the United Nations interest.

The instrumentalities for quiet diplomacy at the United Nations have been varied, though precedents have evidently been useful in choosing the mechanism and the modalities to be followed. In several cases of internal conflict, conciliation commissions composed of governmental representatives were established by the General Assembly or the Security Council (as in the Congo or, earlier, in regard to apartheid in South Africa); in other cases, as in Cyprus or the Dominican Republic, a single individual of high prestige was entrusted with the task of mediation or conciliation.[60] The

---

[59] It is not necessary to assert a direct causal relationship to support a conclusion that "public diplomacy" may have an influence on the positions of Governments. For relevant case studies, see those by Fraleigh, "The Algerian Revolution as a Case Study in International Law," and Corbett, "The Vietnam Struggle and International Law," in Falk, supra note 13. See also Alger, "Non-Resolution Consequences of the United Nations and their Effects on International Conflict," 5 J. Conflict Resolution 127–45 (June 1961); Hoffman, "An Evaluation of the United Nations," in III R. Falk & S. Mendlovitz (eds.), The Strategy of World Order 793, 809–15 (1966); T. Franck & E. Weisband, World Politics (1971), Ch. 6, 8.

[60] See 2 U.N. Repertory of Practice of United Nations Organs (1955), at 195. Other cases include Kashmir, Thailand-Cambodia, Laos, and the Middle East. For documentation and commentary, see I–II R. Higgins, U.N. Peace-Keeping, 1946– 1967: Documents and Commentary v. I (The Middle East) and v. II (Asia) (1969, 1971). See also O. Young, The Intermediaries 9–115 (1967).

Secretary-General himself has played an important "good-offices" role, acting on his own initiative but with the consent of the parties or at the request of one of the political organs.[61] There have also been instances in which representatives at the United Nations have similarly played a role in non-publicized efforts to bring about restraint or cessation of hostilities. Such voluntary friendly intercessions by delegates have occurred in most conflict situations, whether internal or external. The opportunities for such intercessions are available in the United Nations more frequently and often more conveniently than in bilateral diplomatic relationship.

One problem that is presented in internal conflicts arises from the non-recognized character of one or more of the parties to the conflict. These may be leaders of rebellious groups, authorities exercising de facto control of a region, or rival claimants to central government authority who have not been recognized by, or have been recognized by very few, other states. In some cases, there may be reasons to deal with the leader of a particular political organization within the territory of one of the parties or with an outside non-governmental personality. The propriety of dealing with such non-official individuals or de facto authority is often contested because it is assumed that their status and authority will be enhanced or recognized as a consequence of such dealing. United Nations practice contains a number of cases in which third-party mediators (used in the sense) have engaged in formal consultations and even negotiation with persons other than the generally recognized de jure officials. At times it has been considered desirable to state explicitly that such relationships do not imply recognition or acknowledgment of official status. The willingness of mediators to consult with non-official bodies or their leaders has probably been facilitated by the practice of the General Assembly and the Security Council of receiving statements of non-governmental leaders or non-recognized authorities with the understanding that that involves no implications as to recognition.

An even more troublesome question that is often presented in settlement efforts relating to internal conflict is the extent to which the United Nations body or representative should espouse the acceptance of arrangements in conformity with United Nations aims and principles, particularly human rights as expressed in the Declaration and other United Nations resolutions. While recognizing that constitutional and other domestic provisions were to be settled by the country, U.N. representatives and commissions have considered it appropriate to present proposals which embodied fundamental human rights (as, for example, in the Congo and Cyprus). This has been put in the following way by Pechota in his study of peaceful settlement within the United Nations:

---

[61] *See* V. Pechota, *The Good Offices of the Secretary-General* (UNITAR Study, 1972). *See also* A. Rovine, *The First Fifty Years: The Secretary-General in World Politics 1920–1970* 271–463 (1970); Zacher, "The Secretary-General and the United Nations Functions of Peaceful Settlement," 20 *Int'l. Org.* 724–49 (1966).

The parties are expected to accept as part of the mediator's role his concern with the protection of values which are shared by members of the community on whose behalf he is acting. They are also expected to recognize the legitimacy of his initiatives in proposing common grounds for agreement which may not necessarily lie in the intersection of the parties' interests but may be to a great extent determined by the community interest as perceived by the mediator. In the same way the parties are expected . . . to tip the scales within decision-making circles in favor of attitudes compatible with the community interest.[62]

Pechota observes also that while agreement of the contestants remains the objective, the mediator may use "community values to fill the vacuum created by the absence of a common ground between the parties."

3. INQUIRY AND REPORTING

A common and, one might say, characteristic response of the United Nations to cases of internal conflict has been to institute an inquiry by a subsidiary body or, in some cases, by the Secretary-General (or his representative). Such inquiries (called at times "investigations" or "observations") were undertaken in nearly every case in which charges of external involvement (subversion or support of armed rebels) were lodged; examples include the Greek Case (1946–47), Hungary (1956), Lebanon (1958), Laos (1959), Yemen (1963–64), Dominican Republic (1965), Guinea (1970).[63] Although such inquiries involved some form of fact-finding, their political function was rather more complicated than simply ascertaining the facts. In some cases the international inquiries were seen as means of deterring or restraining activities carried out by external groups, in other cases they served to highlight elements in past events which were seen as violations of the Charter or of human rights, and in still others they were instituted as part of the means employed to facilitate conciliation or settlement. The mere institution of an investigation or inquiry was perceived in some cases as detrimental to one side or beneficial to the other. Problems of the composition of the group of inquiry or the character of the individuals delegated to carry out the inquiry were almost always issues of major concern because they had a vital bearing on whether the parties would accept the inquiry.

When such fact-finding inquiries were to be undertaken on the spot, it has been taken for granted that the consent of the de jure government was

---

[62] See V. Pechota, *Complementary Structures of Third-Party Settlement of International Disputes* 28–29 (UNITAR Study, 1971). *See also* O. Young, *supra* note 60, at 116–56.

[63] See the Report of the Secretary-General on methods of fact-finding, 1 May 1964: 20 *U.N. GAOR*, Annexes, agenda items 90 and 94, U.N. Doc. A/5694; D. Wainhouse, *International Peace Observation* (1966); R. Gardner, *In Pursuit of World Order* 84–102 (1964).

necessary;[64] in some cases the agreement of the opposing force was also regarded as essential to practical effectiveness; in one case at least, the investigation was instituted by the General Assembly over the opposition of the government concerned, and that government (as expected) refused entry to the special committee set up by the Assembly. The committee carried out its inquiry outside of the country by examining witnesses of the events as well as by studying relevant documentation.[65] Its report was endorsed by the General Assembly and that body then named a Special Representative who reported to the General Assembly for a few years (1958–63) on the situation despite the opposition of the government. In another case the Security Council and the General Assembly agreed on the establishment of a subcommittee to conduct inquiries though the State concerned, a colonial power, did not consent to the inquiry and refused it entry.[66]

It is difficult to dispute the general feeling that more and better fact-finding by the United Nations may be important in internal conflicts, but this sentiment requires more scrutiny before it can be a basis for precise recommendations. Examples of the success of expert fact-determinations in regard to minor border incidents or in cases of state responsibility for injuries have little if any relevance to the situations under consideration here. In situations of violent conflict between contending factions for governmental authority or involving a threatened secession, fact-finding, no matter how authoritative, can have little significance for bringing the conflict to an end. It may, however, serve as a means for disclosing subversion and perhaps for discouraging such foreign involvements. While this may appear to be best carried out by experts acting in their personal capacity, there is much to be said in favor of a body that carries with it the weight and authority of governments which can exercise influence on the participants. In some situations, the effective mechanism has been the Secretary-General of the United Nations, who with the acquiescence, if not the consent, of major governments can move with dispatch through special representatives or his permanent staff. Constitutional controversies as to the authority of the Secretary-General to institute investigations in matters affecting international peace and security have not precluded such initiatives in the past and most members appear to consider such initiatives as legitimate, particularly on the basis of Article 99 of the Charter.[67] Moreover, the advantages of a

[64] See P. Manin, supra note 37; W. Shore, Fact-Finding in the Maintenance of International Peace (1970).

[65] Interim Report of the Special Committee on the Problem of Hungary, 20 Feb. 1957: 11 U.N. GAOR, Annexes, agenda item 67, U.N. Doc. A/3546; Report of the Special Committee on the Problem of Hungary, 1957: 11 U.N. GAOR, Supp. 18.

[66] Report of the Sub-Committee on the Situation in Angola, 20 Nov. 1961: 16 U.N. GAOR, Supp. 16; id., 14 Nov. 1962: 17 U.N. GAOR, Annexes, Addendum to agenda item 29, U.N. Doc. A/5286.

[67] For criticism of the Secretary-General, see letter, 3 April 1970, from the representative of the U.S.S.R. and reply, 6 April 1970, from the Secretary-General: 25 U.N. SCOR, Supp. April–June 1970, Docs. S/9737 and S/9738. See also statement by the representative of the U.S.S.R., at the 1247th meeting of the Security Council,

large and permanent multinational secretariat with offices in nearly every country of the globe are considerable. Its continuing day-to-day links with the governments of most countries and the relative ease with which consultative or supervisory intergovernmental bodies can be set up are of much greater value than many outside observers recognize. Proposals for creating new permanent fact-finding machinery have not been acceptable and, on the whole, they seem to offer few advantages in comparison with the existing facilities and the potential use of the existing organs and secretariat of the United Nations.

4. ASSISTANCE IN ASCERTAINING THE "WILL OF THE PEOPLE"

A special case of inquiry and fact-finding that is of particular relevance for internal conflict occurs when United Nations organs take part, in one form or another, in the determination of the wishes of the people concerned. This role has been carried out principally in regard to colonial territories which were to be given their independence, and where it was agreed that a United Nations group was either to conduct a plebiscite or supervise the carrying out of a plebiscite by the local authorities. Instances of this occurred in respect to Togo, Cameroon, Rwanda, Burundi, West Irian, and the Cook Islands.[68] Two variants of this role also merit some further attention even though they relate to disputes which did not erupt into violence.

In one case, the Secretary-General was called upon, pursuant to an agreement of the governments of Malaya, Indonesia, and the Philippines (the Manila Accord of August 1963), by the three governments to ascertain the wishes of the people of Sabah (Northern Borneo) and Sarawak with regard to their affiliation with the proposed Federation of Malaysia. In particular, the Secretary-General was to ascertain whether recent elections held under British authority (as the colonial power) had involved the issue of Malaysia and was so understood by the electorate, whether the elections were freely and properly conducted, the registers properly compiled, and the votes properly polled and counted.[69] The team sent by the Secretary-General answered these points in the affirmative, after they had carried out a survey in the territories that included consultation with several hundred persons of all ethnic, religious, and social groups, including a number of people opposed to the Federation of Malaysia (the side which lost the election).[70] Observers from the two governments opposed to the

---

25 Oct. 1965: 20 *U.N. SCOR*, 1247th meeting. Approval of investigation by the Secretary-General was expressed as early as 1946. *See* 1 *U.N. SCOR*, 70th meeting (20 Sept. 1946). For another statement, *see* letter from the representative of Argentina, 30 Sept. 1966: 21 *U.N. SCOR*, Supp. Oct.–Dec. 1966, Doc. S/7522.

[68] A. Papisca, *L'Intervento Delle Nazioni Unite Nelle Consultazioni Popolari* (1969).

[69] *See* Annual Report of the Secretary-General on the Work of the Organization, 1963–1964: 19 *U.N. GAOR*, Supp. 1, Ch. II–14.

[70] Report of the U.N. Malaysia Mission: *U.N. UNST SG* (063.5) M2.

proposed federation, Indonesia and the Philippines, participated in the observation of the mission (but under some restriction). The conclusions of the Secretary-General were generally accepted and given credence, though the two opposing governments rejected the findings on the ground that the mission had been restricted by the British authorities in their "ascertainment" and had prepared its survey in haste.[71] Most independent observers, however, supported the objectivity and impartiality of the mission and gave credence to its findings.[72]

The second case concerned Bahrain, in respect of which a longstanding dispute between the United Kingdom and Iran was in the process of settlement. Both states asked the Secretary-General to exercise his good offices to determine the wishes of the people of Bahrain.[73] The Secretary-General through a senior official of the Secretariat (the Director-General of the European Office) proceeded to consult organizations, institutions, and leaders of opinion in Bahrain and to receive testimony from interested persons. The report of the Special Representative concluded that the great majority of the people favored an independent sovereign state.[74] When objection was raised by the U.S.S.R. against the Secretary-General's undertaking this task simply at the request of two governments without the authorization of the Security Council, the Secretary-General replied that there were precedents for such good-offices missions undertaken at the request of governments, often in confidence, and that in the Bahrain case "the facts will be represented to the Security Council in the form of a report from the Secretary-General. Any substantive action would be taken at that time and only by the Security Council."[75] In the event, the Security Council endorsed the result.[76]

Although these cases are of interest, we should point out that the role of the United Nations in explicitly ascertaining the will of the people as to their future status or government has actually never been carried out in internal conflicts involving large-scale violence within a state. The experience to date has been in respect of situations where conflict has been of much less intensity. (In the Congo, vigorous efforts were made on more than one occasion to encourage leaders of various groups, elected or otherwise, to establish constitutional machinery for representative government, but this

[71] See 18 *U.N. GAOR* 1219th meeting (27 Sept. 1963); *id.*, 1221st meeting (30 Sept. 1963).

[72] Kahin, "Malaysia and Indonesia," 37 *Pac. Aff.* 268 (1964); Starner, "Malaysia and the North Borneo Territories," 3 *Asian Surv.* 533 (1963).

[73] See note from the Secretary-General, 28 March 1970: 25 *U.N. SCOR*, Supp. Jan.–March 1970, Doc. S/9726.

[74] See Report by the Personal Representative of the Secretary-General in Bahrain, 30 April 1970: 25 *U.N. SCOR*, Supp. April–June 1970, U.N. Doc. S/9772.

[75] See U.N. Docs. S/9737 and S/9738, *supra* note 67.

[76] See 1536th meeting of the Security Council, 11 May 1970: U.N. Doc. S/PV. 1536. For a useful note on the Bahrain case, *see* Gordon, "Resolution of the Bahrain dispute," 65 *Am. J. Int'l L.* 560–68 (1971).

did not extend beyond that to a role in respect of the elections.)[77] This fact underlines the difficulties in utilizing the United Nations to help in ascertaining the wishes of the people in situations involving deep and protracted struggles for power or secessionist movements. Nonetheless, it is often observed there may well be occasions in which the termination of a civil war would be facilitated by agreement for United Nations observance or supervision of elections to be held. A role of this kind seems more likely where the conflict has already been settled, but one cannot exclude the possible use of international machinery at an earlier stage of a conflict where the parties see that it would be in their interest to have recourse to plebiscites or elections under international auspices. Plebiscites or elections are, of course, not the only modalities. In some circumstances, the most appropriate and practicable means of ascertaining the wishes of the community would be through consultation of groups or use of traditional procedures. The variety of United Nations experience in this field suggests that diverse means and techniques must be employed to meet different situations, and that a fixed formula for such activities may not work in many situations.

5. ON-THE-SPOT OBSERVATION AND SURVEILLANCE

Military observers have been used by the United Nations in a number of disputes and situations which have included internal conflicts. While such "military observation" is sometimes placed under the general heading of fact-finding or inquiry, it has several distinctive features which make it more useful to deal with as a separate instrument. It is also desirable in this context to distinguish such observation from the peacekeeping activities (to be discussed below) which involve the use of limited force for policing purposes.

The most common example of United Nations observation in the present sense is that undertaken for the supervision or surveillance of a cease-fire truce or armistice arrangement.[78] Such observation may be closely linked in function and presence to cease-fire or demarcation lines. It might also involve a more difficult observation or a combination of both. A somewhat different function of military observation (independently of truce arrangements) is surveillance to detect infiltration of armed bands or their support by external forces. This may be done on a continuing basis or on a more limited basis to check on charges of indirect aggression. A related though separate type is military surveillance to check on the movement of arms, or a particular class of arms, where that has been prohibited, as in a demilitarized zone.

Observation, of course, involves reporting and disclosure. Subsidiary functions may involve aid in determining demarcation lines, arranging for

---

[77] See D. McNemar, supra note 18.

[78] For detailed accounts of U.N. observations activities, see the valuable collection of documents and accompanying commentary by Higgins, supra note 60.

joint inspections, or even assessing whether the construction of a new facility or road has violated a standstill agreement or may be considered as normal economic activity.

Questions of authorization, control and command of military observation operations have given rise to major differences between the major powers from the earliest years to the present and consequently a voluminous documentation on the cases and controversies has come into being. Progress toward agreement on a "model" for military observers (authorized by the Security Council) has been made by a working group of governments, under the aegis of a General Assembly Special Committee on Peacekeeping Operations (established by resolution 2006 [XIX]).[79] It has been evident that the most difficult issues to resolve are those concerning command and control, particularly the extent to which the permanent members would have a decisive voice in operational policy. These differences have given rise to much controversy and have contributed to difficulties in obtaining financial as well as political support. Yet, as occasions have arisen for such military observers when they appeared essential for surveillance of a cease-fire or to check on infiltration, they have been expeditiously authorized and placed in the field. The United Nations experience that has been built up and the expertise developed are valuable assets for future activities.

6. CONSENSUAL PEACEKEEPING AND POLICING

United Nations action in internal conflicts has been most dramatically manifested in the "peacekeeping" operations undertaken by the Security Council in the Congo and in Cyprus. In both cases, this has involved the use of armed forces, made available in national contingents by "contributing" governments who have responded to the Security Council's resolutions. In both cases, the peacekeeping had been requested by the recognized government of the state concerned, in need of assistance in maintaining internal order and forestalling foreign intervention. The U.N. troops were used for what were essentially policing functions, and they did not involve enforcement measures in the generally understood sense of Chapter VII (particularly Article 42). Consequently, these actions were not treated by the Security Council as necessitating the special agreements contemplated by Article 43 of the Charter, nor did they require any role for the Military Staff Committee (I have already referred to the constitutional controversies regarding the creation and control of such Forces).[80]

[79] Report of the Special Committee on Peace-keeping Operations, 3 Nov. 1969: 24 *U.N. GAOR*, Annexes, agenda item 35, U.N. Doc. A/7742; *id.*, 1 Oct. 1970: U.N. Doc. A/8081; *ibid.*, 3 Dec. 1971: U.N. Doc. A/8550.

[80] *Certain expenses of the United Nations (Article 17, para. 2, of the Charter). Advisory Opinion of 20 July 1962*: [1962] I.C.J. 163. For the contrary position, *see* statement by the representative of the U.S.S.R., 18 Feb. 1965: 19 *U.N. GAOR*, Plenary Meetings, 1330th meeting. *See also* Gross, "Expenses of the United Nations for Peace-Keeping Operations: The Advisory Opinion of the International Court of

It is clear enough that the Security Council may institute a United Nations police or surveillance Force, composed of armed troops, to assist in maintaining a cease-fire in an internal conflict or, more broadly, to take measures to prevent outbreaks of violence and disorder. In the Charter sense, the Force is a subsidiary organ of the Security Council. The personnel of the Force—including the members of its national contingents—are required to carry out their duties in accordance with their international status.[81] They are forbidden to seek or accept instructions of their government with respect to their duties in the U.N. Force and to refrain from action which may adversely reflect on the impartiality required by their status.[82]

The most difficult task of the peacekeeping forces in internal conflicts is to preserve the delicate line between maintenance of order and involvement in domestic issues. In the Congo this was tested in the bitter dispute over the autonomy of Katanga as well as time and again in regard to hostilities arising from tribal animosities or pillaging by the troops of the Congolese army.[83] Protection of civilians, and especially of political leaders, against violence similarly brought charges that the action taken, or in some cases the lack of action, favored one side or another in the domestic conflict. A policy of strict neutrality in the internal conflict was especially difficult to maintain in the Congo in the context of the Security Council resolutions which supported the Central Government and where attempts by the U.N. Force to occupy positions in territories controlled by secessionist or dissident authorities resulted in attacks on the U.N. Force. Whatever the merits of the particular issues, it was abundantly clear that the U.N. policeman's lot in a country in a civil war was not a happy one. His right to use arms in self-defense had to be broadened so that the "self" to be defended in-

---

Justice," 17 *Int'l Organ.* 1–35 (1963); Jennings, "International Court of Justice: Advisory Opinion of 20 July 1962 on Certain Expenses of the United Nations (Article 17, paragraph 2, of the Charter)," 11 *Int'l & Comp. L. Q.* 1170 (1962).

[81] For basic statements on the character of the Force and its international status, *see*, relating to the United Nations Emergency Force, the Report of the Secretary-General in pursuance of G.A. Res. 1123 (XI), 24 Jan. 1957: 11 *U.N. GAOR*, Annexes, agenda item 66, U.N. Doc. A/3694 and Add. 1; Summary study of the experience derived from the establishment and operation of the Force: Report of the Secretary-General, 9 Oct. 1958: 13 *U.N. GAOR*, Annexes, agenda item 65, U.N. Doc. A/3843. Relating to the Congo, *see* First Report of the Secretary-General on the implementation of Security Council resolution S/4387, 18 July 1960: 15 *U.N. SCOR*, Supp. July–Sept. 1960, U.N. Doc. S/4389, as well as statements at the 873rd meeting of the Security Council, 13/13 July 1960: 15 *U.N. SCOR*, 873rd meeting, at 7–12. Among the many unofficial commentaries, the following are useful: D. Bowett, *United Nations Force* (1964); L. Bloomfield, *International Military Forces* (1964); A. Burns & N. Heathcote, *Peace-Keeping by U.N. Forces: From Suez to the Congo* (1963); F. Seyersted, *United Nations Forces in the Law of Peace and War* (1966); O. Young, *Trends in International Peacekeeping* (1966); Miller, "Legal Aspects of the United Nations Action in the Congo," 55 *Am. J. Int'l L.* (1961), especially 10–13.

[82] *See* Article 100 of the Charter of the United Nations and U.N. Staff Rules, Regulation 1.4. *See also* M. Harbottle, *The Impartial Soldier* (1970).

[83] *See* C. Hoskyns, *supra* note 18; McNemar, *supra* note 18.

cluded as well civilians under his protection and physical positions which he needed for the performance of his functions.[84] The permissible scope of the use of arms was thus greatly widened.

The role of the peacekeeping forces has also involved measures to prevent the introduction of arms from outside the country to one of the factions involved in the fighting or even, as in the Congo, to the Central Government itself.[85] The exclusion of foreign mercenaries and their apprehension has also been an activity of the peacekeeping forces directed to the maintenance of internal order and the reduction of external intervention.

Despite the relative success of the two principal U.N. peacekeeping missions concerned with internal matters (*i.e.*, Congo and Cyprus), there is considerable uncertainty about prospects in the future. The difficulties encountered—political, constitutional, and financial—have created a climate of pessimism as to the feasibility of such activities in the next decade.[86] The negotiations by the major powers and others, principally in the context of the Special Committee of the General Assembly on Peacekeeping, have not yet brought agreement, by December 1971, on the major issues of a political and constitutional nature. Nor has a viable plan been developed for financing such activities, and it is generally assumed that this will require broad political agreement on such questions as the responsibility of the Security Council for authorization and control and as the principles governing composition and management of the forces. Suggestions have been made for a new role for the Military Staff Committee (established by Article 47 of the Charter) and the use of agreements contemplated by Article 43 for national armed forces and other facilities to be placed at the disposal of the Security Council.[87] Concern has been expressed that such arrangements should not unduly limit the executive functions of the Secretary-General and impose a veto on operational decisions.[88] The question of whether the General Assembly should have residual authority to institute such peacekeeping arrangements has not been resolved by the permanent members and it remains an obstacle to a wider agreement on future peacekeeping arrangements. Notwithstanding the lack of agreement on these constitutional issues, the Security Council has been able to act unanimously in continuing the

[84] *See* Schachter, "The Relation of Law, Politics and Action in the United Nations," 109 *Recueil Des Cours* 169–256 (1963); *id.*, "The Uses of Law in International Peace-Keeping," 50, *Virginia L. Rev.* 107–17 (1964).

[85] *Id.*

[86] *See, e.g.*, Friedmann, "The Reality of International Law," 10 *Colum. J. Transnat. Law* 46, 56 (1971); Morozov *and* Pchelintsev, "Behind the U.N.: Financial Crisis," *Int. Affairs* (Moscow) 23–29 (June 1964).

[87] *See* Memorandum of the U.S.S.R. Government, 16 March 1967, "United Nations operations for the maintenance of international peace and security": 22 *U.N. SCOR*, Supp. April–June 1967, U.N. Doc. S/7841. *See also* 6 *U.N. Mon. Chron.* 91 (Jan. 1969).

[88] *See* statements of the U.S. representative at the 29th meeting of the Special Committee on Peace-keeping Operations, 6 March 1968: U.N. Doc. A/AC. 121/SR. 29, at 23–24.

peacekeeping force in Cyprus (which is under the direct authority of the Secretary-General) and it is assumed by many observers that the Council would institute non-coercive peacekeeping in future cases where there was agreement of the permanent members on the need for a force to meet a threat to international peace.

7. ECONOMIC ASSISTANCE AND TECHNICAL COOPERATION

Economic aid and technical advice tend to have a low visibility against the more dramatic events of civil wars and it is not surprising that they have received relatively little attention as instrumentalities of action in internal conflicts. But it is not difficult to see that they might have an important place in the international organization's repertory of practical measures, not only as "post-operative" rehabilitation but, more importantly, as methods of preventive action. Such preventive action would, to some degree, include the basic measures directed toward meeting the endemic instability and discontent that underlie much of the internal conflict in the less developed areas of the world. Although such United Nations aid is limited in comparison to bilateral programs, multilateral programs may help to reduce external political pressures which are divisive in a country. Perhaps more significantly, they may be able to meet some of the causes of discontent manifested by internal ethnic or linguistic communities by fostering joint endeavors and extending cooperation among mutually suspicious groups. Because they are politically neutral and disinterested, international teams under United Nations aegis engaged in economic and social assistance can be in a good position to stress equitable considerations and conciliatory arrangements. In the Congo, for example, the United Nations agencies provided technical advisers who helped to bring agreement on constitutional arrangements (an expert group worked on the draft constitution), on the fiscal arrangements between the central and provincial governments, on the disposition of external assets, and on a variety of other governmental matters that were in controversy between competing groups in the country. It need hardly be said that this presupposes a policy which would not be manipulated to favor one political group over another and which would be careful to avoid undue sympathy for the elites in power. Although these risks cannot be dismissed, the opportunities for constructive assistance should not be passed over because of the risks. One can readily think of situations in which the influence of an international assistance mission might have had some success in reducing the tensions and grievances that subsequently boiled over into large-scale violence.

8. DETERMINATION OF THE GOVERNMENT ENTITLED TO REPRESENTATION IN THE UNITED NATIONS

In virtually any internal conflict which involves contending claimants to governmental authority, the United Nations is (at least in principle) faced with the issue of passing on the rival contentions for the purpose of determining the "legitimate" representation of that state in the United Nations. The decision on behalf of one or the other of the claimants could of course have an important bearing on the outcome of the conflict.

In actual fact, the United Nations has had relatively few cases in which that issue has been of great import. The most notable example has, of course, been China. Soon after the People's Republic of China was proclaimed, the Central People's Government requested (the precise date was November 18, 1949) that the Nationalist delegation be deprived "of all rights to further represent the Chinese People in the United Nations." That issue was then raised and debated for twenty-two years in the General Assembly as well as in the Security Council and other principal organs of the United Nations. It was finally resolved in October 1971 by the decision of the General Assembly acknowledging that the government of the People's Republic was entitled to the seat of China and that the "Nationalist delegation" was to be excluded.[89]

In the very early stage of the controversy, in March 1950, the Secretary-General issued a memorandum prepared in the Legal Department of the Secretariat on the legal aspects of problems of representation in the United Nations. That memorandum, after distinguishing recognition by States from representation, argued that the proper principle for choosing rival claimants could be derived from Article 4 of the Charter on the obligations of membership. The memorandum reasoned:

> The obligations of membership can be carried out only by governments which in fact possess the power to do so. Where a revolutionary government presents itself as representing a State, in rivalry to an existing government, the question at issue should be which of these governments in fact is in a position to employ the resources and direct the people of the State in fulfillment of the obligations of membership. In essence, this means an inquiry as to whether the new government exercises effective authority within the territory of the State and is habitually obeyed by the bulk of the population. If so, it would seem to be appropriate for the United Nations organs, through their collective action, to accord it the right to represent the State in the Organization, even though individual Members of the Organization refuse, and may continue to refuse, to accord it recognition as the lawful government for reasons which are valid under their national policies.[90]

The position thus stated was criticized for placing all of its emphasis on effective authority and ignoring such criteria as "peaceloving" and the Charter principles on human rights (in particular, the consent of the gov-

---

[89] G.A. Res. 2758 (XXVI) entitled "Restoration of the lawful rights of the People's Republic of China in the United Nations," Oct. 25, 1971.

[90] Memorandum by Secretary-General Trygve Lie, "Legal aspects of problems of representation in the United Nations," 8 March 1950: 5 *U.N. SCOR*, Supp. Jan./ May 1950, U.N. Doc. S/1466.

erned) as an element of legitimacy.[91] When the issue reached the General Assembly at its fifth session in 1950, it did not prove possible to obtain sufficient support for any list of factors to be taken into consideration in choosing between rival claimants. The resolution of the General Assembly as adopted said no more than that the question should be considered in the light of the Purposes and Principles of the Charter and the circumstances of each case.[92] However, it may be said that, in the years that followed, the discussions in the Organization, culminating in the resolution of 1971 at the 26th session, revealed increasing support for applying as a decisive standard the factor of effective control and authority over the territory of the member state.

The question of choosing between rival claimants to governmental authority took a rather different form in the case of the Republic of the Congo (Léopoldville) in October and November 1960. In this case credentials signed by the head of state were challenged on the ground that they had not been drawn in accordance with the fundamental law of the republic and lacked the approval of the legal government.[93] (In effect, the dispute was between the group headed by Kasavubu, the president of the Republic, and the rival group of Lumumba, the prime minister dismissed by Kasavubu.) The contention was that a decision by the General Assembly seating one of the rival delegations over the other would be taking sides in an internal political and constitutional dispute. Despite this argument, the General Assembly accepted the recommendation of its Credentials Committee that the credentials signed by the President were valid.[94]

It is interesting to observe that in neither of the two cases discussed above does it seem that the decision of the United Nations on representation affected in any appreciable way the actual outcome of the conflict. Nevertheless, it would not be unreasonable to conceive of situations in which the action of the United Nations in seating (or refusing to seat) a delegation claiming authority would affect the relative strength and authority of the

[91] *See* discussions at the 18th meeting, 20 Oct. 1950, 19th meeting, 21 Oct. 1950, and 20th meeting, 23 Oct. 1950, of the *Ad Hoc* Political Committee: 5 *U.N. GAOR, Ad Hoc* Political Committee, at 111–34. *See also* Schachter, "Problems of Law and Justice," *Annual Review of United Nations Affairs* 200–204 (1951).

[92] G.A. Res. 396 (V), "Recognition by the United Nations of the representation of a Member State," 14 Dec. 1950: *U.N. GAOR*, Supp. 20, U.N. Doc. A/1775, at 24.

[93] *See* telegram from the President of the Republic of the Congo to the President of the General Assembly, 13 Oct. 1960, Doc. A/4560; note verbale from the President of the Republic of the Congo to the Secretary-General, 9 Nov. 1960, U.N. Doc. A/4569; letters from the President of the Republic of Congo to the President of the General Assembly, 12 Nov. 1960, U.N. Doc. A/4571, and to the Secretary-General, 17 Nov. 1960, U.N. Doc. A/4577. 15 *U.N. GAOR*, Annexes, agenda item 85. *See also* statement by the representative of the U.S.S.R. at the 36th meeting of the Credentials Committee, 9 Nov. 1960: 15 *U.N. GAOR*, Annexes, agenda item 3, U.N. Doc. A/4578. para. 10.

[94] G.A. Res. 1498 (XV), "Credentials of the representatives of the Republic of the Congo (Leopoldville)," 22 Nov. 1960: 15 *U.N. GAOR*, Supp. 16, at 1.

parties in conflict.[95] As a general rule, it would appear to be in keeping with a policy of non-interference in internal affairs for the Organization to follow the criterion suggested by the Secretary-General in 1950, namely, effective authority and control. On the other hand, it can be argued that if this is the only criterion, the decision may run counter to such Charter purposes and principles as those directed to the promotion of human rights or even in some cases the maintenance of international peace and security.[96] Whether the decision of the Organization on representation should be used as a means of implementing these basic Charter purposes is a highly debatable point in circumstances when it would entail loss of representation for a government exercising effective authority. It can be maintained that it opens the way to a type of sanction or enforcement without recourse to the constitutional procedures laid down in the Charter for such action.

9. SANCTIONS AND ENFORCEMENT MEASURES

It is of course elementary that the use of enforcement measures under Chapter VII of the Charter must be premised on a finding by the Security Council that there exists a threat to the peace, a breach of the peace, or an act of aggression. The Council may then decide what measures shall be taken in accordance with Articles 41 and 43 to maintain or restore international peace and security. Such measures are mandatory on member states by virtue of Article 25.

The only clear instance of the adoption of such mandatory measures (at least up to the end of 1971) has occurred in respect of a situation that was in its essential aspects an internal conflict—the case of Rhodesia. That case in its origin involved the action of a regime representing a small minority of whites (about 6 percent) to exclude the black majority in the country from effective participation in the political and economic governance of the country. The regime had imposed a highly restrictive franchise system directed against the blacks and related to the restrictive enfranchisement and supportive of it were numerous restraints on economic,

[95] *See* examples of collective recognition before the United Nations came into being in H. Lauterpacht, *Recognition* 165–74 (1947).

[96] In contending that the General Assembly should refuse to accept the credentials of the representatives of South Africa it was asserted that "the so-called Government of South Africa is composed of white men, it is elected only by white men, it is responsible only to white men, and it is obliged primarily to promote and uphold the interests of white men. Our challenge is also based on the unprecedented record of violations of human rights by the nationalist leaders of South Africa." Statement by the representative of Somalia at the 2027th plenary meeting of the General Assembly, 20 Dec. 1971: U.N. Doc. A/PV. 2027, at 53.—The draft resolution recommended by the Credentials Committee for adoption by the General Assembly, U.N. Doc. A/8625, para. 27, was amended by Somalia, U.N. Doc. A/L. 666, by adding the following sentence to the draft resolution of the Credentials Committee: "except with regard to the credentials of the representatives of South Africa." The draft resolution, as amended, was adopted at the 2027th plenary meeting of the General Assembly, 20 Dec. 1971: G.A. Resolution 2862 (XXVI).

social, educational, and legal rights.[97] The issues came to a head in the United Nations by virtue of the "unilateral declaration of independence" by the governing regime on November 11, 1965, and its rejection by the United Kingdom. Resolutions by the General Assembly and by the Security Council condemned the "usurpation of power by a racist settler minority."[98] The Security Council in November 1965 found that the continuation of the situation brought about by the unilateral declaration of independence would constitute a threat to the peace and it called on states to desist from sending military supplies, including oil and petroleum.[99] Subsequently, in April 1966 it found a present threat to the peace and authorized the United Kingdom to use force, if necessary, to prevent oil from reaching Rhodesia. In December 1966, the Security Council adopted mandatory economic sanctions under Article 41 of the Charter based on its renewed determination of an existing threat to the peace.[100] It adopted more detailed and specific sanctions of a far-reaching character in its resolution 253 of May 29, 1968.[101]

Critics of the Security Council's resolution have attacked its finding of a threat to the peace as contrary to the facts, essentially on the ground that the transgressions of the white minority have occurred wholly within their own country and that no threat to the peace has been made by that regime but rather assisted by its opponents.[102] Moreover, the opposition of other states, though vociferous, was said to involve no credible threat to the international peace. The principal answer to this has been that the "racist" behavior of the white minority has as a matter of demonstrable fact aroused widespread resentment and hostility on the part of the neighboring African countries and that their sympathies for their fellow Africans can be reasonably expected to lead to counteraction with a high probability of violence in support of guerrillas and possibly outright war.[103] Relevant to this is the fact that the unilateral act of independence was declared illegal by the United Kingdom and that virtually all member states regarded the regime as illicit and as a flagrant affront to the conscience of mankind. In these circumstances, it could hardly be said that the unanimous finding of the

---

[97] Higgins, "International Law, Rhodesia and the U.N." 23 *World Today* 94 (March 1967); Perham, "The Rhodesian Crisis: The Background," 42 *Int'l Affairs* (London) 1 (1966).

[98] *See* G.A. Res. 2012 (XX), 12 Oct. 1965; G.A. Res. 2022 (XX), 5 Nov. 1965; G.A. Res. 2024 (XX), 11 Nov. 1965: 20 *U.N. GAOR*, Supp. 14, at 53–56. S.C. Res. 202 (1965), 6 May 1965; S.C. Res. 216 (1965), 12 Nov. 1965; S.C. Res. 217 (1965), 20 Nov. 1965: 20 *U.N. SCOR Resolutions and Decisions of the Security Council* (1964), at 6–9.

[99] *See* S.C. Res. 217 (1965), *supra* note 98, at 8.

[100] *See* S.C. Res. 232 (1966), 16 Dec. 1966: 21 *U.N. SCOR, Resolutions and Decisions of the Security Council* (1966), at 7–9.

[101] *See* S.C. Res. 253 (1968), 29 May 1968: 23 *U.N. SCOR, Resolutions and Decisions of the Security Council* (1968), at 5–7.

[102] Letters of Dean Acheson quoted in Spaeth, "Rhodesia: A Complex and Distant Problem," 3 *Stanford J. Int'l Stud.* 46–50 (1968); *see* Higgins, *supra* note 97.

[103] McDougal & Reisman, "Rhodesia and the United Nations," 62 *Am. J. Int'l L.* 1–19 (1968); *see* Higgins, *supra* note 97.

Security Council that there existed a threat to the peace was unreasonable.[104] Nor could that finding be dismissed as unfounded because it was part of a series of actions by the United Nations aimed at removing the discrimination against the black majority and bringing about their full and unrestricted participation in a government based on the principle of equal rights in the governance of the country.

It was evident by the end of 1971 that the sanctions were not sufficiently effective to bring about a serious deprivation to the economy of the country or to lead to substantial change of position. Numerous violations were reported by a special committee established by the Security Council and the failure of the neighboring countries of South Africa and the Portuguese territories to support the sanction (and indeed their assistance in evading the sanctions) reduced the effectiveness of the embargoes.[105] Toward the end of 1971 the British government reached a settlement with the white ruling group of Rhodesia under which they would gradually widen the enfranchisement of the blacks (though still based on income and property qualifications) with a possibility of eventual majority rule. Under that settlement, the independence of the Rhodesian government would be recognized after certain conditions were met, and economic aid furnished to raise the level of the black population.[106] At the time of this writing (December 1971) the African States have declared the settlement to fall short of the aims of the United Nations and as inadequate to remove the threat to the peace brought about by the Rhodesian regime.[107]

The experience of the United Nations in the Rhodesian case has been regarded as both discouraging and instructive. The widespread violations and loopholes in the sanctions revealed a failure on the part of many states, whether neighbors or distant, to impose strict controls or to undergo the losses resulting from an embargo.[108] The impact on the economy of the target State involved some hardships and higher costs for the business groups but in some respects it brought about favorable economic developments (through import substitution). It also appeared to have little political effect on the elite groups, beyond perhaps fostering their cohesion and resistance. Outside of Rhodesia, the view has been strengthened that "eco-

---

[104] *Id.*

[105] Fourth Report of the Committee established in pursuance of Security Council resolution 253 (1968), 16 June 1971: U.N. Doc. S/10229 and Addenda 1 and 2.

[106] Letter from the Permanent Representative of U.K., 1 Dec. 1971, transmitting text of a White Paper entitled "Rhodesia: Proposals for a Settlement": U.N. Doc. S/10405.

[107] *See* discussions at the Security Council, 1602nd meeting, 25 Nov. 1971: U.N. Doc. S/PV. 1602; 1605th meeting, 2 Dec. 1971: U.N. Doc. S/PV. 1605; 1609th meeting, 8 Dec. 1971: U.N. Doc. S/PV. 1609; 1612th meeting, 13 Dec. 1971: U.N. Doc. S/PV. 1612; 1623rd meeting, 30 Dec. 1971: U.N. Doc. S/PV. 1623.

[108] *See* discussions at the Security Council, 1399th meeting, 19 March 1968: U.N. Doc. S/PV. 1399; 1400th meeting, 20 March 1968: U.N. Doc. S/PV. 1400; 1408th meeting, 26 March 1968: U.N. Doc. S/PV. 1408. *N.Y. Times*, (March 22, 1968) at 2, col. 4.

nomic sanctions are, in the modern day, a romantic delusion."[109] As far as military sanctions are concerned, the reluctance on the part of the United Kingdom government to employ military means and the failure of the Security Council to adopt military sanctions are viewed widely as indications of the ineffectiveness of sanctions in the present circumstances of international life.[110] Yet, it seems most unlikely that demands for stronger sanctions and enforcement measures will disappear as long as some governments follow policies that flout the deeply held convictions of the large majority of states in regard to issues of intense emotional content.

10. THE ELABORATION OF NORMS AND CRITERIA OF CONDUCT

We come to the tenth and last category in our list of the "ways and means" in the United Nations for dealing with internal conflicts, the elaboration by the United Nations of general norms and criteria of conduct for state behavior in respect of domestic conflicts outside of their territory. The endeavor to formulate such norms and criteria—whether of a recommendatory or binding character—has been a continuing activity of the Organization since it began. At the first session of the General Assembly a proposal was made for a draft Declaration on the Rights and Duties of States[111] and soon thereafter other proposals were made for a Draft Code of Offenses against the Peace and Security of Mankind[112] and a Definition of Aggression.[113] When these attempts at developing legal norms did not succeed, the General Assembly turned to the adoption of declaratory resolutions, in particular those entitled "Essentials of Peace" in 1949,[114] and "Peace through Deeds" in 1950.[115] After the large expansion of membership in the 1960's, the General Assembly adopted additional declaratory resolutions, notably the Declaration of the Granting of Independence to Colonial Countries and Peoples in 1960[116] and the Declaration on the Inadmissibility of Intervention in the Domestic Affairs of States.[117] In 1970, after years of committee debate, the General Assembly adopted a Declaration on Principles of

---

[109] G. Ball, *The Discipline of Power* 243 (1968).

[110] *See* Spaeth, *supra* note 102, at 66–69.

[111] G.A. Res. 38 (I), 11 Dec. 1946: U.N. Doc. A/64/Add. 1, at 62; Subsequently, G.A. Res. 178 (II); 21 Nov. 1947: U.N. Doc. A/519, at 112;; G.A. Res. 375 (IV), 6 Dec. 1949: U.N. Doc. 1251 and Corrs. 1 and 2, at 67; G.A. Res 596 (VI), 7 Dec. 1951: 6 *U.N. GAOR*, Supp. 20, at 83.

[112] G.A. Res. 897 (IX), 4 Dec. 1954: 9 *U.N. GAOR*, Supp. 21, at 49; *see also* G.A. Res. 17 (II), "Formulation of the principles recognized in the Charter of the Nürnberg Tribunal and in the judgment of the Tribunal," 21 Nov. 1947: U.N. Doc. A/519, at 111.

[113] G.A. Res. 596 (VI), *see supra* note 111; G.A. Res. 688 (VII), 20 Dec. 1952: 7 *U.N. GAOR*, Supp. 20, at 63.

[114] G.A. Res. 290 (IV), 1 Dec. 1949: U.N. Doc. A/1251 and Corrs. 1 and 2, at 13.

[115] G.A. Res. 380 (V), 17 Nov. 1950: *U.N. GAOR*, Supp. 20, at 13.

[116] G.A. Res. 1514 (XV), 14 Dec. 1960: 15 *U.N. GAOR*, Supp. 16, at 66.

[117] G.A. Res. 2131 (XX), 21 Dec. 1965: 20 *U.N. GAOR*, Supp. 14, at 11.

International Law concerning Friendly Relations.[118] All of these declarations, and especially the last two, bear directly on the issues of intervention by outside States in domestic conflicts. A considerable body of legal literature has developed on the juridical significance of these resolutions, with the major emphasis on whether and to what extent they are declaratory of international law, or presumptive evidence of law or "merely" recommendatory.[119] The jurists, it need hardly be stressed, are far from agreement on these issues, though it can be said that the controversies have stimulated a sophisticated and profound reexamination of the fundamentals of international law.

Whether such declarations are to be regarded as useful for achieving United Nations aims has also been a matter of controversy (though the question of utility has been far less discussed than that of legal effect). Within the United Nations, the adoption of the declarations, generally by near unanimity, has been hailed in exuberant rhetoric as of momentous significance or at the very least as a major achievement in reaching agreement among diverse political and ideological groups.[120] Understandably those who participated in the preparation of the declarations (and who devoted long hours, indeed, years, to an often painful and frustrating negotiation) have been most prominent among the enthusiasts for their achievement. Some of them would readily acknowledge shortcomings and particularly ambiguity and vagueness on many critical concepts. But they nonetheless maintain that the efforts have produced a clarification of standards and that, as a consequence, the policy-makers in national states will have a more enlightened perception of "how far states can go without provoking a reaction of another state's view of what is acceptable."[121]

This optimistic assessment is not always so evident to non-participant

[118] G.A. Res. 2625 (XXV), 24 Oct. 1970: 25 *U.N. GAOR*, Supp. 28 at 121.

[119] *See, e.g.* J. Castaneda, *Legal Effects of U.N. Resolutions* (1971); Falk, "On the Quasi-Legislative Competence of the General Assembly," 60 *Am. J. Int'l L.* 782 (1966); Gross, "The United Nations and the Role of Law," 19 *Int'l Org.* 537 (1966); R. Higgins, *The Development of International Law Through the Political Organs of the United Nations* (1963); Schachter, "Toward a Theory of International Obligation," in S. Schwebel (ed.), *The Effectiveness of International Decisions* (1971); Tammes, "Decisions of International Organs as a Source of International Law," 94 *Recueil Des Cours* 265 (1958); Virally, "La valeur juridique des Recommandations des organisations internationales," *Annuaire Francais de Droit International* 66–97 (1956); *See also* statements in regard to the Declaration on Principles of International Law Concerning Friendly Relations, in particular by Mr. Csatorday (Hungary), and Mr. Yasseen (Iraq), at the 1180th meeting of the Sixth Committee of the General Assembly, 24 Sept. 1970: U.N. Doc. A/C.6/SR. 1180, and by Mr. Riphagen (Netherlands) at the 114th meeting of the Special Committee on Principles of International Law concerning Friendly Relations and Co-Operation among States, 1 May 1970: U.N. Doc. A/AC.125/Sr. 114.

[120] *See* Statements in plenary meetings of the General Assembly at time of adoption of Declaration, G.A. Res. 2625 (XXV), 24 October 1970: U.N. Doc. A/PV. 1883.

[121] *See* R. Rosenstock, *supra* note 9 at 716. *See* also Houben, "Principles of International Law concerning Friendly Relations," 61 *Am. J. Int'l L.* 703 (1967).

observers. Some see the Declarations as a purely verbal exercise that will have little, if any, effect on the behavior of states. They point to the gap between the principles and the actual conduct of states: and to the ambiguities and contradictions in the texts of the Declarations which seem to allow governments to act in whatever way they wish. In one such view, "a norm that operates in such a climate of contradiction is bound to function as mere rhetoric and to erode generally arguments urging for international law."[122] Even harsher judgments have been made by diplomats and political scientists who view such declarations as elaborate self-deception creating an illusion of agreement where none exists. Some have concluded that in a time of revolutionary ferment it is nearly impossible to obtain a consensus on norms that express the interests of states or at least of the major powers.[123] Their self-interest cannot be expressed in either an interventionary or non-interventionary rule; they see themselves as on one side or the other in accordance with their calculations of benefits and costs, which vary from case to case.

The difficult and important question pointed up by these cogent criticisms of U.N. declarations is how to relate general norms to behavior and how to link the norms to specific situations. That problem is elusive because, as diplomats know, in any concrete situation there may be gains and losses and there is hardly ever certainty about the outcome. State action requires balancing risks and opportunities; conflicting goals have to be weighed and "trade-offs" between different alternatives assessed.[124] This does not mean that the effort to set standards is useless. It suggests rather what we must recognize: that governments cannot rely simply on abstract principles and that they must be sensitive to the contextual setting and to the complexities of choice in each concrete case.

It may be no more than a pious hope to believe that the various efforts of the United Nations to elaborate norms relevant to intervention, self-determination, and related concepts have helped the policy-makers to see more clearly the complexity involved. Certainly these Declarations and their protracted preparatory work have brought out the diversity of goals and values that governments must consider in specific cases. But that is only the starting point in the complicated task of developing an adequate normative structure. One needs to go on to achieve a much greater understanding of the types of situations that have to be dealt with and of the procedures that would be effective in the different kinds of cases. The attainment of a satisfactory regulatory system to cope with internal conflicts will not be possible

---

[122] See R. Falk, in "Introduction," supra note 13, at 7.

[123] See J. Rosenau (ed.), International Aspects of Civil Strife (1964); R. Barnet, Intervention and Revolution: The United States in the Third World (1968); W. Friedmann, supra notes 35 and 86; H. Kissinger, A World Restored (1969), Ch. 1.

[124] See L. Bloomfield & A. Liess, Controlling Small Wars: A Strategy for the 1970's (1970), for summaries of policy issues presented in a number of civil-war situations.

without analytic and manipulative concepts and procedures that are adequate to meet the complexities of the actual cases. The incantation of general principles will accomplish little unless governments have effective instruments to understand how they can eliminate international violence and combat its domestic causes in specific cases.

Chapter 17 | **Wars of Liberation—**

as Fought in U.N. Organs | *Stephen M. Schwebel*

"Wars of liberation" have been fought for some years in United Nations organs. The battle of words has been inconclusive. Resultant resolutions, where they have gained universal support, are so general that they lend themselves to conflicting interpretations on the critical issues. Resolutions which are clearer enjoy less support, and certainly lack a support which entitles them to be treated as declaratory of international law.

The debates have been frequent, emotional, and involved. They have been, as United Nations debates tend to be, heavily repetitious. There accordingly is little profit in tracing the details of their course, which is at once labyrinthine and predictable. Their essence is contained in the Goa debate before the Security Council; the deliberations and formulations of the United Nations Special Committee on Principles of International Law Concerning Friendly Relations and Co-operation Among States; and resolutions adopted by the General Assembly in 1972 on colonialism. The inconclusiveness of the outcome is emphasized in the most recent United Nations formulation, that of the Special Committee on the Question of Defining Aggression.

1. THE GOA DEBATE

In December 1961, large Indian forces attacked minuscule Portuguese forces in what Portugal termed "the Portuguese State of India." The attack came after extended, unsuccessful efforts of India to persuade Portugal to follow the path of Britain and France and withdraw peacefully from the Indian subcontinent. Portugal called upon the Security Council to take action against what it termed "aggression" by India.

India's representative in the Security Council bluntly maintained that ". . . this is a colonial question. It is a question of getting rid of the last vestiges of colonialism in India. That is a matter of faith with us. Whatever anyone else may think, Charter or no Charter, Council or no Council, that is our basic faith which we cannot afford to give up at any cost."[1] That is to say, India's representative indicated in this revealing ejaculation that India's act ignored international law and Charter restrictions on the use of force. Nevertheless, India did advance certain arguments. Essentially

[1] *Official Records of the Security Council*, 987th meeting, 18 December 1961, at 9.

they were that Portugal did not have title to territory in the Indian sub-continent, despite 450 years of presence in Goa, since title was unlawfully acquired through conquest in 1510; that Goa was by nature Indian and therefore India could not commit aggression against it; rather, that colonialism was a form of permanent aggression to which India was en-titled to respond in self-defense.

These arguments were treated as astonishing by the majority of the Security Council. Ambassador Adlai Stevenson led the criticism of the Indian position in such vehement terms as to shock the representative of India no less than he had shocked the Council. The United States Rep-resentative held that the most basic Charter norms restricting the use of force in international relations were at stake. The obligations to settle disputes by peaceful means and to refrain from the threat or use of force in international relations were paramount. There was no exception from these obligations which could justify India's assault in these circumstances. India's reply was that "there can be no question of aggression against your own frontier, against your own people, whom you want to liberate. . . . If any narrow-minded, legalistic considerations—considerations arising from international law as written by European law writers—should arise, those writers were, after all, brought up in the atmosphere of colonial-ism. . . ."[2]

The majority of the Security Council voted in favor of a resolution calling for a cease-fire, withdrawal of Indian forces from Goa, and negotia-tion of a permanent solution by peaceful means. That resolution failed of adoption only because of the exercise of the veto power by the Soviet Union. The U.S.S.R. and Ceylon, as well as the United Arab Republic and Liberia, lent vigorous support to the position, and some of the argumentation, of India. In the light of that support, the majority of the Security Council did not refer the matter to the General Assembly (then in session), since it anticipated that the requisite two-thirds vote could not be secured for calling on India to withdraw its forces from Goa.

While the Indian argumentation was rejected by the majority of the Security Council and shredded by as sympathetic a commentator as Quincy Wright,[3] the fact remains that India attacked, occupied, and annexed Goa with impunity. Resolutions and incantations about the in-admissibility of the acquisition of territory by force have been omitted in this case; the world has quietly acquiesced in India's absorption of Goa. In this real sense, the facts of the case arguably support the contention that wars of liberation—viewed, at any rate, as liberation from Western colonialism—are treated by the international community as an exception from Charter prohibitions on the use of force. Insofar as the debate in United Nations organs went, however, the outcome was inconclusive. The

[2] *Ibid.*, at 11.
[3] Wright, "The Goa Incident," 56 *Am. J. Int'l L.* 617 (1962).

majority indicted India; the Soviet Union barred a verdict of guilty; the rhetorical conclusion was uncertain, and the impact on doctrine was unclear.

2. "FRIENDLY RELATIONS"

The battle resumed in Mexico City in 1964 at the First Session of the U.N. Special Committee on Principles of International Law Concerning Friendly Relations and Cooperation among States. The Committee was charged by the General Assembly with preparing a study of specified principles of international law relating to friendly relations among states, "with a view to their progressive development and codification." Among those principles were the principle that states shall refrain in their international relations from the threat or use of force against the territorial integrity or political independence of any state, or in any other manner inconsistent with the purposes of the United Nations; and the principle of equal rights and self-determination of peoples. Wars of liberation were rhetorically fought in the Committee mainly over these principles.

Czechoslovakia proposed to codify the Charter's prohibition of the threat or use of force in international relations by including among the exceptions to that prohibition "self-defense of nations against colonial domination in exercise of the right of self-determination."[4] Yugoslavia joined India and Ghana in proposing that "The prohibition of the use of force shall not affect . . . the right of peoples to self-defense against colonial domination in the exercise of their right to self-determination."[5] The official summary of the debate over these proposals well sets out the fundamentals of the debate repeated in the Committee throughout its five sessions:

> A right of self-defense of peoples and nations against colonial domination, in the exercise of their right of self-determination, was included in the proposals of Czechoslovakia, . . . Ghana, India and Yugoslavia. . . . Some representatives supported the inclusion of such a right in any formulation adopted by the Special Committee. In this respect, reference was made to the Charter of the Organization of African Unity which affirmed the right of African countries still under foreign domination to self-determination and proclaimed, on the part of the independent African States, their "absolute dedication to the total emancipation of the African Territories which are still dependent." Reference was also made to the Declaration of the Heads of State or Government of non-aligned countries adopted at Belgrade in 1961, section III of which demanded that an immediate stop should be put to armed action against dependent peoples and that the integrity of their national territory should be respected.

[4] *Report of the Special Committee on Principles of International Law concerning Friendly Relations and Co-operation among States*, U.N. Doc. A/5746, at 20.
[5] *Ibid.*, at 23.

It was further stated that the practice of the United Nations itself had been against regarding the struggle of colonial peoples for liberation, which was one of the most important phenomena of the modern era, as a violation of the prohibition of the use of force. The Charter provisions undoubtedly covered the right of oppressed peoples to defend themselves against foreign oppression. The United Nations Declaration on the granting of independence to colonial countries and peoples (General Assembly resolution 1514 (XV)) expressly stated that the subjection of peoples to alien subjugation was contrary to the United Nations Charter. The Declaration also reaffirmed that all peoples had the right to self-determination, and called for the cessation of all armed action or repressive measures directed against dependent peoples. Other resolutions of United Nations organs, dealing with specific colonial problems, also supported the application of the principle of self-determination, which should now be considered as a general principle of law.

It was further argued that the right of self-determination would be meaningless if it could not be defended against a colonial Power which attempted by force to deny it. If the Special Committee did not take this into consideration it would jeopardize the progress already achieved by the United Nations in the vital field of decolonization. Were the Special Committee to adopt a proposal along the lines suggested by the United Kingdom, . . . this would be a serious challenge to the whole decolonization movement, for not only was it silent on the sanctity of the right of self-determination but it would brand as indirect aggression any meaningful support to a people acting in self-defense to assert that right, and might entitle colonial Powers to invite other States to aid them in suppressing national liberation movements in their colonies. The work of laying down principles of law banning the use of force would be incomplete if it did not provide for the elimination of colonialism. The use of armed force, which was still being resorted to in a number of territories to repress the aspirations of their peoples to freedom and self-determination, violated the Charter and the resolutions adopted by the United Nations and was a flagrant example of the unlawful threat or use of force prohibited by Article 2, paragraph 4, of the Charter. Colonial rule was in contradiction with contemporary international law, the Charter and resolutions of the General Assembly.

On the other hand, some representatives were opposed to any formulation by the Special Committee which would include reference to a legal right of peoples and nations to self-defense against colonial domination. Some of these representatives stated that, while they were opposed to colonialism and recognized the right of colonial peoples and nations to self-determination, revolution was a political, not a legal, concept. While revolution might be the leaven of law, one could not speak of its intrinsic legality, and, except possibly for the French Constitution of 1793, it had never been regarded as a legal right.

It was further pointed out by some representatives that Article 2, paragraph 4, of the Charter only prohibited the threat or use of force against States, or, in other words, to entities having legal personality in international law. This prohibition did not extend to rebellions against the constituted authorities. A specific mention of a right of self-defense against colonial domination was therefore unnecessary. It would be sufficient, in the case of a genuine war of liberation, for the Security Council or the General Assembly to determine whether aggression by a colonial Power was involved. Furthermore, once a colonial people had won their independence, Article 51 of the Charter, concerning self-defense, granted adequate protection against armed intervention by the former metropolitan Power.

It was also argued that, if express mention were made of a right of self-defense against colonial domination, it would be a move backward towards the traditional concept of the "just war." The Declaration on the granting of independence to colonial countries and peoples, in its paragraph 6, rejected the concept of wars of liberation. Moreover, to sanction a so-called right of self-defense against colonial domination would be to encourage a nation to use force, contrary to the principles of the United Nations, and the reasons in favour of the prohibition of armed force in international relations were equally cogent in regard to the settlement of disputes relating to the exercise of self-determination. To make an exception in this latter case would only have the effect of greatly increasing the existing tensions and would endanger international peace and security. It would give a State complete freedom to wage war provided that it appropriated the charge of colonial domination when so doing. In this latter context, it was relevant to note that Article 2, paragraph 4, of the Charter forbade a State to use force to impair the territorial integrity of another State and "wars of liberation" in many cases would have precisely that result. It would also be strange to restrict the concept of self-defense to cases of colonial domination when there were many other forms of domination, such as ideological domination. The question would also arise whether the right of an ethnic minority to self-defense against oppression by a majority belonging to another race should not also be recognized.

It was further stated that colonial rule, whether by way of the administration of a Trust Territory or otherwise, was not contrary to the Charter, and States administering dependent Territories, in accordance with the Charter, were responsible for the maintenance of law and order in those Territories. If a so-called right of self-defense against colonial domination were to be considered to derogate from the position just stated it would make it all the more unacceptable."[6]

This was one wing of the debate; self-determination was the other. Seven proposed codifications of the principle of self-determination were submitted to the Committee in 1966 and 1967. Among them was a proposal of Czechoslovakia that:

Peoples have an inalienable right to eliminate colonial domination and to carry on the struggle, by whatever means, for their liberation, independ-

[6] *Ibid.*, at 42–45.

ence, and free development. Nothing in this Declaration shall be construed as affecting the exercise of that right.

States are prohibited from undertaking any armed action or repressive measures of any kind against peoples under colonial rule.[7]

A joint proposal by Algeria and nine other States similarly maintained that "peoples who are deprived of their legitimate right of self-determination and complete freedom are entitled to exercise their inherent right of self-defense, by virtue of which they may receive assistance from other States."[8]

Proponents of these provisions maintained that national liberation movements were an outstanding feature of the times. A people striving for independence, it was argued, was a subject of international law and was entitled to international protection. A violation of the rights of such a people in the struggle was alleged to be an international crime.[9] Opponents replied that, while much had been said in the Committee about wars of liberation, all those specified appeared to be taking place in countries whose regimes were not approved of by those who gave such examples. Broad generalizations about movements of national liberation tended to become merely propagandistic assertions.[10] The debate was officially summarized as follows:

> Speaking in support of such a right of self-defense, certain representatives stressed that independence or national liberation movements in the exercise of a people's right of self-determination were not a violation of the Charter. Further, the enunciation of the principle of self-determination in the Charter showed that the right of peoples to self-determination was a matter of international concern, and an international legal right. If peoples were unable to exercise that right, they were entitled to assistance from other States. Accordingly, it could not be said that assistance provided by other States to an independence or national liberation movement constituted an unlawful interference in the internal affairs of the metropolitan power. The provisions of Article 2, paragraph 7, of the Charter were not applicable in such a case. The right of peoples to exercise their right of self-determination and to receive assistance from other States was recognized by the General Assembly in its resolutions 2105(XX), 2107(XX) and 2189(XXI), had been acknowledged by the majority of the Member States of the United Nations, and had been reaffirmed in other important international instruments such as the Charter of the Organization of African Unity, and the declarations of the conferences of the non-aligned countries.

> A number of other representatives stated, however, that the assertion of a right of self-defense in the context of the principle of equal rights and

---

[7] *Report of the Special Committee on Principles of International Law concerning Friendly Relations and Co-operation among States*, U.N. Doc. A/6799, at 87.

[8] *Ibid.*, at 91.

[9] *Ibid.*, at 94.

[10] *Ibid.*, at 95.

self-determination was quite unacceptable. While peoples in dependent territories who were under alien subjugation, domination, and exploitation —which was certainly not the case in all such territories—were clearly being denied fundamental human rights and freedoms in violation of the Charter, recognition of a right of individual and collective self-defense by the use of force against such domination would clearly encourage violence, and could serve as a basis for the intervention of a State in the affairs of another by means of encouraging violent acts against the Government concerned. The right of self-defense belonged, under the Charter, only to sovereign States; the assertion of such a right in respect of peoples was in conflict with the other principles being considered by the Special Committee, such as the prohibition of the threat or use of force, the duty not to intervene in matters within the domestic jurisdiction of any State, and the peaceful settlement of disputes. There was also no basis in the Charter for such a right of self-defense. The Charter, it was said, only authorized resort to force in the case of self-defense under Article 51 or of collective action decided upon in accordance with Chapters VII and VIII. Any unduly broad interpretation of the concept of self-defense, it was observed by one representative, would gravely disturb international peace instead of helping to attain the aims of justice which the concept was intended to serve.[11]

In view of these proposals and the debate upon them, it is of especial interest to consider what emerged. On the proposal of the Committee, a resolution was unanimously adopted by the 25th Session of the General Assembly, containing these provisions:

> Every State has the duty to refrain from any forcible action which deprives peoples . . . of their right to self-determination and freedom and independence. In their actions against, and resistance to, such forcible action in pursuit of the exercise of their right to self-determination, such peoples are entitled to seek and to receive support in accordance with the purposes and principles of the Charter.
>
> Nothing in the foregoing paragraphs shall be construed as enlarging or diminishing in any way the scope of the provisions of the Charter concerning cases in which the use of force is lawful.[12]

The statement that every State has the duty to refrain from forcible action against the exercise of the right of self-determination has a wider application than to wars of liberation (as indeed the full statement of the resolution's section on self-determination makes clear, since it most decidedly and sensibly is not limited to colonial situations). It was also made clear by the United States, the United Kingdom, and other Powers that, in voting for this text, their authority "to employ appropriate measures of police protection in order to maintain law and order in territories"[13] for

---

[11] *Ibid.*, at 104.

[12] General Assembly Resolution 2625 (XXV).

[13] Statement by the U.S. Alternate Representative in the Legal Committee of the General Assembly, Sept. 24, 1970, Press Release USUN–122, at 7.

which they are responsible remains intact. Nevertheless, the provision does declare that states shall not use force to prevent the exercise of self-determination. Moreover, it envisages "actions against, and resistance to, such forcible action"—a fair translation of a genuine war of liberation—and provides that peoples so acting are "entitled to seek and to receive support in accordance with the purposes and principles of the Charter."

These provisions appear to concede much to doctrines of wars of liberation, if not in terms, then in substance. They do indicate that the use of force against the exercise of self-determination is a violation of international law; they contemplate that the victims of that violation may resist and forcibly resist. Indeed, States are under "a duty to refrain from any forcible action" against self-determination and freedom and independence: provisions which plausibly apply, for example, both to the actions of Portugal in Africa and of the Soviet Union in Czechoslovakia.

Insofar as this resolution recognizes a right of internal revolution, it simply codifies what international law has traditionally assumed. Insofar as it lays down the duty of states not to suppress revolutions for self-determination and freedom and independence, it has taken a remarkably bold and progressive step, which, however, is likely to bog down in practice in dispute over what is self-determination, freedom, and independence (not to speak of what is the "alien subjugation, domination, and exploitation" which the resolution proscribes).

Does the resolution indicate that peoples fighting for self-determination and freedom and independence have the right to seek and receive armed support? This plainly was the design of those who argued for the right of self-defense against colonial domination, but it was not a design which this resolution achieves. The language does not specify "armed" support; and the support permitted is that "in accordance with the purposes and principles of the Charter." Thus, in voting for the resolution, the United States representative agreed "fully with the statement by the British representative . . . when he pointed out that the text cannot 'be regarded as affording legal sanction for any and every course of action which might be taken in the circumstances contemplated.' We agree, as the United Kingdom said, that States are not entitled 'under the Charter, to intervene by giving military support or armed assistance in Non-Self-Governing Territories or elsewhere. The support which . . . States were entitled to give peoples deprived of their right to self-determination was . . . limited to such support as was in accordance with the purposes and principles of the Charter and was therefore controlled by the overriding duty to maintain international peace and security.' In short, the Declaration [on Friendly Relations] does not constitute a license for gun-running."[14] Some other Members took the contrary viewpoint, that is, that "freedom fighters" were entitled to armed support from other States. But clearly the Friendly

[14] *Ibid.*

Relations resolution does not settle the question one way or the other—a conclusion that is underscored by the quoted saving clause about the scope of the provisions of the Charter. Particularly in view of that clause, the majority of the Security Council that was prepared to condemn India in the Goa case can maintain its position in the light of the Friendly Relations resolution. There is nothing in that resolution which would have entitled India—however unlawful as suppression of the exercise of the right of self-determination may have come to be—to have sent arms to Goan rebels, still less to have invaded Goa. The resolution would have prohibited Portugal from suppressing a Goan independence movement and would have entitled Goans to fight for one; it would not have given license for an Indian assault.

3. RECENT RESOLUTIONS ON COLONIALISM

More recent resolutions of the United Nations bearing on wars of liberation have gone farther than the Friendly Relations resolution—but without the support of the principal Western Powers. The Friendly Relations resolution declares that the principles it embodies constitute "basic principles of international law." While this is not the same as saying that all the elaborations of the principles contained in the resolution are principles of international law, the fact that the resolution was adopted unanimously, is termed a "Declaration," and was surrounded at adoption with the rhetoric of a resolution declaratory of international law suggests that the international community does regard it as a statement of what the law is. That clearly does not apply to recommendatory resolutions which, while adopted by more than two-thirds of the General Assembly, drew the negative votes of major Powers.

The General Assembly adopted a resolution in November 1972, on the "Implementation of the Declaration on the Granting of Independence to Colonial Countries and Peoples," which reaffirms that "the continuation of colonialism in all its forms and manifestations—including . . . the waging of colonial wars to suppress the national liberation movements of the colonial Territories in Africa—is incompatible with the Charter of the United Nations." It further reaffirmed "its recognition of the legitimacy of the struggle of the colonial peoples and peoples under alien domination to exercise their right to self-determination and independence by all the necessary means at their disposal." It urged "all States" and U.N. organizations "to provide moral and material assistance" to such peoples, "in particular the national liberation movements . . . in Africa."[15] This resolution was adopted by a vote of 99 in favor, 5 against, and 23 abstentions. Those voting negatively were the United States, the United Kingdom, and France, as well as Portugal and South Africa.

[15] Resolution 2908 (XXVII).

Another resolution adopted at the same session looks toward providing "maximum humanitarian and material assistance" to peoples of the liberated areas, colonial territories and territories under alien subjugation.[16] Eight States voted negatively. Still other resolutions of the 27th Session of the General Assembly reiterate the call for material and moral assistance—"all the moral and material assistance necessary to continue their struggle"—[17] to be extended to those seeking to throw off colonial rule in the Portuguese Territories in Africa.

The fact that these resolutions have not attracted universal support in the General Assembly appears to lend weight to the conclusion that the Friendly Relations resolution may not reasonably be interpreted as endorsing support by way of provision of arms—still less, by way of armed support itself—to national liberation movements. The principal Western Powers that endeavored to preserve their positions against such an interpretation at the time of the adoption of the Friendly Relations resolution have reinforced their stand by voting against these resolutions.

It should be noted, however, that those who otherwise interpret both the Friendly Relations resolution and international law have gained since that resolution's adoption a powerful ally: the People's Republic of China. Speaking in plenary session on October 3, 1972, the chairman of the Chinese Delegation stated:

> People condemn war and consider it a barbarous way of settling disputes among mankind. But we are soberly aware that war is inevitable so long as society is divided into classes and the exploitation of man by man still exists. There are two categories of wars, just and unjust. We support just wars and oppose unjust wars. If a socialist still wants to be a socialist, he should not oppose all wars indiscriminately. The non-use of force in international relations can only be conditional and not unconditional. The condition is to realize peaceful coexistence through mutual respect for sovereignty and territorial integrity, mutual non-aggression, non-interference in each other's internal affairs, and equality and mutual benefit. And in order to realize this it is imperative to oppose the policies of aggression and expansion of any imperialism. When imperialism, colonialism and neo-colonialism of various descriptions are still using force to enslave, commit

---

[16] Resolution 2955 (XXVII).

[17] Resolution 2918 (XXVII). The General Assembly's resolution on terrorism, 3034 (XXVII), further "reaffirms the inalienable right to self-determination and independence of all peoples under colonial and racist regimes and other forms of alien domination and upholds the legitimacy of their struggle, in particular the struggle of national liberation movements, in accordance with the purposes and principles of the Charter and the relevant resolutions of the organs of the United Nations." Thus there is a direct affirmation of the legitimacy of wars of liberation, but it is coupled with a reference to the purposes and principles of the Charter. It is not clear whether the purport of that reference is that wars of liberation are consonant with the Charter, or that the legitimacy of such wars is subject to the purposes and principles of the Charter. The former view may be more compelling. But the resolution in any event hardly has the force of law, since 35 states voted against it (including the United States, the United Kingdom, Italy, Japan and Brazil).

aggression against, control and threaten a majority of the countries of the world, it is betrayal to the people of the world to advocate non-use of force in international relations indiscriminately, without regard to conditions and in an absolute way.[18]

Thus the strains of "wars of liberation" and "just wars" are brought together again in a way not unlike that of India in its defense of the Goa invasion. The incompatability of such doctrines with the fundamentals of the United Nations Charter requires no elaboration.

4. THE DEFINITION OF AGGRESSION

The most recent pertinent formulation which has attracted general assent in a United Nations organ is that of the Special Committee on the Question of Defining Aggression. On April 12, 1974, it adopted a definition of aggression which includes the following provision:

> Nothing in this definition . . . could in any way prejudice the right to self-determination, freedom and independence, as derived from the Charter, of peoples forcibly deprived of that right and referred to in the Declaration on Principles of International Law concerning Friendly Relations and Cooperation among States in accordance with the Charter of the United Nations, particularly peoples under colonial and racist regimes or other forms of alien domination; nor the right of these peoples to struggle to that end and to seek and receive support, in accordance with the principles of the Charter and in conformity with the above-mentioned declaration.[19]

Again we see a recognition of the right of revolution. But the support which revolutionaries may seek and receive is no clearer in this definition than it is in that of the Friendly Relations resolution; indeed, it is limited by the terms of that resolution as well as (necessarily) by the terms of the Charter. Moreover, the clause is a saving clause; nothing in the definition limits the scope of the Charter's provisions, which, however, are not defined in respect of self-determination.

5. CONCLUSIONS

What conclusions may be drawn about wars of liberation as fought in U.N. organs?

It is clear that the right of revolution has been recognized more forthrightly and explicitly by the international community than it earlier

---

[18] P.R.C. Mission to the United Nations, Press Release of October 3, 1972, at 10–11.

[19] *The New York Times*, April 13, 1974, at 6.

had been. The illegality of forcible maintenance of colonialism or indeed "subjugation" has been proclaimed. But what has not been accorded to the exponents of wars of liberation is the doctrine that, in international relations (as contrasted with the situation obtaining within a state), force can be used if the cause is that of a war of liberation, if the cause is "just." India, China, and many other states, especially of Africa and Asia, have so maintained, but they have not enacted universal international law in derogation of the United Nations Charter.

Other States have been the less willing to concede privileged status to wars of liberation, not because they support continued imposition of Portuguese rule in Africa but because they are sensitive to the possibilities of abuse of that doctrine. Sukarno's aggression against Malaysia, verbally defended by him as a war of liberation, and so supported by a Soviet veto in the Security Council, is a contemporary case in point. The prohibitions of the Charter against the use of force in international relations cannot be repealed in cases in which the end to be achieved by the application of force is "just." What is "just" in the eyes of some is unjust in the eyes of others. Hitler may have been no less sincere in his desires to unite the German-speaking inhabitants of the Sudetenland with Germany than was Nehru in his desire to unite the Goans with India. Hitler and Nehru were worlds apart; the equities of the two situations profoundly differed; but the doctrine of the use of force "Charter or no Charter" is no more acceptable in this era than comparable doctrine was in the era of the League of Nations.

Chapter 18 | **The Relevance of Regional Arrangements to Internal Conflicts in the Developing World** | *Ellen Frey-Wouters*

INTRODUCTION

It has become increasingly evident that internal conflicts will continue to take place in the developing world for the foreseeable future. At present, we seem to be living in a period of limited political revolt. In most countries, in the short run, internal conflict will at most introduce minor social, economic, and political changes into the society.[1] In the long run, how-ever, radical social change and major structural transformation will be necessary if many countries are to escape from underdevelopment. Internal conflict will therefore continue until substantial social adjustments have been made.

The high level of political and economic competition among countries, along with competing conceptions of appropriate forms of political order, contributes to covert and overt forms of intervention and counter-interven-tion in these internal conflicts. But as Wolfgang Friedmann has pointed out: "Revolution is a time-honored way of effecting political and social change, where either the form of the existing regime or other circumstances do not permit a peaceful change. . . . It would follow from this premise that any attempt by a foreign power to interfere with internal change, either by assisting rebels to overthrow the legitimate government, or by helping the incumbent government to suppress a revolution, is contrary to international law."[2] Continued foreign interference can only delay the process of change, compounding and therefore intensifying the violent elements in that process.[3] Che Guevara spoke for many radicals when he said: "Wherever death may surprise us, it will be welcome, provided that this, our battle cry, reaches some receptive ear, that another hand be extended to take up our weapons and that other men come forward to intone our funeral dirge with the staccato of machine guns and new cries of battle and victory."[4]

---

[1] *See* C. Leiden & K. Schmitt, *The Politics of Violence: Revolution in the Modern World* 213–15 (1968).

[2] W. Friedmann, *The Changing Structure of International Law* 265 (1964).

[3] *See* Edwardes, "Coming to Terms with a Revolutionary World," in N. Houghton (ed.), *Struggle Against History* 301–15 (1968).

[4] Che Guevara, "Message to the Tricontinental," in I. Horowitz, J. de Castro & J. Gerassi (eds.), *Latin American Radicalism* 620 (1969).

Because of the unavoidable slowness of global machinery for the management of conflicts, regional community action may constitute an appropriate response to the problems created by internal conflicts and foreign intervention. Regional involvement in internal conflicts, however, raises a number of fundamental questions: Is effective regional involvement in such situations really possible in the world today? Will existing regional communities continue to develop in the face of major policy differences among their members? Or have they already become the victims of the existing national and international environment? What are the limits of legitimate independent action by regional organizations? During the last few years, it has become clear that norms differentiating legitimate from illegitimate regional response patterns to internal conflict are urgently required. Recent events in the Dominican Republic, Czechoslovakia, and Nigeria make this concern self-evident. The abstractions of the United Nations Charter provide little guidance for determining the legitimacy of regional responses to internal conflict. Certainly not all such responses are censurable, and some are even desirable. The important question is at what point the regional response may be considered to amount to an act of unlawful interference with the sovereignty of a member state.[5]

This chapter attempts to explore and to suggest some tentative answers to the above questions. The notion of "internal conflict" will be defined broadly, to cover any movement which, for economic, social, racial, ideological or other reasons, aims at overthrowing the government by the use of force and at changing the form or structure of the state. The systematic use of military weapons will not be considered an essential element of such conflict, since armed revolution has become difficult in most countries due to the power of the police and army and the development of elaborate counter-guerrilla strategies and capabilities. Further, the traditional criterion of "collective character" will also be considered unessential, since applying this criterion could unjustifiably exclude situations occurring in the initial stages of conflicts. The paper will seek to clarify some of the uncertainties and ambiguities arising when regional organizations tackle internal conflicts. It will briefly analyze the institutional, normative and political factors influencing regional responses; examine the regional role and techniques in selected internal conflicts; and ascertain some of the achievements and failures of existing regional organizations. Finally, it will suggest some institutional, normative and procedural changes to produce more effective regional responses to internal conflict. Even a brief examination of these extremely broad topics may give some insight into the relevance of regional organizations to internal conflicts.

[5] See Friedmann, "Intervention, Civil War, and the Role of International Law," 1965 Proc. Am. Soc. Int'l L. 67–69.

I

Contemporary internal conflict, with its political, social and economic implications, creates regional concerns, but a variety of factors limit the effectiveness of regional organizations in dealing with it.[6] A comparative study of regional involvement in such matters suggests certain factors that more or less consistently affect this involvement in all regions.

1. INSTITUTIONAL FACTORS

The limited character of existing regional institutions shapes their response to internal conflict. The decision-making process of the Organization of American States, the Organization of African Unity, and the League of Arab States is of an intergovernmental character. There is no supranational regional center of power above the member states; the regional system is limited to direct interaction between the power centers of the member units. The regional secretariats are merely administrative organs, exercising no executive power and entrusted with little scope for independent initiative. The organizations rarely possess the material and personnel resources necessary for operative involvement in internal conflict situations. Dynamic and effective organizations do not yet exist in the developing world, nor are they likely to be established there in the immediate future.

2. NORMATIVE FACTORS

The constitutional provisions of the regional institutions set limits to the scope of their legitimate involvement in internal conflicts. The Charters of the O.A.S., the O.A.U., and the Arab League are principally concerned with problems of interstate rather than intrastate violence. Internal conflicts are not mentioned by name or category. The principle of non-intervention is stressed in these charters; internal conflict is considered to be a matter of domestic concern and thus is often shielded from regional scrutiny. The charters, however, also recognize common regional culture and interests, and strive to promote autonomous solutions of local problems. Internal conflicts which appear likely to develop significant international or regional ramifications may therefore fall into this category of relevant problems.

The textual limits of the treaties have proven less important in shaping organizational responses than the political confines within which these treaties operate.[7] The charter provisions are subject to interpretation by

---

[6] For an excellent statement of factors influencing regional responses *see* Miller, "Regional Organization and the Regulation of Internal Conflict," 19 *World Politics* 582 (1967).

[7] *Id.* at 584.

the member states acting in concert, enabling them either to implement or to ignore the basic rules. In addition, the organizations have augmented the legal basis for their involvement in internal conflict by means of specific resolutions. The history of such involvement illustrates the growth of new response patterns. There is often a disparity between solemnly professed principles and the reality of regional behaviour. Internal struggles for supremacy are increasingly seen as parts of larger conflicts of a racial, neo-colonial, or cold-war character that involve the risk of external intervention and thereby constitute threats to regional peace and security. The organizations have actively pursued intervention by declaring that specific domestic circumstances in a country are "undesirable" and hence intervention is legitimate. Different socio-economic and political circumstances in the various regions have led to different trends of treaty usage and interpretation in regional practice.

3. POLITICAL FACTORS

The political and ideological orientation of member states within each region plays an important role in defining each regional response to internal conflict. One reason for limited effectiveness of regions lies in the fact that relevant elites in member states may not be sufficiently oriented toward their regional system, but continue to expect benefits from ties and obligations to outside powers.

The regional response is also influenced by the attitudes of such groups toward the modernization which is taking place within the developing countries. The societies embodied in regional organizations comprise states of different political and ideological orientation. The members, accordingly, may be so intent upon securing a particular outcome of an internal conflict that they ignore its disruptive effects upon regional relations. Even where the regional interest would be best satisfied by an effort at mediation, the differing views of its members may make it impossible for the organization to function as a successful third party. Effective regional involvement requires enough consensus among the elites of member states, a certain compatibility of the major values held by them, a sense of regional unity, the mutual acceptance of a common interest, and mutual perception of an existing threat to regional peace.

The regional response to internal conflict is also influenced by international systemic factors. Various external actors, including governments, international organizations, and nongovernmental actors such as international corporations and revolutionary or antirevolutionary movements can be a cause of regional action or nonaction. For the time being, the regional communities in Latin America, Africa, and the Middle East are open communities which operate under the influence of external elements that are often beyond their control. Foreign interference in their affairs has frequently reduced their effective involvement in internal conflict. It has produced a basic split between the countries which accept and those which reject dependence on the industrialized world. Autonomy, a condition where intra-community actions and responses predominate over external control, is a minimum condition for successful regional response to these internal disorders.

Before examining the regional role in a number of such conflicts, brief note should be taken of the differing institutional, normative and political factors shaping the responses of the Latin American, African, and Middle Eastern regional systems.

The Latin American Regional System

The O.A.S. is an inter-regional political grouping. The great difference between the power of the U.S. and that of the Latin American members enables the former to dominate the Organization and to undermine the cohesion of the associated, largely developing region. The specific interests of the U.S. are too opposed to those of Latin America to permit the rise of a genuine regional political community.

Over the past twenty years, the U.S. has succeeded in establishing norms of conduct within the O.A.S. which have undermined the national sovereignty and integrity of its member states. "A dangerous trend has come to the fore as regards the principle of non-intervention in America. It is the idea that the principle of non-intervention is to be opposed to the action of other states, but not to the collective action which a regional organization may adopt. Thus . . . the measures decreed by the O.A.S. would not be considered intervention."[8]

The U.S. view of the legality of collective intervention is contrary to Article 15 of the O.A.S. Charter, which states that: "No state or group of States has the right to intervene, directly or indirectly, for any reason whatever, in the internal or external affairs of any other State. The foregoing principle prohibits not only armed force but also any other form of interference or attempted threat against the personality of the State or against its political, economic and cultural elements."[9]

The U.S.-sponsored Caracas resolution, adopted by the Inter-American Conference in March 1954, nonetheless authorizes collective action against member states in the event of the domination or control of their political institutions by communism, an issue which clearly belongs within the domestic jurisdiction of states.[10] In May 1965, an even more explicit resolution was passed, stating that the O.A.S., "being competent to assist the member states in: . . . the re-establishment of normal democratic

---

[8] Castenada, "Pan Americanism and Regionalism: A Mexican View," 10 *Int'l Organization* 382 (1965).

[9] Charter of the O.A.S., in R. Lawson (ed.), *International Regional Organizations* 325 (1962).

[10] Tenth Inter-American Conference, March 1–28, 1954, Final Act (Washington, Pan Am. Union), 94–95.

conditions, is also competent to provide the means that reality and circumstances require . . . as adequate for the accomplishment of such purposes."[11]

The U.S. has also made use of certain articles of the Rio Pact. "Aggression" is there stated to include acts against "the inviolability or the integrity of the territory or the sovereignty or political independence of any American State . . . or . . . any other fact or situation that might endanger the peace of America," including an act "which is not an armed attack." By not making an "armed attack" prerequisite to collective self-defense, the Rio Pact seeks to authorize more than permitted by Article 51 of the U.N. Charter. The decision to utilize such measures can be taken by the Organ of Consultation of the Pact "by a vote of two-thirds of the Signatory States which have ratified the Treaty," and this decision is binding, with the sole exception that "no State shall be required to use armed force without its consent."[12]

Under the guise of the above norms, the O.A.S. often serves to carry out the extracontinental objectives of the U.S. Because of the largely negative response to the military intervention in the Dominican Republic, however, Washington will probably turn to more covert forms of coercion involving the indirect management of Latin American military and political establishments rather than direct interventionism. It has, for example, been trying to develop the Central American Defense Council into a military force, which, with a minimum of U.S. personnel, could collectively control any "subversive" movement in the member countries.[13]

This creates a dangerous situation in Latin America, where only a small group of countries, including Argentina, Mexico, and Costa Rica may be able to avoid revolutionary upheavals. The remainder demonstrate various degrees of instability resulting from the desperate impoverishment of Central and South America.

U.S. dominance and intervention can be controlled only if the Latin Americans establish their own Pan-Latin American regional organization. In the short run, no such development will occur since Pan-Latin Americanism does not enjoy decisive political support within the region.[14]

The African Regional System

The O.A.U. is a loose, intergovernmental, cooperative association, its decisions non-binding on a dissenting minority.[15] The Organization has extremely limited material resources and limited leadership for rapid mobiliza-

[11] O.A.S. Resolution of May 1965, *reprinted in* 59 *Am. J. Int'l L.* 987–88 (1965).
[12] Rio Pact, *reprinted in* 42 *Am. J. Int'l L.*, Supp. 53 (1949), *cf.* Arts. 6, 17, 20.
[13] *See* Saxe-Fernandez, "The Central American Defense Council and Pax Americana," in Horowitz, de Castro, Gerassi (eds.), *supra* note 4, at 75.
[14] *See* Slater, "The Limits of Legitimization in International Organizations: The O.A.S. and the Dominican Crisis," 23 *Int'l Org.* 60–73 (1969).
[15] *See* Z. Cervenka, *The Organization of African Unity and Its Charter*, 231–35 (1969).

tion at the time of a crisis. At present, is is controlled by the more traditional African governments, who look upon it as an alliance, one of whose functions is to inhibit revolutionary activities and radical modernization programs. They feel that the Organization should concentrate on political, economic and cultural cooperation. Despite the formal bows to the "One Africa" concept, their loyalties are to the national state, not to Africa. A few more radical governments, on the contrary, would develop the O.A.U. into an all-African political community. They hold that only a supranational body with extended powers of decision and action can solve Africa's problems.

The Charter of the O.A.U. sets up certain norms of permissible involvement in internal conflict. The Organization is dedicated to promote the unity and solidarity of African states, to safeguard their "sovereignty and territorial integrity," to maintain conditions for peace and security, and "to fight against neo-colonialism in all its forms." In pursuit of these purposes, it must adhere to the principle of "non-interference in the internal affairs of states." To judge from its Charter, the O.A.U. is the kind of communal undertaking which could be expected to consider cases of internal conflict threatening the common peace. Since its establishment, a principle of legitimacy has emerged, justifying certain limited, non-coercive regional interventions in internal conflict. During the second Congo crisis and again during the Nigerian internal war, the O.A.U. asserted a legitimate concern with national reconciliation within a member country. The Organization also considers itself authorized to protect its members against foreign subversion, intervention, and indirect aggression.

In such efforts, the O.A.U. has been restricted by its members' ideological and political differences. For the more traditional members the rule of "non-interference in the internal affairs of states" requires that states, within and outside the region, refrain from assisting rebellious elements in a member country, while being permitted to assist an incumbent regime. For the more radical members, intervention is any action taken in the region by non-regional powers for neo-colonialist purposes. According to this view, the concern of a genuinely independent African state about the affairs of another state controlled by neo-colonialism can not be considered an act of intervention. Within the region, all are brothers, and one can give assistance to brothers.[16]

The principle of "respect for the territorial integrity of each state" also affects the regional response to internal conflict. To the majority of African states, this principle is directed not only against external aggression but also against secessionist movements within the state. A few states hold a more limited view of this principle, considering opposition to secessionist movements as a negation of the right to self-determination of peoples. They point out that secession from a state for legitimate reasons,

---

[16] For a comprehensive statement of this view *see* Zartman, "Intervention Among Developing States," 22 *J. Int'l Affairs* 188–98 (1968).

although constitutionally a breach of the law and therefore, from the point of view of the parent state, illegal and an "internal matter" at that, is not contrary to international law.[17]

Because of these conflicting attitudes, a regional consensus is often impossible. In addition, the existence of fundamental differences in political systems, ideological splits, different approaches to the problems of modernization, disparities in the level of political and economic development, and different foreign policy objectives complicate effective regional involvement in internal conflict.[18] Finally, the problems and potential dangers that confront most African leaders from within their societies are likely to deter them from encouraging a stronger role by the O.A.U. in internal conflict. It is to be expected that these various factors will continue to limit the Organization in the near future.

A more effective, responsible, non-partisan O.A.U. involvement in internal conflict will become possible only when a higher level of regional autonomy, consensus and integration has been achieved. The contemporary climate in Africa does not favor an immediate acceleration of this process.

The Middle Eastern Regional System

Like the O.A.U., the League of Arab States is an intergovernmental cooperative association whose major role is that of a coordinator of common political and functional activities. The Arab League Secretariat, however, largely committed to the establishment of supranational regional institutions, provides the Arab world with a dynamic center of regional activity. While the material resources of the organization remain limited, the radical Arab states can provide leadership for rapid regional mobilization. The Pact of the League directs that organization toward the achievement of peace and cooperation between Arab states. In the event of aggression against a member state, the Council of the League can determine self-defense measures, but this decision must be taken unanimously. The only provision relevant to internal conflict *per se* is the stipulation in Article 8 that: "Each member state shall respect the system of government established in the other member states and regard them as exclusive concerns of those states. Each shall pledge to abstain from any action calculated to change established systems of government."[19]

Despite differences between Arab states, identification with the region is stronger in the Middle East than in Africa. The concept of an extended "Arab Nation" exists as a unit of loyalty for all Arab states and has influenced interpretation of the basic Pact as well as the formulation of certain new norms related to internal conflict. The Arab states claim that

[17] See Mazrui, "Violent Contiguity and the Politics of Retribalization in Africa," 23 *J. Int'l Affairs* 102–3 (1969).

[18] See Statements made by African Leaders, in P. Sigmund (ed.), *The Ideologies of the Developing Nations* 212–303 (rev. ed. 1967).

[19] See the Pact of the League in R. Macdonald, *The League of Arab States*, 322 (1965).

regional involvement in internal conflict is legitimate when peace has to be restored and order maintained. They have taken a strong stand against extraregional intervention and indirect aggression. As far as intraregional intervention is concerned, a split has developed among them. According to a majority of League members, the reality of the "Arab Nation" makes any Arab state less than sovereign and authorizes certain forms of "progressive" intraregional intervention. No anti-interventionist resolutions going beyond Article 8 of the League Charter have been passed, nor are any likely to be adopted as long as the more radical Arab governments maintain their present dominant position. Opposed views of the more conservative states have been largely ineffective.[20]

Despite the majority consensus on norms, effective regional involvement in internal conflict has not resulted due to existing divisions in the Middle East. The differences in circumstances and ideologies within the Arab states produce divergent and often conflicting solutions to the complex problems of modernization. As a result of the division of the region into revolutionary socialist, moderate, and traditional monarchical regimes, a lack of unity of purpose exists among the modernizing elites. This division is also reflected in their relationships with outside powers. The location of the League in a contested geopolitical area with considerable strategic importance and resources presents an additional major problem. It weakens the autonomy of the region and provokes interventionary activity on the part of extraregional powers.

The realization of this weakness has created a growing conviction among certain Arab elites that a united Arab community must be established. The differences among contending leaderships are such, however, that the establishment of a common Pan-Arab front seems out of the question for the time being.

II

Before turning to an analysis of the objectives and techniques of regional action patterns, it is useful to give a brief overview of selected examples of regional response to different types of internal conflict in order to illustrate their diversity.

1. THE ORGANIZATION OF AFRICAN UNITY

Five broad categories of internal conflict are discernible in Africa.

a. Internal conflicts resulting from challenges to the legitimacy of the authority in power.

The majority of these disorders have remained domestic in character and the regional institution has not become involved. In some cases which

[20] Zartman, *supra* note 16, at 189.

threatened regional peace and security, however, the African states have chosen to respond collectively. At the time of the first Congo crisis, African leaders, lacking a regional organization through which to act, endorsed a U.N. peacekeeping operation. But in September 1960, when Lumumba was deposed by Kasavubu, the regional unity collapsed.[21] As a result of the division between the radical and the more conservative states, the African group could not function effectively at the United Nations. The installation of Cyrille Adoula as Prime Minister of the Congo, in August 1961, only slightly improved this situation.

The internal conflict was renewed in 1964. The situation was critical: the Tshombe government, relying on American and Belgian military and financial aid and white mercenaries, had launched an offensive into Kwilu and Kivu provinces. Direct support for the Conseil National de Libération (CNL) was facilitated by the existence of friendly states bordering the rebellious regions. The Governments of Congo (Brazzaville), the Sudan, Burundi, and Uganda encouraged the activities of the CNL. Arms and ammunition came from Algeria, Ghana and the U.A.R. The result was a variety of conflicts with the Congo (Leopoldville).[22]

The situation was brought before an extraordinary meeting of the Council of Ministers of the O.A.U., in September 1964. Many normally moderate states joined the radicals in regarding the internal situation in the Congo as a legitimate concern of the O.A.U. At least a third of the O.A.U. members viewed Tshombe as an externally imposed traitor, and detested his use of white mercenaries to combat the rebellion. The Council adopted a resolution asking for withdrawal of mercenaries, requesting a cease-fire, and establishing a nine-nation Congo Conciliation Commission. It also requested non-African states interfering in the Congo to desist.[23]

The Conciliation Commission offered to assist in organizing a round-table discussion with all Congolese leaders and to supervise national elections.[24] On September 23, however, President Kasavubu protested the O.A.U.'s "manifest interference in the Congo's internal affairs" and announced the Congo's withdrawal, which largely destroyed the efforts of the Commission.

Soon the lines of division between African states supporting the CNL and those favoring the Central Government hardened. The Belgian-American Stanleyville operation, in November 1964, only temporarily reunited them. When the Council of Ministers met for its fourth session from February 26 to March 9, 1965, it was so severely split over the legitimacy

[21] See Resolutions of Casablanca and Monrovia Conferences, *reprinted* in C. Legum, *Pan-Africanism* 205–11, 216–20 (rev. ed. 1965).

[22] The best sources of information remain the volumes published by the Centre de Recherche et d'Information Socio-Politique (C.R.I.S.P.) on the Congo. *See also* E. Lefever, *Uncertain Mandate* (1968).

[23] O.A.U. Doc. ECM/Res. 5 (III), September 10, 1964.

[24] Report O.A.U. Ad Hoc Committee, CM/U.N. Doc. 3. Rep. AOM. S.G. *See also* O.A.U. Doc. CL/I/(II), Sept. 1964.

of intervention in the Congo that it could not even pass a cease-fire resolution. Then, on May 23, the Organisation Commune Africaine et Malgache (OCAM) welcomed Tshombe's Congo as a member, before the O.A.U. had worked out an "all-African" attitude toward his regime. The radical states, nonetheless, abandoned neither their opposition to the OCAM nor their condemnation of Tshombe.[25]

b. Internal conflicts arising from secessionist movements.

The Nigerian Civil War was one of the most difficult problems ever faced by the O.A.U. The majority of members supported the federal government's stand of "one Nigeria" and opposed the Biafran challenge to its territorial integrity. The Biafran determination to fight on against overwhelming odds, however, persuaded several other African states to intervene in support of the separatists: Tanzania, Gabon, Zambia, and the Ivory Coast all recognized Biafra as a sovereign state in 1968. They supported President Julius Nyerere's thesis that "Unity can only be based on the general consent of the people involved . . . it should not be imposed by force by one group upon another."[26] But the Nigerian government considered such recognition a hostile act and severed all its links with the four countries.

In addition, foreign military assistance to both the Federal and the secessionist governments widened the scope of the conflict, prolonged the war, multiplied the deaths, and made peaceful settlement more difficult. The injection of arms into the war-torn territory made the African states aware of the dangers of extraregional intervention. They realized that France was fighting British influence in West Africa and was also interested in control over the new flow of oil in Biafra. British, American and Soviet responses were equally determined by political and economic interests.

The first official consideration of the Nigerian crisis by the O.A.U. took place at the Conference of Heads of State and Government at Kinshasa in 1967, where three main principles of the O.A.U. Charter were put to a crucial test: those of "non-interference in the internal affairs of States" and "respect for the territorial integrity of each State," consistently referred to by Nigeria, and "respect for the inalienable right to self-determination" claimed by secessionist Biafra. The Nigerian government held that any O.A.U. involvement would violate the principle of non-interference. At the same time, the Biafran regime was pressing for O.A.U. action in its favor. The resolution finally adopted by the Conference was partisan, fully endorsing the Nigerian view and ignoring the Biafran side. The O.A.U. majority looked upon the conflict as an internal affair, expressed trust and confidence in the Federal Government, and condemned the secession. They also resolved to send an O.A.U. mission to the Nigerian government to assure it

[25] I. Wallerstein, *Africa: The Politics of Unity* 43–55 (1967).
[26] Nyerere, "Why We Recognized Biafra," *The Observer* (April 26, 1968). *See also* Petkovic, "Territorial Integrity and the Right to Self-Determination in Africa— Nigeria and Biafra," 20 *Rev. Int'l Affairs* (Belgrade) 17–20 (May 5, 1969).

"of the Assembly's desire for the territorial integrity, unity, and peace of Nigeria."[27] The countries which had recognized Biafra voted against the resolution.

The O.A.U. Consultative Mission of six Heads of State arrived in Lagos on November 23, 1967. Major-General Yakubu Gowon made clear the terms on which he was prepared to listen to them. He said: ". . . the O.A.U. has rightly seen our problem as a purely domestic affair and, in accordance with the O.A.U. resolution, your Mission is not here to mediate."[28] In its official communiqué, the Mission agreed that, as a basis for a return to peace in Nigeria, the Biafrans should renounce secession and accept the existing administrative structure of the Federation of Nigeria.[29]

The terms of reference of the O.A.U. Mission, as well as the Lagos communiqué, were a bitter disappointment for the Biafrans. Up to the Kinshasa Conference, they had advocated O.A.U. mediation provided that Biafra was invited to the talks as a sovereign state and not as part of Nigeria. They condemned the communiqué and rejected the O.A.U.'s attitude toward the dispute. As a result, the first peace talks between the two parties were held under the auspices of the British Commonwealth Secretariat rather than the O.A.U.

The breakdown of these talks in May 1968, as well as the appalling conditions of the population in the battle area, made any further African inaction impossible. The Consultative Mission convened a meeting of its members in Niamey on July 15, and invited both parties to the conflict. Colonel Ojukwu of Biafra attended, sensing that the Mission was now far more concerned with relief and other humanitarian matters and with ending the war than with its original terms of reference. At this meeting, the Nigerian Federal Government and Colonel Ojukwu agreed to resume peace negotiations under the auspices of the Mission. These took place at Addis Ababa in August and September, 1968. It was soon clear that there was no possibility of reaching agreement on a political settlement of the conflict. From then on, the negotiations were confined to humanitarian aspects of the conflict.[30]

When the Assembly of the Heads of State and Government met on September 4, 1968, at Algiers, the climate had changed, and the O.A.U. had become less partisan. Its final resolution, while still opposing the secession, recognized the Biafran leaders as a party to the conflict and showed greater concern for the welfare of the people in Biafra. It appealed to all concerned to cooperate in the delivery of relief supplies, and asked Nigeria to cooperate with the O.A.U. in ensuring the physical security of all people in

[27] See Z. Cervenka, *supra* note 15, at 196.

[28] Official Publication by the Federal Republic of Nigeria, Nov. 23, 1967, at 4.

[29] Official communiqué of the O.A.U. Consultative Mission, *reprinted in* 4 *Africa Research Bulletin* 901 (1967).

[30] See 5 *Africa Research Bulletin* 1122–24, 1152, 1185 (1968); 1968 *West Africa* 944.

Nigeria alike, until mutual confidence had been restored.[31] The four governments recognizing Biafra again voted against the resolution.

During 1968 and 1969, the Consultative Mission continued to search for ways to give reassurance to the Ibos concerning their future security in a reunited Nigeria. But the tide was turning against Biafra. When the Assembly of Heads of State and Government met in September 1969, it passed its third resolution opposing the secession; Biafra lost all confidence in the Consultative Mission, and all hope for a negotiated settlement faded.[32] The war ended with the sudden collapse of Biafra between January 10 and 12, 1970.

The unwillingness of the O.A.U. to consider the bloody, sixteen-year-old Southern black Sudanese struggle to free themselves from the Arab North is another example of African anti-secessionist feelings. Some 350,000 are claimed to have died from violence or hunger; and thousands of refugees were forced to move to Ethiopia and Uganda.[33] The Southern Sudan Liberation Front has presented petitions to the O.A.U., calling for observer teams to investigate its charges of genocide. The O.A.U. has ignored these petitions and has taken no formal action. An Assistant Secretary-General of the O.A.U., Mohammed Tsahnoun, participated in the negotiations between the Sudanese Government and the Liberation Front at Addis Ababa, in 1972. On February 26, 1972, an agreement providing for regional self-rule was reached ending the rebellion.[34]

The secessionist movement of the Eritrean Liberation Front, in Ethiopia, has likewise been ignored by the O.A.U. This movement, which was launched in 1962, has grown into a full-scale guerrilla war organized by the Front against the Ethiopian Government of Haile Selassie. In December 1970, the Government declared a state of emergency, put most of the province under martial law, and launched a major offensive by the Ethiopian armed forces which killed and injured many.[35] The Liberation Front has attempted to bring the conflict before the O.A.U., but the Organization has never formally discussed it.

c. *Conflicts involving external intervention.*

The O.A.U. has heard a few cases involving accusations of intervention by African states. As noted above, the protest of the Central Congo Government in 1964–65 against alleged interventions by other African states was ignored. In June 1965, the O.A.U. Council of Ministers attempted to

---

[31] *See* Z. Cervenka, *supra* note 15, at 217.

[32] *See* Perham, "Reflections on the Nigerian Civil War," 46 *Int'l Affairs* 231–35 (1970); Dike, "Nigeria—The War of Clichés," 20 *Rev. Int'l Affairs* (Belgrade) 17–20 (May 5, 1969); Hanning, "Nigeria: A Lesson in the Arms Race," 23 *The World Today* 465–68 (1967); 6 *Africa Research Bulletin* 1382, 1517 (1969).

[33] *See N.Y. Times*, Nov. 9, 1970, at 8; *N.Y. Times*, Jan. 4, 1971, at 3.

[34] 6 *Africa Research Bulletin* 1354, 1404–7 (1969); 7 *Africa Research Bulletin* 1302–5, 1676–79, 1814 (1970).

[35] *N.Y. Times*, Dec. 30, 1970, at 3; *N.Y. Times*, Jan. 19, 1971, at 3.

mediate in a quarrel between Ghana and its neighbors—Togo, the Ivory Coast, Upper Volta, and Niger. The Francophone countries had accused Ghana of subversive activity against them. Ghana denied these charges. The Council set up a five-nation subcommittee to mediate the conflict. By June 13, the subcommittee elicited from President Nkrumah assurances that he would expel all refugees who were considered undesirable by any member state.

On a few occasions, the O.A.U. has intervened indirectly in conflicts involving intraregional intervention. In the Chad-Sudan conflict, in 1966–1967, created by Sudanese military support of the so-called Islamic Government of Chad in exile, an accord was finally worked out with the help of President Diori of Niger. President Joseph Mobutu of the Congo (Leopoldville) intervened in 1966 and 1967 as a formal representative of the O.A.U. in the conflict between Rwanda and Burundi, caused by the latter's military support for Tutsi rebels.[36] The conciliation meetings led to agreement and the issue was reported as settled to the 1967 O.A.U. Summit Conference.

The hostile reaction in much of Africa to the Belgian-American paratroop operation in Stanleyville in November 1964 and to the Portuguese intervention in Guinea in November 1970 shows that whenever an extraregional military intervention takes place, a united African front may be established. Such interventions are generally looked upon in racial and neo-colonial terms, and are regarded as an attack on African independence.

The Congo Conciliation Commission tried to intervene in the increasingly dangerous situation in the Congo from September 1964 on. It sent a delegation to Washington to ask the Americans to withdraw their military aid as an essential prerequisite to ending external intervention, but the delegation was not received by President Johnson. The Commission also failed in an attempt to negotiate release of the white civilian hostages, although Gbenye agreed to release them if Tshombe would stop bombing Stanleyville; but neither was willing to make the first move.[37] When Gbenye refused to release the hostages, U.S. aircraft dropped a battalion of Belgian paratroopers at Stanleyville on November 24, 1964. After having safely evacuated the majority of hostages, they seized strategic points of the city and coordinated their operation with Tshombe's advancing columns, who entered Stanleyville on the same day.[38] The combined military operation was enough to bring down the Gbenye regime.

After the Stanleyville operation, the Conciliation Commission condemned the intervention and asked for an emergency meeting of the heads

[36] *See* Segal, "Rwanda: The Underlying Causes," 9 *Africa Report* 4–8 (1964); Matthews, "Interstate Conflicts in Africa: A Review," 24 *Int'l Organization* 353 (1970).

[37] *See* W. Attwood, *The Reds and the Blacks* 191–236 (1967).

[38] For a discussion of the operation *see* E. Van de Walle, *L'Ommegang-Odyssée et Reconquête de Stanleyville* (1970); *also* R. Falk, *Legal Order in a Violent World* 324–36 (1968); Ratsimbazafy, "The Past and Future of the O.A.U.," 19 *Rev. Int'l Affairs* (Belgrade) 20–22 (Oct. 20, 1968).

of state. On December 21, an extraordinary session of the O.A.U. Council of Ministers called upon the U.N. Security Council to condemn the operation. The O.A.U. Council also appealed to all foreign powers to cease interference in the Congo and declared that the Congolese problem would find its best solution within the framework of the O.A.U.[39] Throughout December the Security Council debated the matter at length. The Council resolution of December 30, 1964, asked for an end to foreign intervention and a withdrawal of the mercenaries and called upon the O.A.U. to continue its efforts in the Congo.[40]

The Portuguese-led invasion of Guinea on November 22, 1970, caused an equal outburst of African solidarity. A special session of the Council of Ministers of the O.A.U. was convened in Lagos, which condemned the intervention and charged some of the NATO allies with complicity in the attack. It instructed the O.A.U. Defense Commission to study ways and means of defending African states against foreign attack and set up a special fund to assist Guinea.

The French interventions in Gabon, Cameroun, Chad, Congo (Brazzaville), and Mauritania went uncensured, however. In Gabon, a military coup had succeeded when French paratroopers landed and restored the pro-French president to power. The matter was brought before an emergency meeting of the Council of Ministers. The French action, however, was supported by six U.A.M. states, and the Council did not discuss the issue. When the 1965 rebellion started in Chad, over 3,000 French and Foreign Legion troops were moved in and began military operations against the rebels. As this is being written, the rebellion still continues, and without French assistance the weak Fort Lamy Government would probably collapse. Since 1966, France has used a special division, La Force d'Intervention, on several occasions to support pro-French governments, and the O.A.U. has taken no stand against any of these interventionary activities.

   d. *Conflicts involving "illegitimate" or "racist" incumbent governments.*

The confrontation between a hostile group of independent African states and a recalcitrant alliance of white-controlled states has resulted in a series of conflicts at several levels within the international community. At the United Nations, the diplomatic campaign has been won in the Assembly by the black forces. But they have not been able to command strong Security Council support. Frustrated by this outcome of their campaign, most African states are turning to more direct confrontation with the governments involved. The wide range of positions held by O.A.U. members, however, prevents the Organization from playing an active interventionist role. In addition, the political weakness of the African states limits the organization.

---

[39] O.A.U. Doc. ECM/Res. 6 (IV), Dec. 21, 1964.
[40] *See* 19 *S.C. Off. Rec.*, 1170th–1173rd Meetings; U.N. Doc. S/6129 (1964).

As a result, change in Rhodesia and South Africa remains largely dependent on shifts in the policies of Western states.

e. Non-authority oriented conflicts with some political overtones.

While disorders in Tanganyika, Kenya and Uganda in 1964 were caused essentially by a mutiny of African soldiers against their European officer corps, they were also related to the Zanzibar coup and had some political overtones. An emergency meeting of the Council of Ministers of the O.A.U. was held at the request of President Nyerere, to seek an African alternative to the British troops which he had called in. Agreement was reached to replace the British by Nigerian and Ethiopian soldiers, who played a role in the restoration of order.

2. THE LEAGUE OF ARAB STATES

The League has been involved in relatively few internal conflicts. Only those conflicts involving external intervention have received attention.

a. Conflicts involving intraregional intervention.

The League was involved in the Yemen internal conflict for almost eight years. At first, there was little extraregional intervention. From 1962 to 1965, the United States and the United Kingdom maintained a fairly neutral position, and attempted to bring about Saudi Arabian and Egyptian disengagement in Yemen. From 1965 on, however, extraregional intervention increased. The United States and the United Kingdom became openly more sympathetic to Saudi Arabia. The Yemeni Republicans resented this attitude and turned to the Soviet Union for military and economic assistance.

The split within the Arab League on the Yemen conflict at first paralyzed the organization and led to U.N. action. After failure of the U.N. policy of disengagement in Yemen and termination of the U.N. Yemen Observation Mission (UNYOM) in September 1964, a period of direct diplomatic confrontation between Saudi Arabia and the U.A.R. followed. Although the Council was unable to discuss a case in which two important governments were intervening on opposite sides of an internal dispute, the Secretary-General and the Chairman of the Council visited Arab capitals in an effort to mobilize support for a solution. The U.A.R. and Saudi Arabia finally reached an agreement, in Jeddah, on August 24, 1965, on mutual disengagement. They also agreed that the Yemenis would decide their own future by a plebiscite. But frictions developed within the Republican regime over the plans of Nasser and Faisal to seek a political solution. The conference which was to prepare for the plebiscite broke down. The U.A.R. and Saudi Arabia cancelled their disengagement agreement and the internal war continued.[41]

[41] With respect to the conflict see generally D. Schmidt, Yemen: The Unknown War (1968).

During 1966, Arab mediation efforts intensified, but met with no success. By the meeting of the League Council in September 1966, the majority of Arab states favored the "progressive" intervention of the U.A.R. as against the "reactionary" intervention of Saudi Arabia. They were united, however, in their almost unanimous condemnation of interference by the U.S.A. and Britain.[42]

The Arab summit conference of August 1967 in Khartoum played a more active role in restoring peace to Yemen. Partly as a result of the mediatory efforts of Kuwait and the Sudan, President Nasser agreed with King Faisal to stop their intervention and to cooperate with a League committee comprising officials from Morocco, Iraq, and the Sudan. The Committee was instructed to supervise the withdrawal agreement and to assist the Republicans and the Royalists in negotiating a settlement of their conflict. The withdrawal of U.A.R. forces was completed by December 1967, and Saudi Arabian aid was terminated.[43]

The Khartoum agreement had been arrived at with little consultation with the Yemenis themselves. The Government criticized it and refused to have anything to do with the Committee which was perceived as an attempt to intervene in Yemeni domestic affairs.

In February 1968, Soviet aid, together with the help which Yemen was allegedly receiving from Syria and Southern Yemen, was cited by Saudi Arabia as grounds for the resumption of her aid to the Royalists. On several occasions, the Yemen Republic turned to the League for help against this interference; but the League took no further action.[44] The internal war ended in July 1970, with the formation of a new and more conservative Republican Government of "national unity," including Republicans as well as Royalists.

The League has played only a minor role in the internal conflict in the People's Democratic Republic of Yemen (formerly Southern Yemen), which started in 1967. The Republican Government receives military, financial and technical assistance from the Soviet Union, East Germany and China. Several insurgent forces, armed and financed by Saudi Arabia, are in opposition to the Republican Government.[45] In the fall of 1969, a series of small battles was fought between Yemeni and Saudi Arabian forces, and tension along the border still continues. Some effort to mediate was made at the Arab Summit Conference in Rabat in December 1969, and a fact-finding committee was set up to look into the situation. Since then, the League has taken no formal action, but the Secretary-General of the League has attempted mediation between the parties.

[42] *See* 1966 *Arab Report and Record* 89, 180, 320.
[43] *See* 1967 *Arab Report and Record* 269, 283.
[44] *See* 1968 *Arab Report and Record* 380; 1970 *Arab Report and Record* 133.
[45] *N.Y. Times,* Nov. 10, 1970, at 4; *N.Y. Times,* Feb. 10, 1971, at 4; Bell, "Southern Yemen: 2 Years After Independence," 26 *The World Today* 52–54 (1970).

b.   Conflicts involving extraregional intervention.

The League played a part in the internal conflict in Lebanon in 1958. The Lebanese Government announced, on May 21, that the conflict had arisen from the massive intervention of the U.A.R. in the internal affairs of Lebanon, and requested emergency sessions of both the League Council and the U.N. Security Council. The League Council met in Libya from June 1 to June 6, to consider the Lebanese complaint. Few details were made known of what happened at the meeting, but Lebanon rejected a resolution, submitted by six members, that proposed withdrawal of the Lebanese complaint from the Security Council and instructed the League to use all means at its disposal to put an end to the dispute.

On June 6 the Security Council took up the subject, and soon established an observation group to proceed to Lebanon.[46] The group (UNOGIL) reported in July 1958 that the vast majority of armed men observed were Lebanese nationals and that it found no evidence of massive infiltration.[47] The overthrow of the Iraqi regime at this point led the U.S.A. to support the incumbent Chamoun regime with a unilateral military intervention; concurrently, British troops were moved into Jordan.

The Security Council was convened on July 15, but became deadlocked. An emergency session of the General Assembly was then called in August. In view of prevailing differences in the Assembly, the Arab states decided to meet separately to see if they could evolve a satisfactory formula. Representatives of ten Arab states met on August 20 and agreed on a draft resolution that was unanimously approved by the Assembly on August 21. This provided for withdrawal of foreign troops from Lebanon and Jordan under U.N. supervision. It also instructed the League to use all means at its disposal to end the dispute.

c.   Non-authority oriented conflicts with some political overtones.

The Arab League has dealt with only one such conflict: the continuing strife in Jordan between the Palestinian commandos and the Jordanian armed forces. This conflict is primarily non-authority oriented, but the activities of some of the more radical elements of the Palestinian Liberation Movement are directed against the monarchical and traditional government of King Hussein. Hostilities in September 1970 were provoked by the ousting of the pro-Palestinian civilian government and the creation of a military regime by King Hussein. The Arab League Council, meeting in an emergency session in Cairo from September 4–6, appealed for an immediate end to the fighting and instructed a four-nation committee to find practical means to end the hostilities. This committee, headed by Sudanese Premier Gaafar Al-Nimeiry, went to Jordan and consulted with the com-

---

[46] 13 *Sec. Council Off. Rec.* 825th Meeting 17; Sec. Council Res. 128; *id.*, Resolutions and Decisions at 5, U.N. Doc. S/4023 (1958).

[47] *See* U.N. Doc. S/4040 & Corr. 1 & Add. 1 (1958).

mando leaders and the government. The committee was successful in induc-
ing King Hussein to replace the military regime with a new civilian
administration; but military action against the commandos continued.[48] By
September 15, a full-scale armed conflict had developed. Intraregional intervention in support of the Palestinians was taking place.

On September 22, the Al-Nimeiry committee once more went to Jordan
to confer with King Hussein and Yasir Arafat. The United States and the
Soviet Union made a common front against calling the Security Council
into session and were instrumental in bringing the Arab leaders to Cairo for
a meeting on September 27, 1970. At this meeting, the leaders of nine Arab
countries and Yasir Arafat signed a 14-point agreement that called for an
immediate cease-fire and the appointment of a three-man committee to
restore order in Jordan. The committee, called the Supreme Follow-up
Committee, included one Jordanian and one Palestinian and was headed by
Premier Bahi Ladgham of Tunisia. It formed three subsidiary offices: a
military office, a civilian office, and a relief and assistance office.[49] From
September through December, the committee played a useful role in supervising the application of the peace terms. But by January 1971, the agreement ending the fighting had broken down and renewed hostilities were
reported. Jordan's suppression of the guerrillas in July 1971 terminated
the presence of active bases in the kingdom.

3. THE ORGANIZATION OF AMERICAN STATES

The purpose of the following observations is to show the involvement of the
Latin American states in the Dominican intervention of 1965–66. The
generally conservative regimes of Brazil, Argentina, Guatemala, Panama,
Colombia, El Salvador, Nicaragua, and Honduras fully supported the
U.S.A. However, Chile, Mexico, Peru, Ecuador, and Uruguay opposed all
collective action. Some other states, while supporting collective mediatory
action, were skeptical about an overt O.A.S. role in imposing a Dominican
political settlement, as well as about an inter-American military involvement in the crisis. The Inter-American Peace Force (IAPF) contained
only about 2,000 Latin American troops, most of whom were Brazilians.
The presence of this force may, initially, have prolonged fighting by
strengthening the morale of the pro-junta forces. The Special Committee of
the O.A.S. Council, established in May 1965 to obtain a cease-fire and
composed of Argentina, Brazil, Colombia, Panama, and Guatemala, was
biased against the Constitutionalists, failed in its task, and resigned two
weeks after it was established. After the resignation, the Council authorized
the O.A.S. Secretary-General, José A. Mora, to continue working for a
ceasefire. But the major actors in the conflict were not ready for a settle-

---

[48] *N.Y. Times*, Sept. 7, 1970, at 1; *N.Y. Times*, Sept. 22, 1970, at 1; *N.Y. Times*,
Sept. 25, 1970, at 1.

[49] For the text of the Accord, *see N.Y. Times*, Sept. 29, 1970, at 10.

ment, and Mora also failed.[50] The last O.A.S. body, the Ad Hoc Committee consisting of Ellsworth Bunker of the U.S.A. and representatives of Brazil and El Salvador, took over from Mora in June 1965. This Committee negotiated a settlement based on elections to be conducted by a provisional government.

The only O.A.S. body which played an independent and neutral role in the crisis was the Inter-American Commission on Human Rights, which was instrumental in contributing to a lessening of hostilities between the Dominican parties.[51] The Latin American states thus played only a minor role in the intervention.[52]

III

Regional organizations, as noted above, have responded in a variety of ways to internal conflict: through mediatory operations, preventive operations, nullifying operations, and humanitarian operations. Regional activities do not always fit neatly into this fourfold framework. Sometimes a regional organization has engaged simultaneously in several operations. In other situations, because of the susceptibility of an internal conflict to changing conditions, the organization has played different roles at different times. Moreover, its purpose in setting up a "presence" is not always clear, either in terms of the objectives to be achieved or the strategy to be employed. The mandate given a regional mission is usually a good guide to the role which the Organization wishes it to play: but it is not invariably so.[53]

1. MEDIATORY OPERATIONS

These operations consist of activity intended to bring the parties to the conflict to an agreed political solution, or to assist in the execution of a settlement. Various strategies to foster negotiations and to work for political reconciliation belong within this category: formal discussion and resolution within the regional organization itself; secret or open mediation by a representative of the organization; *ad hoc* missions to engage in investigation, observation or mediation; and supervisory operations to assist in the execution of a settlement.

For a variety of reasons, regional organizations have played only a limited role in the settlement of internal conflict. The main obstacle to an organizational role is that almost all internal wars end in outright victory for either the incumbents or the insurgents. Political reconciliation is a relative

[50] *See* O.A.S. Doc. OEA/Ser. F/II.10 (Doc. 109), May 30, 1965.

[51] Schreiber & Schreiber, "The Inter-American Commission on Human Rights in the Dominican Crisis," 22 *Int'l Organization* 508-28 (1968).

[52] Slater, *supra* note 14, at 57-58.

[53] For a comprehensive discussion of possible responses to conflict situations *see* A. James, *The Politics of Peacekeeping* (1969).

rarity, for the various groups and factions are interested not so much in an agreement as in victory.[54] Or mediatory efforts may be paralyzed because one party strongly opposes regional involvement. In addition, foreign as well as regional intervention may have created competing and irreconcilable interests, making national reconciliation impossible. In most internal conflict situations, therefore, the regional organization must recognize that no realistic prospects for a negotiated settlement exist.

Even if the parties are willing to discuss a policy of national reconciliation, the regional organization's capacity to bring them to an accord is limited. Proposals may be put forward by the intermediaries, but the parties may not be willing to accept them. Rival factions may attempt to use the organization against one another in order to realize internal political aspirations. Temporary agreement may be reached, without necessarily removing the source of conflict. Regional activities of this kind are often in the nature of short-term solutions, the long-term success of which is open to doubt. For example, the agreement drawn up by the Arab Supreme Follow-up Committee, and signed by King Hussein and Yasir Arafat on October 13, 1970, was a dead letter by January 1971.

While regional organizations have engaged in a good deal of mediation, their overall rate of success has been low. Some of their mediatory techniques, however, deserve further consideration. When conditions are appropriate, they may well be successfully resorted to in the future.

a. Debate and resolution.

Both the O.A.U. and the Arab League have been used for debate, the expression of regional concern, and the passage of resolutions calling for an end to the internal conflict. Although often of limited character, sometimes a strong majority has permitted the establishment of a regional presence. The urgings of the organizations have, however, had little effect in improving the climate for settlement.

b. Investigation and observation.

Regional organizations have not been able to put these devices to good use. Internal conflicts are not suitable for resolution by investigation. The parties in conflict do not like their activities, policies or popularity to be the object of an independent appraisal. Sometimes one party to the conflict may ask for a regional investigation, but the other party refuse it. Leaders of the Southern Sudan Liberation Front, for example, have called for an O.A.U. observer team to investigate their charges of genocide, but the Sudanese government has rejected such an investigation.

[54] See Modelski, "International Settlement of Internal War," in J. Rosenau (ed.), International Aspects of Civil Strife 122–53 (1964).

c. Mediation.

The establishment of a permanent and formal organ to mediate between the parties in internal conflicts has not been successful. The O.A.U. Commission of Mediation, Conciliation, and Arbitration has never been utilized. Instead, *ad hoc* committees have been appointed to mediate on occasion, but their effectiveness has been limited. Disagreements between members of a committee may paralyze its efforts. The moment suspicion arises that a committee is working in the interests of one faction and against those of another, support for the committee tends to disappear—as shown by the response of the leaders of Biafra, in November 1967, to the Lagos Communiqué of the O.A.U. Consultative Mission on Nigeria. Even if a committee is truly non-partisan, one or more of the parties may not want to cooperate with it. The response of the Republican Government of Yemen to the Arab League Tripartite Committee shows the fate of an unwanted regional mediatory operation. President Sallal announced, in September 1967, that he would not permit the committee to visit the country. Nonetheless, the mission managed to arrive in Sana on October 3, 1967. The President refused to meet with it. As word spread that the mission had arrived, a menacing crowd gathered, began throwing rocks, and rampaged through the streets. The committee was forced to leave the country within twenty-four hours. Ironically, the mission had shown a certain bias in favor of the Republicans, but this did not diminish the Republican opposition to the committee and its work. From then on, the committee met outside Yemen. When it became clear that it could not accomplish its task of national reconciliation, the committee was terminated in January 1968.[55]

The most successful method of mediation in both Africa and the Middle East has involved the more informal and secret intervention conducted by African or Arab leaders responsible to their organization and trusted and respected by the parties to the conflict. In fact, both organizations have often limited their efforts to requesting some leader to initiate mediation. In this way mediation becomes more flexible and, more important, the possibility of the mediator being suspected of partiality is lessened. The Secretary-General of the Arab League has frequently been involved in mediatory efforts; but the Secretary-General of the O.A.U. does not seem to have played such a vital role in African internal conflicts.

The success of mediatory efforts has depended in part on the objectives sought by the regional organization. The most effective role has been one of a limited, non-partisan character. The intermediaries must pay primary attention to the views of the parties in conflict, and attempt to secure an acceptable compromise. The attempt to formulate and implement a political solution may antagonize one or more of the parties and tensions may be increased rather than eased. The rejection by the Republican Government

---

[55] *See* 1968 *Arab Report and Record* 5.

of Yemen of both the Jeddah and Khartoum agreements illustrates the incapacity of a regional organization to impose a settlement. It is, also, often impossible for the organization to find a suitable solution to the complex problems of a country experiencing internal conflict, especially if that country is a modernizing state. The continuing tense political situation in the Dominican Republic exemplifies the dangers of a foreign-imposed solution not well suited to the internal situation.

Experience has shown that the regional organization should also maintain a non-partisan attitude. Its resolutions and operations should be of a neutral character. The O.A.U. response to the second Congo crisis shows that such a non-partisan attitude can be maintained. The O.A.U. Congo resolution of September 1964 appealed to the parties to settle the war peacefully and did not condemn the rebels. The Congo Conciliation Commission, despite its dislike of Tshombe, maintained a neutral position. In comparison, the 1967 resolution on Nigeria was clearly partisan. The Consultative Mission acted at first as a partisan body; by deciding to consult with only one party to the conflict, it doomed itself to failure from the start. As an ignored and condemned disputant, Biafra was not disposed to accept proposals which seemed only to confirm its suspicions.

d. Supervision.

So far, regional organizations have not often supervised the implementation of an agreement. The activities of the Arab Supreme Follow-up Committee in Jordan, from September 1970 until January 1971, and of the O.A.S. in the Dominican Republic after the establishment of the Provisional Government in the summer of 1965, however, indicate that such a supervisory role is possible under certain circumstances. In the Jordanian case, the promise of regional supervision itself played a part in securing a settlement. Observer teams of one hundred Arab officers, in cooperation with teams of Arab mediators, played a useful role in supervising the army-commando truce. But in the near future, regional organizations will only be able to undertake minor supervisory operations. Quite apart from the possible negative attitude of the parties immediately concerned, the organizations are not well prepared or equipped to undertake such operations.

2. PREVENTIVE OPERATIONS

Whenever conditions fail to offer prospect of a negotiated settlement, action may be undertaken which is designed to prevent the situation from deteriorating. The aims are to limit violence and minimize and censure foreign intervention.

In order to contain the level of violence, various cooling activities have been undertaken by regional organizations, but with extremely limited success. First of all, they basically depend on a desire by the parties to limit violence, a desire which seldom exists. In addition, such cooling activities tend to work against the more radical parties to the conflict who seek necessary internal change. A closely related problem arising from these activities may be the unintended prevention of any solution to the conflict. This may cause a new eruption of fighting once the regional presence is ended. In the Nigerian and Yemeni civil wars, the relevant organizations did have on several occasions a temporary cooling effect, each time interrupted by renewed hostilities.

Outside intervention has been by far the most frequent cause of a regional institution's involvement, becoming the subject of debate, of resolutions of condemnation, and of directives by regional institutions. Resort has also been had to condemnation of the intervention by a global consensus at the United Nations. Use has been made of the device of accusation, by which is meant the collection of facts exposing foreign intervention. Regional *ad hoc* groups have been formed to observe situations in which intervention is alleged or expected. Secret and open mediatory efforts have been undertaken to encourage termination of the intervention. After cessation has been agreed to, supervisory operations have been engaged in. These have been directed at intraregional as well as extraregional interventionary activities.

a. Intraregional intervention

Generally, the control of intraregional intervention has not been very successful. Discussion and resolution by the regional organs has been avoided in most such cases. Investigation and observation, equally, have proven to be limited techniques. Nor have *ad hoc* mediatory bodies been often used. The most successful response pattern has proven to be secret mediatory efforts undertaken by individual leaders. Post-settlement supervisory devices have seldom been used.

The O.A.U. has exerted a favorable, though limited, influence on the attitude of its member states toward intervention. Normatively, it has constituted a collective conscience that no African government can entirely afford to ignore. In certain internal conflicts, such as the second Congo crisis and the Nigerian Civil War, the Organization was unable to prevent intervention by regional states. In the dispute between Ghana and its neighbors, in 1965, a subcommittee of the O.A.U. Council of Ministers attempted mediation. In other cases, such as interventionary activities in Rwanda, Ethiopia, the Sudan, and Chad, secret mediation by African leaders created a climate in which the parties could move toward negotiation limiting or ending the interventions.

Paralysis has often prevailed when the Arab League has dealt with charges of intraregional intervention. As noted, most Arab states tend to discriminate in favor of what they consider "progressive" intervention as against "conservative" intervention. As demonstrated in Yemen, noncooperation by the intervenors, the U.A.R. and Saudi Arabia, and disagreement among its members doomed the League's anti-interventionist operation. Secret mediation, however, played a useful role. Partly as a result of the efforts of the Sudanese Prime Minister, President Nasser agreed with King Faisal, in August 1967, to stop their intervention. Once agreement was reached, the Yemen government refused to have a League supervisory team on its territory. The single instance of successful League action along these lines was the dispatch of an Arab force to Jordan in September 1970, one of the objects of which was to insulate the country against intraregional intervention.

b. *Extraregional intervention*

Debate and resolution have been used in relation to the regulation of extraregional involvement. Investigatory and mediatory operations have also been directed against such intervention. While regional organizations have often undertaken such actions against foreign intervention, the actual effect of these efforts has been minimal. They have had little success in containing internal conflicts so that they do not develop international ramifications which bring in non-regional powers. Success has been least in regard to decisive big-power intervention. The members of the organizations have disagreed on the nature of particular external interventions and have withheld the support necessary to a collective response. Frequently, by the time external interventionary activity is clearly perceived as endangering regional security or regionally recognized interests and values, the foreign countries have been so committed to factions in the conflict that successful regional action is no longer possible.

Thus, in the case of the second Congo crisis, the Belgian-American intervention in November 1964 was brought before the regional organization as a *fait accompli*. The U.N. Security Council resolution on the Congo was moderate in character and the power of the U.S.A. was enough to deter further retaliatory action. The O.A.U. was unable to prohibit foreign intervention in the Nigerian Civil War. In Lebanon and Jordan, the Arab League was unable to ward off the military intervention of the United States and the United Kingdom.

In the near future, regional organizations will be able to deal with foreign intervention only to a limited degree, and it will be largely up to third states to exercise greater restraint in using internal conflict for the achievement of national goals.

3. NULLIFYING OPERATIONS

Regional organizations have also sought to rid the regional community of "illegitimate" incumbent governments or insurgent groups which the majority of the members considered undesirable. They have served as useful political forums for governments wishing to put pressure on odious regimes —witness the use of the human rights issue against the Trujillo government in the O.A.S. Insurgencies considered to be dominated by Cuban or "international" Communism have been condemned in the O.A.S. Colonialist and neo-colonialist adventures in Africa and the Middle East have suffered a similar fate. Nullifying operations have been undertaken against the white-minority governments in Africa. African opposition to secessionist movements resulted, in 1967, in a regional nullifying operation directed against Biafra. The Al-Nimeiry Conciliation Mission engaged in nullifying activities in Jordan, in September 1970, aimed to replace the military with a civilian regime. Regional organizations have both denounced a regime or party to an internal conflict and have given regional legitimacy to the claims of an insurgent faction. Both the O.A.U. and the Arab League have endorsed the principles and objectives of rebellious factions in colonial and neo-colonial situations. The seating of the Provisional Government of Algeria in the Arab League in 1960, for example, strengthened its claims to legitimacy. When denunciation and invalidation have failed to produce results, the employment of coercion has sometimes been used to undermine either incumbents or insurgents. Thus, the O.A.S. engaged in military coercion against the Constitutionalists in the Dominican Republic in 1965, and the O.A.U. has used political, economic and indirect military coercion against the white-minority regimes in Africa.[56]

4. HUMANITARIAN OPERATIONS

Regional organizations have engaged in generally ineffective activities intended to safeguard fundamental human rights, particularly against a threat of widespread loss of life. This consideration was incorporated in regional action with respect to the internal conflicts in the Congo (second crisis), Nigeria, Jordan and the Dominican Republic.

The O.A.U. has played an insignificant role in regard to the humanitarian problems of internal conflict. The broad functions of the O.A.U. Congo Conciliation Commission extended to attempts at safeguarding the lives of the hostages held by the rebels, though this undertaking was complicated by varying interpretations of the Commission's terms of reference. The Commission, however, failed as a rescue mission. In the Nigerian case, from July 1968 on, the emphasis of the O.A.U. Consultative Mission was above all on relief operations in the distressed areas of Biafra; but the Committee was unable to prevent widespread civilian starvation. The failure of the O.A.U., in 1967, to look into the charges of genocide made by the Ibos against the Nigerian Government, demonstrates how an important category of humanitarian problems of internal conflict can elude regional examination. The teams of observers that visited the war-affected areas in 1968 and 1969 and reported that they found no evidence of genocide, were international in composition. Had their work been supplemented by additional observers drawn especially from those African countries with close contacts with the Biafran leaders, the O.A.U. might have influenced the

[56] The legitimacy of nullifying operations will be discussed in Section IV of this chapter.

search for guarantees for the Ibos, short of the promise of secession, under which a truce might have taken place. Like the O.A.U., the Arab League has been generally inactive in the humanitarian area. During the Jordanian internal conflict, however, the Arab states performed a significant emergency relief role. The Civilian Office of the Supreme Follow-up Committee distributed food and medicine and provided further emergency assistance.

Representatives of the Inter-American Commission on Human Rights, on the other hand, performed a valuable role in the Dominican Republic, investigating complaints of police harassment, political imprisonment, and outright murder of Constitutionalist sympathizers. The activities and public reports of the Commission received widespread publicity in the Dominican Republic and the hemisphere at large. The Commission was instrumental in deterring worse atrocities, securing the release of political prisoners, and helping to bring about a more peaceful atmosphere. In the relief sphere the O.A.S. (or, to be precise, the U.S.A., operating through the O.A.S. Dominican Emergency Relief and Recuperation Program) provided emergency relief as well as financial and technical assistance.

Thus a large number of conflicts have been acted upon, in one way or another, by regional institutions. The number and diversity of their undertakings are, however, not paralleled by the extent of their success. It is easier to obtain a registration of concern by the organized regional community than it is to carry through concerted regional action. The complexity of many contemporary internal conflicts, the constitutional limitations of the regional organizations, the divergence of individual national objectives and the lack of regional consensus, the unwillingness to entrust to regional organs the prosecution of even those objectives that might win approval, and, above all, the international environment have limited the accomplishments of regional organizations. The weakness of existing institutions, their meager financial resources, the lack of skilled personnel and other deficiencies have acted as additional restraints on their ability to act in internal conflict.

Some successes have, however, been attained. The efficacy of regional procedures has varied with the type of internal conflict involved. The organizations have moved pragmatically from conflict to conflict, avoiding fixed roles committing them to rigid positions. Over the years, both the O.A.U. and the Arab League have obtained valuable experience in coping with different aspects of internal conflict situations. This experience will enable them to play a continued limited but useful role in the future.

IV

A review of regional efforts in internal conflict management shows that institutional, normative and procedural development are needed for greater effectiveness. Given the infancy of regional machinery, such development holds promise for the future.

1. INSTITUTIONAL DEVELOPMENT

It is important to have stronger institutional mechanisms for effective regional involvement in internal conflict situations. One question to be looked into is whether a radical systemic change will take place in the developing regions or whether we can expect only system-maintaining reform. We can merely speculate about the future of the developing regions. A great many determinants, such as the policies of the super-powers, technological and environmental changes, changes in elite opinion resulting from particular events, new situations, and generational changes will affect the integrative process.

The regions of the developing world face a great crisis, and soon they will have to decide whether to go forward or stagnate. As Frantz Fanon has pointed out: "Africa . . . must understand that . . . like a great body that refuses any mutilation, she must advance in totality, that there will not be one Africa that fights against colonialism, and another that attempts to make arrangements with colonialism."[57] The same holds true for the other regions in the Southern Hemisphere. Strengthening regional systems requires overcoming their present stagnation through a more intensive confrontation of the regionally oriented modernizing elites with the Western dominated national establishments. Regional integration will succeed only if these elites accept the challenge of the era and take resolute steps to overcome the resistance of traditional and Western-oriented forces and to counter Western maneuvers aimed at preventing closer regional unity. This will be a difficult and lonely task. The Soviet Union seldom gives practical support any longer to groups seeking "national liberation," though its rhetorical support for such forces remains unchanged. Its political orientation has become directed toward maintenance of the status quo, which does not preclude political interventionary activity in certain parts of the developing world. On the more positive side, Soviet economic relations with the developing countries are slowly entering a new phase.[58] A more moderate and pragmatic type of economic cooperation, fitting the needs of the developing countries, is bound to bring a certain number of them closer to the Socialist countries and may give them new opportunities to cope with the change-resisting pressures exerted by Western industrialized states.

No radical change may be expected in the developing world in the near future, however. For regional movements in the Southern Hemisphere, the existing world pattern constitutes an obstacle. The development of new foci of world power, the emergence of multi-polarity, is an important condition for the success of their struggle for increased regional autonomy. In this light, a more progressive, neutral, and united Western Europe could

---

[57] F. Fanon, *Toward the African Revolution* 192 (1967).

[58] *See* Valkenier, "New Trends in Soviet Economic Relations with the Third World," 22 *World Politics* 415–33 (1970).

play an important role.[59] China has not yet developed the resources or central world position needed to establish itself as an active power. Eventually, when it can challenge both the U.S.A. and the Soviet Union, progressive forces in the developing world may find an opportunity to develop their own positions and to establish more autonomous regional systems.

In the near future, certain limited institutional, behavioral and operational developments are likely to reform and strengthen the regional systems. The situation will not be the same everywhere, however. In Latin America, new groups with an ideology favorable to change and with developmental and integrationist attitudes are coming into existence. The more radical among them—such as the Organization of Latin American Solidarity and some of the Latin American trade unions—reject the O.A.S.[60] Others, while less hostile to the O.A.S., nevertheless support Latin American integration. The Latin American Parliament, established in 1964, and the Andean Group, established in 1969, are changing the traditional pattern of Latin American political and economic development. There is a feeling also among members of the new managerial elite, the economic bureaucracy, the military, and intellectual and peasant circles that Latin American unity is a fundamental requirement for the development of the region. "The Consensus of Viña del Mar" contains the first formal rejection of the assumption that there is a natural harmony of interest between the U.S.A. and Latin America.[61] On the other hand, the landowning and industrial bourgeoisie and the conservative members of the military, especially in the larger countries—Argentina and Brazil—continue to oppose an integrationist policy. If the U.S.A. can come to terms with the more progressive goals, it should be possible to achieve greater regional integration.

In Africa, the obstacles to continental unity are enormous. It is generally accepted that, for the time being, regional integration can find only limited realization. Efforts are being made on the subcontinental level for the integration of economic and social functions. From the long-range perspective, the emergence of a more dynamic and independent regional community on an all-African scale seems of the utmost importance. In Africa, the process of nation-building and modernization will increasingly create revolutionary and interventionary climates, endangering the region at large. Whether accelerated integration is possible will depend to a large extent on the attitude of the Western European countries. British and Scandinavian membership in a more independent and progressive European Community could weaken the division of the African states into Francophone and Anglophone and result in more fruitful cooperation between Europe and Africa. This

---

[59] Papandreu, "Cold-War Blocs and National Independence," 21 *Rev. Int'l Affairs* (Belgrade) 18–23 (1970).

[60] *See*, for example, the Charter of the Christian Trade Unionists, in Horowitz, de Castro, Gerassi (eds.), *supra* note 13, at 406–7.

[61] *See* Final Document of the Meeting of the Special Committee for Latin American Co-Ordination, Chile, May 1969.

would enable the pro-integration elites to build a bridge between African radicals and conservatives, and lead African regionalism into new and stronger channels.

In the Middle East, the prospects for regional integration are much better. The differences between the more revolutionary and the more traditional regimes are narrowing. It seems likely that with further modernization a mutuality of political and economic interest and a consensus on foreign policy will develop. The existing confederation of Egypt, Libya, and Syria may be joined by the Sudan, Yemen, and the People's Democratic Republic of Yemen, establishing a vital core area as the center of regional activity. In practically every country of the area are groups who believe in a Pan-Arab solution to the problems of the region. This may eventually result in sufficient convergence of aims to permit the evolution of a dynamic regional integrative effort.

2. NORMATIVE DEVELOPMENT

The possible increase in the power of regional institutions makes it essential to develop clear and binding norms for appraising regional involvement in internal conflict and for delineating regional authority in such situations. A number of variables seem relevant to an appraisal of the permissibility of regional response patterns. It would be useful to clarify the norms to be applied in regard to such variables as the context in which the regional response occurs, the objectives sought, and the kind and degree of coercion used.[62] The Charter of the United Nations provides little guidance as to the permissibility of regional involvement in such situations.[63] Recent U.N. resolutions and declarations on internal conflict leave most of the important questions unanswered.[64] This makes normative clarification of the role of regional organizations a difficult task.

a. The context in which the regional response occurs.

The standard of non-intervention should form the foundation of any regional normative structure. Where a people in a state are justly dissatisfied with a government and are engaged in an internal conflict, the process of self-determination may be said to be in evidence. In such a situation, a regional organization would be under obligation not to intervene, even if invited or requested by an incumbent government to save or support that

[62] These criteria are suggested by Burke, "The Legal Regulation of Minor International Coercion: A Framework For Inquiry," in R. Stanger (ed.), *Essays on Intervention* 87–123 (1964).

[63] *See* Eide, "Peace-Keeping and Enforcement by Regional Organizations," 1966 *J. of Peace Research*, No. 2; *also* Frey-Wouters, "The Prospects for Regionalism in World Affairs," in I R. Falk & C. Black (eds.), *The Future of the International Legal Order* 529–43 (1969).

[64] *See*, for example, G.A. Res. 2625, 25 *U.N. GAOR*, U.N. Doc. OPI/424 (1971).

government. Accordingly, most internal conflicts need not come before the organization. Regional involvement in certain cases may even present a threat to self-determination. By regionalizing an internal conflict which is purely domestic in character, the organization may very well magnify the crisis and ensure that regional politics will be waged there. This is especially the case in those institutions, like the O.A.S. and O.A.U., where a majoritarian delimitation of domestic jurisdiction provisions is possible.

The non-intervention standard is in harmony with the general limitations of the principle of domestic jurisdiction. This principle is affirmed in various constitutional documents, as in Article 2(7) of the U.N. Charter. The Declaration on the Principles of International Law concerning Friendly Relations and Co-operation among States, in its interpretation of Article 2(7), states specifically that: "Every state has an inalienable right to choose its political, economic, social and cultural systems, without interference in any form by another state," and also that "no state shall . . . interfere in civil strife in another state."[65] The term "state" must be extended to cover states individually and in groups.

While the non-intervention standard should apply to most internal conflicts, under certain conditions legitimate forms of regional involvement are not only permissible but even desirable. It is in relation to such special categories of internal conflict that regional norms must be developed. These include:

(1) Situations where the parties to the conflict themselves request regional consideration. In most authority-oriented conflicts such a request by all of the parties is unlikely.

(2) Situations in which there is little or no indigenous conflict for the control of internal authority structures—that is, the conflict is externally initiated.

(3) Situations where the current level of crisis is extremely high or where evidence of internationalization or interventionary activity is clear and present. Regional involvement would be justified when a particular conflict sufficiently affects regional peace and security so that it is no longer a matter "essentially within domestic jurisdiction."

(4) Situations involving an extensive and immediate threat to fundamental human rights, particularly a threat of widespread loss of human life.

(5) Situations involving political regimes which deny self-determination on a racial, religious or ethnic basis, such as the discriminatory white-minority regimes in South Africa and Rhodesia.

b. The objectives sought by the regional organization.

Even where regional intervention in internal conflict is justified, certain limitations should be imposed on the powers of the regional organization. In most conflicts, the organization should assume a non-partisan attitude.

[65] *Id.*

Once a politically organized indigenous insurgency breaks out, supported by a sizeable percentage of the population, and the incumbent regime is faced with a serious challenge to its authority, the regional organization should treat the incumbent regime and the insurgents alike and not give partisan assistance to either party. The same holds true for situations where there is no incumbent government or where the competing factions have roughly similar credentials. Partisan response patterns must also be avoided in wars of secession.

Under certain conditions, regional partisan involvement may be considered legitimate. Partisan involvement is permissible in situations involving extensive violations of fundamental human rights. The Declaration on Friendly Relations underlines the legitimacy of a regional partisan involvement in such situations when it states that: "States have the duty to cooperate with one another . . . in the promotion of human rights . . . for all, and in the elimination of all forms of racial discrimination. . . ." Regional partisan involvement also seems justified in proxy war situations. Under these conditions, the regional organization could give collective support to the threatened regime. This would be particularly useful where foreign military personnel participated in tactical operations, but it could also be helpful in more covert types of proxy wars, masked as assistance to an indigenous faction.

A serious problem for regional organizations is the impossibility of maintaining total impartiality in an internal conflict, especially over a period of time. Even if good faith neutrality is aimed at, it is very difficult to achieve, as regional organizations often tend to further the objectives of political moderates over radicals. In most internal conflicts to date, the regional organization attempted to remain neutral in relation to the parties, but soon realized that this was impossible. The very act of establishing a regional presence will probably affect the outcome of an internal conflict. The dilemma of a regional organization in internal conflicts is that, while it should be committed to non-partisan objectives, its actions may turn out to benefit one party more than the other.

Because of the difficulty of maintaining a non-partisan stance, a narrow set of norms regarding the scope of regional involvement and the level of its objectives should be established. Without strict guidelines for the control of regional activities, the dominant position of a super-power in a penetrated system might be strengthened, or an "outsider" within the regional system who does not share the dominant political values, may become the target of a regional intervention. The regional role must remain limited also because regional organizations should not be used to prevent necessary social change. Regional bodies will not invariably exert a positive, liberalizing, and modernizing influence, and the ultimate effects of the regional efforts will long remain unclear. Moreover, internal conflicts for control of internal authority structures are difficult to deal with. Thus, in most cases, the organization should limit itself to being an intermediary between the parties in conflict, encouraging a speedy and just solution or attempting to prevent extreme violence or foreign intervention. Regional activity intended to achieve a particular outcome, or aimed at destroying the independence of the parties to the conflict, or directed at the imposition of a political solution, should be avoided.

c. The kind and degree of coercion used.

Regional coercive activities are regulated by provisions of the U.N. Charter. Three provisions are especially relevant: Article 2(4), concerning the non-use of force; Article 51, authorizing self-defense against armed attack, and Article 53, referring specifically to enforcement action by regional organizations.

Article 2(4), as interpreted by the Declaration on Friendly Relations, instructs states "to refrain from any forcible action which deprives peoples . . . of their right to self-determination and freedom and independence," as well as "to refrain from . . . participating in acts of civil strife . . . in another state . . . when the acts referred to . . . involve a threat or use of force."

One of the main problems facing regional organizations is under what conditions they can invoke Article 51 of the Charter. The article does not, on its face, recognize the existence of newer types of aggression, such as foreign military intervention in internal wars.[66] Regional organizations, in defining their right to retort in instances of indirect military aggression, should be bound by a narrow interpretation of Article 51. They should be permitted to invoke the right of collective self-defense only when the territorial integrity or political independence of one of their member states is threatened by foreign military action. An important variable in determining the legitimacy of regional collective security measures is the level of military coercion of the foreign indirect aggression. In the case of minor military intervention in an internal conflict, the regional organization should have no recourse to the right of collective self-defense. Proxy-war situations, however, where elements of a foreign army have moved across a border to participate in military operations in support of one party to the conflict, could justify resort to the right of collective self-defense.

Any overstepping of the right to collective self-defense could lead to violation of the sovereign rights of states. For example, Article 6 of the Rio Pact defines aggression in a broad sense, including any "fact or situation that might endanger the peace of America." For the sake of regional and international peace and security, such a broad interpretation of Article 51 must be discouraged.

Regional organizations can conduct enforcement operations only under certain specified conditions. According to Article 53 of the U.N. Charter, the Security Council can "utilize regional arrangements . . . for enforcement

---

[66] For an excellent discussion of this problem *see* Franck, "Who Killed Article 2 (4)?," 64 *Am. J. Int'l L.* 809–38 (1970).

action under its authority. . . ." But "no enforcement action shall be taken under regional arrangements or by regional agencies without the authorization of the Security Council. . . ."

The narrow construction of "enforcement action," as asserted by the U.S.A. in the Dominican Republic and by the Soviet Union in Czechoslovakia, should be rejected. For example, in the Dominican case, the U.S.A. took the position that the action was "peace-keeping" not directed against a state, and as such it was not an "enforcement action."

If other regional organizations were to invoke a narrow interpretation, the dangers would be apparent. The eventual emergence of stronger regional communities in the developing world would affect the stability of the international system if these organizations were to declare themselves competent to undertake military intervention in their regions. Thus, new normative restraints on the use of force by regional organizations are needed. First, a much broader definition of "enforcement action" must be accepted. According to a formula adopted by a number of states in recent years, "enforcement action" refers to all coercive action other than valid defensive action.[67] Under this definition, it could not be claimed that military force was being used for "peacekeeping" rather than enforcement. Any use of military force, no matter what the purpose, would have to be considered as enforcement under Article 53 of the Charter. Any form of military coercion by a regional organization would thus be illegal. Moreover, the use of economic, political, or any other measures to coerce a state in order to restrict the exercise of its sovereign rights and to secure from it advantages of any kind should be prohibited. Intensive coercion by a regional organization, whatever its form, should be undertaken only with prior authorization by the Security Council, unless military action under Article 51 is involved.

Limited regional operations, undertaken with the consent of the parties, could be engaged in without involving the United Nations. Such operations should be non-coercive and their purpose should be of a mediatory, preventive, or humanitarian character. Non-military action, in the form of limited economic and diplomatic sanctions, would normally not require Security Council authorization.

One difficult question concerns the legitimacy of the assistance given by the O.A.U. and the Arab League to insurgent movements directed against colonial and racially discriminatory regimes. In the last few years, the General Assembly has passed resolutions authorizing "assistance" to such movements. Such General Assembly authorization would probably be sufficient only for regional political, financial, and economic assistance. In the absence of Security Council authorization, collective direct military involvement in support of such movements should be avoided.

In general, the United Nations should assert more meaningful control

---

[67] See 23 *U.N. GAOR*, U.N. Doc. A/7185/Rev. 1 (1968); and 24 *U.N. GAOR*, Supp. 20, U.N. Doc. A/7620 (1969).

over regional coercive activities. This would require the Organization to become more responsive to the problem of internal conflict and to clarify its relationship with regional organizations. From the point of view of world order, the higher the level of intensity and the broader the scope of regional action, the stricter should be the requirements for U.N. initiation and supervision.

3. PROCEDURAL DEVELOPMENT

Finally, certain suggestions may be made to improve the regional institutions' capacities and procedures. Since operations leading to settlement will remain extremely limited in the near future, a more effective area for regional involvement in internal conflict will be the regulation of foreign interventionary activity. The need for community review and control of intervention suggests that regional organizations should be recognized as having authority to deal with claims of unauthorized intervention. While interventionary situations differ and each case must be judged individually, certain general guidelines may be used in the examination of the intervention. In the absence of an authorization by the General Assembly or Security Council, the neutral non-intervention standard should be basic for a regional appraisal of foreign intervention in internal conflict. The traditional standard, that it is lawful to assist a recognized government at its request, at least until belligerency is attained, should be rejected. The prohibited assistance should include financial and military aid and grants or sales of arms, as well as direct military involvement through the use of troops or para-military personnel.[68] Instigatory, preemptive and precautionary interventionary activity should be prohibited. Except for proxy-war situations, where elements of a foreign army participate in military operations in support of one party to the conflict, counter-interventionary activity should equally be prohibited. As Quincy Wright has pointed out: "It would appear that illegal intervention in the domestic jurisdiction of a state should not be made the occasion for counter-intervention but should be dealt with by the United Nations. . . . Only in this way can illegal counter-intervention designed to stop illegal intervention by another state be avoided."[69]

The use of military measures by one state in the territory of another state, allegedly to protect nationals of the intervening state, must also be rejected. The home state is entitled to intervene on their behalf only by peaceful means not involving armed force. Forceful unilateral intervention to protect the nationals of the target state should equally be prohibited. So far there have been few occurrences of genuine unilateral humanitarian

---

[68] A number of problems related to the non-intervention standard are perceptively explored by Moore, "The Control of Foreign Intervention in Internal Conflict," 9 *Va. J. Int'l L.* 315–39 (1969).

[69] Wright, "Non-Military Intervention," in K. Deutsch & S. Hoffmann (eds.), *The Relevance of International Law* 16 (1968).

action to put an end to inhumane treatment by a government of all or some of its own nationals and it would appear that these situations would remain rare. The recent Indian military involvement in East Bengal seems to fit most closely into this category. While the political and moral justification for the Indian intervention may have been compelling, the intervention must be considered a violation of the non-intervention standard. If the intervention is to be justified, it ought not be on the basis of dangerous legal justifications. Forceful unilateral intervention may have to be practiced in certain extreme genocidal situations, but international law need not authorize or encourage it. The duly established and legally recognized mechanism, at the world or regional level, may or may not function when confronted with human disaster or massive violations of human rights. But forceful unilateral action, however humanitarian in intent, cannot be condoned as legal, even when acting in lieu of the duly established mechanism, lest the abuse of that unilateralism destroy the whole basis for legally constituted process.

The regional organization should permit unilateral humanitarian measures by one state in the territory of another state only under very special circumstances, when there is need to take quick and decisive action in an extreme crisis situation, and when the regional or international community is not able to respond with the same speed. In those cases, the intervention should be authorized by either the parties to the conflict or by the regional organization or the United Nations, and should be nonstrategic, noncoercive, neutral, and strictly humanitarian. An example of such a permissible type of intervention would be the air-lifting of civilians out of battle or disaster areas. Strict guidelines and supervisory techniques will have to be developed if the abuse of such intervention as, for example, during the Belgian-American Stanleyville operation, in November 1964, is to be avoided. In addition, effective international and regional measures against human rights violations and genocidal action within a country must be devised.

To strengthen the role of regional organizations in interventionary situations, certain procedural improvements are required. Such organizations should first try to insulate internal conflicts from competitive intervention by foreign powers. The moment an internal conflict threatens to become internationalized, the organization should attempt secret or open diplomatic interposition, and should serve as a forum for debate and for the expression of regional concern. Once an intervention occurs, regional organizations should attempt to eliminate it. Reliable fact-finding and observation capabilities should be developed and effective review procedures established to scrutinize intervention.[70] There are significant fact-finding problems in appraising most interventions. Was the Stanleyville operation

---

[70] Some of these recommendations for procedural improvement are suggested by Moore, *supra* note 68, at 294–315, 339–43.

primarily a non-authority oriented humanitarian intervention, or was it mainly aimed at the Gbenye regime? What was the extent of British, Soviet, and French involvement in the Nigerian Civil War? Which governments provide military assistance to the insurgents in Chad, the Sudan, and Ethiopia? A neutral investigatory body, relatively shielded from political pressure, is needed to disclose interventionary activity. The establishment of a neutral and specialized observer corps could play a useful role in controlling certain interventionary activities. The corps could also supervise and ensure implementation of specific agreements to control foreign intervention, arrived at under the auspices of the organization and with approval of the parties.

With such procedural improvements, the importance of regional organizations as centers for debate, mediation, and even selective interposition would be enhanced. It is unrealistic to expect regional action in regard to minor interventionary activity, but regional organizations could play a useful role in major cases. As a first step, even limited regional involvement is preferable to the present situation wherein individual states unilaterally assume authority in internal conflict situations. The longer-term effect of continued regional censure of intervention is likely to be more positive. In the Congo case, the bitter denunciations of the Africans probably had some impact on the subsequent behavior of the U.S.A. in Africa. Equally, in the case of Guinea in 1970, the angry response of the Africans may limit future Portuguese interventionary activities. The Arab stand against the American and British intervention in Lebanon and Jordan may affect future intervention in the Middle East. As a result of the response of part of the Latin American community to the Dominican intervention in 1965, and the response of part of the socialist community to the Czechoslovakian intervention in 1968, the U.S.A. and the U.S.S.R. may be more cautious about subsequent ventures. As regional organizations in the developing world expand their authority, independence, and competence, they may be able to maximize pressures to effect a reduction in interventionary activity. Increased regional involvement would also contribute to the development of a new code of rules which has some chance of being followed by a substantial number of national governments.

It is in the interest of the developing countries to press for the strengthening of their regional organizations as agencies for community review of intervention.

Regional pacifying and humanitarian operations aimed to minimize violence may become increasingly important. Escalation of the arms race and military assistance programs tend to intensify violent revolutionary activity. Regional organizations must develop effective procedures for the protection of human rights, so that the unilateral use of force against a member state can be avoided. Regional diplomatic initiatives and cooling-off operations should be undertaken once an internal conflict assumes dangerous military proportions. The regional organization should encourage the parties to respect basic human rights as well as those laws and customs of war applicable to internal conflict. In this respect, a promising trend should be noted toward the application to internal conflict situations of existing humanitarian conventions, so as to afford more effective protection to civilians and prisoners. Because of the limited usefulness of the provisions of Article 3 of the Geneva Conventions, the United Nations, the International Committee of the Red Cross, and other concerned international organizations have recommended the development of law in this area.

Substantive reform alone is not enough to solve some of the existing problems. New techniques of enforcement have to win general acceptance. Unfortunately, the humanitarian problems created by internal wars often elude international and regional regulation. More intensive regional involvement in the task of ensuring compliance with basic humanitarian rules and standards is eminently desirable, especially since the prospects of effective action by the United Nations are presently weak.

Several improvements in this area may be suggested. Regional endorsement of applicable human rights principles could provide a certain measure of protection to non-combatants. Resolutions of regional concern might ensure some respect for the laws and customs of war. More specific resolutions might recommend that the parties to a conflict apply, even unilaterally, relevant humanitarian regulations. Through secret intervention by regional intermediaries, the organization might attempt to humanize as far as possible the treatment of persons affected by armed conflicts.

Specialized regional machinery to ensure implementation of humanitarian rules should be established as permitted by Article 3 of the Geneva Conventions. A specialized, impartial, and sufficiently autonomous regional agency could function not only as agent of the regional community but also as representative of the respective parties in conflict. Such an agency could mediate more effectively than the more politically oriented regional organization itself. The agency could attempt to influence the parties to conform to humanitarian standards of treatment of civilians, combatants, and prisoners; and it could exercise certain investigatory, supervisory, and relief functions. The effectiveness of the Inter-American Commission on Human Rights in the Dominican Republic in 1965 and 1966 is a case in point. The Commission was popular in the Dominican Republic, perhaps in part because it took pains to distinguish itself from other O.A.S. institutions by, for example, *not* flying the O.A.S. flag. In Africa, the establishment of a regional commission on human rights has been proposed, but is not yet generally acceptable because of controversy over such proposed judicial functions for it as fact-finding, conciliation, and consideration of communications from individuals or groups.

Pending establishment of permanent regional agencies, consideration should be given to more frequent use of *ad hoc* machinery. An impartial and autonomous group might be appointed under regional auspices, upon eruption of an internal war, with agreement of both sides. Such machinery should be complementary to existing global machinery, facilitating accommodation to different internal conflict situations in which either the regional agency, a global agency, or several organizations working together would be acceptable to the parties.

CONCLUSION

Regional organizations offer no easy solutions to the problems raised by internal conflicts. Yet, notwithstanding their deficiencies, they seem to be the most suitable institutionalized forms for dealing with internal conflicts in the developing regions. As in the past, the U.N. will probably from time to time be regarded as a more acceptable source of mediation, but not in the majority of cases. The complexity of most internal conflict situations supports some decentralization of international machinery for dealing with these issues.

The institutional, normative, and procedural possibilities discussed above would offer some promise for improvement in regional processes. From a longer-range perspective, a trend toward more genuine partnership within regional arrangements would provide an incentive toward increased regional authority and autonomy. It is understood that future regional involvement in internal war should be compatible with the U.N. Charter, and should build on the effective features of existing international institutions.

While revolution must be allowed to happen when there is no alternative modality of change, regional organizations should encourage efforts at modernization with a minimum of violence. It is crucial for regional organizations in the developing world to participate in a necessary but nonviolent "war on poverty," and to accelerate the economic and social progress of their member states during the 1970's and 1980's. The great challenge to their ingenuity is to find alternative paths to economic and political reconstruction, which can bring basic changes without massive violence. Existing regional political and economic organizations have made little commitment to the peaceful achievement of necessary change on a revolutionary scale. They need to make every possible effort to devise a strategy for helping their members remake their political and economic life. They should encourage the active participation of reform-minded elites and technocrats in regional and national developmental programs. This may facilitate a shift in the value images held by the traditionally educated and motivated politicians and bureaucrats and permit a peaceful transformation of traditional national societies. Only those organizations that can meet this challenge successfully, creating a world environment in which violent revolution will be unnecessary, can hope to survive as dynamic institutions in the emerging world.

PART VI | THE REGULATION OF HOSTILITIES

Chapter 19 | The Applicability of the Laws of War in Civil War | Howard J. Taubenfeld

The acts of persons engaged in civil war, aside, perhaps, from the palace-coup type, have often been of the most violent and ferocious sort. Fratricidal war may normally have these qualities; each side is certain that it is right and acting against "traitors" to the nation. To the psychological impetus towards vile treatment of opponents must be added the confusion over what rules should be applied, indeed, as to whether any international standards properly apply to such an "internal" struggle—and, if they do, which—and who is to supervise their application.

In this chapter we deal only with the application (or lack of application) by the parties concerned of those rules for the conduct of warfare and its aftermath generally accepted as appropriate for the conduct of international warfare, the "laws of war." We do not, therefore, consider the important questions of determining whether the conflict is a "civil" or internal war rather than an "international" conflict, or with rights of or prohibitions against intervention by other states in support of any party. Other chapters of this volume deal with these vital issues. As cases we also use here primarily those "civil" wars already documented in earlier studies of the Civil War Panel; several of these case studies deal expressly with the application of the laws of war in the conflict, making it unnecessary to review those instances in detail here.[1]

THE LAWS OF WAR

In differing ways, for many centuries (certainly since the Middle Ages, when the Church forbade the use of that ultimate weapon—the cross-bow —though only in wars between Christian princes), the notion of limitations, of "laws" on the conduct of warfare, has been with us. Clearly, in war, three basic concepts are in conflict—those of military necessity, humanity, and

[1] R. Falk, (ed.), *The International Law of Civil War* (1971), *see* Wright, "The American Civil War, 1861–65," at 30–109, *esp.* "The Role of the Law of War in Relations Between the Belligerents" at 42–74; Thomas & Thomas, "International Legal Aspects of the Civil War in Spain, 1936–39," at 110–78, *esp.* "The Role of the Laws of War in the Conduct of the Spanish Civil War" at 121–40; Fraleigh, "The Algerian Revolution as a Case Study in International Law," at 179–243, *esp.* "The Conduct of the Belligerents" at 194–207; McNemar, "The Post-independence War in the Congo," at 244–302, *esp.* "Law and the Conduct of Civil War" at 257–71; Boals, "The Relevance of International Law to the Internal War in Yemen," at 303–47; and Corbett, "The Vietnam Struggle and International Law," at 348–404.

chivalry. There has been a long-standing effort to see that "humanity" was not neglected. Thus, in the last two centuries, certain subjects (the treatment of prisoners taken from enemy forces, for example) have been dealt with in many bilateral treaties. In the last hundred years, an international interest in the preservation of at least some semblance of civilization in the midst of war has found expression in a number of multilateral conventions.

In 1864, the representatives of sixteen nations signed, at Geneva, the first such broad agreement, for the "Amelioration of the Condition of Soldiers Wounded in Armies in the Field."[2] With its revisions in 1906 and 1929, protection was provided for the sick and wounded, and provisions also covered the status of medical personnel, the use of the Red Cross and similar emblems on hospitals, etc. Further, conventions signed at the Hague in 1899 and 1907 stated in general that:

> in cases not included in the Regulations . . . the inhabitants and the belligerents remain under the protection and the rule of the principles of the law of nations, as they result from the usages established among civilized peoples, from the laws of humanity, and the dictates of the public conscience.[3]

While almost every term used varies with time and place, the spirit or intent seems clear.

Prisoners of war received protection under the Regulations annexed to the Hague Conventions and under the Geneva Convention of 1929.[4] In addition, the sick and wounded at sea were protected by Hague Conventions of 1899 and 1907, revised in turn by a Geneva Convention of 1949.[5] At the outbreak of World War II, several nations, including Japan and the Soviet Union, were not parties to these later treaties, though Japan specifically stated that it would apply the conventions. Outrage at treatment of prisoners of war and of civilians by some belligerents in World War II, notably Japan and Germany (with respect to Russian prisoners and civilians), led to a major revision of the protective treaties, the 1949 Geneva Conventions.[6]

[2] 55 *British and Foreign State Papers* 43 (1870).

[3] On the Hague Conferences and for texts of the Conventions, *see* Scott, *The Hague Conventions and Declarations of 1899 and 1907* (1918); *see also* 1 *Am. J. Int. L. Supp* 103 *et seq.* (1907) and 2 *Am. J. Int. L. Supp.* 1 *et seq.* (1908).

[4] 47 *Statutes* 2021, G. Hackworth, 6 *Digest of International Law*, at 272–304.

[5] *See* 75 *U.N. T. S.* 85 (1950).

[6] The Geneva Convention for the Amelioration of the Condition of the Wounded and Sick in Armed Forces in the Field; The Geneva Convention for the Amelioration of the Condition of Wounded, Sick and Shipwrecked Members of Armed Forces at Sea; The Geneva Convention Relative to the Treatment of Prisoners of War; The Geneva Convention Relative to the Protection of Civilian Persons in Time of War. All are of August 12, 1949. These Conventions are contained in I *Final Record of the Diplomatic Conference of Geneva of 1949* 205 *et seq.* For discussion of the conventions, *see inter alia* Gutteridge, "The Geneva Conventions of 1949," 26 *Brit. Y.B. Int. L.* 292 (1949); Kunz, "The Geneva Conventions of August 12, 1949," in Lipsky

General rules common to the four Conventions, which are applicable in all cases of international armed conflict, include prohibitions on the taking of hostages, executions without regular trial, torture, cruel and degrading treatment, reprisals on protected persons, and forced renunciation of Convention protection. All protected persons must at all times be able to have resort to a Protecting Power and to the International Committee of the Red Cross (ICRC) or similar agency. In addition, that on the Protection of Civilians in Wartime provides for special protection for the wounded, for children under fifteen, and for pregnant women and the elderly. There is to be no discrimination on racial, religious, national, or political grounds. Civilian hospitals and medical transport are given special protection. Prohibited acts include torture, collective punishment, reprisals, the unwarranted destruction of property, the forced use of civilians for an occupier's armed forces, the failure to feed, and the failure to provide separate camps and protection for civilian internees. The 1949 Convention on Treatment of Prisoners of War includes a pledge to treat prisoners humanely, to feed prisoners adequately, and to permit relief supplies to be addressed to them. They may not be forced to disclose more than minimal information. Of great interest, as we will note below, it extends its protection to members of military organizations and resistance movements, providing they use visible signs of their status and carry arms openly. The other two Conventions expand somewhat the duties of safeguarding wounded and sick in land and naval warfare of the earlier Conventions. Two additional points are common to the four 1949 Conventions and grew out of World War II experence: a nation is not free to "withdraw" from the protection of the Conventions until well after the conflict is indeed over (as German puppet governments did during World War II) and, in each Convention, certain essential principles of protection are extended to "armed conflict not of an international character," making them applicable, for the first time by treaty, to civil wars, although scholars had for two centuries insisted that this was so.

By 1970, over 130 governments, including the United States and the Soviet Union, Communist China, both Koreas, both Germanies, and both Vietnams, had accepted the Conventions, though many reservations and special understandings have been included with ratifications.

In addition, a few non-parties were parties to the earlier humanitarian treaties which remain in force for them. There are also other treaties such as those governing genocide (of December 9, 1949), the conduct of hostilities as such, and the protection of artistic, scientific, and historic property

---

(ed.), *Law and Politics in the World Community* 279 (1953); 10 M. Whiteman, *Digest of Int'l Law*, 131–598 (1968); Pictet, "The New Geneva Conventions for the Protection of War Victims," 45 *Am. J. Int'l L.* 462 (1951); Smith, "The Geneva Prisoner of War Convention," 42 *N.Y.U. L. Rev.* 880 (1967); on POWs, *see also* G. Flory, *Prisoners of War: A Study in the Development of International Law* (1942).

and institutions which are also highly relevant to the humanitarian conduct of hostilities and hence to the aims of the Geneva Conventions.

The scope and content of these rules of warfare accepted by most western nations in the nineteenth and twentieth centuries have been widely discussed and written about; we need not, indeed cannot, repeat that discussion here. As we now all know, generally accepted rules thus provide for some minimum decent standard of treatment for prisoners of war, for the protection of the sick and wounded and those whose job is to care for them, and for the maintenance of some minimum standards for those in territory occupied by hostile military forces and for the protection of noncombatants in general. While the doctrine of "military necessity," the right of a belligerent to apply any amount of force needed to force the enemy to complete submission as rapidly as possible, with minimum loss to itself, remains an overriding right, it does not permit acts of cruelty as such, or *wanton* destruction of property, or murders and assassinations which serve no military purpose, or pillage, or ill-treatment of wounded and prisoners of war.

Despite numerous violations of these generally accepted norms and despite the de facto erosion and elimination of certain rules over time, such as that concerning submarine warfare, there seem to be no nations or quasi-states which claim that, in *international* combat, no rules limit their conduct. Any analysis of the origin and form of *civil* wars makes it readily apparent that, in addition to the ever-present problems of compliance and enforcement, special problems inevitably exist in limiting the forms of combat and in ensuring "humane" treatment for the combatants.

INTERNAL WARS

While formalization began in the American Civil War, the development and eventual codification of rules concerning the conduct of warfare took place in an international setting; it was not until 1949 that conventions specifically were made binding in other than a clear-cut international war.

For several hundred years prior to 1949, it was nonetheless true that writers had insisted that customary norms concerning the conduct of warfare did apply to the parties to civil war. Vattel urged that the parties had an absolute obligation to observe the common laws of war toward each other, for example.[7]

As early as 1912, at an International Conference of the Red Cross, an attempt was made to deal with civil wars. An American motion was made to support a draft international convention which would have permitted aid in the care and nursing of the sick and wounded and of noncombatants with

---

[7] Vattel, *The Law of Nations or the Principles of International Law*, vol. II, Bk. III, Ch. XVIII, secs, 290, 293, 296, III *The Classics of International Law* 336, 338, 340 (Scott, ed., tr. of 1788 ed. by C. G. Fenwick).

"utmost impartiality as between the members of the opposing factors."[8] The motion was opposed by the Russian representative, who argued that: "I consider, in addition, that the Red Cross Societies should have no duty toward insurgents or bands of revolutionaries whom the laws of my country regard as criminals."[9] This view was so widely accepted that not even an exchange of views occurred. The Red Cross did assist in the Russian Revolution of 1918–19 and in the Hungarian Revolution in 1919; in the civil war which raged in Upper Silesia in 1921, the Red Cross not only obtained authorization for care of women, children, the aged, and prisoners of war but persuaded both sides to undertake to apply the Geneva Convention during the hostilities.[10] In the Irish Civil War in 1921–22, however, both sides refused Red Cross offers of aid as "hostile."

After the Second World War, fundamental revisions were proposed in the Geneva Conventions. In addition to many other proposed changes, in 1946, a preliminary Conference of National Red Cross Societies suggested that, in the case of armed conflict in the "interior" of a state, the conventions should be equally applied by all adverse parties, unless one of them expressly declared its refusal to conform.[11] By 1947, a Meeting of Government Experts proposed, instead, that only the "principles" of the Conventions should apply, and this on the basis of reciprocity.[12] At the Geneva Diplomatic Conference in 1949, "heated" arguments occurred over the inclusion of any form of provision concerned with internal wars, arguments which are still heard today, especially with respect to reciprocity and to the standards to be demanded of the rebels to bring them within the scope of any international rules.[13] As a result of the conflict in points of view, each

[8] *See* Schlögel, "Civil War," 108 *Int'l Rev. Red Cross* 123–34, at 124–25. (March, 1970).

[9] *Id.* at 125.

[10] *Id.* at 126. For Red Cross resolutions in 1921 on Civil War, *see id.*, at 125–26.

[11] *Id.* at 127.

[12] *Id.*

[13] *See generally* Swidet, "The Geneva Conventions and Civil War," supplements to 3 *Revue Internationale de la Croix-Rouge*, nos. 8, 9, 11 (August, Sept., Nov., 1950). For a brief review of the divergent viewpoints, *see* Schlögel, *supra* note 8, at 128–30. *See also* I J. Pictet, *Commentary on the Geneva Conventions* 38–61 (1952). On special problems of internal war, *see also* J. Siotis, *Le droit de la guerre et les conflicts armés d'un caratère non-international* (1970); Mameri, "L'application du droit de la guerre et des principes humanitaires dans les opérations de guerila," Brussels Conf., Doc. R/7; Nurick, "Legality of Guerilla Forces, "40 *Am. J. Int'l L.* 563 (1946); Paternogic, "Qualité des individus belligerants," Brussels Conf., Doc. R/2; Farer, "International Armed Conflicts: The International Nature of a Conflict," Brussels Conf., Doc. R. 1 (Jan. 28, 1970); Yingling & Ginnaire, "The Geneva Conventions of 1949," 46 *Am. J. Int'l L.* 393 (1952), esp. 395–96; Ford, "Resistance Movements and International Law," *Int'l Rev. Red Cross* (Oct., Nov., Dec., 1967 and Jan. 1968); Khan, "Guerrilla Warfare and International Law," 9 *Int'l Studies* (New Delhi) 103ff. (Oct. 1967). For comments on current practices, *see,* among many, International Committee of the Red Cross, *Report*, "Reaffirmation and Development of the Laws and Customs Applicable in Armed Conflict (1969); Farer, "The Laws of War 25 Years After Nuremberg, *Int'l Concil.*, no. 583 (May, 1971); Pictet, "The Need to Restore the Laws and Customs Relating to Armed Conflicts," *Int'l Rev. Red*

of the four Conventions adopted in 1949 contains a common Article 3 which provides that:

> In the case of armed conflict not of an international character occurring in the territory of one of the High Contracting Parties, each Party to the conflict shall be bound to apply, as a minimum, the following provisions:
> (1) Persons taking no active part in the hostilities including members of armed forces who have laid down their arms and those placed *hors de combat* by sickness, wounds, detention, or any other cause, shall in all circumstances be treated humanely, without any adverse distinction founded on race, colour, religion or faith, sex, birth or wealth, or any other similar criteria.
> To this end, the following acts are and shall remain prohibited at any time and in any place whatsoever with respect to the above-mentioned persons:
> (a) violence to life and person, in particular murder of all kinds, mutilation, cruel treatment and torture;
> (b) taking of hostages;
> (c) outrages upon personal dignity, in particular humiliating and degrading treatment;
> (d) the passing of sentences and the carrying out of executions without previous judgment pronounced by a regularly constituted court, affording all the judicial guarantees which are recognized as indispensable by civilized peoples.
> (2) The wounded and sick shall be collected and cared for.
> An impartial humanitarian body, such as the International Committee of the Red Cross, may offer its services to the Parties to the conflict.
> The Parties to the conflict should further endeavour to bring into force, by means of special agreements, all or part of the other provisions of the present Convention.
> The application of the preceding provisions shall not affect the legal statue of the Parties to the conflict.

This "armed conflict not of an international character" is now formally covered; not the express provisions of the other Conventions, but rather the general principles of humane treatment and the prohibition of discrimination are to be applied to persons not taking part in the hostilities, including fighting forces who have laid down their arms and those who are sick, wounded, or under detention.[14] Note that acceptance of these standards by

---

Cross, 459–78 (1969); Pictet, "Armed Conflicts: Laws and Customs," *id.* at 22–42; Schwarzenberger, "From the Laws of War to the Law of Armed Conflict," 21 *Current Leg. Prob.* 239–58 (1968); U.N. Report of the Secretary-General, *Respect for Human Rights in Armed Conflicts*, U.N. Doc. A/7720 (20 Nov. 1969); Centre de Droit International de l'Université de Bruxelles, *Conference on Humanitarian Law and Armed Conflicts*, 1970, hereinafter cited as *Brussels Conference*.

[14] In addition, Article 4(2) of the IIIrd Geneva Convention of 1949 provides

a government does not imply any form of recognition of the rebels; there is also no express provision for international supervision.

In a further relevant move, in 1968, the U.N. General Assembly unanimously adopted a Resolution concerning Respect for Human Rights in Periods of Armed Conflict,[15] which recognizes the necessity of applying fundamental humanitarian principles in all armed conflicts. It reaffirms the rule that "the right of the parties to a conflict to adopt means of injuring the enemy is not unlimited," and states that "it is prohibited to launch attacks against the civilian populations as such." Also in 1968, the General Assembly, in a resolution on apartheid, declared that "freedom fighters" should be treated as prisoners of war, called on Portugal to treat prisoners in its territories in accordance with the Geneva Convention on Prisoners of War, and called on the United Kingdom to ensure similar treatment for prisoners taken in Rhodesia.[16]

The very obvious difficulties encountered in giving life to Article 3, in particular, over the last two decades will be noted in part herein, and are discussed in Professor Baxter's Chapter which follows. We turn next to an examination of the treatment of the laws of war by the combatants in several cases, selected to show differing conditions of combat at different times in history.

SOME CASES

THE AMERICAN CIVIL WAR

In the American Civil War, the United States initially declared that Confederate privateers were pirates, and Secretary Seward was reluctant to agree that the Confederates had belligerent rights.[17] Nevertheless, belligerency was in fact recognized and, on the whole, the laws of war as then

---

for prisoner of war status for members of "resistance" movements who meet the conditions: Two main questions were submitted to them:
—the application of the Geneva Conventions to guerrillas, and
—the respect of the Geneva Conventions and the other laws and customs of war of a humanitarian character by these same guerrillas.

For comments on the defects of Article 3 see infra pp. 516–17, Professor Baxter's chapter which follows and, e.g., Schlögel, supra note 8, at 132–34.

[15] Res. 2444 (XXIII), December 19, 1968.

[16] See G.A. Res. 2396, Res. 2345, and Res. 2383, 23 U.N. GAOR (1968). See also G.A. Res. 2446 23 U.N. GAOR (1968). In its 1970 session, as well, draft resolutions proposed that "freedom fighters" in general be treated as prisoners of war and that the assembly affirm minimum rules for the protection of civilians in all armed conflicts. See, e.g., U.N. Docs. A/C.3/L.1798, A/C.3/L.1806 and A/C.3/L.1807.

Calls for treatment as prisoners of war of those captured in internal conflicts are also found in Resolution XVIII of the XXIst International Conference of the Red Cross (Istanbul, 1969). See also Resolution XXVIII of the XX International Conference of the Red Cross (Vienna, 1965), on protecting civilian populations.

[17] On the laws of war and the U.S. Civil War, see Wright, supra note 1, at 42–74.

understood "seem to have been generally observed by both sides."[18] Prisoners were treated as "prisoners of war"; persons and private property were generally spared in "occupied" territory (except for property employed in the service of the rebellion, including slaves and cotton);[19] the "ordinary" acts of the Confederate Government within its territory were considered as valid, and adherents of that Government were not "traitors."[20] Bombardment of cities (*e.g.*, Atlanta in 1864) has been criticized by some later lawyers, but seems in general to have conformed to the international law standards of the time.[21]

Much of the suffering which occurred during the War was occasioned by conditions of the times, not by intentional mistreatment.[22] Some 30,000 of the 200,000 prisoners of war in Northern and Southern prisons died, primarily due to disease, cold weather in the North, inadequate food in the South, and poor medical and sanitary facilities. At the end of the war, the North did seek to proceed against certain Confederate leaders for treason, a course permitted under Lieber's Code.[23] Indictments were issued against Jefferson Davis and members of his Cabinet. While some were held in prison for varying short periods, none were ever tried.[24]

Thus, despite the intensity and bitterness of the conflict, the parties on the whole conformed well to the "civilized" norms as then understood. Comparison with the other cases which follow will be left until the end.

SPAIN, 1936–39

In the course of the Spanish Civil War in 1936–39, it is quite clear that[25] neither side lived up to the humanitarian conventions dealing with armed conflict, despite at least occasional statements by leaders on each side that the rules would be applied.[26] We leave aside here the question of whether or not, in legal theory, the war was one to which the Convention applied at

---

[18] *Id.* at 56.

[19] *See, e.g.*, Mrs. Alexander's Cotton, 2 Wall. 404 (1864).

[20] On the preparation of Lieber's code of land warfare (General Order 100, "Instructions for the Government of the Armies of the United States in the Field,") *see* Wright, *supra* note 2, at 54–55, and, on the code itself and its application *see* at 55*ff*. Gen'l Sherman's "March to the Sea" has given rise to some controversy as to observance of the principle of avoiding unnecessary destruction. *See id.* at 64–65.

[21] O. Spaulding, *Ahriman: A Study in Air Bombardment* 4ff. (1939); 7 J.B. Moore, *Digest of International Law* par. 1170 (1906).

[22] The mistreatment of Union prisoners at Andersonville was scandalous, and the commander, Captain Henry Wirty, was tried and executed for breach of the law of war. *See* S. Morrison, *The Oxford History of the American People* 715 (1965).

[23] Articles 154, 157.

[24] Morrison, *supra* note 22, at 705; Bonner, "War Crimes Trials, 1865–67," *Social Science* 128*ff*. (April 1947).

[25] On the laws of war in the Spanish Civil War, *see* Thomas & Thomas, *supra* note 1, at 121–40. *See also, e.g.*, Garner, "Questions of International Law in the Spanish Civil War," 31 *Am. J. Int'l L.* 66–73 (1937).

[26] On formal declarations by both sides that they would respect the Geneva Conventions, the declarations of Madrid and Burgos, *see* M. Junod, *Warrior Without Weapons* (1951).

all.[27] Looking at POW protection, for example, on August 9, 1936, the Madrid Government announced that the 4,000 military prisoners it then held would be treated according to the military code for the treatment of war prisoners.[28] The Nationalist leaders also declared that they would cause "to be respected, with the utmost scrupulousness, the laws and customs of warfare. . . ."[29] The record indicates, however, that in fact neither side, generally treated prisoners in accordance with any reasonable standards of decency.

On both sides, few prisoners were taken. Those that were, were often shot out of hand or after a summary trial.[30] The captured wounded were often shot. Bodies were mutilated. By 1937, conditions reportedly ameliorated to some degree, at least for prisoners without known specific political affiliations. In 1938, execution of prisoners appears to have dropped off further. Some prisoner exchanges were also arranged by the Red Cross and other groups, but not on a wide scale.

The Red Cross was never able to obtain the consent of either party to those principles of the laws of war relative to the submission of lists of prisoners to that organization and to regular prison visitation, but it was permitted by both sides to establish a message service so that information could be obtained by the families of the fighting men as to whether they were alive or dead.[31] With the end of the war, the Nationalists court-martialed for military rebellion captured and surrendering soldiers, guerrillas, and political prisoners in groups of twenty to thirty persons per day in the camps in which they were held and then executed them by thousands. Thousands of others who had their death sentences commuted to thirty years or life in labor camps died of disease, lack of food, and overwork.[32]

In addition to the widespread abuse of prisoners of war, both sides in Spain committed excesses with respect to non-combatants and property.[33]

---

[27] Several commentators argued that the Conventions were not applicable, since this was not an "international" war. See J. Stone, *Legal Control of International Conflicts* 653 (1959); Padelford, "International Law and the Spanish Civil War," 31 *Am. J. Int'l L.* 226 *ff.* (1937). *See also* II Oppenheim, *International Law* § 59 (H. Lauterpacht, ed., 7th ed. 1952), and M. Greenspan, *The Modern Law of Land Warfare* 18 (1959).

[28] It also declared certain areas to be war zones and subject to blockade, a "warlike" status.

Spain was a party to the 1929 Geneva POW Convention.

[29] *See* Padelford, *supra* note 27, at 597.

[30] For accounts of POW treatment, *see* Thomas & Thomas, *supra* note 1, at 121–26 and sources cited.

[31] The principles are contained in Arts. 77, 79, and 86 of the 1929 Geneva Convention. For discussion of their application in Spain, *see* G. Jackson, *The Spanish Republic and the Civil War, 1931–1939* 435 (1965).

[32] *See id.* at 536–39.

[33] Note that the use of hostages alone was not clearly contrary to international law at the time (nor perhaps now). *See* Thomas & Thomas, *supra* note 1, at 126–27, and sources cited. On civilians and property generally *see id.* at 126 *ff.* and sources cited, *esp.* Toynbee, "The International Repercussions of the War in Spain," *Survey of International Affairs, 1937* 8*ff.* (1938), and Jackson *supra* note 31, at 276*ff.*

Hostages were imprisoned and abused, undefended cities were bombarded, some monuments and works of art were intentionally destroyed. Violence was widespread; widespread attacks against the bourgeoisie, persons in religious orders, and political enemies were not controlled in Republican Spain until 1937. Churches were looted and burned; all were closed. There were many incidents involving the shooting of hostages and prisoners of war. Private property of "enemies" was confiscated. In areas falling to the Nationalists, purges were conducted against freemasons, liberals, members of Popular Front parties, and trade unionists, many of whom were executed. Most former officials of the Republican Government were shot when captured, and this was done at the order of military commanders, not by mobs. Execution by the Nationalists may have amounted to 40,000 or more, and even the semblance of trials was only instituted in 1937. On conquest of an area, Republican sympathizers were accused of conducting military rebellion and were shot by the truckload. Bodies were mutilated; civilians were fired on. In Basque country, there were hundreds of executions with no trial or with only the barest of trials, and this included women and churchmen. It is reported that executions of political "offenders" during and after the war constituted the largest single category of deaths caused by the conflict.[34] The Nationalists, too, confiscated private property of enemies.

One additional major point. Under the Hague Regulations on Land Warfare, attack or bombardment of "undefended cities," etc., is prohibited. Whatever the problems of defining "undefended" and of limiting the use of air warfare, it is clear that, in the Spanish Civil War, bombardment of civilian populations was carried out in several cases solely to kill and terrorize the population, and such acts seem clearly to have been barred at the time.[35] Madrid was bombed and shelled, in part, reportedly, so that German observers could note the civilian reaction to bombing; refugees from Malaga were bombed and shelled; Basque villages were bombed and machine-gunned; Guernica, without defenses, was wiped out by German aviators. In Guernica, the center of the town was destroyed, refugees from the bombing were machine gunned, and a third of the population were killed or wounded in this test of terror bombing.[36] Protests by foreign powers and by the Council of the League of Nations against the bombing of unfortified towns and of civilian populations were ignored by the Nationalists and only modestly responded to, for a while, by the Republicans.

It is quite clear that the Spanish Civil War, fought by organized forces, involved consistent and widespread violations of most generally accepted

[34] Jackson reaches this conclusion *supra* note 31 at 538.

[35] *See* Thomas & Thomas, *supra* note 1, at 135–40. On the rules, *see* II Oppenheim, *International Law* 524–25 (1935); III C. Hyde, *International Law* 1829 (1945). Generally, both sides seem to have respected the Red Cross emblem on hospitals but some bombings did occur. Jackson, *supra* note 31, at 430.

[36] *See* H. Thomas, *The Spanish Civil War* 419–22 (1961); Thomas & Thomas, *supra* note 1, at 138 and sources cited at note 74.

humanitarian limitations on the conduct of armed conflict. It was an internecine war fought almost literally to the death; it was not that the combatants were unaware of the rules, or of the "opinion of mankind." On the
whole, they fought with religious fervor and were uninterested in limits.[37]

ALGERIA

The Algerian conflict occurred after the 1949 Conventions came in existence, but in one of the grave problem areas constantly noted by commentators, that is, where one party—France—insisted that the armed conflict was
nothing but maintenance of internal order and that no internationally imposed restraints were acceptable.[38] The French Parliament, by emergency
measures and special laws, conferred very broad powers on its military
leaders in Algiers. At the same time, the Algerian Revolutionary Front (the
FLN) claimed that it fought to achieve an internationally recognized right,
that of self-determination, that guerrilla methods were all that was available
to it, and that its troops, in or out of uniform, and civilians aiding them,
were not traitors or criminals, but were entitled to treatment as "enemy"
soldiers and/or as political prisoners requiring protection. The FLN acknowledged, in principle, that there were restraints on its conduct of warfare of a type imposed on wartime belligerents but insisted that restraints
could only be reciprocal and hence depended on France's equal commitment.[39] For France, it was not possible to conceive of applying the 1949
Conventions as such since this would have amounted to admitting that a
conflict having an "international character" existed. Yet, while France
initially treated the conflict as a police action subject solely to domestic law,
in practice much of the struggle was admittedly fought by France under the
limited obligations of Article 3 applicable to "armed conflict not of an
international character."[40]

[37] Some have, mystically, attributed the special horrors of the Spanish war to
the Spanish character itself: "From the very first, the war in Spain became a tragic
example of what an English correspondent in Andalusia described as 'the peculiar
attitude—a combination of fatalism, exaltation, and delight in all destruction—which
'Spaniards' have toward death.' " As quoted from the *Manchester Guardian* in Toynbee, *supra* note 33, at 80. Yet other civil wars have also been vicious and bloody.

[38] The French attitude was expressed on May 25, 1955, by Jacques Chevallier,
then French Minister of Defense: "You do not fight rebels with legal means; you
fight rebels with means identical with theirs. It is the *lex talionis*—eye for an eye,
tooth for a tooth; it is the law of self-defense on a country-wide scale." On the
Algerian conflict, *see* Fraleigh, *supra* note 1, at 179–243, *esp.* at 194–207 on "Conduct
of the Belligerents." *See also* International Committee of the Red Cross, *The ICRC
and the Algerian Conflict* (ICRC Doc. D 766b, 1962); ICRC, *Annual Reports*, esp.
1958 at 7–10; 1959 at 8–12; 1960 at 16; Greenberg, "Law and the Conduct of the
Algerian Revolution," 11 *Harv. J. Int'l L.* 37–72, (1970).

Note that France became a party to the 1949 Convention in 1951.

[39] Overall, *see* GPRA, *White Paper on the Application of the Geneva Conventions of 1949 to the French-Algerian Conflict* (1960).

[40] Parliament never termed the situation "a war" though it gave wide powers to
the government. On June 20, 1955, however, Premier Fauré stated that Article 3

As pointed out in the Fraleigh study, in 1954–58, the French in several cases tried, condemned, and executed armed FLN militants for bearing arms against the state[41] while seeming to expect the FLN to offer at least prisoner of war treatment for captured French soldiers. Note that such action by France is not barred by Article 3, providing there is a properly constituted court and a fair trial. In 1958, after the FLN had captured some French troops, the French gave up, on March 19, 1958, the systematic prosecution of FLN militants, and set up POW-like camps for them.[42] On April 12, 1958, the Army of National Liberation (ALN) ordered the strict observance of all the laws of war and of the Geneva Conventions.[43] There were nevertheless some executions of prisoners by both sides thereafter.

In 1958–60, the newly formed provisional government of Algerians, Provisional Government of the Algerian Republic (GPRA), proposed agreements for more humane treatment of captured combatants and detained persons while General DeGaulle's government in fact moved also to according prisoners a POW status. No specific agreements were reached.

In 1960, the GPRA sought in part to improve its international status by "ratifying" the Geneva Conventions. Other governments, including the Swiss, made reservations to the purported accession of the GPRA and France argued that GPRA represented no "state" and could not legally adhere. In 1960 there were some further executions by both sides. No formal agreements concerning humanitarian questions between the sides were ever actually reached.[44]

In this savage war, the total number of war victims has been estimated at about 2,500,000, one fourth the population of Algeria.[45] Here, the principal problems included, on the one side, the use of terror and guerrilla warfare, countered on the other side by terror, bombing, and widespread internment and relocation, plus the refusal of one side to acknowledge, in varying degrees and for varying periods, that the other side had rights requiring protection. The French knew of "the rules"; they did not, in sub-

---

applied, though this was not published in the *Journal Officiel*. Moreover, the French permitted the ICRC to visit French detention camps and accepted reports from the ICRC missions. The ICRC believed that France thus tacitly admitted the applicability of Article 3. See ICRC, *supra* note 38.

[41] The French claimed never to have executed anyone *solely* for bearing arms, alleging that all had been guilty of additional misconduct. Fraleigh, *supra* note 1, at 198.

[42] *Id.* at 196–99.

[43] Note that the ALN claimed the benefits of Article 3 under the terms of Art. 4, that is, that it was organized and disciplined like a national army; its members wore distinctive signs and carried arms openly; it complied with the laws and customs of war. See Algerian Office of the FLN, *White Paper on the Application of the Geneva Conventions of 1949 to the French-Algerian Conflict* at 42–45 (May 1960).

[44] Nevertheless, the ICRC felt that Article 3 had proven its general utility in this conflict. See ICRC, *supra* note 38, at 8. For a survey of some ten ICRC investigative missions 1955–62, *see id.* at 19–20.

[45] *Fraleigh, supra* note 1, at 179, and sources cited there in note 1.

stantial part, consider them applicable here. Their opponents, lacking equal military power, fought in large part the war of subversives and guerrillas.

VIETNAM

As is clear from other Chapters in this book and from numerous studies elsewhere, the conflict in Vietnam from the 1960's to date has been classified by some as an international conflict to which the Geneva Conventions and other humanitarian rules, hopefully, apply; to others, it is a civil war with unwarranted foreign intervention. Without attempting to categorize the conflict, it is interesting to note the stated positions of the competing armed forces with respect to the laws of war. The statement here can be brief; much has been written about legal aspects elsewhere.[46] The four Geneva Conventions of 1949 were accepted by the United States in 1955, by the Republic of Vietnam in 1953 and by the Democratic Republic of Vietnam in 1953. In response to an ICRC request on June 11, 1965, the U.S. and Republic authorities said that they would apply the Conventions as a whole, but Saigon expressed reservations with respect to hostilities south of the 17th parallel.[47] The DRVN limited its reply to a protest against the bombing of its territory. In October, 1965, the National Liberation Front (Vietcong) stated that, since it did not participate in the Conventions, it was not bound by them and that the Conventions contained Sections incompatible with the types of action and form of armed organization it employed. It stated nevertheless that it was observing a humane and charitable policy toward prisoners in its hands.[48] Other governments with armed forces in action, including Australia, New Zealand, and the Republic of Korea, have accepted the binding nature of the four Conventions. The United States has applied the Geneva Convention rules to both the North Vietnamese forces and Vietcong regulars.[49]

Over the years, protests about inhumane actions have been numerous. The DRVN has protested American bombing and the destruction caused by

[46] Six such studies are conveniently reprinted in II R. Falk (ed.), *The Vietnam War and International Law* 361ff. (1969). These include Levie, "Maltreatment of Prisoners of War," 48 *Boston U. Law Rev.* 323–59 (1968); Note, "The Geneva Convention and the Treatment of Prisoners of War in Vietnam," 80 *Harv. L. Rev.* 851–68 (1967); Note, "The Geneva Convention of 1949; Application in the Vietnamese Conflict," 5 *Va. J. Int'l L.* 243–65 (1965); Petrowski, "Law and the Conduct of the Vietnam War," (original printed here at 439–515); Meyrowitz, "Le droit de la guerre dans le conflit Vietnamien," 13 *Annuaire Francais de Droit International* 143–201 (1967) (translated here by Graf as "The Law of War in the Vietnamese Conflict,"); and Note, "International Law and Military Operations against Insurgents in Neutral Territory," 68 *Colum. Law Rev.* 1127–48 (1968).

[47] On the mid-1960's *see* ICRC Information Note, "The International Committee of the Red Cross and the Vietnam Conflict," 1–13 with annex, *passim* (Geneva, Aug. 12, 1966) (hereinafter cited as "ICRC, Note"). In general, *see also* ICRC, *Annual Reports, e.g.*, 1966, at 16; 1967, at 20–28; 1968, at 28–32; 1969, at 33–8.

[48] "ICRC, Note," *supra* note 47, at 2.

[49] *See* Levie, *supra* note 46, at 338–40.

air operations and has protested also the alleged use of poison gas and the use of napalm and defoliants. The DRVN nevertheless refused U.S. offers of international enquiries into some of these allegations.[50] The disclosure of the civilian massacre at My Lai and reports of other though less costly incidents have not helped the image of the U.S.A. as a supporter of international law.

The United States has perhaps been most concerned and most bitter about the fate of prisoners taken by the DRVN and the Vietcong. Initially, while stating that prisoners in its hands were being treated humanely, the DRVN insisted that bombing its territory was a crime, that the prisoners would be tried, and that the Prisoners of War Convention was not applicable to them, especially since it accepted the Conventions with the reservation that it would not apply them to war criminals. While there have been no reported trials, prisoners have been forced to parade publicly, mail to and from them has been delayed or destroyed (or lost), the Red Cross has not been permitted to visit camps, etc.[51]

In the south, the Republic, in August 1965, agreed to grant POW status to NLF fighters who were captured bearing arms. The ICRC has visited prisoners taken by Republic and U.S. forces. Reports of mistreatment of prisoners in South Vietnam have not been uncommon, however.[52] The NLF has itself been almost completely unresponsive to requests for lists of prisoners, for aid to sick prisoners, etc. A few cases of executions of prisoners by the NLF and by the South Vietnamese forces have occurred. In addition, acts of terrorism became a way of life in the Vietcong's technique of guerrilla warfare in South Vietnam.[53] Perhaps it is enough to note Corbett's statement that "on the whole, the record shows little regard for the laws of war as set forth in the Geneva Conventions of 1949."[54]

UNITED NATIONS FORCES

a) KOREA

In a small but potentially significant number of cases in the last two decades, United Nations forces have been involved in civil war situations. While it

---

[50] "ICRC, Note," *supra* note 47, at 3.

[51] *See id.* at 5. *See also* Corbett, *supra* note 1, at 374–76, and, *e.g.*, White House Statements on prisoners of war, *N.Y. Times*, July 18, 1967, at 1, 2. On U.S. complaints as to inhumane treatment by North Vietnam, including the failure to supply information on prisoners' names and health, the irregularity of mail, the refusal to appoint a Red Cross Protecting Power, etc., *see XXI Int'l Red Cross Conference* 90–92 (1966).

[52] "ICRC, Note," *supra* note 47, at 7.

[53] From 1962–65, the U.S. alleged that the Vietcong assassinated nearly 7,000 civilians and kidnapped almost 30,000 more. *See Hearings before the Senate Committee on Foreign Relations on S. 2793*, Annexes 1, 2, 3 *89th Cong., 2d sess.* (1966), pt. 1, 114–15.

[54] Corbett, *supra* note 1, at 376.

is not really necessary to push the notion too far, the Korean War of 1950–53 was in many ways like a civil war situation, if it was not in fact civil war. Both the governments of the Republic of Korea and North Korea argued for a unified country; a third of the seats in parliament were left for North Koreans in the Republic's early elections. With its interest in Korea already established, and at the urging of the U.S.A., the United Nations did form a U.N. Command to resist the North Korean incursion and a substantial U.N. armed force, largely contributed by the U.S.A., was engaged in major hostilities for several years.[55] Without here reviewing the discussions of the time, it is enough to note that, while the United Nations was not (and since it is not a "state," perhaps could not be) a party to any humanitarian treaty, the UN Command promptly announced that it would comply with "the humanitarian principles applied by and recognized by civilized nations involved in armed conflict."[56] The Republic of Korea sent formal word on July 13, 1950 that it would cooperate with the International Red Cross and would abide by the Geneva Conventions to which it adhered on July 6, 1950. On July 13, 1950, as well, the North Korean radio stated that the North Koreans were "strictly observing the terms of the Geneva Conventions regarding prisoners of war."[57] The Chinese Communist government accepted the Conventions on July 16, 1952. In fact, compliance by the U.N. Command and by the Republic was apparently good with the exception perhaps, of the repatriation of North Koreans after the cessation of fighting, when the South Koreans simply released the prisoners. The Red Cross visited camps, etc. On the other hand, no Red Cross observers were ever permitted to observe Communist forces or camps, nor were full prisoner lists sent in.[58]

[55] On U.N. forces, *see, e.g.*, Taubenfeld, "International Armed Forces and the Rules of War," 45 *Am. J. Int'l L.* 671–79 (1951); Report of Committee on Study of Legal Problems of the United Nations, "Should the Laws of War Apply to United Nations Enforcement Action?" 1952 *Proc. Am. Soc. of Int'l Law* 216*ff.*; Seyersted, *United Nations Forces in the Law of Peace and War* 314–98 (1966); D. Bowett, *United Nations Forces* 484–518 (1964); and R. Simmonds, *Legal Problems Arising from the United Nations Military Operations in the Congo* 168–96 (1968).

[56] Statement of Gen. MacArthur, July 4, 1950, *N.Y. Times*, July 5, 1950, at 2, col. 7. On the conduct of the conflict, *see* ICRC, *Annual Reports*, 1950, at 80–87; 1951, at 66–68; 1952, at 52–57; 1953, at 53. *See also* I-II ICRC, *The ICRC and the Korean Conflict* (1952). In the Soviet view, there was no problem. Since this was not a U.N. action but illegal aggression by the U.S. and its allies, the warring nations were of course bound by the Geneva Conventions and similar rules. *See* statement of T. Malik in the Security Council, *U.N. SCOR*, 497th meeting (Sept. 7, 1950) at 9.

[57] *N.Y. Times*, July 14, 1950, at 3, col. 4.

[58] Charges were also made by China and North Korea that the U.S. engaged in bacteriological warfare. The U.S. offered to have the ICRC investigate; North Korea and China never replied to the offers. II ICRC, *The ICRC and the Korean War* (1 Jan.–30 June, 1952) 79–114 (1952), esp. 89, 107, 109.

b) THE CONGO (1960–64)

In the Congo hostilities of the early 1960's, there were both a number of "civil wars" and a direct intervention by U.N. forces as well.[59] At various times, South Kasai, Katanga, and other portions of the Congo were in revolt against the central government.

All of the parties to the fighting accepted the idea that the Geneva Conventions were binding on them. This included the United Nations itself which, as noted above, was not formally a party to any humanitarian convention. Following the precedent of the U.N. force in Korea, the Secretary-General made it clear that the U.N.'s forces would abide by the limitations imposed by the Geneva Conventions.[60]

The Republic of the Congo, which came into existence only five days before the violence began, was considered a Party to the Geneva Conventions by the ICRC by virtue of Belgium's ratification in 1952.[61] In addition, the Congo government declared, on February 20, 1961, that it was a Party to the Conventions.[62] For rebellious Katanga, seeking secession, President Tshombe, in early 1961, informed the Red Cross that the Conventions would be applied, and the Red Cross was invited to visit detention camps in Katanga.[63]

Overall, it has been reported that the military forces involved did comply with the humanitarian principles involved. Thus, in general, captives were detained under acceptable conditions, the Red Cross inspected prison camps and filed reports, prisoners were exchanged and released.[64] There were some violations of humanitarian principles: some 40 Ghanian soldiers serving with ONUC were murdered in 1961, as were 13 Italian airmen; some 92 Baluba tribesmen died after coming into the hands of ONUC's Liberian battalion. These violations were distinct exceptions.[65] Relatively few civilians died due to fighting involving U.N. forces. There were, however, massacres of civilians in tribal struggles which claimed thousands of lives, and armed forces of the government participated in some of these, particularly against the Balubas.[66]

There were also cases of abuse of political prisoners; while the Geneva

---

[59] See McNemar, *supra* note 1, at 257–71. *See also* R. Simmonds, *supra* note 55. *See also* ICRC, *Annual Reports*, 1960, at 7–15; 1961, at 7–15; 1962, at 14–16.

[60] See Art. 43 of the *Regulations for the United Nations Force in the Congo*, U.N. Doc. No. ST/SGB/ONUC/1, July 15, 1963 and 2 *Int'l Rev. Red Cross* No. 10, at 7–8, 29 (Jan. 1962). The U.N. also accepted responsibility for certain damages in the Congo, *e.g.*, in agreements with Belgium (20 Feb. 1965, 535 *U.N.T.S.* 197) Luxembourg (28 Dec. 1966, 585 *U.N.T.S.* 147), Switzerland (28 June 1967).

[61] See ICRC, 2 *Int'l Rev. Red Cross*, No. 13, at 208 (April, 1962).

[62] ICRC, "The Red Cross Action in the Congo," 2 *Int'l Rev. Red Cross*, No. 10, at 7–8 (Jan. 1968).

[63] "The ICRC in the Congo," *Revue Int'l de la Croix-Rouge*, Supplement XIV, No. 3, at 43–45 (March, 1961).

[64] For a summary, *see* McNemar *supra* note 1, at 263–65; and *see* ICRC, *Annual Report*, 1962, at 15.

[65] McNemar, *supra* note 1, at 264–65.

[66] See *id.* at 265–67 and *U.N. SCOR*, 15th Year, 896th Meeting, Sept. 9, 1960, 18.

Conventions do not forbid treason trials, they require a trial with judicial guarantees. The most famous instance of mistreatment involved the execution of Patrice Lumumba; there were other political executions as well.[67]

Other violations of the laws of war occurred: hospitals were assaulted, some Red Cross workers were killed, some non-military targets were bombed. Overall, however, given the horrors of civil war and the bloody tribal battles for dominance, there was a substantial compliance with humanitarian norms by the armed forces involved. This is attributed, *inter alia*, to the limits imposed on ONUC at all times and to the world attention focused on the Congo by the United Nations' involvement.

c) OTHER

There has been a U.N. involvement in a few other civil clashes. In the Cyprus conflict, before U.N. intervention, there were numerous kidnappings, aerial attacks, and a "blockade" by the majority government against the Turkish minority. The U.N. presence has apparently ended most of these problems. The U.N. forces were themselves instructed of their duties under the principles of the Geneva Conventions.[68]

In a different context, the U.N. has taken a position in advance of any wide-scale civil war in the Republic of South Africa and in Rhodesia and in the conflicts in the Portuguese colonies. In this long history of controversy concerning Southern Africa, the U.N. General Assembly has, for example, demanded prisoner of war treatment for captured rebels.[69] In time, the fighting in the Portuguese areas may well resemble that in Algeria. On the one hand, Portugal considers these areas as integral parts of Portugal. On the other hand, the rebels and African and some other states, at least, consider these as wars of liberation and apparently feel free to offer sanctuary and support to the rebellious factions. In the Republic of South Africa and in Rhodesia, it seems clear that "traitors" will be dealt with violently in the foreseeable future.

This survey of the application of the laws of war in civil wars presents a disheartening picture which has been noted and anguished over for decades. In only two kinds of situations have humanitarian rules been applied with some regularity. One is the sort of conflict represented by the American Civil War and, perhaps, by the Nigeria-Biafra situation.[70] Here, the attempt

---

[67] For a summary, *see* McNemar, *supra* note 1, at 266–67.

[68] *See* ICRC, *Annual Report*, 1964.

[69] *See, e.g.*, on the Republic of South Africa and Rhodesia, *G.A. Res.* 2446 XXII (Dec. 19, 1968), and 2396 XXII (Dec. 12, 1968), 23 *U.N. GAOR*. On the Portuguese territories, *see* G.A. Res. 2395 (XXII) of 1968, 23 *U.N. GAOR*.

[70] In the Biafran conflict, both sides alleged compliance with humanitarian rules. *See Int'l Rev. Red Cross*, July, 1968, at 356; Oct. 1968, at 517; Nov. 1968, at 571–72; Jan. 1969, at 4; Feb. 1969, at 83. There have been no post-war reports of slaughters. There was a strenuous "blockade" of Biafra and much reported hunger and starvation. It will be remembered that this form of pressure was also applied by the North against the South.

has been made to prevent a secession; the lines have been clearly marked; the contenders fought in uniform, as armies; covert warfare was not an issue. The other is a conflict in which U.N. armed forces have participated or at least been present. Even so, it is hard to generalize. In Spain, the war was not for secession but for control of a single government. The lines, the territories controlled by the conflicting armies, the ability to distinguish between fighters and civilians were all clear, but the known rules were repeatedly and brutally violated.[71] In wars of "liberation"—in Algeria, for example—mutual threat led to some humanitarian policies on both sides, but again it was not basically a game amenable to the rules created for open armed combat. Despite the existence of Article 3 in each of the 1949 Conventions, internal war has lost little of its savagery in the observed conflicts in the post-1949 period.

In internal conflicts, experience has shown that governments will commonly deny that Article 3 of the 1949 Conventions is applicable; they *do* consider their opponents to be traitors and criminals.[72] Moreover, it also appears that insurgents often refuse to consider themselves bound, particularly when using terrorism, which they may consider an essential technique as a weapon.[73] Article 3 also does not expressly protect Red Cross or medical personnel. It does not bar governments from punishing rebels, though formalities are indicated.[74] The ICRC "may" offer its services; governments are not obliged to accept.[75] Bombardments are but minimally regulated. No

---

[71] In similar manner, in Yemen, while both sides agreed to apply the Conventions, it was reportedly difficult to obtain compliance. In part, there was a tradition of executing prisoners, but a tradition of chivalry existed as well. Katheryn Boals argues that the Geneva Conventions had no modifying effects: both Republicans and Royalists failed to distinguish between civilians and combatants; the Royalists systematically killed prisoners, the Egyptian intervenors used poison gas, etc., etc. *See* Boals, *supra* note 1 *passim*, and ICRC, *the ICRC and the Yemen Conflict* (1964), *passim*.

[72] G.I.A.D. Draper suggests that an "Art. 3 conflict" exists "whenever sustained troop action is undertaken against rebels, even though the rebel organization and control of any area is minimal, and the situation is such that the police are not able to enforce the criminal law in a particular area by reason of rebel action." "Geneva Conventions of 1949," *Recueil des Cours* 94 (1965-I).

[73] For comments on the difficulties, *see* ICRC, "Protection of Victims of Non-International Conflicts," *Report submitted to the XXI Int'l Conf. of the Red Cross* (Istanbul, Sept. 1969), esp. 3, 7; Farer, "The Laws of War 25 Years After Nuremberg," *Int'l Concil.*, No. 583, 25ff. (May, 1971).

[74] Art. 3 does not, in the view of scholars, bar a government from trying, convicting and executing one who bears arms against it. Thus, *e.g.*, in the Algerian crisis, France could urge the legality of trying and executing FLN personnel for bearing arms against France while denying the FLN a similar right against French troops who fought against it. The FLN did not accept this notion.

On hanging for treason, *see also* Draper, "Rules Governing the Conduct of Hostilities —The Laws of War and Their Enforcement," U.S. Naval War College, *Readings in International Law, 1969–1970* at 380.

[75] Even with the 1949 Geneva Conventions available as an indication of an international consensus, a reluctance on the part of states and organizations is still evident to intervene in matters felt to be essentially within a state's domestic concerns. Thus, for example, the International Committee of the Red Cross explained its limited

specific provision exists, as it does in Article 23 of the Fourth Geneva Convention, for making exceptions to a blockade for the benefit of the enemy civilian population.

Suggestions for improvement include, as noted herein and as discussed by Professor Baxter hereafter, the insistence that prisoner of war treatment be given to captured rebels, that executions of "traitors" be forbidden or at least suspended during the conflict, that the Red Cross or similar agency be unequivocally permitted to use its services, that medical personnel, hospitals, etc., receive privileged treatment, that blockades be eased in the event of civilian need, that Article 3 be broadly interpreted to protect as many as possible who could qualify loosely as rebel fighters, including guerrillas, and that a general amnesty be offered by the winner at the end of hostilities.[76]

Difficulties are clear; rebels are faced by a dilemma. Will they not lose if they fight "conventionally," if they are obliged to give up terror, subversion, and secrecy? Yet governments certainly will not observe rules that their opponents ignore. Would a waiver of trials and executions give a free hand to rebels? How does one distinguish a guerrilla from an ordinary bandit?[77] The difficulties as well as the challenge to legal scholars to develop acceptable rules are clear. Even with broader, clearer, more generally known rules, there is no certainty that governments and their internal opponents will, short of the availability of an external policing authority, inevitably be persuaded to abide by restraints in what they consider to be life-and-death issues. Yet the clearer and more universally acknowledged are the constraints, the greater will be the pressure on particular governments and rebels alike to conform.

---

humanitarian role in the Algerian conflict by noting the internal nature of the conflict and the need for special authorizations for each such intervention. The record is not all poor. In 1958–69, the ICRC was authorized by forty-two governments to visit some 100,000 detained persons in twenty cases of internal disorders and twenty-two cases of internal tension. *See* ICRC, *Report to the XXI Conf.*, 6.

[76] *See*, in general, *e.g.*, Farer, *supra* note 73, at 45*ff.*; Veuthey, "The Red Cross and Non-International Conflicts," *Int'l Rev. Red Cross*, Aug., 1970 411–23; ICRC, *Report*, May, 1949, *passim*; R. Falk, *The International Law of Civil War* 27–29 (1971).

[77] On the guerrilla, *see* Farer, *supra* note 73 at 36–44.

Chapter 20 | Ius in Bello Interno:
The Present and Future Law | *Richard R. Baxter*

Prior to 1949, the principal treaties governing the conduct of warfare on land—the Regulations annexed to Convention IV of The Hague of 1907[1] and the Geneva Prisoners of War[2] and Wounded and Sick Conventions[3] of 1929—applied only to war between states and had no bearing, according to their terms, on civil conflicts. If one looks back to the standard treatises of a quarter or half a century ago,[4] one discovers that civil war might be governed by the international law of war under one set of circumstances. If the government of a state resisting the insurrection mounted by rebels were to recognize the belligerency of the rebel faction, then the conflict would be treated as if it were an international one for the purpose of the application of the international law of war. Indeed, that recognition often came in the form of the de facto government's extending to the insurgents the protection of the international law of war. If a third state were to recognize the belligerency of the rebel faction, then the third state would be subject to the same rights and duties of neutrality as in an international armed conflict. The recognition of belligerency by third states would naturally not require the lawful government of the state to recognize the rebels as belligerents, but widespread recognition of belligerency by third states would exercise a certain influence in persuading the lawful government that the time had come to recognize the belligerency of the rebels. As Hyde wrote, paraphrasing the words of Mr. Justice Grier in the *Prize Cases*,[5]

> When the parties in rebellion occupy and hold in a hostile manner a certain portion of territory; have declared their independence; have cast off

[1] Signed Oct. 18, 1907, 36 *Stat.* 2277, *T.S.* No. 539, 1 *Bevans* 631.
[2] Done at Geneva, July 27, 1929, 47 *Stat.* 2021, *T.S.* No. 846, 2 *Bevans* 932.
[3] Done at Geneva, July 27, 1929, 47 *Stat.* 2074, *T.S.* No. 847, 2 *Bevans* 965
[4] *See, e.g.,* W. Hall, *International Law* 36 (8th ed., 1924); II L. Oppenheim, *International Law* 173 (6th ed., 1944); III C. Hyde, *International Law, Chiefly as Interpreted and Applied by the United States* (2d rev. ed., 1945). And *see* as to recognition of belligerency and insurgency H. Lauterpacht, *Recognition in International Law* 175–294 (1948).
[5] C. Hyde, *supra* note 4, at 1698.

This chapter was completed on June 30, 1971 and does not take account of developments after that date.

Although the writer was a member of the United States Delegation to the Conference of Government Experts on the Reaffirmation and Development of International Humanitarian Law Applicable in Armed Conflicts, Geneva, May 24 to June 12, 1971, the views expressed herein are his own and do not necessarily reflect those of the United States Government.

their allegiance; have organized armies; have commenced hostilities against their former sovereign, the world acknowledges them as belligerents, and the contest a war.[6]

Among the important consequences of the recognition of belligerency was that rebels who fell into the hands of the lawful government would be treated as prisoners of war rather than criminals. That the United States had been prepared to treat its own Civil War for many purposes as if it had been an international conflict undoubtedly had a powerful influence on the development of the law.

In the period between the two World Wars, the International Committee of the Red Cross attempted on various occasions to secure the application of the international law of war during civil conflicts.[7] After the Second World War, the International Committee undertook the preparation of new draft conventions for the protection of war victims. The draft treaties approved by the XVIIth International Red Cross Conference at Stockholm and submitted to the Diplomatic Conference of Geneva of 1949 contained a common provision to the effect that:

> In all cases of armed conflict not of an international character which may occur in the territory of one or more of the High Contracting Parties, each of the adversaries shall be bound to implement the provisions of the present Convention.[8]

The broad sweep of this stipulation proved to be too much for the majority of the states represented at the Diplomatic Conference. A compromise formula—that the entire convention would be applicable to internal conflicts only if there had been a recognition of belligerency by the de jure government or if the insurgent faction exercised de facto governmental functions—failed of adoption.[9] The Conference ultimately came around to the view that the most that states could be expected to accept would be a short statement of the basic humanitarian principles that should be given effect in civil conflicts. The result was Article 3, common to the four Geneva Conventions of August 12, 1949 for the Protection of the Wounded and

---

[6] 67 U.S. (2 Black) 635, 666–67 (1862).

[7] J. Pictet, *Commentary on the Geneva Convention for the Amelioration of the Condition of the Wounded and Sick in Armed Forces in the Field* 40 (1952) [hereafter referred to as Pictet].

[8] Art. 2, para. 3, 1 *Final Record of the Diplomatic Conference of Geneva of 1949*, at 47.

[9] Pictet, *supra* note 7, at 45–6. Farer finds textual evidence and "substantial support at the Conference" for the view that all civil conflicts are not necessarily to be held within the limits of Article 3. He concludes that there is thus reason to apply the full Conventions to "serious civil strife." Farer, "Humanitarian Law and Armed Conflicts: Toward the Definition of 'International Armed Conflict,'" 71 *Colum. L. Rev.* 37, 47–48 (1971).

Sick;[10] the Wounded, Sick, and Shipwrecked at Sea;[11] Prisoners of War;[12] and Civilians.[13] The Article is a miniature Bill of Rights for those who are the victims of internal conflict. The portion of the Article here relevant provides:

> In the case of armed conflict not of an international character occurring in the territory of one of the High Contracting Parties, each Party to the conflict shall be bound to apply, as a minimum, the following provisions:
>
> (1) Persons taking no active part in the hostilities, including members of armed forces who have laid down their arms and those placed *hors de combat* by sickness, wounds, detention, or any other cause, shall in all circumstances be treated humanely, without any adverse distinction founded on race, colour, religion or faith, sex, birth or wealth, or any other similar criteria.
>
> To this end the following acts are and shall remain prohibited at any time and in any place whatsoever with respect to the above-mentioned persons:
>
> (*a*) violence to life and person, in particular murder of all kinds, mutilation, cruel treatment and torture;
> (*b*) taking of hostages;
> (*c*) outrages upon personal dignity, in particular, humiliating and degrading treatment;
> (*d*) the passing of sentences and the carrying out of executions without previous judgment pronounced by a regularly constituted court affording all the judicial guarantees which are recognized as indispensable by civilized peoples.
>
> (2) The wounded and sick shall be collected and cared for.

The possibility of applying the Conventions as a whole was not overlooked. Article 3 also provides that:

> The Parties to the conflict should further endeavour to bring into force, by means of special agreements, all or part of the other provisions of the present Convention.

Presumably, this paragraph deals with the application of the Conventions under the circumstances which used to be identified through recognition of belligerency. That institution having fallen into disuse, it seemed appropriate to make the wider application of the Conventions contingent upon the

---

[10] Convention for the Amelioration of the Condition of the Wounded and Sick in Armed Forces in the Field, 6 *U.S.T.* 3114, *T.I.A.S.* No. 3362.

[11] Convention for the Amelioration of the Condition of the Wounded, Sick, and Shipwrecked Members of Armed Forces at Sea, 6 *U.S.T.* 3217, *T.I.A.S.* No. 3363.

[12] Convention relative to the Treatment of Prisoners of War, 6 *U.S.T.* 3316, *T.I.A.S.* No. 3364.

[13] Convention relative to the Protection of Civilian Persons in Time of War, 6 *U.S.T.* 3516, *T.I.A.S.* No. 3365.

agreement of the belligerents, which, for these purposes, would thus be put on a footing of equality.

The deceptively simple expression, "armed conflict not of an international character," has not proven easy to apply to the multiplicity of circumstances under which violence may break out in a state. It was intended that this expression should stand in contrast to the language of common Article 2, defining the scope of application of the Convention as a whole. The Conventions are to "apply to all cases of declared war or of any other armed conflict which may arise between two or more of the High Contracting Parties, even if the state of war is not recognized by one of them."

A number of states in the world are divided by provisional demarcation lines that have led to the establishment of separate governments, each of which effectively exercises jurisdiction over a portion of the territory of the state. Of such character are East and West Germany, North and South Korea, North and South Vietnam, and the People's Republic of China and the Republic of China. Because of the eagerness of the Swiss Federal Council—the depositary of the Geneva Conventions of 1949—to have as many parties to the Conventions as possible, ratifications or accessions have been received from both portions of most of these divided states.[14] If both governments are high contracting parties, then a conflict between them would seem to be a case of "declared war or any other armed conflict which may arise between two or more of the High Contracting Parties," even though for other purposes it might seem that the conflict is an internal one. However, this reading of Article 2, based on a narrowly logical construction, is not free from doubt.

A similar ambiguity exists about the nature of "wars of national liberation." When the Secretary-General was requested by the General Assembly to carry forward the study he had initiated on the adequacy of the existing conventions and on the need for new treaties, he was asked to give "special attention to the need for protection of the rights of civilians and combatants in conflicts which arise from the struggles of peoples under colonial and foreign rule for liberation and self-determination and to the better application of existing humanitarian international conventions and rules to such conflicts."[15] If a "war of national liberation" is defined in these terms, such a conflict may range from an attempt to throw off colonial rule to resistance activities by the local populace against a belligerent occupant. The concept being as amorphous as it is, it cannot fail to provoke controversy. It can be maintained, on the one hand, that if a people under colonial rule is denied the right of self-determination guaranteed by Article 1, paragraph 2, of the Charter of the United Nations and takes up arms in order to secure its independence, then that people is entitled to political independence and

<hr>

[14] See U.S. Department of State, *Treaties in Force, 1971* at 343, 347, and 355 (1971).

[15] G.A. Res. 2597 (XXIV), Dec. 16, 1969, 24 *U.N. GAOR* Supp. 30, at 62, U.N. Doc. A/7630 (1970).

sovereignty and should be treated as if it were a separate state.[16] This right, it is contended, is spelled out in a number of important general resolutions of the General Assembly, such as the Declaration on the Granting of Independence to Colonial Countries and Peoples,[17] as well as of resolutions applicable to particular situations. This view, it may be noted, creates a logical difficulty about the application of the Conventions as a whole under common Article 2, as the people fighting for self-determination is not a high contracting party to the Conventions. If the people constitutes a "Power," then the colonial power is bound by the Conventions in its relations with the other power—the people fighting for self-determination—if "the latter accepts and applies the provisions" of the Conventions. No such problem arises if the "war of national liberation" consists of resistance activity by members of the local population against a belligerent occupant, since in that case the persons involved depend upon high contracting parties to the Conventions, provided of course the parties to the conflict are parties to the Conventions.

The case for saying that a "war of national liberation" is a civil conflict is that the people fighting for self-determination has not yet achieved its independence. That independence would be marked by its recognition as a state by other states and by its becoming a party to the Geneva Conventions of 1949. Prior to that time, the insurgent forces would lack international personality.[18] The characterization of all wars of national liberation waged in pursuit of self-determination as internal conflicts avoids well nigh insoluble problems of characterization of internal conflict. For if a conflict fought within a state in the cause of self-determination is governed by international law but a conflict not legitimately in pursuit of self-determination is governed by Article 3 alone, then a decision concerning what body of law to apply turns on highly subjective value judgments about the nature of the conflict: A war of national liberation will turn out to be the war that I fight; the war you fight will be a colonialist one.

This problem has been recognized by the Secretary-General in his second report on the humanitarian law of war,[19] by the International Committee of the Red Cross,[20] and by the delegates participating in the I.C.R.C. Conference of Government Experts held in May and June of 1971,[21] but has not been resolved.

The two categories of war across provisional demarcation lines and

[16] *Respect for Human Rights in Armed Conflicts*; [Second] Report of the Secretary-General 66–67, U.N. Doc. A/8052 (1970).

[17] G.A. Res. 1514 (XV), Dec. 14, 1960, 15 *U.N. GAOR* Supp. 16, vol. i, at 66, U.N. Doc. A/4684 (1961).

[18] Report cited *supra* note 16, at 66.

[19] *Id.*

[20] 5 Conference of Government Experts on the Reaffirmation and Development of International Humanitarian Law Applicable in Armed Conflicts, *Protection of Victims of Non-International Armed Conflicts* 23–35, Doc. CE/5b (1971).

[21] *Report of Commission II*, at 48–57 (1971).

wars of national liberation do not exhaust the circumstances in which the dividing line between international and internal conflict is obscured. A like problem will arise if the inhabitants of an area the sovereignty over which is in dispute rise in arms against the de facto authority in control of the area. If the area belongs to the territory of the government against which armed force is employed, then the conflict is an internal one. If the area is not subject to the sovereignty of that government, the conflict is an international one. In all of these instances, the perception of the conflict by the participants and by third states will turn on a subjective appraisal of the lawfulness of a government, the existence of a state, and the boundaries of the participants. So long as states and governments are left free to pursue their own recognition policies, just so long will determinations of the nature of the conflict have a highly subjective character.

The classification of a conflict as either internal or international becomes even more difficult when there is participation by a third state or third states in what had theretofore been a civil conflict. How is the conflict in Vietnam to be characterized in the strict terms of Articles 2 and 3 of the four Geneva Conventions of 1949?[22] The Republic of Vietnam, the Democratic Republic of Vietnam, and the United States are all parties to the Geneva Conventions of 1949, and, as pointed out above,[23] conflict between the Republic of Vietnam or the United States and the Democratic Republic of Vietnam is in literal terms an armed conflict between two High Contracting Parties. The Vietcong may supply the domestic element of the conflict.

It is easy enough to say that the participation of the United States internationalizes the conflict[24] so that under Article 2 of the Conventions, the whole of the humanitarian law of war applies. But as one analyzes the various pairings of opposing belligerents,[25] one is forced to give a separate classification to each such pair.

---

[22] The discussion in the text is based on the legal construction of Articles 2 and 3 of the four Geneva Conventions of 1949. The United States and the Republic of Vietnam have expressed their willingness to apply the Conventions in the conflict in Vietnam (5 *Int'l Rev. Red Cross* 477–78 (1965)) in response to the assertion of the International Committee of the Red Cross that "the hostilities raging at the present time in Vietnam both North and South of the 17th parallel have assumed such proportions recently that there can be no doubt they constitute an armed conflict to which the regulations of humanitarian law as a whole should be applied." Letter, June 11, 1965, from the International Committee of the Red Cross to the governments of the Democratic Republic of Vietnam, the Republic of Vietnam, and the United States and to the National Liberation Front of South Vietnam, 5 *id.* at 417. It appears that the International Committee of the Red Cross was merely encouraging the participants to apply the Conventions as a whole, rather than asserting that the Conventions already applied of their own force.

[23] *See* p. 521 *supra.*

[24] Falk, "Janus Tormented: The International Law of Internal War," in J. Rosenau (ed.), *International Aspects of Civil Strife* 185, 218 (1964); Farer, *supra* note 9, at 69; Meyrowitz, "The Law of War in the Vietnamese Conflict," in II R. Falk (ed.), *The Vietnam War and International Law* 516, 532 (1969).

[25] As done by Meyrowitz, *supra* note 24, at 524–33, but with results somewhat different from those reached here.

To start with the easy case, it would seem that the hostilities between the United States and North Vietnam should be regarded as international, calling for the application of the entirety of the Conventions. At the opposite extreme, hostilities between the Republic of Vietnam and the Vietcong seem to be domestic conflict falling within Article 3. However, if, as appears to be the position of the United States, the Vietcong is an arm of the Government of the Democratic Republic of Vietnam, then conflict between South Vietnam and the Vietcong has the same character as conflict between South and North Vietnam. The nature of the conflict between the two governments in Vietnam turns of course on the answer to the questions whether war across a provisional demarcation line is international conflict and when a provisional demarcation line hardens into what amounts to an international frontier. If the conflict between South Vietnam and the Vietcong is internal and the conflict between South and North Vietnam international, then the position of a captured belligerent will turn on the forces in which he serves. If he serves the North Vietnamese forces, he is, in strict law, to be treated as a prisoner of war if he meets the requirements of Article 4 of the Geneva Prisoners of War Convention of 1949. But if he is a member of the Vietcong, then he can be tried and punished, subject only to the safeguards of Article 3 of the Conventions.

If the United States captures a member of the Vietcong, that person is to be held as a prisoner of war if the Vietcong is in actuality an instrument of the Government of North Vietnam. To say that the Vietcong is not such an instrument does not solve the problem. Is conflict between the Vietcong and the United States to be called international because of the foreign participant? The fact that the United States is assisting the Republic of Vietnam and transfers the prisoners that it takes to the Government of the Republic of Vietnam[26] suggests that members of the Vietcong should be treated in the same way as if they had been captured by the South Vietnamese armed forces in the first instance. It could not be expected that persons taken captive should be treated as prisoners of war under Articles 2 and 4 of the Prisoners of War Convention while in the custody of the United States but should lose that status and fall only under the protection of common Article 3 when transferred to South Vietnam.

The government of a state which is attacked by insurgents may, according to the view of a number of authorities, lawfully call upon a third state to assist it, and that state is entitled to aid in the suppression of the rebellion.[27] However, a state which assists the rebels through the use of armed

---

[26] Pursuant to Article 12 of the Geneva Prisoners of War Convention of 1949.

[27] Moore, "The Lawfulness of Military Assistance to the Republic of Viet-Nam," in I R. Falk (ed.), *The Vietnam War and International Law* 237, 265 (1968); and see the statement by Professor Louis B. Sohn concerning the practice of the United Nations, *id.* at 266. The legality of external assistance even to the lawful government is disputed by other authorities. *See, e.g.,* I C. Hyde, *International Law, Chiefly as Interpreted and Applied by the United States* 253 (2d rev. ed. 1945).

force conducts an unlawful intervention in the domestic affairs of the state in which the hostilities are carried on[28] and may by the same token be guilty of "the threat or use of force against the territorial integrity or political independence" of a state in violation of Article 2(4) of the Charter.[29] But these characterizations of the conduct of the external participant proceed on the comfortable assumption that it is possible to identify which is the lawful government and which is the insurgent faction. That simply cannot be done in many circumstances. When the attempt is made, the classification proceeds along the same subjective lines[30] previously mentioned in connection with the complexities of recognition policy.

The foregoing problems arise out of application of Article 3 common to the four Geneva Conventions of 1949 at the upper end of the spectrum of violence. At lower levels of violence, there must obviously be some distinction made between "armed conflict not of an international character" within the meaning of the Conventions and other forms of domestic violence. Students may throw paving stones at policemen. Bandits may hold a rich man for ransom. Gangs of armed men may hold up banks. Communal disorders may break out. Crowds may riot. Tribal or religious differences may lead to outbreaks of violence which the government of a state may be hard pressed to suppress. Civilian and military officials of the government may be assassinated for political purposes. Bombs may be thrown at police stations. The forms of violence are as diverse as the passions, the driving forces, the emotions, the motives, and the ingenuity of man.[31] And even those who are moved by cupidity or by the desire for power will attempt to cloak their actions in the raiment of morality or politics.

In its commentary on the Geneva Conventions of 1949, the International Committee has been able to do no more than to plead for a latitudinarian construction of Article 3, while summarizing the various proposals that had been put forward at the Diplomatic Conference for a more precise formulation of when the Conventions would be applicable to internal conflicts. These proposals—which, it must be emphasized, were not adopted—looked to such criteria as the following:

[28] As stated in the Declaration on Principles of International Law concerning Friendly Relations and Co-operation Among States in Accordance with the Charter of the United Nations, under the rubric of the duty of non-intervention, ". . . [N]o state shall organize, assist, foment, finance, incite or tolerate subversive, terrorist or armed activities directed towards the violent overthrow of the régime of another state, or interfere in civil strife in another state." G.A. Res. 2625 (XXV), Oct. 24, 1970, U.N. Doc. A/RES/2625 (XXV) (1970).

[29] Such conduct is often referred to as "indirect aggression."

[30] I D. O'Connell, *International Law* 326 (1965).

[31] In its report prepared for the Conference of Government Experts on the Reaffirmation and Development of International Humanitarian Law Applicable in Armed Conflicts, the International Committee of the Red Cross referred to some of these forms of low-scale violence as "situations of internal disturbances" and "situations of internal tensions." 5 *Protection of Victims of Non-International Armed Conflicts* 79–94, Doc. CE/5b (1971).

—The party in revolt must possess an "organized military force," "an authority responsible for its acts," territory, and the means of carrying out the Conventions.

—The government is obliged to use its regular military forces against militarily organized insurgents in possession of territory.

—The insurgents have been recognized as belligerents.

—The dispute has been put on the agenda of the General Assembly or Security Council as a threat to the peace, breach of the peace, or act of aggression.

—The insurgents have an organization purporting to have the characteristics of a state, de facto authority over persons within a determinate territory, and armed forces acting under civilian direction and prepared to observe the law of war; and, moreover, agree to be bound by the provisions of the Conventions.[32]

The commentary takes these requirements to be indicative and not exhaustive and then, disregarding the stringency of these requirements, concludes that "the Article should be applied as widely as possible."[33] The justification is that no government could object to carrying out the terms of Article 3; no government should be allowed to claim the right to torture or to carry out a sentence without a previous judgment by a regularly constituted court. The discussion by the International Committee of the Red Cross leaves one with an oddly mixed impression. Those who were struggling with the problem at Geneva in 1949 were apparently thinking in terms very much like the conditions for recognition of belligerency, which would in the past have called for the application of the whole of the international law of war, while the I.C.R.C. pleads for a wide interpretation of the Article. The *ejusdem generis* rule applied to the illustrative examples would seem to point to exactly the opposite conclusion. Of only one thing one may be sure: There is no consensus as to the application of Article 3 to what are, in comparative terms, the lower levels of violence.

These problems of definition, whether at the top or the bottom of the spectrum of domestic violence, reflect, as questions of definition generally do, differences about the substantive law to be applied. Article 3 does not preclude the government of a state from punishing persons, subject to its jurisdiction, for the commission of crimes under the municipal law of that state. The rebel who kills a policeman or a soldier can thus be treated as a murderer, and nothing in Article 3 stands in the way of the imposition of the death sentence, if the trial has been properly conducted. If, on the other hand, the Geneva Prisoners of War Convention of 1949 is to be applied in its entirety, then insurgents captured in combat against the lawful govern-

---

[32] Seventh Report drawn up by the Special Committee of the Joint Committee, July 16, 1949, 2B *Final Record of the Diplomatic Conference of Geneva of 1949*, at 120–23 (1949); Pictet, *supra* note 7, at 49–50.

[33] Pictet *supra* note 7, at 50.

ment gain an immunity, it would seem, from the application of domestic law through their status as prisoners of war. The rebel is a criminal in the eyes of the government, while a prisoner of war is an individual who has violated no rule of municipal law, if he has not acted in contravention of international law. Every state must thus ask itself whether it desires to continue to apply its law for the maintenance of public order to all persons within the territory of the state or whether it is willing to grant an immunity from prosecution and a protected position under international law to those who fight against it. Criminal or protected person?

The dilemma is at its most acute when the position of persons captured in combat is at stake, but a like choice must be made in connection with the Civilians Convention of 1949. If the humanitarian international law of war embodied in that Convention and in the Hague Regulations[34] is applied, the effect is to require treatment of territory under the control of the rebels as if it were the territory of a foreign state and treatment of insurgents and their sympathizers as if they were nationals of an enemy state. The law might even call for treating the territory recovered by the lawful government as belligerently occupied territory, if the whole of the Geneva Civilians Convention is applied. The Geneva Wounded and Sick Convention of 1949 has the least political significance, and a government would be under less embarrassment in applying it to a civil conflict than it would in the case of the Prisoners of War and Civilians Conventions.

The difficulty with the present Conventions of 1949 is thus that Article 3 does not afford enough protection, and the application of the Conventions as a whole tends to be politically unacceptable and unworkable.

Thus far our emphasis has been on the perception of the situation by the lawful government. The position of the insurgents must also be considered. Only states can be parties to the Conventions,[35] so that there is no room for an insurgent faction to become a High Contracting Party. The government of the state, which may be the same government that committed the state to the Conventions by ratification or accession or its successor, is bound according to the usual rule that it is the state, acting through its government, which is bound by a treaty. How then can the insurgents as a "party to the conflict" be bound to carry out duties under an instrument that they have not accepted? One answer is that all nationals of high contracting parties are bound by the Conventions, including Article 3, and that the rebels, qua nationals of a Party, are bound as individuals, who have formed themselves into a political collectivity.[36] A second basis for asserting

---

[34] Regulations annexed to Convention No. IV of The Hague respecting the Laws and Customs of War on Land, signed Oct. 18, 1907, 36 *Stat.* 2277, *L.N. T.S.* No. 539, 1 *Bevans* 631.

[35] Common Articles 56/55/136/151, 57/56/137/152, and 60/59/139/155 of the Geneva Conventions of 1949.

[36] G. Draper, *The Red Cross Conventions* 17 (1958).

that Article 3 is binding on the insurgents is that insurgents must be bound by the obligations of the State to the extent they purport to be the effective government of that State.[37] These propositions may be satisfying to the mind of the international lawyer, but they do not necessarily induce compliance by rebels. The fact is that whether a group of any sort has or has not expressly accepted the obligations of an agreement does have a great deal to do psychologically with the willingness of that group to carry out its purported obligations. The climate for compliance is even less propitious when the insurgents are rebelling against the authority of the very government that has assumed the obligations of the Conventions. And even if the obligations of Article 3 are not particularly onerous for the rebels, they will still see a certain lack of reciprocity in the government's having been afforded the opportunity to determine whether to assume the obligations of the Conventions while they, the rebels, have not been given the occasion for a like decision. Considerations such as these help to explain why it is that the National Liberation Front in Vietnam has refused to apply the Conventions. It asserted that it "was not bound by the international treaties to which others beside itself subscribed."[38]

The position under the "Convention in miniature" of Article 3 is to be contrasted with the situation envisaged under the third paragraph of that article, whereby "The Parties to the conflict should further endeavour to bring into force, by means of special agreements, all or part of the other provisions of the present Convention." In that event there is a desirable mutuality of obligation under an agreement freely entered into by the rebel forces. However, the difficulty of communication and, moreover, of negotiation between a government and insurgents in revolt against its authority is such that little or no use has been made of this provision.

Neither the application of the short bill of rights in Article 3 nor the bringing into force of all or part of the Conventions by means of a special agreement between the parties to a civil war is to "affect the legal status of the parties to the conflict." Nevertheless, governments have shown a reluctance either to acknowledge the existence of internal armed conflict in terms of Article 3 or to conclude a special agreement with the rebels lest that act in any way enhance the status of the insurgents. Thus, the French Government refrained from concluding any agreement with the Gouvernement Provisoire de la République Algérienne, although urged to do so both by the International Committee of the Red Cross and the Provisional Algerian Government.[39] It is not without significance that the Government of Pakistan failed to acknowledge the existence of an internal armed conflict during the recent insurrection in East Pakistan.

The obligations of Article 3 are cast in such general terms and leave so

---

[37] Pictet, *supra* note 7, at 51.

[38] 5 *Int'l Rev. Red Cross* 636 (1965).

[39] Greenberg, "Law and the Conduct of the Algerian Revolution," 11 *Harv. J. Int'l L.* 37, 50–51 (1970).

many things unsaid that they cannot, even under the best of circumstances, be an adequate guide to the conduct of belligerents in civil strife. What legal rules should obtain in internal conflict will be discussed later in this chapter, and several instances of the inadequacies of Article 3 will suffice at this point. The principle that "The wounded and sick shall be collected and cared for" is not enough to guarantee the protection of the wounded and sick and to safeguard the position of those who minister to them. The totality of "judicial guarantees which are recognized as indispensable by civilized peoples" which are required before the "passing of sentences" are not defined. It is not enough to say that captured combatants must "be treated humanely, without any adverse distinction." The protection of non-participants in the civil strife is not spelled out.

The answer that is often given to the inadequacy of Article 3 is to call for the application of the Conventions as a whole, according to the exhortation to the parties "to endeavour to bring into force, by means of special agreements, all or part of the other provisions" of the Conventions. Aside from the difficulties, already alluded to, of negotiation between government and insurgents, there are certain technical difficulties in the application of the Prisoners of War and Civilians Conventions in civil war. Legal machinery designed with a view to its being applied to international conflict will simply not work in internal conflict. The gears of the Conventions do not in a number of respects mesh with those of civil war.

One may start with a key provision of the Prisoners of War Convention, defining the persons who are protected by the Convention. Although Article 4, defining prisoners of war, does not in most instances require that such persons not be of the same nationality as the Detaining Power, case law indicates that a person who is a national of the Detaining Power need not be treated as a prisoner of war and may be tried for treason and other unlawful acts under the law of the state that claims his allegiance.[40] Such a qualification on the broad scope of Article 4 would mean that most rebels could not claim prisoner of war status, except if the protection of the Convention as applied to civil war were to be considered to be wider than the protection of the Convention applied in international conflict. This assumption about the limits placed on Article 4 is borne out by the requirement of Article 87 of the same Convention that "When fixing the penalty [for an offense], the courts or authorities of the Detaining Power shall take into consideration, to the widest extent possible, the fact that the accused, not being a national of the Detaining Power, is not bound to it by any duty of allegiance. . . ."[41]

---

[40] Public Prosecutor v. Oie Hee Koi, [1968] 2 W.L.R. 715 (P.C.), noted in Baxter, "The Privy Council on the Qualifications of Belligerents," 63 *Am. J. Int'l L.* 290 (1969).

[41] *See also* Article 100 of the same Convention requiring that, before the death sentence can be imposed, the attention of the court must be drawn to the fact that a prisoner of war is not a national of the Detaining Power and owes it no allegiance.

A number of the obligations of the Prisoners of War Convention are cast in terms of national treatment under the law of the Detaining Power. This national treatment is then in a number of instances related to the national law or courts of the Detaining Power. Article 102 provides, for example:

> A prisoner of war can be validly sentenced only if the sentence has been pronounced by the same courts according to the same procedure as in the case of members of the armed forces of the Detaining Power, and if, furthermore, the provisions of the present Chapter have been observed.

The other provisions of Section III of Chapter III lay down a number of other stipulations to be observed in judicial proceedings against prisoners of war. The requirement of Article 102 poses no particular difficulty for the lawful government, but insurgents may lack a system of national law and courts and may find it difficult or impossible to observe all of the procedural safeguards called for. Article 51 requires that national legislation concerning the protection of labour be applied to prisoners of war. It is unlikely that any such legislation will have been enacted by insurgents. Many other provisions impose obligations that are too onerous to be borne by insurgents —such as the provision of sufficient food to keep prisoners in a good state of health; regard must be paid to the habitual diet of the prisoners.[42] Prisoners of war are to be interned "in premises . . . affording every guarantee of hygiene and healthfulness."[43] The guerrilla tactics and irregular warfare conducted by insurgents would often make it physically impossible for these obligations to be discharged. And in the absence of reciprocity on the part of the rebels, it is unlikely that the authorities of the state can be expected to comply in all strictness with the Geneva Prisoners of War Convention.

Two key concepts of the Geneva Civilians Convention of 1949 make it fundamentally unworkable in internal conflict. One of these is that the persons protected by the Convention must be of the nationality of another state. The first paragraph of Article 4 of the Convention provides:

> Persons protected by the Convention are those who, at any given moment and in any manner whatsoever, find themselves, in case of a conflict or occupation, in the hands of a Party to the conflict, or Occupying Power of which they are not nationals.

Only fourteen articles,[44] within a section dealing with "General Protection of Populations against Certain Consequences of War," also protect a state's own population. In its literal terms, the Convention, with the exception of these fourteen articles, cannot be applied to civil conflicts because the insurgents are of the same nationality as the state undertaking the obligations of the Convention. It is not possible to say that rebels should be treated *as if*

---

[42] Geneva Prisoners of War Convention of 1949, Art. 26.

[43] *Id.*, at Art. 23.

[44] Arts. 13–26.

they were enemy nationals. In the first place, this is not what the Convention says. In the second place, how can this status by analogy be determined, when the allegiance of civilians is sought by both belligerents and cannot readily be ascertained in individual cases? Nationality is a fixed legal status; loyalty or allegiance is quite another thing.

Other provisions of the Convention apply to "territory of a party to the conflict" and to "occupied territory." In internal conflict, the lawful government and the insurgents will both maintain that there is only "territory of a party to the conflict." Territory cannot be belligerently occupied by the lawful government or the rebels. There is no starting point which divides territory into friendly and enemy areas, so that, when the latter type of area is occupied, it will be belligerently occupied. It surely cannot be maintained that the insurgents should be required to treat all territory over which they exercise control as being belligerently occupied or that the lawful government should be forced to treat territory liberated from the control of rebels as belligerently occupied. It is of the essence of belligerent occupation that it should be exercised over foreign, enemy territory. Such requirements as that of Article 43 of the Hague Regulations that the occupant must respect, "unless absolutely prevented, the laws in force in the country" are simply unworkable in domestic conflict.

Even the machinery for supervision of the operation of the Conventions will not work properly in civil war. Although no Protecting Power has been appointed since the Second World War, the institution still exists.[45] It involves the activity of a third neutral state on behalf of individuals depending on one of the parties to the conflict and in the hands of the opposing belligerent. The Protecting Power maintains communication between two states, and the very appointment of the Protecting Power involves the agreement of high contracting parties to the Conventions. A government asked to designate a Protecting Power to look after its personnel in the hands of the insurgents would justifiably fear that the designation of a Protecting Power would give some degree of international legitimacy to the insurgents themselves.[46] The institution of the Protecting Power, already close to the vanishing point in international conflict, would be under more extreme stress in civil conflict.

It is unfortunate that no serious attempt has ever been made to determine which articles of the four Geneva Conventions of 1949 could work in internal conflicts. If only the "humanitarian" provisions of the law are to be applied in civil war, then it is still necessary to identify what those "humanitarian" principles are and what becomes of the rest of the Conventions. Enough has been said here to indicate that grave difficulties will be encountered in giving full effect to the entirety of the Geneva Conventions of 1949 in civil conflicts.

[45] *See* common Art. 8/8/8/9.

[46] The inability of Israel and the Arab States to designate a Protecting Power is similarly attributable, in part at least, to the fact that the Arab States do not recognize the existence of Israel. That conflict is, of course, international in character.

The generally unsatisfactory state of the law concerning internal conflicts has led the Secretary-General of the United Nations to suggest that this is an area of the law where elaboration of additional rules "in the form of a protocol or of a separate additional convention" is called for.[47] The International Committee of the Red Cross, which has had this subject under consideration for a number of years, submitted a series of proposals to the Conference of Government Experts held at Geneva in May and June of 1971.[48] It was recommended by the Secretary-General that the General Assembly defer further examination of the subject until the International Committee of the Red Cross had had an opportunity to deal with the question.[49]

At the Conference of Government Experts, there was a substantial amount of support for the idea of moving ahead with a protocol—amounting in effect to a new Geneva convention—applicable to internal conflicts.[50] The discussions at Geneva provided some indication of what kind of new obligations States would find acceptable. The delegation of Canada actually submitted a detailed draft,[51] and it would seem that the time has now come for the actual preparation of a draft protocol by the International Committee of the Red Cross or by a group of interested states. If that draft were to be found acceptable at a further conference of government experts, the draft could then be submitted to a diplomatic conference convened either by the Swiss Federal Council, as was the case in the Diplomatic Conference of 1949, or by the General Assembly, by reason of its awakening interest in the humanitarian law of war.

The approach which must be taken in the preparation of a protocol is that protection must be afforded to the human rights of combatants and non-combatants alike during internal conflict. At the same time, due respect must be paid to the need of governments to have at their disposal means of maintaining domestic order and of punishing those who threaten it or attack it. In the reconciliation of these two competing demands lies the principal task of those who must draft the new protocol.

At the outset, the same problem of definition encountered in connection with Article 3 arises again. The new protocol could be given the same scope as Article 3 itself, but so long as the types of conflict to which Article 3 refers are unclear, the imprecision should not be carried over into a new treaty. The alternative is to leave Article 3 as it is and to embark on a new definition of "armed conflict not of an international character" for the pur-

---

[47] *Respect for Human Rights in Armed Conflicts*; [Second] Report of the Secretary-General 51, U.N. Doc. A/8052 (1970).

[48] 5 Conference of Government Experts on the Reaffirmation and Development of International Humanitarian Law Applicable in Armed Conflicts, *Protection of Victims of Non-International Armed Conflicts*, Doc. CE/5b (1971).

[49] Report cited *supra* note 47, at 52.

[50] *Report of Commission II*, at 3 (1971).

[51] Canadian Draft Protocol to the Geneva Conventions of 1949 relative to Conflicts not International in Character, Doc. CE Plen/2 bis (1971).

poses of the protocol alone. The resulting situation is not fully satisfactory, as there would then be three separate bodies of law applicable to different types of internal conflict: (a) the totality or part of the existing conventions brought into force by a special agreement between the belligerents; (b) Article 3 in its present form binding parties to the four Geneva Conventions of 1949; (c) the new protocol applicable to some of the internal conflicts covered by Article 3—or to all of them, or even to more of them. It must be borne in mind that the definition of the types of conflict to which the protocol will apply must depend on the nature of the substantive obligations to be laid down by the protocol. The easier to accept are the duties of the treaty, the more likely states are to apply the agreement to a wide range of circumstances. Correspondingly, the higher the level of performance required, the more limitative the definition will inevitably be.

One possible way of avoiding the problem of definition would be to allow each state, by analogy to the procedure whereby states accept the compulsory jurisdiction of the International Court of Justice by unilateral declaration,[52] to specify the circumstances under which it would be prepared to apply the rules of the protocol. Since the protocol would apply to internal conflicts only, there would be no need of mutuality of obligation with any other state.

But if a definition is called for, it might take the following form:[53]

> This Protocol shall apply to any case of armed conflict not of an international character which is carried on in the territory of a High Contracting Party and in which
> (1)   organized armed forces, subject to a system of military discipline, carry on hostile activities in arms against the authorities in power, and
> (2)   the authorities in power employ their armed forces against such persons.
> This Protocol has no application to situations of internal disturbance or tension.

It will be observed that the definition is cast entirely in terms of objective factors; taking into account the motives or purposes of the insurgents would blunt the edge of the definition and make it much harder to apply. The definition actually goes back to some of the criteria that were suggested for the application of Article 3 at the Diplomatic Conference of 1949.[54] The proposal of the International Committee of the Red Cross that rules should be framed for "internal disturbances" and "internal tensions"[55] does not

---

[52] Statute of the International Court of Justice, Art. 36, para. 2, 59 *Stat.* 1055, *T.S.* No. 993, 3 *Bevans* 1153; see *Report of Commission II*, at 19 (1971).

[53] Based on the Report of the Drafting Committee, Doc. CE/Com. II/13 rev. 1 (1971). The Canadian draft referred to in note 51 *supra* contained no definition.

[54] *See* p. 526 *supra*.

[55] Report cited *supra* note 48, at 79–94.

seem to have elicited much support. The exclusionary clause of the definition assures that it has no application to riots and other like disorders.

The definition makes no attempt to deal with the problem of external participation in a civil conflict. The suggestion that in that event the entire conflict should be regulated by the entirety of the humanitarian law of war[56] is not persuasive. For the government, it would offer a disincentive to acceptance of foreign aid, since the participation even of small forces of a friendly foreign state would require that captured rebels be accorded the status of prisoners of war and thus be immunized from the impact of municipal law. On the other hand, the insurgents would have a strong incentive to seek aid from outside, since they would thereby improve their position by being treated as prisoners of war. The effect would be to stimulate the escalation of internal into international conflict.[57]

If a new protocol on internal conflicts were to be drawn up there would be less reason to think in terms of automatic application of the Geneva Conventions of 1949 as a whole[58] when the conflict assumes the proportions of an inter-state conflict. The possibility should be left open of making the international body of law applicable through special agreements, as now provided by Article 3. However, as has been demonstrated above, the Conventions are not designed to operate effectively in times of civil strife. Indeed, a great service would be done if model special agreements[59] were to be drawn up, identifying those provisions that, subject to modifications in certain respects, could function effectively in time of internal conflict.

Once the hurdle of determining when the protocol on internal conflicts should be applicable has been surmounted, the substantive content of the protocol falls into place with somewhat greater ease. There are certain human rights which obviously do need protection—ones which states would not find it unduly burdensome to guarantee. Other safeguards have political implications and would find less ready acceptance.

Starting with the most obvious and acceptable stipulations, the new protocol or convention should certainly contain wider provisions for the protection of the wounded and sick and of the medical personnel who minister to them.[60] In this respect, there could be a good deal of drawing upon the Geneva Wounded and Sick Convention of 1949 and Part II of the Geneva Civilians Convention of 1949.[61] There are no provisions about relief and the functions of humanitarian organizations in the existing

[56] Report cited *supra* note 48, at 21.

[57] *See Report of Commission II*, at 41–47.

[58] As proposed by the International Committee of the Red Cross in Report cited *supra* note 48, at 15. The expression used by the I.C.R.C.—"the whole of the international humanitarian law"—is itself ambiguous.

[59] As proposed by an expert from France in Doc. CE/Com. II/5 (1971).

[60] *See* Report cited *supra* note 48, at 53; and Canadian Draft Protocol cited *supra* note 51, at 3.

[61] Applicable to "The General Protection of Populations against Certain Consequences of War."

Article 3. There is room for specific rules on this subject, but states will be sensitive to possible infringements upon their sovereignty in connection with relief operations, and those states that have had recent experience of civil war, such as Nigeria, Indonesia, and Pakistan, may be expected to counsel caution in drafting sweeping provisions on this topic.[62]

Without going so far as to grant the status of prisoners of war to captured combatants, provisions should still be inserted which will assure humane treatment of those who have engaged in belligerent acts and are hors de combat. The protocol should not stand in the way of prosecution of those who have engaged in rebellious activities against the state, but it should assure that penal proceedings are conducted with both procedural and substantive due process of law.[63] The internment of individuals who have not engaged in hostilities but are thought to represent a threat to the security of the state should likewise be subject to procedural and substantive safeguards.[64]

The International Committee of the Red Cross proposed three measures to soften the impact of municipal law upon combatants in civil conflict. One would preclude the punishment of a fighter "solely for having belonged to armed forces, unless imperative security requirements make this necessary."[65] The proposal may accomplish both too much and too little—too much in the sense of making it impossible to impose severe punishment on the leaders of an insurrection, and too little because of a general escape clause to deal with "imperative security requirements." The second proposal was to defer the imposition of the death penalty until the termination of the hostilities, again subject to the condition "unless imperative security requirements make this necessary."[66] The proposal has the advantage of avoiding the blood-bath that may come of savage justice and retaliatory killings in war, but it must also be borne in mind that to keep an individual under death sentence for a period running into years can of itself be a cruel and unusual punishment.[67] The third proposal was for a general amnesty at the conclusion of hostilities.[68] The principle is laudable, but it may be too much to put the obligation in the term of a *general* amnesty.

While states and insurgent factions may be in a position, through special agreements, to extend prisoner of war treatment to combatants in civil conflict, the protocol can best avoid offense to the sensitivities of states if it does not speak in the terms employed in the law relating to international

[62] *See, e.g., Report of Commission II* at 28 referring to the fact that developing countries, which had in a number of instances been ravaged by civil conflict, "required stability and order; the very existence of many of them had been in jeopardy."

[63] *See* Canadian Draft Protocol cited *supra* note 51, at 5.

[64] Analogous to those prescribed in Articles 78–135 of the Geneva Civilians Convention of 1949.

[65] Report cited *supra* note 48, at 57.

[66] *Id.* at 59.

[67] *Report of Commission II* at 33.

[68] Report cited *supra* note 48, at 60.

conflict. Instead of granting prisoner of war status to combatants and non-combatants who have engaged in hostile activity, the protocol should provide humane standards for the internment or imprisonment of such individuals. The provisions on internment of civilians in the Geneva Civilians Convention can be heavily drawn upon.[69]

The provisions against inhumane treatment now found in rudimentary form in common Article 3 require expansion.

The question of the protection of the civilian population generally, particularly in connection with aerial bombardment, the use of certain types of weapons (such as napalm), and the danger to civilians posed by certain types of tactics,[70] is intimately related to the protection of the civilian population under similar circumstances in international war. Any stipulations applicable to internal conflict must therefore abide the working out of these problems in the wider context of international armed conflict.

The greatest care must be taken to assure that both the lawful government and the insurgents will be in a position to carry out the provisions of any new protocol. Not only must there be reciprocity of obligation, but the rules must be framed with a realistic understanding of what the capacities and purposes of insurgents are. Since the insurgents will not be parties to the instrument, it is essential that each provision have an inner persuasiveness and reasonableness that commends it as a humane and workable rule of law.

And finally, in light of the widespread noncompliance with the existing Geneva Conventions of 1949, one must cautiously ask whether the new protocol will simply be a number of new provisions adding to the existing bulk of the law or an effective instrument for the protection of human rights and for the amelioration of the conditions of what is often the most savage form of warfare—domestic armed conflict within the borders of a state. The new protocol will in the end be effective only if states wish to make it so.

[69] Arts. 68–135 of the Geneva Civilians Convention.

[70] *See* 3 Conference of Government Experts on the Reaffirmation and Development of International Humanitarian Law Applicable in Armed Conflicts, *Protection of the Civilian Population against Dangers of Hostilities*, Doc. CE/3b (1971).

PART VII | **COMMENTS BY MEMBERS OF THE PANEL**

Comment 1 | Richard A. Falk

I am particularly impressed by the degree to which chapter authors approached this controversial subject-matter without skewing their analysis to reflect the happenchance of national affiliation. I find this degree of universalization of outlook impressive, provided I am correct in my assessment of its existence, and not merely myself exhibiting an inability to discern a set of parochial biases and concerns that would not be regarded as "universal" by "impartial" international law experts in, say, Ghana or India. Nevertheless, I think my assessment on this point is valid, at least as measured against earlier Anglo-American efforts to relate international law to the subject-matter of civil war. I find this increasing capacity for objective analysis to be a very hopeful tendency for those of us who believe that international lawyers can contribute more generally to the emerging debate about the future of world order.

It may also be the case that a redefinition of scholarly identity in more genuinely cosmopolitan terms is an expression of a spreading disenchantment with the capacity of sovereign states to solve the main problems of mankind. Especially in the United States, I think, it is plausible for international law experts to exhibit skepticism about *ex parte* invocations of international law to vindicate an interventionary diplomacy. One would hope, also, that our Soviet colleagues, even if not free now to do so avowedly, would also share this quest for a framework of impartial guidance and restraint that limits state behavior as well as conditions the public rhetoric used by governments to justify controversial foreign policy decisions. I think that many American international lawyers now understand that we serve well neither our prince nor ourselves by a willingness to fashion legal arguments as the national occasion demands.

A PRIOR QUESTION

In my view, no essay in this volume confronts clearly the most fundamental question of all—namely, the relation between the means and ends of military intervention in the modern world within the setting of large-scale counterinsurgency warfare. My own sense is that notions of "proportionality" of relationship between means and end are indispensable to the very existence of law in the area of war and peace. When I contemplate the charred ruins of the villages and cities of Indochina, I wonder what conceivable pattern of justification can possibly vindicate such destruction. In my view, the doctrinal and technological means used to conduct modern counterinsurgency warfare are tending to overwhelm whatever political objectives are relied upon as justifications, especially when the main perpetrator of the destruction is external to the national arena of struggle. For this reason, I would think it becomes important to grant a strong presumption of validity to an absolute norm of non-intervention in relation to this subset of interventionary situations.

Counterinsurgency warfare carried on with high technology weaponry seems inherently intolerable because of its tendency to produce indiscriminate and massive destruction; if "saving" means "destroying," then the *legal* case for responsive violence seems very weak for the same reasons, essentially, that the legal case for torture is weak. Whatever the context, torture is illegal, and no justification, however great in pragmatic terms of alleged military necessity, is regarded as legally sufficient.

But, it might be asked, does not such a prohibition expose the weak to insurgency strategies? Doesn't the prospect of a counterinsurgent response based on modern technology deter risk-taking by external sponsors of insurgency?

These are serious questions, but I find no reason why they vindicate an external locus of counterinsurgent response. External sponsors of insurgency have rarely had notable successes against a *stable* government, whether the sponsor was the United States vis-à-vis Castro's Cuba via the Bay of Pigs in 1961, or Castro vis-à-vis other Latin American governments. It is true, of course, that a minor covert effort can topple foreign governments that enjoy little popular base of support, but I can point to no major revolutionary success in this century that came about as a consequence of massive external sponsorship. Quite the contrary, the major revolutionary victories were secured *despite* overt and massive efforts to help the anti-revolutionary side stay in power. Furthermore, the major governments in the world, regardless of ideology, have generally avoided substantive sponsorship of foreign insurgencies, because they share a major concern with upholding their own statist claims which are based on the legitimacy of governmental control over national territory.

But what of the challenge implicit in the Spanish Civil War? Should one abandon a democratic government confronted by an antidemocratic insurgency sponsored and aided to some extent by external governments? There may arise instances of action so intolerable on one side that prior rules of restraint can be maintained only to an approximate extent. Perhaps in the Spanish Civil War situation, in which high-technology pro-insurgent participation is externally based, there is a sufficient basis for offsetting external help to the incumbent, *i.e.*, we propose a no-first-use approach to high technology intervention in situations of internal war.

I feel that international lawyers, as experts in normative analysis, must not accommodate themselves automatically to the logic of the war system. There may be contexts in which the inefficiency and destructiveness of the military instrument has become so great in moral terms, or its inherent cruelty so evident, that it must be resisted altogether. It is almost immaterial whether this conclusion is put forward as an interpretation of customary international law or as a proposal for new norms. This reasoning extends beyond the counterinsurgency area, and applies even more forcefully, I think, to a consideration of the legitimacy of "first uses" of nuclear weapons. What I am saying is that it seems normatively preferable to risk "losing" a particular struggle than to retain certain military options as part of "the system." Statesmen have agreed with this judgment when it comes to certain tactics such as biological or gas warfare. I am arguing that such a flat prohibition needs to be considered in relation to direct and overt participation by external actors in counterinsurgency warfare.[1]

---

[1] Counterinsurgency warfare exists when a government deploys a substantial portion of its regular armed forces to engage in active combat against internal opposition forces.

It is not a clinching argument against this position to suggest that it might be difficult to delimit or implement the prohibition or to draw a dividing line between high, middle, and low technology weaponry and tactics. I am not proposing an absolute prohibition on intervention, even military intervention, but on *external and overt participation on either side* in one kind of interventionary situation. This categorical prohibition superficially resembles, in effect, the suggestion by Tom Farer of a categorical norm prohibiting tactical military support to either side in a civil war. My emphasis is less on the degree of involvement than on the technological level of sophistication, and therefore it distinguishes high-technology interventions from others. My concern with this prior question is also less motivated by the search for standards of behavior that are as "self-interpreting" and conflict-confining as possible. I do share Professor Farer's judgment that more sophisticated approaches to counterinsurgency options are vulnerable to self-interested manipulation and provide little protection against the sort of "ultra-violence" we have seen on display in Indochina during the last decade. Without a categorical prohibition, it is always possible for a reasonable man to propose "a final solution" as the most efficient, indeed, as the most moral way to pursue a military objective; just as we have no way of knowing whether Hiroshima saved lives and shortened World War II, so we have no way of knowing whether the bombing of the Red River dike system or Hanoi-Haiphong back in 1967, when first proposed, might not have "saved lives" (and won the war), or whether, even in 1972, it might not compel surrender by the other side. Precisely because we have no way of knowing, we need as much protection as possible against the well-documented, distinctive propensities of man to use whatever destructive technology is available. Would you want your doctor to have the power to kill in the name of euthanasia? Or, more aptly, would you want your worst enemy's doctor to have such discretion?

The purpose of raising this "prior question" is to argue that the law of war presupposes a moral foundation of means and ends, and that I find such foundation lacking in many counterinsurgency settings. Governments are even more capable than ordinary men of constructing a clockwork orange.

JOHN NORTON MOORE'S "TOWARD AN APPLIED THEORY . . ."

There are many complexities generated by the interdependence of human affairs in an era of great danger. We are confronted by what I would call "the Bangladesh dilemma," by the stability of totalitarian regimes, and by the prospect of massive overt pro-insurgent intervention of the sort that occurred during the Spanish Civil War. It seems necessary to balance a collective disposition to "liberate" Czechoslovakia against the danger of provoking World War III. We must also distinguish between contexts of global danger and a potential capacity to act effectively on behalf of repressed blacks in Namibia or to prevent a Third World government, such as Burundi, from committing genocide within its own borders. These are not purely moral distinctions—that is, Czechoslovakian repression may be as serious as South African by most yardsticks—but reflect an overall effort to reconcile normative and prudential imperatives. This quest for reconciliation reflects a healthy appreciation by international lawyers of "the art of the possible," but it also introduces a measure of jurisprudential incoherence into a legal order that is decentralized; all law presupposes equality and reciprocity of treatment *in the basic sense that like things should be treated alike.* The international legal order incurs large burdens, it seems to me, when it must absorb rhetorical resolutions in the United Nations that embody categorical prohibitions upon activity that has been selectively engaged in by almost every large governmental actor in the world. International law depends for effectiveness largely upon voluntary acceptance and, hence, upon a widely shared consensus among governments. In the area of intervention there is a self-contradictory consensus arising out of the dual interest of governments in prohibiting interventions that encroach upon *their* sovereignty, while endorsing interventions that promote elsewhere deeply held foreign policy positions. In an interdependent world community, some degree of contradiction is virtually inevitable if behavioral standards are related to single-factor rules.

Professor Moore's approach to intervention, which has gathered sophistication and balance over the years, represents the most significant effort ever made by an international law expert to overcome this kind of incoherence without giving up the game by imposing a single Procrustean rule of prohibition or endorsement. In this sense, Moore's approach contrasts, on the one side, with that of Richard Barnet, who would have international law forbid *all* interventionary undertakings and, on the other side, with that of Dean Acheson, who believed that decisions to intervene were basically not legal questions at all because vital interests of sovereign states were at stake.

I would also recall my effort to raise "the prior question" with reference to external participation in one category of interventionary situations—high-technology counterinsurgency warfare. It is possible that the prior question cannot be satisfactorily resolved, either because there is an insufficient disposition to do so or because the weight of considered opinion is against taking the poison gas or categorical approach. In that event, which I believe, in main, to be the likely response, Professor Moore provides us with a generally enlightened and imaginative approach to the evolution of an interventionary policy. It is even an approach that is coherent to the extent that it incorporates geopolitical prudence into its notion of minimum world order. I believe, also, that Moore's main normative emphases on minimum public order, human rights, and self-determination express an emerging consensus among peoples around the world about the policies at stake in interventionary settings. Such agreement could develop into a general community consensus that might begin to restore a sense of equality to the treatment accorded interventionary claims by most governments on most occasions. His framework for decision is acutely sensitive to the main contextual factors and helps greatly to organize the diversity of interventionary situations into a set of useful categories. The only way to make the equality principle function in a complex series of instances is to evolve discernible standards allowing that reasonably *unlike cases should be treated dissimilarly.*

In the intervention context there is a tendency, usefully decried by Moore in earlier writing, to formulate legal doctrine in an over-generalized way that lumps together diverse situations that raise very different policy choices for government decision-makers. Moore's policy proposals identify policy-relevant diversity in a manner that I find convincing, given the present character of international society. Indeed, his approach to the problems of intervention strikes me as a paradigm for inquiry into almost any complex law/policy setting, a paradigm that could be beneficially extended to many other areas of contemporary concern. I believe that Moore's adaptation of the McDougal/Lasswell framework is a major original contribution of his own that surpasses in important respects earlier efforts associated with the New Haven School to deal with particular problems of substance.

The very excellence of Moore's chapter makes critical commentary seem particularly fruitful. I can mention here only a few areas of concern. To begin, among the seven misperceptions that Moore identifies as those that have "militated against an adequate applied theory," the fifth one is

> (5) In the international system, exaggeration of the effects of decentralized decision.

In his explanatory text Moore says that it is important "to avoid unrealistic despair" that arises from an "exaggerated emphasis on the lack of authoritative third-party judgment in the international system and the related normative relativism sometimes associated with the realization that there are contending world-order systems." It is not clear to me that such despair is "unrealistic." Both national governments and scholars have generally tended to rationalize attitudes that uphold the propriety of national claims and to be quite literally unable to appreciate the adversary's view of the same situation. For instance, can one expect an Indian international lawyer to take a pro-Pakistani view of the Kashmir claim or a Soviet international lawyer to write in support of Chinese border claims? Professor Moore's examples of the American government's reliance on international law *arguments* in various controversial settings is not persuasive even with respect to United States foreign policy. I agree that we, as scholars, can increasingly adopt an impartial position, and I take my "stand" on this where Professor Moore does. However, it seems realistic to emphasize the hazards and significance of decentralization for both the process of interpretation and the prospect of influencing governmental behavior. How many governments at this point really welcome an impartial appraisal of their interventionary undertakings? We have a long way to go before national policy-makers really grasp the extent to which genuine structures of reciprocity—based on notions of principle—really serve national interest in the present world setting. Until this educational job has been substantially accomplished, I think it appropriate for international lawyers to place *due emphasis* on the decentralized character of international society. I would even reverse Moore's fifth precondition and argue that the more common misconception has resulted from insufficient emphasis on and understanding of the extent to which decentralized decision-making influences the pattern of state behavior in interventionary settings.

A second problem I find in Moore's present formulation of a normative theory of intervention is his failure to take account of the inequality of governmental actors within the world system. Unlike protecting ambassadorial immunity or commercial aircraft overflight rights, the interventionary system is available only to the strong in relation to the weak. Are strong actors likely, on balance, to have a beneficial effect when authorized to use force outside their territory? Moore confines national discretion, to some extent, by stressing collective authorization, but I still find the tone of his proposals too sanguine in relation to the constructive potentialities of interventionary policy developed by

Great Powers. I think we need more empirical post-intervention studies in relation to the execution of interventionary claims in such contexts as Bangladesh, Stanleyville Operation (1964), and the Dominican Republic (1965), as well as studies of the effects of non-interventionary postures in relation to strife-torn situations such as Indonesia (1965), the Nigerian Civil War, and Northern Ireland. Until we have such impact studies, recommendations about standards of behavior may be premature. I would, at this point, distinguish between the normative endorsement of interventionary claims and Moore's admirable effort to focus a potential decision-maker's attention on factors that should be taken into account in creating more constructive intervention precedents than heretofore; clear thinking, as Confucius long ago understood, does improve the prospects for enlightened action. Or, making the opposite point, unclear thinking— that is, insufficient clarity about diverse contexts and world order consequences —virtually assures muddled and destructive behavior.

My final critical comment relates to Moore's insufficient sensitivity to "the bull in the china shop" problem. It is hard for me to contemplate a large-scale, high-technology intervention in a low-technology society that does not inflict disproportionate destruction. To press my metaphor, bulls are sometimes "invited" (often the invitations are arranged) into ill-administered china shops that are on the verge of bankruptcy. An isolated political elite may be eager to invite a foreign nation to help it remain in power if opposition forces grow too strong. Uncritical deference to the prerogatives of "widely recognized governments" seems seriously inconsistent with Moore's policy mandate to promote self-determination and human rights. I realize that Professor Moore uses "widely recognized" as a code phrase for political legitimacy that includes a consideration of capacity for internal governance, but I still think his presentation overly legitimates assistance to regimes that are repressive but not quite genocidal. It seems important, especially for American international lawyers, to appreciate the continuity between foreign and domestic policy, especially in a society that itself wants to remain relatively open. When a democratic government betrays its political principles in foreign affairs by intervening on behalf of a repressive regime abroad, then it arouses opposition at home. If this opposition is serious, the regime will seek to neutralize it by persuasion if possible, by deception if necessary, and by intimidation and repression as a last resort.

HUMANITARIAN INTERVENTION: BROWNLIE VERSUS LILLICH

This debate between two leading scholars, although somewhat too concerned for my taste with the comparative merits of personal achievement, is a vivid illustration of the jurisprudential divide between American and English international law techniques that remain, (despite the formidable bridging efforts so graciously carried on within the sedate walls of Chatham House) virtually as wide as the Atlantic Ocean. Professor Brownlie wants clear legal rules substantiated by formal sources—state practice, treaties, doctrinal formulations—to be sharply differentiated from proposals as to what governments ought to be doing. Professor Lillich believes that the legal tradition is ample enough to support his well-reasoned position as to what governments ought to be doing; he argues that there is sufficient "openness" in the formal evidence to support his vindication of a post-Charter doctrine of unilateral humanitarian intervention.

I am all for Lillich on the jurisprudential level of the debate, but I am not persuaded by his examples. He accords India's pro-Bangladesh intervention commanding weight, but he also vindicates the Stanleyville Operation and the Dominican intervention under the "humanitarian" rubric. I wonder whether such a way of thinking could be seriously held outside the hegemonial centers of world power: that is, outside a country that was secure against humanitarian intervention not because it was humane, but because it was big and strong. In an interdependent world where economic and ideological motivation needs to be disguised, I am wondering whether this particular genie should be let out of the bottle, or more accurately, whether we should affix angel's wings to the interventionary genie. Even Hitler, as Brownlie points out, was unscrupulous enough to disguise his aggressions in the garb of humanitarian intervention. I am not convinced that it is desirable to interpret the prohibition on intervention in such an open-textured way as to ease the task of government apologists in controversial contexts.

Brownlie's tantalizing suggestion of euthanasia is attractive on two grounds; first, it keeps up the formal guard against interventionary impulses in Great Power capitals; secondly, it creates an open space for doing what is accepted by the world community as right in exceptional circumstances without explicitly ripping the lid off Pandora's box. As with the status of euthanasia, a doctor is inhibited from ending a patient's life except in the most extreme circumstances of pain and hopelessness, circumstances under which any sensitive law enforcer would avert his eyes.

So much debate in this area comes down to one's attitude toward the impact of the Great Powers on world affairs. Is there still "a white man's burden" to save "the natives" from the agonies of genocide or severe abuses of human rights? Is there "a white man's prerogative" to save their nationals when they are imperiled by strife in "backward" areas? Such questions put these issues in extreme form. If such burdens exist—because it is better to stop some genocide than none—can they be discharged fairly and consistently enough to merit the blessings of international lawyers? Or should we still insist that "humanitarian intervention," to be "legal," must either be mandated by collective action or excused because the circumstances were extreme? Professor Lillich needs to give us more systematic and empirical guidance as to whether the way out of the Bangladesh dilemma is by means of Brownlie's euthanasia approach or by way of his doctrinal pattern of carefully qualified authorization. Such guidance can only be provided after we do a careful cost-benefit analysis of the "cases" that fall within the gambit of the Lillich proposal, as well as after we assess the potential for collective forms of authorization.

Again, however, as with Moore's taxonomy, if we are to have a general tradition of humanitarian intervention, Lillich's effort to explicate guidance criteria is helpful in facilitating restrained execution of an interventionary impulse.

ON PRIVATE ARMIES

Michael Reisman's brilliant and learned chapter exhibits many virtues, and deserves major discussion. I found Professor Reisman's depiction of the war system particularly valuable because it shed so much light on the dangerous and violence-prone ways that are endemic to the state system. In doing so, it raised searching questions about the entire claim by governments to enjoy a legitimated monopoly over the instruments of violence, and it put the position of counter-governmental violence in a more realistic and morally equivalent context.

There are two specific concerns that I would mention: first, the term "private armies" connotes a partiality of orientation that may be functionally and normatively misleading, mainly as it sets up an opposition in the mind to the "public armies" of governments. These governments may be controlled by tiny factions, isolated from popular support, that sustain control by ruthless use of official armies, imported mercenaries, and police capabilities. The counter-government armies, in such settings, may be the more truly "public" actors in the sense of popular support and representativeness. I would prefer the term "unofficial" to "private" as a description of the subject for Reisman's analysis.

Secondly, I would like to grasp more fully Professor Reisman's passing affirmation of a regionalist system of world order. By what criteria of desirability and feasibility? In international legal studies, we require a sub-discipline of comparative systems of world order. I have been working out the preliminary format of such a sub-discipline in the context of a course at Princeton and in connection with the World Order Models Project (syllabus and manuscript available on request). I suspect that Reisman's work with McDougal and Lasswell on constitutive processes will culminate also in a consideration of the emerging structural options for value realization that exist within the world community, and that, perhaps, we will then receive a rationale for the regionalist preferences that are only tantalizingly mentioned in this chapter.

Reisman's chapter is such a trail-blazing venture that he does not provide us with nearly as much policy clarification as is offered in Moore's chapter. Moore was writing against the background of a large literature that was becoming crystallized around his emphasis on systematic categories generating distinct normative standards. I would hope that Reisman's longer work on "private armies" has a final chapter that distills the analysis sufficiently to enable a catalogue of categories and a set of policy-responsive proposals.

Without such an eventual distillation, Reisman would not have created a very usable instrument for policy analysis and guidance. A problem of methodological utopianism has often plagued the McDougal jurisprudence and has been a favorite target for detracting critics. Moore's work is so impressive partly because he has combined McDougal's *sophistication* about *abstract* categories with a very precise and illuminating depiction of *concrete* policy implications. I am confident that Reisman will do the same. Indeed, I think Moore and Reisman are in search of comparable horizons of significance. These horizons are greatly extending our conception of what it is reasonable for practical and decent men to expect from international law.

THE LAWS OF WAR

The highly competent chapters by Professors Baxter and Taubenfeld are not what I believe is primarily called for at this time on this topic. We desperately need, in relation to the laws of war, a reexpression of Kunz's eloquent call for "urgent revision." Existing rules of war are dangerously outmoded, given the character of large-scale civil war and high-technology weapons and tactics. I believe three tasks should be immediately undertaken by international lawyers concerned with this subject:

    1.   An articulation and appraisal of existing principles of customary and treaty international law as they relate to principal battlefield situations;

    2.   An assessment as to whether it is practical and desirable to revise these principles in light of the technological changes in warfare or in response to the dynamics of terror and indiscriminate destruction that are generated by the interplay of insurgent challenges and counterinsurgent responses; and

    3.   A set of policy-responsive proposals for restraint (procedural and substantive) that express an understanding of politico-military imperatives.

On such a basis it might then become possible to mobilize support for a world conference of governments and other concerned actors, organized along the lines of the Hague Conferences of 1899 and 1907. The rise of unofficial armies and international institutions would create the basis for an historic acknowledgment that the international legal order is no longer merely an expression of statist logic. Because of my earlier consideration of "the prior question," it may be virtually impossible to evolve a meaningful framework of second-order restraints in the context of large-scale, high-technology counter-insurgency warfare, but such warfare constitutes only one of several principal categories of interventionary situations.

A SUBSEQUENT QUESTION

This volume of essays suggests the extent to which international lawyers can clarify the structure of choice in complex policy contexts. It remains very important, however, to appreciate the gap that persists between this developing intellectual tradition of scholarly inquiry and the patterns of official decision visible in different portions of the world. In my view, international lawyers should be willing to expose this gap and to make creative proposals for closing it.

    Devising guidelines for interventionary policy is a preoccupation of a few centers of power/authority in the world system. Elsewhere in the world, the subject involves little more than a reaffirmation of non-intervention norms; hence, those United Nations resolutions, endorsed nominally by even the most powerful governments. This dual set of concerns does suggest an underlying tension in the present world order system: the powerful seek guidance frameworks that maintain their ascendant roles; the weak seek barriers against the capabilities of the strong. International law often strikes observers as incoherent because it incorporates both of these political impulses without even acknowledging their contradictory existence.

    I have labeled this concern "the subsequent question" because it complements my earlier consideration of "the prior question." Both questions are generally left out of most analysis of this subject, despite their central significance. It may indeed be time for even international lawyers to think about the unthinkable, *i.e.*, either the total prohibition of all interventionary claims associated with high-technology counterinsurgency or the abandonment of any effort by international law to regulate such interventionary claims. As I have argued, this stark choice is forced upon us by the contradictory logics of military necessity and humanitarian restraint.

In his Introduction and in Chapter I, John Norton Moore has attempted a grand synthesis of six years of more-or-less organized intellectual activity which this volume is intended to culminate. Despite his catholic inquiries and Promethean energies, he has failed. He has failed to comprehend the problem of intervention because he is part of that problem.

I. A REPRESENTATIVE AMERICAN MIND

Moore's work is more interesting and valuable for what it unintentionally reveals about a representative American mind than for its conscious ratiocinations, though they are hardly devoid of significance. Even if the author were anonymous, it would be evident that the Introduction and Chapter I were written by an American. And not just by any United States jurist, but rather by one who is essentially comfortable about the role which his government has been playing in the contemporary world.

Evidence of the peculiarly American vision which informs this work oozes out of its content and its language. One word above all dominates and reveals— the word is "manipulation." Preceded by auguries like "the international law of conflict *management*" and "controllable variables"[1] [emphasis added], it peeps almost shyly out of a concluding page of the Introduction. By the end of Chapter I, such becoming modesty has been eschewed. In its place there is a veritable orgy of self-assertion:

> But development of adequate normative standards is only one policy for realization of the values at stake. It is also important for an adequate applied theory to focus on institutional improvement and the potential for controlling 'undesirable' interventions by *manipulation* of their domestic and systemic causes.
>
> . . .
>
> In addition to suggestions for institutional improvement there are also interesting possibilities for useful policies resulting from recent advances in the theoretical understanding of revolutionary and interventionary phenomena. One hypothesis for exploration is are there key domestic or systemic causes of revolution and intervention which might be *manipulated* to reduce 'undesirable' coercion? Though there is beginning to be an unease among political theorists working in the area with respect to the possible *manipulative* potential of such theories, the answer does not seem to lie in eschewing normative analysis or foregoing further development of theory,

[1] Page xviii of this volume.

but rather in recognition of the inevitability of the normative task. Though present theory has for the most part not advanced to the point where *manipulation* of conditioning factors is either feasible or sufficiently certain to predict the consequences of such *manipulation*, it seems likely that some such factors will emerge as theory is further refined. In fact, present theory is already beginning to focus on a variety of domestic variables which may have significant potential both for *manipulation* and for curtailing undesirable interventions.[2] [emphasis added]

Who, one wonders, is going to do all this managing and controlling and manipulating? Moore refers casually at one point to the need "to strengthen the capability of international institutions to deal with interventionary problems"[3] and to the necessity of "providing more effective community procedures for realization of self-determination, human rights and modernization."[4] But at no point does he suggest how such procedures and institutions are to be strengthened or whether, in light of present trends, there is any prospect for the institutional development he proposes. His essential indifference—or is it perhaps despair?—about institutional development achieves its most amusing expression when, in describing "some of the more useful suggestions for institutional improvement, all of which deserve attention,"[5] he lists the following good-natured banalities:

(1) appraisal of the strengths and weaknesses of particular international organizations as agencies for collective legitimation and the exploration of modalities for strengthening such potential (for example, collective recognition and collective determination of the status of particular conflicts);

(2) the improvement of international machinery for observation and disclosure in interventionary settings;

(3) improvements in arms control measures concerning the proliferation of conventional armaments (for example, proposals for international reporting of military assistance);

(4) improvements in regional and global peacekeeping machinery;

(5) improvements in regional and global machinery for realization of fundamental human rights and for effective response to national and political disasters;

(6) improvements in regional and global machinery for the holding and observation of elections to determine disputed issues of self-determination;

(7) development of a capability for predicting revolutionary and interventory violence based on globally monitored indicators (this is close to being feasible); and

(8) ultimately, development of a comprehensive global response system based on indicators for predicting revolutionary and interventionary vio-

---

[2] *Id.* at 35–37.
[3] *Id.* at 8.
[4] *Id.* at xiii.
[5] *Id.* at 36.

lence coupled to community machinery for alleviating the causes of tension, protecting human rights, promoting self-determination, and confining violence.[6]

This, it seems to me, barely rises above the tautology that international and regional institutional improvements require improved international and regional institutions. When a first-class analytical mind is reduced to that level of generalization, one detects a case of hope unsupported by expectations.

Manipulating, managing, and controlling conflict: This is the vocabulary of the past, of the fool's-gold dawn of the Kennedy era. This is the vocabulary of MacNamara's Pentagon and of its satrapies in Santa Monica and Cambridge, a vocabulary embodying the assumption of a world in which every threat to order is concomitantly a threat to American security. It is the verbal herald of great-power intrusion.

To scholars from developing countries—and even from the more vulnerable developed ones—this would, I am sure, be evident. They entertain few illusions about who will be manipulating and managing, for they deploy the sensitivities instinct in those whose societies have been objects of "international order." I am reminded, in this connection, of a meeting on humanitarian intervention held at the University of Virginia Law School last spring.[7] After a group of eminent United States scholars had passed several hours debating criteria for distinguishing good interventions from bad ones, one Canadian scholar finally observed a little wryly that no one had been moved to ask:

> "Do you want them intervening on [sic] us in these circumstances?"
> Nobody from the U.S. asked that . . . because you never think that anybody is going to intervene in the United States. Who would ever dare . . . ?
> And [anyway, you say to yourselves] "We never deny rights to such an extent that people would want to intervene. . . ." I think that United States thought in part runs rough-shod over what is in the Charter. To my mind, Article 2(4) says exactly what it says—that you shouldn't use force to affect the territorial integrity of a state. . . . [It] . . . keeps the member states from using force . . . to intervene.[8]

While neither Professor Samuels' interpretative technique nor his substantive conclusions may seem finally persuasive, they are hardly eccentric, at least outside the United States. John Norton Moore speaks of an emerging consensus among scholars for a contextual approach, but cites only Yanks and the English legal scholar most deeply influenced by United States intellectual currents.[9] Third World scholars and diplomats cling to a rigid interpretation of the anti-force language of the Charter out of thoroughly rational fears of armed intervention. They share John Norton Moore's concern that rules be policy

---

[6] *Id.*

[7] The Proceedings, as edited by Professor Richard B. Lillich, were published in 1973 (after this article was written) by the University of Virginia Press under the title "Humanitarian Intervention and the United Nations."

[8] Remarks of Professor J. W. Samuels, University of Western Ontario Faculty of Law, at pp. 6–9 of the provisional transcript.

[9] Page 34 of this volume.

responsive; the question, however, is to what policies should the norms of intervention be responsive. For them, protection of the thin fabric of autonomy is the dominant policy. Naturally, they do not share Professor Moore's enthusiasm for the growth of manipulative capacities.

II. THE UNIVERSALIZATION OF AMERICAN VALUES

Language is merely one modest index of the unconscious, national commitments which shape Professor Moore's "synthesis." His conscious perceptions and his proposals are equally illuminating. There is, for instance, his obdurate insistence on the universal appropriateness of political values and institutions which have flourished in the United States.

A dominant theme in United States foreign policy during most of our national history, it is expressed here with admirable clarity in John's "tentative standards for appraisal of the obligation to pursue peaceful settlement of hostilities."[10] There is, of course, no such obligation for parties to *civil conflicts*, except, perhaps, in Moore's mind. What is really interesting, however, is not that little confusion but his procedural and substantive standards designed to measure compliance with the putative obligation. They merit reproduction in full:

Standards of Procedure

(1) The extent to which each belligerent takes the initiative in urging peaceful settlement;

(2) The willingness of the belligerents to negotiate a settlement or at least to negotiate a modality for arriving at settlement: (a) willingness to negotiate at any time without preconditions; (b) willingness to negotiate with all *de facto* belligerents; (c) willingness to negotiate in direct talks; (d) willingness to negotiate with respect to all of the principal issues in dispute;

(3) The willingness of the belligerents to publicly communicate general terms for settlement;

(4) The willingness of the belligerents to suggest specific terms for settlement. Specific suggestions need not always be publicly communicated if public disclosure would inhibit the chances for acceptance;

(5) The willingness of the belligerents to conclude a legally binding settlement, however arrived at, or to agree on a modality for settlement such as arbitration or judicial determination that implies a legally binding outcome.

Standards of Content

(1) The reasonableness of suggested terms for settlement as appraised by reference to fundamental Charter principles including: (a) nonuse of force against the territorial integrity or political independence of any state including: (1) cessation of all belligerent activities and claims of belligerency; (2) nonacquisition of territory (and other values) by force; (3) control of

---

[10] *Id.* at 33.

activities of terrorist or paramilitary forces; (4) measures to strengthen peace; (sic) (b) self-determination of peoples; (c) respect for fundamental human rights; (d) cooperation for economic and social progress;

(2) If self-determination is at issue the willingness of the parties to submit to genuinely free elections;

(3) The willingness of the parties to accept United Nations recommendations for settlement;

(4) In situations in which fundamental Charter principles are uncertain or ambiguous, the willingness of the parties to enter into a compromise settlement.[11]

A. COMPROMISE

As I understand him, Moore assumes that in every national setting, manifestations of tolerance and willingness to compromise are presumptive virtues. There is, in other words, a rebuttable presumption that they will promote the central values of the international system, identified by Moore as minimization of armed conflict, self-determination, and human rights. International community concern with the intensity of domestic conflict is legitimated by the danger of conflict spillover, particularly where it is relatively prolonged, and the risk of injury to alien persons and property. So while it is premature to suggest an "obligation" to pursue a compromise settlement, one may reasonably claim that an important and widely-shared value would be promoted by the recognition of such an obligation.

That is a good deal less clear with respect to the other primary community values which Moore identifies. Indeed, in the case of self-determination, the proposed standard would seem almost inversely related to its achievements, because the community appears to demand total solutions. There is virtually no support for compromise in cases of "salt-water" colonialism, the residue of eighteenth- and nineteenth-century European imperialism. On the other hand, as the toleration of Pakistan's barbarous behavior in Bangladesh grimly demonstrates, there is desperately little sympathy for geographically-contiguous ethnic or other self-conscious groups seeking independence from the often jerry-built national entities that have succeeded the colonial dominion. Shared fear of the precedental effect of a successful secessionist movement has precluded international pressure to compromise with dissidents. To me, at least, it is evident that in conflicts shaped by incompatible claims to a right of self-determination, Moore's preference for compromise, acquired in the cozy setting of United States domestic society, is not favored by many governing elites.

While directly related to the value of conflict minimization and more-or-less inversely related to the value of self-determination, compromise enjoys a haphazard and problematical relationship to the third consensus value, human rights. The chief claim that can be made for compromise as a means for their promotion rests on the terrible lacerations of human rights occasioned by armed conflict. Indeed, since in many eyes the most fundamental human right is freedom from physical harm—a priority formally evidenced by the Genocide Con-

---

[11] *Id.* at 33–34.

vention—one could argue that armed conflict is the polar antagonist of human rights. Hence, a willingness to terminate conflict short of its goals must of necessity promote those rights.

Alas, life is, of course, not so simple. In war, men and women and children die dramatically of bombs and bullets and napalm. The world watches and maybe it weeps. In peace, they die grubbily of disease and hunger and neglect. They die anonymously, too, because the world has other diversions. From time to time, people conclude that responsibility for the physical miseries which can coexist with domestic "peace" lies not in their stars but in their social arrangements. They conclude that the system is blemished by failure in the division or in the production of wealth and they resolve to risk death in order to effect its modification.

We have no way of knowing before the fact and with some degree of certainty whether their calculus of the net potential gain in human rights is accurate. Even if we could predict the length of the conflict and the number of wounds and fatalities it would cause, with what could they be compared? Certainly not only with the human cost of the iniquity or ineptitude which preceded the revolt, for we would also have to take into account the uncertain political and social consequences of either a successful or an unsuccessful rebellion. The calculus is imponderable, obviously, not only at the beginning of conflict but also *during its course*.

It is, I suppose, natural for a white scholar, reared in the cocky middle classes of an affluent and relatively open society, to see compromise as a universal contribution to human rights. His inbred conception of reform is a little more for one group and a little less for another, or a bit of tinkering with the administrative machinery. The notion of root and branch change is frighteningly alien. But for many people it seems the only way to achieve minimally decent standards of living and significantly greater rights of personality. I, for instance, find it plausible to believe that neither goal can be achieved in Santo Domingo until the social structures established by Trujillo are destroyed. As long as the army and police remain intact, the life of its reform politicians and their constituents will tend to be nasty, brutish, and short.

It is similarly difficult to visualize a decent respect in Russia for the autonomy of artistic vision as long as the extant political order survives. Free expression can no more be tolerated in an authoritarian society than can mass poverty in a democratic one. Certain social arrangements are endemically hostile to certain human rights. In such cases, to demand compromise after the commencement of rebellion is to favor losers and hypocrites. For only they will have an incentive to respond.

B. FREE ELECTIONS

In the American Pantheon, "genuinely free elections" rank somewhere between baseball and a good five-cent cigar as a panacea for a muddled world's ills. One of the last times an excessive enthusiasm for the free-elections fix popped up in Moore's writings, I was moved to express a certain scepticism concerning the electoral mechanism as an index of popular will in developing countries:

In desperately poor countries, and some wealthy ones as well, the techniques of political prestidigitation designed to make elections appear free are really quite varied. While these techniques are unlikely to fool anyone in the country where the elections are held, citizens of liberal states located thousands of miles from the scene may prove a good deal more gullible. How many Americans, for example, when informed by a number of straight-faced American governors that the 1967 election in South Vietnam was "free," recalled that persons suspected of an indecent desire for peace were excluded from the list of candidates, that the popular general Big Minh was not even allowed to enter the country, and that all the facilities of the South Vietnamese Government, including the means of transportation, were at the disposal of Generals Thieu and Ky? Careful readers of the *New York Times* might have recalled these phenomena, but did many of them grasp the critical factor of the average individual's overwhelming dependence on the beneficence of a government party which did little to allay the fear that a result which appeared antagonistic to its interests would, in one way or another, be avoided? How many recalled that not long before their departure from Algeria, but before it was clear that they would shortly consent to leave, the French were able to extract a vote of support from the Algerian people for association with France? Given the malleability of the election process in most places, can the announced willingness to submit to the arbitrament of free elections normally be taken very seriously?"[12]

Moore's response to my dour expectations has been to add to his nostrum the word "genuinely." I presume that the resulting verbal overkill is an indication that my agnosticism shook his confidence a bit and that he now sees the more subtle pressures which intimidate a formally free electoral process. What does not seem to have occurred to him is that the staggering difficulties of achieving (even, perhaps, of defining) "genuinely free elections" might reasonably induce participants in civil conflict to reject the electoral mechanism as a technique of self-determination. Moreover, even if they could be assured of the genuine freedom of one election, they might also entertain reasonable doubts about the probability of any future free elections. Multinational intervention might guarantee the former, but after the election, when the conflict is presumably resolved and peace breaks out, international concern will inevitably ebb. Furthermore, the electoral victors will sit astride the high horse of sovereignty and demand the retraction of foreign supervision. Then they may settle down to creating the conditions of permanent peace. Unfortunately, it may be the peace of the graveyard.

This is not inevitable, but it is not unlikely either. Those who loiter on the sidelines may urge risk-taking. After all, they have nothing to lose but their illusions. Still, they ought to appreciate why those who have everything to lose, including their heads, may prefer to submit to the arbitrament of force. And having managed that act of empathy, scholarly observers might develop reservations about the facile employment of the free-election gambit as a test of an elite's commitment to self-determination.

[12] "Harnessing Rogue Elephants: A Short Discourse on Foreign Intervention in Civil Strife," 82 *Harv. L. Rev.* 511, 517 (1969).

Where the alleged struggle for self-determination assumes the shape of secession, there is a more definitive, though equally plain, objection to the free-election standard: It normally will be impossible to define the electorate without simultaneously fixing the result of the election. As often happens in discussions of self-determination, we founder on the question of what is the self to be determined. If in the Nigerian conflict you hold elections throughout the territory of the former colony, one may presume that the Ibos would lose. The self becomes Nigeria. If you confine the genuinely free election to the old Eastern region, the Ibos win. The self becomes Biafra. In such cases, elections merely ratify results determined by other means.

III. THE COUNTER-REVOLUTIONARY INSTINCT

A. METTERNICH'S WORLD

Like his assumption of the universal validity of United States substantive and procedural norms, John Norton Moore's antirevolutionary bias, which prowls throughout his work, is the mark of a representative American Establishment mind. The first plain signs of that bias appear at the virtual outset of Moore's introduction when he lists among the "factors making for increased opportunity for revolution and intervention:

> (7) The increased interventionary activities associated with governments which have recently come to power through revolution, coupled with the significant number and importance of such governments in the present international system. . . ."[13]

If I had any reason to suspect that Moore employed the word "recently" in a leisurely, Toynbeean sense so that it would include our own "Revolutionary" War, his proposition would seem more a self-evident truth than a manifest absurdity. I regret my inability to find grounds for such a comforting suspicion. So we are confronted with the bizarre spectacle of a scholar, ensconced in a state which, since the end of World War II, has attempted with impressive zeal and inimitable resources to create, sustain, or topple governments in every part of the globe, citing as an opportunity factor "governments which have recently come to power through revolution," while omitting the slightest reference to the old U.S. of A. One would suppose that United States marines had never landed in Lebanon or guerrillas in the Bay of Pigs; that governments in Iran and Guatemala and Saigon had been toppled by some uncontrollable natural phenomena; that the Greek Civil War had been determined by the balance of indigenous forces and the Chinese one had self-aborted when it reached the coast opposite Taiwan; that outer-island rebels against Sukarno had manufactured their own weapons and Congolese pilots had flown planes which decimated rebel troops; that in 1954 the people of Hanoi sabotaged their own municipal buses, and that there were no United States advisers assisting throughout the 1960's in the suppression of the Latin American insurgents.

---

[13] Page xii of this volume.

It is tedious for me, as well as for the reader, to recite this somber litany. Yet, is there an alternative when you are examining the work of an author who, unlike the Bourbons, does not appear even to remember everything? What a waste of great talent and energy! Moore carefully collects the contextual features of international society to which his standards for appraisal must be moored and then leaves those standards floating aimlessly in intellectual space because he ignores the most salient of all contextual features—the world role of his and my own state.

His incapacity to recognize the pervasive and often illegitimate interventionist role of the United States seems to be total. In his discussion of self-determination, for example, he lists five types of claims in descending order of "international support." Type V, the weakest claim, is "demands for a particular type of political organization, 'socialist,' 'democratic,' or other." The "paradigm example is Cuban support for wars of national liberation in Latin America for the purpose of establishing 'socialist' regimes."[14] Why, one wonders, is Cuban activity any more paradigmatic than U.S. support for governments and rebels and coups committed to the prevention or termination of "socialist" regimes in Latin America, Asia, or anywhere else? Certainly not because the United States coexists with some "socialist" regimes in some places, since it is also true that Cuba coexists with non-socialist regimes. Cuba has not, for instance, been accused of intervening in Mexico, an authoritarian-capitalist state, or in Canada. And it has recently sought amicable relations with a Peruvian government which, though reformist, is hardly "socialist."

Even where he consciously seeks to be evenhanded, as in his glancing reference to "bloc" politics, Moore's deep, unconscious bias obtrudes. The "contextual threshold"—"avoidance of intervention in a region or nation committed to an opposing bloc"[15]—is evenhanded; but in proceeding to elaborate the threshold, he is moved to contrast Soviet military assistance to Cuba (which is "risky") with "United States avoidance of intervention in Hungary and Czechoslovakia,"[16] thus neglecting the case of the C.I.A.-trained operatives parachuted into Albania where security forces, tipped by Philby, were awaiting them, not to mention United States involvement in covert forays against mainland China.

As a lawyer, I am not interested in Moore's predilections per se; what matters is their influence on his ability to identify and marshall dominant contextual features and to conceive optimal normative and institutional strategies for the promotion of widely-shared values. And in this respect they seem to me to be seriously incapacitating. At an absolute minimum, they discourage balanced appraisal of the risks to value realization associated with his proposed standards.

B. REGIONAL PEACEKEEPING

I have referred already to his settlement criteria as one example of unexamined dangers. Another example is his proposed legitimation of regional peace keeping:

[14] *Id*. at 19
[15] *Id*. at 30
[16] *Id*.

V. Regional peacekeeping is permissible if it meets the following conditions:

(A) authorization by a regional arrangement *acting pursuant to Chapter VIII of the Charter*;

(B) a genuine invitation by the widely recognized government, or, if there is none, by a major faction;

(C) neutrality among factions to the extent compatible with the peacekeeping mission;

(D) immediate full reporting to the Security Council and compliance with Security Council directives;

(E) an outcome consistent with self-determination. Such an outcome is one based on internationally observed elections in which all factions are allowed freely to participate, which is freely accepted by the major competing factions, or which is endorsed by a competent body of the United Nations."[17]

"It is difficult to see," he insists a little plaintively, "how such carefully circumscribed regional action is . . . counter to Article 2(4) of the Charter. . . ."[18] Perhaps, but surely it is not at all difficult to see (if you are not peering through a flawed lense) why, given the real world in which regional action is likely to occur, reasonable men might regard Moore's allegedly impeccable criteria as dangerously susceptible to manipulation. Odd, is it not, that a scholar normally so sensitive to context should omit any reference to the contemporary features and prospects of regional action? There is no specification of existing or prospective regional organizations or, *a fortiori*, of their values, procedures, capacities, or contributions to the achievement of the universal values—conflict minimization, self-determination, and human rights.

If people did bother to consider matters like these, what might they discover? They would discover what most of us, including Moore, already know, in particular that of the three generally-acknowledged regional organizations—the Arab League, the Organization of African Unity (O.A.U.), and the Organization of American States (O.A.S.)—the former two have neither the capacity nor the will to play the "regional peacekeeping" game. The Arab League, enfeebled by the weakness and disunity of its members, appears interested in (although not capable of) "regional peace keeping" to the extent it could serve as a euphemism for the emasculation of Israel. The O.A.U. is, for much the same reasons, more or less equally feeble and, aside from peripheral support of black guerrillas in Southern Africa, is concerned primarily with consolidating a norm of non-intervention by any one under any circumstances anywhere in Black Africa. Hence, when one speaks seriously of "regional peace keeping," either he is thinking like Isaac Asimov of how the world might look in a millenium or so, or he is talking about the O.A.S. which enjoys the peculiar advantage of membership by a nation, the United States, with the capacity and will to intervene.

We have already had at least one sobering indication of the form its "peace keeping" activities are likely to assume. In light of the Dominican affair, it is

---

[17] *Id.* at 27.
[18] *Id.* at 29–30.

difficult for me to visualize O.A.S. involvement in civil strife for any purpose other than assuring the triumph of counter-revolutionary forces, however thuggish. It is useful to recall that the faction invited by United States officials to invite United States intervention constituted the surviving apparatus of Trujillo's terror.

Moore decently enjoins "neutrality among factions *to the extent compatible with the peace-keeping mission*"[19] (emphasis added) and attempts to allay fears about the nature of that mission in part by requiring an outcome consistent with self-determination which he appears to equate with elections. The Dominican Republic experience belies that facile equation. It demonstrates how easy it is for the intervening force to determine the outcome of the election. The force achieves that result in part by determining first the outcome of the armed conflict in which it is intervening.

The sheer fact of intervention at the request of only one of the belligerents enhances that belligerent's position. Protestations of neutrality to the contrary, people will believe that the invitor is favored; after all, he will be collaborating actively with, perhaps even helping to plan, the landings. The more prudent straddlers will quickly join the side which now seems destined to win. There are, moreover, so many ways to appear neutral while being partisan. For example, the intervention may be effected by driving a wedge between the forces of one side, leaving the other free to concentrate its forces on each of the isolated enemy units. The flow of supplies, including ammunition, can be restricted for one belligerent, accelerated for the other. Certain roads can be closed; others left conveniently open. These and similar acts will provoke the victim. He may attempt to force his passage or take other measures which the intervening force can interpret as a threat to "the peace keeping mission." This will provide the rationalization for joint action with the favored belligerent to disable its antagonist.

The final stage is to prepare for the elections. The peace keepers will retire to their barracks while civic order will be maintained by the already victorious faction. It will police election meetings, "investigate" political murders, and in various other ways generate confidence in the victory of its candidate. It may also remind the electorate that after the election the peace keepers will go home.

The likelihood of free elections is peculiarly small when the invitation to intervene is extended by an incumbent elite, whether or not it is recognized as a legitimate government, because it provides an existing structure of government which the intervening army is likely to employ, if for no other reason than just because it is there. An army is not, after all, generally prepared to assume the conduct of civil government. Furthermore, being aware that its mission will be seen as a threat to the prerogatives of national sovereignty, the intervening force will probably attempt to minimize the appearance of wholesale tinkering with indigenous arrangements. Hence the temptation to use existing structures.

You will note that under the terms of John's second condition, regional intervention at the request of insurgents is illegitimate. Only after the incumbents have been so battered that most states have withdrawn recognition can a mere "faction" invite intervention. Is it likely that the anti-establishment group,

---

[19] *Id.* at 27.

having already stripped the incumbents of legitimacy, would call for an intervention?

Even if the O.A.S. were an ideologically neutral or balanced organization, the weight of John's norm would fall on the side of established elites. The contextual point, of course, is that it is not such an organization. It is tilted—not only by the obsession of its hegemonic state, but also by the self-interest of the generally fragile, right-wing governments which preponderate among its members—toward the suppression of revolutionary movements. That tilt provides ample warrant to believe that any "regional peace-keeping" which occurs will bear only the most accidental relationship to self-determination and the conservation of human rights.

Moore might, I suppose, protest that he is not concerned with what regional organizations are likely to do, only with what they should do, and that his standards must be evaluated, therefore, solely on their intrinsic merit. If he did, however, I would be surprised by the incongruity of such a riposte by a scholar who regards the "description of past trends" and the "analysis of conditioning factors and prediction of future trends" as "indispensible for an *applied* theory"[20] (emphasis added). It would, moreover, require Moore to be insensitive to his own perception that "when a standard becomes too non-policy-responsive decision makers will simply not apply it. . . ."[21] Hence I am confident that that is one plea in avoidance Moore would not essay.

On the other hand, what Moore might quite reasonably allege is that the requirement of policy responsiveness is precisely what recommends his norm. If, as I argue, the United States is the effective patron of a strong counter-revolutionary impulse in the Americas, his standard, if followed, might mitigate the harsher consequences of that impulse and, because it seeks merely to domesticate rather than frustrate the impulse, the likelihood of consistent adherence to its conditions is enhanced.

That is a reasonable calculation. It is not mine. I think that the Latin Americans' endemic fear of intervention by the United States (a fear which tends to produce schizophrenia among the conservatives), coupled with the active opposition of a substantial segment of elite opinion in the United States and in extra-hemispheric states to counter-revolutionary adventures, makes it equally reasonable to hope that the preclusion of "peace-keeping" interventions by regional organizations would influence behavior. Conversely, it is also equally reasonable to fear that legitimation of such regional "peace-keeping" interventions would produce a normative fig leaf the existence of which could in a particular case tip the balance toward intervention.

If I believed that Moore shared my concern about, and hostility to, right-wing intervention directed from Washington (he does, of course, share my hostility to counter-revolutionary intervention in Eastern Europe directed from Moscow), I would unhesitatingly attribute our normative difference to different assessments of the most effective means for making the norm work. Regretably, there is ample reason to doubt that we are divided only on the efficacy of alternative normative means. In the two pieces under consideration there are, as I have indicated, other signs of a personal counter-revolutionary impulse. And

---

[20] *Id.* at 7.
[21] *Id.* at 10.

if one looks outside their confines, that impression is only heightened; at least I find no more satisfactory way to explain Moore's contention in a recent discussion of the Dominican affair that it was a "very close case" of permissible and desirable humanitarian intervention.[22]

C. APPRAISING AID TO INCUMBENTS AND REBELS, OR "HEADS—I WIN, TAILS—YOU LOSE"

Moore's proposed standards for appraising the legitimacy of unilateral intervention[23] are fully consistent with the policy preference exhibited at every other point in his work. They have, in fact, remained essentially unchanged since the beginning of the debate over the legality of United States intervention in Vietnam. Under them, while military assistance to incumbents is legitimate, aid to rebels is impermissible at any stage of the struggle. The only apparent shift in Moore's criteria is the preclusion of any increase in preinsurgency levels of assistance.

It is a change in form almost wholly without potential substantive impact: first, because levels of assistance can be increased dramatically at the first signs of rebellion and then sustained after the rebellion reaches the stage of insurgency; and secondly, because any assistance to the rebels by third parties will justify offsetting assistance to the incumbents. Since Moore refers to "assistance to insurgents *or* the use of the military instrument"[24] (emphasis added), he presumably intends the broad definition of assistance to which supporters of United States policy have consistently adhered, a definition that would include arms, ammunition, food, fuel, medical supplies, tactical and strategic advice, training, and sanctuaries. In today's interlocked world with its intense transnational identifications, some degree of foreign assistance—or at least the appearance of such assistance—seems inevitable in virtually every civil conflict.

So after six years of learned debate, accompanied by the decimation of the people of Indo-China, we are back where we started. Aid to rebels, even if qualitatively and quantitatively trivial in comparison to third-party assistance to incumbents, is held to legitimate a joint-venture between incumbents and their patrons for the liquidation of the rebellion, unless Moore has changed his previous view that the offsetting aid should not be limited to the types and amounts of aid received by the rebels. If a third-party's assistance to rebels constitutes an armed attack on the incumbents—which, as Moore's syntax reveals, it may do even though the assisting state does not engage its armed forces—the war may be extended to the third-state's territory. And where we stop nobody knows.

IV. THE PROSPECTS FOR SYNTHESIS

Having on more than one occasion explored the dubious impact of such standards on conflict minimization, self-determination, and human rights,[25] it would

[22] Conference on Humanitarian Intervention, *supra* note 7, at p. 55 of the provisional transcript.

[23] Pages 24–26 of this volume.

[24] *Id.* at 26.

[25] See, *e.g.*, "Harnessing Rogue Elephants," *supra* note 12.

be superfluous for me to cross that terrain again. Anyway, if the slaughter of the innocent in Indo-China does not confirm the perversity of these standards, surely words will be of no avail.

I have argued from the outset that Moore's instinctive political preferences precluded a work of synthesis. I am confident that the tenor of my own comments will convince many readers that I am at least equally incapacitated by policy committments.

They may well be right. Certainly I cannot deny an instinctive sympathy for Third-World rebels when they appear committed to social mobilization or a more equal distribution of values. This sympathy can, I think, be overcome by the concrete circumstances of particular cases; both Moore and I are, I hope, working with rebuttable presumptions, not blind convictions. Even in particular cases, however, the facts are often so complicated and controverted that presumptions play a major role in shaping description and appraisal. And when one is legislating for the assumed average case, presumptions often become determinitive.

It is hard to decide whether one should extract hope or despair from the fact that, despite our sharp disagreements about the salience of various contextual features and the appropriateness of proposed standards for appraisal, Moore and I agree on both the identity of the shared values of international society and on their moral stature. Our agreement might conceivably provide a basis for the increased harmonization of our views as we come to understand more about the relationship between international norms and national decision-making. On the other hand, it may suggest that the consensus necessarily functions at a level of generality more-or-less permanently removed from the passions and assumptions which divide all of us as we struggle in a world of concrete fact.

I incline toward a very modest optimism. Acceptance of human rights and self-determination as major world-order goals offers some prospect of future agreement on specific contexts. My bias towards hope is strengthened by the fact of present agreement on the permissibility of unilateral intervention in at least one specific context—"an immediate threat of genocide or other widespread arbitrary deprivation of human life in violation of international law."[26] Even that modest tangible commitment to human dignity would seem to provide a concrete foundation for the partial reconciliation of different strategies for promoting—and of different weightings of—various human rights.

There is, nevertheless, one particular theme in Moore's work which largely offsets my tenuous optimism. It is announced in his Introduction where, after noting that "[i]nternational law provides a basis for normative appraisal of action by reference to long-run community common interests," he concludes that, "though there are strong reasons why law ought *to be taken into account*, unfortunately it is not always adequately *considered* in national security decisions."[27] (emphasis added) This faint praise of law is then elaborated in the opening pages of the first chapter. "[T]hree perspectives are indispensable in assessing interventionary action,"[28] Moore warns us. They are:

[26] Page 25 of this volume.
[27] *Id*. at xviii–xix.
[28] *Id*. at 5.

International-legal: When is intervention consistent with global interests?

National-political: When is intervention which is consistent with the global common interest (perhaps even inconsistent with the global common interest—taking into account the feedback cost of such inconsistency) also consistent with the national interest (or the interest of an intervening international organization)?

Strategic: When is intervention likely to be successful in achieving the goals set for the action?

All three perspectives are indispensable in assessing interventionary action. By the nature of his discipline an international lawyer is principally concerned with the first perspective. That concern, however, should not be taken as an effort to dictate conclusions on or minimize the importance of the second two perspectives—though an international legal theory will also have relevance for national-political and strategic perspectives. Conversely, international lawyers should not be timid in pointing out the importance of an international-legal perspective and in urging that such a perspective be taken into account by national decision makers. Unless foreign policy is to be purely short term or based on a complete monopoly of power it must take account of the global common interest. In fact, even if foreign policy were implemented with a complete monopoly of power we would still want national goals to be informed by moral or "normative" considerations. An international-legal perspective, which focuses on global common interest, is highly relevant to such normative appraisal.[29]

I wonder whether, if Moore had been advisor to Al Capone, he would have brazenly (not timidly) urged Al to take law into account in assessing the desirability of entering the narcotics trade or murdering shopkeepers who failed to grasp their need for protection. Would Moore have reassured Al that the advice was not to be taken as an effort to dictate his conclusion? I wonder whether, if asked by the Black September group for his professional views on the proposed murder of Israeli Olympians, he would have replied that, while the act's legality must be taken into account, it was indispensable to consider as well the likelihood that the assassination would promote the interests of the Palestine guerrilla movement?

I have clung for many years to the belief that national decision-makers and the states whose resources they deploy are subjects of international law in a sense qualitatively indistinguishable from Al Capone's subjection to the laws of the state of Illinois and Arab terrorists to the homicide law of West Germany. Have I been deluding myself?

Just what is Moore trying to tell us? Why should not every decent man attempt to dictate adherence to law? There will be times when the consensus embodied in law so deeply offends individual conscience that it must be resisted. But that perspective is light-years removed from the "national-political" and "strategic" perspectives which Moore apparently sees not simply as analytic tools but also as standards for appraising the desirability of national behavior.

[29] *Id.*

It is no doubt true that, if one is jostling for position at the ear of the Prince, there may be advantage in discounting the moral claims of obedience to law. But should we encourage the obsessive pursuit of viziership?

As far as I am concerned, while many perspectives are useful for the analysis of national behavior, only two are legitimate for its guidance and assessment: the moral one and the legal one. Moore and other members of the Yale School have often and ably demonstrated that legal standards are not blind to considerations of efficacy or the imperative needs of states; indeed, by the very nature of the process which shapes standards of normative appraisal, those standards must embody national-political and strategic perspectives. When they are so embodied, however, they are compromised or reconciled. To elevate national preference to the plain of international consensus as a standard for appraising behavior is to repudiate the superiority of cosmopolitan perspectives. If Moore is simply trying to tell us that not every legally permissible intervention would be coincidentally prudent, then we have no quarrel. But if he is contending that the legal *im*permissibility of a particular intervention is only one factor which should be "taken into account" in "assessing" it, and that "the national interest" is of coequal concern, then a chasm divides our respective conceptions of the function of law and the obligations of men.

In the course of his chapter, Moore declares that:

> It is the task of international legal scholars to encourage appraisal of national claims rather than to shrink from evaluation. . . . [T]he recognition that contending political systems assert different values or policies need not be paralyzing. Again, the task of the international legal scholar is to identify and reinforce community common interests and to reject special interests: in this determination the scholar must take his stand. . . .[30]

If I were less uncertain of exactly where Moore is taking his stand, I would have higher hopes for an eventual synthesis of competing standards for the appraisal of intervention in civil strife.

[30] *Id.* at 12.

Comment 3 | On Professor Farer's Need
for a Thesis: A Reply* | *John Norton Moore*

Professor Tom Farer says that Chapter One has "failed." He gives his reasons for this generous conclusion with his usual flair and conviction. He also gives them with his usual confusion.

Chapter One seeks to clarify the theoretical underpinnings of an applied theory for the regulation of intervention. Its principal focus is the jurisprudential structure necessary for a comprehensive theory. As one task in the formulation of such a theory it recommends that scholars should seek to identify the values at stake in intervention decisions and, to the extent possible, should operationalize those values through explicit normative and procedural principles. Such principles can then be subject to continuing appraisal and refinement.

In accepting my own advice, Chapter One included a statement of values and specific normative standards which I would recommend. The values and standards, however, though important in their own right, are peripheral to the central purpose of the Chapter, which is to develop an intellectual framework for an adequate applied theory. As such, it was puzzling to learn that Chapter One had "failed" when the thrust of the reasons given for this conclusion related not at all to the four-fifths of the Chapter which develops the central jurisprudential thesis but rather to the less interesting statement of specific normative standards. I would have hoped that a scholar of Tom Farer's creative ability, who has shown glimpses of interest in a more broadly based jurisprudence, would have found more than the black-letter rules on which to lavish his attentions.

Professor Farer's central criticism seems to be that as "a representative American mind" I am incapable of comprehending the problem of intervention or of developing an adequate synthesis of competing values. Elsewhere he more boldly suggests that the bias which he finds is "natural for a white scholar, reared in the cocky middle classes of an affluent and relatively open society . . ." Whether or not the value predispositions which Farer posits are representative of anything but his own images, his underlying point, that scholars are affected by their environmental predispositions, is a commonplace and by now rather dull insight. The important point for the social scientist has long been what to do about such predispositions. Gunnar Myrdal has long ago suggested the only answer, which is that scholars should explicitly set out their values for appraisal by others.[1] Chapter One does so. The values set out are:

(1) The maintenance of world order and the minimization of destructive violence;

---

[1] See generally Miller and Howell, "The Myth of Neutrality in Constitutional Adjudication" 27 *U. Chi. L. Rev.* 661, 669 (1960).

This is a reply to Professor Tom J. Farer's Comment entitled "On Professor Moore's Synthesis." Professor Farer's Comment is a critique of the Introduction and Chapter One of this volume.

(2) Self-determination of peoples; and

(3) The maintenance of basic human rights.

I had not thought these values, which are enshrined in the United Nations Charter, to be peculiarly American. Whatever they are, I accept full responsibility in adopting them as my own. If Tom Farer would prefer some others, he should follow Gunnar Myrdal's advice and tell us which ones.

In a sense, however, Tom Farer is right when he maintains that my views are incompatible with a synthesis of his. For I do not share his apparent true belief in revolutionary violence. Revolution may serve commendable goals or it may serve special interests. It is neither sufficient nor useful to affirm a general revolutionary or counter-revolutionary preference. Moreover, whatever the goal of revolution, the price in human life and social disintegration is usually high. For me, then, revolutionary violence has a considerably higher burden of persuasion than Professor Farer's test of committment "to social mobilization or a more equal distribution of values" would suggest. In this respect, a major difference between us *is* my preference for elections, with all their imperfections, rather than violence as a means of implementing self-determination. And contrary to Tom Farer's understanding, to subject revolutionary violence to a high burden of persuasion is not to support a counter-revolutionary instinct. In this connection Farer might have pointed out that the basic normative standard recommended in Chapter One is:

> It is impermissible to assist a faction engaged in any type of authority-oriented internal conflict or to use the military instrument in the territory of another state (or zone of a divided state) for the purpose of maintaining or altering authority structures.

This basic standard prohibits intervention in a genuine civil conflict either on behalf of a widely recognized government or on behalf of insurgents. Interestingly, a recent review by Eugene V. Rostow takes me to task for *not* permitting assistance to a widely recognized government in a purely civil conflict—the converse of Tom Farer's inaccurate statement of my position.[2]

Aside from the general charge of having "a representative American mind," Farer makes a number of specific criticisms which must bear the burden of his case.

His first criticism is that use of the words "manipulation" and "management" in the introduction and conclusion links me to "the peculiarly American vision" of "McNamara's Pentagon and of its satrapies in Santa Monica and Cambridge. . . ." Further, he urges, this vocabulary embodies "the assumption of a world in which every threat to order is concomitantly a threat to American security." Ignoring the *non sequitur* and considering the merits of the charge, nothing in Chapter One either explicitly or implicitly embodies any assumption that every threat to order is a threat to American security—or, to complete Farer's sand castle, that it would be in the interest of the United States to intervene against every such threat.

To the contrary, Chapter One deals only peripherally with prescriptions for national action and focuses instead on international norms for the appraisal of such action. The Chapter also explicitly points out the need for clear focus on

---

[2] Rostow, "Review of J. N. Moore, *Law and the Indo-China War*" 82 *Yale L. Rev.* 829 (1973).

international-legal, national-political and strategic perspectives. Since it seems a fair assumption that Tom Farer has read Chapter One, I can only assume that he has succumbed to an urge to affirm one of his true beliefs.

Tom Farer's criticism of "management" (as opposed to mismanagement) reveals a dangerous ambivalence akin to the professed normative neutrality of the "new frontiersmen."[3] To accept Farer's criticism of "management" is to accept a world view that man must float like a jellyfish suspended in a watery environment doomed forever to respond instinctively to positive and negative stimuli. But man, unlike the jellyfish, can reflect on how he would like his environment, and, within limits, he can devise policies for achieving change. Moreover, since man *can* reflect, he has no real choice between these models. For both models, the jellyfish (reflexive reaction) or management (deliberate action or inaction) inescapably have value consequences. To assume the role of the jellyfish, as Farer apparently would, is a choice which will have consequences for which he will be responsible as much as any other. In short, Farer must understand the harsh truth that personal commitment is inevitable, and that not to manage is a form of management. As such, there can be no sanctuary in attacking management, but only in attacking mismanagement. In this respect Farer overstates the obvious when he suggests that it would be foolish mismanagement to assume that every threat to civil order is a threat to United States security requiring intervention.

The real issues which Farer should address if he is concerned with appraisal of national action are: are the goals which are being pursued ones which we should support; are the policies which have been devised to achieve them realistic; and, are the policies, though realistic, too costly in terms of other values at stake? Whatever specific praise or criticism one would make of the McNamara approach, it at least avoided Farer's fuzzy "Greening of America" nonsense that somehow there is something wrong—or in fact an alternative to—policy management.[4]

Tom Farer's closing gambit within his first criticism is that a definite rule-oriented approach—which he sweepingly ascribes to "Third-World scholars and diplomats"—will reduce manipulative capacities. I agree up to a point. And that point is that, if definite standards become too non-policy-responsive for the full range of varied contexts in which they are to be applied, they will simply be disregarded. In this respect Farer's discussion ignores the mainstream of the legal realist movement and the detailed discussion in Chapter One as to the choices in operationalizing policy. It also ignores my stated preference for a multiple-rule approach as the first line defense against impermissible intervention.

Farer's second criticism is something called "the universalization of American values." After setting out my tentative recommended standards of content

---

[3] See the discussion of the "new frontiersmen" in Chapter One of this volume at pp. 5–8.

[4] The "Greening of America" refers to a best-selling book written by Yale law professor Charles Reich. Though there is much in the *Greening of America* with which I would agree, it is fundamentally mistaken in its implicit attack on rational decision-making. The causes of the mistaken attack largely seem to lie in a lack of sophistication concerning the decision-process, particularly a confusion about the role of value-choice in that process. See C. Reich, *The Greening of America* (1970). For an even clearer example see T. Roszak, *The Making of a Counter-Culture* (1969). For a good antidote, see H. Lasswell, *A Preview of Policy Sciences* (1971).

and procedure for appraisal of the obligation to pursue peaceful settlement of hostilities—a concept apparently of little interest to him—he selects the last of my four standards of content as specially revealing of this "universalization of American values."[5] According to Farer, "Moore assumes that in every national setting, manifestations of tolerance and willingness to compromise are presumptive virtues." This is a misreading of my position. There is no question that willingness to compromise would, if standing alone, be a poor basis on which to appraise the obligation of parties to settle ongoing hostilities. For example, the Allies were certainly right in refusing to compromise with Hitler to end World War II. Because of this inadequacy of compromise alone, the first standard of content, which Farer does not discuss (and to which he erroneously adds a gratuitious "sic"), specifically sets out all of the fundamental Charter norms as first-line criteria for appraisal of the reasonableness of suggested terms for settlement. And the fourth standard of content, on which Farer relies, states even more explicitly that one looks to willingness to compromise only "in situations in which these fundamental Charter principles are uncertain or ambiguous." That is, one looks first to compliance with the basic Charter principles of maintenance of peace and security, self-determination, and basic human rights. Only when these principles are ambiguous in a particular context does one look to compromise. In those circumstances, willingness to compromise is an important standard for appraising an obligation to end hostilities and I doubt that this would be a peculiarly American judgment. Again, however, whatever it may be, I support it as an important criteria for appraisal. For it is certainly relevant to preventing the further destruction inherent in a continuation of hostilities in a setting where other fundamental goals of self-determination and human rights are unclear.

Paradoxically, Farer seems to himself embrace an unqualified compromise standard when he calls for a "synthesis of competing standards" as the desired goal for intervention standards. I hope that it will comfort Tom Farer to learn that I have no intention of seeking a synthesis with his views. As he quite rightly points out, the test is not compromise alone, but rather commitment to values one supports.

Tom Farer selects the second of my criteria for special obliquy—that of willingness of the parties to submit to free elections if self-determination is at issue. Apparently taken with his insight that elections are subject to a variety of subtle pressures which make them less than perfect, he repeats a lengthy quota-

---

[5] Farer dismisses the concept of standards for the appraisal of the obligation to pursue peaceful settlement of disputes with an airy denial of any such obligation "for parties to civil conflicts." Alas, it seems to have slipped his mind that the normative standards recommended concern civil conflict which have become *internationalized* through external intervention. As such, the obligation reflected in Article 33 of the United Nations Charter is applicable. Even more sadly, Farer seems to have forgotten that a Chapter concerned with developing an applied theory for the regulation of intervention is not a Sears catalogue of present law, but rather an effort to *recommend* an adequate framework. Though the standards set out were developed for internationalized civil conflict, it would, I believe, be useful also to develop criteria for appraisal of the actions of belligerents in purely civil conflicts. The use of force is harsh. It is not to be undertaken lightly and there is no reason why its practitioners, civil as well as international, should escape normative judgment. International law has, of course, already begun to selectively apply the laws of war to purely civil conflicts.

tion from an earlier article which made this point. But the issue is not whether the electoral process is a perfect test of self-determination; rather, whether more often than not it is a better test than "the arbitrament of force." Moreover, if the use of force is to be preferred as a test, it must not only be a better test of self-determination, but a sufficiently better test to offset the intense destruction of values which accompanies it. Far from demonstrating this conclusion, Tom Farer's supporting reasons for his preference for the "arbitrament of force" seem little more than a romantic faith in revolutionary violence. Though he urges that "those who have everything to lose including their heads may prefer to submit to the arbitrament of force," he fails to notice that the innocent bystanders who may lose their heads through the arbitrament of force and who have no voice in this jungle test of survival may prefer even a poor electoral process.[6]

Tom Farer's third principal criticism is that the normative standards which I recommend are the product of an anti-revolutionary bias. If this criticism means that I hold revolutionary and all other violence to a high burden of proof that they are in fact promoting community goals, Tom Farer is right. If, however, it means, as apparently it does, that I support unilateral intervention in genuine civil conflict, Professor Farer is wrong—an error which seems particularly perplexing in view of the pains Chapter One takes to state the contrary. Perhaps he finds an effort to tar with the "Metternich" brush more attractive than fair appraisal.

Aside from the general charge of an "anti-revolutionary bias" "seriously incapacitating" my ability to formulate normative standards, Farer offers specific criticism of only two of my eight standards concerning the initiation of hostilities —a rather sparse harvest for a bias which "prowls" throughout my work. The standards criticized are the basic non-intervention standard (standard III) and the regional peacekeeping standard (standard V).

Farer indicates that under the approach which I propose, "while military assistance to incumbents is legitimate, aid to rebels is impermissible at any stage of the struggle." As previously pointed out, this ignores my basic non-intervention standard (stated as such) that "it is impermissible to assist a faction (any faction—incumbent or insurgent) engaged in any type of authority-oriented internal conflict. . . ." Possibly Tom Farer is confused by the standards concerning pre-insurgency assistance (standard I) and offsetting assistance (standard IV), both of which permit assistance to a widely recognized government under certain circumstances. But, if that is the case, Farer fails to tell us how his approach would deal with the real problems dealt with by these standards: problems of interrelating any normative standard with ongoing military assistance (military assistance reflecting real defense interdependencies existing prior to the outbreak of civil conflict) and the need for assistance to offset impermissible external asistance already being supplied to an insurgency. It has seemed to me that the best answer to the first problem is a rule freezing assistance to pre-insurgency levels once an insurgency breaks out. This is so in spite

---

[6] Farer does articulate one difficulty with an electoral process which is a real problem in wars of secession or unification. That is, the threshold question of identifying the limits of the "self" entitled to determination. A variety of criteria concerning linguistic, ethnic, geographic, historical and economic factors, however, might be fashioned to lend some guidance to solution of this problem. Moreover, despite the difficulty, the "arbitrament of force" does not resolve this problem in any more satisfactory way than the solutions possible through the electoral process.

of the genuine difficulties Tom Farer points out in identifying when an insurgency begins. For the only other viable rule, that all assistance should be withdrawn once an insurgency breaks out, has the same threshold problem as the freeze rule, as well as an element of rapid withdrawal of assistance which may itself amount to an interventionary action. And with respect to the second problem, if there is any normative case for preventing assistance to a widely recognized government to offset prior external assistance to insurgents, Tom Farer fails to make it.[7]

Tom Farer's criticism with respect to the regional peacekeeping standard is more convincing. This standard is debatable and Farer forcefully articulates the case against it. That case includes the high politicization and limited peacekeeping capacity of present regional organizations, the difficulty in achieving genuine neutrality among factions, the temptation to mask partisan intervention as a neutral peacekeeping operation, and the difficulty in ascertaining an outcome supportive of self-determination. These reasons are all valid reasons against such a standard. But Tom Farer has not given us the other side. The real dilemma is whether it is better to accept unrestrained civil violence as the arbiter of self-determination (with, of course, some alleviation possible through an expanded United Nations role), or to attempt a carefully circumscribed role for regional organizations recognizing all the risks Farer articulates. On balance it seems preferable to work toward such a role for regional organizations rather than to throw up one's hands in despair. Perhaps the difference between Farer and me is again largely due to Farer's preference for violence as a more accurate and less costly test of self-determination than the imperfect electoral process.[8]

Tom Farer's final criticism is his most interesting, for it is really the only one which addresses itself to any of the jurisprudential underpinnings of the Chapter. After setting out my discussion of the need to systematically take legal perspectives into account and of the differences between international-legal, national-political, and strategic perspectives, Farer implies that I have lost all decency (or in the equally attractive alternative am jostling for position at the ear of the Prince) by failing to dictate adherence to law. Since I have long had a great interest in upgrading the role of international law in the national foreign-

---

[7] Farer's suggestion that I would place no limitation on permissible counter-intervention is incorrect. Counter-intervention should be limited to that assistance necessary to offset prior impermissible assistance to insurgents. Because of the greater difficulty in defending against guerilla attack than in making the attack, the difficulty in estimating covert assistance to insurgents, and the differing modalities of attack and defense in civil conflict settings, it would not be appropriate to limit offsetting assistance to a man-to-man or weapon-to-weapon comparison. Rather, the assistance should be that necessary to offset the political and military effect of the prior impermissible assistance. For discussion of this point see J. N. Moore, *Law and the Indo-China War*, 115, 206–7 (1972).

The principle of counter-intervention to assist a widely recognized government is recognized by almost all writers on intervention. Not to permit counter-intervention would be to greatly weaken the Charter right of collective defense against armed attack in settings where an attack takes the form of covert assistance rather than open invasion. See *id.* at 205 n. 158.

[8] For a more detailed critique of Professor Farer's approach and a fuller exploration of the supporting and opposing reasons for a regional role, see "The Control of Foreign Intervention in Internal Conflict" and "The Role of Regional Arrangements in the Maintenance of World Order" in J. N. Moore, *supra* note 7 at 115, 258–67, and 296.

policy process, the criticism is especially intriguing.[9] Let me reassure Tom Farer that I do indeed support the thesis that, just because a particular action is legal (or moral) does not necessarily make it wise. In this respect, it seems to me important to supplement an international-legal perspective with national-political and strategic perspectives. In contrast, Tom Farer's statement that only the moral and legal perspectives are "legitimate" for the guidance and assessment of national behavior is simplistic in the extreme. Let me go on, however, to confirm Farer's worst fears. For while he takes the impeccable high road that legal considerations (presumably, when in conflict with other considerations) must *always* determine national behavior, I cannot agree with that absolute either. International law embodies community expectations as to legitimate national behavior. As such, it is entitled to great weight from national decision-makers and it ought to control, in almost every context, when in conflict with other considerations. In fact, I can think of no recent foreign-policy decision where the illegality of a policy should not have been sufficient alone to bar it. Nevertheless, the problem is more difficult than Tom Farer's high road would lead us to believe. Suppose a particular action were clearly illegal under most interpretations of present law but it were certain that to fail to execute it would result immediately in a full-scale nuclear exchange which could kill more than 200 million people.[10] Should the illegality bar the action? The example is admittedly an imaginery horrible—for the real world lacks the certainty and precision of a logical exercise. Nevertheless, it poses the conceptual problem fairly. And in fact, the decisions faced by United States decision-makers in the Cuban missile crisis, and Indian decision-makers in the Bangladesh intervention, presented a not dissimilar dilemma concerning adherence to law, albeit in more ambiguous settings.[11] Since this effort at intellectual honesty may easily frighten, let me reiterate that international law should have great—and in essentially every context imaginable—controlling weight. This is not due to some mystique of adherence to law for its own sake, but out of the compelling long- and short-run reasons why all nations should adhere to law. But conceptually the problem of national adherence to law is not as Farer would have us believe "light years removed" from the problem of individual conscience and adherence to law. Here, as in the need to manage our affairs, the escape from personal responsibility which Farer would find in the principle of legality is an illusion. And the rejection of Farer's absolutist position does not lead to legitimation of the murder of the Israeli Olympians or some such similar action as Farer suggests it would. The importance of human rights for settings of armed conflict is such

[9] See "The Role of Law in the Management of International Conflict," in J. N. Moore, *supra* note 7; Moore, "Law and National Security," 51 *For. Aff.* 408 (1973); Moore, "The Legal Tradition and the Management of National Security" (forthcoming).

[10] In the real world, of course, judgments about legality are frequently cloudy and at least in the more sophisticated systems of jurisprudence one could hardly ignore the catastrophic consequences of a threatened nuclear exchange. In this respect, the nuclear exchange example is oversimplified. Unless a completely configurative approach is taken, however, formal law and community policies may in some settings be inconsistent. Even in those settings one would wish to carefully assess the substantial costs (national and international) inherent in law violation.

[11] For analysis of the legal ambiguities of the missile crisis see McDougal, "The Soviet-Cuban Quarantine and Self-Defense," 57 *Am. J. Int'l L.* 597 (1963).

that no decision-maker should order the deliberate murder of innocent non-combatants to foster a particular political cause. Such a case is "light years removed" from the real and rare dilemmas challenging adherence to law. Farer is free to make a different assessment but he deludes himself if he thinks he can hide behind formal legality to make no assessment at all.

International law, like all law, continues to apply to those who break it—and to the extent that it really is law, lawbreakers, whether nations or individuals, will be subject to real community pressures for compliance. In this sense, of course, international law will always be controlling. Adherence to law will be better served, however, if international lawyers articulate for national decision-makers the multitude of long- and short-run considerations which strongly militate for adherence to law rather than trumpeting righteous but philosophically unsound dogma.[12]

The most disappointing aspect of Farer's Comment is not his charge of personal bias or his oft-repeated disagreement with particular standards, but rather his lack of a thesis for an adequate applied theory of his own. Farer is one of the most articulate and creative of the new breed of international lawyers in the United States. It is a pity that his considerable talents are exhausted in an essentially *ad hominem* attack against "more-or-less organized intellectual activity," "a peculiarly American vision" that "oozes" "good-natured banalities," "obdurate insistence," "the cozy setting of United States domestic 'society' " and "white scholar(s) reared in the cocky middle classes of an affluent and relatively open society."

Even more disappointing, Tom Farer's ambivalence is as total as that of the would-be-revolutionary law student I once observed walking through the halls of the Yale Law School wearing a Che Guevara jacket and clutching tightly to a copy of the Internal Revenue Code. On the one hand, a major burden of his Comment is that the values which I support are peculiarly American and are therefore an unsatisfactory basis for normative development. (Does Farer believe that this would also be so if my values were Nepali or anything else other than American?) He then reverses his field and astonishingly declares: "Professor Moore and I agree on both the identity of the shared values of international society and on their moral structure." How disappointing to discover that Farer, after all, is merely another "white scholar reared in the cocky middle classes of an affluent and relatively open society." Or is it that, rhetoric aside, he does see widespread global support for the principles of world order, self-determination, and human dignity?

As a second example of this moral ambivalence Farer reflects the one-sided myth of the revisionists that the ills of the world are largely a product of United States foreign policy. No mention is made of autocratic or repressive governments in the Third World or elsewhere, except for a fashionable reference to the "authoritarian society" in Russia which he bravely condemns as lacking "decent respect . . . for the autonomy of artistic vision." There is never a hint that decision-makers in Hanoi intervening massively in Laos and Cambodia were anything more than "Third-World rebels" justifiably "committed to social mobilization or a more equal distribution of values." Would Farer have advised the Sri Lanka Maoists that, if only they intended to more evenly distribute

---

[12] For a discussion of the long and short run reasons which collectively militate for adherence to law see J. N. Moore, *supra* note 7 at 20–31.

societal values, they were free to forcefully overthrow the popularly elected government? Does he feel that General Amin, popular at home for his racist and chauvinistic policies, is a desirable model for Third-World development? Or are these cases where "concrete circumstances" would have overcome Farer's presumption for "Third-World rebels"?

There is no escape from the agony of personal choice. Tom Farer must take his stand with a coherent thesis of his own, and defend it if he can. But it cannot be done by random sniping at standards which displease, however dazzling the rhetoric.[13] To take his stand, Farer must further articulate his values and make an effort to operationalize them in context. Does he believe that his preference for "social mobilization" (whatever it may mean) or the "more equal distribution of values" should override a community preference for self-determination? Does he believe that these preferences justify the intense destruction of values which may accompany the use of force? If so, under what circumstances? And how should these and other value preferences which he may articulate relate to normative and institutional means for the control of intervention? When Farer does further specify his preferences, it will be worth reading—not only for the enjoyable Farer wit but also for the insight which, from time to time, he has exhibited in abundance.

[13] It is, of course, gratifying to know that Farer would support a recommendation permitting carefully circumscribed unilateral intervention in cases of an immediate threat of genocide or other widespread arbitrary deprivation of human life in violation of international law. This support is an alteration of Farer's earlier thesis which would have flatly prohibited all external participation in tactical operations. See Farer, "Intervention in Civil Wars: A Modest Proposal," 67 *Col. L. Rev.* 266 (1967). *See also* Farer, "Harnessing Rogue Elephants: A Short Discourse on Foreign Intervention in Civil Strife" 82 *Harv. L. Rev.* 511 (1969).

On humanitarian intervention in general see the interesting exchange between Professors Brownlie and Lillich in this volume. *See also* R. Lillich (ed.), *Humanitarian Intervention and the United Nations* (1973).

Comment 4 | Wolfgang G. Friedmann

The difficulties in arriving at a satisfactory legal theory of intervention in civil wars in the contemporary context—a subject to which this volume is principally devoted—can be simply stated. First, there is the contradiction between the principle of national sovereignty, which is still the cornerstone of contemporary international law and enshrined in numerous documents of the post-war era, from Article 2 of the United Nations Charter to the General Assembly Resolution 2151 of 1965, and the more recent "Declaration of Principles Concerning Friendly Relations and Cooperation Among Nations"—and the obvious fact that the sovereign independence and equality of states is constantly restricted or violated by numerous forms of foreign intervention, from the use of military force to economic pressure. Second, the revolution in modern communications and technology permits many types of intervention unknown to former ages, when the basic alternatives were between peace and war, the latter conducted by land armies or by navies. Third, and most important, the global strategic confrontation—itself an intricate mixture of ideological and power conflicts—has immensely increased the importance of internal conflicts with international implications and participations.

Given this intricate and complex pattern, this brief comment will concentrate on two aspects of intervention in civil war, which represent as it were the polarities: at one end of the spectrum, the relation of intervention to self-defense, *i.e.*, the question of the legitimacy of the unilateral use of force in the contemporary context—dealt with in Dr. Bowett's paper; at the other end, the question of "humanitarian intervention," which is the subject of the dialogue between Professors Brownlie and Lillich. To this, a brief comment on "modernization" will be added. These latter subjects symbolize the deepening range of contemporary international concerns, which have moved far beyond the traditional pattern of international law as a set of rules governing diplomatic relations between states. The question of the legitimacy of intervention in "self-defense" raises one of the basic problems of contemporary international law: to what extent the weakness of the collective organization of international peace and security, as contemplated in the U.N. Charter, has revived the right of the unilateral use of force; the second question is whether it is possible to single out specific areas of international concern as being superior to the principle of "sovereign equality" and national integrity and legitimating outside action against the incumbent governments.

THEORIES OF INTERVENTION AND SELF-DEFENSE

I emphatically agree with Dr. Bowett's observation that, while many attempts have been made to establish numerous categories of conflicts, they are "so replete . . . with sophistication and distinctions that we are in danger of losing the few basic rules of law which inhibit states in resorting to coercion."

Dr. Bowett's basic thesis—formulated before in his important study of

"Self-defense in International Law"—is that to stretch the concept of "individual or collective" self-defense to the point where any state may assist any other state anywhere in the world, regardless of any threat to its own security, and without authorization by the United Nations, "cannot possibly be consistent with a system of collective security" and is "quite contrary to the delegation to the Security Council of 'primary responsibility' for the maintenance of international peace and security in Article 24." We all know that the United Nations, for a variety of reasons which it is neither possible nor necessary to recapitulate here, has failed in its essential task as a guardian of international peace and enforcer of international order that would displace the individual use of force by the nation states. This is deplorable enough. But what is no less deplorable is the spurious and hypocritical use of Article 51 of the U.N. Charter as a pretended manner of "decentralized" enforcement of collective security, when in effect the United Nations neither does nor is expected to play any role whatsoever, and the intervening state makes, in Dr. Bowett's words "a purely unilateral assessment . . . of who is the aggressor. . . ." Whether or not there is a treaty of alliance between the intervening state and the state involved in conflict, "the result is potential global conflict, all on the basis of a so-called right of collective self-defense. The position is thus virtually indistinguishable from the nineteenth-century system of alliances: states have a right to help their allies."

The invocation of Article 51 in the NATO and Warsaw Pacts is dubious enough. Both these alliances have become substitutes for UN actions rather than regional and temporary applications, pending United Nations action. Far more blatant are the invocations of Article 51 in justification of the United States interventions in Vietnam and Cambodia, based on strategic policy decisions, which by no stretch of the imagination were a response to an attack or a threat to the security of the United States, and where the authorization of the United Nations was neither seriously contemplated nor realistically obtainable. What is at issue here is not the political merits of the U. S. action but the perversion of the whole principle of collective security.[1] Unless—writing as scholars, not as government advocates—we wish to use international law merely as rhetoric, we will serve it much better by acknowledging that, except in certain minor conflict situations, the second great attempt to organize collective security has failed and the world has reverted to the unilateral use of force, restrained by the indefinable, but real, weight of world opinion, incalculable dangers of contemporary global war and the balance of power between a few major and larger number of actors.[2]

[1] The present writer has expressed views closely corresponding to those of Dr. Bowett in various publications, some of which are referred to by Dr. Bowett and Professor Lillich in Chapters 2 and 11.

[2] Dr. Bowett's assertion that where an attack by State A on State B, which "also creates a threat to the security of another state that state has an independent right of self-defense which it may exercise in concert, or collectively, with State B . . ." is, I believe, far less controversial than Dr. Bowett believes. He would probably accept the following illustration of his thesis: "Insofar, for example, as the factual or official surrender of Cuban sovereignty to the Soviet Union led to the military control of Cuba by Soviet forces, of dimensions sufficient to constitute a threat to the security of the United States, the . . . principles of self-defense would apply. This, however, is not a matter of political subversion or indirect aggression. It is a question of military, actual or imminent, aggression, and the corresponding right of self-defense." W. Friedmann, *The Changing Structure of International Law* 268 (1964).

I also agree with Dr. Bowett's contention that, in the contemporary context, the right of self-defense justifies "whatever measures are proportionate and necessary to deal with the particular threat to security which would otherwise be illegal." Indeed, it is only by recognizing the multiplicity of the modalities of interventions and counter-interventions made in the exercise of self-defense that we can take account of the complexity of modern international conflict situations and at the same time reduce the danger of the stark alternatives between peace and total war. To Dr. Bowett's mention of the refusal of rights of overflight, the closing of border traffic, the expulsion of nationals, the jamming of broadcasts, etc. we might add the important arsenal of various measures of economic retaliation, *e.g.*, the cutting off or reduction of economic aid, the suspension of trade agreements, or the exclusion of certain imports and exports.

I also concur with Dr. Bowett's rejection of the distinction between incumbent governments and insurgents as a test of legitimacy of intervention. Little need be added to Dr. Bowett's reasons for rejecting the distinction. The subjectivity of recognition is perhaps most blatantly illustrated by the immediate recognition of the Franco Rebellion as the Government of Spain by Hitler's Germany and Mussolini's Italy, and the recognition by the U.S.S.R. of the government which it installed in Hungary in 1956 in order to suppress the successful revolution, as legitimation for intervention; this "legitimacy" doctrine conflicts with the principle of self-determination; and it is an obvious invitation to counter-intervention by another state which supports another faction. Nothing has happened to change the view expressed a few years ago in my controversy with Professor Moore's contention that "the requirements of minimum world public order, *i.e.*, the avoidance of unilateral coercion as a modality of major change, would in most contexts seem more strongly applicable to assistance to insurgent groups than to assistance to the recognized government."[3] Like other countries, the United States has, of course, chosen to assist either incumbent governments or insurgents, in accordance with its policy objectives, not in application of any principle of international law.[4]

Dr. Bowett's analysis exposes the many attempts that have been made to disguise interventions undertaken in furtherance of national policies as exercises in collective security. Prescriptions differ as to how this vacuum can be filled. Perhaps the present writer's conclusion is even more pessimistic than Dr. Bowett's: it is that the only hope in our time for a strengthening of the international order lies in the by-passing of the issue of collective security—since there is little hope of remoulding the United Nations into an effective organ of international security—and concentration of our efforts on organized functional international cooperation in the many fields that will, within decades, or perhaps years, compel worldwide cooperation for the sake of survival (such as the joint conservation and development of resources, pollution control, population control, international redistribution of resources, etc.).

It follows from Dr. Bowett's basic position that he must reject "humanitarian intervention" as a right recognized by contemporary international law. In this he is in essential accord with Dr. Brownlie, and in opposition to Professor

[3] Moore, "The Lawfulness of Military Assistance to the Republic of Vietnam," 61 *Am. J. Int'l L.*, 31 (1967); Friedmann, "Law and Politics in the Vietnamese War: A Comment," 61 *Am. J. Int'l L.*, 776, 781 ff (1967).

[4] For illustrations of U. S. practice, *see id.* at 782.

Lillich's eloquent plea for a recognition of such a right. There is a link between those who, under the guise of Article 51 or for some other reason, advocate a widened right of individual or collective self-defense for states, and those who, like Lillich, Reisman, and others, plead for the recognition of a "right" of humanitarian intervention by individual states in the affairs of other states. In both cases it is the weakness of an effective international legal order that prompts the advocacy of an extension of national rights to fill the gap. If there were an effective international code, backed by a functioning international organization that would not only police the illegal, *i.e.*, the aggressive, use of force in international affairs, but also live under a code of human rights, enforceable as are, for example, the Bills of Rights of the United States, Canada, West Germany, or India, the need would not exist. The suppression of a religious or a racial minority, the persecution or massacres of Greeks, Christians, Armenians, Jews, Gypsies, Bengalis, and others, the suppression of freedom of expression, worship, or assembly, these and many other freedoms as they are embodied in contemporary Bills of Rights—including the unratified Covenants of Human Rights passed by the General Assembly in 1966—would be the subject of organized international supervision and enforcement. The desire to fill the void by extending the rights of individual states to take action where the international community is unable or unwilling to do so is natural enough. But, as both Dr. Bowett and Dr. Brownlie point out, it suffers from the same weakness that makes the extension of self-defense beyond the "clear and present" threat to the security of the actor state so dangerous: the classification of an intervention as "humanitarian" is, in the absence of any impartial determination, a matter of appraisal and decision for the intervening state. Moreover, the concept is even more elastic, and therefore liable to be abused, than that of self-defense—of which it is a kind of specialized sub-concept. Nobody who has been exposed to racial, religious, or national persecution can dismiss the concept of humanitarian intervention lightly. And there are certainly a limited number of instances where intervention by other powers has, at least in part, been prompted by a genuine humanitarian concern rather than as a pretext for power politics. But it is surely significant that the four examples listed by Ganji, in his monograph on *International Protection of Human Rights* (1962), and cited by Professor Lillich, all concern interventions by the major European powers against the decaying Ottoman Empire. And the most ardent defender of the most recent instance of "humanitarian" intervention, *i.e.*, the armed intervention by India against East Pakistan—now Bangladesh—in response to the Pakistan Army's massacres and persecution of Pakistani Bengalis, in December 1971, can hardly deny that this intervention also served India's long-standing purpose of weakening Pakistan and creating a friendly, but necessarily beholden, country on its northeastern frontier. Would India contemplate "humanitarian" intervention, by Pakistan or any other country, against the Biharis—who it is alleged are now subject to comparable persecution by the liberated Bengalis of Bangladesh? Would it react with anything but the use of force against "humanitarian" intervention by another state to insure the right of Kashmiris to freely decide their political allegiance in a plebiscite that India has consistently refused to entertain? These questions only have to be asked to be answered. The right of self-determination—which was at the bottom of the Bangladesh rebellion—is surely one of the most important human rights of our age, from the Peace of Versailles to the abolition of colonies after the Second World War. It has been proclaimed repeatedly, *e.g.*, by the General Assembly Resolutions of 1965 and 1970, both of which have attempted in vain to reconcile this "right" of self-determination with the equally fervently proclaimed principle of non-interference in the sovereignty and integrity of any state. As the new states of Asia and Africa have demonstrated, the right of self-determination, even by clearly defined ethnic or political groups, is vigorously suppressed once the struggle of liberation from colonial domination has been achieved. The new states are as adamant in fighting attempts at secession as the imperialist suppressors of old! Clearly, humanitarian intervention in all its aspects is an infringement of the right of any state to determine its internal affairs and to decide the political, social, and economic regime without dictate or interference from abroad. Nor is it part of the contemporary international order that such determination should be achieved by democratic procedures—a principle that would expose the great majority of contemporary states to foreign intervention.

Whether, as Professor Lillich contends against Dr. Brownlie and many other writers, state practice in favor of humanitarian intervention has been sufficiently frequent and sufficiently accepted to qualify as a custom is a question that appears, to this writer, to be of relatively minor importance, quite apart from the fact that it would be signally difficult to obtain consensus on this point. Far more important is the question how this notably flexible impairment of the principles of state sovereignty and integrity which, for better or worse, dominate the contemporary international system can be accommodated in the international legal order. The present writer firmly sides with Drs. Bowett and Brownlie in the conviction that such concepts as "self-determination," "humanitarian intervention," or the previously discussed enlarged "right" of intervention in aid of any state anywhere against a third state constitute in effect a variety of cloaks for unilateral action. The more of these concepts float around, the greater the latitude of a state to choose the one or the other to pursue its national policy objectives and to adorn them with spurious legal justifications.

Yet, the concept of humanitarian intervention is neither meaningless nor useless. But to appraise its proper place and significance, we shall have to distinguish between law and morality in the present international structure. A weak legal system has a minimum of legal prescriptions, and a correspondingly wider spectrum of moral prescriptions which may eventually harden into legal precepts as the legal system widens its ambit and becomes more effective. In terms of authority and enforceability, the contemporary international legal order is still weak and primitive. Despite two world wars and the world organizations that followed them, the national state remains, with few qualifications, the center of political allegiance and legal power. But, at the same time, the horizon of international society has widened, and the aspirations, if not the achievements, of international law have extended vertically into many domains formerly excluded from the restricted sphere of international law. The advocates of self-determination and of international protection against the violation of elementary human rights are therefore entirely correct in proclaiming these matters to be legitimate international concerns. Ultimately, a comprehensive international legal order will establish and enforce minimum world-wide standards for labor conditions, social welfare, and the basic human freedoms, as is presently the case in municipal legal systems. But at the present time, most or all of these aspirations have at best attained the level of accepted international morality rather than law. The numerous law-making declarations of the United Nations embody such international moral consensus. They often point the way towards a future legal enactment, and they certainly express a moral consensus. Dr. Brownlie refers to the mitigating aspects of a morally excusable—or perhaps acceptable—behavior when he refers to the analogy of euthanasia, "itself a form of humanitarian intervention." In national legal systems, this is a type of behavior that is almost universally condemned by the law, as murder or manslaughter, but is in many circumstances considered as morally justifiable. This may lead to mitigation of punishment or pardon. Even without such legal mitigations, public opinion may regard the legal criminal as a morally guiltless person. In international affairs, such situations will be increasingly frequent. In a recent article,[5] Dr. Bowett has developed this "second-order legality" approach, in an analysis of the Middle Eastern conflict situation. Israel's successive defiances of the U.N. Security Council resolutions since the Six Day War have gradually eroded the once near-universal moral support for a country fighting for survival against overwhelming odds and threats of extermination. Such erosion of moral support is not legally effective as long as the international community lacks muscle. Nevertheless, it is far from irrelevant. Not even the superpowers believe they can afford open defiance of international opinion, except in situations of extreme emergency. To take the more recent example of Bangladesh, the Indian armed intervention was clearly illegal in terms of formal international law, since India occupied parts of another country without being threatened in its own security or integrity. Yet the subsequent Security Council resolution carefully avoided condemnation of India's intervention. This was an expression of the universally felt revulsion against the behavior of the Pakistan forces toward its own citizens, reinforced by the moderation of the Indian occupiers. India's action was illegal, but morally condonable. This is a far cry from the invasion of a helpless and totally non-aggressive Abyssinia by Mussolini's Italy in 1935, the successive assaults on, and annexations of, neighboring countries by Hitler's Germany, or the Japanese attack on the American fleet in Pearl Harbor. In all these cases legal and moral condemnation coincided. In 1935, the inability of the international community to translate its moral condemnation into collective action under League of Nations auspices spelt the doom of the League. In 1939 and 1941, the brutal attacks of the Axis powers gave an immense impetus to the reaction of what later became the United Nations. Obviously, the assessment of morality in international behavior is a fluid and flexible concept. Like many aspects of international conduct at this time, it lacks precision. This does not make it irrelevant. In primitive legal societies, morality, as embodied in social custom, has always occupied a far larger place than law in the strict sense. Gradually, as legal authority was both centralized and expanded, the sphere and the reach of the law expanded with it. Where I differ from Professor Lillich is not in the conviction that the violation of elementary human rights is a vital international concern, but in the assessment of the present state of the international legal system. The aim must be to work towards an international legal order which will be able to develop

[5] Bowett, "Reprisals Involving Recourse to Armed Force," 66 *Am. J. Int'l L.* 1 (1972).

what are at present somewhat imprecise and arbitrary moral criteria into binding legal norms and institutions that will have the support and the authority to enforce these standards.

It is only in this context that I can see any relevance of the theories of "modernization" with which Professor Black's article is concerned. I fully concur with Professor Black's observation that "the path that the peoples of the world appear to be taking toward international integration is therefore not a path of political action, but more of economic and social action." As Professor Black also observes, international economic and social activity takes place to a considerable extent despite state policy. This is in fact a way of describing the "functional" approach to international organization of which this commentator has been an advocate for many years.[6] There can hardly be a *substantive* theory of permissible categories of collective intervention, as an alternative to unilateral intervention, since the range of international concerns expands in proportion to the growth of international law in the domains that have traditionally been the exclusive prerogatives of the national state. But I have great difficulty in regarding "modernization" as even a generally accurate description of the direction in which collective intervention, on behalf of the international community, should develop. Unlike some other writers, Professor Black does not purport to put forward "modernization" as a legitimation of unilateral intervention, and he is not specific on the question whether it should be a ground for multilateral intervention, presumably under the auspices of the United Nations or one of the specialized agencies. The concept of "modernization" shares with that of "humanitarian intervention" the fatal weakness that it would impose a certain mode of behavior on a government, in derogation of the right to determine the social and economic structure, which is an essential aspect of national sovereignty. But "modernization" is an even less precise concept than "humanitarian," and there is a far lesser degree of moral consensus on the desirability of modernization.

What is "modernization"? Is it the replacement of a feudal form of government by a more contemporary type—as, for example, in the Yemen civil struggles? Is the alternative to feudalism a modern autocracy, a democracy, a "capitalist," or a "socialist" system? Does modernization mean the transition from an agricultural to a more or less industrialized economy? Does it mean the replacement of traditional village or tribal communities by urban centers? Even if clear answers could be given to all these questions, it is highly doubtful whether at the present stage of international thinking, as distinct from a decade or two ago, "modernization," would be generally regarded as the desirable objective. Thus, the rapid industrialization of Libya, due to the almost unprecedented oil bonanza, has also meant the disruption of the agricultural economy and the

---

[6] This is also my answer to Professor Lillich's critique (Note 112) that my advocacy of strengthened international procedures of cooperation, as the only alternative to unilateral intervention, is not spelled out. I have attempted to develop in more detail the approaches to institutionalized functional cooperation in various papers, *e.g.*, "The Relevance of International Law to the Processes of Economic and Social Development" in II R. Falk & C. Black (eds.), *The Future of the International Legal Order* 3–35 (1970); "Human Welfare and International Law—A Reordering of Priorities, in *Transnational Law in a Changing Society: Essays in Honor of Philip C. Jessup*, 113–34 (1972); *Joint Fishery Ventures in the Indian Ocean Area* (FAO Fisheries Technical Paper No. 111, 1972).

creation of urban slums. International development aid—which a decade ago seemed to put almost overwhelming emphasis on industrialization—is today more concerned with helping in a proper economic and ecologic balance, between agriculture and industry, villages and towns, social cohesion and social innovation. International development aid—which may be described as a form of intervention in the wider sense—is today in a state of transition and travail. The policies and practices of the World Bank or the various regional development banks, of the FAO, UNCTAD, UNIDO, and others may gradually adjust to the shifting balance of the various group interests and economic conditions involved. But as a legitimation of unilateral intervention, "modernization" is, in this commentator's opinion, totally without merit.

It will have become apparent from the foregoing remarks that this commentator essentially concurs with the observation made in J. L. Brierly's classical *The Law of Nations*[7] that "intervention . . . means dictatorial interference in the domestic or foreign affairs of another state which impairs that state's independence," and that he remains deeply skeptical of any enlargement of justifications for unilateral intervention—which, in the absence of third party adjudication, are usually self-serving and suffering from the kind of imprecision which enlarges the range for unilateral discretion. Intervention is an aspect of restriction of state sovereignty in the name of a higher principle and authority. The only way to achieve this authority is the strengthening of authoritative international institutions. But this cannot be attained without the necessary moral consensus. It is the principal merit of the contributions to this volume to have singled out areas in which it is essential that such consensus be developed and articulated.

[7] J. Brierly, *The Law of Nations* 402 (6th ed., H. Waldock ed. 1963).

Comment 5 | Civil Wars: Guidelines for States and the United Nations | Louis B. Sohn

Looking less to the past and more to the future, there seems to be a great need for more precise guidelines for both states and the United Nations with respect to permissible and prohibited activities in case of civil wars.

CIVIL WARS AND RECOGNITION

Most states have by now abandoned the idea that governments which came to power by the use of force are somehow "unclean," beyond the pale of the international community, and that the only respectable governments are those elected by properly democratic means. In many countries, it has become the new constitutional procedure that, when a particular government has outlived its usefulness, another group replaces it with a minimal use of force and with the blessing or assistance of the local military commanders. The old "palace" revolutions have now been replaced by revolutions originating in military barracks. No longer are such military coups staged in defense of the interests of the ruling classes; they lead often to important economic and social reforms. Consequently, it has become more difficult to attach to such occurrences the stigmas of "undemocratic behavior" or "totalitarianism." The will of the people can be expressed now by this new medium, even if the old oligarchy which has previously controlled the limited electoral process should complain against the illegality of the new government. There is no reason for other governments or the United Nations to be guardians of the national constitutions, which in large areas of the world have never acquired the sanctity of the constitutions in the Western world. Consequently, the requirements for recognition have been considerably relaxed, and in case of revolutions which have been quick, almost bloodless, and acquiesced in by the people without a sign of strong counterrevolutionary currents, the new governments are almost automatically accepted into the family of nations, frequently without need for official recognition. At the United Nations, the issue of new credentials seldom arises in such a situation, and the new government is accepted without unnecessary complications.

CIVIL WARS OF INTERNATIONAL CONCERN

The international community finds it more difficult to deal with two types of situations: when there is a prolonged civil war, and when one or both of the parties to the strife receive considerable military support from one or more foreign states. The first situation becomes a threat to the peace because any prolonged civil war spills in various ways into neighboring countries or even the high seas. In such cases, refugees and defeated armies try to find shelter and help beyond the borders of the war-torn state, and issues of humanitarian assistance become of international concern. The whole burden of such assistance cannot be born simply by the poor State where the victims seek refuge, but needs to be shared by more lucky members of the world community. In other cases, one party to the civil war might try to interfere with the neutral commerce with the other side, and a blockade might be instituted, disrupting normal channels of trade and often impinging on freedom of navigation on the high seas.

The second situation—foreign participation—is often combined with the first, as extensive foreign assistance, especially if received by both parties, is likely to prolong a civil war inordinately. Such foreign assistance might be purely mercenary, in order to earn quick, exorbitant profits, or it might be ideological, based on the assumption that the victory of a particular side would vindicate a particular ideological point of view, would result in desired reforms or social and political changes in the country involved, or would swing the war-torn country toward the group of states to which the assisting states belong.

Should it be desired to adopt some rules to try to limit foreign intervention in civil wars, the following guidelines, distilled from United Nations resolutions and official proposals as well as from recent writings, might be considered:

Possible Guidelines for Non-Intervention in Civil Wars

1. *Basic Principle*

   No military intervention by one state in an internal armed conflict in another state is permissible, except in an extreme emergency requiring instant response and subject to immediate termination of such emergency action on request of the United Nations or an appropriate regional organization.

2. *Non-Intervention in a Civil War*

   The following acts in support of a foreign government or an insurgent group shall be considered as military intervention for the purpose of these guidelines:

   a. Arms sales or grants;

   b. Making available military training at home or abroad;

   c. Making available military advisers to troops engaged in military operations;

   d. Making planes and crews available for air observation;

   e. Providing transportation assistance for troops engaged in military operations;

   f. Limited support of military operations by artillery, air, or naval units;

   g. Participation in military operations by combat units, whether composed of "volunteers" or regular military personnel.

3. *No Assistance to Insurgents*

   In addition, the following acts in support of the insurgent group shall be considered as intervention for the purpose of these guidelines:

   a. Assistance to exile groups, in particular by helping them to organize, finance and equip irregular or volunteer forces or armed bands, including mercenaries, for incursions into the territory of another state; and

  b.   Organizing, supporting, or directing guerrilla activities, or other
        subversive or terrorist activities, in another state.

4.   *Military Assistance in Time of Peace*
      Military assistance shall not be considered as intervention, if it has
      been requested by the national government concerned and a detailed
      report has been presented to the United Nations, except when:
  a.   There is an internal armed conflict of significant size in progress in
        the country requesting assistance; or
  b.   The United Nations or an appropriate regional organization has
        prohibited such assistance in a specific situation or has requested
        that it be terminated.

5.   *Action Authorized by International Organizations*
      Intervention is permissible if specifically authorized by:
  a.   The United Nations; or
  b.   A regional organization, if the United Nations does not request
        that it be terminated.

6.   *Protection against Violations*
      In case of a large-scale violation by a state of these guidelines, tem-
      porary and strictly limited counter-intervention by other states is per-
      missible, subject to termination on request of the United Nations or
      an appropriate regional organization.

7.   *Decisions by the United Nations*
      An authorization, or a request to terminate, may be given on behalf
      of the United Nations by either the Security Council or the General
      Assembly.

COMMENT ON THE GUIDELINES

It will be noted that the basic principle has a provision analogous to the self-
defense principle in Article 51 of the Charter of the United Nations. No attempt
is made here to define what is an "emergency." United Nations practice should
in the long run provide the answer, and one should not try to impose a straight-
jacket on the competent organs of the United Nations or of an appropriate
regional organization.

The enumeration of prohibited acts in paragraph 2 goes beyond the customary list. It tries to prevent a step-by-step involvement and adopts the principle of the slippery slope. If one does not want to land at the bottom of the
slope, it is safer not to take even the first step.

The proposed guidelines depart to some extent from the post-war practice
of allowing assistance to the recognized government, and permitting all kinds of
participation as long as this is done on request, or at the invitation, of that
government. But there have been so many abuses of that practice that it seems
desirable to impose the basic restrictions not only on insurgents but also on the
government fighting for its life. The guidelines thus impose strict neutrality on
third parties and do not permit any exceptions in favor of the government still
officially in power.

It might be necessary, nevertheless, to have some additional guidelines with respect to special assistance to the insurgents. These guidelines, designed to prohibit certain unfortunately rather common practices, are modelled on several United Nations resolutions and declarations.

While it might be difficult to completely abolish military assistance in time of peace, certain parameters for it might be established. Aid given in anticipation of civil war, such as training in counter-insurgency tactics, might be more difficult to prohibit than the parallel training of exiles for a future rebellion. But once a conflict reaches some significant proportions, military aid should be stopped. The United Nations should be informed on a continuous basis about the aid being given, and when a situation seems to be approaching a boiling point, the United Nations should have the power to prohibit further assistance as constituting a threat to the peace.

On the other hand, because of an intervention by other states, a gross and persistent violation of human rights, or the general explosiveness of a particular situation, the United Nations might decide to intervene itself or to authorize an intervention by a state or group of states. Subject to possible United Nations disapproval, such intervention by regional organizations might also be allowed. Similarly, a counter-intervention by a state or group of states might be permissible if another state has grossly violated the guidelines, has intervened on a large scale, and is unwilling to desist from such illegal intervention.

The Charter of the United Nations lodges the primary responsibility for the maintenance of international peace and security in the hands of the Security Council, but it is generally recognized that the General Assembly has at least some secondary powers in this area. In addition, it would facilitate the acceptance of the guidelines by the smaller states if the General Assembly which they control were given clear jurisdiction in this area. As the vast majority of civil wars is likely to occur in states other than the permanent members of the Security Council, and as the crucial question is how to enable the United Nations to act in a case in which two of the major powers are aligned on opposite sides of a civil war, conferring equal powers in this field on the General Assembly would seem eminently desirable. Even as far as the superpowers are concerned, keeping them away from the temptation to intervene is likely to be in their long-run interest, in particular in view of the prevalent estimate that a nuclear war is more likely to arise from an escalation of a minor conflict rather than from a deliberate decision of one superpower trying to destroy the other by a surprise attack.

INTERVENTION BY THE UNITED NATIONS

Apart from the role of the United Nations with respect to the enforcement and interpretation of the guidelines relating to national intervention, there might be some need for guidelines relating to direct intervention by the United Nations in a civil-war situation. They might be as follows:

Guidelines for United Nations Intervention in Civil Wars

1. *Basic Principle*
    The United Nations may intervene in the civil war only to ensure that the situation does not become a threat to the peace.

2. *Intervention to Prevent Foreign Assistance*

The United Nations may establish a blockade of the territory in which the civil war is waged in order to ensure that no foreign assistance would be given to either party to the conflict.

3. *Intervention by Invitation*

When invited by the government of the State in which civil war is taking place, the United Nations may send to that State an observation mission or a peace force for the purpose of assisting in the establishment and maintenance of a cease-fire and the policing of a truce line.

4. *Restoration of Domestic Tranquillity*

When requested by both parties to the conflict, the United Nations may assist:

a. In the establishment of a temporary neutral government drawn from groups not involved on either side of the civil war;

b. In providing administrative, technical, and economic assistance to that temporary government;

c. In the supervision of elections or of a plebiscite;

d. In executing the decisions approved in such plebiscite;

e. In assisting the newly-elected government in restoring order in the country.

5. *Decisions by the United Nations*

Any decisions of the United Nations under these Guidelines may be made on behalf of the United Nations by either the Security Council or the General Assembly.

COMMENT ON THE UNITED NATIONS GUIDELINES

The basic principle limits United Nations intervention to cases of a threat to the peace. Of course, the United Nations has complete discretion in determining what is a threat to the peace, and in particular it may decide that gross violations of human rights by one or the other party to the conflict, or by both of them, constitute a threat to the peace.

One of principal objects of United Nations intervention would be to prevent the fueling of the conflict through foreign assistance to one of the parties or to both of them. For that purpose, the United Nations might establish observation posts on land frontiers and a blockade of ports on the coast.

While an invitation by the government of the war-torn country cannot justify foreign intervention, it might form the basis of United Nations intervention. But the purpose of that intervention cannot be the suppression of the insurgents. The United Nations should merely help to restore peace by arranging a cease-fire and a truce and by supervising their maintenance.

The question has been raised whether the United Nations should not be allowed to come in when invited by the insurgents, especially when they represent the better elements in the population. But such decision would be a very difficult one for the United Nations to make, and no guideline to this effect is proposed.

Only if both parties to the dispute should agree to it, the United Nations might assist in establishing a neutral or coalition government, and the United

Nations might help it to restore the essential public services through administrative, technical and economic assistance. Similarly, if the parties agree, the United Nations might supervise elections or a plebiscite and help in executing the decisions approved by the electorate.

Finally, as in the previous section, it seems desirable to confer the necessary powers not only on the Security Council but also on the General Assembly.

While no special guidelines are proposed here for regional organizations, the United Nations Guidelines can be easily adapted for that purpose, it being always understood that the United Nations would always retain the authority to cancel a regional decision if the United Nations should find it undesirable or ill-advised.

CONCLUSIONS

The suggested two sets of guidelines might be adopted by a General Assembly resolution through consensus rather than voting, thus ensuring for them universal, or almost universal, support. Should it be deemed desirable, the guidelines might be first adopted by the Security Council and recommended by it to the General Assembly for final adoption through a declaration.

The guidelines by themselves are not a panacea. They will not automatically stop all civil wars. But if the United Nations members accept and enact them, the very process of negotiating them and clarifying the issues might contribute to a better understanding of a need for more careful behavior on the part of all concerned. If the United Nations should prove successful in applying the guidelines in a few small cases, and is lucky enough not to have to face a too big problem too soon, its authority in this field might grow sufficiently to enable it to play a more effective role in preventing small threats to the peace from growing into bigger ones.

BIBLIOGRAPHY

Selected Bibliography on Intervention and Civil War | *Frederick S. Tipson*

This bibliography includes a selective listing of writings on intervention and civil war, based on judgments of quality, utility, and accessibility. It is restricted to works in English published or announced as of June 1972. The case studies concern only post-1914 events, as does most of the analytical writing. Due to the complexity of the problems, the volume of recent publications, and the limitations of space, this collection is only suggestive of the relevant literature —particularly with respect to the case studies. In keeping with the contents of the volume itself, the appropriate criteria of coverage have been (a) exposure to a variety of disciplinary approaches and (b) performance of a range of intellectual tasks: historical, scientific, and prescriptive.*

Subject Index to Bibliography

  I. *Basic Works*
     A. Major Collections
     B. Principal Essays
     C. Larger Studies

  II. *Theory and Perspective*
     A. Toward a General Theory
     B. Explanations of Foreign Intervention
        1. Ideological and Economic Imperialism
        2. Structure of the International System
        3. Political and Bureaucratic Decision-Making
        4. Cultural and Psychological Influences
     C. Explanations of Internal Violence
        1. Historical Stages and Patterns
        2. Social Systems and Political Conflict
     D. Prescriptive Theories of Revolution and Counterrevolution
        1. Strategies of Revolution and Insurgency
        2. Strategies of Counterrevolution and Counter-Insurgency

  III. *International Law and Policy*
     A. Normative Standards for Permissible/Impermissible Intervention
     B. International Organizations and Collective Procedures
        1. Global
        2. Regional
     C. The Laws of War

* I would like to thank Professor Cherif M. Bassiouni, Dr. Rosalyn Higgins, and Professor John Norton Moore for their assistance in the preparation of this bibliography.

I. BASIC WORKS

A. MAJOR COLLECTIONS

I–V Black, C., & Falk, R., eds., *The Future of the International Legal Order* (1969–74). (Hereinafter cited by I–V Black & Falk, *Future ILO*).

Falk, R., ed., *The International Law of Civil War* (1971). (Hereinafter cited as Falk, *Civil War*).

I–III Falk, R., ed., *The Vietnam War and International Law* (1968–72). (Hereinafter cited as I–III Falk, *Vietnam*).

Jaquet, L., ed., *Intervention in International Politics* (1971). (Hereinafter cited as Jaquet, *Intervention*).

Moore, J. N., ed., *Law and Civil War in the Modern World* (1974). (Hereinafter cited as Moore, *Civil War*).

I–III Moore, J. N., ed., *The Arab-Israeli Conflict* (1974). (Hereinafter cited as I–III Moore, *Arab-Israeli*).

Rosenau, J., ed., *International Aspects of Civil Strife* (1964). (Hereinafter cited as Rosenau, *Civil Strife*).

B. PRINCIPAL ESSAYS

Burke, "The Legal Regulation of Minor International Coercion: A Framework of Inquiry," in I Falk, *Vietnam* 79.

Falk, "Civil Strife, Intervention and Minor Coercion," in R. Falk, *Legal Order in a Violent World* 97–368 (1968).

Falk, "Janus Tormented: The International Law of Internal War," in Rosenau, *Civil Strife* 185.

Falk, "Introduction," in Falk, *Civil War* 1.

Farer, "Harnessing Rogue Elephants: A Short Discourse on Intervention in Civil Strife," in II Falk, *Vietnam* 1089.

Farer, "Intervention in Civil Wars: A Modest Proposal," in I Falk, *Vietnam* 509.

Firmage, "Summary and Interpretation," in Falk, *Civil War* 405.

Fisher, "Intervention: Three Problems of Policy and Law," in I Falk, *Vietnam* 135.

Friedmann, "Intervention and International Law I," in Jaquet, *Intervention* 40.

Friedmann, "Intervention, Civil War and the Role of International Law," in I Falk, *Vietnam* 151.

Higgins, "Internal War and International Law," in III Black & Falk, *Future ILO* 81.

Hoffmann, "International Systems and International Law," Ch. 4 in S. Hoffmann (ed.), *The State of War: Essays on the Theory and Practice of International Politics* (1965).

Moore, "Toward an Applied Theory for the Regulation of Intervention," Ch. 1 in Moore, *Civil War*.

Moore, "The Control of Foreign Intervention in Internal Conflict," Ch. IV in J. N. Moore, *Law and the Indo-China War* 115–286 (1972).

Rosenau, "The Concept of Intervention," 22 *J. Int'l Aff.* 165 (1968).

Young, "Intervention and International Systems," 22 *J. Int'l Aff.* 177 (1968).

C. LARGER STUDIES

Barnet, R., *Intervention and Revolution: The United States in the Third World* (1968).

Bloomfield, L., & Leiss, A., *Controlling Small Wars: A Strategy for the 1970's* (1970).

Bond, J., *The Law of War and Internal Conflict* (1973).

Castren, E., *Civil War* (1966).

Luard, D., *The International Regulation of Civil Wars* (1972).

O'Brien, W., ed., *The Law of Limited International Conflict* (1965).

Oglesby, R., *Internal War and the Search for Normative Order* (1971).

Schwarz, U., *Confrontation and Intervention in the Modern World* (1970).

Stowell, E., *Intervention in International Law* (1921).

Thomas, A., & Thomas, A., *Non-Intervention* (1956).

Vincent, R., *Non-Intervention and International Order* (1973).

Wehberg, H., *Civil War and International Law* (1938).

II. THEORY AND PERSPECTIVE

A. TOWARD A GENERAL THEORY

Burke, "The Legal Regulation of Minor International Coercion: A Framework of Inquiry," in I Falk, *Vietnam* 79.

Burton, "The Relevance of Behavioral Theories of the International System," Ch. 5 in Moore, *Civil War.*

Eley, "Toward a Theory of Intervention: The Limitations and Advantages of a Transnational Perspective," 16 *Int'l Stud. Q.* 245 (June 1972).

Higgins, "Internal War and International Law," in III Black & Falk, *Future ILO* 81.

Kaplan, "Intervention in Internal War: Some Systemic Sources," in Rosenau, *Civil Strife.*

Kelly, G., & Miller, L., *Internal War and International Systems: Perspectives on Method* (Harvard Center of International Studies, Occasional Paper #21, 1969).

Mitchell, "Civil Strife and the Involvement of External Parties," 14 *Int'l Stud. Q.* 166 (June 1970).

Modelski, "The International Relations of Internal Wars," in Rosenau, *Civil Strife.*

Moore, "Toward an Applied Theory for the Regulation of Intervention," Ch. 1 in Moore, *Civil War.*

Moore, "Intervention: A Monochromatic Term for a Polychromatic Reality," Ch. III in J. N. Moore, *Law and the Indochina War* 83–114 (1972).

Moore, "The Control of Foreign Intervention in Internal Conflict," Ch. IV in J. N. Moore, *Law and the Indo-China War* 115–286 (1972).

Paul, "Toward a Theory of Intervention," 16 *Orbis* 105 (Spring 1972).

Reisman, "Private Armies in a Global War System: Prologue to Decision," Ch. 12 in Moore, *Civil War.*

Rosenau, "Intervention as a Scientific Concept," in II Falk, *Vietnam* 979.

Young, "Intervention and International Systems," in II Falk, *Vietnam* 1016.

B. EXPLANATIONS OF FOREIGN INTERVENTION

1. *Ideological and Economic Imperialism*

Alperovitz, G., *Cold War Essays* (1970).

Barnet, R., *Roots of War* (1972).

Butler, "Soviet Attitudes Toward Intervention," Ch. 15 in Moore, *Civil War.*

Cohen, "China and Intervention: Theory and Practice," Ch. 14 in Moore, *Civil War.*

Dinerstein, H., *Intervention Against Communism* (1967).

Fleming, D., *The Cold War and its Origins* (1961).

Kennan, G., *Memoirs 1925–1950* (1967).

Kolko, G., *The Politics of War: The World and United States Foreign Policy, 1943–1945* (1968).

Kolko, G., *The Roots of American Foreign Policy: An Analysis of Power and Purpose* (1970).

Kolko, J., & Kolko, G., *The Limits of Power: The World and United States Foreign Policy, 1945–1954* (1972).

LaFeber, W., *America, Russia, and the Cold War, 1945–1971* (1971).

Liska, G., *Imperial America: The International Politics of Primacy* (1967).

Marshall, C., *The Cold War: A Concise History* (1965).

Mayer, A., *Wilson vs. Lenin: Political Origins of the New Diplomacy, 1917–1918* (1959).

Mayer, A., *The Politics and Diplomacy of Peacemaking, 1918–1919* (1967).

Moseley, P., *The Kremlin and World Politics* (1960).

Patterson, T., ed., *Cold War Critics* (1970).

Rostow, E., *Peace in the Balance* (1972).

Rostow, E., *Law, Power, and the Pursuit of Peace* (1968).

Shulman, M., *Stalin's Foreign Policy Reappraised* (1963).

Sobel, R., *The Origins of Interventionism* (1960).

Strausz-Hupé, R., *et al., Protracted Conflict* (1959).

Tucker, R., Nation or Empire? *The Debate Over American Foreign Policy* (1968).

Ulam, A., *Expansion and Coexistence: The History of Soviet Foreign Policy, 1917–1967* (1968).

Ulam, A., *The Rivals: America and Russia Since World War II* (1971).

Van Ness, P., *Revolution & China's Foreign Policy: Peking's Support for Wars of National Liberation* (1970).

Williams, W., *The Roots of the Modern American Empire* (1970).

2. *Structure of the International System*

Beloff, "Reflections on Intervention," 22 *J. Int'l Aff.* 198 (1968).

Billington, "Force and Counterforce in Eastern Europe," 47 *For. Aff.* 26 (Oct. 1968).

Black, C., *et al., Neutralization and World Politics* (1966).

Burton, J., *International Relations: A General Theory* (1967).

Burton, J., *Conflict and Communication* (1969).

Claude, I., *Power in International Relations* (1962).

Copeland, M., *The Game of Nations* (1969).

Graber, D., *Crisis Diplomacy: A History of U.S. Intervention Policies and Practices* (1959).

Halle, L., *The Cold War as History* (1967).

Hoffmann, "International Systems and International Law" in S. Hoffmann, *The State of War: Essays on the Theory and Practice of International Politics* (1965).

Hoffmann, "International Organization and the International System," 24 *Int'l Org.* 389 (Summer 1970).

IISS, *Civil Violence and the International System* (Papers of 13th Annual Conference, Stresa, 1971).

Kaplan, M., *System and Process in International Politics* (1957).

Kaplan, M., & Katzenbach, N., *The Political Foundations of International Law* (1961).

Morganthau, H., *Politics Among Nations* (4th ed. 1971).

North & Choucri, "Dynamics of International Conflict: Some Policy Implications of Population, Resources and Technology," 24 *World Pol.* (Supplement) 80 (Spring 1972).

Osgood, R., *et al.*, *America and the World* (1970).

Rapoport, A., *The Big Two: Soviet-American Perceptions of Foreign Policy* (1971).

Rosecrance, R., *Action and Reaction in World Politics* (1963).

Rosenau, J., (ed.), *Linkage Politics: Essays on the Convergence of National and International Systems* (1969).

Scott, "Non-Intervention and Conditional Intervention," 22 *J. Int'l Aff.* 208 (1968).

Singer, "The 'Correlates of War' Project: An Interim Report and Rationale," 24 *World Politics* 243 (Jan. 1972).

Sullivan, D., & Sattler, M., eds., *Revolutionary War: Western Response* (1972).

Wolfers, "The Pole of Power and the Pole of Indifference," in A. Wolfers, *Discord and Collaboration: Essays on International Politics* (1962).

II Wright, Q., *A Study of War* (1942).

Young, "Systemic Bases of Intervention," Ch. 6 in Moore, *Civil War*.

3. *Political and Bureaucratic Decision-Making*

Allison, G., *Essence of Decision: Explaining the Cuban Missile Crisis* (1971).

Barnet, R., *Intervention and Revolution: The United States in the Third World* (1968).

Chomsky, N., *American Power and the New Mandarins* (1969).

Dallin, "Soviet Foreign Policy and Domestic Politics: A Framework for Analysis," 23 *J. Int'l Aff.* 250 (1969).

Ellsberg, D., *Papers on the War* (1972).

Hoffmann, S., *Gulliver's Troubles, or the Setting of American Foreign Policy* (1968).

Hoffmann, "Will the Balance Balance at Home?" 7 *For. Pol.* 60 (1972).

Kissinger, "Domestic Structure and Foreign Policy," in H. Kissinger, *American Foreign Policy: Three Essays* (1969).

Rosenau, J., ed., *Domestic Sources of Foreign Policy* (1964).

————, *The Adaptation of National Societies: A Theory of Political System Behavior and Transformation* (1970).

————, "Foreign Intervention as Adaptive Behavior," Ch. 7 in Moore, *Civil War.*

Triska, J., & Finley, D., *Soviet Foreign Policy* (1968).

Yarmolinsky, "American Foreign Policy and the Decision to Intervene," 22 *J. Int'l Aff.* 233 (1968).

4. *Cultural and Psychological Influences*

Barber, J., *Presidential Character: Predicting Performance in the White House* (1972).

Bozeman, A., *Politics and Culture in International History* (1960).

————, *The Future of Law in a Multicultural World* (1971).

Fairbank, J., ed., *The Chinese World Order* (1968).

Kennan, "The Sources of Soviet Conduct," 25 *For. Aff.* (July 1947).

Lasswell, H., *World Politics and Personal Insecurity* (1935).

DeRivera, J., *The Psychological Dimension of Foreign Policy* (1968).

Schuman, "The Neuroses of the Nations," in Lepawsky, A., Buehrig, E. & Lasswell, H., eds., *The Search for World Order* (1971).

Tucker, R. C., *The Soviet Political Mind* (1963).

C. EXPLANATIONS OF INTERNAL VIOLENCE

1. *Historical Stages and Patterns*

Almond, G., & Powell, G., *Comparative Politics: A Developmental Approach* (1966).

Apter, D., *The Politics of Modernization* (1965).

Black, C., *The Dynamics of Modernization: A Study in Comparative History* (1966).

————, "The Relevance of Theories of Modernization for Normative and Institutional Efforts at the Control of Intervention," Ch. 3 in Moore, *Civil War.*

I–IX Committee on Comparative Politics, Social Science Research Council, "Studies in Political Development," esp. IX Binder, L., *et al.*, *Crisis and Sequences in Political Development* (1971).

Deutsch, K,. *Nationalism and Social Communication* (1954).

————, "Social Mobilization and Political Development," 55 *Am. Pol. Sci. R.* 493 (Sept. 1961).

Eisenstadt, A., *Modernization: Protest and Change* (1966).

Gerschenkron, A., *Economic Backwardness in Historical Perspective* (1962).

Hagen, E., *On the Theory of Social Change: How Economic Growth Begins* (1962).

Huntington, S., *Political Order in Changing Societies* (1968).

————, "The Change to Change: Modernization, Development, and Politics," 3 *Comp. Politics* 283 (April, 1971).

Jowitt, K., *Revolutionary Breakthroughs and National Development: The Case of Romania, 1944–1965* (1971).

I–II Levy, M., *Modernization and the Structure of Society: A Setting for International Affairs* (1966).

Moore, B., *Social Origins of Dictatorship and Democracy* (1966).

Rostow, D., *A World of Nations* (1967).

Rostow, W., *Politics and the Stages of Growth* (1971).

Turner, "Fascism and Modernization," 24 *World Pol.* 547 (July 72).

Wolf, E., *Peasant Wars of the Twentieth Century* (1971).

2. *Social Systems and Political Conflict*

Arendt, H., *On Revolution* (1963).

———, *Crises of the Republic* (1972).

Banks, "Patterns of Domestic Conflict: 1919–39 and 1946–66," 16 *J. Conflict Res.* 41 (March 1972).

Bohannan, P., ed., *Law and Warfare: Studies in the Anthropology of Conflict* (1967).

Brinton, C., *The Anatomy of Revolution* (rev. ed. 1965).

Brogan, D., *The Price of Revolution* (1951).

Crozier, B., *The Rebels: A Study of Post-War Insurrections* (1960).

Dahrendorf, R., *Class and Conflict in Industrial Society* (1964).

Davies, "Toward a Theory of Revolution," 27 *Am. Soc. Rev.* 5 (Feb. 1962).

———, J., ed., *When Men Revolt—And Why* (1971).

Dunn, J., *Modern Revolutions: An Introduction to the Analysis of a Political Phenomenon* (1972).

Eckstein, H., ed., *Internal War: Problems and Approaches* (1964).

Feierabend & Feierabend, "Aggressive Behavior Within Politics; 1948–1962: A Cross-National Study," 10 *J. Conflict Res.* 258 (Sept. 1966).

Fried, M., *et al.*, eds., *War: The Anthropology of Armed Conflict and Aggression* (1968).

Friedrich, C., ed., *Revolution* (1966).

Gottschalk, "Causes of Revolution," 50 *Am. J. Soc.* (1944).

Gurr, "The Relevance of Theories of Internal Violence for the Control of Intervention," Ch. 4 in Moore, *Civil War*.

———, "A Causal Model of Civil Strife: A Comparative Analysis Using New Indices," 62 *Am. Pol. Sci. Rev.* 1104 (Dec. 1968).

———, T., *Why Men Rebel* (1970).

Gurr, T., & Ruttenburg, C., *Cross-National Studies of Civil Violence* (1969).

Higham, ed., *Civil Wars in the Twentieth Century* (1972).

Hunter, R., *Revolution: Why, How, When?* (4th ed. 1953).

Janos, A., *The Seizure of Power: A Study of Force and Popular Consent* (Research monograph #6, Princeton, 1964).

Johnson, C., *Revolution and the Social System* (Hoover Institution Studies #3, 1964).

———, *Revolutionary Change* (1966).

Kelly, G., & Brown, C., eds., *Struggles in the State: Sources and Patterns of World Revolution* (1970).

Leiden, C., & Schmidt, K., *The Politics of Violence: Revolution in the Modern World* (1968).

Leites, N., & Wolfe, C., Jr., *Rebellion and Authority: An Analytic Essay on Insurgent Conflicts* (1970).

Lipset, S., *Revolution and Counterrevolution* (1970).

Lowenthal, R., *Unreason and Revolution* (RAND, 1969).

Marcuse, H., *Reason and Revolution* (1968).

Mazlish, B., *et al.*, eds., *Revolution: A Reader* (1971).

Miller, N., & Aya, R., eds., *National Liberation: Revolution in the Third World* (1971).

Mitchell, "Inequality and Insurgency: A Statistical Study of South Vietnam," 20 *World Politics* 421 (April 1968).

Olson, "Rapid Growth as a Destabilizing Force," 23 *J. Econ. Hist.* 532 (Dec. 1963).

Paige, "Inequality and Insurgency in Vietnam: A Re-Analysis," 23 *World Politics* 22 (Oct. 1970).

Paranzino, "Inequality and Insurgency in Vietnam: A Further Re-Analysis," 24 *World Politics* 565 (July 1970).

Pennock, J., & Chapman, J., eds., *Coercion* (1972).

Pettee, G., *The Process of Revolution* (1938).

Prosterman, R., *Surviving to 3000: An Introduction to the Study of Lethal Conflict* (1972).

Russett, "Inequality of Instability: The Relation of Land Tenure to Politics," 16 *World Politics* 442 (April 1964).

Samson, R., *The Economics of Insurgency in the Mekong Delta of Vietnam* (1970).

Stone, "Theories of Revolution," 18 *World Politics* (Jan. 1966).

Tanter, "Dimensions of Conflict Behavior within Nations, 1955–1960: Turmoil and Internal War," 3 *Papers, Peace Research Society* 159 (1965).

Tanter & Midlarsky, "A Theory of Revolution," 11 *J. Conflict Res.* 271 (Sept. 1967).

Walter, E., *Terror and Resistance: A Study of Political Violence* (1969).

D. PRESCRIPTIVE THEORIES OF REVOLUTION AND COUNTERREVOLUTION

1. *Strategies of Revolution and Insurgency*

Black, C., & Thornton, T., *Communism and Revolution: The Strategic Uses of Political Violence* (1964).

Blackstock, P., *The Strategy of Subversion* (1964).

Bonachea, R., & Valkes, N., *Che: Selected Works of Ernesto Guevara* (1969).

Boorman, S., *The Protracted Game: A Wei-ch'i Interpretation of Maoist Revolutionary Strategy* (1968).

Cross, J., *Conflict in the Shadows: The Nature and Politics of Guerrilla War* (1963).

Debray, R., *Revolution in the Revolution* (1967).

Fanon, F., *The Wretched of the Earth* (1963).

Firmage, "The 'War of National Liberation' and the Third World," Ch. 13 in Moore, *Civil War.*

Giap, Vo-Nguyen, *People's War, People's Army* (1961).

Guevara, Che, *Guerrilla Warfare* (1961).

Hyde, D., *The Roots of Guerrilla Warfare* (1968).

Le Duan, *The August Revolution* (1971).

Lenin, V., *What is to Be Done?* (1902).

Piao, Lin, *Long Live the Victory of the People's War!* (1965).

Tse-Tung, Mao, *On Guerrilla Warfare* (S. Griffith, ed., 1961).

Osanka, F., ed., *Modern Guerrilla Warfare* (1962).

Paret, P., & Shy, J., *Guerrillas in the 1960's* (rev. ed. 1965).

Pye, "The Roots of Insurgency and the Commencement of Rebellions," in H. Eckstein, ed., *Internal War* (1964).

Thayer, C., *Guerrilla* (1963).

Wolfenstein, V., *The Revolutionary Personality: Lenin, Trotsky and Gandhi* (1967).

2. Strategies of Counterrevolution and Counter-Insurgency

Ahmad, "Revolutionary War and Counter-Insurgency," 25 *J. Int'l Aff.* 1 (1971).

Galula, D., *Counterinsurgency Warfare: Theory and Practice* (1964).

Goldsen, J., *Counterinsurgency and Research in 1970* (RAND: P. 3169, May 24, 1965).

Greene, T., ed., *The Guerrilla, and How to Fight Him* (1962).

Heilbroner, "Counterrevolutionary America," *Commentary* (April 1967).

Kelly, "Legal Aspects of Military Operations in Counterinsurgency," 12 *Military L. Rev.* 95 (July 1963).

Marcuse, H., *Counter-Revolution and Revolt* (1972).

Mayer, A., *The Dynamics of Counterrevolution in Europe: 1870–1956: An Analytic Framework* (1971).

Paget, J., *Counter-Insurgency Operations* (1967).

Pustay, J., *Counterinsurgency Warfare* (1965).

Rostow, "Countering Guerrilla Attack," in I Falk, *Vietnam* 127.

Schlesinger, "The Army and the Guerrilla," 4 *Polity* 330 (1972).

Thompson, R., *Defeating Communist Insurgency* (1966).

III. INTERNATIONAL LAW AND POLICY

A. NORMATIVE STANDARDS FOR PERMISSABLE/IMPERMISSABLE INTERVENTION

(See also the works cited in Part I)

Allison, May, & Yarmolinsky, "The Limits to Intervention," 48 *For. Aff.* 245 (Jan. 1970).

Alpert, "Is There an Alternative to Intervention?" 18 *Pub. Pol.* 149.

Bond, "A Survey of the Normative Rules of Intervention," 52 *Military L. Rev.* 51 (1971).

Borchard, E., *The Diplomatic Protection of Citizens Abroad* (1915).

Bos, "Intervention and International Law II," in Jaquet, *Intervention* 69.

Bowett, D., *Self-Defense in International Law* (1958).

———, "The Interrelation of Theories of Intervention and Self-Defense," Ch. 2 in Moore, *Civil War.*

Brierly, J., *The Law of Nations* (6th Waldock ed., 1963).

Brownlie, I., *International Law and the Use of Force by States* (1963).

———, "Humanitarian Intervention," Ch. 10 in Moore, *Civil War.*

Cabranes, "Human Rights and Non-Intervention in the Inter-American System," 65 *Mich. L. Rev.* 1147 (1967).

Claydon, "Humanitarian Intervention and International Law," 1 *Queen's Intra L.J.* (1969).

Dhokalia, "Civil Wars and International Law," *Indian J. Int'l L.* 219 (1971).

Douglas, "Counterinsurgency: A Permitted Intervention," 43 *Military L. Rev.* (1964).

Dunn, F., *The Protection of Nationals* (1932).

Ehrlich, "The Measuring Line of Occasion," 3 *Stanford J. Int'l Stud.* 20 (1968).

Falk, "The Legitimacy of Zone II as a Structure of Domination," in East, M., & Rosenau, J., eds., *The Analysis of International Politics* (1971).

———, "Quincy Wright: On Legal Tests of Aggressive War," 66 *Am. J. Int'l L.* 560 (1972).

Farer, "Law and War," in III Black & Falk, *Future ILO* 15.

———, "Harnessing Rogue Elephants: A Short Discourse on Intervention in Civil Strife," in I Falk, *Vietnam* 1089.

———, "Intervention in Civil Wars: A Modest Proposal," in I Falk, *Vietnam* 509.

Fawcett, "Intervention in International Law: A Study of Some Recent Cases," 103 *Recueil des Cours* 347 (1961).

Firmage, "International Law and the Response of the United States to Internal War," in II Falk, *Vietnam* 89.

Friedmann, "Intervention, Liberalism and Power Politics: The Unfinished Revolution in International Thinking," 83 *Pol. Sci. Q.* 169 (June 1968).

———, "Intervention and the Developing Countries," 10 Va. J. Int'l L. 205 (1970).

Gilmour, "The Meaning of 'Intervention' within Article 2(7) of the United Nations Charter—an Historical Perspective," *Int. & Comp. L.Q.* 330 (1967).

Ginsburg, "Wars of Liberation and the Modern Law of Nations—the Soviet Thesis," 29 *Law & Contemp. Probs.* 910 (1964).

Halpern, "The Morality and Politics of Intervention," in Rosenau, *Civil Strife.*

Henkin, "Force, Intervention, and Neutrality in Contemporary International Law," in II Falk, R., & Mendlowitz, S., eds., *The Strategy of World Order* (1966).

Higgins, R., *The Development of International Law Through the Political Organs of the United Nations* (1963).

———, "The Legal Limits to the Use of Force by Sovereign States: United Nations Practice," 37 *Brit. Yrbk Int'l L.* 269 (1961).

Hoffman, "International Law and the Control of Force," in Deutsch, K., & Hoffman, S., eds., *The Relevance of International Law* (1968).

Hyde, C., *Intervention in Theory and Practice* (1911).

Kelsen, H., *Principles of International Law* (Tucker, ed., 1967).

Lauterpacht, H., *International Law and Human Rights* (1950).

Lillich, "Forcible, Self-Help by States to Protect Human Rights," 53 *Iowa L. Rev.* 325 (1967).

———, "Intervention to Protect Human Rights," 15 *McGill L. J.* 205 (1969).

———, "Humanitarian Intervention: A Reply to Dr. Brownlie and a Plea for Constructive Alternatives," Ch. 11 in Moore, *Civil War.*

Little, D., *American Foreign Policy and Moral Rhetoric* (1969).

McDougal, M., & Feliciano, F., *Law and Minimum World Public Order* (1961).

Moore, "Introduction," in Moore, *Civil War.*

————, "Toward an Applied Theory for the Regulation of Intervention," Ch. 1 in Moore, *Civil War.*

————, "The Control of Foreign Intervention in Internal Conflict," Ch. IV, in J. N. Moore, *Law and the Indo-China War* 115–286 (1972).

O'Connell, D., *International Law* (1965).

Oppenheim, L., *International Law* (8th ed. Lauterpacht (1955).

Osgood, R., & Tucker, R., *Force, Order and Justice* (1967).

Pfeffer, R., ed., *No More Vietnams: The War and the Future of American Foreign Policy* (1968).

Pinto, "The Rules of International Law Governing Civil War," 114 *Receuil des Cours* 454 (1965).

Ramsey, "Ethics of Intervention," 27 *Rev. of Pol.* 287 (July 1965).

Rosenstock, "The Declaration of Principles of International Law concerning Friendly Relations: A Survey," 65 *Am. J. Nat'l L.* 713 (1971).

Schwarz, "Intervention: The Historical Development I," in Jaquet, *Intervention* 29.

Stone, J., *Aggression and World Order* (1958).

————, *Legal Control of International Conflict* (1959).

Waldock, "The Use of Force in International Law," 81 *Recueil des Cours* 458 (1952).

Warnke & Gelb, "Security or Confrontation: The Case for a Defense Policy," 1 *For. Policy* 6 (Winter 1970–71).

Winfield, "The History of Intervention in International Law," *British Yrbk. Int'l L. 1922–23* 130 (1923).

Wright, Q., *The Role of Law in the Elimination of War* (1961).

————, "The Legality of Intervention Under the United Nations Charter," 51 *Proc. Am. Soc. Int'l L.* 79 (1957).

Younger, "Intervention: The Historical Development II," in Jaquet, *Intervention* 12.

B.   INTERNATIONAL ORGANIZATIONS AND COLLECTIVE PROCEDURES

1. *Global*

Bloomfield, L., ed., *The Power to Keep Peace* (1971).

————, "The U.N. and Vietnam," in II Falk, *Vietnam* 281.

Bloomfield, L., & Leiss, A., *Controlling Small Wars: A Strategy for the 1970's* (1970).

Boyd, J., *United Nations Peace-Keeping Operations: A Military and Political Appraisal* (1971).

Bowett, D., *United Nations Forces* (1964).

Claude, "The United Nations and the Use of Force," *Int'l Concil.* #532 (March, 1961).

————, "The United Nations and Collective Security," in R. Gray (ed.), *International Security Systems* (1969).

Fabian, L., *Soldiers Without Enemies: Preparing the United Nations for Peace-keeping* (1971).

Firmage, E., *United Nations Fact-Finding in the Resolution of International Disputes* (1971).

————, "A United Nations Peace Force," 11 *Wayne St. L. Rev.* 717.

Forsythe, "U.N. Peacekeeping and Domestic Instability," 15 *Orbis* 1064 (Winter, 1972).

Ganji, M., *International Protection of Human Rights* (1962).

Gordon, "Vietnam, the United States, and the United Nations," in II Falk, *Vietnam*, 321.

Gottlieb, G., *The U.N. and World Order* (forthcoming).

————, "International Humanitarian Law," 1 *Israel Yrbk. of Human Rights* (1972).

Haas, "Collective Security and the Future of the International System," in I Black & Falk, *Future ILO*, 226.

Higgins, R., *United Nations Peacekeeping, 1946–1967: Documents and Commentary*, Vol. I: *The Middle East* (1969); Vol. II: *Asia* (1971); Vol. III (forthcoming).

Hoffmann, "Sisyphus and the Avalanche: The United Nations, Egypt and Hungary," in M. Kaplan (ed.), *Great Issues in International Politics* (1970).

Horowitz, "The Limited Effectiveness of the United Nations," 3 *Stanford J. Int'l Stud.* 13 (June, 1968).

International Law Association, *Interim Report of the Sub-Committee of the Committee on Human Rights* (1970).

"International Procedures to Protect Human Rights: A Symposium," 53 *Iowa L. Rev.* 268 (1967).

James, A., *The Politics of Peace-Keeping* (1969).

Lefever, "The Limits of U.N. Intervention in the Third World," 30 *Rev. of Pol.* 3 (Jan., 1968).

Legault, A., ed., *Peace-Keeping Operations* (1967).

Lillich, R., ed., *Humanitarian Intervention and the United Nations* (1973).

McDougal & Gardner, "The Veto and the Charter: an Interpretation for Survival," 60 *Yale L.J.* (1951).

McDougal & Reisman, "Rhodesia and the United Nations: The Lawfulness of International Concern," 62 *Am. J. Int'l. L.* 1 (1968).

————, "Response [on Humanitarian Intervention]," 3 *Int'l Lawyer* 438 (1969).

Miller, L., *World Order and Local Disorder: The United Nations and Internal Conflicts* (1967).

Pechota, V., *Complementary Structures of Third-Party Settlement of International Disputes* (1971).

————, *The Good Offices of the Secretary-General* (1972).

Rajan, M., *The United Nations and Domestic Jurisdiction* (1958).

Reisman, M., *Nullity and Revision: The Review and Enforcement of International Judgments and Awards* Part 3 (1971).

————, "Sanctions and Enforcement," in III Black & Falk, *Future ILO* 273.

————, "Memorandum upon Humanitarian Intervention to Protect the Ibos," in R. Lillich ed., *Humanitarian Intervention and the United Nations* (1973).

Schachter, "The United Nations and Internal Conflict," Ch. 16 in Moore, *Civil War.*

————, "The Relation of Law, Politics and Action in the United Nations," 109 *Recueil des cours* 169 (1963).

————, "Intervention and the United Nations," in II Falk, *Vietnam* 273.

Schwebel, "Wars of Liberation in U.N. Organs," Ch. 17 in Moore, *Civil War.*

Seyersted, F., *United Nations Forces in the Law of Peace and War* (1966).

Sohn, "The Role of the United Nations in Civil Wars," in III R. Falk & S. Mendlowitz (eds.), *The Strategy of World Order* (1966).

United Nations Association of the United States of America, *Controlling Conflicts in the 1970's* (1969).

Young, O., *Trends in International Peacekeeping* (1966).

———, *The Intermediaries: Third Parties in International Crises* (1967).

2. Regional

Boutros-Ghali, "The Addis-Ababa Charter," *Int'l Concil.* #546 (Jan., 1964).

Claude, "The OAS, the UN, and the United States," *Int'l Concil.* #547 (March, 1964).

Frey-Wouters, "The Relevance of Regional Arrangements to Internal Conflicts in the Developing World," Ch. 18 in Moore, *Civil War.*

———, "The Prospects for Regionalism in World Affairs," in I Black & Falk, *Future ILO* 463.

Halderman, "Regional Enforcement Measures and the United Nations," 52 *Geo. L.J.* 1 (1963).

Korbonski, "The Warsaw Pact," *Int'l Concil* #573 (May, 1969).

Miller, "The Prospects for Regional Order through Regional Security," in I Black & Falk, *Future ILO* 556.

Moore, "The Role of Regional Arrangements in the Maintenance of World Order," in III Black & Falk, *Future ILO* 122, reprinted as Ch. VI in Moore, J. N., *Law and the Indo-China War* 296–349 (1972).

C. THE LAWS OF WAR

"American Prisoners of War in Southeast Asia, 1971," *Hearings Before the Sub-Committee on National Security Policy and Scientific Developments of the Committee on Foreign Affairs of the House of Representatives 92d Cong. 1st Sess.* (1971).

American Enterprise Institute for Public Policy Research, *The Prisoner of War Problem* (1970).

Baxter, "Jus in Bello Interno: The Present and Future Law," Ch. 20 in Moore, *Civil War.*

Bindschedler-Robert, D., *A Reconsideration of the Law of Armed Conflicts* (1971).

"Bombing Operations and the Prisoner-of-War Rescue Mission in North Vietnam," *Hearings Before the Committee on Foreign Relations of U.S. Senate, 91st Cong., 2d Sess* (1970).

Bond, J., *The Law of War and Internal Conflict* (1973).

———, "Protection of Non-Combatants in Guerrilla Wars," 12 *William & Mary L. Rev.* 787 (1971).

Department of the Army, *The Law of Land Warfare*, FM 27–10 (1956).

———, *Treaties Governing the Law of Land Warfare*, PAM 27–1, (1956).

DeSaussure, "The Laws of Air Warfare: Are There Any?" 23 *Naval War Coll. Rev.* 35 (1971).

Draper, G., *The Legal Classification of Belligerent Individuals* (1970).

————, "The Geneva Conventions of 1949," *Recueil des Cours* 94 (1965).

————, "Human Rights and the Law of War," 12 *Va. J. Int'l L.* 326 (1972).

Esgain & Solf, "The 1949 Geneva Convention Relative to the Treatment of Prisoners of War: Its Principles, Innovations, and Deficiencies," 41 *N. Carolina L. Rev.* 537 (1963).

Falk, "The American POW's Pawns in Power Politics," *Progressive* 13 (March, 1971).

Farer, "The Laws of War 25 Years After Nuremburg," *Int'l Concil.* #584 (May, 1971).

————, "The Humanitarian Laws of War in Civil Strife," 7 *Rev. Belge de Droit Int'l* 20 (1971).

————, "Humanitarian Law and Armed Conflict: Toward the Definition of 'International Armed Conflict,' " 71 *Colum. L. Rev.* 37 (1971).

Ford, "Resistance Movements and International Law, *Int'l Rev. Red Cross* (Oct., Nov., Dec., 1967 & Jan. 1968).

Greenspan, M., *The Modern Law of Land Warfare* (1959).

Havens, "Release and Repatriation of Prisoners of War in the Vietnam Conflict," 57 *A.B.A.J.* 4 (Jan., 1971).

Khan, "Guerrilla Warfare and International Law," 9 *Int'l Stud.* (New Delhi) 103 (Oct., 1967).

Levie, "Civilian Sanctuaries—An Impractical Proposal," in I *Israel Yrbk. on Human Rights* 335 (1971).

————, "Maltreatment of Prisoners of War in Vietnam," in II Falk, *Vietnam* 361.

Mallison, "The Law of War and the Juridicial Control of Weapons of Mass Destruction in General and Limited Wars," 36 *Geo. Wash. L. Rev.* 308 (1967).

Note (*Colum. L. Rev.*), "International Law and Military Operations Against Insurgents in Neutral Territory," in II Falk, *Vietnam* 572.

Note (*Harv. L. Rev.*), "The Geneva Convention and the Treatment of Prisoners of War in Vietnam," in II Falk, *Vietnam* 398.

Note (*Va. J. Int'l L.*), "The Geneva Convention of 1949: Application in the Vietnamese Conflict," in II Falk, *Vietnam* 416.

Nurick, "Legality of Guerrilla Forces," 40 *Am. J. Int'l L.* 563 (1946).

Petrowski, "Law and the Conduct of the Vietnam War," in II Falk, *Vietnam* 439.

Pictet, J., *The Principles of International Humanitarian Law* (1966).

————, "The Need to Restore the Laws and Customs Relating to Armed Conflicts," *Int'l Rev. Red Cross* 459 (1969).

————, "Armed Conflicts: Laws and Customs," *Int'l Rev. Red Cross* 22 (1969).

"Procedures for Protection of Civilians and Prisoners of War in Armed Conflicts: Southeast Asian Examples," 65 *Proc. Am. Soc. Int'l L.* 209 (1971).

Report of the Secretary-General, "Respect for Human Rights in Armed Conflicts," U.N. Doc. Nos. A/7720 (1969) and A/8052 (1970).

Schogel, "Civil War," 108 *Int'l Rev. Red Cross* 123 (March, 1970).

Schwarzenberger, "From the Laws of War to the Law of Armed Conflict," 21 *Current Leg. Probs.* 239 (1968).

Shull, "Counterinsurgency and the Geneva Conventions—Some Practical Considerations," 3 *Int'l Lawyer* 49 (1968).

Swidet, "The Geneva Conventions and Civil War," 3 *Int'l Rev. Red Cross* Supplements #8, 9, & 11 (1950).

Symposium, "War Crimes," 80 *Yale L.J.* 1456 (1971).

Taubenfeld, "The Applicability of the Laws of War in Civil War," Ch. 19 in Moore, *Civil War.*

Trooboff, P., ed., *Applying the International Law of War and Individual Responsibility to the Indochina Conflict* (1973).

D. CRIMINAL RESPONSIBILITY

Adler, "Targets in War: Legal Considerations," in III Falk, *Vietnam* 281.

I Bassiouni, C., & Nanda, V., *A Treatise on International Criminal Law: Crimes and Punishment* (1972).

II Bassiouni, C., & Nanda, V., *A Treatise on International Criminal Law: Jurisdiction and Cooperation* (1972).

Dinstein, Y., *The Defence of "Obedience to Superior Orders" in International Law* (1965).

Falk, "Son My: War Crimes and Individual Responsibility," in III Falk, *Vietnam* 327.

Falk, R., Kolko, G., & Lifton, R., eds., *Crimes of War* (1971).

Ferencz, "War Crimes Law and the Vietnam War," 17 *Amer. U. L. Rev.* 403 (1968).

O'Brien, "The Nuremberg Principles," in III Falk, *Vietnam* 193.

———, "The Law of War, Command Responsibility and Vietnam," 60 *Geo. L.J.* 605 (1972).

Paust, "After My Lai: The Case for War Crime Jurisdiction over Civilians in Federal District Courts," 50 *Texas L. Rev.* 6 (1971).

———, "Legal Aspects of the My Lai Incident—A Response to Prof. Rubin," in III Falk, *Vietnam* 359.

Rubin, "Legal Aspects of the My Lai Incident," in III Falk, *Vietnam* 346.

Taylor, T., *Nuremberg and Vietnam: An American Tragedy* (1970).

Wasserstrom, "Criminal Behavior," 16 *N.Y. Rev. of Books* 8 (June 3, 1971).

Wasserstrom, "The Relevance of Nuremberg," 1 *Phil. & Pub. Aff.* (1972).

Wright, "The Law of the Nuremberg Trial," 41 *Am. J. Int'l L.* 38 (1947).

E. ARMS CONTROL

Bader, "The Proliferation of Conventional Weapons," in III Black & Falk, *Future ILO* 210.

Baxter & Buerganthal, "Legal Aspects of the Geneva Protocol of 1925," 64 *Am. J. Int'l L.* 853 (1970).

Bunn, "Banning Poison Gas and Germ Warfare: Should the United States Agree? 1969 *Wisc. L. Rev.* 375.

Firmage, "The Treaty on the Nonproliferation of Nuclear Weapons,," 63 *Am. J. Int'l L.* 711 (1969).

Frank, L., *The Arms Trade in International Relations* (1969).

Gray, "Traffic Control for the Arms Trade?" 6 *For. Policy* 153 (Spring, 1972).

Hoagland, "Arms in the Developing World," 13 *Orbis* (Spring, 1969).

Kemp, "Dilemmas of the Arms Traffic," 48 *For. Aff.* 272 (Jan. 1970).

——, "Arms Traffic and Third World Conflicts," *Int'l Concil.* (March, 1970).

Kramish, "The Proliferation of Nuclear Weapons," in III Black & Falk, *Future ILO* 224.

Leiss, "The Transfer of Conventional Arms to Less Developed Countries," 1 *Arms Control and National Security* 42 (1969).

Mallison, "The Laws of War and the Juridical Control of Weapons of Mass Destruction in General and Limited Wars," 36 *Geo. Wash. L. Rev.* 308 (1967).

Moore, "Ratification of the Geneva Protocol on Gas and Bacteriological Warfare: A Legal and Political Analysis," 58 *Va. L. Rev.* 419 (1972).

"Report of the Secretary-General on Chemical and Bacteriological (Biological) Weapons and the Effects of Their Possible Use," U.N. Doc. Nos. A/7575; A/7575/Rev. 1 (1969).

Stockholm International Peace Research Institute (SIPRI), *The Arms Trade with the Third World* (1971).

Thayer, G., *The War Business: The International Trade in Armaments* (1970).

Willrich, "Civil Nuclear Power: Conflict Potential and Management," in III Black & Falk, *Future ILO* 252.

F. CONSTITUTIONAL ISSUES

Background Information on the Use of United States Armed Forces in Foreign Countries, 1970 Revision 91st Cong. 2d Sess. (Comm. Print 1970).

Bassiouni, "The War Power and the Law of War: Theory and Realism," 18 *De Paul L. Rev.* 188 (1968).

Committee on Foreign Relations, "Comments on the National Commitments Resolution," in III Falk, *Vietnam* 584.

"Congress, the President, and the War Powers," *Hearings Before the Subcommittee on National Security Policy and Scientific Developments of the Committee on Foreign Affairs of the House of Representatives 91st Cong. 2d Sess.* (Comm. Print 1970).

Faulkner, "War in Vietnam: Is it Constitutional?" 56 *Geo. L.J.* 1123 (1968).

Goldman, "The President, the People, and the Power to Make War," in III Falk, *Vietnam* 489.

Henkin, "Vietnam in the Courts of the United States: 'Political Questions,'" in III Falk, *Vietnam* 625.

Kurland, "The Impotence of Reticence," 1968 *Duke L.J.* 619 (1968).

Lofgren, "War-Making Under the Constitution: The Original Understanding," 81 *Yale L.J.* 672 (1972).

Moore, "The Justiciability of Challenges to the Use of Military Forces Abroad," in III Falk, *Vietnam* 631.

——, "The National Executive and the Use of the Armed Forces Abroad," in II Falk, *Vietnam* 808.

Note, "Congress, the President, and the Power to Commit Forces to Conflict," in II Falk, *Vietnam* 616.

Reveley, "Presidential War-Making: Constitutional Prerogative or Usurpation?," in III Falk, *Vietnam* 521.

———, "Constitutional Aspects of United States Participation in Foreign Internal Conflicts," Ch. 8 in Moore, *Civil War.*

Schwartz & McCormack, "The Justiciability of Legal Objections to the American Military Involvement in Vietnam," in III Falk, *Vietnam* 699.

Stennis, J., & Fulbright, J., *The Role of Congress in Foreign Policy* (1971).

Tigar, "Judicial Power, the 'Political Question Doctrine' and Foreign Relations," in III Falk, *Vietnam* 654.

Velvel, "The War in Vietnam: Unconstitutional, Justiciable, and Jurisdictionally Attackable," II Falk, *Vietnam* 651.

———, "Selected Constitutional Issues Arising From Undeclared Wars," Ch. 9 in Moore, *Civil War.*

"War Powers Legislation," *Hearings Before the Committee on Foreign Relations of the United States Senate, 92d Cong. 1st Sess.* (Comm. Print 1971).

Wilcox, F., *Congress, The Executive, and Foreign Policy* (1971).

Wormuth, "The Vietnam War: The President Versus the Constitution," in II Falk, *Vietnam* 711.

Wright, "The Power of the Executive to Use Military Forces Abroad," in III Falk, *Vietnam* 506.

G. LEGAL RESTRAINTS IN FOREIGN POLICY-MAKING

Acheson, "The Arrogance of International Lawyers," 2 *Int'l Lawyer* 591 (1968).

Barnet, "Toward the Control of International Violence: The Limits and Possibilities of Law," in III Black & Falk, *Future ILO* 370.

Cohen, J., & Chiu, H., *People's China and International Law* (1972).

Dillard, "Some Aspects of Law and Diplomacy," 91 *Recueil des Cours* 447 (1957).

Falk, "Law, Lawyers, and the Conduct of American Foreign Relations," in I Moore, *Arab-Israeli.*

Fisher, R., "Bringing Law to Bear on Governments," in R. Falk and S. Mendlowitz (eds.), *The Strategy of World Order*; Vol. II: *International Law* (1966).

Henkin, L., *How Nations Behave: Law and Foreign Policy* (1968).

Hoffmann, "Introduction," in Scheinman, L., & Wilkinson, D., eds., *International Law and Political Crisis: An Analytic Casebook* (1968).

Hsiung, J., *Law and Policy in China's Foreign Relations* (1972).

Leng, S., & Chiu, H., *Law in Chinese Foreign Policy* (1971).

McDougal, "Law and Power," 46 *Am. J. Int'l L.* 102 (1952).

———, "International Law, Power and Policy: A Contemporary Conception," 82 *Recueil des Cours* 137 (1953).

Moore, "The Legal Tradition and the Management of National Security," (forthcoming).

———, "Law and National Security," 51 *For. Aff.* 408 (Jan. 1973).

———, "The Role of Law in the Management of International Conflict," Ch. 1 in J. N. Moore, *Law and the Indo-China War* 8 (1972).

Oliver, "Reflections on Two Recent Developments Affecting the Function of Law in the International Community," 30 *Texas L. Rev.* 815 (1952).

Outland, J., "Law and the Lawyer in the State Department's Administration of Foreign Policy" (unpublished dissertation, Syracuse, 1969).

IV. CASE STUDIES

A. AFRICA

1. *General*

Grundy, K., *Guerrilla Struggle in Africa: An Analysis and Preview* (1971).
Lee, J., *African Armies and Civil Order* (1969).
Legum, "Africa's Contending Revolutionaries," *Problems of Communism* 2 (March-April 1972).
Mazrui, "Violent Contiguity and the Politics of Retribalization in Africa," 23 *J. Int'l Aff.* 89 (1969).
Mazrui, A., & Patel, H., *Africa and World Affairs; The Next Thirty Years* (1972).
Nielson, W., *The Great Powers and Africa* (1969).

2. *Algeria 1954–61*

Alwan, M., *Algeria Before the United Nations* (1959).
Bedjaoui, M., *Law and the Algerian Revolution* (1961).
Clark, M., *Algeria in Turmoil: A History of the Rebellion* (1959).
Fraleigh, "The Algerian Revolution as a Case Study in International Law," in Falk, *Civil War* 179.
Gordon, D., *The Passing of French Algeria* (1966).
Greenberg, "Law and the Conduct of the Algerian Revolution," 11 *Harv. Int'l L. J.* 37 (1970).
Henissart, P., *Wolves in the City: The Death of French Algeria* (1970).
Hoffmann, "Vietnam: An Algerian Solution?" 2 *For. Pol.* 3 (1971).
Humbaraci, A., *Algeria, a Revolution That Failed* (1966).
International Committee of the Red Cross, *The ICRC and the Algerian Conflict* (1962).
MacDonald, R., *The League of Arab States* (1965).
Merle, R., *Ben Bella* (1967).

3. *Congo 1960–64*

O'Brien, C. Cruise, *To Katanga and Back: A UN Case History* (1962).
Draper, "The Legal Limitations Upon the Employment of Weapons by the United Nations Force in the Congo," 12 *Int'l & Comp. L. Q.* 409 (1963).
Epstein, H., *Revolt in the Congo, 1960–64* (1965).
Grundy, "The Stanleyville Rescue: American Policy in the Congo," 56 *Yale Rev.* 242 (1967).
III Higgins, R., *United Nations Peacekeeping* (1973).
Note, "The Congo Crisis 1964: A Case Study in Humanitarian Intervention," 12 *Va. J. Int'l L.* 261 (1972).

Hoskyns, C., *The Congo Since Independence: January 1960–December 1961* (1965).

Lefever, E., *Crisis in the Congo: A United Nations Force in Action* (1965).

————, *Uncertain Mandate* (1967).

Lemarchand, R., *Political Awakening in the Belgian Congo* (1964).

McNemar, "The Postindependence War in the Congo," in Falk, *Civil War* 244.

Miller (Schachter), "Legal Aspects of United Nations Action in the Congo," 55 *Am. J. Int'l L.* 5 (1961).

Simmonds, R., *Legal Problems Arising From the United Nations Military Operations in the Congo* (1968).

Weiss, H., *Political Protest in the Congo: The Parti Solidaire Africain During the Independence Struggle* (1967).

Young, C., *Politics in the Congo: Decolonization and Independence* (1965).

4. *Nigeria 1966–70*

Carl, "American Assistance to Victims of the Nigeria-Biafra War: Defects in the Prescriptions on Foreign Disaster Relief," 12 *Harv. Int'l L. J.* 191 (1971).

Forsyth, F., *The Biafra Story* (1969).

II Kirk-Greene, A., *Crisis and Conflict in Nigeria: A Documentary Sourcebook 1966–70* (1971).

Melson, R., & Wolfe, H., eds., *Nigeria: Modernization and the Politics of Communalism* (1971).

Niven, R., *The War of Nigerian Unity 1967–1970* (1971).

Nixon, "Nigeria and Biafra," in Spiegel, S., & Waltz, K., eds., *Conflict in World Politics* (1971).

————, "Self-Determination: The Nigeria/Biafra Case," 24 *World Pol.* 473 (July, 1972).

Okpaku, J., ed., *Nigeria: Dilemma of Nationhood; An African Analysis of the Biafran Conflict* (1972).

Panter-Brick, S., *et al.*, *Nigerian Politics and Military Rule: Prelude to the Civil War* (1970).

Uwechue, R., *Reflections on the Nigerian Civil War: Facing the Future* (1971).

5. *Sudan 1967–71*

Albino, O., *The Sudan: A Southern Viewpoint* (1970).

Beshir, M., *The Southern Sudan: Background to Conflict* (1968).

6. *Southern Africa*

Abshire, D., & Samuel, M., eds., *Portuguese Africa: A Handbook* (1969).

Davidson, "The Liberation Struggle in Angola and 'Portuguese' Guinea," 10 *African Q.* 26 (1970).

Marcum, J., *The Angolan Revolution* Vol. I: *The Anatomy of an Explosion, 1950–1962* (1969).

Mondlane, E., *The Struggle for Mozambique* (1969).

Rotberg, R., & Muzrui, A., *Protest and Power in Black Africa* (1970).

Taubenfeld, R., & Taubenfeld, H., *Race, Peace, Law, and Southern Africa* (1968).

B. LATIN AMERICA

1. *General*

Barber, W., & Ronning, N., *Internal Security and Military Power: Counterinsurgency and Civic Action in Latin America* (1966).

Fagen, R., & Cornelius, W., Jr., eds., *Political Power in Latin America: Seven Confrontations* (1970).

Gott, R., *Guerrilla Movements in Latin America* (1971).

Kane, W., *American Involvement in Latin America: A Legal History of U.S. Involvement* (1972).

Martin, C., *The Policy of the United States as Regards Intervention* (1921).

Mecham, L., *The United States and Inter-American Security, 1889–1960* (1961).

Ronning, N., *Intervention in Latin America* (1970).

Stavenhagen, R., ed., *Agrarian Problems and Peasant Movements in Latin America* (1970).

Vega, L., *Guerrillas in Latin America: The Technique of the Counter-State* (1969).

Wagner, R., *United States Policy Toward Latin America* (1970).

2. *Mexico 1914–15*

Clendenen, C., *The United States and Pancho Villa* (1961).

Cline, H., *The United States and Mexico* (1963).

Inman, S., *Intervention in Mexico* (1919).

Link, A., *Wilson: The Struggle for Neutrality, 1914–15* (1960).

Quirk, R., *The Mexican Revolution, 1914–15: The Convention of Aquascalientes* (1960).

Quirk, R., *An Affair of Honor: Woodrow Wilson and the Occupation of Veracruz* (1962).

Womack, J., *Zapata* (1969).

3. *Caribbean 1914–34*

Adler, S., "Bryan and Wilsonian Caribbean Penetration," 20 *Hispanic Am. Hist. Rev.* (1940).

Bemis, S., *The Latin American Policy of the United States* (1943).

Kelsey, C., *The American Intervention in Haiti and the Dominican Republic* (1922).

Munro, D., *Intervention and Dollar Diplomacy in the Caribbean, 1900–1921* (1964).

Perkins, D., *A History of the Monroe Doctrine* (1963).

4. *Guatemala 1954*

Barnet, R., *Intervention and Revolution: The United States in the Third World* 229 (1968).

Bowen & Hughes, "Guatemala, 1954: Intervention and Jurisdiction," 4 *Int'l Relations* 78 (May, 1972).

Fuentes, M., *My War With Communism* (1963).

LaFeber, W., *America, Russia, and the Cold War*, 1945–71 158f (1971).

Schneider, R., *Communism in Guatemala: 1944–54* (1958).

Taylor, "The Guatemalan Affair: A Critique of United States Foreign Policy," 5 *Am. Pol. Sci. Rev.* 787 (Sept., 1956).

U.S. Department of State, *Intervention of International Communism in Guatemala* (1954).

5. Cuba 1959–62

Draper, T., *Castroism: Theory and Practice* (1965).

Falk, "American Intervention in Cuba and the Rule of Law," 22 *Ohio St. L. J.* 546 (1961).

Hilsman, R., *To Move a Nation: The Politics of Foreign Policy in the Administration of John F. Kennedy* Ch. 3 (1964).

"Intervention and Cuba in 1961," 1961 *Proc. Am. Soc. Int'l L.* 2.

Jackson, B., *Castro, The Kremlin, and Communism in Latin America* (1969).

Karol, K., *Guerrillas in Power: The Course of the Cuban Revolution* (1970).

Schlesinger, A., *A Thousand Days: John F. Kennedy in the White House* Ch. 10 (1965).

Suarez, A., *Cuba: Castroism and Communism 1959–1966* (1967).

[Articles on the Cuban Quarantine] 57 *Am. J. Int'l L.* (1963).

6. Dominican Republic 1965

Draper, T., *The Dominican Revolt: Case Study in American Policy* (1968).

Lowenthal, A., *The Dominican Intervention* (1972).

Martin, J., *Overtaken by Events: The Dominican Crisis from the Fall of Trujillo to Civil War* (1966).

Meeker, "The Dominican Situation in Perspective of International Law," 53 *Dept. State Bull.* 60 (1965).

Nanda, V., "The U.S. Action in the 1965 Dominican Crisis: Impact on World Order," 43 *Denver L. Rev.* 439 (1966); 44 *Denver L. Rev.* 225 (1967).

Plank, "The Caribbean Intervention, When and How," 44 *For. Aff.* 37 (Oct. 1965).

Schreiber & Schreiber, "The Inter-American Commission on Human Rights and the Dominican Republic Crisis of 1965," 22 *Int'l Org.* 508 (1968).

Slater, J., *Intervention and Negotiation: The United States and the Dominican Revolution* (1970).

Thomas, A., & Thomas, A., *The Dominican Republic Crisis 1965* (Ninth Hammarskjold Forum, 1967).

Van Tassel, L., "Towards a Perspective of the Concept of Intervention in International Politics: A Case Study of the Dominican Intervention" (Unpublished dissertation, Claremont, 1970).

Wiarda, H., *The Dominican Republic: Nation in Transition* (1969).

C. EAST ASIA

1. China 1911–49

Brandt, C., *Stalin's Failure in China, 1924–1927* (1958).

Ch'en, J., *Mao and the Chinese Revolution* (1967).

Feis, H., *The China Tangle: The American Effort in China from Pearl Harbor to the Marshall Mission* (1953).

Isaacs, H., *Tragedy of the Chinese Revolution* (rev. ed. 1951).

Johnson, C., *Peasant Nationalism and Communist Power: The Emergence of Revolutionary China, 1937–1945* (1962).

North, R., *Moscow and the Chinese Communists* (1963).

Schwartz, B., *Chinese Communism and the Rise of Mao* (1951).

Snow, E., *Red Star Over China* (rev. ed. 1968).

Thomson, J., *While China Faced West: American Reformers in Nationalist China, 1928–1937* (1969).

II Tsou, T., *America's Failure in China, 1941–50* (1963).

Tuchman, B., *Stillwell and the American Experience in China, 1911–1945* (1971).

U.S. Department of State, *United States Relations with China with Special Reference to the Period 1944–1949* (1949). [This is the famous "China White Paper."]

Whiting, A., *Soviet Policies in China, 1917–1924* (1954).

2. *Korea 1950–53*

Acheson, D., *Present at the Creation: My Years at the State Department* Chs. 44–55 (1969).

Goodrich, L., *Korea: A Study of United States Policy in the United Nations* (1956).

Guttman, A., ed., *Korea and the Theory of Limited War* (1967).

II Higgins, R., *United Nations Peacekeeping* 153f (1971).

Leckie, R., *Conflict: The History of the Korean War, 1950–53* (1962).

Osgood, R., *Limited War* (1957).

Paige, G., *The Korean Decision* (1968).

Rees, D., *Korea: The Limited War* (1964).

Shulman, M., *Stalin's Foreign Policy Reappraised* Ch. VI–VII (1963).

II Truman, H., *Memoirs* 316f. (1956).

Whiting, A., *China Crosses the Yalu: The Decision to Enter the Korean War* (1960).

D. SOUTHEAST ASIA

1. *General*

Benda, H., & Bastin, J., *A History of Modern Southeast Asia* (1968).

Gordon, B., *The Dimensions of Conflict in Southeast Asia* (1966).

Gordon, B., *Toward Disengagement in Asia* (1969).

Gurtov, M., *China and Southeast Asia—The Politics of Survival* (1971).

Kahin, G., ed., *Governments and Politics of Southeast Asia* (2nd ed. 1964).

Steinberg, D., ed., *In Search of Southeast Asia: A Modern History* (1971).

2. *Malaya 1948–60*

Barber, N., *The War of the Running Dogs: The Malayan Emergency, 1948–1960* (1971).

Bartlett, V., *Report from Malaya* (1954).

Clutterbuck, R., *The Long War: The Emergency in Malaya, 1948–1960* (1967).

Hanraham, G., *The Communist Struggle in Malaya* (1954).

O'Ballance, E., *Malaya: The Communist Insurgent War, 1948–1960* (1966).

Purcell, V., *Malaya: Communist or Free?* (1954).

Pye, L., *Guerrilla Communism in Malaya* (1956).

Short, A., (forthcoming official history of the Communist "emergency.")

Stenson, M., *Repression and Revolt: The Origins of the 1948 Communist Insurrection in Malaya and Singapore* (1968).

Thompson, R., *Defeating Communist Insurgency: The Lessons of Malaya and Vietnam* (1966).

3. *Philippines 1946–54*

Baclagon, V., *Lessons from the Huk Campaign in the Philippines* (1960).

Pomeroy, W., *The Forest: A Personal Record of the Huk Guerrilla Struggle in the Philippines* (1963).

Scaff, A., *The Philippines Answer to Communism* (1955).

Taruc, Luis, *Born of the People* (1953) [by the leader of the Hukbalahap (Huk) movement].

4. *Vietnam 1946–72*

Buttinger, J., *Vietnam: A Dragon Embattled* (1967).

Cameron, A., ed., *Viet-Nam Crisis: A Documentary History* (1971).

Chaliand, G., *The Peasants of North Vietnam* (1969).

Chin, Truong, *The August Revolution* (1958).

Cooper, C., *The Lost Crusade: America in Vietnam* (1970).

Corbett, "The Vietnam Struggle and International Law," in Falk, *Civil War* 348.

Devillers, P., & Lacouture, J., *End of a War: Indochina, 1954* (1969).

Duncanson, D., *Government and Revolution in Vietnam* (1968).

Ellsberg, D., *Papers on the War* (1972).

I–III Falk, R., *Vietnam.*

Fall, B., *The Two Vietnams: A Political and Military Analysis* (2nd ed. 1967).

Hammer, E., *The Struggle for Indo-China, 1940–55* (1954).

Hoopes, T., *The Limits of Intervention* (1968).

Hosmer, S., *Viet Cong Repression and Its Implications for the Future* (1970).

Kahin, G., & Lewis, J., *The United States in Vietnam* (enlarged ed. 1967).

Lacouture, J., *Vietnam: Between Two Truces* (1966).

Lancaster, D., *The Emancipation of French Indochina* (1961).

Littaver, R., & Uphoff, N., eds., *The Air War in Indochina* (rev. ed. 1972).

McAlister, J., *Vietnam: The Origins of Revolution* (1969).

McAlister, J., & Mus, P., *The Vietnamese and Their Revolution* (1970).

Moore, J. N., *Law and the Indochina War* (1972).

Osborne, M., *Strategic Hamlets in South Vietnam* (1965).

Pike, D., *The Viet Cong* (1965).

———, *War, Peace, and the Viet Cong* (1969).

Randle, R., *Geneva 1954: The Settlement of the Indochinese War* (1969).

Raskin, M., & Fall, B., eds., *The Viet-Nam Reader: Articles and Documents* (rev. ed. 1967).

Shaplen, R., *The Lost Revolution* (1966).

———, *Time Out of Hand* (1969).

———, *The Road From War* (1971).

Schlesinger, A., *The Bitter Heritage* (1966).

Schurmann, F., Scott, P., & Zelnick, R., *The Politics of Escalation in Vietnam* (1966).

Thompson, R., *No Exit from Vietnam* (1969).

5. *Laos, Cambodia, Thailand 1960–72*

Adams, N., & McCoy, A., eds., Laos: *War and Revolution* (1971).

Branfman, F., *Voices from the Plain of Jars: Life Under an Air War* (1972).

Darling, F., *Thailand and the United States* (1965).

III Falk, R., *Vietnam.*

Fall, B., *Anatomy of a Crisis* (1969).

Grant, J., *et al.*, *Cambodia: The Widening War in Indochina* (1971).

Hilsman, R., *To Move A Nation* Pt. IV (1964).

Langer, P., & Zasloff, J., *North Vietnam and the Pathet Lao: Partners in the Struggle for Laos* (1970).

Leifer, M., *Cambodia: The Search for Security* (1967).

Moore, "Legal Dimensions of the Decision to Intercede in Cambodia," Ch. X in J. N. Moore, *Law and the Indochina War* 479–530 (1972).

Moss, L., & Unger, J., eds., *Cambodia in the Expanded War* (1972).

Neuchterlein, D., *Thailand and the Struggle for Southeast Asia* (1965).

Poole, P., *Cambodia's Quest for Survival* (1969).

Schlesinger, A., *A Thousand Days* Ch. VIII (1965).

Smith, R., *Cambodia's Foreign Policy* (1965).

Wilson, D., *The United States and the Future of Thailand* (1970).

E. SOUTH ASIA

1. *General*

Barnds, W., *India, Pakistan and the Great Powers* (1972).

Hodson, G., *The Great Divide* (1969).

Menon, V., *The Transfer of Power in India* (1957).

Siddiqui, K., *Conflict, Crisis and War in Pakistan* (1972).

Spear, P., *India, Pakistan and the West* (1967).

Tinker, H., *India and Pakistan: A Political Analysis* (1962).

Wilcox, "India and Pakistan," in Spiegel, S., & Waltz, K., eds., *Conflict in World Politics* (1971).

2. *Kashmir 1947–72*

Birdwood, L., *Two Nations and Kashmir* (1956).

Brecher, M., *The Struggle for Kashmir* (1953).

———, "Kashmir: A Case Study in United Nations Mediation," *Pac. Aff.* (1963).

Gupta, J., *Jammu and Kashmir* (1968).

Gupta, S., *Kashmir: A Study in India-Pakistan Relations* (1966).

II Higgins, R., *United Nations Peacekeeping* 315f (1971).

Korbel, J., *Danger in Kashmir* (1954).

Lamb, A., *The Kashmir Problem* (1967).

Lockwood, "Resolving the Problem of Kashmir," 133 *World Aff.* 215 (Dec. 1970).

Menon, V., *The Integration of the Indian States* (1956).

Miller, "The Kashmir Dispute," in Scheinman, L., & Wilkinson, D., eds., *International Law and Political Crisis: An Analytic Casebook* (1968).

3. *Ceylon 1970*

Morgan, I., "Intervention by Government Invitation: A Case Study of the Conflict in Ceylon" (unpublished paper in University of Virginia Law School Library, 1972).

4. *Bangladesh 1971–72*

Ahmad, F., *East Bengal: Roots of Genocide* (1971).

Bangladesh: Contemporary Events and Documents (published by the People's Republic of Bangladesh, 1971).

Barnds, "Pakistan's Disintegration," 27 *World Today* 319 (Aug. 1971).

————, "Moscow and South Asia," *Problems of Communism* 12 (May–June 1972).

Gottlieb, "The United Nations and Emergency Humanitarian Assistance in India-Pakistan," 66 *Am. J. Int'l L.* 362 (1972).

Hussein, S., S.J.D. dissertation on the Emergence of Bangla Desh and the India-Pakistan War of 1971, University of Virginia (forthcoming).

Jack, H., *The India-Pakistan Crisis of the United Nations* (1971).

————, *Dacca Diary* (1971).

Khan, "Legal Aspects," in Khan, R., ed., *Bangla Desh, A Struggle for Nationhood* (1971).

Leff, "Bengal, Biafra & the Bigness Bias," 3 *For. Pol.* 129 (Summer 1971).

Mason, E., Dorfman, R., & Marglin, S., *Conflict in East Pakistan* (1971).

Nanda, "Self-Determination in International Law: The Tragic Tale of Two Cities—Islamabad (West Pakistan) and Dacca (East Pakistan)," 66 *Am. J. Int'l L.* 321 (1972).

Nawaz, "Bangla Desh and International Law," *Indian J. Int'l L.* 251 (1971).

Rashiduzzaman, "The Awami League in the Political Development of Pakistan," 10 *Asian Survey* 574 (1970).

Saltzburg, "The United Nations and the Bangladesh Crises," in *The United Nations: A Reappraisal* (1973).

F. PERSIAN GULF

1. *General*

Watt, "The Persian Gulf-Cradle of Conflict?" 21 *Probs. of Comm.* 32 (May–June 1972).

Halpern, "The Middle East and North Africa," in C. Black and T. Thornton (eds.), *Communism and Revolution* (1964).

2. *Iran 1953*

Barnet, R., *Intervention and Revolution* 226f. (1968).

Engler, R., *The Politics of Oil* (1957).

Lafeber, W., *America, Russia, and the Cold War, 1945–1971* 155f. (1971).

3. *Yemen 1963*

Boals, "The Relevance of International Law to the Internal War in Yemen," in Falk, *Civil War* 303.

Brown, "The Yemeni Dilemma," 17 *Middle East J.* 349 (Autumn 1963).

Guldescu, "Yemen: The War and the Hardh Conference," 28 *Rev. of Pol.* 322 (July 1966).

I Higgins, R., *United Nations Peacekeeping* 609 (1969).

O'Ballance, E., *The War in the Yemen* (1971).

Schmidt, D., *Yemen: The Unknown War* (1968).

von Horn, C., *Soldiering for Peace* (1966).

Wenner, M., *Modern Yemen, 1918–1966* (1967).

G. MIDDLE EAST

1. *General*

Bassiouni, C., *Storm Over the Arab World* (1972).

Draper, T., *Israel and World Politics: Roots of the Third Arab-Israeli War* (1967).

Hurewitz, J., ed., *Soviet American Rivalry in the Middle East* (1969).

Feinberg, N., *The Arab-Israel Conflict in International Law* (1970).

Klieman, A., *Soviet Russia and the Middle East* (1970).

Helderman, J., ed., *The Middle East Crisis: Test of International Law* (1969).

Laqueur, W., ed., *The Israel-Arab Reader* (1968).

————, *The Struggle for the Middle East: The Soviet Union in the Mediterranean 1958–1968* (1969).

I–III Moore, J. N., ed., *The Arab-Israeli Conflict* (1973) (including a selected bibliography by Helen Philos in vol. III.)

Polk, W., *The United States and the Arab World* (1965).

Sharabi, H., *Nationalism and Revolution in the Arab World* (1966).

Stone, J., *No Peace-No War in the Middle East* (1970).

Young, "Intermediaries and Interventionists: Third Parties in the Middle East Crisis," 23 *Int'l J.* 52 (Winter 1967–68).

2. *Suez 1956*

Burns, E., *Between Arab and Israeli* (1962).

Friedmann & Collins, "The Suez Canal Crisis of 1956," in Sheinman, L., & Wilkinson, D., eds., *International Law and Political Crisis: An Analytic Casebook* (1968).

Henkin, L., *How Nations Behave: Law and Foreign Policy* Chs. 13–14 (1968), *reprinted in* I Moore, *Arab-Israeli.*

I Higgins, R., *United Nations Peacekeeping* 221f. (1969).

Lauterpacht, E., ed., *The Suez Canal Settlement—A Selection of Documents* (1960).

Love, K., *Suez: The Twice Fought War: A History* (1969).

Moncreiff, A., ed., *Suez Ten Years After* (1967).

Robertson, T., *Crisis: The Inside Story of the Suez Conspiracy* (1965).

Rosner, G., *The United Nations Emergency Force* (1963).

Thomas, H., *Suez* (1967).

3. *Lebanon 1958*

Agwani, M., *The Lebanese Crisis 1958: A Documentary Study* (1965).

Bostani, E., *The Lebanon, A Dissection of the Current Situation* (1959).

Curtis, "The UN Observation Group in Lebanon," *Int'l Org.* (Autumn 1964).

Eisenhower, D., *The White House Years: Waging Peace* (1965).

Barnet, R., *Intervention and Revolution* Ch. 7 (1968).

I Higgins, R., *United Nations Peacekeeping* 535f. (1969).

Humbaraci, A., *Middle East Indictment: From the Truman Doctrine, the Soviet Penetration and Britain's Downfall to the Eisenhower Doctrine* (1958).

Leo, L., *Lebanon: Improbable Nation* (1965).

Murphy, R., *Diplomat Among Warriors* (1964).

Potter, "Legal Aspects of the Beirut Landings," 52 *Am. J. Int'l L.* (1958).

Qubain, F., *Crisis in Lebanon* (1961).

Seale, P., *Struggle for Syria: A Study of Post-War Arab Politics, 1948–1958* (1965).

Thayer, C., *Diplomat* (1960).

Wright, "United States Intervention in the Lebanon," 53 *Am. J. Int'l L.* 112 (1959).

H. SOUTHERN EUROPE

1. *Spain 1931–39*

Bolloten, B., *The Grand Camouflage* (1961).

Borchard, " 'Neutrality' and Civil War," 31 *Am. J. Int'l L.* 304 (1937).

Cattell, D., *Soviet Diplomacy and the Spanish Civil War* (1957).

Cattell, D., *Communism and the Spanish Civil War* (1955).

Chomsky, "Objectivity and Liberal Scholarship," in O'Brien, C. Cruise, & Vanech, W., eds., *Power and Consciousness* (1969).

Garner, "Question of International Law in the Spanish Civil War," 31 *Am. J. Int'l L.* 66 (1937).

Jackson, G., *The Spanish Republic and the Civil War, 1931–1939* (1965).

Murrow, F., *Revolution and Counter-Revolution in Spain* (reissued 1963).

O'Rourke, "Recognition of Belligerency and the Spanish Civil War," 31 *Am. J. Int'l L.* 398 (1937).

Padelford, N., *International Law and Diplomacy in the Spanish Civil Strife* (1939).

Puzzo, *Spain and the Great Powers: 1936–1941* (1962).

Richards, U., *Lessons of the Spanish Revolution* (1953).

Thomas, & Thomas, "International Legal Aspects of the Civil War in Spain, 1936–39," in Falk, *Civil War* III.

Thomas, H., *The Spanish Civil War* (1961).

2. *Greece 1943–49*

Barnet, R., *Intervention and Revolution* Ch. 6 (1968).

Condit, D., *Case Study in Guerrilla War: Greece During World War II* (Special Operations Research Office, American University 1961).

Kolko, G., *The Politics of War* Ch. 8 (1968).

Kousoulos, D., *Revolution and Defeat: The Story of the Greek Communist Party* (1965).

Jones, J., *The Fifteen Weeks* (1955).

McNeil, W., & McNeil, E., *Report on the Greeks* (1948).

O'Ballance, E., *The Greek Civil War* (1966).

Stavrionos, L., *Greece: American Dilemma and Opportunity* (1952).

Xydis, S., *Greece and the Great Powers* (1963).

3. *Cyprus 1954–72*

Adams, T., & Cottrell, A., *Cyprus Between East and West* (1968).

Ierodiakonov, L., *The Cyprus Question* (1971).

III Higgins, R., *United Nations Peacekeeping* (1973).

Miller, L., *Cyprus: The Law and Politics of Civil Strife* (Occasional Paper #19, Harvard Center for Int'l Aff. 1968).

Stegenga, J., *The United Nations Force in Cyprus* (1968).

Stephens, R., *Cyprus: A Place of Arms* (1966).

Windsor, P., *NATO and the Cyprus Crisis* (Adelphi Paper #14, 1964).

Xydis, S., *Cyprus: Conflict and Conciliation, 1954–1958* (1967).

I. EASTERN EUROPE

1. *Soviet Union 1917–21*

Footman, D., *The Russian Civil War* (1961).

Hoover, H., *The Ordeal of Woodrow Wilson* Ch. 10 (1958).

Kennan, G., *Soviet American Relations, 1917–1920* Vol. I: *Russia Leaves the War* (1956); Vol. II: *The Decision to Intervene* (1958).

Levin, N., *Woodrow Wilson and World Politics: America's Response to War and Revolution* (1968).

Luckett, R., *The White Generals: An Account of the White Movement and the Russian Civil War* (1971).

Mayer, A., *Wilson vs. Lenin: Political Origins of the New Diplomacy, 1917–1918* (1959).

Mayer, A., *The Politics and Diplomacy of Peacemaking, 1918–1919* (1967).

Morley, W., *The Japanese Thrust into Siberia* (1957).

Pipes, R., *The Formation of the Soviet Union, Communism and Nationalism, 1917–1923* (1954).

Thompson, J., *Russia, Bolshevism, and the Versailles Peace* (1966).

Ullman, R., *Anglo-Soviet Relations, 1917–1921: Intervention and War* (1961).

For a survey of Soviet historiography on the intervention as of 1962, *see* Thompson, "Allied and American Intervention in Russia, 1918–1921," in Black, C., ed., *Rewriting Russian History* (1962).

2. *Hungary 1956*

Barber, N., *A Handful of Ashes* (1957).

Brzezinski, Z., *The Soviet Bloc: Unity and Diversity* (rev. ed. 1967).

Fryer, P., *The Hungarian Tragedy* (1957).

International Commission of Jurists, *The Hungarian Situation and the Rule of Law* (1957).

Lasky, M., ed., *The Hungarian Revolution* (1957).

Lettis, R., & Morris, W., *The Hungarian Revolt* (1961).

Loeber, "Hungary and the Soviet Definition of Aggression," *Internationales Recht and Diplomatie* 46 (1957).

Michener, J., *The Bridge at Andau* (1957).

Mikes, G., *The Hungarian Revolution* (1957).

Sohn, L., ed., *Cases on United Nations Law* 634–79 (1967).

Zinner, P., ed., *National Communism and Popular Revolt in Eastern Europe* (1956).

3. Czechoslovakia 1968

Czechoslovakia and the Brezhnev Doctrine (prepared by the Subcommittee on National Security and International Operations, Senate Committee on Government Operations, 90th Cong., 1st Sess. 1969).

Czerwinski, E., & Pickelkiewicz, J., eds., *The Soviet Invasion of Czechoslovakia: Its Effects on Eastern Europe* (1972).

Ello, P., ed., *Czechoslovakia's Blueprint for "Freedom"* (1968).

Golan, G., *The Czechoslovak Reform Movement* (1972).

Goodman, "The Invasion of Czechoslovakia: 1968," 4 *Int'l Lawyer* 42 (1969).

Hayter, W., *Russia and the World* (1970).

Kusin, V., *The Intellectual Origins of the Prague Spring: The Development of Reformist Ideas in Czechoslovakia* (1971).

Levine, I., *Intervention: The Causes and Consequences of the Invasion of Czechoslovakia* (1969).

Littell, R., ed., *The Czech Black Book* (1969).

Parrish, M., ed., *The 1968 Czechoslovak Crisis: A Bibliography 1968–1970* (1971).

Remington, R., ed., *Winter in Prague* (1969).

Rothschild, "The Soviet Union and Czechoslovakia," in Spiegel, S., & Waltz, K., eds., *Conflict in World Politics* (1971).

Shawcross, W., *Dubcek* (1971).

Svitak, I., *The Czechoslovak Experiment, 1968–1969* (1971).

Szulc, T., *Czechoslovakia Since World War II* (1971).

Windsor, P., & Roberts, A., *Czechoslovakia 1968: Reform, Repression and Resistance* (1969).

Zeman, Z., *Prague Spring* (1969).

NOTES ON CONTRIBUTORS

Notes on Contributors

John Norton Moore is Professor of Law and Director of the Graduate Program at the University of Virginia School of Law. He is Chairman of the American Bar Association Committee on International Law and the Use of Force, Rapporteur of the American Society of International Law Panel on the Role of International Law in Civil Wars, and a member of the Council on Foreign Relations and the Board of Editors of the *American Journal of International Law*. During 1971–72 he was a Sesquicentennial Associate of the Center for Advanced Studies at the University of Virginia. Since 1970 he has served as a member of the U.S. Department of State Advisory Panel on International Law and during 1972–73 he was on leave from the University of Virginia to serve as Counselor on International Law to the Department of State. At present, Professor Moore is on leave from the University of Virginia serving as Chairman of the National Security Council's Interagency Task Force on the Law of the Sea, and Deputy Special Representative of the President of the United States for the Third United Nations Conference on the Law of the Sea. He is the author of *Law and the Indo-China War* (1972), the editor of a forthcoming three-volume study of the *Arab-Israeli Conflict*, and has written extensively on conflict management and the theory of international law.

Derek W. Bowett is President of Queen's College, Cambridge and a Lecturer in the Faculty of Law at Cambridge. He is a member of the English Bar and has served as a Legal Officer in U.N. Headquarters from 1957–59 and as General Counsel of UNRWA from 1966–68. His writings include *Self-Defence in International Law* (1958), *The Law of International Institutions* (1964; 2d ed. 1970), *United Nations Forces* (1964), *The Law of the Sea* (1967), and *Search for Peace* (1972).

Cyril E. Black is Duke Professor of Russian History and Director of the Center of International Studies at Princeton University. During World War II he was an officer of the U.S. Department of State and has since served on several official delegations to Eastern Europe and the Soviet Union. He is author or co-author of several books, including *Twentieth Century Europe* (with E.C. Helmreich, 2d ed. 1959), *The Transformation of Russian Society* (1960), *Communism and Revolution: The Strategic Uses of Political Violence* (co-editor with T.P. Thornton, 1964), *The Dynamics of Modernization: A Study in Comparative History* (1966), and co-editor (with R.A. Falk) of *The Future of the International Legal Order*, (vols. I–V, 1969, 1970, 1971, 1972 & 1974).

Ted Robert Gurr is Professor of Political Science at Northwestern University and Research Associate of the Center of International Studies, Princeton University. He is interested primarily in the comparative analysis of political order, conflict, and change. His principal monographs and books on the subject include *The Conditions of Civil Violence* (1967), *Political Performance: A Twelve-Nation Study* (with M. McClelland, 1971), and *Why Men Rebel*, which received the American Political Science Association's Woodrow Wilson Prize for best book of 1970 in political science. In 1968–69 he was co-director of the History Task Force of the National Commission on the Causes and Prevention of Violence, for which he co-authored the report *Violence in America: Historical and Comparative Perspectives* (with H.D. Graham, 1969).

John W. Burton is Director of the Centre for the Analysis of Conflict, London, and was previously the Permanent Secretary of the Australian Foreign Office. He has been developing graduate and post-graduate courses in international relations at University College London since 1963, endeavoring to incorporate the sociological literature on change and conflict with an emphasis on transactions across state boundaries other than those of the inter-state system. His books include *The Alternative* (1954), *Peace Theory* (1962), *International Relations: A General Theory* (1965), *Nonalignment* (1966) (editor and contributor), *System, States, Diplomacy and Rules* (1968), *Conflict and Communication* (1969), and *World Society* (1972).

Oran R. Young is Professor of Government at the University of Texas, Austin. His books include *The Intermediaries: Third Parties in International Crises* (1967); *The Politics of Force: Bargaining During International Crises* (1968); *Systems of Political Science* (1968); and *Political Leadership and Collective Goods* (with N. Frohlich and J.A. Oppenheimer). He has edited and contributed to a forthcoming theoretical work entitled *Bargaining*, and he is currently working on the development of formal models of political choice.

James N. Rosenau is Professor of Political Science and International Relations and Director of the Institute for Transnational Studies at the University of Southern California. He was formerly Profesor of Political Science at Ohio State University. From 1949 to 1970 he taught at Rutgers University. His books include *Public Opinion and Foreign Policy* (1961) and *National Leadership and Foreign Policy*, (1963), *The Adaptation of National Societies*, (1970), *The Scientific Study of Foreign Policy*, (1971), *International Studies and the Social Sciences*, (1972), and *The Dramas of Politics*, (1973). He has edited *International Aspects of Civil Strife*, (1964), *Domestic Sources of Foreign Policy*, (1967), *Linkage Politics*, (1969), *Contending Approaches to International Politics*, (with Klaus Knorr), (1969), *International Politics and Foreign Policy*, (2d ed. 1969), and *The Analysis of International Politics* (with Vincent Davis & Maurice East) (1971).

W. Taylor Reveley, III is an associate with the law firm of Hunton, Williams, Gay & Gibson. He received his A.B. from Princeton University and his J.D. from the University of Virginia. After a year as Assistant Professor of Law at the University of Alabama Law School, he clerked at the Supreme Court for Mr. Justice Brennan. During 1972–73 he studied the war powers as a Joint Fellow of the Council on Foreign Relations and the Woodrow Wilson International Center for Scholars. He also served as the Rapporteur of a panel of the American Society of International Law on constitutional aspects of foreign relations.

Lawrence R. Velvel is Professor of Law at the Catholic University of America and prior to joining Catholic University was a Professor of Law at the University of Kansas. He specializes in constitutional law and has written several articles on the constitutionality of the Indo-China War. He is also the author of a book on the same subject, *Undeclared War and Civil Disobedience: The American System in Crisis* (1970). He aided in the enactment of the Shea-

Wells Massachusetts anti-war bill in 1970, and he subsequently formed and became chairman of, and one of the two principal attorneys for, "The Constitutional Lawyers' Committee on Undeclared War." This Committee of over thirty-five legal experts has filed *amicus curiae* briefs in several of the most important cases challenging the constitutionality of the Indo-China War. In other cases, Professor Velvel has acted as counsel for reservists, soldiers, Congressmen and others who have challenged the legality of the War. He also is a member of the Civil War Panel of the American Society of International Law, and of the Consultative Council of The Lawyers' Committee on American Policy Towards Vietnam.

Ian Brownlie is a Fellow of Wadham College, Oxford, and a Lecturer in the University of Oxford. He is currently a co-Editor and member of the Editorial Committee of the *British Year Book of International Law*. His writings include *International Law and the Use of Force by States* (1963; reprinted 1969), *Principles of Public International Law* (1966; 2d ed. 1973), and of numerous articles.

Richard B. Lillich is Professor of Law at the University of Virginia School of Law and Director of the Procedural Aspects of International Law Institute. He is the author of *International Claims: Their Adjudication by National Commissions* (1962), *International Claims: Their Preparation and Presentation* (with Gordon A. Christenson) (1962), *The Protection of Foreign Investment: Six Procedural Studies* (1965), *International Claims: Postwar British Practice* (1967), and *International Claims: Their Settlement by Lump Sum Agreements* (with Burns H. Weston) (1973). Editor of the Procedural Aspects of International Law Series since 1964 and a Member of the Board of Editors of the *American Journal of International Law* since 1969, he also has edited and contributed to three volumes on *The Valuation of Nationalized Property in International Law* (1972–74).

W. Michael Reisman is Professor of Law at the Yale Law School. He is the author of *Nullity and Revision: The Review and Enforcement of International Judgments and Awards* (1971); *The Art of the Possible: Diplomatic Alternatives in the Middle East* (1970); and a forthcoming two-volume work with Myres S. McDougal and Harold D. Lasswell on the world constitutive process.

Edwin Brown Firmage is Professor of Law at the University of Utah College of Law, where he has taught since 1966. He was graduated magna cum laude from Brigham Young University with a baccalaureate degree in political science and a master's degree in history. He was National Honors Fellow at the University of Chicago Law School and received the J.D. degree from Chicago in 1963. At Chicago he was an editor of the *University of Chicago Law Review* and pursued a course of graduate study in international law and international relations which led to the LL.M. and S.J.D. degrees. He was White House Fellow in 1965–66 and in that capacity served on the staff of Vice-President Hubert Humphrey, with responsibility in the areas of civil rights and urban problems. He was named an International Affairs Fellow of the Council on Foreign Relations for 1970–71 and attended the conference of the Committee on Disarmament at Geneva. During 1970–71 he was also a Visiting Scholar at the United Nations.

Jerome Alan Cohen is Professor of Law and Director of the East Asian

Legal Studies Program at the Harvard Law School. His books include *The Criminal Process in the People's Republic of China 1949–1963* (1968), and *People's China and International Law* (with Hungdah Chiu) (1974). He is also the editor of *Contemporary Chinese Law: Research Problems and Perspectives, China's Practice of International Law: Some Case Studies* (1970), and other works.

William E. Butler is the Reader in Comparative Law at the University of London, being associated with University College London, where he teaches courses on Soviet law and socialist legal systems. He is the author of *The Soviet Union and the Law of the Sea* (1971), *The Merchant Shipping Code of the USSR 1968* (with J.B. Quigley) (1970), and two bibliographies of Soviet law, as well as numerous journal articles and reviews. Since 1969 he has edited *Soviet Statutes and Decisions*. During 1971–72 he spent a semester at the Department of International Law of Moscow State University as a member of the U.S.-U.S.S.R. Senior Scholar Exchange Program.

Oscar Schachter, a past President of the American Society of International Law, has been a United Nations official since early 1946. He is at present the Director of Studies of the United Nations Institute for Training and Research (UNITAR). He was previously the Director of the General Legal Division of the United Nations Secretariat and he has served as representative of the Secretary-General and as a legal adviser to many international conferences. He is an associate of the Institut de Droit International and editor of the *American Journal of International Law* and he has written extensively on problems of international organization. He has been a visiting professor at several universities and for some fifteen years conducted seminars on international organization at Yale Law School. Before joining the United Nations he was Assistant General Counsel of the United Nations Relief and Rehabilitation Administration and prior to that he served in the U.S. Department of State and in other government posts. He received his law degree at Columbia University in 1939 where he was the Editor-in-Chief of the *Columbia Law Review*.

Stephen M. Schwebel is Executive Vice President of the American Society of International Law and Burling Professor of International Law and Organization at the School of Advanced International Studies of The Johns Hopkins University. He has served as United States Representative in sessions of the United Nations Special Committees on the Question of Defining Aggression and on Principles of International Law Concerning Friendly Relations and Cooperation among States. He is the editor of *The Effectiveness of International Decisions* (1971) and the author of *The Secretary-General of the United Nations* (1952), and numerous articles on the United Nations and the Middle East. Since 1973 he has been on leave from The American Society of International Law to serve as the Counselor on International Law to the Department of State.

Ellen Frey-Wouters is Professor of Political Science at the City University of New York. Formerly she was a member of the United Nations Educational, Scientific, and Cultural Organization and the United Nations Secretariat. She has authored "The Prospects for Regionalism in World Affairs" in III C. Black & R. Falk (eds) *The Future of the International Legal Order* (1971), as well as numerous other articles on the United Nations and regional organizations.

Howard J. Taubenfeld is Professor of Law and Director of the Institute of Aerospace Law at Southern Methodist University School of Law. His books include *Race, Peace, Law and Southern Africa* (with Rita F. Taubenfeld) (1968), *The Law Relating to Activities of Man in Space* (with S. H. Lay) (1970), and *Controlling the Weather: A Study of Law and Regulatory Procedures* (1970). He is engaged in continuing studies with Rita F. Taubenfeld on the international implications of weather modification activities and on the effects of non-military international sanctions.

Richard R. Baxter is Professor of Law at Harvard University and Editor-in-Chief of the *American Journal of International Law*. He has served as a Regular Army officer, as an attorney in the Office of the General Counsel, Department of Defense, and as Counselor on International Law to the Department of State. He was a member of the United States Delegation of Experts to the first and second Conferences on International Humanitarian Law, convened by the International Committee of the Red Cross in 1971 and 1972. He was co-editor of Army Manual 27–10, *The Law of Land Warfare*, is the author of *The Law of International Waterways* (1964), and has written extensively on the law of war.

Richard A. Falk is Albert G. Milbank Professor of International Law and Practice at Princeton University. He is acting as Research Director of the North American Section of the World Order Models Project and as Co-director with Cyril E. Black of a project to study the future of the international legal order. His books include *Legal Order in a Violent World* (1968), *The Status of Law in International Society* (1970), and *This Endangered Planet* (1971). He has edited *Security in Disarmament* (with R. J. Barnet) (1961) I–IV *The Strategy of World Order* (with Saul H. Mendlovitz) (1966), I–V *The Future of the International Legal Order* (with C. E. Black) (1969–73), and I–III *The Vietnam War and International Law* (1968–72).

Tom J. Farer is Professor of Law at the Rutgers Law School, Camden. Prior to joining the Rutgers law faculty he served as a Special Assistant to the General Counsel of the Department of Defense and as a Legal Adviser to the Somali Police. From 1966–71 he taught at the Columbia Law School. He was the editor of *Financing African Development* (1969), and his writings include *The Laws of War Twenty-Five Years After Nuremberg* (1971), and numerous articles in scholarly journals.

Wolfgang G. Friedmann was Professor of International Law and Director of International Legal Research at Columbia University. Prior to this post he held professorships at the Universities of London, Melbourne and Toronto. He was a visiting professor at Paris and Calcutta, where he delivered the Tagore Lectures in 1967 and 1969. He was adviser to the Allied Military Government of Germany (SHAEF and the British Control Commission) from 1944–47, and in 1954 acted as United Nations Consultant for Public Industrial Enterprise. His major publications include *Law In A Changing Society* (1959, 2d ed., 1972), *The Changing Structure of International Law* (1964), *Legal Theory* (5th ed., 1967), *Joint International Business Ventures in Developing Countries* (with J. P. Beguin) (1971), and *The Future of the Oceans* (1971). He also was the author of numerous articles which have appeared in American and foreign journals.

Louis B. Sohn is Bemis Professor of International Law at Harvard University. He has served as a Legal Officer in the United Nations Secretariat, a Consultant to the U.S. Arms Control and Disarmament Agency, a Consultant to the Department of Defense, and as Counselor on International Law in the U.S. Department of State. His writings include *Cases on World Law* (1950); *World Peace Through World Law* (with G. Clark) (1958; 3d ed. 1966); *Cases on United Nations Law* (1956; 2d ed. 1967); *Basic Documents of African Regional Organizations* (1972); and numerous articles in scholarly journals.

Frederick S. Tipson is a law student and a graduate student in foreign affairs at the University of Virginia. During 1973–74 he was the Editor-in-Chief of the *Virginia Journal of International Law*.

INDEX

Index

Acquiescent societies, interventionary behavior of, 147–148

African regional system, 463–65. *See also* Organization of African Unity (OAU); Regional organizations

Aggression: charges of indirect, investigated by UN, 432; coercion as, 15; definition of, 62, 92–93, 456; distinguished from interference by Soviet Union, 388–90; uninvited intervention as, 100; UN sanctions on, 439–42

Aid to insurgents: denied until status of belligerency has been attained, 344; guidelines for, 22, 29, 524, 583–84. *See also* Collective intervention; Economic and technical aid; Military assistance; Recognition of governments; Regional organizations; Regulation of intervention

Aircraft, commercial overflight rights, 543

Airlift of civilians, as legal humanitarian intervention, 493

Air warfare, code of, xvi, 32

Algeria: absence of agreement between France and Provisional Government of, 528; counter-insurgency theories of, 82; non-intervention in, by Western powers, 355; seating of Provisional Government of, in Arab League, 483

Algerian Civil War, applicability of laws of war during, 509–11

Algerian Revolutionary Front, 509

Alliance systems: increased demand for intervention because of, xii; international law based on, 575. *See also* Regional organizations; Treaties

Al-Nimeiry Conciliation Mission in Jordan, 483

Ambassadorial immunity, 543

American Civil War: laws of war during, 502, 505–6; treated by US as international conflict, 519

Amnesty, 535

Angola, guerrilla conflict against Portuguese control of, 325–26

Anticipatory defense, permissibility of, 14

Anti-colonial wars: initiation of hostilities in, 22; modernization theories of, 64; as type of intervention, 21. *See also* Colonialism; National liberation wars; Self-determination

Apartheid: and non-intervention, 224; UN conciliation commission on, 426; UN condemnation of, 20, 396–97, 413–14; UN resolution on, 505

Arab League. *See* League of Arab States

Arbitration, 103

"Armed conflict not of an international character", definition of, in laws of war, 521, 532–33

Armies: Chinese army, Mao's organization of, 321; mobilization techniques of, 266; modern nation-state and, 252–54. *See also* Armies, private

Armies, private: basis of power for, 274, 295; *caudillo* politics and, 279–80; Communist states' rejection of traditional rule of, in Third World, 258; conditions leading to, 278–83; contextuality and, 288–96; counter-private armies, 291–92; current state system and, 283–84; decision-making (*see* Decision-making); Falk view of Reisman's article on, 545–46; as force for order, 259–60; international law and, 255–60; international problems because of, 259, 294–95; legitimate targets of, 274; participants in, 290; peasant revolt in 17th century Europe and Asia and, 280–81; perspectives of, 273, 290; public order features of, 270–77, 293–94; regional systems and, 292; as responsible community structure, 301; revolutionary and interventionary violence because of, xii; social systems of, 286; Spanish *padrones* system of, 280; strategies of, 295; territorial community identified with, 291; "unofficial," 546; value demands of, 293; war system and, 269–70. *See also* Private army claims; Private army rule

Arms control: improvements in, 36; prevention of conventional war as focus of, xvi

Art works, destruction of during Spanish Civil War, 508

Asia, internal political violence in, 328–33

Asian-African Conference, in Bandung, 354, 374

Authority-oriented conflict, determination of insurgency in, 24

Autonomy and regional response to internal disorders, 462

Library of Congress Cataloging in Publication Data

Main entry under title:
Law and civil war in the modern world.

"Published under the auspices of the American Society of International Law and the International Legal Research Fund of the Columbia Law School, and prepared in collaboration with Wolfgang G. Friedmann."
    Bibliography: p.
    1. Civil war—Addresses, essays, lectures. 2. Intervention (International law)—Addresses, essays, lectures. I. Moore, John Norton, 1937–   ed. II. Friedmann, Wolfgang Gaston, 1907–1972. III. American Society of International Law.
JX4541.L38   341.6′8   73-19338

ISBN 0-8018-1509-6
ISBN 0-8018-1598-3 (pbk.)